STAIRS 2010

Frontiers in Artificial Intelligence and Applications

FAIA covers all aspects of theoretical and applied artificial intelligence research in the form of monographs, doctoral dissertations, textbooks, handbooks and proceedings volumes. The FAIA series contains several sub-series, including "Information Modelling and Knowledge Bases" and "Knowledge-Based Intelligent Engineering Systems". It also includes the biennial ECAI, the European Conference on Artificial Intelligence, proceedings volumes, and other ECCAI – the European Coordinating Committee on Artificial Intelligence – sponsored publications. An editorial panel of internationally well-known scholars is appointed to provide a high quality selection.

Series Editors:
J. Breuker, N. Guarino, J.N. Kok, J. Liu, R. López de Mántaras,
R. Mizoguchi, M. Musen, S.K. Pal and N. Zhong

Volume 222

Recently published in this series

Vol. 221. A.V. Samsonovich, K.R. Jóhannsdóttir, A. Chella and B. Goertzel (Eds.), Biologically Inspired Cognitive Architectures 2010 – Proceedings of the First Annual Meeting of the BICA Society
Vol. 220. R. Alquézar, A. Moreno and J. Aguilar (Eds.), Artificial Intelligence Research and Development – Proceedings of the 13th International Conference of the Catalan Association for Artificial Intelligence
Vol. 219. I. Skadiņa and A. Vasiļjevs (Eds.), Human Language Technologies – The Baltic Perspective – Proceedings of the Fourth Conference Baltic HLT 2010
Vol. 218. C. Soares and R. Ghani (Eds.), Data Mining for Business Applications
Vol. 217. H. Fujita (Ed.), New Trends in Software Methodologies, Tools and Techniques – Proceedings of the 9th SoMeT_10
Vol. 216. P. Baroni, F. Cerutti, M. Giacomin and G.R. Simari (Eds.), Computational Models of Argument – Proceedings of COMMA 2010
Vol. 215. H. Coelho, R. Studer and M. Wooldridge (Eds.), ECAI 2010 – 19th European Conference on Artificial Intelligence
Vol. 214. I.-O. Stathopoulou and G.A. Tsihrintzis, Visual Affect Recognition
Vol. 213. L. Obrst, T. Janssen and W. Ceusters (Eds.), Ontologies and Semantic Technologies for Intelligence
Vol. 212. A. Respício et al. (Eds.), Bridging the Socio-Technical Gap in Decision Support Systems – Challenges for the Next Decade
Vol. 211. J.I. da Silva Filho, G. Lambert-Torres and J.M. Abe, Uncertainty Treatment Using Paraconsistent Logic – Introducing Paraconsistent Artificial Neural Networks

ISSN 0922-6389 (print)
ISSN 1879-8314 (online)

STAIRS 2010

Proceedings of the Fifth Starting AI Researchers' Symposium

Edited by

Thomas Ågotnes

*Department of Information Science and Media Studies,
University of Bergen, Norway*

Press

Amsterdam • Berlin • Tokyo • Washington, DC

© 2011 The authors and IOS Press.

All rights reserved. No part of this book may be reproduced, stored in a retrieval system, or transmitted, in any form or by any means, without prior written permission from the publisher.

ISBN 978-1-60750-675-1 (print)
ISBN 978-1-60750-676-8 (online)
Library of Congress Control Number: 2010940335

Publisher
IOS Press BV
Nieuwe Hemweg 6B
1013 BG Amsterdam
Netherlands
fax: +31 20 687 0019
e-mail: order@iospress.nl

Distributor in the USA and Canada
IOS Press, Inc.
4502 Rachael Manor Drive
Fairfax, VA 22032
USA
fax: +1 703 323 3668
e-mail: iosbooks@iospress.com

LEGAL NOTICE

The publisher is not responsible for the use which might be made of the following information.

PRINTED IN THE NETHERLANDS

Preface

The Fifth Symposium for Artificial Intelligence Researchers (STAIRS 2010) took place in conjunction with the 19th European Conference on Artificial Intelligence (ECAI 2010), as well as the Sixth Conference on Prestigious Applications of Intelligent Systems (PAIS 2010), in Lisbon, Portugal, 16–20 August 2010.

STAIRS is an international meeting intended to support AI researchers from all countries at the beginning of their career: PhD students or those who have held a PhD for less than one year. STAIRS offers doctoral students and young post-doctoral AI fellows a unique and valuable opportunity to gain experience in presenting their work in a supportive scientific environment, where they can obtain constructive feedback on the technical content of their work as well as advice on how to present it, and where they can also establish contacts with the broader European AI research community.

Papers selected by the program committee through a peer-review process were presented at the conference. The topics covered a broad spectrum of subjects in the field of AI: learning and classification, ontologies and the semantic web, agent programming and planning, logic and reasoning, economic approaches, games, dialogue systems, user preferences and recommender systems.

This book contains revised versions of most of the peer-reviewed papers presented at the conference. The final versions of the papers were submitted after the conference, giving the authors an opportunity to take account of any feedback they received during the conference, and improve their contributions accordingly.

I would like to thank the ECAI chairs for supporting STAIRS and for creating a perfect environment for it, as well as the local organisers and the STAIRS participants. Last but not least, I am grateful to the STAIRS program committee for their work in selecting papers and providing feedback to the authors. They were:

Natasha Alechina
Sylvain Bouveret
Fabio Gagliardi Cozman
Sarah Jane Delany
Daan Fierens
Ian Kash
Nicolas Lachiche
Weiru Liu
Peter McBurney
Nardine Osman
Henri Prade
Carles Sierra
Heiner Stuckenschmidt
Kalliopi Zervanou

Josep Lluis Arcos
Rui Camacho
Claudia d'Amato
Clare Dixon
Chiara Ghidini
Udo Kruschwitz
Nada Lavrac
Alessio Lomuscio
Elena Montiel-Ponsoda
Hector Palacios
Marta Sabou
Matthijs Spaan
Anni-Yasmin Turhan
Wamberto Vasconcelos

Yoram Bachrach
Hubie Chen
Eric de la Clergerie
Esra Erdem
Wojtek Jamroga
Oliver Kutz
Francesca Alessandra Lisi
Peter Lucas
Eva Onaindia
Jeff Z. Pan
David Schlangen
Kostas Stergiou
Menno van Zaanen
Stefan Woelfl

Bergen, September 2010
Thomas Ågotnes

Contents

Preface *Thomas Ågotnes*	v
First-Order Multi-Class Subgroup Discovery *Tarek Abudawood and Peter Flach*	1
Improving the Efficiency of Ontology Engineering by Introducing Prototypicality *Xavier Aimé, Frédéric Fürst, Pascale Kuntz and Francky Trichet*	13
Towards Effective 'Any-Time' Music Tracking *Andreas Arzt and Gerhard Widmer*	24
Relaxing Regression for a Heuristic GOLOG *Michelle L. Blom and Adrian R. Pearce*	37
POMDP Solving: What Rewards Do You Really Expect at Execution? *Caroline Ponzoni Carvalho Chanel, Jean-Loup Farges, Florent Teichteil-Königsbuch and Guillaume Infantes*	50
Generative Structure Learning for Markov Logic Networks *Quang-Thang Dinh, Matthieu Exbrayat and Christel Vrain*	63
Learning Fuzzy Models of User Interests in a Semantic Information Retrieval System *Mauro Dragoni, Célia da Costa Pereira and Andrea G.B. Tettamanzi*	76
Ontology-Based Document and Query Representation May Improve the Effectiveness of Information Retrieval *Mauro Dragoni, Célia da Costa Pereira and Andrea G.B. Tettamanzi*	89
"Do You Trust Me or Not?" – Trust Games in Agent Societies *Rui Figueiredo, João Carmo and Rui Prada*	101
Modal Access Control Logic: Axiomatization, Semantics and FOL Theorem Proving *Valerio Genovese, Daniele Rispoli, Dov M. Gabbay and Leendert van der Torre*	114
Probabilistic Logic with Conditional Independence Formulae *Magdalena Ivanovska and Martin Giese*	127
Difficulty Rating of Sokoban Puzzle *Petr Jarušek and Radek Pelánek*	140
The Decidability of RPTL *Fahad Khan*	151
Confluent Term Rewriting for Only-Knowing Logics *Espen H. Lian, Einar Broch Johnsen and Arild Waaler*	162

A Much Better Polynomial Time Approximation of Consistency in the $\mathcal{LR}$ Calculus 175
Dominik Lücke and Till Mossakowski

Fair Mechanisms for Recurrent Multi Unit Combinatorial Auctions 186
Javier Murillo and Beatriz López

Onto.PT: Automatic Construction of a Lexical Ontology for Portuguese 199
Hugo Gonçalo Oliveira and Paulo Gomes

MEC – Monitoring Clusters' Transitions 212
Márcia Oliveira and João Gama

Dealing with the Dynamics of Proof-Standard in Argumentation-Based Decision Aiding 225
Wassila Ouerdane, Nicolas Maudet and Alexis Tsoukias

Domain Independent Goal Recognition 238
David Pattison and Derek Long

Maintaining Arc Consistency in Non-Binary Dynamic CSPs Using Simple Tabular Reduction 251
Matthieu Quéva, Christian W. Probst and Laurent Ricci

User-Based Collaborative Filtering: Sparsity and Performance 264
Jennifer Redpath, David H. Glass, Sally McClean and Luke Chen

Merging and Splitting for Power Indices in Weighted Voting Games and Network Flow Games on Hypergraphs 277
Anja Rey and Jörg Rothe

Cancer Classification Using SVM-Boosted Multiobjective Differential Fuzzy Clustering 290
Indrajit Saha, Ujjwal Maulik, Sanghamitra Bandyopadhyay and Dariusz Plewczynski

Performance Analysis of Class Noise Detection Algorithms 303
Borut Sluban, Dragan Gamberger and Nada Lavrač

Relational Graph Mining for Learning Events from Video 315
Muralikrishna Sridhar, Anthony G. Cohn and David C. Hogg

A Workbench for Anytime Reasoning by Ontology Approximation – With a Case Study on Instance Retrieval 328
Gaston Tagni, Stefan Schlobach, Annette ten Teije, Frank van Harmelen and Giorgios Karafotias

Obligationes as Formal Dialogue Systems 341
Sara L. Uckelman

On-Line ADL Recognition with Prior Knowledge 354
Jonas Ullberg, Silvia Coradeschi and Federico Pecora

Subject Index 367

Author Index 369

First-Order Multi-class Subgroup Discovery

Tarek ABUDAWOOD [1] and Peter FLACH [2]
Intelligent Systems Laboratory
University of Bristol [3]

Abstract. Subgroup discovery is concerned with finding subsets of a population whose class distribution is significantly different from the overall distribution. Previously subgroup discovery has been predominantly investigated under the propositional logic framework. This paper investigates multi-class subgroup discovery in an inductive logic programming setting, where subgroups are defined by conjunctions in first-order logic. We present a new weighted covering algorithm, inspired by the Aleph first-order rule learner, that uses seed examples in order to learn diverse, representative and highly predictive subgroups that capture interesting patterns across multiple classes. Our approach experimentally shows considerable and statistically significant improvement of predictive power, both in terms of accuracy and AUC, and theory construction time, by considering fewer hypotheses.

Keywords. Subgroup Discovery, Inductive Logic Programming, Machine Learning

1. Introduction

Rule induction is a common form of machine learning and data mining often used in classification and association rule learning. It can either be done in a propositional framework, where examples are represented by attribute-value pairs, or in the more expressive framework of first-order logic, where examples, rules and background knowledge are described by logical formulae, allowing the rule learner to deal with complexly structured data.

Classification rule learning is a predictive task aimed at constructing a set of rules that predict the class of future examples. On the other hand, association rule learning, e.g. Apriori [4], is a form of descriptive induction aimed at the discovery of individual rules that express interesting patterns in data. In classification rule learning a target concept is pre-defined and so the search heuristic is usually some form of accuracy. On the other hand, no target concept is given in descriptive rule learning and the search heuristic evaluates measures of interestingness and unusualness in the data, e.g., support and confidence. Subgroup discovery can be seen as being halfway between predictive and descriptive rule learning, as there is a target concept but the goal of subgroup discovery is

---

[1] E-mail: Dawood@cs.bris.ac.uk
[2] E-mail: Peter.Flach@bristol.ac.uk
[3] Address: Intelligent Systems Laboratory, Department of Computer Science, Faculty of Engineering, University of Bristol, Merchant Venturers Building, Woodland Road, BRISTOL BS8 1UB, United Kingdom

not necessarily to achieve high accuracy, but rather to find subsets of a population whose class distribution is significantly different from the overall distribution. In this way, the target concept helps us to achieve a trade-off between accuracy and interestingness.

In [15] this trade-off was achieved using weighted relative accuracy, but their propositional CN2-SD algorithm is restricted to two classes. The work of [1] extended the approach to more than two classes by introducing different multi-class search heuristics that take into account the distribution of all the involved classes. The induced multi-class subgroups were also shown to be highly predictive when used as features in a meta-level learner, resulting in considerably smaller models with comparative performance in terms of accuracy and area under ROC curve (AUC). Their work motivated us to investigate multi-class subgroup discovery in a first-order logic framework. Our main contribution is a new weighted covering algorithm that takes advantage of learning from seed examples inspired by Aleph first-order rule learner [21]. In a rigourous experimental evaluation we show that the use of seed examples leads to considerable and statistically significant improvement of predictive power, both in terms of accuracy (3 percent points on average over the data sets) and AUC (7 percent points).

The paper is structured as follows. Section 2 review some relevant work in subgroup discovery, propositional and first-order logic frameworks. In Section 3 we discuss the benefits of first-order multi-class subgroup discovery. Section 4 describes the ingredients of our Aleph-MSD++ algorithm. An empirical evaluation of multi-class subgroup discovery for feature construction over 11 data sets is presented in Section 5. Finally, we discuss possible future work and conclude the paper in Section 6.

2. Previous Work on Subgroup Discovery

Early work on propositional subgroup discovery included Klösgen's generic pattern discovery system Explora [13, 14], incorporating various search strategies (exhaustive or heuristic), refinement methods and evaluation measures for predictive as well as descriptive learning. PRIM [10] is another system that searches for subgroups by top-down specialisation followed by a bottom-up generalisation on the induced subgroups. PRIM exhaustively examines all possible solutions which makes it unsuitable for large data sets. More recent work includes the CN2-SD rule learner which learns two-class subgroups based on the CN2 inductive rule learner [6]. Where CN2 employed a covering algorithm, removing training examples as soon as they were covered by a rule, CN2-SD demonstrated the advantages of using a weighted covering algorithm, in which example weights were decreased according to the number of rules that covered them. The evaluation measure used was weighted relative accuracy (WRAcc), which compares the precision of a rule with the overall class distribution, weighted by the coverage. CN2-MSD [1] generalised the approach to multi-class subgroup discovery, theoretically and experimentally comparing a range of different subgroup evaluation measures.

Previous work on relational or first-order subgroup discovery includes MIDOS [22], which adapts an evaluation measure from Explora and uses it together with a minimal support criterion when evaluating subgroups. MIDOS uses sampling to estimate these evaluation measures in order to reduce the computational cost of querying multiple tables. Another subgroup discovery study in a relational setting has been conducted in [16]. Their RSD system extracts propositionalised first-order features from a given domain and discovers subgroups amongst them where the binary WRAcc search heuristic and the weighted covering algorithm were used as in CN2-SD. In such a two-stage approach, the quality of the subgroups depends on the quality of the features constructed at the first stage, but RSD constructs these in a non-heuristic manner. In this paper we induce subgroups directly from multi-class relational data and we show that the induced subgroups have higher predictive performance when compared to classification approaches.

3. Benefits of First-Order Multi-class Subgroup Discovery

We argue that the key difference between the induction process in classification systems and subgroup discovery systems lies in the search heuristics. In classification tasks, accuracy-based heuristics are typically employed because the ultimate goal is to have models that achieve high predictive accuracy. However, in subgroup discovery a trade-off between accuracy and interestingness is to be achieved. A single subgroup can cover examples from several classes whereas the conventional classification rules try to avoid covering examples from several classes which could lead to overfitting the training model.

Most ILP induction systems use binary evaluation measures that evaluates the class of the rule being learned against one or more other classes. If the problem consists of two classes only, then it is sufficient to induce rules for the positive class only while a default rule is assigned for the negative class. However, there is a difficulty in dealing with multi-class problems and previous research [9, 11, 12, 19] has investigated methods of multi-class classification that usually decompose a multi-class problem into several binary problems either by considering all pairwise combinations of classes (one-vs-one) or considering each class against the union of the other classes (one-vs-rest). The same approach is typically applied in ILP where the rules of the final model are, in practice, a combination of multiple binary models that sometimes can be obtained by applying the induction process on each one of those binarised problems individually.

The search heuristics of the Multi-class subgroup discovery, Definition 3.1, take the distribution of all classes into account when evaluating a subgroup clause during the induction process and does not evaluate a discovered subgroup in a multi-class problem as in a two-class problem. Unlike classification models, a subgroup discovery model comprises headless rules which can be regarded as boolean features representing interesting and statistically unusual patterns. In propositional subgroup discovery such features can be seen as a transformation of the original propositional feature space into a new propositional complex feature space. However, in first-order subgroup discovery the transformation is done from a complex relational feature space into a new propositional complex feature space.

Definition 3.1 (Multi-class Subgroup Discovery). *A multi-class subgroup discovery task can be defined as a process of finding interesting patterns, called* subgroups, *describing subsets of the population such that they are sufficiently large and statistically unusual w.r.t. the distribution of all classes.*

The advantages of multi-class subgroup discovery in first-order logic may outperform its advantages in propositional logic and could be much more desirable. This is because the multi-class relational data can be very large and complex, and the needs for techniques to extract interesting and significant features across all relations and over all the classes is indeed crucial. The results of such approach can also produce simple symbolic representation of a complex relational problem and that would make it easier to understand and interpret.

We argue that subgroups can be used to form a classification model when used as binary features for a meta-level learner providing that the subgroups cover sufficient amount of the population and identify a variety of significant features. As a result of using subgroup discovery heuristics and the weighted covering algorithm, the resulting subgroups tend to overlap considerably. If a classification model is desired, we propose the use of decision tree as a meta-level learner as it has the ability, following divide-and-conquer paradigm, to make the best use of the information hidden between the subgroup features and construct a predictive decision tree with leaves representing all possible overlapping and non-overlapping regions across all the binary subgroup features as will be seen in Section 5.

One would expect the presence of overlaps is limited when using classification heuristics together with the covering algorithm. This is because a set of independent rules are derived for each class and also training examples covered by newly induced rules are removed immediately before the induction progresses. Still a subsequent rule may cover some of the removed examples in practice. In theory, if classification rules are used as features for a decision tree meta-level learner, this would result in a smaller tree than a tree of subgroups features applied to the same problem.

4. First-Order Multi-class Subgroup Discovery with Aleph-MSD++

In this section we describe our main contribution, the Aleph-MSD++ first-order multi-class subgroup discovery algorithm. Just as CN2-SD and CN2-MSD were derived from an existing propositional rule learner, we started from an existing inductive logic programming (ILP) learning system. There are many ILP systems, including FOIL [20], PROGOL [17] and GOLEM [18]; they are mostly restricted to binary classification. The starting point for our study was Aleph, a Prolog-based inductive logic programming rule learner that induces first-order classification rule models. Aleph is similar to PROGOL but incorporates additional search strategies and some extra options.

A classification rule in first-order logic is normally represented by a clause consisting of a head literal assigning the class and a body consisting of a conjunction of literals. A subgroup does not assign a class, and hence can be alternatively seen as a conjunction of literals, a headless rule, or a query.

4.1. From Aleph to Aleph-MSD++

Aleph conducts general-to-specific search in the θ-subsumption lattice of a single clause hypothesis. It restricts the search by first computing the Most-Specific-Clause (MSC) or bottom-clause from a single seed example. This technique bounds the search space from below. The mode declarations determine which atoms can be used as body literals when constructing the hypothesis clause.

More specifically, learning a single clause starts by picking a single uncovered seed example and generating its MSC. Next, the generalisation step begins from the empty clause guided by a heuristic function and restricted to literals from the MSC and the mode declarations. A typical search heuristic in `Aleph` is the *Compression* that maximises the positive coverage and minimises the negative coverage and the number of literals in a hypothesis clause when refining the hypothesis lattice. The search for a clause stops if the heuristic evaluation score could not be improved further. Each time a search for a clause is done, several clauses are considered and the clause with the highest evaluation score is accepted for the final theory. Once a new clause is accepted, all examples it covers are removed from the training examples due to the use of the covering algorithm. The learning proceeds by picking a new seed example from the remaining training examples and the same procedure is applied until no training examples are left or no clauses can be induced for the remaining training examples.

We present a new algorithm which extends `Aleph` in a number of ways: by incorporating multi-class subgroup discovery search heuristics; by using a novel weighted covering algorithm; by implementing a significance test to be applied on nominated subgroups; as well as some other, smaller modifications. These extensions are discussed in the following sections.

4.2. An Improved Weighted Covering Algorithm

Most ILP induction systems implement the covering algorithm in the induction process where every time a new rule is induced, the training examples covered by this rule are removed from the training set and the induction as well as the statistical evaluation of new rules is restricted to the remaining training examples. This approach clearly biases the rules induced later in the induction process due to the limitation of examples and background information available with the remaining training examples. The weighted covering algorithm comes as a suitable remedy to this problem. In weighted covering, each example is assigned initial weight, typically a value of 1, and that weight gets reduced every time the example is covered by a new induced rule. Weighted covering was introduced to subgroup discovery in [15].

The weight is decreased according to one of the following two schemata: additive or multiplicative. Let $w_t(x)$ denote the weight of example x after being covered by t number of rules: with respect to the additive weight method we have $w_t(x) = \frac{1}{1+t}$ while in the multiplicative method $w_t(x) = \gamma^t, 0 \leq \gamma \leq 1$. Two special cases are worth noting. If $\gamma = 0$ then this is equivalent to the use of covering algorithm where the examples are removed from training once new induced rule covers them. In contrast, if $\gamma = 1$ then no change happens to the weights of the covered examples which means that all the training examples are kept.

Similarly to `CN2-SD` and `CN2-MSD`, the weights of all the examples covered by a newly induced subgroup rule in `Aleph-MSD` is decreased according to the chosen weighting schema when applying the weighted covering algorithm. In `Aleph-MSD++`, on the other hand, *only the weights of examples matching the class of the selected seed example are decreased*. Restricting the weight reduction in `Aleph-MSD++` is a crucial point in our paper. It ensures that we can learn diverse subgroups representing examples from all the different classes. The importance of this issue is magnified when encountering class imbalance since the minority classes may get ignored during the discovery process.

The advantages conveyed by seed examples are not available when using `CN2`-based classifiers. We will demonstrate these advantages by comparing the new weighted covering algorithm `Aleph-MSD++` against a `CN2`-like version called `Aleph-MSD`. In the latter algorithm, the weights of *all* training examples covered by a newly induced clause are reduced – not just the ones from the same class as the seed example. The experimental results in Section 5 show that the `CN2`-like approach leads to subgroups that are no more predictive than the rules learned by `Aleph`. In contrast, the use of seed examples in `Aleph-MSD++` leads to considerable and statistically significant improvement of predictive power, both in terms of accuracy (3 percent points on average over the data sets) and AUC (7 percent points).

4.3. Multi-class Subgroup Discovery Search Heuristics

We employed four of the six evaluation methods for subgroup discovery proposed in [1].[4] Let T be a training set of examples labeled by n classes $C_1, \ldots, C_n$. We denote the total number of examples in the training set by E and the number of examples belonging to class C_i by E_i. The number of examples in T covered by a subgroup b is denoted by e, and the number of examples belonging to C_i and covered by b is denoted by e_i.

Definition 4.1 (Weighted Multi-class WRAcc). *The weighted multi-class weighted relative accuracy score of a subgroup b is defined as* $WMWRAcc(b) = \frac{1}{E^3} \sum_{i=1}^{n} E_i |e_i E - eE_i|$.

Definition 4.2 (Mutual Information). *The mutual information score of a subgroup b is defined as* $MI(b) = \sum_{i=1}^{n} \left(\frac{e_i}{E} \log \frac{e_i}{E} + \frac{E_i - e_i}{E} \log \frac{E_i - e_i}{E} \right) - \sum_{i=1}^{n} \frac{E_i}{E} \log \frac{E_i}{E} - \frac{e}{E} \log \frac{e}{E} - \frac{E-e}{E} \log \frac{E-e}{E}$

Definition 4.3 (Gini-split). *The Gini-split score of a subgroup b is defined as* $GS(b) = \frac{1}{nE^2} \sum_{i=1}^{n} \frac{[eE_i - e_i E]^2}{e(E-e)}$

Definition 4.4 (Chi-Squared). *The Chi-squared score of a subgroup b is defined as* $Chi^2(b) = \sum_{i=1}^{n} \frac{[e_i E - eE_i]^2}{eE_i(E-e)}$

These measures are adapted to take advantage of example weights in the obvious way: e.g., e_i is the total weight of examples of class C_i covered by the subgroup.

4.4. Other Improvements

Other improvements to `Aleph` implemented in `Aleph-MSD++` are:

Selecting Seed Examples To emphasise learning subgroups from various examples and classes, the selection of seed examples is done randomly but only on examples that have never been considered as seed examples before, and that have never been covered by any subgroup induced from a seed example of the same class.

Significance Testing In order to reduce the number of subgroups during the learning and maintaining high quality subgroups at the same time, we apply Chi^2 significance testing at significance level $p = 0.95$. This is important especially when using a weighted covering algorithm since the number of subgroups can be large

---

[4] The remaining two were variants of WRAcc that performed equally well or worse in our experiments.

as the examples covered by previously induced subgroups do not get removed. [5] suggested the use of significance testing to reduce the number of induced rules in their `CN2` rule learning system, and it was used in `CN2-SD` for the same reason.

Rule Construction `Aleph-MSD++` rules are constructed based on a heuristic search of combination of literals appear in the MSC as in `Aleph`. Despite the use of new seed examples in every iteration of the induction process, the same rule can be induced several times due to the use of the weighted covering algorithm; therefore, `Aleph-MSD++` algorithm checks whether the new rule is not θ-subsumed by a previously induced rules before accepting it.

Stopping Criteria The learning is terminated according to one of the following conditions: if all examples were covered at least once or if all the remaining uncovered training examples were considered as seed examples even if none of the induced subgroups cover them. This is an advantage over [15] and [1] in the sense that there are no minimum evaluation thresholds imposed in `Aleph-MSD++`; instead, we ensure that all the examples are at least considered as seed examples in case that they do not get covered by any induced subgroup generated from a seed example of the same class.

Pseudo-code for the `Aleph-MSD++` algorithm is given as Algorithm 4.4. We only show the Pseudo-code for `Aleph-MSD++` due to the space limitation but we would like to emphasise that `Aleph-MSD` is our genuine algorithm as well.

5. Empirical Evaluation

In this section we study the behaviour of the proposed subgroup discovery algorithm and examine its usefulness for feature generation in a classification context. We used the 11 data sets listed in Table 1 with our implementation of `Aleph-MSD++` and also its variant `Aleph-MSD` where the latter uses the standard weighted covering algorithm.

Name	Class distribution	Name	Class distribution
Alzheimer-Amine	1026, 343	Diterpene	447, 355, 352, 155, 71
Alzheimer-Choline	1026, 343	English	50, 50, 50
Alzheimer-Scopolamine	1026, 343	Mutagenesis	125, 63
Alzheimer-Toxic	1026, 343	Protein	116, 115, 77, 73
Car	1210, 384, 69, 65	Ecoli	143, 77, 52
Scale	288, 288, 49		

Table 1. Data sets used in the experiments. The first group are first-order data sets (obtained from various sources), the second group are propositional (obtained from UCI [8] repository).

For the purpose of evaluating the quality and utility of the induced first-order subgroup rules, we used them as boolean features and applied a decision tree learner (J48, the Weka implementation of C4.5). We also used the classification rules induced by standard `Aleph` using the Compression search heuristic as features for J48 in order to compare the performance and behaviour of subgroup discovery methods against a typical classification method.

We evaluated the performance of `Aleph-MSD++` using the four search heuristics from Section 4.3 and the following six settings of the weighted covering algorithm:

Algorithm 1 Aleph-MSD++

Require: *X* (Examples), *BK* (Background Knowledge), *MD* (Mode Declarations) and *WSat* (Weight Setting);
1: let seed examples $X_{seed} = X$;
2: let subgroup rules $SR = \{\}$;
3: let weights W be initialised to 1;
4: **while** $X_{seed} \neq \{\}$ and $\exists w_i \in W : w_i = 1.0$ **do**
5:    let $x_i = select\_example\_randomly(X_{seed})$;
6:    let $MSC = construct\_MSC(x_i, BK, MD)$;
7:    let rule $r = \{\}$ and score $s = -\infty$;
8:    **while** search limit not exceeded **do**
9:       $r^{new} = construct\_subgroup\_rule(MSC, MD)$;
10:      ensure $\forall sr \in SR$, sr does not θ-subsume r^{new};
11:      $[X_{covered}, s^{new}] = evaluate(r^{new}, X, BK, W)$;
12:      **if** $significant(r^{new})$ and $s^{new} > s$ **then**
13:        $r = r^{new}$ and $s = s^{new}$;
14:      **end if**
15:    **end while**
16:    **if** $r \neq \{\}$ **then**
17:      $SR = SR \cup \{r\}$;
18:      **for all** $x_j \in X_{covered}$ such that $class(x_j) = class(x_i)$ **do**
19:        $w_j = recompute\_weight(w_j, WSat)$;
20:        $X_{seed} = X_{seed} \setminus \{x_j\}$;
21:      **end for**
22:    **else**
23:      $X_{seed} = X_{seed} \setminus \{x_i\}$;
24:    **end if**
25: **end while**
   Output Subgroup Rules *SR*;

- setting 0: unweighted covering algorithm, $\gamma = 0.00$;
- setting 1: multiplicative weights, $\gamma = 0.25$;
- setting 2: multiplicative weights, $\gamma = 0.50$;
- setting 3: multiplicative weights, $\gamma = 0.75$;
- setting 4: multiplicative weights, $\gamma = 1.00$ (no weight reduction);
- setting 5: additive weights.

For each data set, cross-validated results were recorded for various aspects (accuracy, AUC, size of decision tree, number of leaves, number of induced first-order clauses, number of considered first-order clauses and average size of a induced first-order clauses). Since averaging across data sets has limited meaning as the values may not be commensurate, for each performance aspect we report the average values as well as its average rank (1 is best, 6 is worst). We use the Friedman Test (FT) on these average ranks at $p = 0.10$ with Bonferroni-Dunn post-hoc test to check significance against Compression method as a control learner. The FT records wins and losses in the form of ranks ignoring the magnitude of these wins and losses. FT is considered to be more appropriate when comparing multiple classifiers on multiple data sets. The reader is referred to [7] for more details about the Friedman Test.

5.1. Results and Discussion

Tables 2 and 3 shows the average accuracies and AUCs for `Aleph-MSD` and `Aleph-MSD++` algorithm respectively against the control learner (Compression) when applying J48 on the subgroups and classification rules. Regarding to all the weighted covering algorithm settings (setting 1-5), subgroup discovery methods in `Aleph-MSD++` show higher accuracies and significantly better AUCs when compared against Compression (control learner). On the other hand, the same methods reported significantly worse accuracy and comparative AUCs to Compression in `Aleph-MSD`. It is clear that the use of the new weighted covering (in `Aleph-MSD++`) outperforms the standard weighted covering (in `Aleph-MSD`) with regards to both performance aspects.

setting	algorithm	WMWRAcc	MI	Chi^2	GS	Comp
$\gamma = 0.00$	Standard Covering	76.99 (3.86)	77.74 (2.77)	77.38 (3.14)	77.49 (2.73)	**77.76 (2.50)**
$\gamma = 0.25$	Aleph-MSD++	80.07 (3.18)	79.66 (2.68)	79.77 (3.27)	**79.97 (2.64)**	77.76 (3.23)
	Aleph-MSD	76.03 (3.45)	74.80 (4.18)	76.46 (2.82)	**77.79 (2.27)**	**77.76 (2.27)**
$\gamma = 0.50$	Aleph-MSD++	80.50 (3.05)	80.52 (2.64)	80.48 (2.91)	**80.45 (2.55)**	77.76 (3.86)
	Aleph-MSD	75.87 (3.00)	75.69 (3.41)	76.69 (2.73)	75.71 (3.18)	**77.76 (2.68)**
$\gamma = 0.75$	Aleph-MSD++	80.66 (2.95)	80.95 (2.68)	80.85 (2.86)	**80.75 (2.41)**	77.76 (4.09)
	Aleph-MSD	74.73 (3.68)	75.28 (2.91)	75.43 (3.05)	76.71 (3.00)	**77.76 (2.36)**
$\gamma = 1.00$	Aleph-MSD++/MSD	79.71 (2.91)	**79.73 (2.77)**	**79.84 (2.77)**	79.78 (3.05)	77.76 (3.50)
additive	Aleph-MSD++	80.62 (2.95)	80.32 (2.91)	80.75 (2.68)	**80.62 (2.55)**	77.76 (3.91)
	Aleph-MSD	74.53 (4.18)	76.90 (2.41)	76.13 (3.00)	76.36 (3.05)	**77.76 (2.36)**

Table 2. Comparison of average accuracies (ranks in brackets) when using subgroups of `Aleph-MSD++` and `Aleph-MSD` (columns 3-6) against classification rules (column 7) as features for J48.

setting	algorithm	WMWRAcc	MI	Chi^2	GS	Comp
$\gamma = 0.00$	Standard Covering	0.80 (3.32)	0.81 (2.91)	0.81 (3.14)	**0.81 (2.68)**	0.79 (2.95)
$\gamma = 0.25$	Aleph-MSD++	0.85 (2.82)	0.84 (2.91)	0.84 (2.91)	**0.85 (2.55)**	0.79 (3.82)
	Aleph-MSD	0.80 (3.55)	0.79 (3.82)	**0.81 (2.55)**	**0.81 (2.55)**	**0.79 (2.55)**
$\gamma = 0.50$	Aleph-MSD++	0.86 (2.64)	0.85 (3.55)	**0.86 (1.82)**	0.86 (2.27)	0.79 (4.73)
	Aleph-MSD	0.79 (3.41)	**0.80 (2.64)**	0.80 (2.91)	0.79 (3.32)	0.79 (2.73)
$\gamma = 0.75$	Aleph-MSD++	0.86 (2.64)	**0.86 (2.50)**	0.86 (2.73)	0.86 (2.77)	0.79 (4.36)
	Aleph-MSD	0.80 (3.23)	0.80 (2.86)	0.80 (3.27)	**0.80 (2.82)**	**0.79 (2.82)**
$\gamma = 1.00$	Aleph-MSD++/MSD	0.85 (2.95)	**0.85 (2.59)**	0.85 (2.77)	0.85 (2.77)	0.79 (3.91)
additive	Aleph-MSD++	**0.86 (2.55)**	0.86 (2.73)	**0.86 (2.55)**	**0.86 (2.55)**	0.79 (4.64)
	Aleph-MSD	0.79 (4.09)	**0.81 (2.55)**	0.80 (2.82)	0.80 (2.73)	0.79 (2.82)

Table 3. Comparison of average AUCs (ranks in brackets) when using subgroups of `Aleph-MSD++` and `Aleph-MSD` (columns 3-6) against classification rules (column 7) as features for J48.

A graphical illustration of the post-hoc test results on accuracy and AUC of the `Aleph-MSD++`'s subgroup discovery methods and the control methods is given in Figure 1. For each weight setting the corresponding critical difference diagram is shown vertically (the lower the rank the higher the performance). The figure indicates a supe-

setting	WMWRAcc	MI	Chi^2	GS	Comp
$\gamma = 0.00$	27.91 (3.05)	21.20 (2.91)	27.58 (2.68)	**27.51 (2.59)**	31.69 (3.77)
$\gamma = 0.25$	34.60 (3.41)	**32.91 (2.36)**	33.13 (2.73)	34.84 (3.32)	31.69 (3.18)
$\gamma = 0.50$	39.98 (3.00)	41.44 (2.77)	41.62 (3.45)	41.16 (3.50)	**31.69 (2.27)**
$\gamma = 0.75$	42.56 (3.05)	45.56 (3.55)	45.07 (3.68)	41.76 (2.64)	**31.69 (2.09)**
$\gamma = 1.00$	44.91 (3.50)	42.51 (3.50)	43.20 (2.86)	42.95 (2.95)	**31.69 (2.18)**
additive	40.53 (2.86)	42.22 (3.27)	42.09 (3.32)	40.73 (3.18)	**31.69 (2.36)**

Table 4. Average tree size (ranks in brackets) when using `Aleph-MSD++`'s subgroups (columns 2-5) and classification rules (column 6) as features for J48.

setting	WMWRAcc	MI	Chi^2	GS	Comp
$\gamma = 0.00$	**42,056 (1.86)**	42,538 (2.45)	50,896 (3.32)	50,940 (3.14)	138,949 (4.23)
$\gamma = 0.25$	**40,713 (2.55)**	49,782 (3.27)	**43,048 (2.55)**	41,162 (2.64)	138,949 (4.00)
$\gamma = 0.50$	**32,661 (1.91)**	34,144 (2.64)	35,103 (2.82)	34,299 (3.55)	138,949 (4.09)
$\gamma = 0.75$	**30,721 (1.09)**	33,009 (3.55)	32,457 (2.91)	33,272 (3.09)	138,949 (4.36)
$\gamma = 1.00$	**33,242 (1.77)**	31,163 (3.00)	33,460 (2.95)	33,466 (3.05)	138,949 (4.23)
additive	**32,385 (1.91)**	32,908 (2.82)	33,576 (3.36)	33,387 (2.55)	138,949 (4.36)

Table 5. Average number of considered first-order subgroups in `Aleph-MSD++` and classification rules (Comp) in `Aleph`.

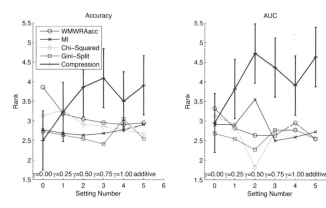

Figure 1. Average ranks achieved by `Aleph-MSD++` with regard to accuracy and AUC (lower is better), using different search heuristics over 11 data sets. The left-most setting is the default covering algorithm, while the other settings use different variants of weighted covering. Vertical lines show the critical difference with the control method (Compression): differences outside the critical difference are statistically significant.

riority of subgroup discovery methods over Compression in almost all weighted covering algorithm settings. This demonstrates the high quality of the subgroups induced in `Aleph-MSD++`. *GS* achieves the best accuracy in all weighted covering settings except setting 4 ($\gamma = 1$) where the weights of covered training examples are not decreased. A striking result on AUC is reported for Chi^2 in setting 2 ($\gamma = 0.5$).

It deserves to be mentioned that not removing the covered examples nor reducing their weights (setting 4) still achieves better accuracy and significantly better AUC than the control.

Apart from the predictive performance, `Aleph-MSD++` in general considers 3 to 4 times fewer hypotheses (Table 5) which contributes to faster building of a clausal theory (with 30 percent fewer number of clauses and 4 times higher coverage on average, results not reported here) when compared against the control method. Among all, the WMWRAcc method was fastest and produced the smallest number of clauses in its models.

The subgroups tend to produce about 25% larger trees, Table 4, when used as features for J48 meta-level learner. This is because the subgroups are highly overlapping due to the use of weighted coverage, and J48 exploits these overlaps to produce superior predictive performance. We should note that the statistical significance of the subgroups, their diversity, high coverage and the overlaps amongst them have all contributed to this significant findings.

6. Conclusion and Future Work

In our previous work [1] we investigated multi-class subgroup discovery in propositional logic framework. In this paper we investigate multi-class subgroup discovery in the inductive logic programming framework, where the induced subgroups are defined by conjunctions in first-order logic. We presented a novel algorithm, `Aleph-MSD++`, implementing a new weighted covering algorithm based on learning from seed examples and over multi-class domains. One major observation is that example-driven approach in ILP appears to be more suitable for subgroup discovery task than feature-driven approach in propositional learning as the former not only employs a better strategic and structural search mechanisms but also gives a chance to learn subgroups over all examples of all classes even when classes are imbalanced.

We demonstrated the usefulness and the high quality of the subgroups produced by `Aleph-MSD++` algorithm and compared it with the standard covering algorithm and also classification rules when used as features for a decision tree learner (J48). At a small increase in the size of the decision tree, we showed that our algorithm is four times faster and produces more accurate predictions in both performance aspects (accuracy and AUC). If one is to maximise the accuracy, it is recommended to use the combination of setting 2 ($\gamma = 0.5$) and *Chi*^{2} heuristic in `Aleph-MSD++` while *GS* is preferred when the AUC is to be maximised though it is very close to the other multi-class subgroup discovery heuristics.

In the future we intend to investigate probabilistic multi-class subgroup discovery in both propositional logic and first-order logic. We also would like to exploit more subgroup discovery search heuristics and enhance the discovery of subgroups.

References

[1] Tarek Abudawood and Peter Flach. Evaluation Measures for Multi-class Subgroup Discovery. In *The European Conference on Machine Learning and Principles and Practice of Knowledge Discovery in Databases (ECML PKDD'09)*, pages 35–50. Springer-Verlag Berlin Heidelberg, September 2009.

[2] Tarek Abudawood and Peter Flach. Learning Multi-class Theories in ILP. In *The 20th International Conference on Inductive Logic Programming (ILP'10)*. Springer, 2010.

[3] Tarek Abudawood and Peter Flach. The Advantages of Seed Examples in First-Order Multi-class Subgroup Discovery. In *The 19th European Conference on Artificial Intelligence (ECAI'10)*, pages 1113–1114. IOS Press, August 2010.

[4] Rakesh Agrawal and Ramakrishnan Srikant. Fast Algorithms for Mining Association Rules. In *In Proceedings of the 20th International Conference on Very Large Data Bases*, pages 487–499, 1994.
[5] Peter Clark and Robin Boswell. Rule Induction with CN2: Some Recent Improvements. In *Proc. 5th European Conference on Machine Learning*, volume 482 of *LNAI*, pages 151–163. Springer, 1991.
[6] Peter Clark and Tim Niblett. The CN2 Induction Algorithm. *Machine Learning*, 3:261–283, 1989.
[7] Janez Demšar. Statistical Comparisons of Classifiers Over Multiple Data Sets. *Journal of Machine Learning Research*, 7:1–30, 2006.
[8] A. Frank and A. Asuncion. UCI machine learning repository, 2010.
[9] Jerome H. Friedman. Another approach to polychotomous classification. Technical report, Stanford University, Department of Statistics, 1996.
[10] Jerome H. Friedman and Nicholas I. Fisher. Bump Hunting in High-dimensional Data. *Statistics and Computing*, 9:123–143, 1999.
[11] Chih-Wei Hsu and Chih-Jen Lin. A comparison of methods for multiclass support vector machines. *Neural Networks*, 13:415–425, March 2002.
[12] Boonserm Kijsirikul, Nitiwut Ussivakul, and Surapant Meknavin. Adaptive Directed Acyclic Graphs for Multiclass Classification. In *The 7th Pacific Rim International Conference on Artificial Intelligence: Trends in Artificial Intelligence*, volume LNAI 2417, pages 158–168. Springer, 2002.
[13] Willi Klösgen. Subgroup discovery. In Willi Klösgen and Jan M. Zytkow, editors, *Handbook of Data Mining and Knowledge Discovery*, pages 354–361. Oxford University Press, June 2002.
[14] Willi Klösgen. Explora: A Multipattern and Multistrategy Discovery Assistant. In Usama M. Fayyad, Gregory Piatetsky-Shapiro, Padhraic Smyth, and Ramasamy Uthurusamy, editors, *Advances in Knowledge Discovery and Data Mining*, pages 249–271. MIT Press, 2004.
[15] Nada Lavrač, Branko Kavšek, Peter Flach, and Ljupco Todorovski. Subgroup Discovery with CN2-SD. *Journal of Machine Learning Research*, 5:153–188, 2004.
[16] Nada Lavrač, Filip Zelezny, and Peter Flach. RSD: Relational Subgroup Discovery Through First-order Feature Construction. In *In 12th International Conference on Inductive Logic Programming*, pages 149–165. Springer, 2002.
[17] Stephen Muggleton. Inverse Entailment and Progol. In *Proceedings of the Sixth International Workshop on Inductive Logic programming*, volume 13, pages 245–286. Springer, 1995.
[18] Stephen Muggleton and Cao Feng. Efficient Induction Of Logic Programs. In *New Generation Computing*. Academic Press, 1990.
[19] John C. Platt and Nello Cristianini. Large margin DAGs for multiclass classification. In *Advance in Neural Information Processing Systems*, volume 12. MIT Press, 2000.
[20] J. R. Quinlan and R. M. Cameron-Jones. FOIL: A Midterm Report. In *In Proceedings of the European Conference on Machine Learning*, pages 3–20. Springer-Verlag, 1993.
[21] Ashwin Srinivasan. The Aleph Manual. Technical report, University of Oxford, 2001.
[22] Stefan Wrobel. An Algorithm for Multi-Relational Discovery of Subgroups. In *Principles of Data Mining and Knowledge Discovery (PKDD'97)*, pages 78 – 87. Springer Verlag Berlin, 1997.

Improving the efficiency of ontology engineering by introducing prototypicality

Xavier AIMÉ [a], Frédéric FÜRST [b], Pascale KUNTZ [c] and Francky TRICHET [c]

[a] *LINA, University of Nantes & Tennaxia, France, xaime@tennaxia.com*
[b] *MIS, University of Picardie, France, frederic.furst@u-picardie.fr*
[c] *LINA, University of Nantes, France, pascale.kuntz,francky.trichet@univ-nantes.fr*

Abstract. This paper introduces the notion of prototypicality in Ontology Engineering. Three kinds of prototypicality are considered: a concept can be more or less representative of its super-concept (conceptual prototypicality); a term can be more or less associated to a concept (lexical prototypicality); an instance can be more or less representative of its concept (instance prototypicality). Prototypicalities are modeled as order relations which allow to modulate links between concepts, terms and instances within an ontology. To calculate prototypicality gradients used to quantify these orders, we advocate a specific method which is based on all the components of an ontology (i.e. concepts, properties and instances) and a corpus. This paper also underlines the relevance of prototypicality for improving the efficiency of Ontology Engineering processes, in particular Ontology Personalization and Semantic-based Information Retrieval.

Keywords. Ontology, Prototypicality, Personalization, Semiotic

Introduction

Currently, a lot of Information Systems exploit ontologies which are defined as conceptual representations of knowledge related to a given field and are built according to a consensus shared by the members of an ingroup[1]. Classically, an ontology is composed of ordered sets of concepts and properties[2]. But such an ontology does not capture all the knowledge the members of the ingroup have on the domain. In particular, it does not specify how a concept is representative of its upper concept. Nevertheless, this notion, called *prototypicality* in cognitive psychology, underlies all conceptual categorisation [10,4]. For example, parrots, sparrows and chicken are all considered as birds, but the concept of sparrow is more close to the concept of bird than those of parrot and chicken (at least for european people). In other words, thinking to a bird leads more to think to a sparrow than to a parrot or a chicken.

We propose to introduce this notion in ontology, as a supplementary knowledge layer above existing models. We introduce prototypicalities between two concepts hierarchically linked (directly or not), but also between concepts and their terms, and between

---

[1] The term *ingroup* comes from sociology. We use it to denote the set of individuals who share the conceptualisation expressed in the ontology O, and not only the set of individuals who have built O.
[2] We call property both concept attributes and binary relations between concepts.

concepts and their instances. In practice, prototypicalities are represented by weights added on the links defined between the considered elements (*isa* links between concepts, *instanciation* links between concepts and instances, *namming* links between concepts and terms). To perform the calculation of these weights, we have defined semi-automatic and automatic methods which are based on (1) the semantics expressed in the ontology, (2) a textual corpus of the domain which is considered and (3) a population of concept instances. Our work falls within the scope of the semiotic approach of Knowledge Engineering, which takes the three dimensions of knowledge [6,7] (*i.e.* intensional, extensional and expressional dimension) into account.

Various applications of prototypicality can be considered in Ontology Engineering and Knowledge-Based Systems (KBS). The main issues we focus on are KBS personalization and information retrieval, mainly in the context of industrial projects.

The rest of this paper is structured as follows. Section 2 introduces the model we advocate to equip ontology with prototypicality. Each type of prototypicality (*i.e.* conceptual, lexical and instance prototypicalitty) is associated with a specific gradient and the method used to compute it. This section also presents how an emotional state can be used to modulate the gradients. Section 3 describes how prototypicality can be used to refine information retrieval and KBS personalization. Section 4 shows the results of two experiments respectively dedicated to environment legal intelligence and environment policy.

1. Introducing prototypicality in ontology

To formalize the notion of prototypicality, we consider an ontology O (related to a domain D and an ingroup G) as a tuple:

$$O_{(D,G)} = \{\mathcal{C}, \mathcal{P}, \mathcal{I}, \leq^C, \leq^P, dom, codom, \sigma, L\} \text{ where}$$

- $\mathcal{C}, \mathcal{P}$ et $\mathcal{I}$ are respectively the sets of concepts, properties and instances;
- $\leq^C$: $\mathcal{C} \times \mathcal{C}$ et $\leq^P$: $\mathcal{P} \times \mathcal{P}$ are partial orders which organize the hierarchies of concepts and properties[3];
- $dom : \mathcal{P} \to \mathcal{C}$ and $codom : \mathcal{P} \to (\mathcal{C} \cup Datatypes)$ associates to each property its domain and co-domain;
- $\sigma : \mathcal{C} \to \wp(\mathcal{I})$ associates to each concept its instances;
- $L = \{L_C \cup L_P \cup L_I, term_c, term_p, term_i\}$ is the vocabulary of the language used by G to speak about the domain D, where L_C, L_P and L_I are the sets of terms associated to $\mathcal{C}$, $\mathcal{P}$ and $\mathcal{I}$, and where $term_c : \mathcal{C} \to \wp(L_C)$, $term_p : \mathcal{P} \to \wp(L_P)$ and $term_i : \mathcal{I} \to \wp(L_I)$ are the fonctions which associate to each concept, property or instance the terms used to denote them.

We introduce the prototypicality by weighting the different kinds of links of the ontology. These weights form numerical gradients which express two kinds of prototypicality:

- **conceptual prototypicality** defined on links $\leq^C$: two concepts, with one inherits from the other, can be more or less close together. More precisely, in a sibship of

---

[3]$c_1 \leq^C c_2$ means that the concept c_2 is subsuming the concept c_1.

concepts, some of them are more prototypical of their father than the others. For example, among all plane types, the most representative, about which we tend to think when we think to the concept of plane, is rather a modern and commercial plane, and not the first biplane or a plane propeled by muscular strength.
- **lexical prototypicality** defined on links $term_c$ and $term_p$: for a given concept (or a property) with several terms used to name it, some terms are most often used than the others. For example, *plane* is rather used than *aeroplane* or *heavier-than-air*.

1.1. Conceptual prototypicality gradient

From a semiotic perspective, the conceptual prototypicality gradient, that we call *Semiotic-Based Conceptual Prototypicality Gradient* (SPG), is composed of three components: (1) an **intensional component**, based on the comparison between the concept intensions (*i.e* the properties of concepts), (2) an **extensional component**, based on the comparison between concept instances and (3) an **expressional component**, based on the comparison between concept terms which appears in a corpus. The calculation of the extensional component requires a set of concept instances, which must be representative of the cognitive universe of the ingroup. The calculation of the expressional component requires a corpus of documents representative of the cognitive universe of the ingroup. And the calculation of the intensional component requires that properties exist in the ontology.

Moreover, the intensional component can be refined by weighting links between properties and concepts: these weights express, for each concept and each property, the significance of the property in the definition of the concept. At present, these weights have to be specified manually. For each property, all the concepts which own the property have to be ordered on the interval [0,1]. For example, for the property *has_author*, the concept *Scientific article* will be placed first (close to 1), the concept *Press article* will be placed after (because to have an author is less important for this concept) and the concept *Instructions leaflet* will be placed close to 0.

Of course, all these resources (instances, corpus, property weights) are not always available, but the method we propose to calculate prototypicalities remains valid whatever resources we have. For example, if there is no instance, only the intensional and expressional components are calculated. If the ontology is the only available resource, with no instance, no weight on properties and no corpus, only the intensional component is calculated, with all the weights equal to 1.

Then, the model we advocate allows to weight each component of the SPG, in order to take the domination of the intensional, extensional and/or expressional aspects in the conceptualisation of the domain into account. These dominations are conditioned by the domain, the ingroup and the applicative context. For example, in the field of mathematics, the intensional aspect prevails. In the domain of biological species, a biologist builds its conceptualisation on biological properties (the intensional aspect prevails), but most of people usually use extensional conceptualisations, based on the animals encountered during their lifes.

Formally speaking, the SPG is a function $spg : \mathcal{C} \times \mathcal{C} \to [0, 1]$ that, to each pair of concepts $(c, c_f) \in \mathcal{C} \times \mathcal{C}$ such that $c \leq^C c_f$, associates the value:

$$spg(c, c_f) = \alpha.int(c, c_f) + \beta.ext(c, c_f) + \gamma.exp(c, c_f)$$

The int, ext and exp functions are respectively presented in the following sections. α, β and γ are positive coefficients which weight each component of the SPG. To normalize the values, we impose the SPG and each of its component to be between 0 (minimum representativeness) and 1 (maximum representativeness), and $\alpha + \beta + \gamma = 1$. The values of these 3 coefficients can be set arbitrarily or experimentally; we also provide a method to set them automatically.

Because the ratios between α, β and γ express the cognitive coordinates of the ingroup in the semiotic triangle, it is impossible to set independently the 3 values. We chose to calculate the ratios γ/α and γ/β, then α, β and γ are infered from these ratios and the above constraints.

γ/α represents the ratio between what is conceptualized by the ingroup and what is expressed in the corpus, *i.e.* the ratio between what is purely intensional (concepts of the ontology which are not expressed in the corpus) and what is purely expressionnal (terms which appear in the corpus but which name concepts missing from the ontology). But we suppose that the ontology covers all the corpus, *i.e.* each term of the corpus denotes at least a concept, a property or an instance of the ontology. Then, γ/α is estimated by the cover rate of concepts in the corpus, that is the number of concepts which at least one term appears in the corpus, divided by the total number of concepts. Similarly, γ/β is estimated by the cover rate of instances in the corpus, that is the number of instances which at least one term appears in the corpus divided by the total number of instances.

When no corpus is available, only α/β is calculated. A concept that owns very significant properties, but with few instances (for example *Dragon*) is conceptualized more in an intensional way. Conversely, a concept with ordinary properties but which owns a lot of instances (for example *Car*) is conceptualized in an extensionnal way. So, α/β is estimated by the average ratio, for all concepts, between the significance of properties owned by a concept and the number of instances of this concept.

1.1.1. Intensional component

The intensional component of the SPG assesses how much a concept c is representative of its father c_f, by comparing properties of the two concepts. Like in [1], concepts are represented by vectors in the vectorial space of properties. But [1] uses fuzzy truth values as vector coordinates, whereas our coordinates are values which assesses the significance of properties in the definitions of concepts. Formally speaking, to each concept $c \in \mathcal{C}$ is associated the vector $\vec{v_c} = (v_{c1}, v_{c2}, ..., v_{cn})$ with $n = |\mathcal{P}|$ and $v_{ci} \in [0, 1], \forall i \in [1, n]$. v_{ci} is the weight fixed for the concept c with respect to the property i ($v_{ci} = 1$ if the weight is not fixed).

The prototype of the upper concept c_f is calculated as a vector $\vec{p_{c_f}}$, and the intensional prototypicality between c and c_f is the euclidian distance between $\vec{p_{c_f}}$ and $\vec{v_c}$, the vector that represents c.

The prototype of a concept c_f has been introduced in [1] as the average of the vectors which represents the children of c_f. But [1] only considers the concepts which directly inherit from c_f, whereas we extend the calculation to all the descendants of c_f, because properties wich appear only in a indirect descendant of c_f can nevertheless appear in the prototype of c_f. For example, to wear a white coat is not a property of the concept *Researcher*, but the prototype of *Researcher* can have this property. The prototype vector $\vec{p_{c_f}}$ is a vector in the vectorial space of properties, with the coordinate for the property i

is the average of all the coordinates of the c_f descendants for this property. With $i \in \mathcal{P}$ and $S_i(c) = \{c_j \leq^C c, c_j \in dom(i)\}$:

$$\vec{p_{c_f}}[i] = \frac{\sum\limits_{c_j \in S_i(c_f)} \vec{v_{c_j}}[i]}{|S_i(c_f)|}$$

The intensional component is $int(c, c_f) = 1 - d(\vec{v_c}, \vec{p_{c_f}})$ with d the euclidian distance in the space of properties.

1.1.2. Extensional component

The extensional component of the SPG assesses how much a concept c is representative of its father c_f by estimating the space occupied by the instances of c in the extension of c_f. More this space is wide, more c is prototypical of c_f. For example, someone who owns a dozen of cats considers a cat more prototypical with respect to the concepts *Animal* than someone who owns a goldfish. Calculating this component supposes that instances are fixed in the ontology. We use a logarithmic function in order to obtain a behavior of the extensional component close to human evaluation (prototypicalities of concepts with very few instances are not too close to 0). The extensional component is:

$$ext(c, c_f) = 1 / \left(1 - \log \left(\frac{|\sigma(c)|}{|\sigma(c_f)|} \right) \right)$$

1.1.3. Expressional component

The expressional component of the SPG assesses how much a concept c is representative of its father c_f by comparing the way they are expressed. More c is expressed, more it is representative of c_f. A first estimation of the expressional prototypicality of c is based on the number of terms: more c has terms, more the place that c occupies in the cognitive universe of the ingroup is wide. For example, the concept *Horse*, that has a lot of synonyms (*e.g. cob, nag, gee-gee* or *jade*) is more prototypical of the concept *Animal* than the concept *Raccoon* that has only one term. This first estimation is given by the ratio between the number of terms that name c and the maximum number of terms that name each direct child of c_f.

$$exp_{syn}(c, c_f) = \frac{|term_c(c)|}{\max\limits_{c_i \leq^C c_f, not \exists c_j, c_i \leq^C c_j \leq^C c_f}(|term_c(c_i)|)}$$

This estimation is based on terms which appear in the ontology. If a corpus considered as representative of the domain is available, it can be used to refine the expressional component: the more the terms of c or its descendants are present in the corpus, the more c is expressed in the cognitive universe of the ingroup, and the more c is prototypical of c_f. The occurences of terms are weighted according to structures of the documents. For example, an occurence that appear in a title or in a keyword list counts more than an occurence that appears in a paragraph. We also want to take into account the distribution of occurences between documents, because a term that appears often but in few documents should have smaller weight than one which appears not very often but in most documents.

We measure the pregnance of a term l in the corpus with the function $pregnance_l(t)$: $L_C \rightarrow [0, 1]$ defined as follows:

$$pregnance_t(t) = \frac{count_{occ}(t)}{N_{occ}} * \frac{count_{doc}(t)}{N_{doc}}$$

with $count_{occ}(l)$ is the weighted occurrence number of t in the documents, $count_{doc}(t)$ the number of documents where t appears, N_{occ} the sum of all weighted occurences of all terms in the corpus and N_{doc} the number of documents in the corpus.

The function $pregnance_c(c)$ represents the pregrance of concepts and is defined as follows ($S_{term}(c)$ is the set of terms that name c or one of its descendant):

$$pregnance_c(c) = \sum_{t \in S_{term}(c)} pregnance_t(t)$$

The expressional component is $exp(c, c_f) = exp_{syn}(c, c_f) \times \frac{pregnance_c(c)}{pregnance_c(c_f)}$ (or $exp(c, c_f) = exp_{syn}(c, c_f)$ if no corpus is available).

1.2. Lexical prototypicality gradient

The Lexical Prototypicality Gradient (LPG) estimates, for a given concept C and a term T used to name C, the representativeness of T to name C. The calculation of the LPG requires a corpus. The principle is that the more the ratio between occurence number of the term and occurence number of one of the terms used to name the concept is close to 1, the more the term is prototypical of this concept. Occurences of terms are weighted according to the structure of corpus and their distributions in the documents. The function $lpg(t, c) : L_C \times C \to [0, 1]$ is defined as follows, for each couple (t, c) with c the concept named by t:

$$lpg(t, c) = 1 / \left(1 - \log\left(\frac{pregnance_t(t)}{\sum_{m \in term_c(c)} pregnance_t(m)}\right)\right)$$

1.3. Emotional factor

Works in cognitive psychology show that the emotional state of a person influences his perception of categories: more the person is stressed, more his mind is concentrated on objects cognitively close to those which concern him [5,8]. Then, we introduce an emotional factor, represented by a coefficient δ, that can vary from 0 to 1, for an open state of mind, and from 1 to ∞, for a closed state of mind. SPG, LPG and IPG are elevated to the power $1/\delta$, in order to modulate the gradients according to a state of mind: for an open state of mind, weak values of prototypicality are increased and for a closed state of mind, they are decreased.

2. Applications of prototypicality

We introduce the notion of prototypicality as an additional cognitive element above existing ontology models. Thus, as the basics elements of a domain ontology (e.g. concepts, properties or axioms), prototypicalities can be applied (at the operational level) to various tasks.

2.1. Application to ontology engineering

Prototypicality gradients can be used as a tool to facilitate *ontology building*. Indeed, the expressional component of the SPG can be calculated from a corpus for all couples of concepts of an ontology, and subsumption links automatically added between each couple of concepts c_1 and c_2 such that $exp(c_1, c_2)$ is higher than a given threshold. This can help to automatically extract concept hierarchies from text, as long as the concepts have been extracted using text-mining techniques. If properties of concepts are also available, the intensional component can also be used to complete the estimation of the SPG, in order to refine the automatic building of the hierarchy.

Prototypicality can also be used for *ontology validation* and *ontology evolution*. Given an ontology and a corpus representative of the domain, SPG, LPG and IPG can be calculated. If some values of SPG are very low, the corresponding *isa* links should be considered as inadequate. Perhaps the child concept could inherit from another concept, or an additionnal concept could be inserted between the two initial ones, in order to smooth the distribution of SPG within the ontology. Similarly, if the value of a LPG (resp. IPG) is very low, the term (resp. instance) would be allocated to another concept.

2.2. Application to information retrieval

The first application of SPG to ontology-based information retrieval is the improvement of request expansion. Given a concept c in a request, the request can be expanded to all subconcepts of c such that $spg(c, c_f)$ is higher than a given value. Request expansion can then be modulated according to prototypicalities. For example, a request about *Bird* can be expanded to *Sparrow*, *Partridge* and *Duck*, but not to *Ostrich*. An horizontal expansion can also be considered: given a concept c in a request, the request can be expanded to each concept c' that inherits from the same concept c_f than c and such that $spg(c, c_f)$ and $spg(c', c_f)$ are close enough. For example, a request about *Cat* can be expanded to *Dog*, which is as representative of *Domestic animal* as *Cat*, but not to *Crocodile*. Moreover, prototypicality can be used to sort results of a expanded request c. Of course, results can be graded from more to less prototypical one, according to how the concept used to annotate the result is prototypical of c.

Information retrieval is a good application to exploit the emotional factor. The coefficient δ is close to 0 if the user of an ontology-based information retrieval system wants a broad search, and then the request expansion will be large. If the user wants to focus on the concept he puts himself in the request, δ is a very high value, and few concepts are added to the request. In an other way, if we suppose that the user stress level is automatically obtained from a device, δ can be fixed as inversely proportional to this level. So if the user is stressed, the system will open the search space, in order to reduce its stress, and inversely, if the user is too relaxed, the system will restrict the results set in order to favour the user concentration.

2.3. Application to KBS personalization

The personalization of an Information System (IS) mainly consists in adapting its behavior to the user profile and the user activity, in order to allow the user accessing to information that are only relevant for its activity. This personalization process is more and more crucial, because of the ceaseless growth in data volume managed by IS. Moreover, IS are more and more open to various users, especially IS that operates on the Web [2]. Personalization is often based on user preferences in the system interface which is enable to modify and expand requests, to filter results and to adapt the presentation of the results. But, in the case of IS that include knowledge representation, we propose to use the ontology as the support of the personalization process: the ontology captures the consensual knowledge that is shared by the end user, and the personalization of the system can be done by adding to the ontology supplementary knowledge that depends on the cognitive universe of the end user. Ontologies, as sets of concepts, properties and axioms that express the semantics of a domain, are considered as consensual and shared conceptualisations of a domain [3]. We use the term *ingroup* to denote the set of people who share such a conceptualisation. But, within a single ingroup, cognitive elements that are not modeled in the ontology can not be the same from an ingroup member to another one. If concepts are the same in member minds, the instances can be different. For example, in the case of an ontology about trading activity, two marketing men can agree with the ontology, but the instances they know will be different: they do not meet the same customers, they do not sell the same goods and so on. In a similar idea, documents representative of what ingroup members know about the domain are inevitably not the same for all the members. For example, teachers of mathematics agree with what is Pythagoras' theorema, but each of them can advise to read a particular book to study this theorema. In section 1.1, we have introduced properties weigths in order to express the importance of each property in the conceptualization. If ingroup members agree with concepts, properties and links between them that appear in the ontology, they can attribute different weigths to properties. For instance, everybody agree that all birds have two feet. But a biologist who studies bird locomotion will judge this property very important, while most of us will consider it of secondary importance. Thus, resources that we use to calculate prototypicality gradients can vary within the ingroup from which the members agree with the ontology. Of course, to reach a consensus about prototypicality, the ingroup can be reduced to people who agree about concept instances, documents representative of the domain and property weights. This can be done if we want to use the ontology enriched with prototypicality as consensual knowledge resource in a KBS. But the prototypicality can be used to adapt the basic ontology, with gradients that vary from a user to another. Prototypicality is then used to personalize the ontology, and the KBS, according to personal cognitive elements such that instances known by the user, documents the user usually reads or writes, and importance he attributes to properties in the definition of concepts. For a given Domain Ontology (DO), gradients of conceptual, lexical and/or instance prototypicality are calculated from instances, corpus and property weigths peculiar to a user (or to a group of users). DO enriched with prototypicality is called Personnalized Domain Ontology (PDO) and several PDO can be derived from one DO.

Supplementary resources used to calculate prototypicality gradients can be get in different ways. Instances can be specified manually by the user, or discovered in texts he supplies. The corpus can be explicitly supplied by the user, or automatically built from external resources. For example, the corpus can be built from documents produced by the user in Web 2.0 applications such that blogs or wikis. But property weigths have to be set manually by the user.

3. Experimental results

Our method is implemented in TOOPRAG (*a Tool for Pragmatics in ontology*), dedicated to the automatic calculation of our gradients. This tool, written in Java, uses Lucene[4] and Jena[5]. TooPrag takes as inputs (1) an ontology represented in OWL 1.0, where each concept and relation is associated with a set of terms defined via the primitive *rdfs:label* and (2) a corpus composed of text files. The corpus is first indexed by Lucene. Then the ontology is loaded by Jena and the SPG, LPG and IPG gradients are calculated. These results are stored in an OWL file whose format extends the current specification of OWL 1.0. A SPG value is represented by a new attribute *xml:spg* associated to the *rdfs:subClassOf* link. For example, the SPG values of the *is-a* links between the concept *working_population_engaged_in_agriculture* and its sub-concepts *agricultural_labour_force* and *farmer* are respectively 0.0074 and 0.9841. And a LPG value is represented by a new attribute *xml:lpg* associated to the *rdfs:label* link. For instance, the LPG values of the terms *grower* and *peasant*, used to denote the concept *agricultural_labour_force*, are respectively 0.375 and 0.

3.1. Experiment in environment legal intelligence

The first evaluation of our work is done in the context in the project THESEUS[6] devoted to semantic and personalized information retrieval. This project aims at improving the efficiency of an information system dedicated to management of legal texts in the domain of environment. A first ontology of the Health, Security, Safety and Environment domain (HSE) has been built from both expert interviews and legal texts produced by the european and french parliaments. This ontology includes about 10.000 concepts structured in a lattice of depth 12 and maximum width 1500; it also includes 20 properties structured in a lattice of depth 3. To calculate the SPG gradients (which is the more interesting gradient for this project), a corpus of 1100 legal texts extract from LegiFrance (*www.legifrance.gouv.fr*) and Eur-Lex (*eur-lex.europa.eu*) has been used. The average value of SPG is 0.128, 30.2% of these values are not null and 3.34% are equal to 1. The values of SPG have been validated by the experts, who are consultants in the company which funds the project. This experiment clearly indicates that our model and method is in accordance with the way the experts perceive prototypicality. Our gradients are currently used to expand requests and to grade results of requests in the software proposed by the company.

3.2. Experiment in environment policy

We set-up a second experiment in the context of environment policy, with a group of engineering students as subjects. First, these 25 engineers have built (by hand and from scratch) an ontology from various texts produced by different french political organisations about their choices concerning the domain of environment. About 15 texts

---

[4]Lucene is a high-performance, full-featured text search engine distributed as an open-source Java library *http://lucene.apache.org/*.
[5]Jena is an open-source Java framework for building Semantic Web applications *http://jena.sourceforge.net/*.
[6]THESEUS is funded by Tennaxia, a company which offers service and software for legal intelligence in the domain of environment, *www.tennaxia.com*.

per organisation were collected on web sites such that *www.lemouvementpopulaire.fr*, *www.parti-socialiste.fr*, *www.fondation-nicolas-hulot.org* or *www.greenpeace.org/france*. The ontology contains 130 concepts named by 350 terms, organized in a lattice of depth 3 and maximum width 9. All the students agree with the hierarchy, although they do not attach the same importance to each concept. Then, each student has chosen 10 texts from any kind of sources (not necessarily the web sites used for building the ontology), which he considers to be representative of his own ideas about environment policy. He also manually grades, for each concept of the ontology, all its sub-concepts, according to the representativeness of sub-concepts. Finally, the SPG gradients are calculated for each student, by using their personal corpus of 10 texts. In 89% of the cases, the calculated prototypical order and the manually set order clearly coincide. This experiment confirms the relevance of our model with non-experts. However, our approach is more efficient when the corpus used to calculate the gradients is close to the conceptualisation of the user; for instance, using texts directly written by the end user such that blogs or emails is a relevant way. Moreover, considering instances and properties when calculating the extensional and intensional components of the gradients also improve the results. This experiment also underlines that the use of prototypicality to personalize a domain ontology seems justified, because even among a little group of person (25 students were involved in the experiment), the SPG gradients vary from a student to another and can be used to clearly personalize the ontology and adapt information retrieval. However, we should experiment prototypicality-based personalization in the context of a more consensual knowledge domain. For this purpose, we plan to lead the same experiment with the experts of legal intelligence.

4. Conclusion

The main objective of our work is to introduce prototypicality in the current ontology models, in order to refine knowledge description. Prototypicality is used to weigth *isa* links between concepts but also links between concepts and terms that name them, and between concepts and their instances. We propose a method to calculate these 3 kinds of prototypicality. This method is based on the use of three kinds of resource: the ontology for which the prototypicality values are calculated, a corpus and a set of instances. The method is still applicable if only one of these resources is available. Prototypicality has already been studied in Ontology Engineering. In particular, [1] proposes to calculate prototypicality values only from properties of concepts. But the weights they use are fuzzy truth values. This approach is not coherent with the formal semantics underlying an ontology, where all the properties of a concept are fully shared by all the instances of the concept. The weights we propose to use express the importance of the properties in the concept definition. This approach respects the formal semantics and is more coherent with the prototypicality notion. Moreover, to calculate the intensional component of our gradients, we extend the method proposed by [1] by considering the properties of all the concepts belonging to the descendance of the considered concept, and not only those of the direct sub-concepts. Our approach is closer to cognitive process. The calculation of the expressional component of our gradients is quite similar to the Resnik's semantic measure which uses information content [9]. But Resnik considers the corpus as a whole, whereas we propose to exploit the granularity of the corpus by taking the number of documents where a given term appears into account. We also consider that a concept is more present in the corpus if the term that names the concept is few present but in a lot of documents, than if a lot of occurence of the term appear in few texts. Comparing to Resnik, we also consider the structure of documents to weight the occurences, according to they appears in a title, an abstract or other kind of text element. The main applications we have studied concern information retrieval. Prototypicality can be used to extend requests, to grade and filter results. Calculating prototypicality gradients from peculiar resources of each user allows us to personalize the ontology and the system that exploits it. The experiments presented in this paper clearly demonstrate that our gradients are close to expert and non-expert human judgements. But prototypicality can also be applied to ontology engineering for ontology validation or evolution. A very low prototypicality value between two concepts could indicate that the *isa* link between them is not correct, or that a third concept should be inserted. Calculating the gradients between two concepts whose one inherits from the other whithout beeing one of its direct subconcepts is also possible. If the obtained value is high, it means that the child concept should be placed higher in the hierarchy. Prototypicality can also be calculated between two concepts that are not linked by an *isa* link. The intensional component is the same, but extensional and expressional components of the gradient must be modified. Using this extension of our method for ontology validation could reveal missing *isa* links in ontology. Generally speaking, the prototypicality gradients represent a semantic measure of concepts parentage within an ontology. We work on the definition of such a measure which combines the semiotic approach and our model of prototypicality.

References

[1] C. M. Au Yeung and H. F. Leung, 'Ontology with likeliness and typicality of objects in concepts', in *Proceedings of the 25th International Conference on Conceptual Modeling (ER'2006)*, volume 4215, pp. 98–111. Springer - LNCS, (2006).

[2] P. Brusilovsky and A. Kobsa, *The Adaptive Web: Methods and Strategies of Web Personalization*, Springer, 2007.

[3] Thomas Gruber, 'A translation approach to portable ontology specifications', *Knowledge Acquisition*, **5**(2), 199–220, (1993).

[4] Stevan Harnad, 'Categorical perception', *Encyclopedia of Cognitive Science*, **LXVII**(4), (2003).

[5] M. Mikulincer, P. Kedem, and D. Paz, 'The impact of trait anxiety and situational stress on the categorization of natural objects', *Anxiety Research*, **2**, 85–101, (1990).

[6] C.W. Morris, *Foundations of the Theory of Signs*, Chicago University Press, 1938.

[7] C. K. Ogden and I.A. Richards, *The Meaning of Meaning: A Study of the Influence of Language Upon Thought and of the Science of Symbolism*, Harcourt, 1989.

[8] J. Park and M. Nanaji, 'Mood and heuristics: The influence of happy and sad states on sensitivity and bias in stereotyping', *Journal of Personality and Social Psychology*, (78), 1005–1023, (2000).

[9] Philip Resnik, 'Using information content to evaluate semantic similarity in a taxonomy', in *Proceedings of the 14th International Joint Conference on Artificial Intelligence (IJCAI'95)*, volume 1, pp. 448–453, (1995).

[10] E. Rosch, 'Cognitive reference points', *Cognitive Psychology*, (7), 532–547, (1975).

Towards Effective 'Any-Time' Music Tracking

Andreas ARZT [a] and Gerhard WIDMER [a,b]

[a] Department of Computational Perception, Johannes Kepler University Linz, Austria
[b] Austrian Research Institute for Artificial Intelligence, Vienna, Austria

Abstract. The paper describes a new method that permits a computer to listen to, and follow, live music in real-time, by analysing the incoming audio stream and aligning it to a symbolic representation (e.g, score) of the piece(s) being played. In particular, we present a multi-level music matching and tracking algorithm that, by continually updating and evaluating multiple high-level hypotheses, effectively deals with almost arbitrary deviations of the live performer from the score – omissions, forward and backward jumps, unexpected repetitions, or (re-)starts in the middle of the piece. Also, we show that additional knowledge about the structure of the piece (which can be automatically computed by the system) can be used to further improve the robustness of the tracking process. The resulting system is discussed in the context of an automatic page-turning device for musicians, but it will be of use in a much wider class of scenarios that require reactive and adaptive musical companions.

Keywords. Music Tracking, Real-Time Systems

1. Introduction

Computers that can listen to music and follow it in real time promise to be useful in a wide range of applications, from synchronisation tasks to automatic monitoring of radio stations or web streams, from live music visualisation in artistic contexts to real-time accompaniment of soloists. A specific application example was given in [2], where an *automatic sheet music page turner* (a real mechanical device) for musicians is controlled by a computer that listens to the musicians (e.g., a pianist), aligns the incoming audio stream to an internal (audio) representation of the printed score of the music, follows the musician through the performance and autonomously decides when to trigger the page turner. Such a system would be especially useful during practicing, where instrumentalists generally don't have human page turners at their disposal[1] and also need to focus on the sheet music, as they have not yet memorised the piece.

For the purposes of this paper, then, we define *'music tracking'* as follows: for a machine to listen to live music through a microphone, to identify and track the corresponding positions in the printed score, and, in this way, to always 'know' where the musicians are in the piece, even if the live performance varies in tempo and sound and perhaps even deviates from the score in certain places. In this paper, we present a new,

---

[1] Note, by the way, that music page turners are highly trained and specialised professionals!

extremely robust algorithm for score-based music tracking, where the live music takes the form of an audio stream, and the system has an audio representation of the printed score of the piece being played (produced using synthesiser software). Thus, the tracking problem is one of real-time audio-to-audio alignment.

The specific *goal* we wish to achieve with our algorithm is robustness in the face of almost arbitrary disruptions or re-starts within a performance, where current music tracking algorithms would simply 'get lost'. For instance, in a practicing scenario this will be the norm: the musician will want to repeat difficult passages an arbitrary number of times, stop after a mistake and re-start somewhere, skip some parts, or take a break and then re-start somewhere in the middle of the piece – all of these without having to tell the system the precise starting position each time.

The two *key aspects of the solution* we propose are: (1) a two-level hypothesis tracking process, with a high-level tracker constantly evaluating *all possible* (!) positions in the score as potential 'current points', and more detailed hypothesis evaluators checking, selecting from, and refining these hypotheses – all in real time; and (2) the additional introduction of knowledge about the structure of the piece being played (which, as we will show, can be computed by the system itself), which facilitates heuristic guesses as to the most likely points of continuation.

As the experiments will show, the resulting system is indeed capable of quickly reacting to jumps, omissions, or performers starting at arbitrary points in the middle of a piece. For lack of a better term, we chose to call this *'Any-time Music Tracking'*: continuously being ready to receive input and to revise one's hypothesis as to what the performers are doing.

2. Related Work

While there has been quite some work on real-time music tracking, starting as early as 1984 [4,10] and including some recent publications on very advanced systems (e.g. [3,9]), the problem of how to deal with changes to the structure of a piece on-line has so far been largely neglected (in contrast to the off-line case, see [6]), with two notable exceptions.

In [8] HMMs are used to model the structure of the piece. This is a very static approach as only deviations which are modeled beforehand can be detected. The same applies for the method devised in [2], where multiple instances of matching algorithms are started at predefined positions (e.g. notated repeats) to detect deviations via the alignment costs. The finding that it is possible to recognise which instance of the matching algorithm is working at the correct position by comparing their alignment costs sets the ground for our new and more dynamic approach.

3. Preliminaries: Data Representation and Basic Matching Algorithm

3.1. Data Representation

Rather than trying to transcribe the incoming audio stream into discrete notes and align the transcription to the score, we first convert a MIDI version of the given score into a sound file by using a software synthesizer. Due to the information stored in the MIDI file, we know the time of every event (e.g. note onsets) in this 'machine-like', low-quality rendition of the piece.

The audio streams to be aligned are represented as sequences of analysis frames, using a low-level spectral representation, at two different resolution levels. This approach and the way the lower-resolution features are computed are very much inspired by [7].

The high-resolution features are computed via a windowed FFT of the signal with a hamming window of size 46ms and a hop size of 20ms. The data is mapped into 84 frequency bins, spread linearly up to 370Hz and logarithmically above, with semitone spacing. In order to emphasize note onsets, which are the most important indicators of musical timing, only the increase in energy in each bin relative to the previous frame is stored.

The low-resolution features are computed by convolving the sequence of high-resolution features component-wise with a Hann window with length 30 (or 600ms). This new sequence is down-sampled by a factor of 15, resulting in a hop-size of 300ms, and each vector is normalized to sum up to 1.

For both feature resolutions the cost of aligning two feature vectors is computed as the Euclidean distance of two vectors. While the feature extraction from the live audio signal can of course only be done on-line, the feature extraction from the score representation is done beforehand, so that information about the whole piece of music is available during the matching process.

3.2. On-line Dynamic Time Warping (ODTW)

This algorithm is the core of our real-time audio tracking system; slight variants of it are used at both levels of our system. ODTW takes two time series describing the audio signals – one known completely beforehand (the score) and one coming in in real time (the live performance) –, computes an on-line alignment, and at any time returns the current position in the score.

ODTW is based on the original DTW algorithm, which works as follows: Given 2 time series $U = u_1, ..., u_m$ and $V = v_1, ..., v_n$, an alignment between U and V is a path $W = W_1, ..., W_l$ (through a cost matrix) where each W_k is an ordered pair (i_k, j_k) such that $(i, j) \in W$ means that the points u_i and v_i are aligned. W is constrained to be monotonic and continuous. A local cost function $d(i, j)$ assigns costs to the alignment of each pair (u_i, v_i). The cost of a path W is the sum of the local alignment costs along the path. The $m \times n$ path cost matrix D is computed using the recursion:

$$D(i,j) = d(i,j) + min \left\{ \begin{array}{l} w_a * D(i, j-1) \\ w_a * D(i-1, j) \\ w_b * D(i-1, j-1) \end{array} \right\} \quad (1)$$

$D(i, j)$ is the cost of the minimum cost path from $(1, 1)$ to (i, j), $D(1, 1) = d(1, 1)$, $w_a = 1$ and $w_b = 2$. The weights w_a and w_b are used to normalize paths of different lengths to make them comparable. After the computation of the matrix the path itself is obtained by tracing the recursion backwards from $D(m, n)$.

Originally proposed by Dixon in [5], the ODTW algorithm is based on this algorithm, but has two important properties making it useable in real-time systems: it has linear time and space complexity and the alignment (a *'forward path'*) is computed incrementally.

For every iteration the number of cells calculated is given by a search width parameter $c = 500$, e.g. for a new column i the local distances $d(i, j - c), d(i, j - (c - 1)), ..., d(i, j)$ are calculated, where j is the index of the current row. The calculation of the minimum cost paths using formula 1 is restricted to using only calculated cells, thus reducing time and space complexity from quadratic to linear.

During every iteration the minimum path cost matrix is expanded by either calculating a new row or a new column. Calculating a row (column) means incrementing the pointer to the next element of the respective time series, calculating the new local distances within the defined search width c, and updating the cost matrix D by using formula 1.

To decide if a row or a column should be computed (i.e., which of the two time series to advance), the minimum path cost for each cell in the current row j and column i is found. If this occurs in the current position (i, j) both a new row and column are calculated. If this occurs elsewhere in row j a new row is calculated and if this occurs elsewhere in column i a new column is calculated. If one time series has been incremented more than $MaxRunCount = 3$ times, the other series is incremented. In our musical setting, this embodies the assumption that a given performance will not be more than 3 times faster or slower than the reference score, and prevents the alignment algorithm from 'running away' too far.

At any time during the alignment it is possible to compute a *'backward path'*, i.e. a path starting at the current position and computed backwards in time, leading to an off-line alignment of the two time series which generally is much more accurate.

Improvements to this algorithm, focusing both on adaptivity and robustness, were presented in [2] and are incorporated in our system. That includes the 'backward-forward strategy', which reconsiders past decisions and tries to improve the precision of the current score position hypothesis, and the utilization of onset information derived from the MIDI score.

Both of these strategies aim at an improvement in alignment precision. In the present paper, we provide a more dynamic and more general solution to the third problem discussed in [2], namely the problem of how to deal with structural changes effectively on-line.

4. 'Any-time' Music Following via Two-level Tracking

While previous systems – if they did deal at all with serious deviations from the score – had to rely on explicitly provided information about the structure of a piece of music and points of possible deviation (e.g., notated repeats, which a performer might or might not obey), our system does without any such information and continuously checks all (!) time points in the score as alternatives to the currently assumed score position, thus theoretically being able to react to arbitrary deviations (jumps etc.) by the performer.

The overall structure is shown in Figure 1. A *'Rough Position Finder'* continually evaluates every possible score position by computing a very rough alignment of the last few seconds of the live audio input to the score at that point; that is done at the level of low-resolution features and $600ms$ frames. A *'Decision Maker'* takes these candidate

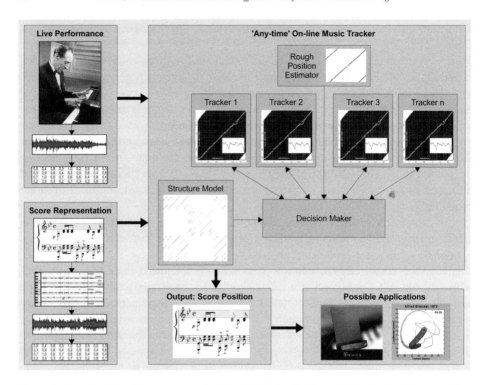

Figure 1. Overview of our 'Structure-aware Any-Time Music Tracking System' showing the different modules and the data flow.

score positions and tries to verify or falsify them via *several parallel ODTW matchers* at the detailed, high-resolution level. At any time one instance of the matching algorithm is marked as 'trusted', representing the system's current belief about the correct position. A model of the structure of the piece, which is computed automatically, proves to be very useful during this process, as will become clear later.

4.1. Rough Position Estimator (RPE)

The task of the Rough Position Estimator (RPE) is to continually provide our system with rough but reliable hypotheses about possible current positions in the score. It takes two low-resolution time series (with frame size $600ms$ and hop time $300ms$; thus a piece of, say, 10 minutes will consists of 2,000 such frames) as input. At any time the RPE has a set of hypotheses about possible score positions. The number of hypotheses is not limited, but they are ordered by a value representing the 'probability' that the score position in question is corresponding to the current position in the live input.

For every new incoming low-resolution audio frame the RPE is updated in the following way. First the local 'low resolution' cost matrix, which contains the Euclidean distances of the frames of the live input series to every frame of the score representation, is updated. As the live input stream sits on the x-axis this means adding a new column to the matrix.

Next, starting in every new cell rough backward alignments on the last $n = 9$ seconds of the live performance are computed using a greedy local search algorithm constrained to step at most 3 times in a row into a single direction. The alignment costs of the resulting paths are normalized by the number of steps and then scaled to lie between 0 and 1. The result is a vector giving the similarity values of rough alignments of the last n seconds of the live audio to score passages ending at any possible score position (with a resolution of 600ms).

To reduce the computational complexity and to add some robustness to the algorithm, only the cells ('score positions') with a similarity value of at least 0.95 are selected as possible hypotheses to be passed on to the lower-level matchers for evaluation (see 4.2 below).

As only the last n seconds on the live input axis are needed and due to the low resolution of the two streams, the necessary computations are easily done in real time, even for pieces as long as 30 minutes.

4.2. Detailed Matching Algorithm (DMA)

Our system maintains a fixed number of instances of the ODTW matching algorithm, working on the high-resolution features (frame size $46ms$, hop time $20ms$ – thus a piece of 10 minutes consists of $30,000$ frames), which are managed by the 'Decision Maker' (see below). The number of matcher instances is limited by the computing power of the computer in use, but usually 3 or 4 instances are sufficient. The matching algorithm is identical to the one described in 3.2 above, including all extensions proposed in [2] with one notable difference: In [1] we introduced a simple reactive *tempo model* based on the performed tempo relative to the score representation, computed over the last couple of seconds of the live performance. This model is used to stretch or compress the score representation accordingly and therefore reduce differences in absolute tempo between the score representation and the live performance. This increases robustness in the face of global and local tempo deviations.

4.3. Decision Maker (DM)

The Decision Making Component (DM) decides on which hypotheses to investigate in detail, and which to accept or reject. To achieve this it manages instances of the DMA of which at any time at least one is active. One of the active instances is marked as 'trusted', representing the system's current belief about the score position.

If there is an idle DMA instance available, the first step in every iteration is to analyse the output of the RPE and to find the best hypothesis for which further investigation is not in progress. The idle DMA instance is initialised accordingly, but not with the current time points in score and live audio, but with points a few seconds in the past – the end positions of the rough backward alignment leading to this hypothesis, as computed by the RPE. The DMA then starts aligning there. That gives the DMA more context for evaluating the current hypothesis and accelerates the DM's decision making process (because it will not have to wait for several seconds of new live audio until the hypothesis can be evaluated).

Next, the DM iterates through the instances of the DMA, trying to decide, for each matcher, whether to reject it, to accept it as the new 'trusted' one, or to postpone the decision. Only matching algorithms that have tracked at least 5 seconds of audio input are considered here, as of course no decision should be made without sufficient grounding.

A matcher may need some time to converge on the correct alignment path as the RPE's hypotheses are only rough estimates.

The decision itself is made as follows: for each matcher i, the difference d_i between the current alignment cost of matcher i and the alignment cost c_t of the currently 'trusted' matcher is computed; these differences are summed up over the whole lifetime of the matcher. After every iteration the sums are compared to two heuristic thresholds. If the sum is lower than $t_r = -rc_t$ the hypothesis is rejected and the matcher is set to idle. If the sum exceeds $t_a = sc_t$, the hypothesis is accepted and the matcher is marked as the new 'trusted' one. In our system we use $r = 2$ and $s = 10$, which gives a good trade-off between fast response times and overall robustness.

5. Adding Musical Knowledge

Music is a highly structured artifact, and most music exhibits a certain degree of repetition – a significant motif may reappear many times, a refrain is a repeated part by definition, whole sections are sometimes repeated. Thus, we generally have repeating passages at many levels – from short segments of just a few beats, to segments lasting several minutes.

Repetition in music presents a problem to a music following system that always considers all possible positions in the score: which of the instance of a repeating pattern corresponds to the passage currently played by the performer? In order to cope with this problem, we introduce knowledge about the structure of the current piece, by way of a *Structure Model (SM)* that identifies repeated parts at all levels and builds an equivalence relation that specifies which parts are instances of the same class. As shown in 6.2 below, without such knowledge it is not possible to distinguish these parts and make musically sensible decisions about the current position in the score. Furthermore the SM also adds to the robustness of our system.

The SM is extracted automatically from the score by computing a *self-similarity matrix* based on the rough feature representation of the score. In this matrix the diagonal represents a performance of the piece as annotated in the score. Simple image processing techniques are used to identify connected lines with maximum similarity which are parallel to the diagonal. These represent repetitions of the same part at another time in the score (see Figure 1, which shows the structure model computed for the Impromptu in A-flat major D.935-2 by Franz Schubert).

This additional knowledge proves useful for several tasks in our system: It is used to (1) prune the list of hypotheses by identifying equivalent hypotheses and discarding all hypotheses equivalent to positions that are already checked in detail. This greatly reduces computation time and gives the system the ability to track more different hypotheses at once. Furthermore, the DM is used to (2) control the pruning process by introducing a configurable matching strategy. Therewith it is possible to affect the behaviour of the system, e.g. by using the strategy 'always prefer the shortest jump in the score'. And (3) we use information from the model to double the acceptance threshold t_a if an active hypothesis supports (i.e., belongs to the same class as the segment processed by) the 'trusted' matcher, which add to the robustness of the system.

6. Evaluation

Our system was evaluated on 3 classical piano pieces: the Valse brillante Op. 34 No. 1 by Frédéric Chopin, the Impromptu in A♭ major D 935-2 by Franz Schubert and the Prelude in G minor Op. 23 No. 5 by Sergei Rachmaninoff. For each piece we selected as least 5 different performances by well-known classical pianists, including e.g. Vladimir Horowitz, Evgeny Kissin, and Vladimir Ashkenazy. The pieces are of considerable complexity, with a rich structure of repetitions at various levels and, belonging to the romantic piano genre, they are generally played with a lot of expressive freedom (in terms of tempo changes etc.), which is a challenge to the ODTW matching algorithms. The experiments were performed off-line but, except for a very small latency, the results are the same for on-line alignments.

For a quantitative evaluation a correct reference alignment is needed. As the goal of our experiments was not to evaluate the overall accuracy of the alignments – this was already done in [2] – but the performance of the multi-level approach in reacting to structural changes to the piece, data acquired by off-line alignments was sufficiently accurate as ground truth for this task. Manual examination guaranteed that no large errors were included in the reference alignments. As shown in [5] these alignments are generally very accurate.

6.1. Evaluation of the 'Rough Position Estimator'

The overall performance of our system depends heavily on the accuracy of the RPE. If its hypotheses about possible score positions are poor, the whole system will rarely detect jumps during a performance or, even worse, may get confused even in the course of a 'normal' performance. The RPE, which at any time gives an ordered list of possible current score positions, was first evaluated in isolation, by analysing the output at every note onset in our test set. For every output the minimum distance to the actual score position or an equivalent position (e.g. due to a repetition) was computed.

As Table 1 shows, the performance of the RPE is sufficient for the task we have in mind. In general, due to the robustness of the ODTW matching algorithm, even hypotheses with an error of up to 5 bars are useable as a starting point for our detailed matchers.

6.2. Evaluation of the Any-Time Music Tracker

In the following the basic system without the SM will be referred to as 'Any-Time Music Tracker' (AMT), and the system including the SM will be referred to as 'Structure-aware Any-Time Music Tracker' (SAMT). The evaluation of the systems is based on versions of the performances in our data set which were edited by removing parts of various length, ranging from 10 to 250 bars.

6.2.1. 'Starting in the Middle'

For the first experiment we deleted the first $x = 10, 15, 20, \ldots$ bars from the performances, resulting in performances where the pianist skips some bars at the beginning, thus simulating 'random' starts somewhere in the score. In total we computed alignments on 600 performances, with x ranging from 10 up to 250 (the larger value of course de-

Error ≤	Selecting 'best' of top n hypotheses				
	1	2	3	4	5
0 bars	41%	56%	58%	60%	60%
1 bar	70%	78%	83%	85%	86%
2 bars	78%	83%	87%	89%	90%
3 bars	80%	85%	89%	91%	92%
4 bars	82%	87%	90%	92%	93%
5 bars	83%	87%	91%	93%	94%

Table 1. Cumulative percentages of the best of the top n proposed hypotheses of the RPE with an error up to the given value – e.g. cell (3,2) should be read as 'at 83% of all note events in the performances, the best of the top 3 hypotheses proposed by the RPE is at most 1 bar away from the correct position (or an equivalent position according to the structure model)'.

pending on the total number of bars of the piece), amounting to about 38 hours of live performance. We provide 2 different measures for the performance of the algorithm:

- **Measure 1 (M1):** The time spent matching wrong positions until the algorithm actively jumps to a bar in the score corresponding to the actual performance. It is important to note that this might not be the exact same position as in the performance, as parts often occur more than once in a piece completely identical and without some context it is impossible, even for humans, to decide which instance of a part is currently being played.
- **Measure 2 (M2):** The time spent matching wrong positions until the algorithm reaches (possibly by jumping more than once) the exact bar corresponding to the live performance.

In both cases time spent matching positions which according to the structure model are equivalent is not added to this measure.

The results of this experiment can be found in Tables 2 and 3. Just for comparison, Table 3 also shows the results of the system described in [2], on the same data. The latter can only detect predefined structural changes and thus has no means to cope with the arbitrary changes we made to the performances. Loosely speaking, it is mere chance if the correct position is ever detected, which becomes more improbable as the changes grow bigger (see also Figure 2).

The performance of the AMT (the system without Structure Model) depends on the characteristics of the piece in question. While the results on the Chopin and Rachmaninov pieces are quite similar – especially considering M2 as shown in Table 3 – the results for the Schubert piece are considerably worse. Considering the structure of this piece, which consists of a lot of repetitions, this does not come as a surprise as the AMT has no means to distinguish these parts and does not use any context that would allow for musically sensible decisions. This leads to a very annoying behaviour, which is not reflected in these tables: The algorithm sometimes jumps between different instances of the repetion in the score – not only while trying to find the correct position, but also after such a position is found (see Table 4).

This behaviour, which for musicians is very tiresome, finally led us to introduce the Structure Model (see Section 5). For our experiments we used the structure model to

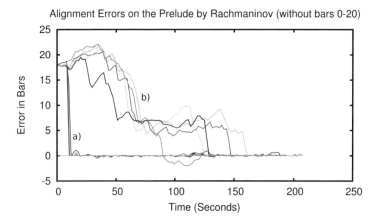

Figure 2. 'Starting in the middle': A visual comparison of the capabilities of the old and the new AMT real-time tracking system. 5 performances of the Prelude by Rachmaninov, with bars 0-20 missing, are aligned to the score by the old and the new system. For all performances, the new one (a) almost instantly identifies the correct position, while the old one (b) finds the correct position by mere chance.

	AMT			SAMT		
	C	R	S	C	R	S
Best	3.52	5.18	0.12	3.51	4.98	4.60
Quartile 1	6.78	8.10	7.52	6.62	8.88	7.36
Median	7.42	10.32	10.44	7.16	10.52	8.74
Quartile 3	10.18	14.56	30.70	8.04	15.76	11.92
Worst	60.26	51.96	128.86	56.18	56.04	68.7

Table 2. Statistics about the erroneous matching time (in seconds) until the system actively jumps to the next correct score position (error measure M1). The data is computed on performances of the pieces by Chopin (C), Rachmaninov (R) and Schubert (S) starting somewhere in the middle of the score instead of at the beginning (see text).

make SAMT prefer the linearly next segment if several alternative positions pertaining to a class of repeated segments are available. As discussed in Section 7, other strategies are entirely possible and in fact depend on the usage scenario of the system.

As can be seen in Tables 2 and 3 the introduction of a SM leads to a similar performance on the pieces by Chopin and Rachmaninov while reducing the time needed to adapt to deviations in the Schubert piece, which is rich in repetitions. But even more important is the increase in robustness, as shown in Table 4. There still occurred some erroneous jumps in the Chopin piece, but over all aligned performances a wrong jump or an unnecessary jump roughly occurs only once every 2 hours of a live performance. Moreover, due to the ability of the algorithm to identify equivalent hypothesis, SAMT needs only half of the computation time of AMT.

	Old System (ECAI 08)			AMT			SAMT		
	C	R	S	C	R	S	C	R	S
Best	15.98	24.74	25.08	4.74	5.18	0.86	4.64	4.98	4.60
Quartile 1	130.8	106.88	243.14	7.14	8.10	7.84	7.2	8.88	8.16
Median	–	–	–	8.36	10.32	14.32	8.34	10.52	13.04
Quartile 3	–	–	–	15.42	14.56	43.66	13.09	15.76	19.04
Worst	–	–	–	60.26	51.96	128.86	56.18	56.04	82.36

Table 3. 'Starting in the Middle': Statistics about the erroneous matching time (in seconds) until the system reaches the exact same position in the score as in the live performance (error measure M2). The data is computed on performances of the pieces by Chopin (C), Rachmaninov (R) and Schubert (S) starting somewhere in the middle of the score (with omissions up to 250 bars) instead of at the beginning (see text).

	AMT			SAMT		
	C	R	S	C	R	S
J_{wrong}	2%	0%	28%	2%	0%	0%
J_{equiv}	4%	2%	30%	3%	0%	0%

Table 4. 'Starting in the Middle': Percentage of performances in which AMT/SAMT jumps to a completely wrong position (J_{wrong}), or 'unnecessarily' jumps to equivalent parts after reaching the correct position (J_{equiv}), which is also musically wrong.

6.2.2. 'Leaving out Parts'

In the course of a second experiment we simulated performances where an arbitrary part in the middle of the piece is skipped. In total we used 394 performances in which parts with lengths from 20 to 200 bars were removed at different positions. The results (see Table 5) show that it generally takes a little bit longer to find the correct position than in the first experiment. Closer investigation showed that this is caused by the extra (and misleading) context given by the last couple of seconds of the live performance which increases the time the RPE needs to supply the correct position as hypothesis. This also accounts for the noticeably bigger difference in the results between the two experiments for the piece by Rachmaninov. It seems that the similarity of many short segments of this pieces makes the task of the algorithm more difficult. A possible improvement may be to make the thresholds t_a and t_r adaptive, thus speeding up the detection. Of course there is a trade-off between detection speed and robustness.

6.3. Conclusions from the Experiments

Although during the evaluation we focused on cases where parts from the score are left out during the performance, insertions or backward jumps should make no difference. This estimation is also supported by preliminary experiments.

In general the performance of our approach depends very much on how a piece of music is performed and where jumps occur. The performance decreases with extreme tempo changes within a performance, and with large differences in absolute tempo between the (audio representation of) the score and the live performance. Problems are es-

	M1			M2		
	C	R	S	C	R	S
Best	3.98	3.08	3.26	3.98	3.08	3.26
Quartile 1	6.38	8.86	6.12	7.30	10.42	6.12
Median	9.62	14.68	9.28	12.82	15.20	9.28
Quartile 3	15.38	20.60	13.46	19.6	23.72	15.84
Worst	55.02	41.48	86.76	55.02	55.62	86.76

Table 5. 'Leaving out Parts': Statistics about the erroneous matching times (in seconds) until SAMT actively jumps to the (next) correct score position (M1 and M2). The data is computed on performances of the pieces by Chopin (C), Rachmaninov (R) and Schubert (S) which skip parts of different length somewhere during the performance (see text).

pecially apparent at phrase boundaries, where huge differences in timing occur. Jumps to these areas account for many of the bigger errors found in Tables 2, 3 and 5.

Depending on the scenario one could think of a different alignment strategy than we used for our experiments, e.g. if it is known beforehand that the musician is practicing and therefore may repeat parts multiple times the strategy 'always jump to the nearest hypothesis' instead of 'always jump to the linearly next hypothesis' would be more appropriate.

7. Conclusion and Future Work

The paper has presented an robust on-line audio alignment algorithm which is capable of coping with arbitrary structural changes during a musical performance. The algorithm may also prove useful for other domains that need robust on-line alignment of time series which possibly include structural deviations.

A possible future scenario would be to extend this algorithm to operate on a whole database of musical pieces, automatically recognising both the piece being played, and the current position. An off-line matching/retrieval scenario related to this has been described in [7]. Practically this will require a clever indexing scheme based on musically relevant high-level features to quickly find those pieces and time points most likely to match the ongoing sound stream.

More directions for future work are to find ways to cope with phrase boundaries and more elaborate methods to determine the actually played part from a number of equivalent hypotheses (e.g. by analysis of the musical context). To achieve the latter the additional use of high-level musical features for the RPE should be considered.

Acknowledgements

This research is supported by the City of Linz, the Federal State of Upper Austria, the Austrian Federal Ministry for Transport, Innovation and Technology, and the Austrian Science Fund (FWF) under project number TRP 109-N23.

References

[1] Andreas Arzt and Gerhard Widmer. Simple tempo models for real-time music tracking. In *Proc. of the Sound and Music Computing Conference (SMC)*, Barcelona, Spain, 2010.

[2] Andreas Arzt, Gerhard Widmer, and Simon Dixon. Automatic page turning for musicians via real-time machine listening. In *Proc. of the 18th European Conference on Artificial Intelligence (ECAI)*, Patras, Greece, 2008.

[3] Arshia Cont. A coupled duration-focused architecture for realtime music to score alignment. *IEEE Transactions on Pattern Analysis and Machine Intelligence*, 99, 2009.

[4] Roger Dannenberg. An on-line algorithm for real-time accompaniment. In *Proc. of the International Computer Music Conference (ICMC)*, San Francisco, 1984.

[5] Simon Dixon. An on-line time warping algorithm for tracking musical performances. In *Proc. of the 19th International Joint Conference on Artificial Intelligence (IJCAI)*, Edinburgh, 2005.

[6] Meinard Mueller and Daniel Appelt. Path-constrained partial music synchronization. In *Proc. of the International Conference on Acoustics, Speech, and Signal Processing (ICASSP)*, Las Vegas, 2008.

[7] Meinard Mueller, Frank Kurth, and Michael Clausen. Audio matching via chroma-based statistical features. In *Proc. of the 5th International Conference on Music Information Retrieval (ISMIR)*, London, 2005.

[8] Bryan Pardo and William Birmingham. Modeling form for on-line following of musical performances. In *Proc. of the 20th National Conference on Artificial Intelligence (AAAI)*, Pittsburgh, 2005.

[9] Christopher Raphael. Current directions with music plus one. In *Proc. of the Sound and Music Computing Conference (SMC)*, Porto, 2009.

[10] Barry Vercoe. The synthetic performer in the context of live performance. In *Proc. of the International Computer Music Conference (ICMC)*, San Francisco, 1984.

Relaxing Regression for a Heuristic GOLOG

Michelle L. BLOM and Adrian R. PEARCE [1]
NICTA Victoria Research Laboratory
Department of Computer Science and Software Engineering
The University of Melbourne, Australia

Abstract. GOLOG is an agent programming language designed to represent complex actions and procedures in the situation calculus. In this paper we apply relaxation-based heuristics – often used in classical planning – to find (near) optimal executions of a GOLOG program. In doing so we present and utilise a theory of relaxed regression for the approximate interpretation of a GOLOG program. This relaxed interpreter is used to heuristically evaluate the available choices in the search for a program execution. We compare the performance of our heuristic interpreter (in terms of the quality of executions found) with a traditional depth-first search interpreter and one guided by a greedy heuristic without a look-ahead on three domains: spacecraft control, mine operations planning, and task scheduling.

Introduction

GOLOG [7] is an agent programming language grounded in the situation calculus [10]. The aim of a GOLOG interpreter is to find an execution of a GOLOG program – a sequence of actions for an agent to perform. To increase the applicability of GOLOG as a tool for programming agents, we do not want an interpreter to find just any execution, but one that satisfies desirable properties (eg. minimising resource utilisation). In this paper we consider the application of relaxation-based heuristics (often used in classical planning) to find an optimal or near optimal execution of a GOLOG program.

Relaxation-based heuristics have been used in classical planning to find optimal or near-optimal plans (w.r.t plan length) with great success [2,6]. The choices available during the search for a plan are evaluated by solving a relaxed version of the planning problem. This relaxed problem typically ignores the negative effects of actions (such as the depletion of a resource). For each choice, a relaxed plan is formed representing what an actual (legal) plan might look like if that choice is made. The properties of this relaxed plan (eg. length) are used to select the most promising choice for further exploration.

We consider the relaxation-based heuristics explored in [2,6] and adapt them for use in the interpretation of GOLOG programs. In doing so we develop a heuristic GOLOG interpreter. We assume that we have a numeric evaluation function f_e that assesses the quality of an execution, and that the aim of our heuristic interpreter is to find an execution

---

[1] Corresponding Author: Michelle Blom, E-mail: mlblom@csse.unimelb.edu.au.

that minimises this function. This function can be derived from factors such as execution cost, resource utilisation, and the achievement of weighted goals or desires.

A GOLOG interpreter is faced with choices each time it comes across a non-deterministic construct (eg. a branch). A typical Prolog implementation of a standard interpreter selects the first available choice (eg. the first program in a branch). In contrast, our heuristic interpreter evaluates each choice by: making the choice, and then finding a relaxed execution of the remaining program. We develop a relaxed GOLOG interpreter for this purpose, relying on a relaxed form of (situation calculus) regression to optimistically determine whether an action is possible in any given situation. This relaxed execution is designed to represent what desirable future may exist by making this particular choice in the interpretation of the program. The evaluation function f_e applied to each relaxed execution assigns a heuristic value to the corresponding choice. Our interpreter opts to pursue the choice with the best (smallest) evaluation.

To assess the performance of our heuristic interpreter, we conduct experiments on three domains. Among these is a domain presented in [12] in which a spacecraft is required to maximise the number of scientific observations made of celestial targets during a limited time window. Given a GOLOG program controlling the agents of these domains, we show that our interpreter is able to find executions that are higher in quality than those found by both a traditional interpreter and one guided by a greedy heuristic without a look-ahead by relaxation.

In the next section we review GOLOG, the situation calculus, and a traditional GOLOG interpreter. We then describe regression, and how it can be altered to operate in a relaxed manner. Following this, we develop our relaxed and heuristic GOLOG interpreters. We present these interpreters within the context of offline planning. We conclude by considering the use of our interpreter in an online setting, and with an analysis of related work. To the best of our knowledge, this is the first work to consider the application of relaxation-based heuristics in the GOLOG interpretation process, without requiring compilation of the problem for use with a classical planner.

1. GOLOG and the Situation Calculus

The situation calculus [10] is a formalism for reasoning about dynamically changing worlds. Key elements in the situation calculus are: *actions*, which change the state of a world; *situations*, which describe a sequence of actions applied to an initial state; and *fluents*, which represent properties of a world. A fluent is *relational* if it represents a true or false value, and *functional* if it evaluates to an alternative value type (such as a number or a coordinate). We describe a world in the situation calculus with a set of: precondition, successor state, initial state and domain independent axioms. These axioms, in conjunction with a set of unique names axioms for actions, form a basic action theory $\mathcal{D}$.

Definition 1. (Action Preconditions) A precondition axiom for an action $A(\vec{x})$ describes the conditions (Π_A) that must be satisfied before $A(\vec{x})$ can be performed in a given situation s, and assumes the form:

$$Poss(A(\vec{x}), s) \equiv \Pi_A(\vec{x}, s)$$

□

a	primitive action		$\delta*$		execute δ 0 or more times
$\phi?$	test if ϕ holds		**if** ϕ **then** δ_1 **else** δ_2		synchronised conditional
$\delta_1 : \delta_2$	execute program δ_1 then δ_2		**while** ϕ **do** δ **end**		synchronised loop
$\delta_1 \mid \delta_2$	choose to execute δ_1 or δ_2		**proc** $P(\vec{v})$ δ **end**		procedure
$\pi\, v.\delta$	choice of argument v in δ				

Table 1. GOLOG constructs [3].

Definition 2. (Successor State Axioms) A successor state axiom for a fluent defines how its value changes. A relational fluent F has a successor state axiom of the form:

$$F(\vec{x}, do(a, s)) \equiv \Phi_F(\vec{x}, a, s) \equiv \gamma_F^+(\vec{x}, a, s) \vee F(\vec{x}, s) \wedge \neg \gamma_F^-(\vec{x}, a, s)$$

where: $\gamma_F^+(\vec{x}, a, s)$ denotes how F is made true by action a in situation s; $\gamma_F^-(\vec{x}, a, s)$ denotes how F can be made false by a in s; and $do(a, s)$ denotes the situation that results after action a is performed in situation s.

A successor state axiom for a functional fluent G has the form:

$$G(\vec{x}, do(a, s)) = y \equiv \Psi_G(\vec{x}, y, a, s) \equiv \delta_G(\vec{x}, y, a, s)$$
$$\vee\; G(\vec{x}, s) = y \wedge \neg(\exists y').\delta_G(\vec{x}, y', a, s)$$

where: $\delta_G(\vec{x}, y, a, s)$ denotes the conditions that must hold for G to evaluate to y in $do(a, s)$; $G(\vec{x}, s) = y$ holds iff G evaluates to y in the situation s; and $\neg(\exists y').\delta_G(\vec{x}, y', a, s)$ indicates that the action a did not change this evaluation to another value y'. □

The constructs of the GOLOG programming language are listed in Table 1. These elements are combined to produce programs. In Example 1, a GOLOG program is defined that controls the operation of a spacecraft charged with observing celestial targets.

Example 1. Consider a spacecraft designed to observe celestial targets within a limited time window [12]. These targets are located in clusters within a 3D space. The spacecraft has an instrument capable of making observations (which must be calibrated prior to its first observation). Making an observation requires turning the instrument to a target (consuming an amount of fuel and time dependent on the magnitude of the turn), and taking an image (consuming power). Fuel is limited, while power is renewable at a constant rate[2]. An execution of the GOLOG program SPACE, below, defines a plan for the craft.

    proc SPACE
        switchOn : $\pi\, t_1$. [caltrgt(t_1)? : turnto(t_1) : calibrate(t_1)] :
        while $\exists$ t. (trgt(t) $\wedge$ ¬ obsd(t)) $\wedge$ timeleft **do**
            (π tg. [(trgt(tg) $\wedge$ ¬ obsd(tg))? : turnto(tg) : takeimage(tg)] | wait)
        end :
        switchOff
    end

where: *trgt(t)* denotes that t is a celestial target; *obsd(t)* denotes that target t has been observed; *timeleft* denotes that there is ≥ 1 unit of time left; *caltrgt(t)* denotes that t is a calibration target; and *switchon, calibrate(t), switchoff, turnto(t), wait*, and *takeima-*

---

[2]This is a simplification of the example in [12] in which the power renewal rate is dependent on the orientation of the craft with respect to the sun.

$$trans(a, s, \delta', s') \equiv Poss(a, s) \wedge \delta' = nil \wedge s' = do(a, s)$$
$$trans(\delta_1|\delta_2, s, \delta', s') \equiv trans(\delta_1, s, \delta', s') \vee trans(\delta_2, s, \delta', s')$$
$$trans(\textbf{while}\,\phi\,\textbf{do}\,\delta, s, \delta', s') \equiv \exists \gamma.\delta' = (\gamma : \textbf{while}\,\phi\,\textbf{do}\,\delta) \wedge \phi[s] \wedge trans(\delta, s, \gamma, s')$$
$$trans(\pi v.\delta, s, \delta', s') \equiv \exists x.trans(\delta_x^v, s, \delta', s')$$

Table 2. A selection of transition axioms [3].

ge(t), are primitive actions. The craft selects a target to observe until the available time has elapsed. If there is time left but it is not possible to observe a target (due to limited resources) the craft waits for one unit of time before repeating this process.

□

1.1. A Traditional GOLOG Interpreter

We now describe a traditional depth-first search GOLOG interpreter (using the transition semantics of [3]). These semantics define when an agent can transition from one configuration (δ, s) to another (δ', s') by performing one step in the program δ in situation s, resulting in the situation s' and program δ' left to perform.

For each GOLOG construct of Table 1, δ_f, a *trans* axiom defines which configurations can be transitioned to from (δ_f, s) by performing a single step of δ_f in situation s. A configuration (δ_f, s) is final (*final*(δ_f, s)) if no steps remain to be performed in δ_f. A selection of *trans* axioms are shown in Table 2. We find a legal execution of a program δ in situation s_0 by repeatedly applying these *trans* axioms, starting with the configuration (δ, s_0), until we reach a final configuration. In Table 2, $\phi[s]$ holds iff ϕ holds in situation s (as determined by regression), and δ_x^v denotes that v has been replaced with x in δ. We refer the reader to [3] for a description of the final axioms for each δ_f.

2. Regression and Relaxed Regression

Regression takes a query involving a situation s and transforms it into an equivalent query that is uniform in the initial situation s_0. A formula W is uniform in the initial situation if the only situation term mentioned in W is s_0 (and several other conditions are satisfied, as described in [9]). This query can then be proven with respect to a set of initial state axioms with a first order theorem prover.

When finding an execution of a GOLOG program, we use regression to determine: if an action a is possible in a situation s ($Poss(a, s)$); and whether a condition within a test, while, or if ... else construct holds. The regression operator R is defined by a series of rules. These rules look at the structure of a formula and tell us how it can be shifted one step closer to being uniform in the initial situation. For a definition of regressable formulae (situation calculus formulae that can be regressed) we refer the reader to [9].

Example 2. Consider a regressable relational fluent $F(\vec{t}, do(\alpha, s))$, and let $F(\vec{x}, do(a, \sigma)) \equiv \Phi_F(\vec{x}, a, \sigma)$ denote the successor state axiom for the fluent F (as defined in Definition 2). The regression rule for this fluent is [9]: $R[F(\vec{t}, do(\alpha, s))] = R[\Phi_F(\vec{t}, \alpha, s)]$.

□

We would like to estimate whether such formulae hold without expending the effort required by an exact regression. This estimation can be used to find an approximate execution of a GOLOG program. To perform this estimation, we define a *relaxed regression* operator RR. To do so we combine the concept of relaxation used in classical planning [2,6] with the regression rules of standard regression.

In classical planning relaxation is typically conducted by ignoring the effects of actions that cause propositions (aspects of the planner's environment) to be false. Propositions that are true in the initial state, or that become true by performing an action, persist. We employ this idea in our formalisation of relaxed regression. A relational fluent F holds in a situation $do(\alpha, s)$, for example, if it holds in situation s or the action α has made it hold. We do not consider whether α causes the fluent to be false. We now describe the required properties of RR.

Definition 3. Given a regressable formula W, and a basic action theory $\mathcal{D}$:

1. $RR[W]$ is uniform in the initial situation s_0; and,
2. If $\mathcal{D} \models W$ then $\mathcal{D}_{s_0} \cup \mathcal{D}_{una} \models RR[W]$,

where $\mathcal{D}_{s_0}$ and $\mathcal{D}_{una}$ are the set of initial state and unique names axioms of $\mathcal{D}$.

□

Property 2 above states that if a regressable formula W holds given $\mathcal{D}$, then the transformation of W under relaxed regression holds given $\mathcal{D}_{s_0} \cup \mathcal{D}_{una}$. The converse will not necessarily be the case. If $RR[W]$ holds we infer that W *might* hold, not that it *does* hold. If $RR[W]$ does not hold, we infer that W does not hold. Contrast these properties with those of R [9]. R is both sound and complete as the property $\mathcal{D} \models W$ iff $\mathcal{D}_{s_0} \cup \mathcal{D}_{una} \models R[W]$ holds. RR is designed to be complete but not sound.

Definition 4 outlines the rules of RR, presented alongside their R counterpart (defined as in [9]). It is clear that we need to regress negated formulae and non-negated formulae with different perspectives under relaxed regression. $RR[\neg W]$ is an optimistic determination of whether W does not hold. It is not the case that $RR[\neg W] \equiv \neg RR[W]$ as in traditional regression. To avoid the addition of a new rule for the negation of each type of compound formula, formulae are converted to *negation normal form* (NNF) prior to the application of RR. In this form: implications ($p \rightarrow q$) are eliminated by replacing them with their equivalent representation ($\neg p \vee q$); negation operators are moved inward using De Morgan's laws; and double negations are eliminated. The result is a formula in which the negation operator appears only before atomic sub-formulae.

Definition 4. Let: W denote a regressable situation calculus formula in NNF; $\phi_n(\psi)$ the result of converting a formula ψ into NNF; σ and s situations; and α and a actions.

1. W is a situation independent atom or is uniform in s_0.

$$RR[W] = W \qquad R[W] = W$$

2. W is a possibility predicate $Poss(A(\vec{t}), s)$ where $A(\vec{t})$ is an action. Let $Poss(A(\vec{x}), \sigma) \equiv \Pi_A(\vec{x}, \sigma)$ (as in Definition 1).

$$RR[W] = RR[\phi_n(\Pi_A(\vec{t}, s))] \qquad R[W] = R[\Pi_A(\vec{t}, s)]$$

3. W is a relational fluent $F(\vec{t}, do(\alpha, s))$. Let $F(\vec{x}, do(a, \sigma)) \equiv \Phi_F(\vec{x}, a, \sigma)$ (as described in Definition 2).

$$RR[W] = RR[\phi_n(F(\vec{t}, s) \vee \gamma_F^+(\vec{t}, \alpha, s))] \qquad R[W] = R[\Phi_F(\vec{t}, \alpha, s)]$$

4. W is an atomic formula mentioning a functional fluent $G(\vec{t}, do(\alpha, s))$. Let $G(\vec{x}, do(a, \sigma)) = y \equiv \Psi_G(\vec{x}, y, a, \sigma)$ be defined as in Definition 2. $W|_{\phi'}^{\phi}$ denotes the formula that results from replacing all instances of ϕ in W with ϕ'.

$$RR[W] = RR[\phi_n((\exists y).(\delta_G(\vec{t}, y, \alpha, s) \vee G(\vec{t}, s) = y) \wedge W|_y^{G(\vec{t}, do(\alpha, s))})]$$
$$R[W] = R[(\exists y).(\delta_G(\vec{t}, y, \alpha, s) \vee G(\vec{t}, s) = y \wedge$$
$$\neg(\exists y').\delta_G(\vec{t}, y', \alpha, s)) \wedge W|_y^{G(\vec{t}, do(\alpha, s))}]$$

5. W is a negated possibility predicate $\neg Poss(A(\vec{t}), s)$ where $Poss(A(\vec{x}), \sigma) \equiv \Pi_A(\vec{x}, \sigma)$ (defined as in Definition 1).

$$RR[W] = RR[\phi_n(\neg \Pi_A(\vec{t}, s))] \qquad R[W] = \neg R[\Pi_A(\vec{t}, s)]$$

6. W is the negation of a relational fluent $F(\vec{t}, do(\alpha, s))$. Let $F(\vec{x}, do(a, \sigma))$ be defined as in Definition 2.

$$RR[W] = RR[\phi_n(\neg F(\vec{t}, s) \vee \gamma_F^-(\vec{t}, \alpha, s))] \qquad R[W] = \neg R[\Phi_F(\vec{t}, \alpha, s)]$$

7. W is the negation of an atomic formula W_1 involving a functional fluent $G(\vec{t}, do(\alpha, s))$. Let $G(\vec{x}, do(a, \sigma))$ be defined as in Definition 2.

$$RR[W] = RR[\phi_n((\exists y).(\delta_G(\vec{t}, y, \alpha, s) \vee G(\vec{t}, s) = y) \wedge \neg W_1|_y^{G(\vec{t}, do(\alpha, s))})]$$
$$R[W] = \neg R[W_1]$$

8. W is a compound formula. RR is defined in the same manner as R (refer to [9]).

□

Theorem 1. *(Completeness of RR) Let W be a regressable situation calculus formula and $\mathcal{D}$ a basic action theory. $RR[W]$ is a formula uniform in the initial situation s_0, and:*

$$\mathcal{D} \models (\forall)(W \rightarrow RR[W])^3$$

Consequently, if $\mathcal{D} \models W$ then $\mathcal{D}_{s_0} \cup \mathcal{D}_{una} \models RR[W]$.

Proof: For space reasons we do not include the proof. In this proof we follow the basic steps of the completeness proof for R ([9]).

3. A Heuristic GOLOG Interpreter – Preamble

A GOLOG interpreter makes a sequence of choices in the search for a program execution. These choices are: selecting a path to pursue given a branch ($\delta_1 \mid \delta_2$); how to instantiate a variable v in $\pi v.\delta$; and whether to execute a program δ zero times or at least once in δ^*. When faced with a choice, a standard GOLOG interpreter selects the first available option (eg. δ_1 given the branch $\delta_1 \mid \delta_2$). When search reaches a dead-end, the interpreter backtracks to the last choice made and makes a different choice in its place.

Hence, a standard interpreter does not consider the impact of its choices on the quality of executions found. We develop a heuristic interpreter that evaluates available choices when faced with a non-deterministic construct. We assume: that there exists an

---
[3] As in [9], $(\forall)\phi$ denotes the universal closure of ϕ w.r.t its free variables.

evaluation function f_e that returns the numeric quality of an execution; and that the aim of our interpreter is to find an execution that minimises this function.

Example 3. Consider the spacecraft control domain of Example 1. Let $f_e(s) = -num\_obs(s)$ denote the number of observations made in the execution s of the given program. The goal in this domain is to maximise the number of targets observed.

□

Our heuristic GOLOG interpreter is constructed by adapting the ideas described in [2,6]. When faced with a non-deterministic construct, the interpreter has the option of transitioning to one of a number of configurations $[(\delta_{c_1}, s_{c_1}), \ldots, (\delta_{c_n}, s_{c_n})]$. For each of these choices, we solve a relaxed version of the problem – we use a relaxed interpreter (defined in Section 4) to find a relaxed execution (δ_{r_i}, s_{r_i}) of δ_{c_i} in s_{c_i}. We then assign to (δ_{c_i}, s_{c_i}) a numeric evaluation given by $f_e(s_{r_i})$. The available choices are ordered from best (smallest) evaluation to worst (largest). The best configuration is transitioned to, and if that choice leads to a dead-end, the next best configuration is considered upon backtracking. Section 5 presents an implementation of our heuristic interpreter.

4. A Relaxed GOLOG Interpreter

We use relaxed regression to approximate the interpretation of a GOLOG program. A relaxed interpreter finds a program execution while approximately deciding if an action is possible or not. The result is a relaxed execution of a program in a given situation.

The purpose of the relaxed interpreter is to determine what desirable future may result from making a particular choice in the interpretation of a program. To achieve this, we assume that we have an evaluation function f_p that assesses the quality of a configuration – which may or may not be the same as f_e (the evaluation function for executions). When faced with a range of configurations to transition to, our relaxed interpreter selects the configuration that minimises this function. If this configuration leads to a dead-end, the next best configuration is selected upon backtracking.

Example 4. In the spacecraft control domain (Example 1), our relaxed interpreter selects targets for observation that require the least degree of movement of the craft's instrument. The intuition is that small movements allows for the observation of more targets.

□

Relaxed interpretation must terminate if we are to extract from it a heuristic value. Hence, we assume that: we have a finite domain (ie. v in $\pi\ v.\ \delta$ has a finite range); there is a finite horizon of actions h over which the interpreter searches for an execution[4]; and all paths through a while or iteration construct involve an action being performed. We discuss the implications of an action horizon at the conclusion of this section.

4.1. A Relaxed Transition Semantics

Our relaxed interpreter uses the same *trans* and *final* clauses as the traditional interpreter (with additional bookkeeping for the finite action horizon h), with the exception of the

---
[4]The relaxed interpreter will find relaxed executions of up to h actions long.

trans clause for actions, branches, argument selection, and iteration. The modified versions of these clauses (called *transR*) are defined below. In these clauses, $\delta, \delta_1, \delta_2, \delta'$ denote programs, while s and s' denote situations.

In the *transR* clause for a primitive action: *primAct(a)* holds if a is a primitive action, and *possR(a, s)* holds if a is possible in s where its preconditions have been evaluated by relaxed regression.

transR(h, a, s, δ', s', h') :-
  $h > 0$, *primAct(a), possR(a, s)*, δ' = *nil*, s' = *do(a, s)*, h' is *h-1*.

In the *transR* clause for a branch: *transR'(h, δ, s, list)* finds the *list* of configurations that can be transitioned to from (δ, s) under *transR*. The predicate *best(list, δ', s', h')* uses f_p to select the best configuration (δ', s') in *list* (where horizon h' remains).

transR(h, $\delta_1|\delta_2$, s, δ', s', h') :-
  transR'(h, δ_1, s, list$_1$), transR'(h, δ_2, s, list$_2$),
  append(list$_1$, list$_2$, list), best(list, δ', s', h').

In the *transR* clauses for argument selection and iteration, *transR''(h, δ, s, list)* finds the *list* of configurations that can be transitioned to from (δ, s) under *transRS*, defined below. *sub(v, _, δ, δ_1)* replaces v in δ with an unbound variable to produce δ_1.

transR(h, prog, s, δ', s', h') :-
  (prog = $\pi v.\delta$; prog = δ^*),
  transR''(h, prog, s, list), best(list, δ', s', h').

transRS(h, $\pi v.\delta$, s, δ', s', h') :-
  sub(v, _, δ, δ_1), transR(h, δ_1, s, δ', s', h').

transRS(h, δ^*, s, $\delta':\delta^*$, s', h') :- transR(h, δ, s, δ', s', h').

Definition 5. The *transR* clauses defined in this section are used to find a relaxed execution s' of a program δ in situation s with horizon h as follows (where *transR** is the reflexive transitive closure of *transR*).

doR(δ, s, s', h) :- transR*(h, δ, s, δ', s', h'), ($h' = 0$; finalR(δ', s')).

□

In classical planning, action horizon selection can be difficult. As we shall see in Section 5.1, the structure of a GOLOG program provides a basis from which h can be derived. Given our intended use of the relaxed interpreter as a tool for generating heuristic values, h selection need not be agonised over. A h value that is too low will only yield a (potentially) less informed heuristic. As we shall discuss in Section 7, the use of this look-ahead bound allows us to use our heuristic interpreter in an online setting.

5. An Implementation of a Heuristic GOLOG

Our heuristic interpreter finds an execution of a GOLOG program in the same way as a traditional interpreter – with a set of transition axioms. Our interpreter utilises the same final axioms as the standard interpreter but defines new transition axioms for most of the GOLOG constructs of Table 1. The *transH* clauses for the primitive action, test, if …

else, and procedure constructs are the same as those in a traditional interpreter[5]. Let *prog* = $\delta_1 : \delta_2$, $\delta_1|\delta_2$, $\pi v.\delta$, δ^*, or **while** ϕ **do** δ **end**. The *transH* clauses in our heuristic interpreter for each of the *prog* constructs have the following form:

transH(prog, s, δ', s', h) :- *transH'(prog, s, list)*, *best'(list, h, δ', s')*.

where *transH'(prog, s, list)* finds the *list* of configurations that can be transitioned to from *(prog, s)* (under *trans*), and *best'(list, h, δ', s')* selects the best configuration in *list* to transition to. It does so by finding a relaxed execution of each configuration with *doR* and applying the evaluation function f_e to this execution resulting in a heuristic value for the corresponding choice.

Definition 6. The *transH* clauses defined in this section are used to find an execution s' of a program δ in situation s with horizon h as follows (where *transH** is the reflexive transitive closure of *transH*).

doH(δ, s, s', h) :- *transH*(δ, s, δ', s', h)*, *finalH(δ', s')*.

□

Remark 1. *Our heuristic interpreter is not optimal (admissible).*

Executions found by our relaxed interpreter are not necessarily the best or even possible. The heuristic values assigned to configurations that our heuristic interpreter can choose from do not necessarily represent which choices will definitely lead to the best legal executions. In addition, once a choice is made by the search algorithm, we do not backtrack until we arrive at a dead-end.

5.1. Experimental Results

We compare our heuristic interpreter with a traditional interpreter, and an interpreter in which choices are made according to a greedy heuristic without look-ahead by relaxation. Each of our test domains demonstrate situations in which the choices made during interpretation affect the quality of the execution found, and where some choices (that may not appear at first to be favourable) need to be made to find the best executions.

Our first collection of experiments is conducted in the spacecraft control domain of Examples 1, 3 and 4. In this domain, executions are evaluated with respect to the number of targets observed. Our relaxed and greedy interpreters select targets for observation that require the least degree of movement of the craft's instrument. The effect of relaxation on the preconditions of actions in this example removes the need to check for adequate resources and time to turn to and take images of targets.

A set of test cases have been generated with a specific number of celestial and calibration targets, fuel, power, and time limits (Table 3 shows the results of a subset of these tests). The locations of the target clusters were randomly defined – each coordinate (x, y, and z) assigned a random integer between -100 and 100. The position of each target within a cluster was randomly defined and lies within a small deviation of this location. The action horizon was set to the number of time steps available in each test case. In 33/50 (46/50) of the tests, our heuristic interpreter found executions that made more observations than those found by the greedy (traditional) interpreter. In the remainder, the compared interpreter pairs yielded executions with equal observation counts.

---

[5]With the addition of an action horizon h to pass to our relaxed interpreter when evaluating configurations.

N_T	FUEL	POWER	TIME	N_{CL}	O_S	O_G	O_H
10	500	200	150	6	4	6	6
10	500	200	150	6	1	1	4
20	600	300	250	9	4	4	10
20	600	300	250	9	1	3	7
30	700	200	350	11	4	5	16
30	700	200	350	11	4	10	17
40	800	300	450	14	9	21	21
40	800	300	450	14	8	17	24
50	900	400	550	18	8	20	30
50	900	400	550	18	7	22	28

Table 3. Observations made in executions found by the standard (O_S), greedy (O_G), and heuristic (O_H) interpreters. N_T and N_{CL} denote the number of celestial targets and clusters in each test.

Example 5. Consider an iron ore mine consisting of a series of iron ore blocks located across the mine landscape. A mining robot is designed to travel to a block, blast the block, collect the ore, and transfer the ore to a stockpile. Each block has a percentage amount of iron, silica, alumina, and phosphorus. Some blocks are dependent on others and cannot be mined until they are mined. A mining robot can only travel between a block and the stockpile if there is a safe (non-hazardous) path between the two. The robot is designed to build a stockpile of a desired tonnage and target defining the desired bounds on the percentages of iron, silica, alumina, and phosphorus. A plan for the miner is determined by finding an execution of the GOLOG program MINEOP.

    proc MINEOP
        powerup :
        while stockrequired **do**
            π blk, [available(blk)? : moveto(blk) · blast(blk) : mine(blk) :
            moveto(stockpile) : combine(blk)]
        end :
        powerdown
    end

where: *stockrequired* denotes that the stockpile requires more ore; *available(blk)* denotes that blk is a block that is available for mining (ie. it has not been previously mined and all blocks it depends on have been mined); and *powerup, moveto(object), blast(blk), mine(blk), combine(blk)*, and *powerdown* are primitive actions.

□

Let $f_e(s) = distance(s, target)$ denote how far away from the desired $target$ the stockpile is in execution s. Distance is defined as the sum of differences between each stockpile component value and its target divided by its acceptable range. Our relaxed and greedy interpreters select blocks to mine that are closest in composition to this target. The relaxation of action preconditions removes the need to check for hazards along the paths between blocks and the stockpile.

A set of test cases have been generated with a specific number of blocks (of equal tonnage) and hazards (Table 4). Each block, hazard, and the stockpile, is located at a coordinate whose components are assigned a random integer between 0 and 500. The blocks are divided into groups, forming a chain of blocks that can only be mined in

N_{Blocks}	R_{To}	N_G	N_H	D_S	D_G	D_H
5	1500	3	5	6.12	6.97	2.55
10	2500	5	5	3.27	5.90	0.75
15	3500	6	5	4.29	1.78	1.70
20	4500	6	10	1.85	1.43	2.11
25	5500	8	10	2.62	4.09	0.86
30	6500	11	15	1.54	4.10	0.36
35	7500	10	15	1.23	2.58	0.34
40	8500	12	20	2.37	1.58	0.81
45	8500	17	20	4.68	3.91	0.33

Table 4. Distance from stockpile target in executions found by the standard (D_S), greedy (D_G), and heuristic (D_H) interpreters. N_{Blocks}, R_{To}, N_G, and N_H denote the number of blocks, required stockpile tonnage, number of block groups, and hazards.

sequence. The stockpile target is randomly configured, and the composition of each block is defined by adding or subtracting a random deviation from the stockpile target. The action horizon chosen in each test is 5× the number of its blocks.

In 51/60 (56/60) of the tests, executions found by our heuristic interpreter led to a closer-to-target stockpile than those found by the greedy (traditional) interpreter. In 3/60 (1/60) of the tests, executions found by our heuristic interpreter resulted in a lower quality stockpile than those found by the greedy (traditional) interpreter.

Example 6. Consider a set of workers W, each $w_i \in W$ with a set of skills S_i. A scheduling agent is designed to select a set of jobs for the workers to perform within a limited time window, where each job consumes one unit of time. Each job consists of a set of tasks, each task requiring a specific subset of skills to complete. Only one job can be scheduled at a time, and only if there is a worker able to perform each of its tasks (where each worker can only perform one task per job). Jobs have dependencies such that some jobs can only be scheduled if other jobs have been performed before them. An execution of the GOLOG program SCHEDULE defines a plan for the scheduler.

proc SCHEDULE
    while timeleft **do**
        π job. [available(job)? : { π tk. [(task(tk, job) $\wedge \neg$ assigned(tk, job))? :
        π w. [worker(w)? : assign(w, tk, job)]] }* : scheduled(job)?]
    end
end

where: *timeleft* denotes that there is ≥ 1 unit of time left; *available(job)* holds if *job* has not been scheduled and each of its dependencies have been scheduled; *task(tk, job)* denotes that *tk* is a task of *job*; *assigned(tk, job)* denotes that *tk* in *job* has been assigned to a worker; *worker(w)* denotes that *w* is a worker; *scheduled(job)* holds if all the tasks in *job* have been assigned a worker; and *assign(w, tk, job)* is a primitive action assigning *tk* (of *job*) to worker *w*.

□

Let $f_e(s) = -tasks(s)$ describe the number of tasks that have been assigned to workers in execution s. Our relaxed and greedy interpreters select jobs to schedule that consist of the most tasks for assignment. In this example, relaxation of action preconditions removes the need to check whether a worker has already been assigned to a task on a job before assigning them to another.

A set of test cases have been generated with a specific number of workers, jobs, and maximum number of tasks per job. The number of tasks in each job is a randomly generated number between 1 and this maximum. The jobs are divided into groups forming a chain of jobs that can only be scheduled in sequence (with jobs later in the sequence more likely, but not necessarily, to have more tasks). Each worker is assigned a randomly selected subset of skills (from a set of 10), and each task is assigned a set of skills such that there are at least two workers able to complete it. The action horizon in each test is the number of jobs × the maximum number of tasks per job.

Due to space limitations, we only summarise the results of these tests. In 31/40 (38/40) of the tests, executions found by our heuristic interpreter resulted in more task assignments than those found by the greedy (traditional) interpreter. In 2/40 of the tests, the heuristic interpreter could not find a solution within 15 minutes. On the remainder, the compared interpreter pairs resulted in equally good executions.

5.2. Speed Comparison

Traditional interpretation is much faster than our heuristic interpreter. In each of the test cases in Table 3, traditional interpretation takes at most 2 seconds. In the most complex test case of this example (with 50 targets) our heuristic interpreter takes 98 seconds to find a solution. The average time required to find a solution in the set of 50 target test cases was 71 seconds.

In each domain, we also compared our heuristic interpreter to one that uses actual interpretation (not relaxed) to evaluate choices. On test cases in Table 3, this interpreter was on average 8× (at most 19 and at least 5×) slower than our heuristic interpreter.

6. Related Work

There are several existing techniques that combine GOLOG and classical planning. In [1], GOLOG programs are compiled into PDDL – a domain description language used by many classical planners. A classical planner can then be used to find an action sequence that is an execution of the GOLOG program. The underlying action theory in [1] must be described in PDDL, rather than a (more expressive) situation calculus basic action theory (BAT)[6]. Our approach allows the domain to be characterised by a BAT. In addition, the compilation of a GOLOG program into PDDL has potential limitations (highlighted in [8]), such as the addition of new fluents and actions (increasing state-space size). As we remain within the situation calculus and GOLOG, our approach does not suffer from these limitations.

The embedding of classical planning within a GOLOG program is considered in [4]. This work looks at problems that in part are suited for representation in GOLOG, but have stages in which general planning is required (such as the navigation of an entity across a grid). While this approach and ours combine GOLOG and classical planning, our technique looks at applying classical planning techniques to the whole interpretation process (rather than individual steps) to find an optimal or near optimal program execu-

---

[6]Relative expressiveness of BATs and PDDL is analysed in [5,11].

tion (while the other does not). Our interpreter is designed to work with problems that are suited for representation in GOLOG, while still involving combinatorial optimisation, and not the kind of general planning described above.

7. Conclusion and Future Work

In this paper we have described a heuristic GOLOG interpreter that is able to simulate the interpretation of a GOLOG program as a means of evaluating the available choices in the search for an execution. This simulation uses a relaxed form of regression (relaxed regression), developed in this paper. We have considered the successful relaxation-based heuristics used in classical planning [2,6] and described how they can be used to find a (near) optimal execution of a GOLOG program given an evaluation function.

We have presented our interpreter within an offline setting. The interpreter can be extended for use in an online setting by adding techniques to handle sensing actions during relaxed interpretation (which is conducted offline). Within our relaxed interpreter, we can view sensing actions as being a choice construct, where each possible sensing result is a choice. The interpreter can then select the sensing result most beneficial for it (ie. it assumes the best case scenario), just as it would a choice between actions. As a finite action horizon bound is used during relaxed interpretation, our interpreter can be used even with non-terminating programs (in an online setting).

As future work, we plan to investigate the relative performance of our interpreter with the compilation approach of [1] on the subset of GOLOG programs and BATs that are suitable for compilation into PDDL.

References

[1] J. Baier, C. Fritz, M. Bienvenu, and S. McIlraith. Beyond classical planning. In *AAAI*, pages 1509–1512, 2008.
[2] B. Bonet and H. Geffner. Planning as heuristic search. *Artificial Intelligence*, 129:5–33, 2001.
[3] G. de Giacomo, Y. Lespérance, and H. J. Levesque. ConGolog, a concurrent programming language based on the situation calculus. *Artificial Intelligence*, 121(1-2):109–169, 2000.
[4] J. Claßen, P. Eyerich, G. Lakemeyer, and B. Nebel. Towards an integration of Golog and planning. In *IJCAI*, pages 1846–1851, 2007.
[5] P. Eyerich, B. Nebel, G. Lakemeyer, and J. Claßen. GOLOG and PDDL: What is the relative expressiveness? In *PCAR*, 2006.
[6] J. Hoffmann and B. Nebel. The FF Planning System: Fast Plan Generation Through Heuristic Search. *JAIR*, 14:253–302, 2001.
[7] H. J. Levesque, R. Reiter, Y. Lespérance, F. Lin, and R. B. Scherl. Golog: A logic programming language for dynamic domains. *Journal of Logic Programming*, 31(1-3):59–83, 1997.
[8] Ronald P. A. Petrick. P^2: A baseline approach to planning with control structures and programs. In *ICAPS 2009 Generalized Planning*, pages 59–64, 2009.
[9] Fiora Pirri and Ray Reiter. Some contributions to the metatheory of the situation calculus. *Journal of the ACM*, 46(3):325–361, 1999.
[10] Raymond Reiter. The frame problem in situation the calculus. *Artificial Intelligence and Mathematical Theory of Computation*, pages 359–380, 1991.
[11] G. Röger, M. Helmert, and B. Nebel. On the Relative Expressiveness of ADL and Golog: The Last Piece in the Puzzle. In *KR*, 2008.
[12] D. E. Smith, J. Frank, and A. K. Jónsson. Bridging the Gap Between Planning and Scheduling. *Knowledge Engineering Review*, 15, 2000.

POMDP solving: what rewards do you really expect at execution?

Caroline Ponzoni Carvalho CHANEL [a,b] Jean-Loup FARGES [a] and
Florent TEICHTEIL-KÖNIGSBUCH [a] and Guillaume INFANTES [a]
[a] *ONERA - Office National d'Etudes et de Recherches Aérospatiales,
Toulouse, France. Email: name.surname@onera.fr*
[b] *ISAE - Institut Supérieur de l'Aéronautique et de l'Espace*

Abstract. Partially Observable Markov Decision Processes have gained an increasing interest in many research communities, due to sensible improvements of their optimization algorithms and of computers capabilities. Yet, most research focus on optimizing either average accumulated rewards (AI planning) or direct entropy (active perception), whereas none of them matches the rewards actually gathered at execution. Indeed, the first optimization criterion linearly averages over all belief states, so that it does not gain best information from different observations, while the second one totally discards rewards. Thus, motivated by simple demonstrative examples, we study an additive combination of these two criteria to get the best of reward gathering and information acquisition at execution. We then compare our criterion with classical ones, and highlight the need to consider new hybrid non-linear criteria, on a realistic multi-target recognition and tracking mission.

Keywords. POMDP, active perception, optimization criterion.

Introduction

Many real-world AI applications require to plan actions with incomplete information on the world's state. For instance, a robot has to find its way to a goal but without perfect sensing of its current localization in the map. As another example, the controller of a camera must plan the best optical tasks and physical orientations to precisely identify an object as fast as possible. If action effects and observations are probabilistic, Partially Observable Markov Decision Processes (POMDPs) are an expressive but long-neglected — due to prohibitive complexity — model for sequential decision-making with incomplete information [5]. Yet, new recent strides in POMDP solving algorithms [8,12,13] have revived an intensive research on algorithms and applications of POMDPs.

A POMDP is a tuple $\langle S, A, \Omega, T, O, R, b_0 \rangle$ where S is a set of states, A is a set of actions, Ω is a set of observations, $T : S \times A \times S \to [0;1]$ is a transition function such that $T(s_t, a, s_{t+1}) = P(s_{t+1} \mid a, s_t)$, $O : \Omega \times S \to [0;1]$ is an observation function such that $O(o_t, s_t) = P(o_t \mid s_t)$, $R : S \times A \times S \to \mathbb{R}$ is a reward function associated with transitions, and b_0 is a probability distribution over initial states. We note

B the set of probability distributions over the states, named *belief state space*. At each time step t, the agent updates its *belief state* defined as an element $b_t \in B$.

The aim of POMDP solving is to construct a policy function $\pi : B \to A$ such that it maximizes some criterion generally based on rewards or belief states. In robotics, where symbolic rewarded goals must be achieved, it is usually accepted to optimize the long-term average discounted accumulated rewards from any initial belief state [2,11]: $V^\pi(b) = E_\pi\left[\sum_{t=0}^{\infty} \gamma^t r(b_t, \pi(b_t)) \mid b_0 = b\right]$. Following from optimality theorems, the optimal value function is piece-wise linear, what offers a relatively simple mathematical framework for reasoning, on which most, if not all, algorithms are based. However, as highlighted and explained in this paper, the linearization of belief states' average value comes back to flatten observations and finally to loose distinctive information about them. Therefore, the optimized policy does not lead the agent to acquire sufficient information about the environment before acting to gather rewards: as discussed in this paper, such a strategy unfortunately results in less reward gathering at execution than expected if the initial belief state is very far from actual state.

This confusing but crucial point deserves more explanations for better understanding of what is at stake in this paper. At first, it may seem strange that the strategy which maximizes accumulated rewards is not optimal at actual execution: in what sense are the optimized criterion and the rewards gathered at execution different? In fact, the average accumulated rewards criterion is defined over belief states (because the agent applies a strategy based only on its belief), whereas the rewards gathered at execution are accumulated on the basis of the actual successive states, hidden from the agent. With total observability (MDP case), such issue does not arise since actual states are observed, so the criterion is averaged over actual probabilistic execution paths. But in the POMDP case, the criterion is *averaged over probabilistic believed paths*, which are generally different from the *actual* execution paths. Strangely enough, this bias between optimized criterion and actual rewards gathered at execution has not been much studied: to our knowledge, most robotics research on POMDPs has considered more and more efficient methods to optimize this average accumulated rewards criterion, despite the lack of explicit separation between possible observations during optimization.

In spite of better explaining the idea raised here, we seek to show the existence of a Δ, more or equal à zero, defined by 1, that expresses the difference between the criterion optimized by the classical POMDP framework and the rewards cumulated at policy execution.

$$\Delta = \left| E\left[\sum_{t=0}^{\infty} \gamma^t r(s_t, \pi(b_t)) | b_0\right] - E\left[\sum_{t=0}^{\infty} \gamma^t r(b_t, \pi(b_t)) | b_0\right] \right| \qquad (1)$$

b_t represents de belief state, i.e. the probability distribution over states at an instant t (at each time step b_t updated with the Bayes' rule after each action done and observation perceived). And s_t represents de hidden state of the system, and depends only on the dynamic of the system. The difference is more or equal to zero every time step. Equal to zero for anytime step in which the agents' belief is a Dirac's delta over a state of the system ($b_t = \delta_{s_t}$), and more than zero otherwise

($b_t \neq \delta_{s_t}$). Formally, $r(b_t, \pi(b_t))$ is defined by: $r(b_t, \pi(b_t)) = \sum_s r(s, \pi(b_t)) b_t(s)$, and we introduce it in the Eq. (1):

$$\Delta = \left| E\left[\sum_{t=0}^{\infty} \gamma^t r(s_t, \pi(b_t)) | b_0 \right] - \sum_{t=0}^{\infty} \gamma^t \left(\sum_s r(s, \pi(b_t)) b_t(s) \right) | b_0 \right| \quad (2)$$

Using the norm and the expected value properties, we get:

$$\Delta = \left| E\left[\sum_{t=0}^{\infty} \gamma^t \left(r(s_t, \pi(b_t)) - \left(\sum_s r(s, \pi(b_t)) b_t(s) \right) \right) | b_0 \right] \right|$$

$$\leq \left| E\left[r(s_0, \pi(b_0)) - \left(\sum_s r(s, \pi(b_0)) b_0(s) \right) | b_0 \right] \right| + \cdots +$$

$$\gamma^t \left| E\left[r(s_t, \pi(b_t)) - \left(\sum_s r(s, \pi(b_t)) b_t(s) \right) | b_0 \right] \right|, \ t \to \infty \quad (3)$$

$\sum_s r(s, \pi(b_t)) b_t(s)$ clearly average rewards $r(s, \pi(b_t))$ over states. More precisely, for a given state s_n and a given time step t, if $b_t = \delta_{s_n}$, the reward will be $\sum_s r(s, \pi(b_t)) b_t(s) = r(s_n, \pi(b_t))$, on the contrary for a $b_t \neq \delta_{s_n}$ the reward will be different of $r(s_n, \pi(b_t))$. Denoting:

$$\triangle R_t(s_t, b_t) = E\left[r(s_t, \pi(b_t)) - \left(\sum_s r(s, \pi(b_t)) b_t(s) \right) | b_0 \right]$$

and re-writing Eq. (3), we obtain:

$$\Delta \leq \triangle R_0(s_0, b_0) + \gamma \triangle R_1(s_1, b_1) + \cdots + \gamma^t \triangle R_t(s_t, b_t), \text{ with } t \to \infty \quad (4)$$

If for a given time step $t = k$ we have $b_k = \delta_{s_k}$, it is easy to see that $\triangle R_k(s_k, b_k) = 0$. This allows us to infer that if $b_0 \neq \delta_{s_0}$, i.e, the probability distribution over states is not a Dirac's delta over the initial hidden state s_0, the difference Δ is more than zero already in $t = 0$. And successively, for all time steps where $b_t \neq \delta_{s_t}$.

On the other hand, researchs on active sensing aim at maximizing knowledge of the environment [3,4,7]; thus minimizing *Shannon's entropy* criterion, which assesses the accumulated quantity of information in the initial belief state b_0: $H(b_0) = \sum_{t=0}^{+\infty} \gamma^t \sum_{s \in S} b_t(s) \log(b_t(s))$. Contrary to the previous criterion, this criterion is non-linear over belief states so it makes a clear distinction between observations to promote one that update the belief state in the right direction. But this criterion does not take into account rewards, so it is not appropriate for goal reaching problems.

Thus, considering approaches from both research communities, it is natural to search for new non-linear reward-based optimization criteria by aggregating the average accumulated rewards criterion and the entropy one into a single mixed criterion. This way, optimized strategies would consist in alternating information acquisition and state-modification actions to maximize reward gathering at execution, provided both criteria are appropriately balanced. Formally, noting $J_\lambda(V,H)$ a mixed criterion depending on some $\lambda \in \Lambda$ parameter, the *general problem we address* is formalized as follows:

$$\max_{\lambda \in \Lambda} E\left[\sum_{t=0}^{+\infty} \gamma^t r_t \mid s_0, \pi_\lambda\right] \text{ such that } \pi_\lambda = \underset{\pi \in A^S}{\operatorname{argmax}} J_\lambda(V(b_0), H(b_0))$$

In other words, what is the value λ balancing $V(b_0)$ and $H(b_0)$ that maximizes the average accumulated rewards gathered at execution, starting from an initial state s_0 unknown to the agent, when applying the policy that maximizes the mixed criterion based on the agent's initial belief state? Solutions to this problem depend on the class of functions to which J_λ belongs. Yet, even for simple classes like $\{J_\lambda : J_\lambda(V,H) = (1-\lambda)V + \lambda H, 0 \leqslant \lambda \leqslant 1\}$, we could not find algebraic general solutions. Some authors studied applications of such criterion for some fixed λ with 1-step optimization of the entropy [1]. Others formalized active sensing problems as POMDP optimization based on the previous class, but without solving them nor studying the impact of λ on rewards gathered at execution [6].

A recent work [10] considers the problem of dynamical sensor selection in camera networks based on user-defined objectives, such as maximizing coverage or improved localization uncertainty. The criterion optimized is the POMDP classical one, but the key of this work relies in the model of the reward function. For exemple, for improving localization uncertainty, the authors use the determinant of the variance matrix as additional information in the reward function. This variance matrix is obtained for each sensor and possible location of the target. In this way, the reward function continues to be linear, and the classical criterion is applied.

Therefore, in the next section, we highlight the importance of mixed nonlinear criteria as introduced above on a simple but illustrative example. We show the impact of different values of λ on rewards gathered at execution, depending on the initial belief state. Then, in the next section, we formally define an additive criterion that may be of interest for better optimization of POMDP robotics problems. Finally, before concluding the paper, we point out the relevance of considering non-linear mixed criteria on a realistic multi-target recognition and tracking robotics mission, which we solved with a state-of-the-art POMDP planner modified for our new criterion.

1. Illustrative Examples

This section intends to study the difference of behavior obtained at execution by modifying the classical POMDP's criterion on a given problem. The objective is to show that the change of criterion induces agent caution in relation to its belief state, reducing the chances of mistake at policy execution.

Let us define a problem with four states $\{s_0, s_1, s_2, s_3\}$ and two observations $\{o_1, o_2\}$. Initially, the agent can be in s_0 or s_2, so that $b_0(s_0) = 1 - b_0(s_2)$, and o_1 (resp. o_2) corresponds to observe if it is in s_0 (resp. s_2). It can perform three actions: a_0 is a perception action that costs c and does not change the state, while a_1 and a_2 deterministically lead to absorbing states as shown in Figure 1. Depending on the actual state s_0 or s_2, actions a_1 and a_2 give opposite rewards (either R or $-R$), meaning that a_1 should be chosen if actual state is s_0, a_2 if it is s_2. Note that $R > c > 0$.

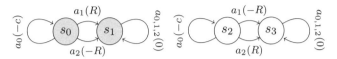

Figure 1. Transitions of the POMDP (rewards between parenthesis)

Intuitively, there are two "good" strategies here, depending on the initial belief state:
- try to avoid the observation cost and directly choose a_1 or a_2;
- first observe with action a_0 then act with action a_1 or a_2.

The observation matrix is defined as: $p(o|s') = \begin{bmatrix} 1 & 0.5 & 0 & 0.5 \\ 0 & 0.5 & 1 & 0.5 \end{bmatrix}$ We can compute the Q-values over $b(s)$, which are the best values of each action if the optimal policy is applied next. Note that, in this simple example, the optimal policy is obvious after the first action, starting either in s_0 or s_2. Q-values depend on $b_0(s_0)$ and $b_0(s_2)$:

$$Q^\pi(b, a_0) = (R - c)(b_0(s_0) + b_0(s_2))$$
$$Q^\pi(b, a_1) = R(b_0(s_0) - b_0(s_2))$$
$$Q^\pi(b, a_2) = R(b_0(s_2) - b_0(s_0))$$

Q-values over $b_0(s_0)$ are shown in Figure 2-left along with the value function, which is the best Q-value (for $R = 1$ and $c = 0.5$). We see that the optimal policy depends on the initial belief state, as expected. Also, is represented the actual value gathered by the agent according to its initial belief when the initial state of the system is s_0.

1.1. Criterion Modification

Now, we add Shannon's entropy of $b(s)$ to the criterion at every time step, i.e. we add the expected entropy $H^\pi(b)$ denoted by : $H^\pi = \sum_{t=0}^{N} H(b_t)$. And so as, the new criterion becomes: $J^\pi(b, \lambda) = (1 - \lambda)V^\pi(b) + \lambda H^\pi(b)$ The value of the belief state entropy $H(b)$ almost does not change when the first strategy is executed. In other hand, when the second strategy is chosen, the entropy lowers to zero at the second step. After taking action a_1 or a_2, the entropy value decreases, but less than after action a_0 which brings the entropy to zero. So, the mixed criterion of the first strategy is more penalized than the one of the second strategy, because it takes into account the total value of entropies (at $t = 0$ and $t = 1$).

$$Q^\pi(b, a_0) = (1 - \lambda)(R - c)(b_0(s_0) + b_0(s_2)) + \lambda H(b_0)$$
$$Q^\pi(b, a_1) = (1 - \lambda)R(b_0(s_0) - b_0(s_2)) + \lambda(H(b_0) + H(b_1))$$
$$Q^\pi(b, a_2) = (1 - \lambda)R(b_0(s_2) - b_0(s_0)) + \lambda(H(b_0) + H(b_1)))$$

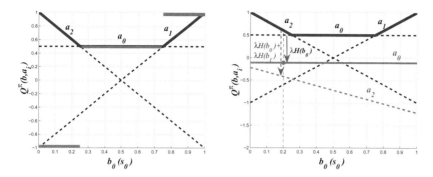

Figure 2. Left: Q-values (in blue), value function (in red), also actual value gathered by the agent (in green) when system's initial state is s_0, all over $b_0(s_0)$. Right: Q-values for $b_0(s_0) = 0.2$ before (blue) and after (green) criterion modification.

In order to illustrate the change in the criterion, we have computed the α-vectors for a given belief state. In the Figure 2-right the Q-values for the classical criterion and the Q-values for the modified criterion are presented for a $b_0(s_0) = 0.2$. It can be verified that the addition of the weighted entropy changes the gradient of the α-vectors. The new criterion penalizes much more the first strategy than the second one. In other words, when the weighted entropy is taken into account for this belief, the new criterion reflects in the Q-value for this belief the uncertainty, and brings on the α-vector for a_0 as dominant.

To show the change in the criterion and as a consequence, the change in the shape of the value function, we have computed the best mixed criterion in function of $b_0(s_0)$ for different values of λ. Figure 3-left shows that the mixed criterion's shape changes a lot while varying the value of λ from zero to one: the higher the λ value is, the more the first strategy gets penalized. It also shows that the criterion is no longer linear.

Some assumptions can be overcome with this change. Figure 3-right presents the actual rewards gathered by the agent when it acts based on $b(s)$, without knowing it is actually in state s_0 at the beginning. Note the differences with

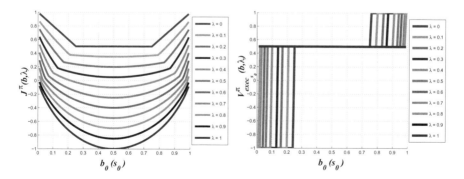

Figure 3. Left: best mixed-criterion based on the agent's initial belief for different λ values (λ increases from top curves to bottom ones); Right: rewards gathered at execution for different λ values depending on the agent's initial belief when the initial state of the system is s_0– which determines its policy (λ increases from inside to outside).

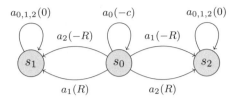

Figure 4. Counter example of entropy addition in criterion.

the average rewards which the agent believes to gather on Figure 2-left. The closer λ is to one, the more the agent prefers observing first, so that it is less penalized if its initial belief is wrong (0.5 instead of -1). But the rewards gathered if it is right decrease also (0.5 instead of 1). So, we would like to establish some degree of confidence over $b(s_0)$ and then figure out the appropriate λ for the problem. For this simple example, we can calculate a function $\lambda = f(b_{s_0})$, with $b_{s_0} = b_0(s_0)$, using the point where $Q^\pi(b, a_0) = Q^\pi(b, a_2)$ and taking advantage that $H(b_1) = H(b_0)$ when action a_2 is done.

$$\lambda(b_{s_0}) = \frac{2Rb_{s_0} - c}{2Rb_{s_0} - c + b_{s_0}\ln(b_{s_0}) + (1-b_{s_0}))\ln(1-b_{s_0}))}$$

This kind of modification of criterion is necessary when the agent's initial belief (or prior) $b_0(s)$ does not correspond to real frequencies of the initial states. In real situations, this kind of mistake often happens: the $b_0(s)$ used for the policy calculation may not be the best approximation of the reality.

A counter example is detailed in Figure 4. We see that there is no gain in adding the belief state entropy value at every time-step, because there is no ambiguity in the initial state this case. The value function only depends on the arrival state and it will be equally penalized by the belief state entropy for each action.

$$Q^\pi(b, a_0) = R|b_0(s_1) - b_0(s_2)| - cb_0(s_0)$$
$$Q^\pi(b, a_1) = Q^\pi(b_0, a_2) = R|b_0(s_1) - b_0(s_2)|$$

In the following, a mixed non-linear criterion for POMDPs is presented and the modification we made to the state-of-the-art algorithm Symbolic-PERSEUS [9] to optimize it. The next sections present some results obtained by modeling and solving a simple realistic problem which confirms the intuitions raised in this example.

2. Hybrid Optimization Criterion for POMDPs

The criterion proposed in this section models the expected cumulative discounted reward, attributed to the chosen actions, added to the expected cumulative discounted entropy of the belief (computed over the successive stochastic belief states), both in infinite-horizon. This two values are themselves weighted by a constant λ:

$$J^\pi(b) = (1-\lambda)V^\pi(b) + \lambda H^\pi(b), \text{ with} \tag{5}$$

$$V^\pi(b) = E_\pi\left[\sum_{t=0}^{\infty} \gamma^t r(b_t, \pi(b_t)) \mid b_0 = b\right]$$

$$H^\pi(b) = E_\pi\left[\sum_{t=0}^{\infty} \gamma^t H(b_t) \mid b_0 = b\right]$$

Theorem : Bellman's equation of the additive criterion. *The optimal value function of the additive criterion is the limit of the vector sequence defined by:*

$$J_{n+1}(b) = \max_{a \in A}\left\{(1-\lambda)r(b,a) + \lambda H(b) + \gamma \sum_{o \in \Omega} p(o|b,a) J_n(b_a^o(s'))\right\} \tag{6}$$

Proof. The equation 5 can be rewritten as:

$$J^\pi(b) = E_\pi\left[\sum_{t=0}^{\infty} \gamma^t \left(\beta r(b_t, \pi(b_t)) + \rho H(b_t)\right) \mid b_0 = b\right] \tag{7}$$

This shows that this criterion corresponds to the classic γ-discounted criterion which is the current reward added to the current entropy of the belief. It is therefore a maximization problem over γ-discounted artificial rewards equals to the real rewards plus the actual belief's entropy. □

This new Bellman's equation permits *via* dynamic-programming the computation of a policy that weights the immediate reward by the immediate entropy of the belief.

Heuristic. Symbolic-PERSEUS uses a heuristic function to determine the set of reachable belief states. It initializes the belief states search with $V_{degrad}^\pi = \max_{s,a} r(s,a)$, calculated from a depleted model, e.g. with an admissible heuristic whose value must be smaller than the optimal value. The definition of the new criterion therefore requires to change this heuristic as well, in order to take into account a minimal value for H in the initialization of the reachable beliefs search calculation. The heuristic is now defined by J_0 shown below.

Theorem: Heuristic for the additive criterion. *An admissible heuristic to the additive criterion is given by:*

$$J_0 = \frac{(1-\lambda)V_{degrad}^\pi - \lambda \log_{10}(n)}{1 - \gamma} \tag{8}$$

Proof. The minimal value to $H(b)$ constrained by $\sum_{i=1}^{n} b(s_i) = 1$ is given by the Lagrangian optimization:

$$H(b)_{min} = n\frac{1}{n}\log_{10}\left(\frac{1}{n}\right) = -\log_{10}(n) \tag{9}$$

$$\text{So: } J^\pi \geq \frac{(1-\lambda)V_{degrad}^\pi - \lambda \log_{10}(n)}{1-\gamma} = J_0 \qquad (10)$$

□

Discussion. The criterion presented in this section is no more piecewise linear, but algorithms such as PBVI [8], PERSEUS [11] and Symbolic-PERSEUS [9], which approach the criterion by stochastic generation of local belief states, can approximate this nonlinear criterion, given that every function can be approximate by a piecewise linear function.

3. Robotics Example

The studied model deals with an autonomous helicopter that tries to identify and track two targets. These targets are of different types, A or B. Objective of the helicopter is to land onto the target of type A, without initially knowing types of targets . This scenario combines both mission and perception objectives. Thus, this is relevant for this work because the reward optimization (implicitly) implies reducing the belief's entropy: actually, it is necessary to reduce uncertainty over the nature of targets in order to achieve the mission. Initially, the autonomous helicopter has an *a priori* knowledge about the targets. It needs to track and identify each target by its actions in order to accomplish its goal. In the simulations studied in this work, the agent was given an initial belief state weighted and not uniforme over all possible combinations of targets types. The initial belief's values with respect to the targets types are shown in table 1.

Table 1. Initial belief about the targets.

Targets	A	B
target 1	0.2	0.8
target 2	0.8	0.2

The motion space of the helicopter is modeled by a $3 \times 3 \times 3$ grid, and the one of the targets by a $3 \times 3 \times 1$ grid: the targets moves only on the ground (see Figure 5). The helicopter can do 7 actions: forward in x, y and z (go up), backward in x, y and z (go down), and land. It cannot realizes more than one action at any time-step. Motions of helicopter can fail with a 10% probability, except the land action which always succeeds. Target positions are completely observable to the helicopter agent. Nevertheless, the targets change position in x and/or y, 1 time for 20 helicopter motions, but the latter cannot predict the evolution. Helicopter is allowed to land only if it is directly above a target ($z = 2$, as ground is $z = 1$). Once the helicopter has landed on the target (A) or (B), neither the helicopter nor the targets can move, and helicopter is not allowed to take-off. The observation model of the type of the targets depends on the euclidean distance from helicopter to targets as show below.

$$p(o' = A \mid s' = A) = \frac{1}{2}\left(e^{\frac{-d}{D}} + 1\right) \text{ and } p(o' = A \mid s' = B) = \frac{1}{2}\left(1 - e^{\frac{-d}{D}}\right)$$

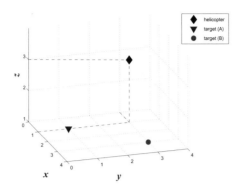

Figure 5. Initial position of helicopter, target 1 (A) and target 2 (B).

where d is the euclidean distance between helicopter and target, and D a factor of adjustment of the exponential. This observation function allows to model the gain of information when the helicopter comes near to the target : the closer the helicopter is from the observed target, the higher the probability to observe the actual nature of the target is. The helicopter completely observes others state variables, as the positions of targets. Note that, this model does not aim at testing the effectiveness of an algorithm in terms of time of calculation nor memory used, but it is meant to illustrate different optimization criteria for the same problem.

3.1. Experimental Protocol

The optimization criterion for the POMDP is a function of the agent's belief state, so it is optimized in terms of agent's pessimistic and subjective belief, which have not access to the actual state of world.

On the other hand, the criterion proposed is based on rewards which *really* are accumulated at policy execution, weighting only the uncertainty over effects of actions. Thus we want to measure the criterion optimality from an external viewpoint i.e. from an observer outside the system, who knows perfectly the state of environment at any moment. In this paper, this omniscient observer based on a policy simulator.

For each optimized policy, we have performed 500 simulations for a 50 horizon time, i.e. for 50 successive actions executed. For $\gamma = 0.9$, this horizon is considered large enough to obtain a good approximation of the criterion for an infinite horizon. The objective value function, which depends only on the current state of the environment is compute by means of Eq. (11).

$$V^\pi(s_t) = \frac{1}{500} \sum_{500\,simulations} \left[\sum_{k=0}^{t} \gamma^k r^\pi(s_k) \mid s_t \right] \qquad (11)$$

In this paper the optimized policies with different optimized criteria are compared on the basis of the same objective value, which, whatever the optimization criterion is, will always be the rewards actually collected by the agent at policy execution. To study convergence speed of the entropy of the agent's belief, the current entropy of the belief entropy was calculated (statistically averaged over the runs), as shown in Eq. (12).

$$H^\pi(b_t) = \frac{1}{500} \sum_{500\,simulations} \left[\sum_{k=0}^{t} \gamma^k H^\pi(b_k) \mid b_t \right] \quad (12)$$

Note that this measure is subjective, specific to the agent, unlike the previous measure which is objective and specific to the simulator.

3.2. Simulation and Results

Policies have been computed for different λ values : $0, 0.5$ and 1. The first value is the γ-weighted classic criterion. Note that this criterion tries to optimize only the expected cumulative discounted reward assigned to the actions and task completion. The second λ value seeks to give the same importance to the accomplishment of the mission and information acquisition. And the third one optimizes only the information gain, i.e. the reduction of the entropy of the belief.

On Figure 6-left, the average of the value functions $V^\pi(s_t)$, Eq. (11), for the 3 values of λ are presented. In the first case ($\lambda = 0$), the value function $V^\pi(s_t)$ starts with negatives value; this is because the landing actions on the correct target (achieved after more than 10 simulation steps) weight less than those on the wrong one (done after 3 or 4 steps simulation) in the calculation of $V^\pi(s_t)$ due to γ-weighting. The authors think that the landing actions on the wrong target are probably due to the small size of the grid preventing the autonomous helicopter to acquire more information before the landing happens. The helicopter, which starts with a belief state weighted towards the type of the targets, leads to land as fast as possible over a target of type (B) after only 4 or 5 steps because, at this point, it still believes that this one can be a correct target of type (A). On the other side, in simulations in which the autonomous helicopter has acquired more information from its environment, the autonomous helicopter has inverted its belief state (not presented in this section due to space) and lands on the correct target of type (A). Hence the observed reversal of the value function, which shows that the agent reacts well even to the worst case.

For the second λ value, the criterion value starts also with negative values, corresponding to the same reasons raised above. The main difference reposes on the total value gathered when $t \to 50$. The value for the $\lambda = 0.5$ is more important than the value for $\lambda = 0$. Here the landing actions are made earlier than with the classical criterion, and so they weight more in the calculation of the $V^\pi(s_t)$ because of the γ-weighting. The paper contribution is here illustrated, since the agent now explicitly tries to acquire more information from its environment, allowing it to reverse earlier its belief and finally to land more frequently (402 times *versus* 390) on the correct target of type (A). A problem with the classical criterion is actually its linearity in $b(s)$: it considers that a belief state with 60% of chance of giving a reward actually brings 60% of this reward in. The non-linearity of this new criterion allows to better evaluate the value of $b(s)$, giving less weight to smaller uncertainties. Thus we conclude that taking into account actual belief state entropy at every time-step in policy computation forces the autonomous

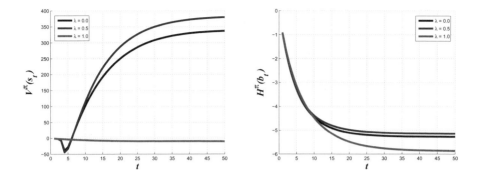

Figure 6. Averaged value function of current state $V^\pi(s_t)$ (left); And cumulated weighted entropy of belief state $H^\pi(b_t)$ (right).

agent to better sense its environment and then, carry out its mission and receive more rewards at policy execution, which is the overall objective for the designers of an autonomous system.

With the third value of λ, the criterion optimizes only the information gain. The Figure 6-left shows that the average of $V^\pi(s_t)$ remains close to zero: the helicopter does not try to land, it only gathers information. This is because the reward related with the task completion (landing on the target of type (A)) is no longer taken into account.

The Figure 6-right shows comparison of the subjective criterion $H^\pi(b_t)$, Eq. (12), for the 3 values of λ. Note that in the second case, average of the sum of entropy is bigger than with the classical criterion. Actually, the helicopter needs to observe its environment before task completion, which makes him reduce uncertainty over its belief state faster. This Figure also shows that the optimization of $J^\pi(b)$ allows to reduce the uncertainty faster than optimizing only $H^\pi(b)$, because it is implicitly necessary to reduce uncertainty in order to land on the correct target. Furthermore, this work shows that the $H^\pi(b)$ optimization does not necessarily optimizes its rate of growth at strategy execution. The mission objective, integrated to the additive criterion, gives a faster lowering of uncertainty by optimizing only $H^\pi(b)$.

To conclude, the additive criterion is as good as the purely entropic criterion in terms of information gathering, and it converges to a bigger value than the two others criteria (purely entropic or classic γ-weighted). This is due to a second fundamental fact: the additive criterion, by forcing the optimized policy to choose actions to gain rewards over actions to gain information from time to time, actually accumulates more rewards than running the classical criterion.

4. Conclusions and Future Works

In this paper have been presented a new mixed optimization criterion for POMDPs, which aggregate the cumulative information gain (perception) and the cumulative rewards gain (mission), weighted and averaged over an infinite horizon. Optimality of Bellman's equation has been underlined and proved for this new criterion. Furthermore new admissible heuristic have been proposed for this criterion in order to use with algorithms such as Symbolic-PERSEUS.

We have experimentally demonstrated that this criterion allows the autonomous agent to gather information about this environment and to estimate faster its real state, compared to classic criteria (which take into account only either information gain, or rewards). Furthermore, for the additive criterion, the agent accumulates more rewards at policy execution than when it executes a policy obtained with a classical criterion (which does not explicitly take into account the information gain). In some way, explicit consideration of the entropy of the belief state in addition to rewards makes the autonomous agent acquire more information in order to weight his subjective view of the rewards, that it believes receiving, but may not due to its imperfect knowledge of the environment.

In the future, the influence of the λ coefficient in the additive criterion will be studied in more details. The authors believe that there is an optimal λ coefficient depending on the problem model, allowing to maximize the objective rewards actually accumulated at policy execution. The authors may also propose an optimization algorithm that optimizes policy and λ coefficient at the same time with respect to the modeled problem.

References

[1] W. Burgard, Dieter Fox, and Sebastian Thrun. Active mobile robot localization. In *Proceedings of IJCAI-97*. Morgan Kaufmann, 1997.

[2] A.R. Cassandra, L.P. Kaelbling, and J.A. Kurien. Acting under uncertainty: Discrete Bayesian models for mobile-robot navigation. In *In Proceedings of IEEE/RSJ*, 1996.

[3] F. Deinzer, J. Denzler, and H. Niemann. Viewpoint selection-planning optimal sequences of views for object recognition. *Lecture notes in computer science*, pages 65–73, 2003.

[4] R. Eidenberger, T. Grundmann, W. Feiten, and RD Zoellner. Fast parametric viewpoint estimation for active object detection. In *Proceeding of the IEEE International Conference on Multisensor of Fusion and Integration for Intelligent Systems (MFI 2008), Seoul, Korea*, 2008.

[5] L.P. Kaelbling, M.L. Littman, and A.R. Cassandra. Planning and acting in partially observable stochastic domains. *Artificial Intelligence*, 101(1-2):99–134, 1998.

[6] L. Mihaylova, T. Lefebvre, H. Bruyninckx, K. Gadeyne, and J. De Schutter. Active sensing for robotics – a survey. In *5th Intl Conf. On Numerical Methods and Applications*, pages 316–324, 2002.

[7] Lucas Paletta and Axel Pinz. Active object recognition by view integration and reinforcement learning. *Robotics and Autonomous Systems*, 31:71–86, 2000.

[8] J. Pineau, G. Gordon, and S. Thrun. Point-based value iteration: An anytime algorithm for POMDPs. In *Proc. of IJCAI*, 2003.

[9] P. Poupart. *Exploiting structure to efficiently solve large scale partially observable Markov decision processes*. PhD thesis, University of Toronto, 2005.

[10] M.T.J. Spaan and P.U. Lima. A decision-theoretic approach to dynamic sensor selection in camera networks. In *Int. Conf. on Automated Planning and Scheduling*, pages 279–304, 2009.

[11] M.T.J. Spaan and N. Vlassis. A point-based POMDP algorithm for robot planning. In *IEEE International Conference on Robotics and Automation*, volume 3, pages 2399–2404. IEEE; 1999, 2004.

[12] M.T.J. Spaan and N. Vlassis. Perseus: Randomized point-based value iteration for POMDPs. *JAIR*, 24:195–220, 2005.

[13] M. Sridharan, J. Wyatt, and R. Dearden. HiPPo: Hierarchical POMDPs for Planning Information Processing and Sensing Actions on a Robot. In *Proc. of ICAPS*, 2008.

Generative Structure Learning for Markov Logic Networks

Quang-Thang DINH [a,1], Matthieu EXBRAYAT [a] and Christel VRAIN [a]
[a] *LIFO, Université d'Orléans, Orléans, FRANCE*

Abstract. In this paper, we present a generative algorithm to learn Markov Logic Network (*MLN*) structures automatically, directly from a training dataset. The algorithm follows a bottom-up approach by first heuristically transforming the training dataset into boolean tables, then creating candidate clauses using these boolean tables and finally choosing the best clauses to build the *MLN*. Comparisons to the state-of-the-art structure learning algorithms for *MLNs* in two real-world domains show that the proposed algorithm outperforms them in terms of the conditional log likelihood *(CLL)*, and the area under the precision-recall curve *(AUC)*.

Keywords. Markov Logic Network, Structure Learning, Relational Learning.

Introduction

In the Machine Learning community, Markov Logic Networks can be viewed as the most recent cross-fertilization of logic and statistical learning. A Markov Logic Network [20] is a structure, which aims at describing a given world with a set of weighted logical formulas.

Let us first remind the definitions of Markov Networks and Markov Logic Networks. A Markov Network *(MN)* is a graphical model, that consists of a set of vertices representing random variables, these vertices being connected by edges. There exists an edge linking two nodes if the corresponding random variables are conditionally dependent. A weight is associated to each clique of this graph. Given the actual value of a subset of the variables, the value of the remaining ones can be inferred using some sampling technique such as a Markov-Chain Monte-Carlo *(MCMC)* algorithm [20].

A Markov Logic Network (MLN) L consists of a set of pairs (F_i, w_i), where F_i is a formula in first order logic to which a weight w_i is given. This latter is a real number, which expresses the "probability" of this formula to be true, in the sense that the higher w_i, the more likely a grounding of F_i to be true. From a MLN and a set of constants $C = \{c_1, c_2, \ldots c_{|C|}\}$ a Markov Network can be generated. The nodes (vertices) of this MN correspond to all the ground predicates that can be generated with the predicates appearing in the formulas and C. This set can be restricted when constants and variables are typed. Nodes are connected by features, each feature corresponding to the grounding of a formula F_i. A node takes value *1* if the corresponding ground predicate is true,

---

[1] LIFO, Université d'Orléans, Rue Léonard de Vinci, B.P. 6759, F-45067 ORLEANS Cedex 2, France; Email: {thang.dinh,matthieu.exbrayat,christel.vrain}@univ-orleans.fr

0 otherwise; a feature takes value *1* when the corresponding ground formula is true, 0 otherwise.

Both generative and discriminative learning can be applied to Markov Logic Networks. In this paper we focus on generative learning. We propose a heuristic method based on propositionalization, that aims at transforming the database into boolean tables expressing the combinations of literals that exist in the training database. From these boolean tables we extract a set of *template* clauses from which we build the set of candidate clauses to form the MLN structure. These candidate clauses are evaluated according to the weighted pseudo-log-likelihood *(WPLL)* measure.

This paper is organized as follows: in Section 1 we propose a state-of-the-art overview of generative learning of MLNs. In Section 2 we present our approach and compare it to related work. Section 3 is devoted to experiments and in Section 4, we sum up and propose some extensions to this work.

1. Generative Learning of Markov Logic Networks

Generative approaches try to induce a global organization of the world and thus, in the case of a statistical approach, optimize the joint probability distribution of all the variables. Concerning MLNs, generative approaches optimize the log-likelihood or the pseudo-log-likelihood as proposed in [20]. Weights might be learned using the iterative scaling algorithm [18]. However, using a quasi-Newton optimization method such as the *L-BFGS* algorithm [29] has recently showed to be much faster [21].

Regarding generative structure learning, the original algorithm in Alchemy [12] consists of two steps. First, it uses the CLAUDIEN [5] system to learn a set of clauses. Then it learns the weights by maximizing pseudo-likelihood [20]. In [11], the authors propose a method that combines ideas from the ILP [30] and the feature induction of Markov Networks. This algorithm involves a beam or shortest first search in the space of clauses guided by the weighted pseudo-log-likelihood *(WPLL)* [11] measure. These two systems follow a top-down paradigm where many potential candidate structures are systematically generated without considering data and then evaluated using a statistical measure of their fitness to the data. In [15], an algorithm called *BUSL* follows a bottom-up approach in order to reduce the search space. The structure of *BUSL* is composed of three main phases. In the first phase, BUSL creates a boolean table *MP* for each predicate *P* in the domain. In the second phase, *BUSL* applies the *Grow-Shrink Markov Network (GSMN)* algorithm (Bromberg et al, 2006) on *MP* to find every clique of the template network structure, from which it builds candidate clauses. Finally, *BUSL* considers candidate clauses to put into the *MLN* one-by-one, using the *WPLL* measure to choose clauses and the *L-BFGS* algorithm to set parameters. The most recent proposed algorithms are the *ILS* (Iterated Local Search) [1] and the *LHL* (Learning via Hyper-graph Lifting) [9]. *ILS* is based on the iterated local search meta-heuristic that explores the space of structures through a biased sampling of the set of local optima. The algorithm focuses the search not on the full space of solutions but on a smaller subspace defined by the solutions that are locally optimal according to the optimization engine. In more details, it starts by randomly choosing a unit clause CL_C in the search space. Then it performs a greedy local search to efficiently reach a local optimum CL_S. At this point, a perturbation method is applied leading to the neighbor CL'_C of CL_S and then a greedy local search is applied to CL'_C to reach another local optimum CL'_S. The algorithm has to decide whether the search must continue from the previous local optimum CL_C or from the last found local optimum CL'_S. *LHL* is a different approach, that directly utilizes data in order to construct candidates. From the training dataset, *LHL* builds a hyper-graph from which it forms clauses, that are evaluated using the *WPLL* [9]. Through experiments on two real-world domains, both *ILS* and *LHL* have shown improvement over the state-of-the-art algorithms. Although, as far as we know, there is no direct comparison between *ILS* and *LHL*.

2. Generative Structure Learning

Let us first recall some basic notions of first order logic and make precise the task at hand. We consider a function-free first order language composed of a set $\mathcal{P}$ of predicate symbols, a set C of constants and a set of variables. An *atom* is an expression $p(t_1, \ldots, t_k)$, where p is a predicate and t_i are either variables or constants. A *literal* is either a positive or a negative atom; it is a *ground literal* when it contains no variable; it is a *variable literal* when it contains all variables. A *clause* is a disjunction of literals; a *Horn clause* contains at most a positive literal. Two ground atoms are said to be connected if they share at least one ground term (or argument). A clause (resp. a ground clause) is *connected* when there is an ordering of its literals $L_1 \vee \ldots \vee L_p$, such that for each L_j, $j = 2 \ldots p$, there exists a variable (resp. a constant) occurring both in L_j and L_i, $i < j$. A *variabilization* of a ground clause e, denoted by $var(e)$, is obtained by assigning a new variable to each constant and replacing all its occurrences accordingly.

We have as inputs a database composed of true/false ground atoms. We are looking for a set of clauses with their weights. We describe in this section our algorithm for Heuristic Generative Structure learning for *MLNs*, called *HGSM*.

In our approach we use the concept of Markov Blanket (*MB*), where the *MB* of a node is the set of all its neighbors. If two literals L_i and L_j occur in a same clause, then they are conditionally dependent and L_i must be in the *MB* of L_j, and vice versa.

As a basis of our algorithm, candidate clauses will be extracted from template clauses. We define a template clause as a disjunction of positive variable literals. This suggests that a *MLN* (or its template) can be built from the training dataset by first forming such sets of possible variable literals, and then finding links among them. Clauses will thus be generated from the template clauses.

We sketch the global structure of *HGSM* in Algorithm 1. *HGSM* tries to find global existing clauses by considering all predicates in the domain in turn. For a given predicate QP, it correspondingly builds a set *SL* of variable literals, then it forms template clauses from several subsets of *SL*, each of them containing at least an occurrence of QP. To build the set *SL* of variable literals, *HGSM* constructs the largest possible set of connected ground atoms corresponding to every true ground atom of QP, then heuristically variabilizes them. We describe the way this set *SL* is built in Subsection 2.1. For each literal $L_{QP} \in SL$, *HGSM* generates a set of template clauses from which it extracts a set of relevant candidate clauses to add into the *MLN*. A template clause is built from the variable literal L_{QP} and its *neighbors*. Once every predicate has been considered we get a set of template clauses *STC*. From each template clause, *HGSM* generates all possible candidate clauses (flipping the sign of each literal) and then keeps the best one according

Algorithm 1 Generative Structure Learning (DB, MLN)

Set of template clauses $STC = \emptyset$;
for each predicate QP **do**
  Form a set of possible literals SL (Algorithm 2);
  for each literal $L_{QP} \in SL$ **do**
    Find $MB(L_{QP})$ (Algorithm 3);
    Create template clauses TC (Algorithm 4); $STC = STC \cup TC$;
  end for
end for
Add clauses from STC into the MLN (Algorithm 5);
$Return(MLN)$;

Algorithm 2 Form literals (DB, QP)

$index = -1$;
for each true ground atom tga of QP **do**
  $index = index + 1$; $Chains[index] = MakeChain(tga)$;
end for
Sort $Chains$ by decreasing $length$; $SL = Variablize(Chains[0])$;
$SL = SL \cup CaptureLiteral(Chains[i])$, $1 \leq i \leq maxIndex$;
$Return(SL)$;

---

to a given measure (i.e. *WPLL*). When every template clause has been considered, we get a set of the best clauses, a subset of which will form the final *MLN*. We present techniques to determine neighbors in Subsection 2.2 and detail how template clauses are composed in Subsection 2.3. In Subsection 2.4 we present how the set *STC* of template clauses can be used to learn the final *MLN*.

We must emphasize that our approach is, at a first glance, somewhat similar to the principle underlying *BUSL* [15]. Both of them consist of three mains steps: Transforming the relational dataset into a boolean table corresponding to each predicate in the domain, Building candidate clauses using these boolean tables and Putting clauses into the *MLN*. Methods used in the first phase can be viewed as different propositionalization approaches [30] in *ILP*. As it is shown in [30], they are a kind of incomplete reduction, hence the quality of the boolean table affects the results of the next steps of both approaches. Our approach differs from *BUSL* not only in the first step but also in the remaining ones. In Subsection 2.5 we will discuss these differences in more detail.

2.1. Forming Variable Literals

We use a heuristic technique to form variable literals described in Algorithm 2. Given a training database DB and a predicate QP, Algorithm 2 returns a set SL of variable literals. For each true ground atom tga of QP in *DB*, the set of ground atoms of *DB* connected to tga is built. Such a set is called a *chain*, the length of a chain being the number of ground atoms in it. The set *SL* is then built so that for each chain, there exists a variabilization of it with all variable literals belonging to *SL*.

The longest chain is first chosen and variabilized to initialize the set *SL*. It is then completed by capturing all the relations of the other shorter chains. By variabilizing chains in order of decreasing length, reasonably and intuitively, we can expect that the algorithm can reuse more variable literals for the shorter chains, hence the number of variable literals created in *SL* is as small as possible. In the variabilization process, the algorithm ensures that different constants in a chain are replaced by different variables.

In order to illustrate our approach, let us consider a training database consisting of 13 ground atoms as follows: *stu(Bart), prof(Ada),advBy(Bart,Ada), pub(T1,Bart), pub(T1,Ada), pub(T2,Ada), pub(T2,Bart), stu(Betty), prof(Alan), advBy(Betty,Alan), advBy(Bob,Alan), pub(T3,Betty), pub(T4,Alan)*.

Let *QP*={advBy}. Let us start from the true ground atom *advBy(Bart,Ada)*. The longest chain that can be built starting from this ground atom contains 7 atoms as *{advBy(Bart,Ada), stu(Bart), pub(T1,Bart), pub(T2,Bart), prof(Ada), pub(T1,Ada), pub(T2,Ada)}*.

The algorithm then variabilizes this chain by assigning each constant to a precise variable to get the following set of literals: *SL={advBy(A,B), stu(A), pub(C,A), pub(D,A), prof(B), pub(C,B), pub(D,B)}*.

Let us consider now the true ground atom *advBy(Betty,Alan)*, then we get the chain: *{advBy(Betty,Alan), stu(Betty), prof(Alan), advBy(Bob,Alan), pub(T3,Betty), pub(T4,Alan)}*. The above set of literals *SL* is not sufficient to capture the relation among the two ground atoms *{advBy(Betty,Alan), advBy(Bob,Alan)}*, and one more literal *advBy(E,B)* is added to *SL*.

Let us describe this heuristic technique in more detail here. Having got the initialized set *SL*, the algorithm scans for every shorter chain to capture additional variable literals. During the scan process the algorithm follows precisely the two following principles:

• **Check for a new relation:** It happens when there is a new relation between two ground atoms in the considered chain. For example, the relation between the two ground atoms *{advBy(Betty,Alan), advBy(Bob,Alan)}* is the new one. As the ground atom *advBy(Betty,Alan)* is already variabilized by the variable literal *advBy(A,B)* and variables *C,D* are already used for other relations in *SL*, a new variable *E* is introduced to form a new variable literal *advBy(E,B)* to variabilize the true ground atom *advBy(Bob,Alan)*. It guarantees the link between *advBy(Betty,Alan)* and *advBy(Bob,Alan)* by the shared variable *B* between *advBy(A,B)* and *advBy(E,B)*.

• **Check for the existing relations:** It happens when there are several similar relations (which have occurred in some previous considered chain) but there does not exist any variabilization of it. For example, we assume that the dataset in our example contains one more true ground atom *pub(T5,Alan)*. The relation between *advBy(Betty,Alan)* and *pub(T5,Alan)* is similar to the relation between *advBy(Betty,Alan)* and *pub(T4,Alan)*, both of them sharing the term *Alan* at the same positions. The set *SL* is sufficient to variabilize the relations among the three ground atoms *advBy(Betty,Alan), pub(T3,Betty), pub(T4,Alan)* (respectively by *advBy(A,B), pub(C,A), pub(D,B)*) but it is not sufficient to variabilize relations among the four ground atoms *advBy(Betty,Alan), pub(T3,Betty), pub(T4,Alan), pub(T5,Alan)*. In this case, a new variable literal *pub(F,B)* is used to variabilize *pub(T5,Alan)*.

Repeating this process until the last true ground atom of the given predicate *advBy*, algorithm 2 produces the set of 8 variable literals as: *SL={ advBy(A,B) stu(A) pub(C,A) pub(D,A) prof(B) pub(C,B) pub(D,B) adv(E,B)}*.

Algorithm 3 Find Markov Blanket (DB, SL, L_{QP})

$MatrixForGS = \emptyset$; Find $SLPL(L_{QP})$;
for each true/false ground atom qga of QP **do**
　fillchar($OneRowOfMatrix, 0$); Find $Slpga(qga)$;
　for each $lpga \in Slpga(qga)$ **do**
　　if $lpga$ fits some $LPL \in SLPL(L_{QP})$ **then**
　　　$OneRowOfMatrix[L] = 1$ **for** each literal L in LPL;
　　end if
　end for
　$MatrixForGS.append(OneRowOfMatrix)$;
end for
$GSMN(MatrixForGS)$;
$Return(MB(L_{QP}))$;

2.2. Finding Neighbors of a Variable Literal

The next step of our approach performs the task of finding relevant connections among variable literals in the set *SL*. For this purpose we find the set of neighbors (Markov Blanket) of a variable literal. For this purpose we propose, as in [15], to use the Grow-Shrink Markov Network algorithm (*GSMN*) [25]; it is based on the Pearson's conditional independence chi-square (χ^2) statistic test (see [26] for details of its computation) to determine whether two variables are conditionally independent or not.

In order to apply the *GSMN* algorithm, we first build a boolean table, called *Matrix-ForGS*. From this boolean table, $GSMN$ can easily arrange contingency tables needed to compute the (χ^2) tests. *MatrixForGS* is organized as follows: each column corresponds to a variable literal; each row corresponds to a true/false ground atom of the considered predicate. *MatrixForGS[r][c]* being true means that there exists at least a linked-path vc of connected variable literals containing variable literal at column c, a linked-path of connected ground atom gc starting from the ground atom at row r, and a variabilization of gc such that $var(gc) \subseteq vc$. Here, a linked-path is related to the relational pathfinding [32] and the relational cliché [33]. Figure 1 presents a part of such a boolean table in our example.

Let us consider a connected clause $C = A_1 \vee A_2 \vee ... \vee A_k$ where k is the maximum number of literals per clause. Since the clause is connected, from some literal A_i we can reach some other literal A_j with at most k links. For example, considering the clause $P(x) \vee !Q(x,y) \vee R(y,z)$, $R(y,z)$ can be reached from $P(x)$ through two links: the link *{P(x), Q(x,y)}* by the term *x* and the link *{Q(x,y),R(y,z)}* by the term *y*. This implies that to find links from a given variable literal L_{QP} to the others, we only need to consider the subset of *SL* that can be reached from L_{QP} with at most *k* links. We can reasonably expect that this subset is much smaller than *SL* when the dataset is large, hence the size of the boolean table is reduced considerably. Without considering the time and the space, *k* can be set as large as needed. Our algorithm uses this value as a parameter to limit the search space. For the sake of simplicity, we henceforth omit this parameter in the presentation.

In the following, a *linked-path* of variable literals denotes a connected clause and $SLPL(L_{QP})$ denotes the set of all linked-paths of variable literals starting from L_{QP}.

Literals Groundings	AdvBy (A,B)	Stu (A)	Pub (C,A)	Pub (D,A)	Prof (B)	Pub (C,B)	Pub (D,B)	AdvBy (E,B)
advBy(Bart,Ada)	1	1	1	1	1	1	1	0
advBy(Betty,Alan)	1	1	1	1	1	1	1	1
advBy(Bob,Alan)	1	0	0	0	1	1	1	1
advBy(Betty,Bob)	0	1	1	1	0	0	0	0
advBy(Alan,Bart)	0	0	1	1	0	1	1	0
...	...	...	...	...	...	...	...	...

Figure 1. A part of the boolean table

Algorithm 3 describes the steps for finding the Markov Blanket of a variable literal L_{QP}. For each *true/false* ground atom qga of QP, HGSM creates a row in the *MatrixForGS*. It builds every linked-path $lpga$ of true ground atoms starting from qga. If $lpga$ satisfies a linked-path of variable literals LPL in $SLPL(L_{QP})$, then for each variable literal L in LPL, value at row qga column L in the *MatrixForGS* is set to *true*. $Slpga(qga)$ denotes the set of all $lpga$. During the process for filling boolean values, the algorithm heuristically, greedily focuses on variable literals that are not yet filled with true values to decide whether they are true or not. Algorithm 3 returns the Markov Blanket of the input literal L_{QP}.

Let us continue our example by starting from the variable literal *advBy(A,B)*. From *advBy(A,B)*, the algorithm can reach any element in the set *{stu(A), pub(C,A), pub(D,A), prof(B), pub(C,B), pub(D,B), adbBy(E,B)}*. In this case, it is the whole set SL, but as we mentioned above, it could be much smaller than SL when the dataset is large. *MatrixForGS*, each column corresponds to an element in this set, each row corresponds to a true/false ground atom of the predicate *advBy*. Figure 1 shows several rows of the boolean table *MatrixForGS* in our example starting from the variable literal *advBy(A,B)*. We consider, for example, the row corresponding to the false ground atom *advBy(Betty,Bob)*. There exists a linked-path of true ground atoms *{advBy(Betty,Bob), stu(Betty)}* that satisfies the linked-path of variable literals *{advBy(A,B),stu(A)}*, and a linked-path of true ground atoms *{advBy(Betty,Bob), publication(T3,Betty)}* that satisfies the two linked-path of variable literals *{advBy(A,B), pub(C,A)}* and *{advBy(A,B), pub(D,A)}*. The values at columns corresponding to variable literals *stu(A), pub(C,A), pub(D,A)* are thus set to *true*. The others are set to *false*.

By applying the *GSMN* algorithm on this boolean table we get the MB of the variable literal *advBy(A,B)* is *{stu(A), prof(B), advBy(E,B)}*.

2.3. Creating Template Clauses

A set of template clauses is created from the starting variable literal L_{QP} and its neighbors, given by its Markov Blanket $MB(L_{QP})$, computed by Algorithm 3. The *Pseudo-code* of this task is detailed in Algorithm 4. At each iteration, by fixing the number of literals per clause $j, 2 \leq j \leq k$, where k is the maximum number of variable literals per clause, HGSM collects every subset S of $(j-1)$-$elements$ ($S \subseteq MB(L_{QP})$)

Algorithm 4 Create template clauses $(L_{QP}, MB(L_{QP}), k)$

$TC = \emptyset$;
for $j = 2$ **to** k **do**
    for each subset $(j-1)$-*elements* $S \subseteq MB(L_{QP})$ **do**
        $c = CreateTempClause(L_{QP}, S)$ **if** $CheckLink(L_{QP}, S)$; $TC = TC \cup c$;
    end for
end for
$Return(TC)$;

Algorithm 5 Add clauses to the MLN (DB,MLN,STC,modeClause)

$AddUnitClauseIntoMLN()$; $LearnWeightsWPLL(MLN, DB)$;
$BestScore = measureWPLL(MLN, DB)$; $CanClauses = \emptyset$;
for each template clause $Tc \in STC$ **do**
    $Clauses = CreateClauses(Tc, modeClause)$;
    for each clause $c_i \in Clauses$ **do**
        $LearnWeightsWPLL(c_i, MLN, DB)$; $c_i.gain = measureWPLL(c_i, MLN, DB)$;
    end for
    $CanClauses = CanClauses \cup c$ where $c.gain = max\{c_i.gain\}$;
end for
Choose $BestClauses$ from $CanClauses$;
for each clause c in $BestClauses$ **do**
    $LearnWeightsWPLL(c, MLN, DB)$; $NewScore = measureWPLL(c, MLN, DB)$;
    if $NewScore > BestScore$ **then**
        Add clause c into MLN; $BestScore = NewScore$;
    end if
end for
$PruneClauseFromMLN(MLN, DB)$;
$Return(MLN)$;

---

and L_{QP} to form a template clause c. The boolean function $CheckLink(L_{QP}, S)$ ensures that each variable literal in c can reach the other ones. Algorithm 4 returns a set of template clauses TC.

We finish this step by illustrating the set of template clauses created from the starting variable literal *advBy(A,B)* and its neighbors in Subsection 2.2. Among template clauses, we found $advBy(A, B) \vee stu(A)$, $advBy(A, B) \vee prof(B)$, $advBy(A, B) \vee advBy(E, B)$, $advBy(A, B) \vee stu(A) \vee prof(B)$, etc.

2.4. Adding Clauses into the MLN

Algorithm 5 describes the task of putting clauses into the MLN from the set of template clauses STC. For each template clause $Tc \in STC$ of length n, HGSM generates a set *Clauses* of clauses by flipping the sign of each variable literal. Depending on the goal (or on time constraints), *HGSM* can restrict the search to *Horn clauses* or consider all *arbitrary* clauses (2^n possible clauses). In [20,11], the authors have shown that it is useful to start the generative learning of a MLN structure by adding all unit clauses. Thus for each clause $c_i \in Clauses$, HGSM first learns weights for a *MLN* composed of all unit clauses *plus* c_i, and then computes the $WPLL$ of this MLN. Then $HGSM$ chooses the clause in *Clauses* that leads to the best $WPLL$ and adds it into the set *CanClauses* of candidate clauses. As proposed in [20,11], we eliminate several clauses from *CanClauses* by keeping only clauses improving *WPLL* measures and having a weight greater than a given threshold; this allows time saving during the next steps. The final set of candidate clauses is stored into *BestClauses*.

The learned *MLN* is initialized with the set of unit clauses. Clauses in *BestClauses* are sorted by decreasing gain, and then checked one-by-one to test whether they can be put into the learned *MLN*: when a clause allows improving the *WPLL* it is added into the *MLN*. As adding a clause into the *MLN* might drop down the weight of the clauses added before, once every clause in *BestClauses* has been considered, we try to prune some clauses of the *MLN*, as was done in [11].

2.5. Comparing to BUSL

The outline of our method, at a first glance, is similar to the generative structure learning algorithm *BUSL* [15]. Nevertheless, it differs deeply in all three steps: the way propositionalization is performed, the way to build the set of candidate clauses and the way to put clauses into the learned *MLN*:

- **Propositionalization:** The boolean tables respectively constructed by *BUSL* and *HGSM* are different in the meaning of columns, hence in the meaning of values of entries. Each column in the table *MP* of *BUSL* corresponds to a *TNode* which can be either a single variable literal or a conjunction of several variable literals, while each column in the table *MatrixForGS* of *HGSM* corresponds to a variable literal. For instance, starting from the ground atom *stu(a)*, knowing *advBy(b,a)* and then *pub(t,b)*, *BUSL* would produce three *TNodes* $t1 = \{stu(A)\}$, $t2 = \{advBy(B,A)\}$ and $t3 = \{AdvBy(C,A), Pub(D,C)\}$, while *HGSM* would produce tree separated variable literals $l1 = \{stu(A)\}$, $l2 = AdvBy(B,A)$ and $l3 = Pub(T,B)$. The number of *TNodes* in *BUSL* can be very high, depending on the number of atoms allowed per *TNode*, the size of the database and the links existing between ground atoms. On the contrary, *HGSM* produces just a set of variable literals, enough to reflect all possible links between ground atoms. For the *r-th* ground atom of the target predicate, $MP[r][t] = true$ if and only if the conjunction of the set of variable literals in *t* is true, while $MatrixForGS[r][l] = true$ if there exists at least a linked-path of ground atoms starting from the *r-th* true ground atom and containing a true ground atom of *l*. These differences influence the performance when applying the *GSMN* algorithm.
- **Composing the set of candidate clauses:** *BUSL* uses *GSMN* to determine edges amongst *TNodes* and composes candidate clauses from cliques of *TNodes*. *HGSM* uses just the MB of the considered variable literal in order to get a little more clauses. Moreover, candidate clauses in *BUSL* must contain all the literals appearing in a *TNode*, meaning that, concerning our example, both *AdvBy(C,A)* and *Pub(D,C)* of TNode *t3* occur together in the clause. This might not be flexible enough as it might occur that a relevant clause contains only one of these two literals.
- **Adding clauses into the *MLN*:** For each clique, *BUSL* creates all possible candidate clauses, then removes duplicated clauses and finally considers them one-by-one to put into the MLN. *HGSM* just keeps at most one clause per template clause in the set of candidate clauses.

3. EXPERIMENTS

3.1. Datasets

We used *UW-CSE* and *CORA*, the two publicly-available datasets from the web page http://alchemy.cs.washington.edu/. The *UW-CSE* dataset, prepared by Richardson and Domingos (2006), describes an academic department. The published dataset consists of 15 predicates as $Student(person)$, $Professor(person)$, $AdvisedBy(person, person)$, $Publication(paper, person)$, etc. The dataset contains a total of 2673 true ground atoms with the remainder assumed to be $false$. The *CORA* dataset is a collection of citations of computer science papers, created by Andrew McCallum, and later processed by Singla and Domingos (2006) into 5 folds. The dataset contains a total of 70367 true and false ground atoms with the others assumed to be false.

3.2. Systems and Methodology

HGSM has been implemented on top of the Alchemy package [12]. We used the APIs implementation of *L-BFGS* to learn the maximum *WPLL* weights. We ourself perform experiments to answer the following questions:

1. Does *HGSM* outperform *BUSL*?
2. Does *HGSM* perform better the state-of-the-art generative systems?
3. How does *HGSM* perform for only Horn clauses?

To answer question 1, we directly compare *HGSM* to *BUSL*. To answer question 2, we compare *HGSM* to the state-of-the-art generative system *ILS* and also refer to the results of *LHL* published in [9]. Finally, for question 3, we configured *HGSM* to limit to Horn clauses, named *HGSM-H*.

For all domains, we performed *5-fold cross-validation*. For each system on each test set, we measured the *CLL* and the area under the precision-recall curve *(AUC)* for every predicate. The advantage of the *CLL* is that it directly measures the quality of the probability estimates produced. The advantage of the *AUC* is that it is insensitive to true negatives (i.e., ground atoms that are false and were predicted to be false). In other words, the *AUC* is useful because it demonstrates how well the algorithm predicts the few positives in the data. The *CLL* of a predicate is the average over all its groundings of the ground atoms log-probability given evidence. The precision-recall curve for a predicate is computed by varying the *CLL* threshold above which a ground atom is predicted to be true. Parameters for *ILS* and *BUSL* were set as in [1]. To guarantee the fairness of comparison, we set the maximum number of literals per clause to 5 for all systems as it is shown in [1]. We used the package provided in [4] to compute *AUC*. For each test set, we ran each system on a Dual-core AMD 2.4 GHz CPU - 4GB RAM machine.

3.3. Results

Having learned the *MLN*, we performed inference for every predicate on the test folds for both datasets, using the *Lazy-MC-SAT* algorithm. *Lazy-MC-SAT* produces probability for every grounding of the query predicate on the test fold. These probability values were used to compute the average *CLL* over all the groundings and the related *AUC*. The *CLL* and *AUC* of a test fold are averaged over all predicates of the domain.

Table 1. CLL, AUC measures

	UW-CSE		CORA	
ALGORITHM	CLL	AUC	CLL	AUC
BUSL	-0.358 ± 0.019	0.291 ± 0.021	-0.341 ± 0.014	0.435 ± 0.010
ILS	-0.180 ± 0.015	0.257 ± 0.019	-0.131 ± 0.011	0.501 ± 0.018
HGSM-H	-0.138 ± 0.017	0.292 ± 0.022	-0.108 ± 0.013	0.701 ± 0.014
HGSM	**-0.103 ± 0.020**	**0.311 ± 0.014**	**-0.087 ± 0.016**	**0.762 ± 0.015**

Table 2. Number of clauses and training time

	UW-CSE			CORA		
Alg	NOC	FC	TT	NOC	FC	TT
BUSL	362.00	**37.00**	360.85	188.60	17.75	3412.08
ILS	**3104.20**	23.40	191.84	**1755.00**	18.25	1730.08
HGSM-H	570.20	23.20	281.43	114.60	17.00	1963.74
HGSM	1520.00	23.60	**521.40**	143.40	**20.25**	**3849.52**

Table 1 reports the *CLL* and *AUC* measures for all approaches on both databases. These are the average of *CLLs* and *AUCs* over all test folds. It must be noted that, while we used the same parameter setting, our results do slightly differ from the ones in [1]. This comes from the fact that we conducted inference using the *Lazy-MC-SAT* instead of the *MC-SAT*. Table 2 exposes the average number of candidate clauses *(NOC)* and final learned clauses *(FC)* and the training time (in minutes) *(TT)* over all train folds.

First, let us compare *HGSM* respectively to *BUSL* and *ILS*. *HGSM* outperforms *BUSL* and *ILS* in terms of both *CLL* and *AUC*. We would like to emphasize that *HGSM* dominates them not only on average values, but also for each test fold of each dataset. However, *HGSM* is slower than *BUSL* and *ILS* is the fastest system. We can answer to question 1 that *HGSM* performs better than *BUSL* in the sense of *CLL* and *AUC*. Referring to results of *LHL* [9], *HGSM* gets better *CLL* values and worse *AUC* values for *CORA* dataset. In spite of the lower *AUC*, with the better results than *ILS* and the better *CLL* values than *LHL* for the large dataset *CORA*, we believe in the domination of our method compared to the state-of-the-art generative structure learning algorithms for *MLNs*, especially for the task of classification. This is the answer to question 2. Since the *CLL* determines the quality of the probability predictions output by the algorithm, *HGSM* outperforms *ILS* and *BUSL* in the sense of the ability to predict correctly the query predicates given evidences. Since the *AUC* is insensitive to the large number of true negatives (i.e., ground atoms are false and predicted to be false), *HGSM* enhances the ability to predict the few positives in the data.

Last, let us compare all systems together. *HGSM* is the best system in terms of *CLL* and *AUC* measures, and *ILS* is the best one in terms of runtime. However, in theory, all algorithms have involved the *L-BFGS* to set weights for clauses, hence the times all depend on the performance of the weights learning algorithm. In practice, as revealed in [31], the presence of a challenging clause like $AdvisedBy(s,p) \land AdvisedBy(s,q) \rightarrow SamePerson(p,q)$ for the *UW-CSE* dataset will have a great impact on optimization as well as on inference. Runtime therefore depends mostly on the number of candidate clauses and the occurrence of literals together in each clause. From practice we also verify that the time used for finding candidate clauses is much less than the time for weight learning and inference. From Table 2 we can see that, although *BUSL* and *HGSM* evaluate fewer candidates than *ILS*, they are both slower than *ILS*. It is because *BUSL* and *HGSM* change the *MLN* completely at each step, calculating the *WPLL* thus becomes very expensive. In *ILS* this does not happen because at each step the *L-BFGS* is initialized with the current weights (and zero weight for a new clause) and it converges in a few iterations [2]. Regarding *HGSM* and *BUSL*, for the *Cora* dataset, despite *HGSM* evaluates fewer candidate clauses than *BUSL*, it gives better *CLL* and *AUC* and unfortunately it runs slower than *BUSL*. This implies that the set of candidate clauses created by *HGSM* is better than the one created by *BUSL*, furthermore our method to create candidate clauses is better than the one in *BUSL*. This issue also urges us to apply a method like it is done in *ILS* to accelerate *HGSM*. It is very interesting that *HGSM-H* takes much less time than *HGSM* does with arbitrary clauses while it also outperforms both *ILS* and *BUSL* in terms of both *CLL* and *AUC*. *HGSM-H* gets only a little loss in the sense of *CLL* and *AUC* compared to *HGSM* with arbitrary clauses. From the logic point of view, a Horn-clause *MLN* might integrate easier in further processing than a *MLN* based on arbitrary-clauses. These results give us belief in restricting our system to solve with *Horn clauses* in a more acceptable runtime. This is the answer to question 3.

4. CONCLUSION

We have presented a heuristic algorithm for the generative learning of *MLN* structure. For each predicate in the domain, the algorithm first heuristically builds a set of variable literals from which to heuristically transform the relational dataset into boolean tables, each of its columns corresponds to a variable literal. Then candidate clauses are built from these boolean tables, which are added into the *MLN* as long as they improve its measure (i.e. *WPLL*). Comparisons show that the proposed algorithm outperforms the state-of-the-art algorithms. From the execution-time point of view, we also noticed that our algorithm runs much faster on Horn clauses than on arbitrary ones, at the price of a small loss in terms of *CLL* and *AUC*. In the future we plan to improve the performance of our algorithm in terms of measures and of execution time. We also plan to apply it to richer and more complex domains and also to compare directly to *LHL*.

Acknowledgements

We would like to thank Marenglen Biba for his assistance on ILS and ILS-DSL. We also thank the anonymous reviewers for their comments which helped us to improve this paper considerably.

References

[1] M. Biba, S. Ferilli, F. Esposito: Structure Learning of Markov Logic Networks through Iterated Local Search, *ECAI'08, IOS Press* (2008), 361–365.

[2] M. Biba, S. Ferilli, F. Esposito: Discriminative Structure Learning of Markov Logic Networks, *ILP'08*, Springer-Verlag (2008), 59–76.
[3] M. Collins: Discriminative training methods for hidden Markov models: theory and experiments with perceptron algorithms, *EMNLP'02, Association for Computational Linguistics* (2002), 1–8.
[4] J. Davis, M. Goadrich: The relationship between Precision-Recall and ROC curves, *ICML'06*, ACM (2006), 233–240.
[5] D. L. Raedt, L. Dehaspe: Clausal Discovery, *Mach. Learn.*, (1997), 99–146.
[6] N. T. Huynh, R. J. Mooney: Max-Margin Weight Learning for Markov Logic Networks, *ECML PKDD'09*, Springer-Verlag (2009), 564–579.
[7] N. T. Huynh, R. J. Mooney: Discriminative structure and parameter learning for Markov logic networks, *ICML'08*, ACM (2008), 416–423.
[8] K. Henry, S. Bart, J. Yueyen: A General Stochastic Approach to Solving Problems with Hard and Soft Constraints, *The Satisfiability Problem: Theory and Applications*, American Mathematical Society (1996), 573–586.
[9] S. Kok, P. Domingos: Learning Markov logic network structure via hypergraph lifting, *ICML'09*, ACM (2009), 505–512.
[10] S. Kok, P. Domingos: Statistical predicate invention, *ICML'07*, ACM (2007), 433–440.
[11] S. Kok, P. Domingos: Learning the structure of Markov logic networks, *ICML'05*, (2005), 441–448.
[12] S. Kok, M. Sumner, M. Richardson, P. Singla, H. Poon, D. Lowd, J. Wang, P. Domingos: The Alchemy system for statistical relational AI, *Technical report, Univ. of Washington.* (2009), http://alchemy.cs.washington.edu.
[13] L. John, M. Andrew, F. Pereira: Conditional Random Fields: Probabilistic Models for Segmenting and Labeling Sequence Data, *ICML '01*, Morgan Kaufmann, San Francisco, CA (2001), 282–289.
[14] D. Lowd, P. Domingos: Efficient Weight Learning for Markov Logic Networks, *PKDD '07*, Springer-Verlag (2007), 200–211.
[15] L. Mihalkova, R. J. Mooney: Bottom-up learning of Markov logic network structure, *ICML '07*, ACM (2007), 625–632.
[16] L. Mihalkova, M. Richardson: Speeding up Inference In Statistical Relational Learning by Clustering Similar Query Literals, *ILP '09*, (2009).
[17] M. F. Møller: A scaled conjugate gradient algorithm for fast supervised learning, *Neural Netw.*, Elsevier Science Ltd. (1993), 525–533.
[18] S. D. Pietra, V. D. Pietra, J. Lafferty: Inducing Features of Random Fields, *Carnegie Mellon University* (1995).
[19] H. Poon, P. Domingos: Sound and efficient inference with probabilistic and deterministic dependencies, *AAAI* (2006), 458–463.
[20] M. Richardson, P. Domingos: Markov logic networks, *Mach. Learn.*, Kluwer Academic Publishers (2006), 107–1363.
[21] F. Sha, F. Pereira: Shallow parsing with conditional random fields, *NAACL* (2003).
[22] P. Singla, P. Domingos: Discriminative training of Markov logic networks, *AAAI'05*, (2005), 134–141.
[23] S. Ashwin: The Aleph manual, *http://web.comlab.ox.ac.uk/oucl/research/areas/machlearn/Aleph* (2001).
[24] M. C. Bishop: Pattern Recognition and Machine Learning, *Inf. Sci. and Statistics*, Springer (2007).
[25] B. Facundo, D. Margaritis, V. Honavar: Efficient Markov Network Structure Discovery Using Independence Tests, *SIAM DM*, (2006), 449–484.
[26] A. Agresti: Categorical Data Analysis (Second Edition), *John Wiley and Sons* (2002).
[27] H. Poon, P. Domingos, M. Sumner: A general method for reducing the complexity of relational inference and its application to MCMC, *AAAI'08*, AAAI Press (2008), 1075–1080.
[28] P. Singla, P. Domingos: Memory-efficient inference in relational domains, *AAAI'06*, (2006), 488–493.
[29] D. C. Liu, J. Nocedal: On the limited memory BFGS method for large scale optimization, *Math. Program.*, Springer-Verlag New York, Inc (1989), 503–528.
[30] L. D. Raedt: Logical and relational learning, *Springer* (2008).
[31] J. Shavlik, S. Natarajan: Speeding up inference in Markov logic networks by preprocessing to reduce the size of the resulting grounded network, *IJCAI*, (2009), 1951–1956.
[32] B. L. Richards, R. J. Mooney: Learning Relations by Pathfinding, *AAAI*, (1992).
[33] G. Silverstein, M. Pazzani: Relational clichés: Constraining constructive induction during relational learning, *The 8-th International Workshop on ML*, (1991).

Learning Fuzzy Models of User Interests in a Semantic Information Retrieval System

Mauro DRAGONI, Célia da Costa PEREIRA and Andrea G.B. TETTAMANZI

Università degli Studi di Milano, Dipartimento di Tecnologie dell'Informazione, Via Bramante 65, I-26013 Crema (CR), Italy, email:
mauro.dragoni,celia.pereira,andrea.tettamanzi@unimi.it

Abstract. We propose an approach to user model-based information retrieval which uses an evolutionary algorithm to learn fuzzy models of user interests and to dynamically track their changes as the user interacts with the system. The system is ontology-based, in the sense that it considers concepts behind terms instead of simple terms.

The approach has been implemented in a real-world prototype newsfeed aggregator with search facilities called IFeed. Experimental results show that our system learns user models effectively. This is proved by both the convergence of the interest degrees contained in the user models population and the increase of the users' activities on the set of proposed documents.

1. Introduction

An Information Retrieval (IR) system aims at retrieving, from a collection of documents, those which are perceived by the user as containing information of value with respect to his personal information need. There are some problems which, if solved, could lead to a real improvement of the set of retrieved documents in terms of information value. For example, conventional IR systems do not consider that users are not always able to specify correctly their information need; that user experiences, goals, knowledge, etc., may significantly affect their judgment in defining a document as relevant or not and that the user's information need may vary over time, for example as a result of interacting with the system.

The earliest approaches to IR claimed that "IR systems should not attempt to understand the content of a document" [12]. Systems constructed upon this hypothesis use a keyword approach to individuate documents which are pertinent with respect to the keywords representing the user query. However, as stated by Giger [6] and later by others, these approaches do not take into consideration that the users invariably associate a meaning with each keyword in order to express their information need. Another inconvenient with keyword-based approaches is that they do not take into account the fact that there are terms which are syntactically independent but which can have the same meaning (synonyms). Ontology-based information retrieval approaches [1,14] promise to increase the quality of responses since they aim at capturing within computer systems some part of the semantics of documents, leading to more effective information retrieval systems. This paper presents a User-Modeling-based IR system which attempts to solve the above-mentioned problems with the result of improving the document's information value for the user and with the advantage of increasing the precision of query results. The system considers a set of parameters from the user environment to learn the user's degree of interest toward different sets of document.

The original contribution of the work described is a synthesis of two research directions that are being actively pursued in the field of information retrieval:

1. the use of machine-learning techniques;
2. automated user model acquisition.

The paper is organized as follows: Section 2 begins with an overview of proposed IR methods that use User Modeling, Machine Learning, and Ontologies; Section 3 describes the evolutionary algorithm used for evolving models and implemented in our system; Section 4 presents the experiments that we have carried out and discusses their results. Section 5 concludes.

2. Related Work

Many approaches for improving the effectiveness of IR systems have been proposed in the past years. Among them, we can distinguish those which determine term importance by exploiting concept-based information found in ontologies; those which construct an user profiling thanks to the interaction between the user and the system; and those which predict users' interests by using learning algorithms. In this section, a description of some of such approaches proposed in the literature is provided.

Shen and colleagues [10] introduce a domain-specific concept information retrieval system to facilitate the retrieval of organizational internal documents like technical reports, professional references and even e-mails. The domain knowledge of the proposed system is organized using taxonomy for ease of knowledge storage and sharing.

Baziz [1] introduced an approach to document content representation by ontology-document matching. His approach detects concepts in a document by means of a general-purpose ontology, namely WordNet, and uses two criteria to calculate the weight of a concept: co-occurrence of concepts in a document, and their semantic similarity to compute semantic relatedness and then disambiguate them. The result is the set of scored concepts-senses with weighted links called *semantic core of document* which best represents the semantic content of the document. A survey of concept-based approaches in information retrieval has been carried out by Haav and Lubi [8].

User modeling can be defined as the process of constructing, maintaining and using user models. The development of user models offers the possibility of individuating users' interests by tracking their information-seeking behavior and evolving information needs over time.

Crabtree and colleagues, [2] derive user interest profiles automatically by monitoring user web and email habits. A clustering algorithm is employed to identify interests, which are then clustered together to form interest themes.

Soltysiak and colleagues [11] describe experimental work conducted to investigate user profiling within a framework for personal agents. In particular, the authors aimed at discovering whether user interests could be automatically classified through the use of several heuristics.

Kelly and colleagues [9] propose a user modeling system for personalized interaction and tailored retrieval that (1) tracks interactions over time, (2) represents multiple information needs, both short and long term, (3) allows for changes in information needs over time, (4) acquires and updates the user model automatically, without explicit assistance from the user, and (5) accounts for contextual factors such as topic familiarity and endurance of need.

Goldman and colleagues [7] propose a system that carries out highly effective searches over collections. The system is comprised of two major parts. The first part consists of an agent, MUSAG, that learns to relate concepts that are semantically "similar" to one another. In other words, this agent dynamically builds a dictionary of expressions for a given concept. The second part consists of another agent, SAg, who is responsible for retrieving documents, given a set of keywords with relative weights. This retrieval makes use of the dictionary learned by MUSAG, in the sense that the documents to be retrieved for a query are semantically related to the concept given.

3. Evolutionary Algorithm

Evolutionary algorithms (EAs) [3,5] are a broad class of stochastic optimization algorithms, inspired by biology and in particular by those biological processes that allow populations of organisms to adapt to their surrounding environment: genetic inheritance and survival of the fittest.

An EA maintains a population of candidate solutions for the problem at hand, and makes it evolve by iteratively applying a (usually quite small) set of stochastic operators, known as *mutation, recombination*, and *selection*.

Mutation randomly perturbs a candidate solution; recombination decomposes two distinct solutions and then randomly mixes their parts to form novel solutions; and selection replicates the most successful solutions found in a population at a rate proportional to their relative quality.

The initial population may be either a random sample of the solution space or may be seeded with solutions found by simple local search procedures, if these are available.

The resulting process tends to find, given enough time, globally optimal solutions to the problem much in the same way as in nature populations of organisms tend to adapt to their surrounding environment.

In the proposed system, an individual of the population is a vector of as many components as the document clusters in the repository; each component is the fuzzy degree to which the user is interested in the relevant cluster (0 = not interested at all, 1 = absolutely interested).

3.1. Fitness Function

By definition, the quality of a model should be measured as the degree to which the relevant user is satisfied, overall, with the answers to his queries. However, such overall user satisfaction cannot be measured in a single interaction. The only thing that can be indirectly estimated is user satisfaction with respect to an actual query. Therefore, the fitness of a user model can only be estimated incrementally, by subsequent refinements, every time an answered filtered by it is given feedback by the user. At each moment, the fitness of a user model is known with imprecision, which, by its nature, may be represented as a fuzzy interval [13] in the interval $[0, 1]$, where 0 represents complete user dissatisfaction and 1 indicates complete user satisfaction, which would occur if all queries were answered with the desired set of documents ordered by decreasing user interest.

This fuzzy interval can be represented by means of a trapezoid (a, b, c, d) where (a, d) is the support interval and (b, c) the core interval.

When a random user model is created, there is complete ignorance on its fitness; this is represented by a fuzzy fitness of $(0, 0, 1, 1)$, i.e., the whole $[0, 1]$ interval.

Every time a user submits a query, a model is selected from the relevant population and used to filter the answer; then an implicit feedback is calculated based on the actions the user takes: these are reading a document and spending time on a document. The fuzzy fitness of the model is then updated based on two coefficients:

$r \in [0, 1]$: the rating (implicitly) given by the user (0 = completely negative, 1 = completely positive);

$w \in [0, 1]$: the confidence of the rating.

The updated trapezoid is calculated as follows:

$$a' = (a + wr)/(1 + w); \tag{1}$$
$$b' = (b + wr)/(1 + w); \tag{2}$$
$$c' = (c + wr)/(1 + w); \tag{3}$$
$$d' = (d + wr)/(1 + w). \tag{4}$$

A positive rating moves the trapezoid to the right, a negative rating to the left, and both shrink it, i.e., make it less uncertain. In addition, also the recombination and mutation operators, as explained below, change the fuzzy interval of fitness.

3.2. Recombination

The recombination operator is implemented by means of uniform crossover, whereby the new individual is created by selecting, for each cluster interest, the corresponding interest from either parent with $\frac{1}{2}$ probability.

Following recombination, the fitness of the offspring is calculated from those of the two parents (a_1, b_1, c_1, d_1) and (a_2, b_2, c_2, d_2) as follows:

$$a = b - (b_1 + b_2 - a_1 - a_2)/2; \tag{5}$$
$$b = \min\{0.95b_1, 0.95b_2\}; \tag{6}$$
$$c = \max\{1.05c_1, 1.05c_2\}; \tag{7}$$
$$d = c + (d_1 + d_2 - c_1 - c_2)/2. \tag{8}$$

The rationale behind these formulas is that the fitness of the offspring can be anything in between the fitness of the parents, or even slightly better or worse. The 1.05 and 0.95

factors represent a 5% expansion of the core of the fitness of the parents, which models a slight decrease of precision. The actual value of these factors is not critical, as previous experiments revealed.

3.3. Mutation

The mutation operator perturbs every cluster interest in a user model. In addition, to speed up convergence, an *intelligent* mutation has been used, that has already been applied with success to a similar problem [4]. The main idea behind intelligent mutation is to inject single, larger perturbations and observe the improvement they bring about: if the fitness increases, the perturbation is maintained, otherwise it is discarded.

In this case, intelligent mutation uses user feedback directly to modify the interest of the cluster whose centroid is closest to the query results.

Following mutation, the trapezoid of fitness is updated as follows:

$$a' = \max\{0, b' - (b-a)(1+s)\}; \tag{9}$$
$$b' = b(1-s); \tag{10}$$
$$c' = c(1+s); \tag{11}$$
$$d' = \min\{1, c' + (d-c)(1+s)\}, \tag{12}$$

where $0 \leq s < 1$ is the strength of the perturbations undergone by the mutated user model. The idea is that the fitness of a mutated model is more uncertain than the fitness of the original model.

3.4. Selection

Probabilistic tournament selection is used to select individuals for reproduction. A number of individuals are picked at random to play a tournament. A deviate from a probability distribution obtained by normalizing the fuzzy fitness interval of each individual is extracted and the individual whose deviate is greatest wins the tournament and is inserted in the population for the next generation.

Elitism is implemented: the best individual in the population is passed on unchanged to the next generation. Another slot in the new population is taken by the last individual used for filtering a query answer; the rationale for this choice is that the fitness of that individual incorporates the most recent information on user interests.

4. Experiments and Results

To validate the proposed approach, we have implemented a small but working real-world prototype newsfeed aggregator with search facilities, called IFeed[1]. IFeed is a web-based newsfeed aggregator that is able to crawl news from RSS feeds, to monitor the user's activities (such as queries, clicks, etc.) in order to estimate implicit feedbacks, and to learn user profiles without requesting explicit interactions from users. IFeed is composed of the modules briefly described below.

---
[1] http://www.genalgo.com/IFEEDINT

1. Crawler: this module fetches RSS feeds from the web, extracts news from the XML file containing them, translates them into a conceptual document representation, and stores the news in the database. Documents are represented by means of a conceptual representation which is out of the scope of this paper.
2. User Profile Reader (UPR): when a user logs into the system, the UPR loads the models associated with the logged user, selects one of such models, composes a set of 20 documents that are most interesting with respect to the selected model, and proposes them to the user.
3. User Profile Analyzer (UPA): this module updates the user models based on the implicit feedbacks stored in the database. The UPA implements the evolutionary algorithm explained in Section 3.
4. Web Interface: this is the interface used by the users to interact with the system through their browser.

IFeed is implemented by using two different programming languages: the crawler, the UPR, and the web interface have been implemented in PHP, while the UPA has been developed in Java. Documents and other data are kept in a MySQL database.

The experiments have focused on three different aspects:

- convergence of the algorithm: we measure the distance between the user models in the population and we show that this distance decreases; this is indicative of how the system learns the real user interests;
- learning the user models: we analyze the correlation between the evolution of the user models and the activities performed by the users of the system.
- quality of the proposed documents: the main aim of the proposed approach is that the more the users interact with the system, the more the quality of the documents proposed by the system increases. We have analyzed this aspect by investigating if the documents read by the users have been proposed by the UPR module or not.

IFeed was launched on September 1st, 2009. Since then, it has been running 24 hours a day and, as of December 10th, more than 500 users had signed up to this project. Not all the registered users have performed the same amount of activity. Therefore, for the purpose of evaluation, we have considered only the 50 most active users. For each user, we have considered his or her first 100 sessions. In each session, a user generally reads more than one document. A brief statistic analysis related to the users activities illustrates that the total number of documents read by users is 12,578, the average documents per user is 251.56 with a standard deviation of 120.79.

The feeds are grouped in 9 different categories based on different topics (*Politics, Economics, Science, Sports*, etc.). The considered users have been assigned to each category by observing their activities. For instance, if most documents read by a user come from the science feeds, the user is assigned to the *Science* category. For each category, we have computed the graphs related to the users' activities in order to study the correlation between the behavior of the evolutionary algorithm and the way the users interact with the system. Moreover, we have analyzed the ability of the system to propose interesting documents to the users. Due to lack of space, in this paper we present and discuss the results obtained for one of the categories, namely *Politics*. However, the considerations below hold for the other categories as well. We will consider five users who have been assigned to the considered category. Nonetheless, the graphs presented represent the convergence of the algorithm with respect to all of the 50 most active users.

	Model 1		Model 2		Model 3
Feed	Interest	Feed	Interest	Feed	Interest
1	0.79	1	0.60	1	0.32
2	0.24	2	0.90	2	0.09
3	0.55	3	0.33	3	0.21
4	0.12	4	0.01	4	0.49
5	0.89	5	0.77	5	0.94

Table 1. Examples of user models.

	Model 2 Norm.	Documents published	
Feed	Int. Norm	Coarse value	Published
2	0.34	6.8	7
5	0.30	6.0	6
1	0.23	4.6	5
3	0.13	2.6	$3 \rightarrow_{pub} 2$
4	0.00	0.0	0

Table 2. Normalization and document publishing.

4.1. Creation of the Proposed Document Set

In this section, we describe in more detail how the UPR module works. This module is executed each time a user logs into the system. It aims at retrieving information about the user's profile and at creating a set of 20 documents to propose to the user. Here, for illustrative purpose, we consider a simple example. We assume to have a user with the models shown in Table 1.

When the user logs into the system, the UPR module chooses randomly one among the models associated to the user, for example Model 2. Then, the interest of each feed in the model is normalized with respect to the sum of all interests of the chosen model. Subsequently, the feeds are ranked in descending order with respect to the feed interests. In order to present the user with documents distributed in a way to be proportional to the user's interests, we then calculate the number of such documents by multiplying the normalized interests by 20. Finally, the UPR module extracts and publishes documents until the limit of 20 documents has been reached. All the above considerations are illustrated in Table 2. We can notice that only two among the tree documents coming from Feed 3 will be published by the UPR module, because the limit of 20 documents has already been reached.

4.2. Learning Curve

In this section, the results related to the convergence of the system are presented. The system was set with a population of 30 individuals, the selection of individuals uses a tournament strategy with size 3, and the probabilities of crossover and mutation were respectively 0.75 and 0.10.

The value of 3 for the tournament size is to keep the selective pressure very low and to avoid premature convergence; with a probability of 0.75 for the crossover operator, we favor the exchange of user interests between the models and, finally, with a mutation probability of 0.10 we allow the system to explore more possible solutions. As said above, we have considered only the first 100 sessions for each user, each session corresponds to a generation of the evolutionary algorithm.

The formula used to calculate the sum of all the distances between all models is:

$$\text{Dist} = \sum_{k=1}^{m-1} \sum_{j=k+1}^{m} \sum_{i=1}^{n} |I_{F_i}^k - I_{F_i}^j|, \tag{13}$$

where n is the number of feeds in the system, m is the population size, $I_{F_i}^k$ is the interest in feed F_i of the model k, and $I_{F_i}^j$ is the interest in feed F_i of the model j. Thus, Dist represents the "overall distance" between the evolved user models present in the population and should be interpreted as an index of population diversity.

Figure 1 illustrates the learning curve obtained by analyzing the system's logs for the 50 users considered. We can notice that, for the first 30 generations, the algorithm converges quickly, then, after the 50th generation, the distance between models tends to remain constant. The value of zero is never reached due to the mutation operator. Indeed, the mutation operator introduces perturbations that maintain a small diversity even between individuals with similar interest degrees. Instead, a possible reason for the fact that the graph does not change after 50 generations is that we have supposed that the considered users are only interested in one category.

The models that have high interest degrees receive positive feedback. Therefore, such models have a higher probability of being chosen during the selection phase. After a given number generations the population is composed by similar individuals, therefore, the distance between the models is hardly conditioned by the perturbations applied by the mutation operator.

In general, since the interest for each feed is encoded as a separate gene in the genotype of a model, learning user interests gets harder as the number of feeds available to the users increase. If a user is interested in a restricted subset of feeds, however, it is relatively easy for the evolutionary algorithm to set the genes of the uninteresting feeds to zero and to focus on the few interesting feeds. This is why, when the number of feeds associated to each category is small, as it is the case with the *Politics* category here, the number of generations required by the system to learn satisfactory interest degrees is small too.

On the contrary, when users are interested in different categories, the convergence speed is slower than the situation described above, because the evolutionary algorithm needs to search a larger space of candidate user models.

4.3. Statistics of User Activity

In this section we present some statistical data about the user models. This data represents the correlation between the way the users interact with the system and how the user models evolve as a result of these interactions. The presented values correpond to the average of the results obtained for the five users associated to the choosen category. In addition, for completeness, we illustrate in each graph the standard deviation of such results.

Figures 2, 3, and 4 show, respectively, the average, the maximum, and the minimum of the following values:

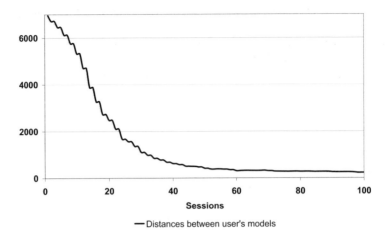

Figure 1. System's learning curve.

- the user's interest degrees at the initialization of the user models;
- the user's interest degrees after the last evolutionary generation considered;

Moreover, in Figure 5 we present the statistics of the documents read by the users for each feed. The x-axis represents the feed number, while the y-axis represents the percentage of read documents coming from the corresponding feed. The lines with markers represent the percent standard deviation calculated over the considered users.

We can notice that most of the read documents come from Feeds 1 and 14, which are the feeds associated with the *Politics* category considered in this example. However, the users also read, in a lesser proportion, documents coming from different categories, although we do not study this aspect in depth. We can observe that the average, the minimum, and the maximum value of the interest degrees related to those feeds are very similar. This is due to the ability of the system to learn the user's profiles. Indeed, when a user reads documents coming always from the same two or more sources alike, the models associated with the user's profile tend to assume similar interest degrees for those sources.

Moreover, we can observe that the more a user reads documents coming from a given feed, the less is the standard deviation associated with that feed. Indeed, for Feeds 1 and 14, the standard deviation is very small in every graph. The interest degrees of the other feeds exhibit a higher standard deviation than the two feeds cited above do. This happens for two reasons. The first is that a small number of documents coming from those feeds has been read, so that the system does not have enough information to learn the exact interest degrees. The second is that the genetic operators constantly apply perturbations on all genes, thereby causing the seldom used interest degrees, which are less sensitive to the pressure of selection, to drift away from their optimal values in time. Surprisingly, Feed 18 too presents a small standard deviation. However, after a more in-depth analysis of the results we concluded that this case must be just a coincidence.

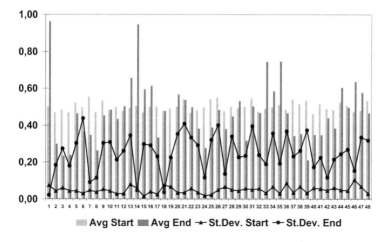

Figure 2. Average interest degrees for each feed calculated on the user profiles.

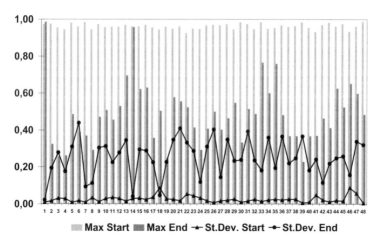

Figure 3. Maximum interest degrees for each feed calculated on the user profiles.

4.4. System Evaluation

In this section we discuss how the system improves the quality of the document set proposed to the users. As explained previously, every time a user logs into the system, the UPR module presents the user with a set of 20 documents. The aim of our approach is to present the users with documents that are as much as possible in line with their interests. To evaluate this aspect we have considered how many documents, out of those proposed to the user by the system, have been read by users with respect to the total number of documents read. To compare the five users considered above, we have taken the first 200 documents read by each user into account.

The results are shown in Figure 6. The graph represents the ratio between the number of documents read belonging to the set of the documents proposed by the system and the total number of documents read. Each point is calculated as follows:

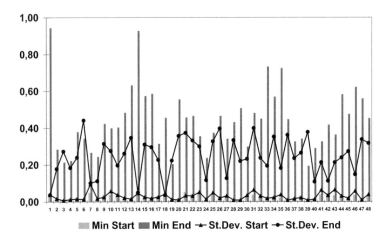

Figure 4. Minimum interest degrees for each feed calculated on the user profiles.

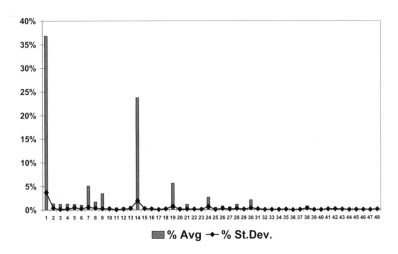

Figure 5. Statistics about the percentage of documents read for each feed.

$$R_j = DRP_j/j, \tag{14}$$

where DRP_j is the number of documents proposed by the system read when the jth document has been read and R_j is the value of the ratio after the user has read the jth document. We can observe that the more the users interact with the system, the more this ratio increases. This means that the system is able to propose an increasing number of documents that are interesting to the users. We can also notice that the system's behavior is not the same for all users. The reason behind that is quite obvious: the implicit feedbacks received by the system for each document read are not the same for all users; therefore, for each user, the time required by the system to learn the user's profile may vary.

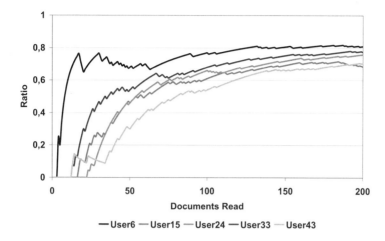

Figure 6. Trend of the quality of the set of the documents proposed by the system.

5. Conclusions

This paper describes an approach to user model-based information retrieval which exploits a concept-based representation and a machine learning technique, namely evolutionary algorithms, to evolve models of user interests. The evolved models are used to propose documents to users, that are in line with their interests. The approach is also capable of dynamically tracking changing user interests.

Experiments have been performed on a real-world prototype newsfeed aggregator with search facilities called IFeed, to validate the approach with respect to two criteria: the first is the capability of learning user interests: the results show that the distance between the evolved models decreases as the user interacts with the system. The second is the increase of precision of the set of documents proposed to the users, indeed, the results show that, as the evolved models get closer to the real user interests, the users increase their activities on the set of documents proposed by the system.

References

[1] M. Baziz, M. Boughanem, N. Aussenac-Gilles, and C. Chrisment. Semantic cores for representing documents in ir. In *SAC '05*, pages 1011–1017. ACM, 2005.
[2] B. Crabtree and S. Soltysiak. Identifying and tracking changing interests. *International Journal on Digital Libraries*, 2(1):38–53, 1998.
[3] K. A. DeJong. *Evolutionary Computation: A unified approach*. MIT Press, Cambridge, MA, 2002.
[4] M. Dragoni and A. Tettamanzi. Evolutionary algorithms for reasoning in fuzzy description logics with fuzzy quantifiers. In *Proceedings of GECCO 2007*, volume 2, pages 1967–1974, London, UK, 2007.
[5] A. E. Eiben and J. E. Smith. *Introduction to Evolutionary Computing*. Springer, Berlin, 2003.
[6] H. P. Giger. Concept based retrieval in classical ir systems. In *SIGIR '88*, pages 275–289. ACM, 1988.
[7] C. Goldman, A. Langer, and J. Rosenschein. Musag: an agent that learns what you mean, 1996.
[8] H. M. Haav and T. L. Lubi. A survey of concept-based information retrieval tools on the web. In *ADBIS'01*, Advances in Databases and Information Systems, pages 29–41. Vilnius "Technika", 2001.
[9] D. Kelly and N. J. Belkin. A user modeling system for personalized interaction and tailored retrieval in interactive IR. In *Proceedings of the American Society for Information Science and Technology*, pages 316–325, 2002.

[10] L. Shen, Y. Lim, and H. Loh. Domain-specific concept-based information retrieval system. In *Proceedings of the IEEE International Engineering Management Conference*, volume 2, pages 525–529, 2004.
[11] S. Soltysiak and B. Crabtree. Automatic learning of user profiles — towards the personalisation of agent service, 1998.
[12] C. J. van Rijsbergen. *Information Retrieval*. Butterworths, London, 1979.
[13] L. A. Zadeh, G. J. Klir, and B. Yuan. *Fuzzy Sets, Fuzzy Logic and Fuzzy Systems: selected papers by A. L. Zadeh*. World Scientific, Singapore, 1996.
[14] J. Zakos and B. Verma. Concept-based term weighting for web information retrieval. In *ICCIMA'05*, pages 173–178. IEEE Computer Society, 2005.

Ontology-Based Document and Query Representation May Improve the Effectiveness of Information Retrieval

Mauro DRAGONI, Célia da Costa PEREIRA and Andrea G.B. TETTAMANZI

Università degli Studi di Milano, Dipartimento di Tecnologie dell'Informazione, Via Bramante 65, I-26013 Crema (CR), Italy, email: mauro.dragoni,celia.pereira,andrea.tettamanzi@unimi.it

Abstract. This paper presents a vector space model approach to representing documents and queries, which considers concepts instead of terms and uses WordNet as a light ontology. This representation reduces information redundancy with respect to conventional semantic expansion techniques. Experiments carried out on the MuchMore benchmark and on the TREC-7 and TREC-8 Ad-hoc collections demonstrate the effectiveness of the proposed approach.

1. Introduction

This paper presents an ontology-based approach to the conceptual representation of documents. Such an approach is inspired by a recently proposed idea presented in [8], and uses an adapted version of that method to standardize the representation of documents and queries. The proposed approach bears some similarity to the classic query expansion technique. However, additional considerations have been taken into account and some improvements have been applied as explained below.

Query expansion is an approach used in Information Retrieval (IR) in order to improve the system's performance. It consists of the expansion of the content of the query by adding the terms that are semantical correlated with the original terms of the query. Several works demonstrated the enhanced performance of IR systems that implement query expansion approaches [22] [3]. However, the query expansion approach has to be used carefully because, as demonstrated in [7], expansion might degrade the performance of some individual queries. This is due to the fact that an incorrect choice of terms and concepts for the expansion task might harm the retrieval process by drifting it away from the optimal correct answer [1].

Document expansion applied to IR has been recently proposed in [2]. In that work, a sub-tree approach has been implemented to represent concepts in documents and queries. However, when using a tree structure, there is a redundancy of information because more general concepts may be represented implicitly by using only the leaf concepts they subsume.

This paper presents a new representation for documents and queries. The proposed approach exploits the structure of the well-known WordNet machine readable dictionary in order to reduce the redundancy of information generally contained in a concept-based document representation. The second improvement is the reduction of the computational time needed to compare documents and queries represented using concepts. This representation has been applied to the *ad-hoc* retrieval problem. The approach has been evaluated on the Muchmore benchmark and on the TREC-7 and TREC-8 Ad-hoc collection, and the results demonstrate its viability.

The paper is organized as follows. In Section 2 an overview of the environment in which ontology has been used is presented. Section 3 presents the tools used for this work. Section 4 illustrates the proposed approach to represent information, while Section 5 compares this approach with other two well-known approaches used in conceptual representation of documents. In Section 6 the experimental results are discussed. Finally, Section 7 concludes.

2. Related Works

An increasing number of recent information retrieval systems make use of ontologies to help the users clarify their information needs and come up with semantic representations of documents. Many ontology-based information retrieval systems and models have been proposed in the last decade. An interesting review on IR techniques based on ontologies is presented in [10]. Model for the exploitation of ontology-base knowledge bases are presented in [6] and [19]. The aim of these models is to improve search over large document repositories. Both models include an ontology-based scheme for the annotation of documents, and a retrieval model based on an adaptation of the classic vector-space model.

The implementation of ontology models has been also investigating using fuzzy models, an approaches is presented in [5].

Ontology-based semantic retrieval is very useful for specific-domain environments. A general IR system to facilitate specific domain search is illustrated in [13]. The system uses fuzzy ontologies and is based on the notion of information granulation, a novel computational model is developed to estimate the granularity of documents. The presented experiments confirm that the proposed system outperforms a vector space based IR system for domain specific search.

In IR, the user's input queries usually are not detailed enough, so the satisfactory query results can not be brought back. Query expansion of IR can help to solve this problem. However, the common query expansion in IR cannot get steady retrieval results. Ontologies play a key role in query expansion research. A common use of ontologies in query expansion is to enrich the resources with some well-defined meaning to enhance the search capabilities of existing web searching systems.

In [21] the authors propose and implement query expansion method which combines domain ontology with the frequent of terms. Ontology is used to describe domain knowledge; logic reasoner and the frequency of terms are used to choose fitting expansion words. This way, higher recall and precise can be gotten as user's query results.

A natural language processing approach is presented in [14]. In this work the authors have developed ontology-based query processing to improve the performance of design information retrieval. In [9] the authors present an approach to expand queries that consists in searching terms from the topic query in an ontology in order to add similar terms.

One of the vital problems in the searching for information is the ranking of the retrieved results. Users make typically very short queries and tend to consider only the first ten results. In traditional IR approaches the relevance of the results is determined only by analyzing the underlying information repository. On the other hand, in the ontology-based IR the querying process is supported by an ontology. In [17] a novel approach for determining relevance in ontology-based searching for information is presented.

3. Preliminaries

The roadmap to prove the viability of a concept-based representation of documents and queries consists in two main tasks: to choose a method that permits to represent all documents terms using the same set of concepts and to implement an approach that permits to index and to evaluate each concept, in both documents and queries, with an appropriate weight.

To represent documents, the method described in Section 4 has been used, combined with the use of the WordNet Machine-Readable Dictionary (MRD). From the WordNet database, the set of terms that do not have hyponymy has been extracted, each term is named "base concept". A vector, named "base vector", has been created and, to each component of the vector, a base concept has been assigned. This way, each term is represented using the base vector of the WordNet ontology.

The representation described above has been implemented on top of the Apache Lucene open-source API.[1]

In the pre-indexing phase, each document has been converted in its ontology representation. After the calculation of the importance of each concept in a document, only concepts with a degree of importance higher than a fixed cut-value have been maintained, while the others have been discarded. The cut-value used in these experiments is 0.01. This choice has a little drawback, namely that an approximation of representing information is introduced due to the discard of some minor concepts. However, we have experimentally verified that this approximation does not affect the final results.

During the evaluation activity, queries have been also converted into the ontological representation. This way, weights have to be assigned to each concept to evaluate all concepts with the right proportion. One of the features of Lucene is the possibility of assigning a boost to each term of the query. Therefore, to each element present in the concept-based representation of the query, the assigned boost value is the concept weight.

4. Document Representation

Conventional IR approaches represent documents as vectors of term weights. Such representations use a vector with one component for every significant term that occurs in the document. This has several limitations, for example:

1. different vector positions may be allocated to the synonyms of the same term; this way there is an information loss because the importance of a determinate *concept* is distributed among different vector components;

---
[1] See URL http://lucene.apache.org/.

2. the size of a document vector have to be at least equal to the total number of words of the language used to write the document;
3. every time a new set of terms is introduced (which is a high-probability event), all document vectors must be reconstructed; the size of a repository thus grows not only as a function of the number of documents that it contains, but also of the size of the representation vectors.

To overcome these weaknesses of term-based representations, an ontology-based representation has been used [15].

An ontology-based representation has been recently proposed in [8] which exploits the hierarchical *is-a* relation among concepts, i.e., the meanings of words. For example, to describe with a term-based representation documents containing the three words: "animal", "dog", and "cat" a vector of three elements is needed; with an ontology-based representation, since "animal" subsumes both "dog" and "cat", it is possible to use a vector with only two elements, related to the "dog" and "cat" concepts, that can also implicitly contain the information given by the presence of the "animal" concept. Moreover, by defining an ontology base, which is a set of independent concepts that covers the whole ontology, an ontology-based representation allows the system to use fixed-size document vectors, consisting of one component per base concept.

Calculating term importance is a significant and fundamental aspect for representing documents in conventional information retrieval approaches. It is usually determined through term frequency-inverse document frequency (TF-IDF). When using an ontology-based representation, such usual definition of term-frequency cannot be applied because one does not operate by keywords, but by concepts. This is the reason why it has been adopted the document representation based on concepts proposed in [8], which is a concept-based adaptation of TF-IDF.

The quantity of information given by the presence of concept z in a document depends on the depth of z in the ontology graph, on how many times it appears in the document, and how many times it occurs in the whole document repository. These two frequencies also depend on the number of concepts which subsume or are subsumed by z. Let us consider a concept x which is a descendant of another concept y which has q children including x. Concept y is a descendant of a concept z which has k children including y. Concept x is a leaf of the graph representing the used ontology. For instance, considering a document containing only "xy", the occurrence of x in the document is $1 + (1/q)$. In the document "xyz", the occurrence of x is $1 + (1/q(1 + 1/k))$. As it is possible to see, the number of occurrences of a leaf is proportional to the number of children which all of its ancestors have. Explicit and implicit concepts are taken into account by using the following formulas:

$$N(c) = \text{occ}(c) + \sum_{c \in \text{Path}(c,\ldots,\top)} \sum_{i=2}^{\text{depth}(c)} \frac{\text{occ}(c_i)}{\prod_{j=2}^{i} ||\text{children}(c_j)||}, \quad (1)$$

where $N(c)$ is the number of occurrences, both explicit and implicit, of concept c and $\text{occ}(c)$ is the number of lexicalizations of c occurring in the document.

Given the ontology base $I = b_1, \ldots, b_n$, where the b_is are the base concepts, the quantity of information, $\text{info}(b_i)$, pertaining to base concept b_i in a document is:

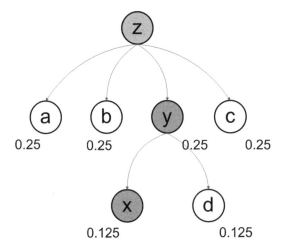

Figure 1. Ontology representation for concept 'z'.

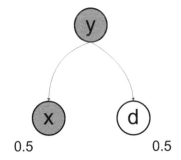

Figure 2. Ontology representation for concept 'y'.

$$\text{info}(b_i) = \frac{N_{\text{doc}}(b_i)}{N_{\text{rep}}(b_i)}, \qquad (2)$$

where $N_{\text{doc}}(b_i)$ is the number of explicit and implicit occurrences of b_i in the document, and $N_{rep}(b_i)$ is the total number of its explicit and implicit occurrences in the whole document repository. This way, every component of the representation vector gives a value of the importance relation between a document and the relevant base concept.

A concrete example can be explained starting from the ontology represented in Figures 1 and 2, and considering a document D_1 containing concepts "$xxyyyz$".

In this case the ontology base is:

$$I = \{a, b, c, d, x\}$$

and, for each concept in the ontology, the vectors N_{doc} are:

Verb	Noun sense
navigate#1	voyage, voyager, sail, navigation
drink#1	drink, drinker, imbiber

Adjective	Noun sense
high#1	highness
small#1	smallness, littleness

Table 1. Examples of "derivationally related forms" relations.

$$\vec{z} = (0.25, 0.25, 0.25, 0.125, 0.125)$$
$$\vec{a} = (1.0, 0.0, 0.0, 0.0, 0.0)$$
$$\vec{b} = (0.0, 1.0, 0.0, 0.0, 0.0)$$
$$\vec{c} = (0.0, 0.0, 1.0, 0.0, 0.0)$$
$$\vec{y} = (0.0, 0.0, 0.0, 0.5, 0.5)$$
$$\vec{d} = (0.0, 0.0, 0.0, 1.0, 0.0)$$
$$\vec{x} = (0.0, 0.0, 0.0, 0.0, 1.0),$$

so the document vector associated to D_1 is:

$$D_1 = (2 * \vec{x}) + (3 * \vec{y}) + \vec{z} = (0.25, 0.25, 0.25, 1.625, 3.625). \qquad (3)$$

In Section 5, a comparison between the proposed representation and other two classic concept-based representation is discussed.

4.1. Issues about Verbs, Adjectives, and Proper Names

The representation described above is chiefly suited to representing nouns. However, a different representation is in order to handle verbs, adjectives, and proper-names.

In WordNet, verbs and adjectives are structured in a different way than nouns. The role of the hyperonymy and hyponymy relations (that make MRD comparable to light ontologies) is different for verbs and adjectives [11,18]. To overcome this issue, we have exploited the "derivationally related form" relation existing in WordNet. This kind of relation links each verb and adjective to the semantically closest noun sense. By such device, for each verb and adjective, the semantically correlated noun sense can be extracted. This enables us to represent the verb (or adjective) information in the same way as nouns. Examples of "derivationally related form" verb-noun relations are reported in Table 1.

A similar approach has been followed for proper-names. These entities, which are part of the WordNet dictionary, are not linked in the WordNet hyperonymy/hyponymy light ontology. All these entities have an "instance of" relationships with nouns that describes the kind of the entity. It is then possible to represent each proper-name by using the concept base associated to the noun linked to it through the "instance of" relationship. Examples of "instance of" relationships are reported in Table 2.

Of course, the issue of proper names is much more complicated than that, and we consider this but a preliminary approximation to a satisfactory solution for handling them, whose main purpose is to enable us to run experiments on a collection of real-world documents and queries, which are highly likely to contain proper names, besides nouns, verbs, and adjectives.

Proper-name	"Instance Of" Noun
Yellowstone	river
George Bush	President of the United States

Table 2. Examples of "instance of" relations.

5. Representation Comparison

In Section 4, the approach used to represent nouns, verbs, adjectives, and proper-names has been described. In this section, we aim at illustrating the improvements obtained, by applying the proposed approach, with respect to the information redundancy and computational time. We also make a comparison between the results obtained by using the proposed approach and those obtained by other two approaches commonly used in conceptual document representation.

Information Redundancy Approaches that apply the expansion of documents and queries use correlated concepts to expand the original terms of documents and queries. A problem with expansion is that information is redundant and there is not a real improvement of the representation of the document (or query) content. With the proposed representation this redundancy is eliminated because only independent concepts are taken into account to represent documents and queries. Another positive aspect is that the size of the vector representing the document content by using concepts is generally smaller than the size of the vector representing document content by using terms.

In [12], the authors propose an indexing technique that takes WordNet synsets into account instead of terms. For each term in documents, the synsets associated to that term are extracted and then used as a token for the indexing task. Therefore, the computational time needed to perform a query does not increase. However, there is a significant overlap of information because different synsets might be semantically correlated, as introduced in Section 4.

Computational Time When IR approaches are applied in a real-world environment, the computational time needed to evaluate the match between documents and the submitted query has to be considered. It is known that systems using the vector space model have higher efficiency. Conceptual-based approaches, such as the one presented in [2], generally implement a non-vectorial data structure which needs a higher computational time than a vector space model representation does. The approach proposed in this paper overcomes this issue, because the document content is represented by using a vector and, therefore, the computational time needed to compute the document score is comparable to the computational time needed when using the vector space model.

6. Experiments

In this section, the impact of the ontology-based document and query representation is evaluated. The experiments have been divided in two different phases:

1. in the first phase, the proposed approach has been compared to the most well-known state of the art kinds of semantic expansion techniques: document representation by synsets and document representation by semantic trees;

Systems	Precisions				
	P5	P10	P15	P30	MAP
Baseline	0.544	0.480	0.405	0.273	0.449
Synset Indexing proposed by [12]	0.648	0.484	0.403	0.309	0.459
Conceptual Indexing proposed by [2]	0.770	0.735	0.690	0.523	0.449
Proposed Ontology Indexing approach	**0.784**	**0.765**	**0.728**	**0.594**	**0.477**

Table 3. Comparisons table between semantic expansion approaches.

2. in the second phase, the proposed approach has been validated with systems that use semantic expansion presented at the TREC7 and TREC8 conferences.

The evaluation method follows the TREC protocol [20]. For each query, the first 1,000 documents have been retrieved and the precision of the system has been calculated at different points: 5, 10, 15, and 30 documents retrieved. Moreover, the Mean Average Precision of the system has been calculated. The document assessment has been computed by adopting the Vector Space Model with the slightly variance of using the Conceptual-IDF proposed in [8] instead of the classic IDF.

The first part of the experiments has been performed by using the MuchMore [2] collection [4], which consists of 7,823 abstracts of medical papers and 25 queries with their relevance judgments. Table 3 illustrates the results obtained by applying the synset indexing approach, the semantic approach proposed by [2], and the approach proposed in this paper. We have considered the classic term-based representation as baseline.

The results show that the proposed method obtains better performances than the two approaches it is compared to. We can notice that the improvement increases with the increment of the retrieved documents considered.

The second part of these experiments has been performed by using the TREC collections. In particular, the TREC Ad-Hoc Collection Volumes 4 and 5 (containing over 500,000 documents) has been used. The approach has been evaluated on topics from 351 to 450. These topics correspond to two editions of the TREC conference, namely TREC-7 and TREC-8.

The approach is also compared to the approaches presented in the TREC-7 and TREC-8 conferences.

For each conference, dozens of runs have been submitted; therefore we have chosen the three systems implementing a semantic expansion that obtained higher precision values at lower recall levels. The rationale behind this decision is the fact that the majority of search result click activity (89.8%) happens on the first page of search results [16], that is, generally, users only consider the first 10 to 20 documents.

Another aspect that we have taken into account is the way queries are composed by each system and which kind of information has been used to do that. Two possible query composition methods are used in the TREC conferences: manual and automatic. Queries are formed completely automatically if the used software already exists at the time of query evaluation; in all other cases, the queries are considered to be manual. Automatic

---

[2]http://muchmore.dfki.de

Systems	Precisions				
	P5	P10	P15	P30	MAP
Term-Based Representation	0.444	0.414	0.375	0.348	0.199
AT&T Labs Research (att98atdc)	0.644	0.558	0.499	0.419	0.296
AT&T Labs Research (att98atde)	0.644	0.558	0.497	0.413	0.294
City University, Univ. of Sheffield, Microsoft (ok7am)	0.572	0.542	0.507	0.412	0.288
Proposed Approach	**0.656**	**0.588**	0.501	0.397	**0.309**

Table 4. Precision@X and Mean Average Precision results obtained on TREC7 Topics.

Systems	Precisions				
	P5	P10	P15	P30	MAP
Term-Based Representation	0.476	0.436	0.389	0.362	0.243
IBM T.J. Watson Research Center (ibms99a)	0.588	0.504	0.472	0.410	0.301
Microsoft Research Ltd (ok8amxc)	0.580	0.550	0.499	0.425	0.317
TwentyOne (tno8d3)	0.500	0.454	0.433	0.368	0.292
Proposed Approach	**0.616**	**0.572**	0.485	0.415	0.315

Table 5. Precision@X and Mean Average Precision results obtained on TREC8 topics.

queries provide a reasonably well controlled basis for cross-system comparison, although they are typically representative of only the first query in an interactive search process. On the contrary, manual queries are used to demonstrate the retrieval effectiveness that can be obtained after interactive optimization of the query. Examples of manual queries are queries in which stop words or stop structure are manually removed.

Each topic (query) is composed of three main fields: title, description, and narrative. A query might consist of one or more of these fields. The proposed approach builds queries using only the title and the description fields; therefore, it has been compared only to systems that used the same fields. Because documents are represented using an ontology, also each topic has been converted into the corresponding ontological representation.

The precision/recall graph shown in Figure 3 illustrates the comparison between the proposed approach (heavy gray curve), the classical term-based representation (black curve), and the three systems presented at the TREC-7 Ad-Hoc Track (light gray curves). As expected, for all recall values, the proposed approach obtained better results than the term-based representation.

By comparing the proposed approach with the three TREC-7 systems, we can notice that the results obtained by our approach are better than the results obtained by the other approaches. Indeed, we obtained better results for the recall levels between 0.0 and 0.4, the best results being at recall levels 0.0 and 0.2. At recall levels 0.5 up to 1, the pro-

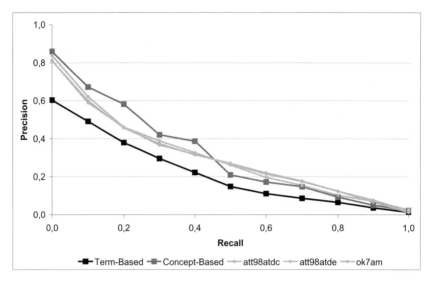

Figure 3. Precision/recall graph for TREC-7 topics.

posed approach is slightly worst, but substantially in line with the other concept-based approaches. A possible explanation for this scenario is that, for documents that are well related to a particular topic, the adopted ontology-based representation is able to improve the representation of the document contents. However, for documents that are partially related to a topic or that contain many ambiguous terms, the proposed approach is not able to maintain a high precision of the results. At the end of this section, a couple of improvements that may overcome this issue are discussed.

In Table 4, all systems are compared for the Precision@X and MAP values. The results confirm that the proposed approach obtains better results for the top 10 retrieved documents. Indeed, the values for Prec@5 and Prec@10 are the best results. The same consideration holds for the MAP value. However, the Prec@15 value is in line with the other systems, while the Prec@30 value does not outperform the values obtained by the three TREC-7 systems.

The same evaluations have been carried out for the topics of the TREC-8 Ad-Hoc Track. The precision/recall graph in Figure 4 shows how the concept-based representation curve approaches and overtakes the curves of the three TREC-8 systems for recall levels between 0.0 and 0.4. The behavior of the proposed approach is similar to the one shown by using the TREC-7 topics, however, in this case the gain is reduced. It is also interesting to observe that, with the TREC-8 topics, the results of all presented systems are closer to the ones obtained on the TREC-7 topics.

The Precision@X and the MAP values shown in Table 5 confirm the impression described above.

Inspecting the precision/recall curve obtained by the system with both TREC-7 and TREC-8 topics, we can notice that the performance of the system decreases in both cases. We think that this situation can mainly be due to two reasons:

- Absence of some terms in the ontology: some terms, in particular terms related to specific domains (biomedical, mechanical, business, etc.), are not defined in the MRD because WordNet does not cover all possible terms of the English language.

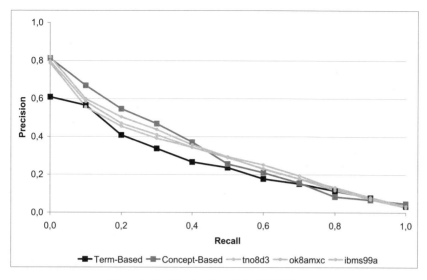

Figure 4. Precision/recall graph for TREC-8 topics.

Therefore, in some cases there is a loss of information that can affect the final retrieval result.
- Term ambiguity: the concept-based representation can introduce an error given by not using a word sense disambiguation algorithm. This could cause concepts associated to incorrect senses being discarded or weighted less.

We are convinced that improving the actual model with the above considerations would yield significantly better results in forthcoming experiments. This positive view is motivated by the fact that, by expanding semantically each term, the ambiguity plays a significant role in the representation of document content.

7. Conclusion

This paper has discussed an approach to indexing documents and to representing queries for information retrieval purposes which exploits a conceptual representation based on ontologies. Experiments have been performed on the MuchMore Collection and on TREC Ad-Hoc Collection to validate the approach with respect to problems like term-synonymity in documents.

Preliminary experimental results show that the proposed representation improves the ranking of the documents in the first positions. Investigation on results highlights that further improvement could be obtained by integrating WSD techniques to avoid the error introduced by considering incorrect word senses, and a better usage of linguistic resources to overcome the absence of domain-specific terms.

References

[1] A. Abdelali, J. Cowie, and H. Soliman. Improving query precision using semantic expansion. *Inf. Process. Manage.*, 43(3):705–716, 2007.
[2] M. Baziz, M. Boughanem, G. Pasi, and H. Prade. An information retrieval driven by ontology: from query to document expansion. In *RIAO*. CID, 2007.

[3] B. Billerbeck and J. Zobel. Techniques for efficient query expansion. In *SPIRE*, volume 3246 of *Lecture Notes in Computer Science*, pages 30–42. Springer, 2004.

[4] M. Boughanem, T. Dkaki, J. Mothe, and C. Soulé-Dupuy. Mercure at trec7. In *TREC*, pages 355–360, 1998.

[5] S. Calegari and E. Sanchez. A fuzzy ontology-approach to improve semantic information retrieval. In *URSW*, volume 327 of *CEUR Workshop Proceedings*. CEUR-WS.org, 2007.

[6] P. Castells, M. Fernández, and D. Vallet. An adaptation of the vector-space model for ontology-based information retrieval. *IEEE Trans. Knowl. Data Eng.*, 19(2):261–272, 2007.

[7] S. Cronen-Townsend, Y. Zhou, and W. Croft. A framework for selective query expansion. In *CIKM*, pages 236–237. ACM, 2004.

[8] C. da Costa Pereira and A. G. B. Tettamanzi. *Soft computing in ontologies and semantic Web*, chapter An ontology-based method for user model acquisition, pages 211–227. Studies in fuzziness and soft computing. Ed. Zongmin Ma, Springer, Berlin, 2006.

[9] M. Díaz-Galiano, M. G. Cumbreras, M. Martín-Valdivia, A. M. Ráez, and L. Ureña-López. Integrating mesh ontology to improve medical information retrieval. In *CLEF*, volume 5152 of *Lecture Notes in Computer Science*, pages 601–606. Springer, 2007.

[10] O. Dridi. Ontology-based information retrieval: Overview and new proposition. In O. Pastor, A. Flory, and J.-L. Cavarero, editors, *RCIS*, pages 421–426. IEEE, 2008.

[11] C. Fellbaum and G. Miller. Folks psychology or semantic entailment? a reply to rips and conrad. *The Psychology Review*, 97:565–570, 1990.

[12] J. Gonzalo, F. Verdejo, I. Chugur, and J. Cigarrán. Indexing with wordnet synsets can improve text retrieval. *CoRR*, cmp-lg/9808002, 1998.

[13] R. Lau, C. Lai, and Y. Li. Mining fuzzy ontology for a web-based granular information retrieval system. In *RSKT*, volume 5589 of *Lecture Notes in Computer Science*, pages 239–246. Springer, 2009.

[14] Z. Li and K. Ramani. Ontology-based design information extraction and retrieval. *AI EDAM*, 21(2):137–154, 2007.

[15] L. Shen, Y. Lim, and H. Loh. Domain-specific concept-based information retrieval system. In *Proceedings of the IEEE International Engineering Management Conference*, volume 2, pages 525–529, 2004.

[16] A. Spink, B. Jansen, C. Blakely, and S. Koshman. A study of results overlap and uniqueness among major web search engines. *Inf. Process. Manage.*, 42(5):1379–1391, 2006.

[17] N. Stojanovic. An approach for defining relevance in the ontology-based information retrieval. In *Web Intelligence*, pages 359–365. IEEE Computer Society, 2005.

[18] L. Talmy. Lexicalization patters: Semantic structure in lexical forms. *Language Typology and Syntactic Description*, 3:57–149, 1985.

[19] D. Vallet, M. Fernández, and P. Castells. An ontology-based information retrieval model. In *ESWC*, volume 3532 of *Lecture Notes in Computer Science*, pages 455–470. Springer, 2005.

[20] E. Voorhees and D. Harman. Overview of the sixth text retrieval conference (trec-6). In *TREC*, pages 1–24, 1997.

[21] F. Wu, G. Wu, and X. Fu. Design and implementation of ontology-based query expansion for information retrieval. In *CONFENIS (1)*, volume 254 of *IFIP*, pages 293–298. Springer, 2007.

[22] J. Xu and W. Croft. Query expansion using local and global document analysis. In *SIGIR*, pages 4–11. ACM, 1996.

"Do you trust me or not?" - Trust games in agent societies

Rui FIGUEIREDO [a,1], João CARMO [a,2] and Rui PRADA [a,3]
[a] *INESC-ID, Instituto Superior Técnico, Lisboa, Portugal*

Abstract. Multi-agent simulation provides a way to explore results from social studies and provide hints on how these results scale. One particular class of studies that is interesting to explore are economic-related studies. We developed a multi-agent system that simulates an investment game and incorporates the results from economic-related social studies into the design of the agents. We analyzed how several factors, such as trust and reputation influence the outcome of the agents in terms of distribution of wealth and total generated money.

Keywords. Agent Societies, Trust, Reputation, Autonomous Agents

Introduction

Several social studies have been performed to assess how people behave in group situations. These studies are hard to organize and often can only involve a small number of participants. One particular type of studies that is hard to orchestrate is related to economics (especially because of cost issues). Generally, in these studies, the participants are handed money upon which they have to make decisions that will, depending on several factors that are not controlled by the individual holding the money, affect the nature of their outcome as participants.

One particular area of interest in economics is how markets can be made efficient. The mechanisms that allow individuals and corporations to perform efficient transactions lie at the basis for that efficiency [9]. Low-cost transactions or transactions with no associated costs can be achieved in reputation-based markets, where reputation ensures trust from the individuals investing. Reputation itself becomes an asset that is in the interest of the holder to maintain [9]. Using multi-agent simulations with data provided by social studies it is possible to analyze the effects reputation and trust have on how the market evolves, and furthermore it allows us to provide hints on how the results from studies involving small numbers of participants scale when applied to large populations.

In order to explore these results from economics and also results from social studies that describe how people act in economic-related games, we developed a multi-agent system that simulates several interactions of the investment game [2]. The agents in the sim-

---
[1] email: rui.figueiredo@gaips.inesc-id.pt
[2] email: joao.carmo@inesc-id.pt
[3] rui.prada@gaips.inesc-id.pt

ulation were built using results from social studies [2] [12] [5] [9] concerning the dictator and investment game [2] [12], and taking into account economic-inspired definitions [9] of trust and reputation in their behavior.

1. Related Work

Several work has been developed that explores the use of trust as a regulatory mechanism in multi-agent systems. In [8] a trust assessment process is described where an agent (*truster*) computes trust based on the quality of direct interactions with another agent (*trustee*) and by the information provided from a group of consulting agents (comprised of a selected group of trustworthy agents by the truster, and a group of advocating agents selected by the trustee). The temporal and frequency characteristics of the interactions are also taken into account, as discounting factors, when computing trust.

In [1] a belief revision process based on trust and reputation is explored and applied to agents' information sources (which can be sensory information or information provided by other agents) in non-deterministic settings.

In [13] a formal model of trust that focuses on a statistical measure of trust is described. Trust is defined over a probability distribution of the probability of positive outcomes together with an explicit measure of certainty. This particular work has the advantage of providing measures of trust that are independent of the agents' rationale and the particular object of trust.

Also, multi-agent system design based on information about human societies has been explored in several studies as a way to provide insight on several social phenomenons. It has been used as an alternative to more traditional approaches where mass amounts of social data are analyzed in order to find patterns which are then theorized in terms of underlying individual behaviors [3] [7].

Using this approach a multi-agent system was built to study social mobility [4]. The agents in the simulation were modeled using several attributes (Class, Education, Status, etc.) which influence their outcome in the simulations (directly and indirectly through interactions with other agents). The results provide insights on the population evolves in terms of its constituents and their particular characteristics (demographics, distribution of education, average education and class levels, etc).

In [6] Doran describes a simulation where possible benefits of collective misbelief are explored in an agent society. A multi-agent system is used to verify that there are situations where collective agent misbelief might be beneficial to the agent society as it is sometimes the case in human societies.

In [11] a multi-agent simulation was developed to provide insight as how people might fair in mixed human-agent societies. The multi-agent system runs a dictator game where human-like agents (based on a social study of how human act in a dictator game [12]) interact between themselves and a set of rational agents.

2. Trust Games

A game that is commonly used in experimental economics is the dictator game which is comprised of two players, the first ("the proposer") determines how much of an initial endowment to split between himself and the other player (the second player's role is entirely passive). The purpose of this game is to rebut the homo economicus model of individual behavior, where each individual is only concerned with his/her own economical well-being.

The trust game extends the dictator game in that the allocation provided by the first player is increased by some factor before given to the second player, who then has the choice of giving part of that factored allocation back or keeping it all as profit. This game's subgame perfect Nash equilibrium states that both players should give nothing, but several studies show that is rarely the case [2] [12]. The fact that people give something even when there is no guarantee of getting anything back indicates that trust must exist a priori to any transaction [2].

Following on that are theories that define reputation as how an individual/organization is expected to fulfill an implicit contract, and as an asset that is in the interest of its holder to maintain [9]. Using reputation as a way of facilitating transactions provides a way of performing exchanges of values that do not involve the costs of elaborating and enforcing contracts that describe how to deal with all the possible contingencies that can occur during the transaction, and thus making the market itself more efficient and free of transaction costs related to enforcing the agreed upon terms of how contingencies should be dealt with [9].

In [2] an experiment is devised to explore in a one time interaction the role of trust in a two-person (that never meet) exchange. This study not only shows that people have a natural tendency to trust, but also provides insight on how much they are willing to give. The game described in [2] is similar to the trust game, it is played only once between two players, where each is given an equal amount of money. The first player has the choice to give part of his/her amount to the second player. If he/she chooses to do this, that amount is multiplied by three, and the second player can then decide how much of that factored amount to keep to himself and how much to return to the first player.

In [12] a distinction is made on the population, people are classified a priori as Altruists or Egoists based on a "social value orientation" questionnaire [10]. Two studies were performed, where on the first a dictator game was played and as expected, altruists had a natural tendency to give more than egoists. A second study followed where indirect reciprocity was taken into account by having a third player reward the dictator of the first game based on his/her offering to the second player. In the second study, the amount given back by the altruists was essentially the same, but in contrast the egoists gave more.

3. Simulation

The simulation (Figure 1) runs a trust game that is repeated several times. In each iteration several steps take place. We have named the first step role-setting, in which half of the agents are given the role of investor, and the remaining half the role of idealists. An investor represents an agent who wants to invest some of its money in an idealist. An idealist is an agent that has an idea the can generate profit. For the sake of simplicity, all idealists make, as profit, the money invested on them multiplied by a factor of three.

After the role-setting step comes the coupling phase, where each investor is paired with an idealist. Following that, the transaction starts. Each player is handed an equal amount (c.f. trust game [2]), then the investment phase takes place where the investor

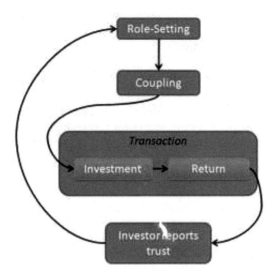

Figure 1. Simulation Cycle

decides how much of the handed money to invest in the idealist. The idealist then, in the return phase, decides how much of the generated money to return to the investor. Finally, the investor informs all agents in the simulation of how good of an investment the idealist was. And the cycle repeats.

Each agent's decisions are driven by one of two profiles, Egoist or Altruist, inspired by [12]. Although [12] describes a dictator game, where there is no return phase, we decided to look at the investment game as a two-time dictator game (where the return phase can be seen as another dictator game), we based our decision on the fact that there is some evidence that the return in an investment game is unrelated to the amount invested [2]. We are also aware that this is a weak assumption given that if past interaction history exists, the amount invested seems to influence the amount that is returned [2].

4. The Agents

The agent's role is to make decisions in each of the phases of the simulation cycle based on the role they are assigned at each iteration. The role each agent has is assigned randomly at the beginning of each cycle (the simulation ensures that half the agents are idealists and the other half investors).

As an investor, the first decision to be made is in whom to invest. The investor is aware of all the available idealists and can choose one based on previous interaction history and on the information made available by other agents.

As an idealist, if there are several interested investors, a choice is made on whom to accept investment from.

As there are always an even number of agents, the coupling phase is repeated for the uncoupled agents until all investors have an idealist to invest in.

Following the coupling phase, the investors must decide how much to invest in their idealist, the decision is made based on how much money they have available, and also from previous interaction history information provided by other investors regarding the idealist.

The idealist decides how much of the received money to return based on how much money was invested in him.

In the last step of the simulation the investor updates his trust regarding the idealists based on the payback received from its investment, and reports the updated trust to the other agents.

Each investor stores past information history regarding an idealist as a value that represents trust. As defined by [9], trust is maintained if the party that was trusted acts in a way that is expected by the trustee. In our case, we have defined trust as a positive integer that is computed by:

$$TransactionTrust = \min\left(\frac{Ar}{Ai} \times \frac{MaxTrust}{2}, MaxTrust\right) \quad (1)$$

Where Ai is the amount invested, Ar the amount returned and $MaxTrust$ the maximum trust value that an investor can assign to an idealist.

As it is defined, $\frac{MaxTrust}{2}$ represents the neutral value for trust (the investor neither wins nor loses any money). Values below that indicate negative and values over represent positive trust. Maximum trust is achieved when the amount returned is twice the amount invested, which represents the best possible outcome for both agents where they end up profiting the same amount (for example, if both are handed 10 at the beginning of the transaction, if the investor invests 5, the idealist gets 15 and returns 10, both end up with 15).

After each transaction the investor updates his trust over the idealist by averaging his previous trust with the trust computed from the current transaction:

$$Trust = \frac{Trust + TransactionTrust}{2} \quad (2)$$

4.1. Egoist

As an investor, an egoist agent will choose an idealist randomly. Conversely, as an idealist in the situation where several investors are competing for investment, the idealist chooses one investor randomly.

The egoist agents represent an agent type that has the tendency to keep most of the profit for itself. People classified as Egoists [12] have a tendency to give less in the dictator game and reciprocate less in the indirect reciprocity game (the indirect reciprocity game consists in having a third player observe the dictator behavior and then deciding how much to "reciprocate" to the dictator [12]).

In [12], the experiment where the dictator game is played without the possibility of reciprocation is called *private*, and where reciprocation is possible is named *public*. In the private experiment egoists gave an average of 22% of the money they had available. In the public experiment they gave on average 46% of the available money.

At the transaction phase, an egoist agent invests a percentage that is given by a normal probability distribution with mean 0.22 (22%) and variance 0.1. These values were inspired by the private experiment described in [12] since the investment is not covered by any form of indirect reciprocation.

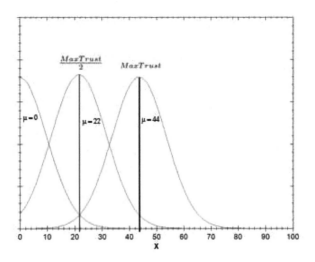

Figure 2. Egoist investment distribution

As the simulation progresses and the agent interacts repeatedly with other agents, it as an investor will adjust the mean of the probability distribution accordingly to the trust it has on the investor. With neutral trust the agent invest on average 22% (private experiment results described in [12]), but as it loses or gains trust in the idealist its probability distribution changes accordingly. The investment is computed by the following equation:

$$I_{Ag_k}(Ag_j) = Mi \times P_{prv} \times 2 \times \frac{Trust_{Ag_k \to Ag_j}}{MaxTrust} \qquad (3)$$

Where $I_{Ag_k}(Ag_j)$ represents the investment agent Ag_k will perform in agent Ag_j, Mi is the available money to invest, P_{prv} is the private random variable with normal distribution, $\mu = 0.22$ and $\sigma^2 = 0.1$, $Trust_{Ag_k \to Ag_j}$ is the value that represents the investor's (Ag_k) trust in the idealist (Ag_j) and $MaxTrust$ is the maximum value for trust. In neutral trust ($\frac{MaxTrust}{2}$) situations the agent behaves as in [12], however as the trust evolves favorably the average investment increases until twice the value of the neutral situation. As the trust decreases, so does the average investment until the extreme (no trust) of an average of 0% investment (Fig. 2).

When the egoist has the role of idealist, it returns an average of 22% of the value that the idealist invested in it. This value is inspired by the donations made in private conditions in the dictator game described in [12], since in these conditions the returned money is not subjected to indirect reciprocation. The equation for the returned money is given by:

$$R_{Ag_j}(Ag_k) = M_r \times P_{prv} \qquad (4)$$

Where $R_{Ag_j}(Ag_k)$ is the amount returned by agent Ag_j to agent Ag_k, M_r is the amount agent Ag_j received from agent Ag_k's investment (in our simulation it is $I_{Ag_k}(Ag_j) \times 3$), and P_{prv} is a normal probability distribution with $\mu = 0.22$ and $\sigma^2 = 0.1$.

Table 1. Example of agent Ag_1's reputation table. $Ag_{i(ide)}$ represents Ag_i as an idealist and $Ag_{i(inv)}$ represents agent Ag_i as an investor. (−) means that the agents in question have not interacted previously.

	$Ag_{1(ide)}$	$Ag_{2(ide)}$	$Ag_{3(ide)}$	$Ag_{4(ide)}$
$Ag_{2(inv)}$	6	×	2	8
$Ag_{3(inv)}$	5	−	×	10
$Ag_{4(inv)}$	5	−	4	×

4.2. Altruist

Regarding the coupling phase, the altruist agent behaves as the egoist. It will choose a random idealist when assigned the role of investor, and will choose a random investor if several are interested in investing in it when it has the role of idealist.

Altruist represent agents that act prosocially in all situations, meaning they will tend to give more (regardless of the existence or not of future benefits) [12]. An altruist agent in our simulation is an agent that will on average, invest more and return more than an egoist agent. In [12] people classified as altruists, gave on average 40% in the private experiment and 51% in the public experiment (where future benefits are possible via indirect reciprocity).

At the transaction phase, an altruist agent invests a percentage that is given by a normal probability distribution that ensures it invests 40% on average. As with the egoist agent, these values were inspired by the private experiment described in [12]. The equation used to compute the value to invest is equivalent to the egoist agent (Eq. 3), the diference being in that P_{prv} is a normal probability distribution with $\mu = 0.4$ and $\sigma^2 = 0.1$. The same applies to the return equation (Eq. 4).

4.3. Reputation

Reputation can be seen as a mechanism that allows future trading partners to observe the fulfillment (or lack of) of an (implicit) agreement [9]. Each time the trusted entity honors the trust ascribed in it its reputation grows, and every time it dishonors it, its reputation diminishes. From this perspective reputation can be looked upon as an asset, that is in the interest of the holder to maintain [9].

At the end of each transaction, the agent that has the role of investor tells all other agents its updated trust regarding the idealist (Eq.1 and Eq.2). The agents who receive this information store it as a triplet containing the investor, the idealist and the trust value. As the simulation progresses each agent will build up information regarding what is the level of trust each agent, as an investor, has in other agents, as idealists (Table 1).

We compute reputation as the average of the reported trust values(Eq. 5), for example, imagine Table 1 represents the information agent Ag_1 has about the other agents present in the simulation. Agent Ag_1 will assign agent Ag_3's a reputation value of 3 ($\frac{Trust_{Ag_2 \to Ag_3} + Trust_{Ag_4 \to Ag_3}}{2}$), and for agent Ag_4 a reputation value of 9.

$$Reputation_{Ag_k}(Ag_j) = \frac{\sum_{Ag_i \in (A \setminus \{Ag_k\})} Trust_{Ag_i \to Ag_j}}{|A \setminus \{Ag_k\}|} \quad (5)$$

Where $Reputation_{Ag_k}(Ag_j)$ is the reputation agent Ag_k computes for agent Ag_j, A is the set of agents that have reported a trust value in Ag_j and $Trust_{Ag_i \to Ag_j}$ is the trust agent Ag_i reported concerning agent Ag_j.

4.3.1. Egoist

The way the egoist agent performs investments now takes into account the reputation together with trust (both are given equal weights). The investment is given by:

$$I_{Ag_k}(Ag_j) = Mi \times P_{prv} \times 2 \\ \times \left(\frac{\frac{Trust_{Ag_i \to Ag_j}}{MaxTrust} + Reputation_{Ag_k}(Ag_j)}{2} \right) \quad (6)$$

Where $I_{Ag_k}(Ag_j)$ represents the amount Ag_k invests in Ag_j, Mi is Ag_k's available money to invest and P_{prv} is a random variable with normal distribution ($\mu = 0.22$ and $\sigma^2 = 0.1$).

Note that when investing the egoist does not take into account its reputation, since the amount invested has no effect on it. Hence, we used the same probability distribution as in Eq. 3.

Introducing reputation in the simulation is a way of making the transactions public in the way that the reported outcome (via the trust reported by the investor) will have an influence on all future investments. Because of this and because egoists are defined by the influence that (possible) future benefits have on their behavior [12], when reputation is introduced the egoists change their return behavior (so as to ensure a positive reputation). In [12], in the public setting experiment (where there was indirect reciprocity) people classified as egoists invested on average 46% (in contrast with the 22% invested in private settings).

Regarding the return, the egoist will tend to return more in order to protect its reputation:

$$R_{Ag_j}(Ag_k) = M_r \times P_{pub} \quad (7)$$

Where again $R_{Ag_j}(Ag_k)$ is the amount returned by Ag_j to Ag_k, M_r the amount Ag_j received from Ag_k's investment and P_{pub} is a random variable governed by a normal probability distribution with $\mu = 0.46$ and $\sigma^2 = 0.1$ (in contrast with P_{prv} where μ was 0.22).

4.3.2. Altruist

Altruists do not respond as markedly to the presence of possible future benefits as egoists, however in [12] there were subtle differences - altruists gave on average 51% when faced with possible future benefits (in contrast with 40% when no future benefits were accounted for).

Since there is no effect on reputation when investing, an altruist uses Eq. 6, the difference being that P_{prv} is now a normal random variable with $\mu = 0.4$ and $\sigma^2 = 0.1$.

Also, when performing the return on an investment, the altruist agent uses the same equation as the egoist (Eq. 7), where P_{pub} is a normal random variable with $\mu = 0.51$ and $\sigma^2 = 0.1$.

4.4. Weighted Reputation

In an exploratory effort to provide an alternative calculation for reputation we took into account that agents represent explicitly what level of trust each agent as an investor has on the idealists they invested in, and we incorporated those explicit representations in the computation of reputation. The agents can weigh the information provided by the level of trust they have in the provider. Defining reputation this way makes it a subjective view from the agent who is assigning it to the idealist. The reputation is now given by:

$$Reputation_{Ag_k}(Ag_j) =$$

$$\frac{\sum_{Ag_i \in A_T} \left(\frac{Trust_{Ag_k \to Ag_i}}{MaxTrust} \times Trust_{Ag_i \to Ag_j} \right)}{|A \setminus \{Ag_k\}|} + \frac{\sum_{Ag_i \in (A \setminus A_T) \setminus \{Ag_k\}} Trust_{Ag_i \to Ag_j}}{|A \setminus \{Ag_k\}|} \quad (8)$$

Where the first term of the sum represents the average of the weighted trust reports from the agents the agent already has invested in, and the second term the average of the trust reports from the agents it has not interacted with as investor yet.

$Reputation_{Ag_k}(Ag_j)$ is the reputation agent Ag_k ascribes to agent Ag_j, $\frac{Trust_{Ag_k \to Ag_i}}{MaxTrust}$ is the weight (in the form of percentage) agent Ag_k devotes to the trust reported by agent Ag_i regarding agent Ag_j ($Trust_{Ag_i \to Ag_j}$). A_T is the set of agents with whom agent Ag_k has invested in (therefore having a trust value for them) and A is the set of agents that have have interacted with Ag_j as investors.

4.4.1. Egoist

By computing an agents' reputations using Eq. 8, more credit is given to agents that the calculating agent trusts. Therefore, agents that are globally more trusted have a bigger influence "in their saying" in another agent's reputation. Egoist agents can take advantage of this by using a more egoistic strategy when faced with an investor that has bad reputation (less than $\frac{MaxTrust}{2}$) and a less egoistic strategy otherwise (by deceiving an agent with a low reputation, the egoist reputation should be less affected than when deceiving an investor with high reputation).

When investing, an egoist agent behaves the same way as in Eq. 6, the difference being that reputation is now computed using Eq. 8.

When returning in a transaction the egoist now takes into account the reputation of the investor. If the investor has a good reputation, that is seen by the egoist as a sign that the investor has many trustees, on the other hand if it has a bad reputation its disclosure regarding the egoist performance in the transaction is less likely to affect significantly its reputation. The return is computed by:

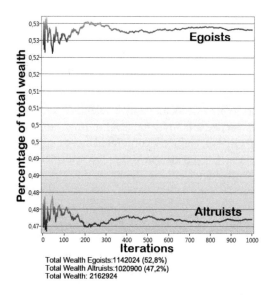

Figure 3. Agents using only results from social studies

$$R_{Ag_j}(Ag_k) = \begin{cases} M_r \times P_{pub} \text{ if } Reputation_{Ag_j}(Ag_k) \geq \phi; \\ M_r \times P_{prv} \text{ if } Reputation_{Ag_j}(Ag_k) < \phi. \end{cases} \quad (9)$$

Where $R_{Ag_j}(Ag_k)$ is the amount returned by Ag_j to Ag_k, M_r the amount Ag_k received from Ag_j's investment, P_{pub} is a random variable governed by a normal probability distribution with $\mu = 0.46$ and $\sigma^2 = 0.1$, P_{prv} is also a random variable with normal distribution, $\mu = 0.22$ and $\sigma^2 = 0.1$, $Reputation_{Ag_j}(Ag_k)$ the reputation computed by agent Ag_j relative to agent Ag_k and ϕ is $\frac{MaxTrust}{2}$ which represents neutral trust.

4.4.2. Altruist

As altruists have the characteristic of being less influenced by the prospect of future benefits they do not take advantage of the investor when it has a low reputation.

As like egoists, altruists use weighted reputation (Eq. 8) to decide how much to invest (Eq. 7) when having the role of investor.

However, when returning an altruist does not take into account any of the investor's characteristics, it behaves the same was as before (using Eq. 7).

5. Simulation Results

To assess the effect of introducing trust and reputation in a population of agents performing the trust game we have run 1000 iterations of the game (where each of the agents is handed 100 units of money per round) using several configurations. The first configuration was composed of an equal amount of egoist and altruist agents (10 each) using only the results from the social studies [2] [12]. The simulation (Figure 3) shows that, as expected, this is a favorable setting for the egoist agents.

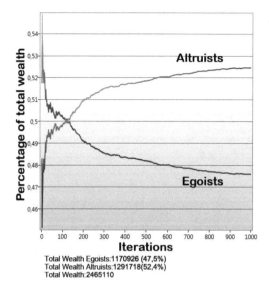

Figure 4. Agents using trust

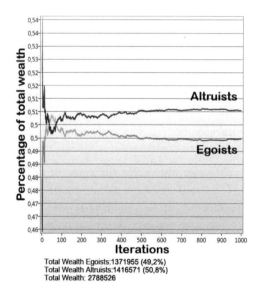

Figure 5. Agents using reputation

Upon introducing trust (Figure 4) there is an inversion of the situation. The altruists now thrive since egoists are rapidly identified as bad investments.

With the inclusion of reputation (Figure 5) a balance is achieved. This is the situation where wealth is better distributed and where the whole agent population generates more money. This is an interesting result since it mirrors the benefits of reputation, described as a tool for generating efficient markets [9].

Using weighted reputation (Figure 6) proved to yield a big difference in the distri-

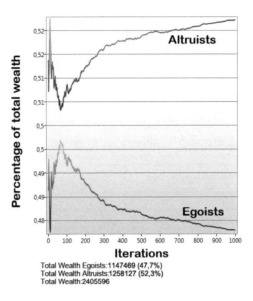

Figure 6. Agents using weighted reputation

bution of wealth between egoist and altruist agents, similar to the one observed when we use only trust (cf. Figure 4). In this setting the egoist agents although using a more elaborate return strategy still end up with bad reputation after a sufficient number of iterations.

6. Conclusions and Future Work

We have developed a multi-agent system that simulates the trust game based on results from social studies [12] [2]. Based on interpretations of trust and reputation taken from an economics market perspective [9] we simulated several runs of the trust game and were able to show the effect trust and reputation had on the way that the wealth was distributed. The introduction of reputation confirmed the expected result of being a good mechanism to regulate markets [9].

We also included an alternative computation for reputation that takes into account a subjective view of the agent that is computing it. We believe this can become useful if we include dishonesty in the simulation. We are presently modeling trust as a measure of the quality of the agent as an idealist, and not as a measure of its honesty when reporting its trust on transactions. We would like to explore this issue more, including dishonesty in the simulation and using results like [13] to handle it.

There were other aspects that we would like to address as future work in order to achieve a richer simulation environment. Issues such as the ability for the agents to choose who to invest in and who to accept investment from and other measures of trust [8] [13].

Acknowledgements

This work was partially supported by two scholarships (SFRH / BD / 31362 / 2006 and SFRH / BD / 31877 / 2006) granted by the Fundação para a Ciência e a Tecnologia (FCT). The authors are solely responsible for the content of this publication. It does not represent the opinion of FCT, which is not responsible for any use that might be made of data appearing therein.

References

[1] K. Suzanne Barber and Joonoo Kim, 'Belief revision process based on trust: Agents evaluating reputation of information sources', *Trust in Cyber-societies, LNAI 2246*, 73–82, (2001).
[2] Joyce Berg, John Dickhaut, and Kevin Mccabe, 'Trust, reciprocity, and social history', *Games and Economic Behavior*, **10**(1), 122–142, (July 1995).
[3] E. Chattoe, 'Building empirically plausible multi-agent systems: A case study of innovative diffusion', in *Socially Intelligent Agents: Creating Relationships with Computers and Robots, K. Dautenhahn, A. H. Bond, L. Canamero, and B. Edmonds, Ed. Kluwer Academic Publishers, Norwell, MA, 109-116.*, (2002).
[4] E. Chattoe and A. Heath, 'A new approach to social mobility models: Simulation as "reverse engineeringt't'', in *Presented at the BSA Conference, Manchester Metropolitan University*, (2001).
[5] J. Coleman, *Foundations of Social Choice Theory*, Cambridge, MA: Harvard Univ. Press, 1990.
[6] J. Doran, 'Simulating collective misbelief', *Journal of Artificial Societies and Social Simulation*, **1**, (1998).
[7] N. Gilbert, *Emergence in Social Simulation In Gilbert, N. and Conte, R. (eds.) Artificial Societies*, UCL Press, London, 1995.
[8] Babak Khosravifar, Maziar Gomrokchi, Jamal Bentahar, and Philippe Thiran, 'Maintenance-based trust for multi-agent systems', in *AAMAS '09: Proceedings of The 8th International Conference on Autonomous Agents and Multiagent Systems*, pp. 1017–1024, Richland, SC, (2009). International Foundation for Autonomous Agents and Multiagent Systems.
[9] D.M. Kreps, 'Corporate culture and economic theory', in *Perspectives on Positive Political Economy*, (1990).
[10] Paul A.M. Van Lange, 'The pursuit of joint outcomes and equality in outcomes: An integrative model of social value orientation', in *Journal of Personality and Social Psychology*, (1999).
[11] A. Ruvinsky and M. N. Huhns, 'Simulating human behaviors in agent societies', in *In proceeding of Autonomous Agents and Multi-agent Systems (AAMAS)*, (2008).
[12] Brent Simpson and Robb Willer, 'Altruism and indirect reciprocity: The interaction of person and situation in prosocial behavior', *Social Psychology Quarterly*, **71**(1), 37–52, (March 2008).
[13] Yonghong Wang and Munindar P. Singh, 'Formal trust model for multiagent systems', in *IJCAI'07: Proceedings of the 20th international joint conference on Artifical intelligence*, pp. 1551–1556, San Francisco, CA, USA, (2007). Morgan Kaufmann Publishers Inc.

Modal Access Control Logic
Axiomatization, Semantics and FOL Theorem Proving

Valerio GENOVESE [a,b], Daniele RISPOLI [b], Dov M. GABBAY [c], and
Leendert VAN DER TORRE [b]

[a] *University of Luxembourg - Luxembourg*
[b] *University of Torino - Italy*
[c] *King's College London - UK*

Abstract. We present and study a Modal Access Control Logic (M-ACL) to specify and reason about access control policies. We identify canonical properties of well-known access control axioms. We provide a Hilbert-style proof-system and we prove soundness, completeness and decidability of the logic. We present a sound and complete embedding of Modal Access Control Logic into First-Order Logic. We show how to use SPASS theorem prover to reason about access control policies expressed as formulas of Modal Access Control Logic, and we compare our logic with existing ones.

Keywords. Access Control, Theorem Proving, Intuitionistic Modal Logic

Introduction

Access control is concerned with the decision when to accept or deny a request from a principal (e.g., user, program) to do an operation on an object. In practice, an access control system is a product of several, often independent, distributed entities with different policies that interact in order to determine access to resources. In order to specify and reason about such systems, many formal frameworks have been proposed [10,13,14].

A common feature of almost all well-known approaches is the employment of formulas of the form "K says φ", intuitively meaning that principal K *asserts* or *supports* φ to hold in the system. On top of the says operator many other constructs have been proposed, a central one is the speaks-for relationship to model delegation between principals. More precisely, we say that a principal "K speaks-for K'" if K says φ implies that also K' says φ.

Recently the increasing need to evaluate, combine and integrate different access control architectures motivated researchers to study logics themselves [1,8,9,10]. This research trend shifted the attention from ad-hoc formalisms to the identification of common foundations for access control logics by studying their formal, mainly unexplored, properties (e.g., axiomatizations, expressiveness, decidability and semantics). Even if there is some agreement on looking at the says construct as a *modal* operator, the correspondence theory between its axiomatizations and the underlying (Kripke-style) semantics is often left unexplored.

In this paper we address the following research question: *can Kripke semantics be employed to specify and reason about access control policies?* This breaks down in two sub-questions:

- what is a sound and complete axiomatization of well-known access control axioms with respect to a Kripke semantics?
- how can Kripke semantics be used to employ state-of-the-art theorem provers to reason about policies?

These questions raise several challenges. First of all, axioms of access control are not standard in modal literature and their correspondence with the underlying semantics is mainly unexplored. Identifying canonical properties for well-known axioms for access control permits to study them separately and naturally yields completeness for logics that adopt *any* combination of them. This approach is significant if we want logic to be employed to compare different access control models, because different systems adopt different axioms depending on the specific application domain.

Moreover, one emergent trend is the use of intuitionistic logics for authorization (see Section 6), therefore we need to concentrate on a new *constructive* modal logic. In order to directly employ semantics in the reasoning process we present an embedding of our logic into First-Order Logic (FOL) and then we show how to use a theorem prover to carry out sound and complete deductions.

In this paper we present a novel intuitionistic access control logic called Modal Access Control Logic (M-ACL), we establish a tight correspondence between axioms of the logic and semantics (via soundness and completeness proofs), we exploit this correspondence by relying on the semantics to embed M-ACL into FOL, we prove decidability and then we show how to employ SPASS theorem prover to reason about access control policies expressed in M-ACL.

The paper is structured as follows: Section 1 presents the syntax and axiomatization of M-ACL. Section 2 introduces the constructive semantics while Section 3 and 4 are devoted to prove completeness and decidability, respectively. Section 5 presents the parser from M-ACL syntax into First Order Logic and how to use the translation to reason with SPASS theorem prover. Section 6 underlines related work and Section 7 ends the paper with conclusions and future work.

1. Modal Access Control Logic

M-ACL is an access control logic based on intuitionistic multi-modal logic which extends intuitionistic propositional logic with two operators:

- A binary modality $\Box_K$ indexed by a principal, where $\Box_K \varphi$ has to be read as "K says φ".
- A binary operator between principals $\Rightarrow$, were $K \Rightarrow K'$ stands for "K speaks-for K'".

Definition 1 (M-ACL syntax) *Formulae of M-ACL are defined by the following grammar*

$$\varphi ::= p \mid \bot \mid \neg \varphi \mid (\varphi \vee \varphi) \mid (\varphi \wedge \varphi) \mid (\varphi \to \varphi) \mid (K \Rightarrow K') \mid \Box_K \varphi$$

where,

- *p ranges over a set of Boolean variables Φ_0,*
- *K and K' range over a set of principals $\mathcal{P}$.*

Definition 2 (M-ACL Axiomatization) *The axiomatization of M-ACL consists of all axioms of intuitionistic propositional logic plus axioms and rules for the says ($\Box$) and speaks-for ($\Rightarrow$) operators.*

all axioms of intuitionistic propositional logic	*(IPC)*
If $\vdash \varphi$ *then* $\vdash \Box_K \varphi$	*(N)*
If $\vdash \varphi$ *and* $\vdash \varphi \to \psi$, *then* $\vdash \psi$	*(MP)*
$\vdash \Box_K(\varphi \to \psi) \to \Box_K \varphi \to \Box_K \psi$	*(K)*
$\vdash \varphi \to \Box_K \varphi$	*(Unit)*
$\vdash \Box_K(\Box_K \varphi \to \varphi)$	*(C)*
$\vdash K \Rightarrow K$	*(S-refl)*
$\vdash (K \Rightarrow K') \to (K' \Rightarrow K'') \to (K \Rightarrow K'')$	*(S-trans)*
$\vdash K \Rightarrow K' \to \Box_K \varphi \to \Box_{K'} \varphi$	*(speaking-for)*
$\vdash \Box_{K'}(K \Rightarrow K') \to (K \Rightarrow K')$	*(handoff)*

(N) and (K) are standard for normal modal logics, (Unit) is a well known axiom in access control and states that for every formula φ, if it holds, then it is supported by every principal K. (C) has been employed in authorization logics [8] and comes from doxastic logic. Intuitively, (C) means that every principal says that all its statements have to hold. (S-refl),(S-trans) and (speaking-for) come from [9] and model the speaks-for relationship. (handoff) states that whenever K' says that K speaks-for K', then K does indeed speak for K' (i.e., every principal can decide which principals speak on its behalf).

The above axioms are not new in the access control literature and, as shown in [8], most of the logic-based security policy systems are based on (a subset of) them. However, M-ACL is the first access control logic that combines them in a unique system, for this reason it can be seen as a generalization of both logics presented in [8] and [9].

Theorem 1 (Deduction Theorem for M-ACL) *Given two wff φ and ψ*

$$\varphi \vdash \psi \text{ implies } \vdash \varphi \to \psi$$

where $\varphi \vdash \psi$ means that assuming φ we can derive (in the axiomatic proof-system of Definition 2) ψ.

Proof. This theorem follows from the deduction theorem of intuitionistic propositional logic (IPC) and the fact that M-ACL is an axiomatic extension of IPC. $\square$

We conclude this section by providing a simple example of how policies can be represented in M-ACL

Example 1 (Taken literally from [9]) *Consider the following scenario with three principals* Admin, Bob, Alice *and one file (*file1*) together with the following policy:*

(1) *If the administrator (*Admin*) says that* file1 *should be deleted, then this must be the case.*
(2) Admin *trusts* Bob *to decide whether* file1 *should be deleted.*
(3) Bob *delegates its authority to* Alice.

(4) Alice *wants to delete* `file1`.

The policy can be encoded in M-ACL[1] as follows:

(1) admin *says* `delete_file1` → `delete_file1`
(2) admin *says* ((Bob *says* `delete_file1`) → `delete_file1`)
(3) Bob *says* (Alice ⇒ Bob)
(4) Alice *says* `delete_file1`

The question of whether `file1` *should be deleted corresponds to prove* `delete_file1`, *which follows from (2)-(4),(Unit),(K),(handoff) and (speaking-for).*

2. M-ACL Constructive Semantics

Semantics for M-ACL is based on standard semantics for constructive modal logic, defined as follows

Definition 3 *An intuitionistic model $\mathcal{M}$ for M-ACL is a tuple $(S, \leq, \{R_K\}_{K \in \mathcal{P}}, h)$ where*

- $(S, \leq)$ *is a preordered set.*
- R_K *is a binary relation on S.*
- h *is an assignment which, for each boolean variable q, assigns the subset of worlds $h(q) \subseteq S$ where q holds. Moreover, we require h to be monotone w.r.t $\leq$ i.e., $x \in h(q)$ and $x \leq y$ then $y \in h(q)$.*

An *interpretation* for the logic is a pair $\mathcal{M}, t$ where $\mathcal{M}$ is a model and t a state (or world) in $\mathcal{M}$. The satisfaction relation "$\models$" holds between interpretations and formulae of the logic, and it is defined as follows (we omit ∧ and ∨):

- $\mathcal{M}, t \models q$ iff $t \in h(q)$
- $\mathcal{M}, t \not\models \bot$
- $\mathcal{M}, t \models \varphi \rightarrow \psi$ iff for all $s, t \leq s$ and $\mathcal{M}, s \models \varphi$ implies $\mathcal{M}, s \models \psi$
- $\mathcal{M}, t \models \neg\varphi$ iff for all $s, t \leq s$ implies $\mathcal{M}, s \not\models \varphi$
- $\mathcal{M}, t \models K' \Rightarrow K$ iff for all s, $tR_K s$ implies $tR_{K'} s$
- $\mathcal{M}, t \models \Box_K \psi$ iff for all s such that $tR_K s$ we have $\mathcal{M}, s \models \psi$

Moreover, we force all models $\mathcal{M}$ of M-ACL to satisfy the semantical conditions reported in Definition 4.

Definition 4 (Semantical Conditions) *For any two principals K and K', we impose on $\leq$, R_K and $R_{K'}$ the following conditions to hold:*

(a) $\forall x, y((xR_K y \rightarrow xR_{K'} y) \rightarrow (\forall s, z(x \leq s \rightarrow (sR_K z \rightarrow sR_{K'} z))))$
(b) $\forall x, y, z((x \leq y \wedge yR_K z) \rightarrow xR_K z)$
(c) $\forall x, y(xR_K y \rightarrow x \leq y)$
(d) $\forall x, y(xR_K y \rightarrow yR_K y)$
(e) $\forall x, y((xR_K y \rightarrow \forall z(yR_K z \rightarrow yR_{K'} z)) \rightarrow \forall s(xR_K s \rightarrow xR_{K'} s))$

---
[1] For the sake of readability we write "A *says* φ" instead of "$\Box_A \varphi$".

Conditions (a) and (b) ensure monotonicity for speaks-for and modal formulas (see Lemma 1), conditions (c), (d) and (e) are the semantic conditions associated with axiom (Unit), (C) and (handoff) respectively. In Section 3 we show that each condition is canonical for the corresponding axiom, i.e., it is *necessary* and *sufficient* for the corresponding axiom to hold.

We now show that condition (e) is implied by conditions $(b), (c)$ and (d), but we prefer to make it explicit. In fact, having canonical conditions for each of the axioms permits to study them separately from each other and naturally yields completeness for logics which adopt *any* combination of them. For instance, $Unit$ is a strong axiom adopted in both [9,8], but not every access control system adopts it. With our methodology we can provide soundness and completeness for a weaker logic without $Unit$ by removing the corresponding axiom from Definition 2 and condition (c) from Definition 4.

Observation 1 *The semantical condition corresponding to (handoff) is implied by conditions* $(b), (c)$ *and* (d) *in Definition 4.*

Proof. Given a model $\mathcal{M}$, suppose we are in a world x in which the antecedent of (e) holds i.e., $\mathcal{M}, x \models \Box_K(K' \Rightarrow K)$ and suppose, for the sake of contradiction, that the consequent does not hold. Then, there is a world s such that $xR_K s$ and $\neg(xR_{K'}s)$. By hypothesis and with condition (d) we have that for every R_K accessible world y from x, $yR_K y$ and $yR_{K'}y$. But then, by conditions (b) and (c) we have that for any world y, $xR_K y$ implies $xR_{K'}y$, so it must be $xR_{K'}s$, which is a contradiction. □

Lemma 1 (Monotonicity) *For any wff φ and an interpretation $\mathcal{M}, t$, such that $\mathcal{M}$ satisfies semantical conditions of Definition 4 we have that, if $\mathcal{M}, t \models \varphi$ and $t \leq s$ then $\mathcal{M}, s \models \varphi$*

Proof. By structural induction on φ, we show the modal case:

$(\varphi = \Box_K \psi)$, suppose $\mathcal{M}, t \models \Box_K \psi$, we want to show that for any s, such that $t \leq s$ we have $\mathcal{M}, s \models \Box_K \psi$. By contradiction suppose that there exists a state t', such that $s \leq t'$ and $\mathcal{M}, t' \not\models \Box_K \psi$. Then it exists a world r K-accessible from t' (i.e., $t'R_K r$) such that $\mathcal{M}, r \not\models \psi$, but by condition (b) we have also that $sR_K r$ so, by hypothesis $\mathcal{M}, r \models \psi$, which is a contradiction. □

Theorem 2 (Soundness for M-ACL) *If $\vdash \varphi$ then $\models \varphi$.*

Proof. By structural induction on φ. □

3. Completeness

Definition 5 (Consistency) Γ *is consistent iff* $\Gamma \not\vdash \bot$. *If* Γ *has an infinite number of formulas, we say that* Γ *is consistent iff there are no finite* $\Gamma_0 \subset \Gamma$ *such that* $\Gamma_0 \vdash \bot$.

Definition 6 (Saturation) *Let* Γ *be a set of well formed formulas, we say that* Γ *is saturated iff*

1. Γ *is consistent,*
2. *For all principals* K, K' *either* $(K \Rightarrow K') \in \Gamma$ *or* $\neg(K \Rightarrow K') \in \Gamma$

3. If $\Gamma \vdash \varphi$ then $\varphi \in \Gamma$
4. If $\Gamma \vdash \varphi \vee \psi$ then $\Gamma \vdash \varphi$ or $\Gamma \vdash \psi$

Lemma 2 (Saturated Extensions) *Suppose $\Gamma \nvdash A$, there is a saturated extension Γ^* such that $\Gamma^* \nvdash A$.*

Proof. This is proved by standard Lindenbaum construction. We obtain Γ^* as $\bigcup \{\Gamma^k : k \in \mathcal{N}\}$, with $\Gamma_0 = \Gamma \cup \{\neg A\}$, $\Gamma^k \setminus \Gamma$ is finite. We now provide an inductive definition of Γ^{k+1}. Let $\{\beta_1, \ldots \beta_n, \ldots\}$ be an enumeration of formulas of M-ACL and define Γ^{k+1} to be

- Γ^k if $\Gamma^k \cup \beta_i$ is inconsistent
- $\Gamma^k \cup \beta_i$ otherwise

We now prove that $\Gamma^* \nvdash A$. Suppose that $\Gamma^* \vdash A$, then Γ^* is inconsistent since $\neg A \in \Gamma_0$, hence $\neg A \in \Gamma^*$. Now, at every stage Γ_k is, by construction, consistent and by compactness, if Γ^* is inconsistent then some finite subset is inconsistent, which means that some Γ_k is inconsistent, which is a contradiction. □

Lemma 3 *Let Γ be a set of formulas and let $\Delta = \{\alpha : \Box_K \alpha \in \Gamma\}$. If $\Delta \vdash \beta$, then $\Gamma \vdash \Box_K \beta$*

Proof. Suppose there is a derivation of β from Δ. Then, there must be a finite set of formulas $\{\alpha_1, \ldots, \alpha_n\} \subseteq \Delta$ such that $\{\alpha_1, \ldots, \alpha_n\} \vdash \beta$. By Theorem 1, $\vdash \alpha_1 \wedge \ldots \wedge \alpha_n \rightarrow \beta$. By (N) and (K), $\vdash \Box_K \alpha_1 \wedge \ldots \wedge \Box_K \alpha_n \rightarrow \Box_K \beta$. As $\Box_K \alpha_i \in \Gamma$ for all $i = 1, n$, by modus ponens, $\Gamma \vdash \Box_K \beta$. □

Definition 7 (Canonical model construction) *Let Γ_0 be any theory (set of formulas). Then we define $\mathcal{M}^* = (S, \leq, \{R_K\}_{K \in \mathcal{P}}, h)$, where*

- *S is the set of all saturated $\Gamma \supseteq \Gamma_0$.*
- *$\Gamma_1 \leq \Gamma_2$ iff $\Gamma_1 \subseteq \Gamma_2$.*
- *$\Gamma_1 R_K \Gamma_2$ iff $\{\alpha \mid \Box_K \alpha \in \Gamma_1\} \subseteq \Gamma_2$*
- *$\Gamma \in h(q)$ iff $q \in \Gamma$*

Lemma 4 *For all $\Gamma \in S$ and each wff formula φ*

$$\Gamma \models \varphi \Leftrightarrow \varphi \in \Gamma$$

Proof. By induction on the complexity of φ, we look at some cases

- *Case 1.*: For φ atomic the lemma holds by definition.
- *Case 2.*: Let $\varphi \equiv \Box_K \beta$, and suppose $\Gamma \models \Box_K \beta$. Hence, for all Γ' such that $\Gamma R_K \Gamma'$, $\Gamma' \models \beta$ By inductive hypothesis, $\beta \in \Gamma'$, let $\Delta = \{\alpha : \Box_K \alpha \in \Gamma\}$. By construction, $\Gamma' \supseteq \Delta$. Assume, by absurdum, that $\Box_K \beta \notin \Gamma$. By the saturation condition (2), $\Gamma \nvdash \Box_K \beta$. Then, by Lemma 3, $\Delta \nvdash \beta$. By Lemma 2, there is a saturated extension Δ^* such that $\Delta^* \nvdash \beta$. This contradicts the fact that, for all Γ' such that $\Gamma R_K \Gamma'$, $\beta \in \Gamma'$, i.e., that (by construction of the canonical model) for all saturated sets Γ' such that $\Gamma' \supseteq \Delta$, $B \in \Gamma'$. The converse is trivial.
- *Case 3.*: Let $\varphi \equiv K \Rightarrow K'$, it then follows from Definition 6 that $K \Rightarrow K' \in \Gamma$

□

To show that the canonical model $\mathcal{M}^*$ defined above is indeed a model of M-ACL, we have to prove that it satisfies the conditions in Definition 4.

Lemma 5 *Let $\mathcal{M}^*$ be the canonical model as defined in Definition 7. $\mathcal{M}^*$ satisfies conditions (a), (b), (c), (d) and (e) of Definition 4.*

Proof. We have to prove that

(a) $\forall \Gamma_1, \Gamma_2((\Gamma_1 R_K \Gamma_2 \to \Gamma_1 R_{K'} \Gamma_2) \to (\forall \Gamma_3, \Gamma_4 (\Gamma_1 \leq \Gamma_3 \to (\Gamma_3 R_K \Gamma_4 \to \Gamma_3 R_{K'} \Gamma_4))))$

(b) $\forall \Gamma, \Gamma', \Gamma'' \in S$, if $\Gamma \leq \Gamma'$ and $\Gamma' R_K \Gamma''$ then $\Gamma R_K \Gamma''$

(c) $\forall \Gamma, \Gamma' \in S$, if $\Gamma R_K \Gamma'$ then $\Gamma \leq \Gamma'$

(d) $\forall \Gamma, \Gamma' \in S$, if $\Gamma R_K \Gamma'$ then $\Gamma' R_K \Gamma'$

(e) $\forall \Gamma_1, \Gamma_2((\Gamma_1 R_K \Gamma_2 \to \forall \Gamma_3(\Gamma_2 R_K \Gamma_3 \to \Gamma_2 R_{K'} \Gamma_3)) \to \forall \Gamma_4(\Gamma_1 R_K \Gamma_4 \to \Gamma_1 R_{K'} \Gamma_4))$

The proof of points (a) and (b) is trivial and follows from that for any two worlds Γ_1, Γ_2, if $\Gamma_1 \leq \Gamma_2$ then $\Gamma_1 \subseteq \Gamma_2$.

Let us prove point (c). We want to show that if $\Gamma R_K \Gamma'$ then $\Gamma \leq \Gamma'$. Take a world $\Delta \in S$, for any formula $\varphi \in \Delta$ we have that $\Box_K \varphi \in \Delta$ (by Unit and MP) which means that for every Δ' such that $\Delta R_K \Delta'$ $\varphi \in \Delta'$, which means that $\Delta \leq \Delta'$.

Relating point (d) we have to show that if $\Gamma R_K \Gamma'$ then $\Gamma' R_K \Gamma'$. Take a world $\Delta \in S$, for any formula φ we have that $\Box_K(\Box_K \varphi \to \varphi) \in \Delta$ (by C), so for any world $\Delta' \in S$ such that $\Delta R_K \Delta'$ and $(\Box_K \varphi \to \varphi) \in \Delta'$, we have to show that $\Delta' R_K \Delta'$. By definition of R_K in the canonical model, this means that we must prove that if $\Box_K \varphi \in \Delta'$ then φ, but this follows from $\Box_K \varphi \to \varphi \in \Delta'$, so we are done.

Concerning point (e) we have to show that, for any world $\Gamma \in S$ if $\Gamma \models \Box_K(K' \Rightarrow K)$ then $\Gamma \models K' \Rightarrow K$. This follows from the fact that, by (handoff), $(\Box_K(K' \Rightarrow K) \to K' \Rightarrow K) \in \Gamma$ and that Γ is saturated. $\square$

Theorem 3 (Strong completeness for M-ACL) *If $\Gamma \models \varphi$ then $\Gamma \vdash \varphi$*

Proof. Suppose $\Gamma \not\vdash \varphi$, and let Γ_0 be a saturated extension of Γ, $\varphi \notin \Gamma_0$; construct a canonical model $\mathcal{M}^*$ as in Definition 7, then $\mathcal{M}^*, \Gamma_0 \not\models \varphi$. This yields completeness. $\square$

4. Decidability

In this section we prove decidability of M-ACL using a technique introduced in [2] which generalizes a decidability result reported in [7]. Following [2], we first show that M-ACL semantics can be embedded into a monadic two-variable guarded fragment (GF^2_{mon}) of classical first-order logic, and then we show that M-ACL identifies a class $\mathcal{C}$ of Kripke models defined by an acyclic set of monadic second-order (MSO) definable closure conditions on relations $\leq$ and $\{R_K\}_{K \in \mathcal{P}}$.

We start by defining GF^2_{mon}. In the following $FV(\varphi)$ stands for the set of free variables of φ, and $\overline{x}$ stands for a sequence of variables. We assume a first order language which contains predicate letters of arbitrary arity, including equality, and no constants or functional symbols.

Definition 8 *The guarded fragment GF of first-order logic is the smallest set containing all first-order atoms, closed under boolean connectives and the following rule: if ρ is an atom, $\varphi \in GF$, and $\bar{x} \subseteq FV(\varphi) \subseteq FV(\rho)$, then $\exists \bar{x}(\rho \wedge \varphi)$ and $\forall \bar{x}(\rho \to \varphi) \in GF$ (in such a case ρ is called a guard).*

Definition 9 *The monadic two-variable guarded fragment GF^2_{mon} is a subset of GF containing formulas φ such that (i) φ has no more than two variables (free or bound), and (ii) all non-unary predicate letters of φ occur in guards.*

Now we show that M-ACL semantics can be translated into GF^2_{mon}. In line with [2] we define, by mutual recursion, two translations, τ_x and τ_y, so that a first-order formula $\tau_v(\varphi)$ ($v \in \{x, y\}$) contains a single free variable v, which intuitively stands for the world at which φ is being evaluated in the Kripke model.

Definition 10 (M-ACL embedding into GF^2_{mon}) *We define $\tau_x(\varphi)$[2] by structural induction on the complexity of φ*

- $\tau_x(p) = P(x)$
- $\tau_x(\neg \varphi) = \forall y(x \leq y \to \neg \tau_y(\varphi))$
- $\tau_x(\varphi \wedge \psi) = \tau_x(\varphi) \wedge \tau_x(\psi)$
- $\tau_x(\varphi \vee \psi) = \tau_x(\varphi) \vee \tau_x(\psi)$
- $\tau_x(\varphi \to \psi) = \forall y(x \leq y \to \neg \tau_y(\varphi) \vee \tau_y(\psi))$
- $\tau_x(K \Rightarrow K') = \forall y(x \leq y \to \forall x(yR_{K'}x \to yR_K x))$
- $\tau_x(\Box_K \varphi) = \forall y(x \leq y \to \forall x(yR_K x \to \tau_x(\varphi)))$

The translation of the modality and speaks for (i.e., $\tau_x(\Box_K \varphi)$ and $\tau_x(K \Rightarrow K')$) forces directly monotonicity of $\Box$ and $\Rightarrow$. It is equivalent (in the sense of Theorem 4) to the definition of $\mathcal{M}, x \models K \Rightarrow K'$ and $\mathcal{M}, x \models \Box_K \varphi$ satisfying respectively conditions (a) and (b) of Definition 4.

Theorem 4 *Let φ be a M-ACL formula and $\mathcal{C}$ be a class of models of M-ACL. Let $\mathcal{M} \in \mathcal{C}$. Then, $\mathcal{M}, w \models \varphi$ iff $\mathcal{M} \models \tau_x(\varphi)[x/w]$[3].*

Proof. By structural induction of φ. □

Definition 11 *Let W be a non-empty set. A unary function C on the powerset of W^n is a **closure operator** if, for all $\mathcal{P}, \mathcal{P}' \subseteq W^n$,*

1. $\mathcal{P} \subseteq C(\mathcal{P})$ *(C is increasing)*
2. $\mathcal{P} \subseteq \mathcal{P}'$ *implies* $C(\mathcal{P}) \subseteq C(\mathcal{P}')$ *(C is monotone)*
3. $C(\mathcal{P}) = C(C(\mathcal{P}))$ *(C is idempotent)*

*An $m + 1$-ary function C on the powerset of W^n is a **parametrised closure operator** if, given any choice of m relations $\mathcal{P}_1, \ldots, \mathcal{P}_m \subseteq W^n$, it gives rise to a unary function $C^{\mathcal{P}_1, \ldots, \mathcal{P}_m}$ (parametrised by $\mathcal{P}_1, \ldots, \mathcal{P}_m$) that is a simple closure operator on the powerset of W^n*

---

[2] τ_y is defined analogously, switching the roles of x and y.
[3] Where $\mathcal{M}$ is taken as a model of first order logic with relations $\leq$ and $\{R_K\}_{K \in \mathcal{P}}$ respecting properties of M-ACL semantics, and $\varphi[x/w]$ is the result of substituting w for the free variable x.

In order to characterize M-ACL models we need the following closure operators[4]: A reflexive and transitive closure operator $TC(\mathcal{P})$; A parametrized inclusion operator $Incl^{\mathcal{P}'}(\mathcal{P}) = \mathcal{P}' \cup \mathcal{P}$; A one step reflexivity operator $1SR(\mathcal{P})$;

Definition 12 *A condition on relation $\mathcal{P}$ is a **closure condition** if it can be expressed in the form $C(\mathcal{P}) = \mathcal{P}$, where C is a closure operator.*

The following are the closure conditions for relations $\leq$ and $\{R_K\}_{K \in \mathcal{P}}$ of M-ACL: $TC(\leq) = \leq$ (reflexivity-and-transitivity closure condition); $Incl^{R_K}(\leq) = \leq$ (R_K is subset of $\leq$); $1SR(R_K) = R_K$ (one-step-reflexivity closure condition).

Definition 13 *Let S be a set of relations and $\mathbf{C}$ a set of closure conditions on relations in S. Let us say for $\mathcal{P}, \mathcal{P}' \in S$, that $\mathcal{P}$ depends on $\mathcal{P}'$ if $\mathbf{C}$ contains a parametrised condition of the form $C^{\mathcal{P}_1,\ldots,\mathcal{P}',\ldots,\mathcal{P}_m}(\mathcal{P}) = \mathcal{P}$. A set of closure conditions $\mathbf{C}$ is **acyclic**, if its "depends on" relation is acyclic.*

Theorem 5 (proof in [2]) *Let $\mathbf{M}$ be a class of intuitionistic modal models defined by an acyclic set of MSO closure conditions on its relations (e.g. $\leq$, accessibility modal relations,...) so that at most one closure condition is associated with each relation, and let φ be an intuitionistic modal formula. Then, it is decidable whether φ is satisfiable in $\mathcal{M}$.*

Now, on the basis of 5 we show that all the conditions reported above can be expressed in Monadic Second-Order Logic.

Definition 14 *The closure operators of M-ACL can be represented in Monadic Second-Order Logic as follows:*

- *Closure operator TC is definable by the MSO formula $TC_{\leq}(z_1, z_2) = \forall X(X(z_1) \land \forall x, y(X(x) \land x \leq y \to X(y)) \to X(z_2))$*
- *Closure operator $Incl^{R_K}(\leq)$ is definable by the MSO formula: $Incl^{\leq}_{R_K}(z_1, z_2) = R_K(z_1, z_2) \lor z_1 \leq z_2$*
- *The one-step reflexivity operator $1SR(R_K)$: $1SR_{R_K}(z_1, z_2) = R_K(z_1, z_2) \lor \exists x(R_K(x, z_1) \land z_1 = z_2)$*

Theorem 6 (M-ACL Decidability) *M-ACL is decidable*

Proof. M-ACL is an intuitionistic modal logic with indexed modalities $\Box_K$, defined by the class of models where the following closure conditions on R_K (for each $K \in \mathcal{P}$) and $\leq$ are specified: $TC(\leq) = \leq$; $Incl^{R_K}(\leq) = \leq$; $1SR(R_K) = R_K$. This set of conditions is acyclic and each condition is MSO definable. However there are two constraints associated with $\leq$. To satisfy the conditions of Theorem 5 we need to combine them into one MSO definable closure condition. Alechina et al. report in [2] that $TC \circ Incl^{\mathcal{P}'}$ is a closure operator with the property that for any relation $\mathcal{P}$,

$$TC(Incl^{\mathcal{P}'}(\mathcal{P})) = \mathcal{P} \Leftrightarrow TC(\mathcal{P}) = \mathcal{P} \text{ and } Incl^{\mathcal{P}'}(\mathcal{P}) = \mathcal{P}$$

---

[4]The formal specification of these operators is given in Definition 14.

```
list_of_formulae(axioms)
[](admin,deletefile1) -> deletefile1.
[](admin, ([](bob, deletefile1) -> deletefile1)).
[](bob, deletefile1).
end_of_list
list_of_formulae(conjectures)
deletefile1.
end_of_list
```

Figure 1. `example.macl`

If we look at semantical conditions in Definition 4 we notice that there are no closure conditions for constraints $(a), (b)$ and (e). We prove that the closure conditions on TC, $Incl^{R_K}(\leq)$ and $1SR(R_K) = R_K$ are sufficient to characterize M-ACL semantics. We previously noticed that (a) and (b) are redundant with the adopted equivalent definition of $\tau_x(K \Rightarrow K')$ and $\tau_x(\Box_K \varphi)$ (see Definition 10) while, in Observation 1, we show that (e) is implied by conditions $(b), (c)$ and (d). □

5. FOL Theorem Proving for M-ACL

SPASS[5] is an automated theorem prover for full first-order logic with equality [16], in this section we show how to employ SPASS to reason about M-ACL access control policies.

The use of SPASS theorem prover is based on the soundness and completeness results of M-ACL and, in particular on the identification of the canonical properties of its axioms which can be expressed as first-order constraints on Kripke structures. Moreover, in Definition 10 we showed an embedding of M-ACL formulas into FOL by relying on the definition of satisfiability. In order to use SPASS to do sound and complete deductions in M-ACL, we developed a parser called `macl2spass` which translates M-ACL formulas into first-order formulas. The translation is similar to the one in Definition 10 and it is based on standard embedding of modal logic into FOL [15].

Example 2 *We illustrate how to use* `macl2spass` *to reason about access control policies with a (very simple) example*[6]. *Consider a file-scenario with an administrating principal* admin, *a user* Bob, *one file* file1, *and the following policy:*

(1) *If* admin *says that the* file1 *should be deleted, then this must be the case.*
(2) admin *trusts* Bob *to decide whether* file1 *should be deleted.*
(3) Bob *wants to delete* file1.

In Figure 1 we report the content of file `example.macl` which represents Example 2 using M-ACL syntax[7]. The file is divided in two parts, the policies (represented as `axioms`) and the `conjectures` which are the formulas that we want to prove from the axioms.

---

[5] SPASS is available at http://spass.mpi-sb.mpg.de

[6] More complex examples can be found in the source package of macl2spass which is available at http://www.di.unito.it/~genovese/tools.html .

[7] `[](bob,deletefile1)` stands for $\Box_{bob} deletefile1$.

Once we have the M-ACL specification of the policy we can translate it into SPASS syntax with `$ ./macl2spass example.macl > exmaple.dfg`. The above command translates the M-ACL example into a first-order problem in DFG syntax[8]. The `example.dfg` can be directly given as input to SPASS theorem prover to check if the conjectures follow from the axioms.

6. Related Work

The formal study of properties of access control logics is a recent research trend. As reported in [11], constructive logics are well suited for reasoning about authorization, because constructive proofs preserve the justification of statements during reasoning and, therefore, information about accountability is not lost. Classical logics, instead, allows proofs that discard evidence. For example, we can prove G using a classical logic by proving $F \to G$ and $\neg F \to G$, since from these theorems we can conclude $(F \vee \neg F) \to G$, hence $\top \to G$.

Abadi in [1] presents a formal study about connections between many possible axiomatizations of the says, as well as higher level policy constructs such as delegation (speaks-for) and control. Abadi provides a strong argument to use constructivism in logic for access control, in fact he shows that from a well-known axiom like Unit in a classical logic we can deduce K says $\varphi \to (\varphi \vee K$ says $\psi)$. The axiom above is called *Escalation* and it represents a rather degenerate interpretation of says, i.e., if a principal says φ then, either φ is permitted or the principal can says *anything*. On the contrary, if we interpret the says within an intuitionistic logic we can avoid Escalation.

Even if there exist several authorization logics that employ the says modality, a limited amount of work has been done to study the formal logical properties of says, speaks-for and other constructs. In the following, we report the three different approaches adopted to study access control logics themselves.

Garg and Abadi [9] translate existing access control logics into S4 by relying on a slight simplification of Gödel's translation from intuitionistic logic to S4, and extending it to formulas of the form A says φ.

Garg [8] adopts an ad-hoc version of constructive S4 called DTL_0 and embeds existing approaches into it. Constructive S4 has been chosen because of its intuitionistic Kripke semantics which DTL_0 extends by adding *views* [8], i.e., a mapping from worlds to sets of principals.

Boella et al. [5] define a logical framework called FSL[9], based on Gabbay's Fibring methodology [6] by looking at "says" as a (fibred) modal operator.

However, adopting a fixed semantics like S4 does not permit to study the *correspondence theory* between axioms of access control logics and Kripke structures. Suppose we look at says as a principal indexed modality $\Box_K$, if we rely on S4 we would have as an axiom $\Box_K \varphi \to \varphi$, which means: *everything* that K says is permitted. To overcome this problem, both in [8,9], Kripke semantics is sweetened with the addition of *views* which relativize the reasoning to a subset of worlds. Although this approach provides sound and complete semantics, it breaks the useful bound between modality axioms and relations of Kripke structures.

---

[8] http://www.spass-prover.org/webspass/help/syntax/index.html
[9] Fibred Security Language.

Name	Problem	LEO	SPASS
unit	s -> [](A, s)	0.031	0.02
K	[](A, s -> t) -> [](A, s) -> [](A, t)	0.083	0.02
idem	[](A, [](A, s)) -> [](A, s)	0.037	0.02
refl	A => A	0.052	0.02
trans	(A => B) -> (B => C) -> (A => C)	0.105	0.08
sp.-for	(A => B) -> [](A, s) -> [](B, s)	0.062	0.07
handoff	[](B, A => B) -> A => B	0.036	0.02
Ex.1	Example 1	3.494	0.18
Ex.2	Example 2	0.698	0.21

Figure 2. Comparison of SPASS performance against LEO-II

The third approach, instead, shows a precise connection between axioms of access control logics and the underlying fibred semantics, but suffers from being generally undecidable and from not having an efficient methodology to reason about policies.

In [3], the higher-order theorem prover LEO-II [4] is used to reason about access control logics presented in [9] by exploiting an embedding from modal logic S4 into simple type theory. In our approach, the direct mapping of M-ACL semantics into FOL allows us to use a pure FOL theorem prover like SPASS which is generally faster than LEO-II. In Fig. 2 we compare time performance of LEO-II (taken from [3]) with SPASS[10]. We notice that in Ex.1 and Ex.2, which require more deductive steps than proving single axioms, SPASS is significantly faster then LEO-II.

7. Conclusions

In this paper we introduce Modal Access Control Logic, a constructive propositional multimodal logic to reason about access control policies.

We formalize a standard (i.e., without views) Kripke semantics for Modal Access Control Logic. We provide canonical properties for well known access control axioms like (Unit), (C), (handoff) and (speaking-for). We give a semantical interpretation of the speaks-for construct and we study how it relates with the says modality. We provide soundness and completeness results for M-ACL by employing a *standard* constructive semantics. We show a new application of the technique presented in [2] to prove decidability of M-ACL. We present an embedding of M-ACL into FOL and use it to reason with SPASS theorem prover.

M-ACL is the result of a new methodology in studying access control logics. In M-ACL we do not translate existing approaches into another logic (like S4 in [9]), or enrich the semantics with ad-hoc functions (like views in [8]). We show that by looking at the says operator as an universal modality we can use Kripke semantics not only to map axioms with structural properties on models, but also to use state-of-the-art theorem provers to reason about access control. By means of the translation into SPASS we show that semantics can be directly employed to reason about access control policies and that a semantics-based study of access control can benefit foundations and applications.

As future work we plan to extend M-ACL with compound principals by using semantics of conditional logics. Another line of research is to apply M-ACL to proof-

---

[10] All the experiments with SPASS were conducted with SPASS version 3.0 on a computer with an Intel Pentium 2.53 GHz processor with 1.5GB memory running Linux.

carrying authorization, by developing a sequent calculus for M-ACL to exchange compact proofs about access control in a distributed environment.

Acknowledgments Valerio Genovese is supported by the National Research Fund, Luxembourg. The authors would like to thank Christoph Weidenbach, Renate Schmidt for their help with SPASS. Gian Luca Pozzato, Laura Giordano and Valentina Gliozzi for useful comments and suggestions about the completeness proof which is based on a joint work with the first author reported in [12]. Finally, the authors thank the reviewers for their comments, which proved to be helpful for improving the clarity of the paper.

References

[1] Martín Abadi, 'Variations in access control logic', in *9th International Conference on Deontic Logic in Computer Science (DEON)*, pp. 96–109, (2008).

[2] Natasha Alechina and Dmitry Shkatov, 'A general method for proving decidability of intuitionistic modal logics', *J. Applied Logic*, **4**(3), 219–230, (2006).

[3] Christoph Benzmüller, 'Automating access control logics in simple type theory with LEO-II', in *Emerging Challenges for Security, Privacy and Trust, 24th IFIP TC 11 International Information Security Conference, SEC*, pp. 387–398, (2009).

[4] Christoph Benzmüller, Lawrence C. Paulson, Frank Theiss, and Arnaud Fietzke, 'LEO-II - a cooperative automatic theorem prover for classical higher-order logic (system description)', in *Automated Reasoning, 4th International Joint Conference, IJCAR*, pp. 162–170, (2008).

[5] Guido Boella, Dov M. Gabbay, Valerio Genovese, and Leendert van der Torre, 'Fibred security language', *Studia Logica*, **92**(3), 395–436, (2009).

[6] Dov M. Gabbay, 'Fibring logics', *Oxford University Press*, (1999).

[7] Harald Ganzinger, Christoph Meyer, and Margus Veanes, 'The two-variable guarded fragment with transitive relations', in *14th Annual IEEE Symposium on Logic in Computer Science (LICS)*, pp. 24–34, (1999).

[8] Deepak Garg, 'Principal centric reasoning in constructive authorization logic', in *Informal Proceedings of Intuitionistic Modal Logic and Application (IMLA)*, (2008). Full version available as Carnegie Mellon Technical Report CMU-CS-09-120.

[9] Deepak Garg and Martín Abadi, 'A modal deconstruction of access control logics', in *11th International Conference on Foundations of Software Science and Computation Structures (FoSSaCS)*, pp. 216–230, Budapest, Hungary, (2008).

[10] Deepak Garg, Lujo Bauer, Kevin D. Bowers, Frank Pfenning, and Michael K. Reiter, 'A linear logic of authorization and knowledge', in *European Symposium on Research in Computer Security (ESORICS)*, pp. 297–312, (2006).

[11] Deepak Garg and Frank Pfenning, 'Non-interference in constructive authorization logic', in *19th IEEE Computer Security Foundations Workshop, (CSFW-19), 5-7 July 2006, Venice, Italy*, pp. 283–296, (2006).

[12] V. Genovese, L. Giordano, V. Gliozzi, and G. L. Pozzato, 'A constructive conditional logic for access control: a completeness result.', in *Technical Report 125/2010, Dipartimento di Informatica, Università degli Studi di Torino, Italy*, (2010).

[13] Yuri Gurevich and Arnab Roy, 'Operational semantics for DKAL: Application and analysis', in *Trust, Privacy and Security in Digital Business, 6th International Conference (TrustBus)*, pp. 149–158, (2009).

[14] Ninghui Li, Benjamin N. Grosof, and Joan Feigenbaum, 'Delegation logic: A logic-based approach to distributed authorization', *ACM Trans. Inf. Syst. Secur.*, **6**(1), 128–171, (2003).

[15] Hans Jürgen Ohlbach, 'Semantics-based translation methods for modal logics', *J. Log. Comput.*, **1**(5), 691–746, (1991).

[16] Christoph Weidenbach, Dilyana Dimova, Arnaud Fietzke, Rohit Kumar, Martin Suda, and Patrick Wischnewski, 'SPASS version 3.5', in *Automated Deduction, 22nd International Conference on Automated Deduction (CADE)*, pp. 140–145, (2009).

[17] F. Wolter and M. Zakharyaschev, 'Intuitionistic modal logic', in *A. Cantini, E. Casari, and P. Minari, editors, Logic and Foundations of Mathematics. Kluwer Academic Publishers*, pp. 227–238, (1999).

Probabilistic Logic with Conditional Independence Formulae[1]

Magdalena IVANOVSKA and Martin GIESE [2]
Department of Informatics, University of Oslo, Norway

Abstract. We investigate probabilistic propositional logic as a way of expressing and reasoning about uncertainty. In contrast to Bayesian networks, a logical approach can easily cope with incomplete information like probabilities that are missing or only known to lie in some interval. However, probabilistic propositional logic as described e.g. by Halpern [1], has no way of expressing conditional independence, which is important for compact specification in many cases. We define a logic with conditional independence formulae. We give an axiomatization which we show to be complete for the kind of inferences allowed by Bayesian networks, while still being suitable for reasoning under incomplete information.

Keywords. probabilistic logic, Bayesian networks, conditional independence

Introduction

We report work carried out within the CODIO project on COllaborative DecisIon support for Integrated Operations. The goal of this project is to develop a decision support system for petroleum drilling operations. Decisions in drilling operations are characterized by a high degree of uncertainty (geology, reservoir size, possible equipment failure, etc.) and certain temporal aspects, like parts of the information about downhole happenings only being available after drilling fluid has been circulated up. In modern days, this is complemented by overwhelming amounts of sensor data, and the collaboration of several people on- and off-shore in decision making processes.

As one part of the CODIO project, we have designed a system based on a Bayesian network [2] model to provide assistance in operational decisions based on real-time sensor readings for a specific kind of typical situation [3]. While this effort was largely successful when tested on case data from a major oil company, the use of Bayesian networks as a modelling tool also had some shortcomings. It seems as if a logic-based approach to decision support would make it possible to resolve some of the issues:

- It was hard to elicit complete information about all probabilities required in the Bayesian network. Some of the values had to be guessed without feedback on the impact of those guesses. By contrast, it is typical for logic-based approaches that information irrelevant to a certain conclusion does not need to be given in a specification. If the specification is not precise enough to arrive at some conclu-

---
[1] A short version of this paper is published as an ECAI 2010 short paper.
[2] magdalei/martingi@ifi.uio.no

sion, then no conclusion is inferred. For instance, knowing only that some value or probability lies within a certain range, instead of having a concrete number, is not a problem in a logical setting.
- The temporal aspects of the problem could be included in the description of the uncertainties by using temporal logic operators.
- The fact that different people with different information are involved in the decision making could be taken into account by using a multi-modal logic of knowledge or belief. One could for instance reason about the necessary knowledge transfer needed to make all involved parties come to the same conclusion.

Though attempts have been made to cope with time, imprecise information, etc. in Bayesian networks, we believe that a logical approach can be a natural framework to merge many different aspects.

We are currently in the process of investigating logics to express decision problems, similarly to influence diagrams. The topic of this paper is a small but important part of this endeavor, namely the combination of quantitative reasoning about uncertainty with the qualitative reasoning about conditional independence which is central to approaches based on Bayesian networks, but which has received comparatively little attention from the logical side. More specifically, in contrast to the related work mentioned in Sect. 7 for instance, we consider a purely logical approach, where the whole specification takes the shape of logical formulae, and inference is done with an axiomatic system. This is important if the formalism is to be combined with temporal, epistemic, or other kinds of reasoning.

We begin in Sect. 1 by reviewing some results on probabilistic logic without independence statements. In Sect. 2, we introduce syntax and semantics of a logic with formulae expressing conditional independence. Sect. 3 briefly reviews the definition of Bayesian networks and shows how to transform them into sets of axioms in our logic. We then show two completeness results for this transformation, a semantical one in Sect. 4, and a syntactical one in Sect. 5. In Sect. 6, we discuss reasoning with conditional independence under incomplete information. An account of various related work is given in Sect. 7. We conclude with an outlook on future work in Sect. 8.

1. Probabilistic Propositional Logic

Let a set $\mathbf{P} = \{X_1, X_2, \ldots\}$ of propositional letters be given. Following Fagin, Halpern, and Megiddo ([4], see also [1]), we consider a probabilistic propositional logic obtained by augmenting the propositional logic over the alphabet $\mathbf{P}$ with *linear likelihood formulae*

$$a_1 \ell(\varphi_1) + \cdots + a_k \ell(\varphi_k) \geq a \quad ,$$

where $a_1, \ldots, a_k, a$ are real numbers and $\varphi_1, \ldots, \varphi_k$ are *pure propositional formulae*, i.e. formulae which do not themselves contain likelihood formulae. The intention is that $\ell(\varphi)$ expresses the probability of φ being true, and the language allows expressing arbitrary linear relationships between such probabilities.

This logic is interpreted over (simple, measurable)[3] *probability structures* $M = (W, \mu, \pi)$, where W is a set of possible worlds, μ is a probability measure that assigns a value in $[0,1]$ to any subset of W, and π is an interpretation function. To each element $w \in W$, the function π assigns a truth-value function $\pi_w : \mathbf{P} \to \{0,1\}$. The interpretation π_w is extended to arbitrary formulae in the usual way, where the interpretation of linear likelihood formulae is defined as follows:

$\pi_w(a_1 \ell(\varphi_1) + \cdots + a_k \ell(\varphi_k) \geq a) = 1$ iff $a_1 \mu(\varphi_1^M) + \cdots + a_k \mu(\varphi_k^M) \geq a$,
where $\varphi^M := \{w | \pi_w(\varphi) = 1\}$ for any formula φ.

Conditional likelihood formulae can be introduced as abbreviations as follows: $\ell(\varphi/\psi) \geq c$ is defined as $\ell(\varphi \wedge \psi) - c\ell(\psi) \geq 0$ and $\ell(\varphi/\psi) \leq c$ is defined as $\ell(\varphi \wedge \psi) - c\ell(\psi) \leq 0$. We also define $\ell(\varphi/\psi) = c$ to be an abbreviation for the conjunction of the previous two formulae. Note that linear combinations of conditional likelihood terms are not allowed.

Fagin et al. [4] give a sound and complete axiomatization consisting of the following axioms:

Prop All the substitution instances of tautologies in propositional logic,
QU1 $\ell(\varphi) \geq 0$,
QU2 $\ell(\top) = 1$,
QU3 $\ell(\varphi) = \ell(\varphi \wedge \psi) + \ell(\varphi \wedge \neg \psi)$, where φ and ψ are pure propositional formulae,
Ineq All substitution instances of valid linear inequality formulae,

and two inference rules:

MP From f and $f \Rightarrow g$ infer g,
QUGen From $\varphi \Leftrightarrow \psi$ infer $\ell(\varphi) = \ell(\psi)$.

From this axiomatization, an NP decision procedure for the logic can be derived.

What is *not* expressible in this logic is stochastic independence of formulae. In fact, it is not hard to see that any statement about independence leads to non-linear statements about probabilities. Fagin et al. discuss an extension of their formalism which includes *polynomial likelihood formulae*, and in which independence can easily be expressed. Unfortunately, this increases the complexity of the satisfiability problem to PSPACE.

To give a complete specification of a large probabilistic system, it is vital to be able to express conditional independence of variables. This is one of the main assets of Bayesian networks. This is our motivation for looking at other ways to include statements about independence in a probabilistic logic.

2. Probabilistic Propositional Logic with Independence Formulae

To the probabilistic propositional logic defined in the previous section, we add *conditional independence formulae* (CI-formulae)

$$I(\mathbf{X}_1, \mathbf{X}_2 / \mathbf{X}_3) \quad ,$$

---
[3]Halpern and others define variants where not all events need to be measurable, and also variants where several separate subjective probability measures are dealt with. We consider neither of these here.

where $\mathbf{X}_1$, $\mathbf{X}_2$, and $\mathbf{X}_3$ are sets of propositional letters.

If any of the sets $\mathbf{X}_i$ is a singleton set, we will omit the braces around it, for example, we will write $I(A, \{B,C\}/D)$ instead of $I(\{A\}, \{B,C\}/\{D\})$. We denote the set of all formulae by $\mathbf{F}$.

Before assigning a semantics to CI-formulae, we recall the definition of conditional independence from probability theory:

Definition 1 *Given a probability space* (W, μ), *we say that events A and B are independent conditional on an event C*, $I_\mu(A, B/C)$, *iff*

$\mu(B \cap C) \neq 0$ *implies* $\mu(A/C) = \mu(A/B \cap C)$ *or, equivalently,*
$\mu(A \cap C) \neq 0$ *implies* $\mu(B/C) = \mu(B/A \cap C)$.

We extend this to sets of events $\mathbf{A}_i$ *by defining that* $I_\mu(\mathbf{A}_1, \mathbf{A}_2/\mathbf{A}_3)$ *iff* $I_\mu(B_1, B_2/B_3)$ *for all intersections* $B_i = \bigcap_{A \in \mathbf{A}_i} A^{(C)}$ *of possibly complemented events from* $\mathbf{A}_i$.

We then define the interpretation of CI-formulae in a structure $M = (W, \mu, \pi)$ in the following way:

$$\pi_w(I(\mathbf{X}_1, \mathbf{X}_2/\mathbf{X}_3)) = 1 \text{ iff } I_\mu(\mathbf{X}_1^M, \mathbf{X}_2^M/\mathbf{X}_3^M), \text{ where } \mathbf{X}_i^M = \{X^M \mid X \in \mathbf{X}_i\}.$$

We denote the logic given by this syntax and semantics by $\mathbf{L}$.

We will use the following terminology and notations:

A *literal* is a propositional letter (*positive literal*) or a negation of a propositional letter (*negative literal*).

Given a propositional letter X, an *X-literal* is either X or $\neg X$. An *S-atom* for some set $S \subseteq \mathbf{P}$ is a conjunction of literals containing one X-literal for each $X \in S$.

A formula f from the language $\mathbf{L}$ is *true (satisfied)* in the structure M, written $M \models f$, if $\pi_w(f) = 1$ for every $w \in W$. If S is a set formulae *satisfied* in the structure M, we denote that by $M \models S$.

We say that the set of formulae S *semantically entails* the formula f from the language $\mathbf{L}$, if $M \models f$ for every model with $M \models S$. We denote that by $S \models f$.

Note that according to the previous definitions, the conditional likelihood formula $\ell(\varphi/\psi) \geq c$, i.e. $\ell(\varphi \wedge \psi) - c\ell(\psi) \geq 0$, is true in M if and only if $\mu(\varphi^M \cap \psi^M) - c\mu(\psi^M) \geq 0$, which is equivalent to $\mu(\varphi^M/\psi^M) \geq c$ only in the case when $\mu(\psi^M) \neq 0$. If $\mu(\psi^M) = 0$, then $\mu(\varphi^M \cap \psi^M) = 0$ as well, and $\mu(\varphi^M \cap \psi^M) - c\mu(\psi^M) \geq 0$ is true for any real number c. Hence, if $\mu(\psi^M) = 0$, then for arbitrary c, $\ell(\varphi/\psi) \geq c$ is true in the structure, but it does not really mean that $\mu(\varphi^M/\psi^M) \geq c$, since the mentioned conditional likelihood is not even defined in that case. The same observation holds for the other two types of conditional likelihood formulae. The attentive reader will see in the following that this fits nicely with the role of conditional likelihoods for zero-probability conditions in Bayesian networks.

3. Expressing Bayesian Networks

In $\mathbf{L}$, it is possible to express the content of a Bayesian network using a similar amount of space. We will make this precise in the following definitions. To keep the presentation as simple as possible, we restrict ourselves to Bayesian networks where each variable can only have two states. Instead of talking about variables, we talk about events, identified by propositional letters. Our results could be generalized to variables with many states by using one propositional letter per state and adding some more axioms.

Definition 2 *A binary Bayesian network BN is a pair (G, f) where $G = (V, E)$ is a DAG (directed acyclic graph) whose nodes $V \subseteq \mathbf{P}$ are propositional letters. We denote by $Pa(X)$ resp. $ND(X)$ the sets of parents resp. non-descendents of $X \in V$ in G. f is a function that associates with each node X in G a cpt (conditional probability table) which contains an entry $f(X)(\delta) \in [0, 1]$ for each $Pa(X)$-atom δ.*

A cpt entry of a node X gives the probability of (the degree of belief in) the proposition X, under the assumption that the $Pa(X)$-atom corresponding to that entry takes a true value.

Given a binary Bayesian network BN with nodes V, let W_{BN} be the set of all V-atoms, and define $\pi_w(X) = 1$ iff X occurs positively in w. In other words, W_{BN} has exactly one world for each combination of the propositions in BN being true or false. We define a probability measure μ_{BN} on W_{BN} by defining for any elementary outcome $w \in W_{BN}$:

$$\mu_{BN}(\{w\}) = \prod_{X \text{ pos. in } w} f(X)(w_{Pa(X)}) \cdot \prod_{X \text{ neg. in } w} (1 - f(X)(w_{Pa(X)})) \quad (1)$$

where $w_{Pa(X)}$ is the unique $Pa(X)$-atom consisting of a subset of the conjuncts of w. It is easy to see that this really defines a probability measure on W_{BN}. Let $M_{BN} = (W_{BN}, \mu_{BN}, \pi_{BN})$.

Definition 3 *We say that a DAG $G = (V, E)$ qualitatively represents or is qualitatively compatible with a probability structure $M = (W, \mu, \pi)$ if the Markov condition $I_\mu(X^M, ND(X)^M / Pa(X)^M)$ is satisfied for every node $X \in V$.*

For any network $BN = (G, f)$, it can be shown that μ_{BN} as defined in (1) satisfies the Markov condition, i.e. that G qualitatively represents M_{BN}.

Definition 4 *The Bayesian network $BN = (G, f)$ quantitatively represents or is quantitatively compatible with a probability structure $M = (W, \mu, \pi)$, if G qualitatively represents M, and the cpts agree with μ: for each node $X \in V$ and $Pa(X)$-atom δ with $\mu(\delta^M) \neq 0$, $\mu(X^M / \delta^M) = f(X)(\delta)$. (It does not matter what $f(X)(\delta)$ is when $\mu(\delta^M) = 0$.)*

Due to definition (1), M_{BN} is also *quantitatively represented* by $BN = (G, f)$ in this sense. The usual formulation of Bayesian networks with random variables leads to the result that a Bayesian network quantitatively represents a *unique* probability distribution (See e.g. [1]). A corresponding result for our formulation with events is the following:

Lemma 1 *Any models $M = (W, \mu, \pi)$ and $M' = (W', \mu', \pi')$ quantitatively represented by a Bayesian network BN agree in the probabilities assigned to any combination of events described by letters from V, i.e. $\mu(\delta^M) = \mu'(\delta^{M'})$ for all V-atoms δ.*

This means that in a given network $BN = (G, f)$, the graph G captures qualitative information about a probability distribution: existence of independencies between events (absence of arrows) and the cpts present the quantitative information about the strength of the probabilistic dependencies.

Both qualitative and quantitative information embedded in the network can be appropriately represented in our logical language **L**.

For example, if a network consists of the nodes A, B, and C, and edges (B,A) and (C,A) and the cpt contains the following information: $f(B) = b_1$, $f(C) = c_1$ $f(A)(B \wedge C) = a_1$, $f(A)(B \wedge \neg C) = a_2$, $f(A)(\neg B \wedge C) = a_3$ and $f(A)(\neg B \wedge \neg C) = a_4$, then this information can be given in our language in the following way: $\ell(A/B \wedge C) = a_1$, $\ell(A/B \wedge \neg C) = a_2$, $\ell(A/\neg B \wedge C) = a_3$ and $\ell(A/\neg B \wedge \neg C) = a_4$.

The qualitative information from the graph structure of the network is represented by conditional independence formulae. In the case of the previous example we will have: $I(A, \{B,C\}/\{B,C\})$, $I(B,C/\emptyset)$ and $I(C,B/\emptyset)$.

We generalize the whole idea with the following definition:

Definition 5 *Let* **BN** *be the class of all binary Bayesian networks and* **F** *be the set of all formulae in* **L**. *The* specific axioms function, $Ax : \mathbf{BN} \to 2^{\mathbf{F}}$ *is a function that to each Bayesian network* $BN = (G, f)$ *with* $G = (V, E)$ *assigns the set of formulae containing*

- $\ell(X/\delta) = c$ *for every node* $X \in V$ *and every* $Pa(X)$-*atom* δ *such that* $f(X)(\delta) = c$, *and*
- $I(X, ND(X)/Pa(X))$ *for every node* $X \in V$.

4. Theorem for Semantic Entailment

Bayesian networks capture only the probabilities of combinations of certain events identified by the nodes, and not a probability measure on some underlying set of worlds or elementary outcomes. Also the formulae in our logic only describe certain properties of models. It is easy to show however that the inferences possible from a Bayesian network are also logical consequences of the network's set of specific axioms.

By inferences in BNs, we mean the computation of probabilities of arbitrary conjunctions of literals, conditional on other conjunctions of literals. Due to Lemma 1, such a conditional probability follows for *one* model quantitatively represented by the Bayesian network iff it follows for *all* such models.

Theorem 1 *Let BN be a Bayesian network with nodes V and M a probability structure quantitatively represented by BN. If the formula* $\ell(\varphi/\psi) = b$, *where* φ *and* ψ *are conjunctions of literals of letters from V, is satisfied in M, then it is entailed by the specific axioms of BN,* $Ax(BN) \models \ell(\varphi/\psi) = b$.

Proof: Let $M = (W, \mu, \pi)$ be quantitatively represented by BN, and $M \models \ell(\varphi/\psi) = b$. It is sufficient to show that $M' \models \ell(\varphi/\psi) = b$ for an arbitrary but fixed structure $M' = (W', \mu', \pi')$ with $M' \models Ax(BN)$.

The axioms in $Ax(BN)$ are a direct encoding of the conditions for qualitative and quantitative representation, so it is easy to see that BN also quantitatively represents M'. Due to Lemma 1, we have $\mu(\delta^M) = \mu'(\delta^{M'})$ for all V-atoms δ.

For an arbitrary conjunction ξ of literals of letters from V and any structure M'',

$$\xi^{M''} = \bigcup_{\substack{\delta \text{ a } V\text{-atom} \\ \xi \text{ a sub-conjunction of } \delta}} \delta^{M''}$$

and since the sets $\delta^{M''}$ are disjoint, additivity of the probability measure gives us:

$$\mu''(\xi^{M''}) = \sum_{\substack{\delta \text{ a } V\text{-atom} \\ \xi \text{ a sub-conjunction of } \delta}} \mu''(\delta^{M''})$$

for any probability measure μ''. Together with Lemma 1 it follows in particular that $\mu(\varphi^M \cap \psi^M) = \mu'(\varphi^{M'} \cap \psi^{M'})$ and $\mu(\psi^M) = \mu'(\psi^{M'})$.

Now $M \models \ell(\varphi/\psi) = b$, i.e. $\mu(\varphi^M \cap \psi^M) - c\mu(\psi^M) = 0$ and therefore also $\mu'(\varphi^{M'} \cap \psi^{M'}) - c\mu'(\psi^{M'}) = 0$, i.e. $M' \models \ell(\varphi/\psi) = b$. **Q.E.D.**

While Theorem 1 guarantees the semantic connection between a Bayesian network BN and its axiomatization $Ax(BN)$ in our logic **L**, it says nothing about the derivability of conditional likelihood formulae. This will be covered in the following section.

5. Axiomatic System and Theorem for Syntactic Entailment

The axiomatic system given in Sect. 1 is complete for reasoning in a logic without CI-formulae. To accommodate those, we need to add some extra axioms. The axiomatization of conditional independence has been the subject of a certain amount of research, see e.g. [5] for a survey. In particular, it has been shown (see [6] and [7]) that there is no finite complete axiomatization of conditional independence, if the language contains nothing but CI statements. On the other hand, Fagin et al. [4] show that complete reasoning about conditional independence is possible if one is willing to pay the price of reasoning about polynomials.

In this work, we are less interested in deriving new CI formulae. We want to mimic the kind of reasoning possible with a Bayesian network, so we want a system that allows to derive arbitrary statements about conditional likelihood of propositional formulae from the specific axioms $Ax(BN)$ of a Bayesian network.

We will use an axiomatic system that consists of four parts, each dealing with a different type of reasoning: propositional reasoning, reasoning about probability, reasoning about linear inequalities, and reasoning about conditional independence. For the first three parts, we use the axioms from the system AX_{MEAS} in [4], as given in Sect. 1. For conditional independence reasoning, we add the following inference rules:

SYM From $I(\mathbf{X}_1, \mathbf{X}_2/\mathbf{X}_3)$ infer $I(\mathbf{X}_2, \mathbf{X}_1/\mathbf{X}_3)$
DEC From $I(\mathbf{X}_1, \mathbf{X}_2 \cup \mathbf{X}_3/\mathbf{X}_4)$ infer $I(\mathbf{X}_1, \mathbf{X}_2/\mathbf{X}_4)$
IND From $I(\mathbf{X}_1, \mathbf{X}_2/\mathbf{X}_3)$ and $\ell(\varphi_1/\varphi_3) \leq (\geq)a$ infer $\ell(\varphi_1/\varphi_2 \wedge \varphi_3) \leq (\geq)a$, where φ_i is an arbitrary $\mathbf{X}_i$-atom, for $i \in \{1,2,3\}$.

We say that a set of formulae S *syntactically entails* a formula f in this axiomatic system (including the axioms and rules from Sect. 1) if f can be derived from S by using the given axioms and inference rules. We denote this by $S \vdash f$.

It can be checked that this system is sound, in the sense that only semantically valid entailments can be inferred: If $S \vdash f$, then $S \models f$.

Before we state our restricted completeness theorem, we show how to use the calculus by proving the following proposition:

Proposition 1 *Let $\mathbf{X}_1$, $\mathbf{X}_2$ and $\mathbf{X}_3$ be sets of propositional letters. Then we can derive the following syntactic entailments:*

a) $\{I(\mathbf{X}_1, \mathbf{X}_2/\mathbf{X}_3), \ell(\varphi_1/\varphi_3) = a, \ell(\varphi_2/\varphi_3) = b\} \vdash \ell(\varphi_1 \wedge \varphi_2/\varphi_3) = ab$
b) $\{I(\mathbf{X}_1, \mathbf{X}_2/\mathbf{X}_3), \ell(\varphi_1/\varphi_3) = a, \ell(\varphi_3/\varphi_2) = b\} \vdash \ell(\varphi_1 \wedge \varphi_3/\varphi_2) = ab$

where φ_i are arbitrary $\mathbf{X}_i$-atoms for $i \in \{1,2,3\}$.

Proof: a) We have the following derivation:

1. $I(\mathbf{X}_1, \mathbf{X}_2/\mathbf{X}_3), \ell(\varphi_1/\varphi_3) = a$ .... (premises)
2. $\ell(\varphi_1/\varphi_2 \wedge \varphi_3) = a$ .... (1 and IND)
3. $\ell(\varphi_1 \wedge \varphi_2 \wedge \varphi_3) = a\ell(\varphi_2 \wedge \varphi_3)$ .... (2, def. of cond. likel., Ineq)
4. $\ell(\varphi_2/\varphi_3) = b$ .... (premise)
5. $\ell(\varphi_2 \wedge \varphi_3) = b\ell(\varphi_3)$ .... (4, def. of cond. likelihood, Ineq)
6. $\ell(\varphi_1 \wedge \varphi_2 \wedge \varphi_3) = ab\ell(\varphi_3)$ .... (3, 5, Ineq)
7. $\ell(\varphi_1 \wedge \varphi_2/\varphi_3) = ab$ .... (6, def. of conditional likelihood)

b) The derivation is as in a) until step 3, and then

4. $\ell(\varphi_3/\varphi_2) = b$ .... (premise)
5. $\ell(\varphi_3 \wedge \varphi_2) = b\ell(\varphi_2)$ .... (4, def. of cond. likelihood, Ineq)
6. $\ell(\varphi_1 \wedge \varphi_2 \wedge \varphi_3) = ab\ell(\varphi_2)$ .... (3, 5, Ineq, Prop)
7. $\ell(\varphi_1 \wedge \varphi_3/\varphi_2) = ab$ .... (6, def. of conditional likelihood)

Q.E.D.

The following lemma is required for the proof of the restricted completeness theorem:

Lemma 2 *Let φ, ψ and ν be pure propositional formulae. Then the following syntactic entailment holds:* $\{\ell(\varphi \wedge \nu/\psi) = a_1, \ell(\varphi \wedge \neg \nu/\psi) = a_2\} \vdash \ell(\varphi/\psi) = a_1 + a_2$.

Proof: We have the following derivation steps:

1. $\ell(\varphi \wedge \nu/\psi) = a_1$ .... (premise)
2. $\ell(\varphi \wedge \nu \wedge \psi) = a_1 \ell(\psi)$ .... (1, def. of cond. likelihood)
3. $\ell(\varphi \wedge \neg \nu/\psi) = a_2$ .... (premise)
4. $\ell(\varphi \wedge \neg \nu \wedge \psi) = a_2 \ell(\psi)$ .... (3, def. of cond. likelihood)
5. $\ell(\varphi \wedge \psi) = \ell(\varphi \wedge \nu \wedge \psi) + \ell(\varphi \wedge \neg \nu \wedge \psi)$ .... (QU3)
6. $\ell(\varphi \wedge \psi) = a_1 \ell(\psi) + a_2 \ell(\psi)$ .... (3, 4, 5, Ineq)
7. $\ell(\varphi \wedge \psi) = (a_1 + a_2)\ell(\psi)$ .... (6, Ineq)
8. $\ell(\varphi/\psi) = a_1 + a_2$ .... (7, def. of cond. likelihood)

Q.E.D.

We are now ready to state our limited completeness theorem for the derivation of conditional likelihoods from $Ax(BN)$.

Theorem 2 *Let $BN = (G, f)$ be a Bayesian Network. If the formula $\ell(\varphi/\psi) = b$, where φ and ψ are conjunctions of literals of letters from V, is satisfied in models quantitatively represented by BN, then $Ax(BN) \vdash \ell(\varphi/\psi) = b$.*

Proof: We prove this by deriving $Ax(BN) \vdash \ell(\varphi \wedge \psi) = m$, $\ell(\psi) = n$, where $\ell(\varphi \wedge \psi) = m$ and $\ell(\psi) = n$ are formulae that are satisfied in every model of $Ax(BN)$. If $n = 0$, then also $m = 0$, and therefore $\ell(\varphi \wedge \psi) - b\ell(\psi) = 0$ is an instance of Ineq independently of b. Otherwise, $b = m/n$, and the conclusion follows from the following derivation steps:

1. $\ell(\varphi \wedge \psi) = m$, $\ell(\psi) = n$
2. $\ell(\varphi \wedge \psi) - (m/n)\ell(\psi) = 0$ .... (1 and Ineq)
3. $\ell(\varphi/\psi) = m/n$ .... (2, def. of cond. likelihood)

We will describe the procedure of deriving $\ell(\psi) = n$. A similar one can be used for the derivation of $\ell(\varphi \wedge \psi) = m$.

Let $\mathbf{Y} = \{Y_1, Y_2, \ldots, Y_s\}$ be ancestors in G of all the propositional letters occurring in ψ. Applying QU3 and Ineq, we perform the following derivation steps:

1. $\ell(\psi) = \ell(\psi \wedge Y_1) + \ell(\psi \wedge \neg Y_1)$
2. $\ell(\psi \wedge Y_1) = \ell(\psi \wedge Y_1 \wedge Y_2) + \ell(\psi \wedge Y_1 \wedge \neg Y_2)$
3. $\ell(\psi \wedge \neg Y_1) = \ell(\psi \wedge \neg Y_1 \wedge Y_2) + \ell(\psi \wedge \neg Y_1 \wedge \neg Y_2)$
4. $\ell(\psi) = \ell(\psi \wedge Y_1 \wedge Y_2) + \ell(\psi \wedge Y_1 \wedge \neg Y_2) + \ell(\psi \wedge \neg Y_1 \wedge Y_2) + \ell(\psi \wedge \neg Y_1 \wedge \neg Y_2)$

...

j. $\ell(\psi) = \sum_{\delta \text{ is a } \mathbf{Y}\text{-atom}} \ell(\psi \wedge \delta)$

Let $\psi \wedge \delta = Z'_1 \wedge \cdots \wedge Z'_k$ be one of the conjuncts in the last step, where $Z'_i = Z_i$ or $Z'_i = \neg Z_i$, for some propositional letters $Z_1, \ldots, Z_k$. We put the Z_is into a topological order with respect to G, i.e. if Z_i is a descendent in G of Z_j, then $i > j$.

If we can derive a formula $\ell(Z'_1 \wedge \cdots \wedge Z'_k) = c$ such that $\ell(Z'_1 \wedge \cdots \wedge Z'_k) = c$ is true in every model of $Ax(BN)$, for all conjuncts, then we have derived $\ell(\psi) = n$ as desired. To do this, we start with Z_k. All of $Z_1, \ldots, Z_{k-1}$ are non-descendants of Z_k, hence, by application of DEC to $I(Z_k, ND(Z_k)/Pa(Z_k))$, we obtain that $I(Z_k, \{Z_1, \ldots, Z_{k-1}\}/Pa(Z_k))$ holds. Since $Z'_1 \wedge \cdots \wedge Z'_k$ is a full conjunction (together with a propositional letter, it contains all of its ancestors), all the parents of Z_k are in $\{Z_1, \ldots, Z_{k-1}\}$. Let us denote by $\varphi_{Pa(Z_k)}$ the $Pa(Z_k)$-atom which is a sub-conjunction of $Z'_1 \wedge \cdots \wedge Z'_k$. Then we proceed with the following derivation:

1. $I(Z_k, \{Z_1, \ldots, Z_{k-1}\}/Pa(Z_k))$, $\ell(Z'_k/\varphi_{Pa(Z_k)})) = z_k$

   (If $Z'_k = Z_k$, then $z_k = a_k$, where $\ell(Z_k/\varphi_{Pa(Z_k)}) = a_k$ is a premise. If $Z'_k = \neg Z_k$, then, by using Lemma 2 and Ineq, we obtain $\ell(Z'_k/\varphi_{Pa(Z_k)}) = 1 - a_k$, from the premise $\ell(Z_k/\varphi_{Pa(Z_k)}) = a_k$)

2. $\ell(Z'_k/\varphi_{Pa(Z_k)} \wedge Z'_1 \wedge \cdots \wedge Z'_{k-1}) = z_k$ .... (1 and IND)
3. $\ell(Z'_k/Z'_1 \wedge \cdots \wedge Z'_{k-1}) = z_k$ .... (2, Prop, QUGen)
4. $\ell(Z'_1 \wedge \cdots \wedge Z'_{k-1} \wedge Z'_k) = z_k \ell(Z'_1 \wedge \cdots \wedge Z'_{k-1})$ (3 and the definition of conditional likelihood)

This process can be inductively repeated for the letters $Z_1, \ldots, Z_{k-1}$ to obtain:

5. $\ell(Z'_1 \wedge \cdots \wedge Z'_{k-1}) = z_{k-1} \ell(Z'_1 \wedge \ldots \wedge Z'_{k-2})$
6. $\ell(Z'_1 \wedge \cdots \wedge Z'_{k-1} \wedge Z'_k) = z_k z_{k-1} \ell(Z'_1 \wedge \cdots \wedge Z'_{k-2})$ .... (4, 5, Ineq)

for a number $z_{k-1} = \ell(Z'_{k-1}/\varphi_{Pa(Z_{k-1})})$, obtained similarly like z_k, and so on inductively, until we obtain

$$\ell(Z'_1 \wedge \cdots \wedge Z'_{k-1} \wedge Z'_k) = z_k z_{k-1} \cdots z_1 \quad ,$$

where the $z_i = \ell(Z'_i/\varphi_{Pa(Z_i)})$ are directly determined by the axioms in $Ax(BN)$. This is easily seen to be in direct correspondence to the product given in (1), so we derived $\ell(Z'_1 \wedge \cdots \wedge Z'_k) = c$ for the same c that can be computed from the Bayesian network.
Q.E.D.

6. Beyond Bayesian Networks

So far, we have proved that using our language we can completely imitate the reasoning in Bayesian networks, and derive the same probabilistic statements as from a BN. To do this, we worked only with formulae expressing conditional probabilities of conjunctions of literals, and we did not make use of the possibility to express inequalities in our language. In our logic, it is easy to use complex formulae in axioms and conclusions to be derived, which can lead to more natural formulations in some cases. One can show that our axiomatization is complete also for conditional likelihoods of arbitrary pure propositional formulae, since these can be computed from the conditional likelihoods of conjunctions of literals.

Expressing inequalities for conditional probabilities can also be very useful. For instance, in many contexts in modeling using Bayesian networks, it is very hard to elicit the numbers in the cpts, which determine the probability distribution expressed by the network. In some cases, it may be possible to give a range of the cpt entry (or, not to give information about it at all, in which case the range will be [0,1]), instead of a precise value. Reasoning with such a range is then preferable to using an imprecise guess. In Bayesian network research, *credal networks* [8] have been developed for this purpose. Our logic **L** in its current form can be used to express imprecise information about probabilities by using conditional likelihood inequality formulae. The following example shows that our axioms can be used to infer bounds on conditional probabilities, but not necessarily tightest bounds. In other words, the axiomatization is not complete for the combination of inequality reasoning and conditional independence. In future work, we hope to be able to extend our axiom system to be complete also for the inference of tightest bounds on conditional inequalities.

Figure 1. The DAG part of the three-node Bayesian network BN_3.

Example: Let us consider a three-node Bayesian network BN_3 given with the DAG on Figure 1, and with the following information provided in its cpts:

$f(B) \in [b_1, b_2], f(C) \in [c_1, c_2],$
$f(D)(B \wedge C) = d_1, f(D)(B \wedge \neg C) = d_2, f(D)(\neg B \wedge C) = d_3, f(D)(\neg B \wedge \neg C) = d_4.$

We translate the given input information about BN_3 into the logical language in the following way:

$\ell(B) \geq b_1, \ell(B) \leq b_2, \ell(C) \geq c_1, \ell(C) \leq c_2,$
$\ell(D/B \wedge C) = d_1, \ell(D/B \wedge \neg C) = d_2, \ell(D/\neg B \wedge C) = d_3, \ell(D/\neg B \wedge \neg C) = d_4,$
$I(B,C/\emptyset), I(C,B/\emptyset), I(D, \{B,C\}/\{B,C\}).$

To derive a probability statement of type $\ell(D) \geq d$, for some d, we follow a similar procedure as described in Theorem 2, using axioms and inference rules for linear likelihood inequality formulae:

1. $\ell(D) = \ell(D \wedge B \wedge C) + \ell(D \wedge B \wedge \neg C) + \ell(D \wedge \neg B \wedge C) + \ell(D \wedge \neg B \wedge \neg C)$
2. $\ell(D \wedge B \wedge C) = d_1 \ell(B \wedge C)$
3. $\ell(D \wedge B \wedge \neg C) = d_2 \ell(B \wedge \neg C)$
4. $\ell(D \wedge \neg B \wedge C) = d_3 \ell(\neg B \wedge C)$
5. $\ell(D \wedge \neg B \wedge \neg C) = d_4 \ell(\neg B \wedge \neg C)$
6. $\ell(D) = d_1 \ell(B \wedge C) + d_2 \ell(B \wedge \neg C) + d_3 \ell(\neg B \wedge C) + d_4 \ell(\neg B \wedge \neg C)$

For each $\ell((\neg)B \wedge (\neg)C)$ we can derive two bounds that can be expressed as *linear* likelihood formulae:

7. $\ell(B \wedge C) \geq \ell(B)c_1$
8. $\ell(B \wedge C) \geq b_1 \ell(C)$
9. $\ell(B \wedge \neg C) \geq \ell(B)(1 - c_2)$
10. $\ell(B \wedge \neg C) \geq b_1 \ell(\neg C)$
11. $\ell(\neg B \wedge C) \geq \ell(\neg B)c_1$
12. $\ell(\neg B \wedge C) \geq (1 - b_2)\ell(C)$
13. $\ell(\neg B \wedge \neg C) \geq \ell(\neg B)(1 - c_2)$
14. $\ell(\neg B \wedge \neg C) \geq (1 - b_2)\ell(\neg C)$

Depending on $d_1, \ldots, d_4$, these can be used to derive different lower bounds for $\ell(D)$.
On the other hand, for any structure $M = (W, \mu, \pi)$, such that $M \models Ax(BN)$, we have:

$$\mu(D^M) = d_1 \mu(B^M)\mu(C^M) + d_2 \mu(B^M)\mu((\neg C)^M) +$$
$$d_3 \mu((\neg B)^M)\mu(C^M) + d_4 \mu((\neg B)^M)\mu((\neg C)^M)$$

Assuming for instance that $d_1 < d_2, d_3 < d_4$, it is not hard to see that this expression has a greatest lower bound of

$$\mu(D^M) \geq d_1 b_2 c_2 + d_2 b_2 (1 - c_2) + d_3 (1 - b_2) c_2 + d_4 (1 - b_2)(1 - c_2)$$

which is larger than any bound that can be obtained as a sum of the individual bounds in formulae 7 to 14.

7. Related work

We are certainly not the first who attempt to combine the expressiveness and the inference mechanisms of probabilistic logics and probabilistic networks. There are several other lines of work with the same or similar goals. Haenni et al. [9] use inference networks (Bayesian networks as well as credal networks [8] for the case with incomplete information) as a calculus for probabilistic logic in general – they provide a network model for a set of (linear inequality) probabilistic statements that describes the problem domain and then make inference using Bayesian and credal network inference algorithms. Cozman et al. [10] also propose inference with imprecise probabilities, but they represent the independence statements by introducing a graph-theoretic model called probabilistic propositional logic network consisting of a DAG and linear inequality probabilistic statements corresponding to its nodes; for inferencing, they construct a credal counterpart of the DAG. In both mentioned approaches the independence structure is captured by a qualitative BN, which means that independence statements are implied by missing edges, according to the Markov condition. We prefer explicitly stating independence statements in the logic because that requires conscious thought while building a specification. In a graph representation, a missing arrow that expresses a conditional independence might be missing by accident. Another advantage of this representation could be the possibility of expressing conditional independencies of a probability distribution that can not be entailed by any graph.

The work on 'Bayesian logic' by Andersen and Hooker [11] is perhaps that which is most closely related to ours. The independence statements there are encoded in a standard probabilistic logic by using polynomial likelihood formulae that come from the definition of independence and Bayes' rule; these formulae together with formulae that come from the cpts and some general probability constraints are used as a basis for a linear programming inference to infer the tightest range for a probability in question. They also go beyond Bayesian networks, considering probabilistic inequality statements. Note that the representation of independence in polynomial likelihood formulae has also been suggested by Fagin and Halpern [4].

What these approaches have in common, and what separates them from our work is that we do not recur to existing Bayesian or credal network algorithms, or linear or non-linear programming for inference. These surely give efficient means of reasoning within their respective limits, but we were interested in a purely logical characterization, i.e. not only are all aspects of a specification expressed as formulae with a standard model semantics, but also inference is done using an axiomatic system. While this surely doesn't give the most efficient reasoning, we consider the sufficiency of a relatively small axiomatic system to be interesting in its own right. And the axiomatic approach should make it easier to combine the logic with epistemic, temporal, and other logics.

8. Conclusion and Future Work

A logical approach to reasoning about uncertainty has a number of advantages over approaches based on Bayesian networks, including the ease of accommodating incomplete knowledge, and the possibility of combining uncertainty reasoning with logics for reasoning about time, knowledge of multiple agents, etc.

Conditional independence is a crucial element for the compact and efficient representation of a system of uncertainties. This is naturally expressed in Bayesian networks, but not usually a part of logics dealing with probabilities. We have introduced a probabilistic logic with conditional independence formulae that allows representing the information in a Bayesian network in a comparable amount of space. We have discussed the difficulties of complete quantitative reasoning in the presences of conditional independence, but we have given an axiom system and shown it to be complete for a small class of problems, including at least the conditional probability statements derivable from a Bayesian network.

Topics for future work include the extension of the calculus to obtain completeness also for ranges of probabilities. It would also be interesting to investigate efficient, maybe approximate, reasoning algorithms for Bayesian networks and try to recast them into an optimized axiom system or other logical calculus, allowing more efficient inference in practice.

Introducing the conditional independence statements directly in the language, and the choice of CI axioms we have made also allows for other choices of semantics, for example, model structures with a possibility instead of a probability measure, or with a more general belief measure, so we consider that as another possibility for extending the scope of our work.

We are currently in the process of extending the given logic with a mechanism for expressing decision scenarios, including options and utilities, which will make it possible to infer optimal strategies from a set of observations.

Acknowledgements

The authors would like to thank the anonymous reviewers of STAIRS and ECAI 2010 for many useful suggestions on previous versions of this paper. The CODIO project is partially funded by grants from the Research Council of Norway, Petromaks Project 175899/S30, 2007–2010.

References

[1] Joseph Y. Halpern, *Reasoning about Uncertainty*, MIT Press, 2003.
[2] R. E. Neapolitan, *Learning Bayesian Networks*, Prentice Hall, 2003.
[3] M. Giese and R. B. Bratvold, *Probabilistic Modelling for Decision Support in Drilling Operations, SPE 127761*, in Proc. SPE Intelligent Energy Conference, 2010.
[4] R. Fagin, J. Y. Halpern and N. Megiddo, *A Logic for Reasoning about Probabilities*, Information and Computation, vol.87, 78–128, 1990.
[5] D. Geiger and J. Pearl, *Logical and Algorithmic Properties of Conditional Independence and Graphical Models*, Ann. Statist., vol.21, n.4, 2001–2021, 1993.
[6] Milan Studený, *Conditional independence relations have no finite complete characterization*, 11th Prague Conf. on Information Theory, Statistical Decision Functions and Random Processes, vol.B, 377–396, Kluwer, 1992.
[7] Sanjiang Li, *Causal models have no complete axiomatic characterization*, CoRR, abs/0804.2401, 2008.
[8] F. G. Cozman, *Credal networks*, Artif. Intell., vol.120, n.2, 199–233, 2000.
[9] R. Haenni, J. W. Romeijn, G. Wheeler and J. Williamson, *Probabilistic Logic and Probabilistic Networks*, December 2008, Draft
[10] F. G. Cozman, C. P. de Campos, and J. C. Ferreira da Rocha, *Probabilistic logic with independence*, Int. J. Approx. Reasoning, vol.49, n.1, 3–17, 2008.
[11] K. A. Andersen, and J. N. Hooker, *Bayesian logic*, Decis. Support Syst., vol.11, n.2, 191–210, 1994.

Difficulty Rating of Sokoban Puzzle[1]

Petr Jarušek and Radek Pelánek

Abstract. Sokoban puzzle is very challenging problem for both humans and computers. It also illustrates differences between human and artificial intelligence – different problems are difficult for humans and for computers. Whereas algorithmic techniques for Sokoban solving have been intensively studied by previous research, factors determining difficulty for humans have not been sufficiently explained so far. We describe two methods for difficulty rating of Sokoban puzzle – a problem decomposition metric and a computational model which simulates human traversal of a state space. We evaluate these metrics on large scale data on human solving (2000 problems solved, 785 hour of problem solving activity).

Keywords. Sokoban puzzle, State space, Difficulty rating, Computational model

1. INTRODUCTION

Human problem solving is influenced by many parameters, e.g., formulation of rules, number of items that need to be held in working memory, or familiarity with problem domain. But even when all of these intuitive parameters are fixed, there can still be large differences in problem difficulty. We study human behaviour during Sokoban problem solving and we show that even for a set of very similar problems the differences in difficulty are significant and not explained by any simple problem parameter. Why do these differences occur?

Understanding this phenomenon is important not just for providing insight into human cognition, but it also has several applications. Humans and computers solve problems in different ways and have complementary strengths [22]; to built tools for human-computer collaboration we need to understand what makes problems difficult for humans. Another application is for teaching and training (e.g., with intelligent tutoring systems [2]). Humans enjoy problem solving, but only when faced with problems of adequate difficulty, i.e., neither too boring nor too difficult. To recommend appropriate instance of problem we need to be able to evaluate its difficulty.

1.1. Sokoban

In this paper we report on experiments with the Sokoban puzzle. Sokoban is a logic puzzle which has simple rules and yet incorporates intricate dynamics and great complexity for both humans and computers. Example of the puzzle is in Figure 1. There is a simple maze with several boxes and one man. The goal is to get the boxes into the target squares by pushing one box at a time.

---

[1]Supported by GA ČR grant no. P202/10/0334.

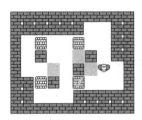 

Figure 1. Example of two difficult Sokoban puzzles. The median solving time for the left problem (further denoted example 1) is 43 minutes, for the right one (denoted example 2) it is 49 minutes.

We have chosen Sokoban puzzle for several reasons. The first reason is interestingness. Sokoban has simple rules and intuitive visual setting; hence it is very simple to understand. Most people find it interesting and challenging and thus are willing to solve it voluntarily.

The second reason is availability of resources. There is a very large number of levels of the puzzle freely available on the Internet. These available levels span wide range of difficulty. Sokoban is also used by artificial intelligence community as a testbed for developing single agent search techniques, with many techniques and results are described in research literature (see e.g., [5,6,11,12,13]).

The third reason is complexity. Despite the simplicity of the rules, Sokoban can be very challenging for both humans and computers (Sokoban is PSPACE-complete problem [5]). The puzzle also illustrates differences between humans and computers. There exist small instances that can be quickly solved by computer (using a trivial brute force algorithm) but take humans hours to solve (see Figure 1). At the same time, there are also instances of the puzzle, which humans can solve but which are beyond capabilities of the state-of-the-art artificial intelligence solvers [11].

1.2. Human Problem Solving

Problem solving encompasses many different activities. The main classification is into well-structured problems and ill-structured problems [23]. Well-structured problems have clear boundaries and sharply defined situations, rules, and goals (e.g., proving mathematical statement, optimizing logistic operation). Ill-structured problems are defined more vaguely (e.g., writing a book).

A typical example of well-structured problem are logic puzzles. Puzzles contain all important information in the statement of the problem (and hence do not depend on knowledge), are amenable to automated analysis, and are also attractive for humans. The use of puzzles has a long tradition both in computer science (particularly artificial intelligence) [20] and cognitive psychology [21,23].

Human problem solving has been studied for a long time, starting by a seminal work by Simon and Newell [21]; for a recent overview see [17]. Relevant to this work is particularly research concerned with puzzles which can be directly expressed as state space traversal, e.g., Tower of Hanoi puzzle [14], river crossing problems [9], Water jug puzzle [3], Fifteen puzzle [18], and Chinese ring puzzle [15].

This work is concerned with analysis of human problem solving activity on the Sokoban puzzle with the special focus on the issue of problem difficulty. As opposed to previous research, which has been based only on small samples of human problem solving activity in laboratory setting, we employ large scale data collection through Internet. The data are collected via web portal which contains a simulator of the puzzle. People log into this portal and try to solve provided puzzles. All their actions (including their timing) are saved and stored into a database on the server.

This approach has certainly some disadvantages over the standard 'laboratory' approach to experiments with human problem solving, particularly we do not have a direct control over our subjects. Nevertheless, we believe that the advantages significantly outweigh these disadvantages. We have been able to collect large number of data about human problem solving activity: more then two thousand completed games. Almost three hundred people solved Sokoban on the portal and spent 785 hours with solving. This is much more than would be feasible with the classical laboratory approach. Moreover, the experimental setting is cheap and the data collection rather fast.

1.3. Problem Difficulty

We focus on the issue of problem difficulty. Previous research on the problem difficulty (e.g., [7,9,14,15,18]) was focused particularly on the following concepts:

- hill-climbing heuristic, which was studied for example for river crossing problems [9], Fifteen puzzle [18], and Water jug puzzle [3,4],
- means-end analysis, which was proposed as a key concept in the "General Problem Solver" [16] and was studied for example for Tower of Hanoi puzzle,
- differences between comprehension of isomorphic problems, which focus on the difficulty of successor generation and were studied for example for Tower of Hanoi [14] and Chinese ring puzzle [14].

However, these concepts are not sufficient to explain differences in difficulty in Sokoban problems. In our experiment there are very similar problems with large difference in difficulty (more than 10-fold) – whereas the problems in Figure 1 took human on average nearly one hour, other problems were solved in within few minutes. Yet with respect to the above mentioned concepts the problems are nearly the same. Hill-climbing is not applicable for solving Sokoban problems (except very easy ones). Means-end analysis is applicable only in very limited sense and it is not clear how this concept could explain large differences in difficulty of different Sokoban problems. Differences between comprehension of isomorphic problems and successor generation also cannot be responsible for differences in difficulty, because all instances are stated in the same way.

1.4. Contributions

We describe a novel type of experiment with human problem solving using large scale data collection of human problem solving activity over the Internet. Using the collected data on Sokoban puzzle, we identify differences in problem difficulty that are not explained by previous research. To explain these differences, we develop an abstract computational model of human behaviour during search through a problem state space. We also describe a successful difficulty metric which is based on problem decomposition. Full version of the paper, which contains more detailed analysis of collected data, is available as a technical report [10].

2. PRELIMINARIES AND METHODOLOGY

In this section we describe the Sokoban problem, its state space, and methodology of our data collection on human problem solving. We also provide an analysis of the collected data.

2.1. Sokoban and Its State Space

Sokoban is a single player game that was created around 1980 in Japan[2]. Example of the puzzle is in Figure 1. There is a simple maze with several boxes and one man. The goal of the puzzle is to get the boxes into the target squares. The only allowed operation is a push by a man; man can push only one box. For more precise description of rules see, e.g., [1].

To analyze behavior of humans during problem solving, we explore their movement in the underlying problem state space. State space of the game is then formalized as a directed graph $G = (V, E)$ where V is the set of game states and E is the set of edges corresponding to a move of single box[3]. State of the game is thus given by a position of boxes in the maze and by area reachable by a man. We denote s_0 the vertex corresponding to the initial position of the game. In our discussion we consider only states reachable from the initial state.

There can be several states corresponding to a solved problem – all boxes have to be on given position in the final state, but there can be more final states due to the position of the man. Nevertheless, in nearly all cases there is just one final state; thus to simplify the discussion in the following we assume just one final state denoted s_f[4]. We say that a state s is "live" if there exists a path from s to s_f; otherwise we call the state s "dead".

2.2. Data Collection

To obtain data about human Sokoban solving, we used a web portal with a game simulator. Simulator was implemented in Javascript; all moves during the game were sent to the server, where they were stored into a database. We logged description of each move and time spent before the move.

For the experiment we used 35 problems, all of them had 4 boxes and similar size. To avoid bias from learning, we randomized order of problems for each player. Level were given non-explanatory names (fixed prefix + random looking three digit number). Moreover there were 4 sample training problems which players solved to gain the understanding of the problem; these training problems are not included in our analysis.

Participants were not paid and we did not have a direct control over them since the whole experiment run over the Internet. As a motivation to perform well there was a public results list – this is for most people sufficient motivation, and at the same time it is sufficiently weak so that there is not a tendency to cheat.

Table 1. Summary information about data collection.

participants who solved all 35	6
participants who solved at least 20	35
participants who solved at least 1 level	294
successful attempts to solve a problem	2071
all attempts to solve a problem	21511
total time spent solving	785 hours

Summary statistics about the experiment are given in Table 1. In the next section we provide the analysis of data and show that they are sufficiently robust to be used for research purposes.

2.3. Data Analysis

Our aim is to explain and predict difficulty of individual problems. As the first step it is necessary to specify a fair and robust measure of difficulty. There are several natural measures of difficulty: time taken to solve a problem, number of moves necessary to solve a problem, number of solvers who successfully solved a problem. It turns out that all these measures are highly correlated (see [10]), i.e., it seems plausible that any single of them sufficiently captures a concept of problem difficulty. In the rest of the paper we use as a difficulty measure the median solving time of successful attempts.

Figure 2 shows the distribution of solving time using the boxplot method; problems are sorted by the median time (our measure of difficulty). The solving time median varies from one minute to almost one hour. This result is interesting because we are working with very similar Sokoban problems – all levels have exactly four boxes and the size and topology of the underlying maze is in all cases also very similar.

In our experiment we saved information about all moves performed by solvers (including time taken to make the move). Although 73.8% of game-configuration are dead (i.e. states from which is impossible to reach the goal), humans usually do not spent much time in dead states (14.5% on the average). They can relatively quickly discover that they are in bad configuration and restart the game. Humans spent more time far from goal position. Once humans get to one half of the distance between the start and goal state, they finish the problem rather quickly.

3. COMPUTATIONAL MODEL OF HUMAN SOLVER

In this section we describe a simple computational model of human Sokoban solving. Our goal is to replicate only the human behavior in terms of state space traversal characteristics. We do not try to model the actual human cognitive processes while solving the problem, i.e., this is cognitive engineering model rather than cognitive science model [8]. Our model is very abstract and is based only on information about underlying problem

---

[2] Sokoban is Japanese for "ware-house keeper"

[3] A naive formulation of a state space is to consider as a move each step of a man. This formulation does not add any important information to the analysis and leads to unnecessary large state spaces.

[4] This simplification is only for sake of readability of the text. Implementations of all our techniques work correctly in the general case of multiple final states.

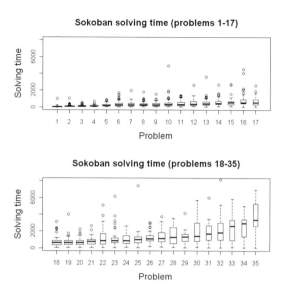

Figure 2. Boxplot of time to solve the Sokoban problems.

state space, i.e., the model is not specific for Sokoban. In the next section we use the model for difficulty rating.

3.1. Basic Principle

Our model is based on the analysis of human behaviour as discussed in Section 2.3. At the beginning humans explore the state space rather randomly, later, as they get closer to the solution, they move more straightforwardly to the goal. Since humans spent most time at live states, the basic model works only with these states and completely avoids dead states.

The model starts at the initial state and then repeatedly selects a successor state. This selection is in the basic model local and very simple – it is a combination of two tendencies:

- random walk – select a random successor,
- optimal walk – select a successor which is closer to the goal state.

Human decisions are usually neither completely random, nor completely optimal. Nevertheless, the model assumes that a weighted combination of these two tendencies can provide a reasonable fit of human behaviour.

3.2. Model Formalization

The general principle of our model is the following. In each step the model considers all successors s' of the current state s. Each successor s' is assigned a value $score(s')$, the sum of all $score$ values is denoted $SumScore$. The model moves to a successor which is selected randomly according to a probabilistic distribution:

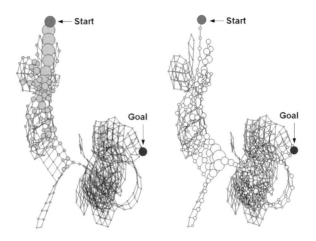

Figure 3. Comparison of human visits (left) and model visits (right) for the example 2. Vertexes represent states of the game, edges represents transitions between states. Size of each vertex is proportional to visits spent by human solvers / model.

$$P(s') = score(s')/SumScore$$

This general model is specified by a selection of a *score* function. In this report we evaluate the basic version of the model which uses a simple function based on distance $d(s)$ of a state s from the goal state. The function is defined as follows (B is a single parameter of the model – 'optimality bonus'):

$$score(s') = \begin{cases} 0 & d(s') = \infty \\ d(s) & d(s') \neq \infty, d(s') \geq d(s) \\ d(s) + B & d(s') < d(s) \end{cases}$$

Let us discuss the intuition and rationale behind this formula. The first case means that dead states have zero probability of being visited, i.e., the model visits only live states. The second and third case means that successors that lead to the solution get an 'optimality bonus', i.e., they have higher chance of being selected. The use of distance from the goal in the formula has the consequence that the relative advantage of 'bonus' increases as the model gets closer to the goal, i.e., the model behaves less randomly when it is close to the goal (as do humans).

If $B = 0$ than the model behaves as a pure random walk (within live states). As B increases the behaviour of the model converges to the optimal path. Hence by tuning the parameter B the model captures continuous spectrum of behaviour between randomness and optimality.

Figure 3 gives an example of a comparison of human and model state space traversal.

3.3. Possible Extensions

In this work we discuss and evaluate just the simplest reasonable version of the model. Nevertheless, the model can be further extended in several ways. The extensions are quite natural and can be done simply by extending the scoring function:

- Hill climbing heuristic (specific for the particular problem, i.e., Sokoban). For Sokoban the natural heuristic is the total distance of boxes from goal positions.
- Use of memory (loop avoidance heuristic). The model would remember states that were already visited and in the scoring function would prefer unvisited states.
- Exploration of dead states (with lower, but non-zero, probability than live states).
- Penalization of long back edges. Humans can recognize not just moves which lead to dead states, but also moves which lead "backwards".

Each of these extensions incorporates at least one additional parameter into the model. With the size of our testing data (35 problems) it could be misleading to evaluate versions of the model with more parameters due to the potential overfitting of data [19].

The model can be easily used as a basis for a difficulty metric. We just run the model repeatedly and take the number of steps it took the model to reaching the goal state. The average number of steps is used as a difficulty metric.

4. METRICS BASED ON THE SHORTEST PATH

In this section we describe metrics based on the shortest path.

4.1. Basic Metrics

The most intuitive difficulty metric is the 'number of steps necessary to reach a solution', i.e., the length of the shortest path from initial to goal state in the state space. Other metrics can be obtained as variations on this basic principle.

One of the concepts which was intensively studied in previous research on problem solving is the hill-climbing heuristics [3,4,18]. This concept can be quite directly applied as a difficulty metric. The straightforward hill-climbing heuristic for Sokoban is to minimize the total distance of boxes from their goal positions. Given this heuristic, we can define the metric 'counterintuitive moves' as a number of steps on the shortest path which go against this hill-climbing heuristic.

4.2. Problem Decomposition

Another intuitively important concept in problem solving is problem decomposition. Humans are not good at systematic search, but they are good at tasks such as abstraction, pattern recognition, and problem decomposition. If a problem can be decomposed into several subproblems it is usually much simpler (for humans) than a same type of problem which is highly interwoven and indecomposable (see example in Figure 4). The concept of problem decomposition is however more difficult to grasp than the hill-climbing heuristic.

We propose a way to formalize problem decomposition for a Sokoban puzzle. A natural unit of 'composition' is a single box. Thus we can consider decomposition of a problem into single boxes and than count as a single move any series of box pushes. We can also generalize this idea and decompose the problem into two pairs of boxes[5] and than count as a single move any series of box pushes within the group.

---

[5]Remember that all our problems contain 4 boxes.

problem	decomposition			
	ABCD	**AABB**	ABAB	ABBA
left problem	10	**2**	6	5
right problem	14	**7**	12	10

Figure 4. Example of two Sokoban puzzle; the first one can be easily decomposed into two subproblems and is thus easy (median solving time 3:02 minutes), the second one is rather indecomposable and thus very difficult (median solving time 53:49 minutes). The table gives the number of 'steps' for different decomposition (see text). The bold column corresponds to the decomposition provided in the figure.

Let D be a division of n boxes into several groups (at most n), in our case $n = 4$ and we denote the division by 4 letter string; e.g., 'ABAB' is a division in which the first and the third box are in group A, the second and the fourth box are in group B; 'ABCD' is a division in which each box is in a separate group. Each edge in the state space is labelled by identification of the group to which the moved box belongs. Let p be a path in a state space (a sequence of valid moves). We are interested in the number of label alternations $a(p, D)$ along the path.

Optimal solution of the problem with respect to a division D (denoted $s(D)$) is the minimum $a(p, D)$ along all paths from the initial to the goal state. This optimal solution can be computed by the Dijkstra algorithm over an augmented state space – vertices are tuples (s, g) where s is a state in the state space and g is an identification of a group and edges have weights 0 or 1. Figure 4 gives results for different decompositions of the two provided examples.

For our evaluation we use two metrics based on these concepts. At first, we use the 'box change' metric which is based on the division 'ABCD', i.e., each box is a single group. At second, we use the '2-decomposition' metric, which is the minimum number of steps over all possible division into two groups (division 'AABB', 'ABAB', 'ABBA'). We also tried other types decompositions (e.g., 3-1 decomposition such as 'AAAB'), but the results were similar to 2-decomposition and we do not report them explicitly.

5. Evaluation

Based on results from Section 2.3, we take as a 'real' measure of problem difficulty a median solving time of human solvers.

To quantify the quality of a metric we use correlation coefficients. Except for the standard Pearson correlation coefficient, we also measure Spearman correlation coefficient, which gives the correlation with respect to ordering of values – for practical application of difficulty metrics the ordering is often more important than absolute values.

Table 2 provides overview of all results. The results shown for metric based on model correspond to the optimal choice of the bonus parameter B. We have done sensitivity

Table 2. Correlation coefficients for different difficulty metrics, results given in bold are statistically significant ($\alpha = 0.05$).

type	metric	Pearson	Spearman
state space	size	-0.11	-0.07
shortest paths	shortest path	0.30	**0.47**
	counterintuitive moves	**0.52**	**0.69**
problem	box change	**0.51**	**0.74**
decomposition	2-decomposition	**0.63**	**0.82**
model	avg. steps, $B = 25$	**0.76**	**0.66**

analysis of the metric based on the computational model with respect to the parameter – Spearman coefficient is quite stable, but Pearson coefficient is not (for details see [10]).

We also evaluated the most straightforward approach based on the size of state space, which was initially proposed by Newell and Simon [21]. This metric, however, does not achieve statistically significant correlation. Similar results were obtained for other metrics based on global state space parameters (see [10]).

The intuitively plausible metric based on length of the solution also provides rather poor results. An improvement is brought by Sokoban specific extension of shortest paths (counterintuitive moves) and the best results are obtained by the metric based on problem decompositions and by the metric based on computational model. We believe that the results of the computational model can be further improved by extensions discussed in Section 3.3, but at the moment we do not have enough data to fairly evaluate a model with several free parameters.

6. CONCLUSIONS AND FUTURE WORK

In this paper we study methods for difficulty rating of a Sokoban puzzle. We describe two successful methods of difficulty rating – computational model based on the problem state space and problem decomposition based on division of a given problem into several subproblems. Using these methods, we are able to partially predict the difficulty of the given puzzles and thus to explain the large differences of the recorded Sokoban solving time. We believe that both techniques should be applicable to other problems as well.

There are many direction for future research:

- evaluation of the computational model on other transport puzzles (Rush hour, Replacement puzzle),
- development of the score function without whole state space knowledge,
- a more detailed study of data on human problem solving, particularly study of differences among individual solvers (comparison between experts and average solvers),
- application of studied metrics to improve recommender systems in intelligent tutoring systems (evaluation of unsolved puzzles),
- development of a tutor system devoted to problem solving skill acquisition.

Acknowledgement

We thank Ondřej Bouda for assistance with the web experiment and Aymeric du Peloux, David W. Skinner, M. Hiroshi, and Mart Homs Caussa for creating some of the Sokoban problems which were used in our experiments.

References

[1] Sokoban wiki. http://www.sokobano.de/wiki.
[2] J.R. Anderson, C.F. Boyle, and B.J. Reiser, 'Intelligent tutoring systems', *Science*, **228**(4698), 456–462, (1985).
[3] M.E. Atwood and P.G. Polson, 'Further explorations with a process model for water jug problems', *Memory & Cognition*, **8**(2), 182–192, (1980).
[4] H.P. Carder, S.J. Handley, and T.J. Perfect, 'Counterintuitive and alternative moves choice in the Water Jug task', *Brain and Cognition*, **66**(1), 11–20, (2008).
[5] J. Culberson, 'Sokoban is PSPACE-complete, Technical Report', Department of Computing Science, The Univerzity of Alberta, 1997.
[6] D. Dor, U. Zwick, 'Sokoban and other motion planning problems', 1996.
[7] M. Dry, M.D. Lee, D. Vickers, and P. Hughes, 'Human performance on visually presented traveling salesperson problems with varying numbers of nodes', *Journal of Problem Solving*, **1**(1), 20, (2006).
[8] W. D. Gray, *The Cambridge Handbook of Computational Psychology*, chapter Cognitive Modeling for Cognitive Engineering, 565–588, Cambridge University Press, 2008.
[9] J.G. Greeno, 'Hobbits and orcs: Acquisition of a sequential concept', *Cognitive Psychology*, **6**(2), 270–292, (1974).
[10] P. Jarušek, R. Pelánek *Human Problem Solving: Sokoban Case Study*, Technical Report, Masaryk Univerzity, Faculty of Informatics, 2010.
[11] A. Junghanns, *Pushing the limits: New developments in single-agent search*, Ph.D. dissertation, University of Alberta, Department of Computing Science, 1999.
[12] A. Junghanns, S. Jonathan, 'Sokoban: A Challenging Single-Agent Search Problem', Department of Computing Science, The Univerzity of Alberta, 1997.
[13] A. Junghanns, J. Schaeffer, 'Sokoban: Enhancing general single-agent search methods using domain knowledge', Department of Computing Science, The Univerzity of Alberta, 2000.
[14] K. Kotovsky, J.R. Hayes, and H.A. Simon, 'Why are some problems hard? Evidence from tower of Hanoi', *Cognitive psychology*, **17**(2), 248–294, (1985).
[15] K. Kotovsky and H.A. Simon, 'What Makes Some Problems Really Hard: Explorations in the Problem Space of Difficulty.', *Cognitive Psychology*, **22**(2), 143–83, (1990).
[16] A. Newell and H.A. Simon, 'GPS, a program that simulates human thought', *Computers and thought*, 279–293, (1963).
[17] Z. Pizlo, 'Human Problem Solving in 2006', *The Journal of Problem Solving*, **1**(2), 3, (2007).
[18] Z. Pizlo and Z. Li, 'Solving combinatorial problems: The 15-puzzle', *Memory and Cognition*, **33**(6), 1069, (2005).
[19] S. Roberts and H. Pashler, 'How persuasive is a good fit? A comment on theory testing.', *Psychological Review*, **107**(2), 358–367, (2000).
[20] J. Schaeffer and H.J. Van den Herik, 'Games, computers, and artificial intelligence', *Artificial Intelligence*, **134**(1-2), 1–8, (2002).
[21] H.A. Simon and A. Newell, *Human problem solving*, Prentice Hall, 1972.
[22] L.G. Terveen, 'Overview of human-computer collaboration', *Knowledge Based Systems*, **8**(2), 67–81, (1995).
[23] R.A. Wilson and F.C. Keil, *The MIT encyclopedia of the cognitive sciences*, MIT Press, 1999.

The Decidability of RPTL

Fahad KHAN [1],
University of Nottingham

Abstract. In this paper we look at regular path temporal logic, RPTL, a modal logic which combines the ability to quantify over (finite) paths described by regular expressions (a property which characterises PDL) with the addition of temporal operators. The formulation of RPTL was inspired by agent programming verification considerations. In this paper we prove the decidabilty of RPTL and establish complexity bounds on the satisfiability problem for RPTL by translating it into the theory of alternating tree automata on infinite trees.

Keywords. PDL, Regular Path Temporal Logic, Alternating Tree Automata, CTL, SimpleAPL

Introduction

In this paper we look at regular path temporal logic abbreviated as RPTL, a modal logic which combines the ability to quantify over (finite) paths described by regular expressions (a property which characterises PDL) with the addition of temporal operators. RPTL is based on aspects of Claßen and Lakemeyer's situation calculus variant ESG, as described in [3], and was initially adapted from ESG by Alechina and Logan[2]. Their motivation was to enable the formulation and verification of properties that arise during the executions of agent programs, in particular those properties which hold prior to the termination of a program.

In the 2007 paper *A Logic of Agent Programs* [1], Alechina et al., were able to define a sound and complete logic for reasoning about agent programs written in the agent programming language SimpleAPL. SimpleAPL's operational semantics are defined in terms of a transition system, with each transition corresponding to a single execution step between agent configurations.

The sound and complete logic which was defined in [1] and into which SimpleAPL programs were translated was based on PDL and this allowed the formal specification of various properties of SimpleAPL programs under different execution strategies. However while this enabled the expression of, for example, goal achievement at the end of some/every program execution, it was difficult to use this PDL based logic to check for properties which held while the program was executing.

This signalled the usefulness of expressions such as $\langle \pi \rangle Fp$ where $\langle \pi \rangle$ stands for 'there exists a path described by a regular expression π' and Fp stands for 'somewhere on this path, p holds'. However in PDL we are limited to using existential modalities in

---

[1] University of Nottingham, England; E-mail: afk@cs.nott.ac.uk
[2] Personal Communication.

expressions of the form $\langle \pi \rangle \phi$ - there is a path described by π and at the last state of this path ϕ holds, and in CTL we can use them in expressions of the form EFp - there exists some path and somewhere on this path p holds, without being able to say that this path is described by π. And this led to the adaption and simplification of ESG which resulted in RPTL.

RPTL is very similar to both PDL and CTL, the obvious question was how it stood in relation to both of these logics. Initially an attempt was made to translate RPTL into PDL to show that it was a fragment of that logic. However, there seems to be no obvious or straightforward way of doing so. However, PDL can be easily embedded into RPTL (see below). This gives us an EXPTIME lower bound on the complexity of the satisfiability problem for RPTL. RPTL does not contain CTL, unlike related logics RCTL which is an extension of CTL with regular expressions [2], and ECTL which is also an extension of CTL [4].

The central aim of this report is to prove the decidability of RPTL. We achieve this by translating each formula of RPTL into an alternating tree automaton on infinite trees (ATA) and making use of the fact that the non emptiness problem for ATA is in EXPTIME. The translations are based on Thomas Wilke's translation of the μ-calculus into ATA in [8]. So that RPTL is a fragment of L_μ, though a direct translation from RPTL to L_μ is difficult. As with PDL we can add tests to our RPTL program expressions. For the sake of simplification we do not add them, but the proof for RPTL with tests is a straightforward extension of the current proof.

RPTL is related to Process Logic. Process Logics also allow us to quantify over paths and to talk about what happens during them – see especially Vardi and Wolper's YAPL [6] and PL [5] both of which extend PDL by allowing us to talk about what happens within a path. However these logics tend to be slightly too strong for our purposes with higher complexity than is desirable.

As for the rest of this paper. We start in Section 1 with a definition of the syntax and semantics of RPTL and in Section 2 we give a definition of ATA's and MAR's. In Section 3.1 we give a basic outline of the proof of decidability given in the rest of the paper.

1. Syntax and Semantics of RPTL

RPTL has four temporal operators, two of them are unary next operators corresponding to the next operators of CTL but labelled with a regular expression, $[\![\pi]\!]X$, $\langle\pi\rangle X$, the other two are ternary 'untiltil' (three place until) operators, box untiltil $[\![\pi]\!]\mathcal{U}\mathcal{T}$ and diamond untiltil $\langle\pi\rangle\mathcal{U}\mathcal{T}$. The intuition behind untiltil $p\mathcal{U}q\mathcal{T}r$, for some triple of proposition variables, p, q, r, is that given a path $x = (w_0, ..., w_k)$ we want to determine whether either the proposition p holds in the path x until q for the subpath $x1 = (w_0, ..., w_{k-1})$, or p holds at each point in $x1$ and r holds at w_k. We introduce the untiltil because it is a natural generalisation of the until temporal operator for finite paths, where we know that there is an end point, and because it simplifies the proof of decidability.

Definition 1 *Given a fixed, infinite, set of proposition symbols, $\Phi = \{p, q, ...\}$, we can inductively define the set of RPTL formulae as follows:*

- *$\bot, p \in \Phi$ are both formulae of RPTL,*
- *if ϕ, ψ are formulae of RPTL then so are $\neg\phi$ and $(\phi \wedge \psi)$,*

- if ϕ, ψ and χ are formulae of RPTL and π is a program expression, as defined below, then $[\![\pi]\!]X\phi$, $\langle\pi\rangle X\phi$, $[\![\pi]\!]\phi\mathcal{U}\psi\mathcal{T}\chi$, $\langle\pi\rangle\phi\mathcal{U}\psi\mathcal{T}\chi$ are also formulae of RPTL.

Assuming a fixed set of basic programs $\Psi_0 = \{a, b, ...\}$ we inductively construct the set of program expressions, Ψ, used in the previous definition, in the following manner:

- each basic program $a \in \Psi_0$ is a program,
- if α and β are programs, then so too are $\alpha \cup \beta, \alpha; \beta$, and α^*.

Definition 2 Let $\mathfrak{M}$ be a structure, $\mathfrak{M} = (W, \tau, \kappa)$, then $\mathfrak{M}$ is a model for RPTL if:

- W is a set of states,
- $\tau(a) \subseteq (W \times W)$ gives us the set of state transitions for $a \in \Psi_0$. We can extend this inductively to give us a set of paths $\tau(\pi) \subseteq (W \times W)^*$ corresponding to any program expression π in M:
  * $\tau(\pi_1 \cup \pi_2) = \{z : z \in \tau(\pi_1) \cup \tau(\pi_2)\}$,
  * $\tau(\pi_1; \pi_2) = \{z_1 \circ z_2 : z_1 \in \tau(\pi_1), z_2 \in \tau(\pi_2)\}$, where $\circ$ is a concatenation of paths operator,
  * $\tau(\pi_1^*)$ is the set of all paths consisting of zero or finitely many concatenations of paths in $\tau(\pi_1)$.
- $\kappa(p) \subseteq W$ is a function that for each $p \in \Phi$ gives us the set of states in W at which p holds. We can extend κ to map formulae ϕ to sets of states $\kappa(\phi)$ in W in the usual way.

Assume state $w \in W$ and that ϕ, ψ, and χ are RPTL formulae and π is a program expression. The relation $\Vdash$ of a formula being true in a state of a model is defined inductively as follows:

- $(\mathfrak{M}, w) \Vdash p$ iff $w \in \kappa(p)$,
- $(\mathfrak{M}, w) \Vdash \neg\phi$ iff $\mathfrak{M}, w \nVdash \phi$
- $\mathfrak{M}, w \Vdash (\phi \wedge \psi)$ iff $\mathfrak{M}, s \Vdash \phi$ and $\mathfrak{M}, w \Vdash \psi$,
- $(\mathfrak{M}, w) \Vdash [\![\pi]\!]X\phi$ iff for all paths $x = (w_0, ..., w_l) \in \tau(\pi)$ where $w_0 = w$ we have that $\mathfrak{M}, w_1 \Vdash \phi$,
- $(\mathfrak{M}, w) \Vdash \langle\pi\rangle X\phi$ iff there exists a path $x = (w_0, ..., w_l) \in \tau(\pi)$ such that $w_0 = w$ and $\mathfrak{M}, w_1 \Vdash \phi$,
- $(\mathfrak{M}, w) \Vdash [\![\pi]\!]\phi\mathcal{U}\psi\mathcal{T}\chi$ iff for all paths $x = (w_0, ..., w_l) \in \tau(\pi)$ such that $w_0 = w$ and we have that either: for some initial prefix $(w_0, ..., w_k)$ of x it is the case that $\mathfrak{M}, w_k \Vdash \psi$ and $\mathfrak{M}, w_i \Vdash \phi$ for $i < k < l$; or $\mathfrak{M}, w_i \Vdash \phi$ for all $i < l$ and $\mathfrak{M}, w_l \Vdash \chi$.
- $(\mathfrak{M}, w) \Vdash \langle\pi\rangle\phi\mathcal{U}\psi\mathcal{T}\chi$ iff there exists a path $x = (w_0, ..., w_l) \in \tau(\pi)$ where $w_0 = w$ such that either: for some initial prefix $(w_0, ..., w_k)$ of x we have that and $\mathfrak{M}, w_k \Vdash \psi$ and $\mathfrak{M}, w_i \Vdash \phi$ for $i < k < l$; or $\mathfrak{M}, w_i \Vdash \phi$ for all $i < l$ and $\mathfrak{M}, w_l \Vdash \chi$.

It is clear from the preceding definitions that we have the following equivalences:

- $[\![\pi]\!]Xp \equiv \neg\langle\pi\rangle X\neg p$, and $\langle\pi\rangle Xp \equiv \neg[\![\pi]\!]X\neg p$,
- $[\![\pi]\!]p\mathcal{U}q\mathcal{T}r \equiv \neg\langle\pi\rangle\neg q\mathcal{U}(\neg p \wedge \neg q)\mathcal{T}\neg r$, and $\langle\pi\rangle p\mathcal{U}q\mathcal{T}r \equiv \neg[\![\pi]\!]\neg q\mathcal{U}(\neg p \wedge \neg q)\mathcal{T}\neg r$,

We can easily define a binary until operator $\mathcal{U}$ corresponding to the temporal until operator, using the untiltil operator, so that for example $[\![\pi]\!]p\mathcal{U}q$ is shorthand for $[\![\pi]\!]p\mathcal{U}q\mathcal{T}q$. We can then define the F operator by translating formulae such as $\langle\pi\rangle Fp$ as $\langle\pi\rangle\top\mathcal{U}p$.

The embedding of PDL into RPTL is also straightforward, so for example formulae of the form $\langle \pi \rangle p$ can be written as $\langle \pi \rangle \top \mathcal{U} \bot \mathcal{T} p$.

2. Alternating Tree Automata

Definition 3 *An alternating tree automaton (ATA) is a tuple $\mathcal{A} = (S, s_I, \delta, \Psi, \Omega)$ such that S is a finite set of states, $s_I \in S$ is an initial state, δ is a transition function defined below, Π is a finite set of path labels, and $\Omega : S \to \omega$ is a function that assigns a whole number priority to each state*

We define the transition function as follows:

Definition 4 *The transition function δ maps each state $s \in S$ to a transition condition over S, where the set of all transition conditions over S is defined by:*

- *0 and 1 are transition conditions over S,*
- *p and $\neg p$ are transition conditions over S for every $p \in \Phi$,*
- *s, $[a]s$, and $\langle a \rangle s$ are transition conditions over S, for every $s \in S$ and $a \in \Psi$,*
- *$s \wedge s'$ and $s \vee s'$ are transition conditions over S, for $s, s' \in S$.*

Note that we are dealing exclusively with ATA which accept infinite trees (although they will also accept finite trees too). We have a notion of run specific to ATA's:

Definition 5 *A run of $\mathcal{A}$ on a pointed Kripke structure[3] $(\mathfrak{M}, w)$ where $\mathfrak{M} = (W, \tau, \kappa)$, is a $(W \times S)$-vertex-labeled tree $r = (V^r, E^r, \lambda^r)$ such that the root ρ^r is labeled (w_0, s_I) by the function λ^r and for every vertex v with label (w, s) assigned by λ^r the following conditions are satisfied, we write this as λ when no confusion is possible. In the following definition we will use the notation $\Delta_r(v)$ to refer to the E-successors of the vertex v in W, and $\Delta_a(v)$ to refer to the a- successors of v in $\mathfrak{M}$:*

- *$\delta(s) \neq 0$,*
- *if $\delta(s) = q$, then $w \in \kappa(q)$, and if $\delta(s) = \neg q$, then $w \notin \kappa(q)$,*
- *if $\delta(s) = s'$, then there exists $v' \in \Delta_r(v)$ such that $\lambda(v') = (w, s')$,*
- *if $\delta(s) = \langle a \rangle s'$, then there exists $v' \in \Delta_r(v)$ such that $s^r(v') = s'$ and $w^r(v') \in \Delta_a(w)$,*
- *if $\delta(s) = [a]s'$, then for every $w' \in \Delta_a(w)$ there exists $v' \in \Delta_r(v)$ such that $\lambda(v') = (w', s')$,*
- *if $\delta(s) = s' \vee s''$, then there exist $v', v'' \in \Delta_r(v)$ such that $\lambda(v') = (w, s')$ or $\lambda(v'') = (w, s'')$,*
- *if $\delta(s) = s' \wedge s''$, then there exist $v', v'' \in \Delta_r(v)$ such that $\lambda(v') = (w, s')$ and $\lambda(v'') = (w, s'')$.*

We will only be interested in minimal run trees in the paper, in which case the conditions for any vertex v with label (w, s) are altered as follows:

- $\delta(s) \neq 0$,
- if $\delta(s) = q$, then $w \in \kappa(q)$, and if $\delta(s) = \neg q$, then $w \notin \kappa(q)$,

---

[3] A pointed Kripke structure is a pair $(\mathfrak{M}, w)$, where $\mathfrak{M} = (W, \tau, \kappa)$, and $w \in W$.

- if $\delta(s) = s'$, then there exists $v' \in \Delta_r(v)$ such that $\lambda(v') = (w, s')$, and there is only one such successor,
- if $\delta(s) = \langle a \rangle s'$, then there exists $v' \in \Delta_r(v)$ such that $s^r(v') = s'$ and $w^r(v') \in \Delta_a(w)$, and there is only one such successor,
- if $\delta(s) = [a]s'$, then for every $w' \in \Delta_a(w)$ there exists $v' \in \Delta_r(v)$ such that $\lambda(v') = (w', s')$, and for each $w' \in \Delta_a(w)$ there is exactly one succesor labelled with (w', s').
- if $\delta(s) = s' \vee s''$, then there exist $v', v'' \in \Delta_r(v)$ such that $\lambda(v') = (w, s')$ or $\lambda(v'') = (w, s'')$, and there is only one such successor,
- if $\delta(s) = s' \wedge s''$, then there exist $v', v'' \in \Delta_r(v)$ such that $\lambda(v') = (w, s')$ and $\lambda(v'') = (w, s'')$, and we assume that there are exactly two such successors.

For each vertex $v = (w, s)$ of r, we use v^W to denote the first component of v and v^S to refer to the second component of v, so that $v^W = w$ and $v^S = s$.

Also with minimal run trees r we impose the condition that for any vertex u with state component s if u has an edge leading from it, then the transition condition $\delta(s)$ contains one or more states.

Note that in the rest of this paper we will allow as transition conditions basic multi-modal formulae over Ψ_0, Φ, and S. This does not lead to an increase in expressive power, see [8].

We call an infinite branch b of r accepting if the largest value in X, the set of whole numbers n such that n is allocated to the state component of a vertex $v \in W$ by Ω for an infinite number of vertices, is even. A run r is accepting if all infinite branches are accepting. (If there are no infinite branches then the run is trivially accepting).

We use the acronym MAR to refer to a minimal accepting run and denote the set of pointed Kripke structures accepted by an ATA $\mathcal{A}$ by $\|\mathcal{A}\|$.

3. The Decidability of RPTL

We can 'translate' any formula of RPTL into an ATA enabling us to prove the decidability of RPTL. In other words for any formula ϕ of RPTL we can find an ATA $\mathcal{A}(\phi)$ such that for any pointed Kripke structure $(\mathfrak{M}, w)$, $(\mathfrak{M}, w) \Vdash \phi$ iff $(\mathfrak{M}, w) \in \|\mathcal{A}(\phi)\|$.

3.1. Outline of Proof

The proof is based on the idea of translating limited fragments of the language into ATA's. So that for formulae of the form $[\![\pi]\!]Xp$, $\langle\pi\rangle Xp$, $[\![\pi]\!]p\mathcal{U}q\mathcal{T}r$, and $\langle\pi\rangle p\mathcal{U}q\mathcal{T}r$, where π is a regular expression and p, q and r are propositional variables, it is possible corresponding ATA's of the form $\mathcal{D}[\![\pi]\!]Xp, \mathcal{D}\langle\pi\rangle Xp, \mathcal{D}[\![\pi]\!]p\mathcal{U}q\mathcal{T}r$, and $\mathcal{D}\langle\pi\rangle p\mathcal{U}q\mathcal{T}r$. So that for all pointed Kripke structures $(\mathfrak{M}, w)$, a RPTL formula satisfies $(\mathfrak{M}, w)$ iff $(\mathfrak{M}, w)$ belongs to its corresponding ATA, e.g., for each pointed Kripke structure $(\mathfrak{M}, w), \mathcal{D}[\![\pi]\!]Xp$ iff $(\mathfrak{M}, w) \in \|\mathcal{D}[\![\pi]\!]Xp\|$. However in this paper we omit the $\mathcal{D}[\![\pi]\!]Xp$ and $\mathcal{D}\langle\pi\rangle Xp$ cases for reasons of space they are however fairly easy.

In Section 3.2 we define a new kind of ATA, the Double Alternating Tree Automaton (DATA). DATA's keep track of a so called final state, and also have two states corresponding to a pair of propositional variables p, q.

We then construct for any regular expression π and pair of propositional variables p,q, a DATA $\mathcal{D}[\![\pi]\!]^- p\mathcal{U}q$ such that for any pointed Kripke structure $(\mathfrak{M}, w)$ where $\mathfrak{M} = (W, \tau, \kappa)$, the DATA $\mathcal{D}[\![\pi]\!]^- p\mathcal{U}q$ enables us to keep a track of all paths in $x = (w_0, ..., w_k) \in \tau(\pi)$ – or at least their first and last points – such that either $w_i \Vdash p \wedge \neg q$ for all $i < k$ or $w_j \Vdash \neg p \wedge \neg q$ and $w_i \Vdash p \wedge \neg q$.

This will enable us to define, given one extra propositional variable r, an ATA $\mathcal{D}[\![\pi]\!]p\mathcal{U}q\mathcal{T}r$ for which given any pointed Kripke structure $(\mathfrak{M}, w)$ satisfies the RPTL expression $[\![\pi]\!]p\mathcal{U}q\mathcal{T}r$ if and only if $(\mathfrak{M}, w) \in \|\mathcal{D}[\![\pi]\!]p\mathcal{U}q\mathcal{T}r\|$, thereby relating an untiltil formula of the form $[\![\pi]\!]p\mathcal{U}q\mathcal{T}r$ to a corresponding ATA $\mathcal{D}[\![\pi]\!]p\mathcal{U}q\mathcal{T}r$.

We also state a corresponding theorem for untiltil formulae of the form $\langle\pi\rangle p\mathcal{U}q\mathcal{T}r$ and their corresponding ATA's $\mathcal{D}\langle\pi\rangle p\mathcal{U}q\mathcal{T}r$.

Finally in Section 3.3 we put the results from the previous few sections together. For any formula ϕ of RPTL we can find an equivalent formula ϕ' of RPTL We then define an ATA $\mathcal{A}(\phi)$ which is the translation of ϕ'. Since negation of ATA's can lead to an exponential blowup, we are careful to define a special ATA $\mathcal{N}(\phi)$ which we use in the definition of $\mathcal{A}(\phi)$.

3.2. $\mathcal{D}[\![\pi]\!]p\mathcal{U}q\mathcal{T}r$ and $\mathcal{D}\langle\pi\rangle p\mathcal{U}q\mathcal{T}r$

We will define a new kind of alternating tree automaton, the double-alternating tree automaton.

Definition 6 *A Double-alternating tree automaton (DATA) for any pair of proposition symbols p,q is a tuple $\mathcal{D}(p,q) = (\mathbf{R}, \mathbf{r}_I, \mathbf{r}_f, r_p, r_{\neg p}, r_q, r_{\neg q}, \delta, \Omega)$ where $\mathbf{R}$ is a disjoint pair of finite sets of states $\mathbf{R} = (R^1, R^2)$; $\mathbf{r}_I = (r_I^1, r_I^2)$ is a pair of states, where $r_I^1 \in R^1$ is the initial state of the automaton, and $r_I^2 \in R^2$ is a special marked state; $\mathbf{r}_f = (r_f^1, r_f^2)$ is a pair of states, where $r_f^1 \in R^1$ and $r_f^2 \in R^2$ are marked states.*

We also single out four more states $r_p, r_{\neg p}, r_q, r_{\neg q} \in R^1$. Additionally δ is a transition function that maps each state $r \in R^1 \cup R^2$ to a complex transition condition over $R^1 \cup R^2$. Finally $\Omega : (R^1 \cup R^2) \to \omega$ is a function that assigns a whole number priority to each state in $R^1 \cup R^2$.

A run of the DATA $\mathcal{D}(p,q)$ on a pointed Kripke Structure $(\mathfrak{M}, w)$ is simply a run of the ATA $\mathcal{A}(p,q) = (R^1 \cup R^2, r_I^1, \delta, \Omega)$ on $(\mathfrak{M}, w)$.

DATA's are mere notational conveniences and we can view a DATA $\mathcal{D} = (\mathbf{R}, \mathbf{r}_I, \mathbf{r}_f, r_p, r_{\neg p}, r_q, r_{\neg q}, \delta, \Omega)$ as essentially being a ATA, $\mathcal{F}(\mathcal{D}) = (S, s_I, \delta', \Omega')$ where each $s \in S$ is a tuple $(s', s_p, s_{\neg p}, s_q, s_{\neg q}, s_f)$, where $s' \in R^1 \cup R^2$, and the other components are used to determine whether, for example $s' = s_f$. We alter the transition function δ accordingly; we can also easily alter the runs of the DATA's to get the runs of their equivalent ATAs.

We construct the DATA $\mathcal{D}[\![\pi]\!]^- p\mathcal{U}q = (\mathbf{R}, \mathbf{r}_I, \mathbf{r}_f, r_p, r_{\neg p}, r_q, r_{\neg q}, \delta, \Omega)$, for a program expression π, and a fixed pair of propositional variables p, q, by induction:

- (Base case: $\pi = a$) For any $a \in \Psi_0$ we define the DATA $\mathcal{D}[\![a]\!]^- p\mathcal{U}q = (\mathbf{R}, \mathbf{r}_I, \mathbf{r}_f, r_p, r_{\neg p}, r_q, r_{\neg q}, \delta, \Omega)$ where $\mathbf{R} = (\{s_0, s_1, s_2, s_3, s_4, s_5\}, \{t_0, t_1\})$, Ω assigns 1 to all states, and the assignments are: $\mathbf{r}_I = (s_0, t_0), \mathbf{r}_f = (s_1, t_1), r_p = s_2, r_{\neg p} = s_3, r_q = s_4$ and $r_{\neg q} = s_5$.
  The transition function δ is defined as follows: $\delta(r_I^1) = r_q \vee (r_p \wedge r_{\neg q} \wedge [a]r_f^1) \vee (r_{\neg p} \wedge r_{\neg q} \wedge r_I^2)$, $\delta(r_f^1) = 1$, $\delta(r_q) = q, \delta(r_{\neg q}) = \neg q, \delta(r_{\neg p}) = \neg p, \delta(r_p) = p$, $\delta(r_I^2) = [a]r_f^2$, and $\delta(r_f^2) = 1$.

- (Inductive case: $\pi = \pi_1; \pi_2$) Here we assume we have already defined the DATA's $\mathcal{D}[\![\pi_1]\!]^-p\mathcal{U}q = (\mathbf{S}, \mathbf{s}_I, \mathbf{s}_f, s_p, s_{\neg p}, s_q, s_{\neg q}, \delta_\mathbf{S}, \Omega_\mathbf{S})$, $\mathcal{D}[\![\pi_2]\!]^-p\mathcal{U}q = (\mathbf{T}, \mathbf{t}_I, \mathbf{t}_f, t_p, t_{\neg p}, t_q, t_{\neg q}, \delta_\mathbf{T}, \Omega_\mathbf{T})$ for the program expressions π_1 and π_2. Then we can construct $\mathcal{D}[\![\pi_1; \pi_2]\!]^-p\mathcal{U}q = (\mathbf{R}, \mathbf{r}_I, \mathbf{r}_f, r_p, r_{\neg p}, r_q, r_{\neg q}, \delta, \Omega)$ as follows. We assume S^1 and T^1 are disjoint and set R^1 to be their union; similarly we assume that S^2 and T^2 are disjoint and let R^2 be their union. Set $\mathbf{r}_I = \mathbf{s}_I$, $\mathbf{r}_f = \mathbf{t}_f$, and $r_p = s_p, r_{\neg p} = s_{\neg p}, r_q = s_q, r_{\neg q} = s_{\neg q}$.
  Let $\Omega(r) = \Omega_\mathbf{S}(r)$ for $r \in S^1 \cup S^2$, $\Omega(r) = \Omega_\mathbf{T}(r)$ for $r \in T^1 \cup T^2$. Finally the transition function $\delta(r)$ for $r \in R^1 \cup R^2$, is defined as follows:
$$\delta(r) = \begin{cases} \delta_\mathbf{S}(r) & \text{if } r \in S^1 \cup S^2 - \{s_f^1, s_f^2\}, \\ \delta_\mathbf{T}(r) & \text{if } r \in T^1 \cup T^2, \\ t_I^1 & \text{if } r = s_f^1, \\ t_I^2 & \text{if } r = s_f^2. \end{cases}$$
  and for each formula $\delta(r)$, we replace each instance of s_p or t_p by r_p, similarly s_q or t_q are replaced by r_q, $s_{\neg p}$ or $t_{\neg p}$ are replaced by $r_{\neg p}$ and $s_{\neg q}$ or $t_{\neg q}$ are replaced by $r_{\neg q}$.

- (Inductive case: $\pi = \pi_1 \cup \pi_2$) Again we assume we have already defined the DATA's $\mathcal{D}[\![\pi_1]\!]^-p\mathcal{U}q = (\mathbf{S}, \mathbf{s}_I, \mathbf{s}_f, s_p, s_{\neg p}, s_q, s_{\neg q}, \delta_\mathbf{S}, \Omega_\mathbf{S})$, $\mathcal{D}[\![\pi_2]\!]^-p\mathcal{U}q = (\mathbf{T}, \mathbf{t}_I, \mathbf{t}_f, t_p, t_{\neg p}, t_q, t_{\neg q}, \delta_\mathbf{T}, \Omega_\mathbf{T})$ for the program expressions π_1 and π_2. Then we construct $\mathcal{D}[\![\pi_1 \cup \pi_2]\!]^-p\mathcal{U}q = (\mathbf{R}, \mathbf{r}_I, \mathbf{r}_f, r_p, r_{\neg p}, r_q, r_{\neg q}, \delta, \Omega)$ as follows. We assume S^1 and T^1 are disjoint and set R^1 to be their union with two new states r_1 and r_2; and let R^2 be the disjoint union of S^2 and T^2 with two new states r_3 and r_4. We set $\mathbf{r}_I = (r_1, r_3)$, and $\mathbf{r}_f = (r_2, r_4)$. We set $\Omega(r_1), \Omega(r_2), \Omega(r_3), \Omega(r_4)$ to be 1, the rest of the states as above. The transition function $\delta(r)$ for $r \in R^1 \cup R^2$, is defined as follows:
$$\delta(r) = \begin{cases} \delta_\mathbf{S}(r) & \text{if } r \in S^1 \cup S^2 - \{s_f^1, s_f^2\}, \\ \delta_\mathbf{T}(r) & \text{if } r \in T^1 \cup T^2 - \{t_f^1, t_f^2\}, \\ r_f^1 & \text{if } r = s_f^1 \text{ or } r = t_f^1, \\ ((r_{\neg p} \wedge r_{\neg q}) \wedge r_I^2) \vee (r_p \wedge s_I^1 \wedge t_I^1) & \text{if } r = r_I^1, \\ r_f^2 & \text{if } r = s_f^2 \text{ or } r = t_f^2, \\ s_I^2 \wedge t_I^2 & \text{if } r = r_I^2, \\ 1 & \text{if } r = r_f^1 \text{ or } r = r_f^2. \end{cases}$$
  and for each formula $\delta(r)$, we replace each instance of s_p or t_p by r_p, similarly s_q or t_q are replaced by r_q, $s_{\neg p}$ or $t_{\neg p}$ are replaced by $r_{\neg p}$ and $s_{\neg q}$ or $t_{\neg q}$ are replaced by $r_{\neg q}$.

- (Inductive case: $\pi = \pi_1^*$) We assume that we have already defined the DATA $\mathcal{D}[\![\pi_1]\!]^-p\mathcal{U}q = (\mathbf{S}, \mathbf{s}_I, \mathbf{s}_f, s_p, s_{\neg p}, s_q, s_{\neg q}, \delta_\mathbf{S}, \Omega_S)$ for the regular expression π_1. Then we can construct $\mathcal{D}[\![\pi_1^*]\!]^-p\mathcal{U}q = (\mathbf{R}, \mathbf{r}_I, \mathbf{r}_f, r_p, r_{\neg p}, r_q, r_{\neg q}\delta, \Omega)$ as follows. We let R^1 be the disjoint union of S^1 with two new states r_1 and r_2, and R^2 be the disjoint union of S^2 with two new states r_3 and r_4. We set $\mathbf{r}_I = (r_1, r_2)$ and $\mathbf{r}_f = (r_3, r_4)$. We set $\Omega(r_1), \Omega(r_2), \Omega(r_3), \Omega(r_4)$ to be 1 and $\Omega(s_f^1) = \Omega(s_f^2) = 2$ and the rest as above. The transition function $\delta(r)$ for $r \in R^1 \cup R^2$, is defined as follows:

$$\delta(r) = \begin{cases} \delta_{\mathbf{S}}(r) & \text{if } r \in S^1 \cup S^2 - \{s_I^1, s_I^2\} \\ ((r_{\neg p} \wedge r_{\neg q}) \wedge r_I^2) \vee (r_p \wedge s_I^1 \wedge r_f^1) & \text{if } r = r_I^1, \\ s_I^1 \wedge r_f^1 & \text{if } r = s_f^1, \\ s_I^2 \wedge r_f^2 & \text{if } r = r_I^2 \text{ or } r = s_f^2, \\ 1 & \text{if } r = r_f^1 \text{ or } r = r_f^2. \end{cases}$$

and for each formula $\delta(r)$, we replace each instance of s_p or t_p by r_p, similarly s_q or t_q are replaced by r_q, $s_{\neg p}$ or $t_{\neg p}$ are replaced by $r_{\neg p}$ and $s_{\neg q}$ or $t_{\neg q}$ are replaced by $r_{\neg q}$.

Proposition 1 *For any pointed Kripke structure $(\mathfrak{M}, w)$, there exists exactly one MAR of $\mathcal{D}[\![\pi]\!]^- p\mathcal{U}q$ on $(\mathfrak{M}, w)$ (up to isomorphism).*

Lemma 1 *Let $\mathcal{D}[\![\pi]\!]^- p\mathcal{U}q = (\mathbf{R}, \mathbf{r}_I, \mathbf{r}_f, r_p, r_{\neg p}, r_q, r_{\neg q}, \delta_R, \Omega_R)$ be a DATA, and $\mathcal{D}[\![\pi]\!] p\mathcal{U}q\mathcal{T}r$ be the corresponding ATA, where $p, q, r \in \Psi_0$, and $(\mathfrak{M}, w)$ be a pointed Kripke structure with $w_0 = w$ then:*

$(\mathfrak{M}, w_0) \Vdash [\![\pi]\!] p\mathcal{U}q\mathcal{T}r$ if and only if $(\mathfrak{M}, w_0) \in \|\mathcal{D}[\![\pi]\!] p\mathcal{U}q\mathcal{T}r\|$.

We construct the DATA $\mathcal{D}\langle\pi\rangle^- p\mathcal{U}q = (\mathbf{R}, \mathbf{r}_I, \mathbf{r}_f, r_p, r_{\neg p}, r_q, r_{\neg q}, \delta, \Omega)$, for a program expression π, and a fixed pair of propositional variables p, q, by induction:

- (Base case: $\pi = a$) For any $a \in \Psi_0$ we define the DATA $\mathcal{D}\langle a \rangle^- p\mathcal{U}q = (\mathbf{R}, \mathbf{r}_I, \mathbf{r}_f, r_p, r_{\neg p}, r_q, r_{\neg q}, \delta, \Omega)$ where $\mathbf{R} = (\{s_0, s_1, s_2, s_3, s_4, s_5\}, \{t_0, t_1\})$, Ω assigns 1 to all states, and the assignments are: $\mathbf{r}_I = (s_0, t_0), \mathbf{r}_f = (s_1, t_1), r_p = s_2, r_{\neg p} = s_3, r_q = s_4$ and $r_{\neg q} = s_5$.
  The transition function δ is defined as follows: $\delta(r_I^1) = (r_q \wedge r_I^2) \vee (r_p \wedge r_{\neg q} \wedge \langle a \rangle r_f^1)$, $\delta(r_f^1) = 1$, $\delta(r_q) = q$, $\delta(r_p) = p$, $\delta(r_{\neg q}) = \neg q$ $\delta(r_I^2) = \langle a \rangle r_f^2, \delta(r_f^2) = 1$.

- (Inductive case: $\pi = \pi_1; \pi_2$)
  Here we assume we have already defined the DATA's $\mathcal{D}\langle\pi_1\rangle^- p\mathcal{U}q = (\mathbf{S}, \mathbf{s}_I, \mathbf{s}_f, s_p, s_{\neg p}, s_q, s_{\neg q}, \delta_\mathbf{S}, \Omega_\mathbf{S})$, $\mathcal{D}\langle\pi_2\rangle^- p\mathcal{U}q = (\mathbf{T}, \mathbf{t}_I, \mathbf{t}_f, t_p, t_{\neg p}, t_q, t_{\neg q}, \delta_\mathbf{T}, \Omega_\mathbf{T})$ for the regular expressions π_1 and π_2.
  Then we can construct $\mathcal{D}\langle\pi\rangle^- p\mathcal{U}q = (\mathbf{R}, \mathbf{r}_I, \mathbf{r}_f, r_p, r_{\neg p}, r_q, r_{\neg q}, \delta, \Omega)$ as follows. We assume S^1 and T^1 are disjoint and let R^1 be their union; similarly we assume that S^1 and T^2 are disjoint and let R^2 be their union. Set $\mathbf{r}_I = \mathbf{s}_I$, $\mathbf{r}_f = \mathbf{t}_f$, and $r_p = s_p, r_{\neg p} = s_{\neg p}, r_q = s_q, r_{\neg q} = s_{\neg q}$.
  Let $\Omega(r) = \Omega_\mathbf{S}(r)$ for $r \in S^1 \cup S^2$, $\Omega(r) = \Omega_\mathbf{T}(r)$ for $r \in T^1 \cup T^2$. Finally the transition function $\delta(r)$ for $r \in R^1 \cup R^2$, is defined as follows:

$$\delta(r) = \begin{cases} \delta_1(r) & \text{if } r \in S^1 \cup S^2 - \{s_f^1, s_f^2\}, \\ \delta_2(r) & \text{if } r \in T^1 \cup T^2, \\ t_I^1 & \text{if } r = s_f^1, \\ t_I^2 & \text{if } r = s_f^2. \end{cases}$$

and for each formula $\delta(r)$, we replace each instance of s_p or t_p by r_p, similarly s_q or t_q are replaced by r_q, $s_{\neg p}$ or $t_{\neg p}$ are replaced by $r_{\neg p}$ and $s_{\neg q}$ or $t_{\neg q}$ are replaced by $r_{\neg q}$.

- (Inductive case: $\pi = \pi_1 \cup \pi_2$) Again we assume that we have already defined the DATA's
  $\mathcal{D}\langle\pi_1\rangle^- p\mathcal{U}q = (\mathbf{S}, \mathbf{s}_I, \mathbf{s}_f, s_p, s_{\neg p}, s_q, s_{\neg q}, \delta_\mathbf{S}, \Omega_\mathbf{S}), \mathcal{D}\langle\pi_2\rangle^- p\mathcal{U}q = (\mathbf{T}, \mathbf{t}_I, \mathbf{t}_f, t_p, t_{\neg p},$

$t_q, t_{\neg q}, \delta_{\mathbf{T}}, \Omega_{\mathbf{T}})$. Then we can construct $\mathcal{D}\langle\pi_1 \cup \pi_2\rangle^- p\mathcal{U}q = (\mathbf{R}, \mathbf{r}_I, \mathbf{r}_f, r_p, r_{\neg p}, r_q, r_{\neg q}, \delta, \Omega)$ as follows. We assume S^1 and T^1 are disjoint and set R^1 to be their union with two new states r_1 and r_2; and let R^2 be the disjoint union of S^2 and T^2 with two new states r_3 and r_4. We set $\mathbf{r}_I = (r_1, r_3)$, and $\mathbf{r}_f = (r_2, r_4)$. We set $\Omega(r_1), \Omega(r_2), \Omega(r_3), \Omega(r_4)$ to be 1, the rest of the states as above. The transition function $\delta(r)$ for $r \in R^1 \cup R^2$, is defined as follows:

$$\delta(r) = \begin{cases} \delta_1(r) & \text{if } r \in S^1 \cup S^2 - \{s_f^1, s_f^2\}, \\ \delta_2(r) & \text{if } r \in T^1 \cup T^2 - \{t_f^1, t_f^2\}, \\ r_f^1 & \text{if } r = s_f^1 \text{ or } r = s_f^2, \\ (r_q \wedge r_I^2) \vee (r_p \wedge r_{\neg q} \wedge (s_I^1 \vee t_I^1)) & \text{if } r = r_I^1, \\ 1 & \text{if } r = r_f^1, \\ r_f^2 & \text{if } r = s_f^2 \text{ or } r = t_f^2, \\ s_I^2 \vee t_I^2 & \text{if } r = r_I^2, \\ 1 & \text{if } r = r_f^2, \end{cases}$$

and for each formula $\delta(r)$, we replace each instance of s_p or t_p by r_p, similarly s_q or t_q are replaced by r_q, $s_{\neg p}$ or $t_{\neg p}$ are replaced by $r_{\neg p}$ and $s_{\neg q}$ or $t_{\neg q}$ are replaced by $r_{\neg q}$.

- (Inductive case: $\pi = \pi_1^*$) We assume that we have already defined the DATA $\mathcal{D}\langle\pi_1\rangle^- p\mathcal{U}q = (\mathbf{S}, \mathbf{s}_I, \mathbf{s}_f, s_p, s_{\neg p}, s_q, s_{\neg q}, \delta_S, \Omega_S)$ for the regular expression π_1. Then we can construct $\mathcal{D}\langle\pi_1^*\rangle^- p\mathcal{U}q = (\mathbf{R}, \mathbf{r}_I, \mathbf{r}_f, r_p, r_{\neg p}, r_q, r_{\neg q}, \delta, \Omega)$ as follows. We let R^1 be the disjoint union of S^1 with two new states r_1 and r_2, and R^2 be the disjoint union of S^2 with two new states r_3 and r_4. We set $\mathbf{r}_I = (r_1, r_3)$ and $\mathbf{r}_f = (r_3, r_4)$. We set $\Omega(r_1), \Omega(r_2), \Omega(r_3), \Omega(r_4)$ to be 1 and $\Omega(s_f^1) = \Omega(s_f^2) = 2$ and the rest as above. The transition function $\delta(r)$ for $r \in R^1 \cup R^2$, is defined as follows:

$$\delta(r) = \begin{cases} \delta_1(r) & \text{if } r \in S^1 \cup S^2 - \{r_I^1, r_I^2\} \\ (r_q \wedge r_I^2) \vee (r_p \wedge r_{\neg q} \wedge (s_I^1 \vee r_f^1)) & \text{if } r = r_I^1, \\ s_I^1 \vee r_f^1 & \text{if } r = s_f^1, \\ 1 & \text{if } r = r_f^1, \\ s_I^2 \vee r_f^2 & \text{if } r = r_I^2 \text{ or } r = s_f^2, \\ 1 & \text{if } r = r_f^2. \end{cases}$$

and for each formula $\delta(r)$, we replace each instance of s_p or t_p by r_p, similarly s_q or t_q are replaced by r_q, $s_{\neg p}$ or $t_{\neg p}$ are replaced by $r_{\neg p}$ and $s_{\neg q}$ or $t_{\neg q}$ are replaced by $r_{\neg q}$.

Lemma 2 *Let $\mathcal{D}\langle\pi\rangle p\mathcal{U}q\mathcal{T}r = (S, s_I, s_p, s_{\neg p}, s_q, s_{\neg q}, s_r, \delta, \Omega)$ be a DATA, where $p, q, r \in \Phi$, and $(\mathfrak{M}, w)$ be a pointed Kripke structure with $w_0 = w$ then: $(\mathfrak{M}, w_0) \Vdash \langle\pi\rangle p\mathcal{U}q\mathcal{T}r$ if and only if $(\mathfrak{M}, w_0) \in \|\mathcal{D}\langle\pi\rangle p\mathcal{U}q\mathcal{T}r\|$.*

3.3. The Translation of RPTL into Alternating Tree Automata

In the following definition and two propositions we work with the ATA's $\mathcal{A}^1 = (S^1, s_I^1, \delta^1, \Omega^1)$ and $\mathcal{A}^2 = (S^2, s_I^2, \delta^2, \Omega^2)$.

Definition 7 *We define the ATA $\mathcal{A}^1 \cdot \mathcal{A}^2 = (S^1 \cup S^2 \cup \{s_I\}, s_I, \delta, \Omega)$, where s_I is a new state, $\delta(s_I) = s_I^1 \wedge s_I^2$, and $\Omega(s_I) = 1$, and $\Omega(s_1) = \Omega^1(s)$ for $s \in S^1$, $\Omega(s) = \Omega^2(s)$ for $s \in S^2$. We can similarly define $\mathcal{A}^1 + \mathcal{A}^2 = (S^1 \cup S^2 \cup \{s_I\}, s_I, \delta, \Omega)$, where s_I is a new* state, $\delta(s_I) = s_I^1 \vee s_I^2$, and $\Omega(s_I) = 1$, and $\Omega(s_1) = \Omega^1(s)$ for $s \in S^1$, $\Omega(s) = \Omega^2(s)$ for $s \in S^2$.

Proposition 2 *For any pointed Kripke Structure* $(\mathfrak{M}, w)$ *where* $\mathfrak{M} = (W, \tau, \kappa)$ $(\mathfrak{M}, w) \in \|\mathcal{A}^1 \cdot \mathcal{A}^2\|$ *if and only if* $(\mathfrak{M}, w) \in \|\mathcal{A}^1\|$ *and* $(\mathfrak{M}, w) \in \|\mathcal{A}^2\|$ *and* $(\mathfrak{M}, w) \in \|\mathcal{A}^1 + \mathcal{A}^2\|$ *if and only if* $(\mathfrak{M}, w) \in \|\mathcal{A}^1\|$ *or* $(\mathfrak{M}, w) \in \|\mathcal{A}^2\|$.

Definition 8 *We define $\mathcal{A}(\phi)$ inductively for any RPTL formula ϕ as follows (for this definition we assume that we can define $\mathcal{N}(\chi)$ for any formula χ of RPTL of lower complexity than ϕ where $\mathcal{N}$ is defined below):* $\mathcal{A}(p) = (\{s\}, s, \delta, \Omega)$ *where* $\delta(s) = p, \Omega(s) = 1$; *for* $\phi = \neg \psi$ *)* $\mathcal{A}(\phi) = \mathcal{N}(\psi)$ *where $\mathcal{N}(\psi)$ is defined below; for* $\phi = \psi_1 \wedge \psi_2$*)* $\mathcal{A}(\phi) = \mathcal{A}(\psi_1) \cdot \mathcal{A}(\psi_2)$. *For the inductive case:* $\phi = [\![\pi]\!]\psi_1 \mathcal{U} \psi_2 \mathcal{T} \psi_3$ *we have the following definition*

By induction that we already have $\mathcal{A}(\psi_1) = (S^{\psi_1}, s_I^{\psi_1}, \delta^{\psi_1}, \Omega^{\psi_1})$, $\mathcal{A}(\psi_2) = (S^{\psi_2}, s_I^{\psi_2}, \delta^{\psi_2}, \Omega^{\psi_1})$, and $\mathcal{A}(\psi_3) = (S^{\psi_3}, s_I^{\psi_3}, \delta^{\psi_3}, \Omega^{\psi_3})$, and by assumption we have $\mathcal{N}(\psi_1) = (S^{\neg\psi_1}, s_I^{\neg\psi_1}, \delta^{\neg\psi_1}, \Omega^{\neg\psi_1})$, $\mathcal{N}(\psi_2) = (S^{\neg\psi_2}, s_I^{\neg\psi_2}, \delta^{\neg\psi_2}, \Omega^{\neg\psi_2})$. But as we saw above we can also define the ATA $\mathcal{D}[\![\pi]\!]p\mathcal{U}q\mathcal{T}r = (S', s_I', s_p', s_{\neg p}, s_q', s_{\neg q}, s_f', \delta', \Omega')$, where p, q and r can be any triple of distinct propositional variables not in ϕ (it doesn't matter which distinct triple we choose the resulting DATAs will be isomorphic to each other). We assume that $S^{\psi_i}, S^{\neg \psi_i}$, and S' are disjoint. Then $\mathcal{A}([\![\pi]\!]\psi_1 \mathcal{U}\psi_2 \mathcal{T}\psi_3) = (S^{\phi_1} \cup S^{\phi_2} \cup S^{\phi_3} \cup S^{\neg\phi_1} \cup S^{\neg\phi_2} \cup S', s_I', \delta, \Omega)$ where $\Omega(s) = \Omega^{\phi_i}(s)$ for $s \in S^{\phi_i}$, $\Omega(s) = \Omega^{\neg\phi_i}(s)$ for $s \in S^{\phi_i}$ and $\Omega(s) = \Omega'(s)$ for $s \in S'$. The transition function δ is defined as follows:

- $\delta(s) = \delta^{\neg\psi_i}(s)$ if $s \in S^{\neg\psi_i}$ where $i \in \{1, 2, 3\}$
- $\delta(s) = \delta^{\neg\psi_i}(s)$ if $s \in S^{\neg\psi_i}$ where $i \in \{1, 2\}$
- $\delta'(s) = \delta'(s)$ if $s \in S' - \{s_p', s_{\neg p}', s_q', s_{\neg q}', s_f'\}$
- $\delta(s) = s_I^{\psi_1}$ if $s = s_p'$ and $\delta(s) = s_I^{\neg\psi_1}$ if $s = s_{\neg p}'$
- $\delta(s) = s_I^{\psi_2}$ if $s = s_q'$ and $\delta(s) = s_I^{\neg\psi_2}$ if $s = s_{\neg q}'$
- $\delta(s) = s_I^{\psi_3}$ if $s = s_f'$

Definition 9 *We can define $\mathcal{N}(\phi)$ for any RPTL formula ϕ (under the assumption that we can define $\mathcal{A}(\chi)$ for any formula χ of RPTL of lower complexity than ϕ) making the following changes to the above definition:* $\mathcal{N}(p) = (\{s\}, s, \delta, \Omega)$ *where* $\delta(s) = \neg p, \Omega(s) = 1$; $\mathcal{N}(\phi) = \mathcal{A}(\psi)$, *where* $\phi = \neg \psi$; $\mathcal{N}(\phi) = \mathcal{N}(\psi_1) + \mathcal{N}(\psi_2)$ *where* $\phi = \psi_1 \wedge \psi_2$. *For* $\phi = [\![\pi]\!]\psi_1 \mathcal{U}\psi_2 \mathcal{T}\psi_3$ *we have the following definition:*

By induction that we already have $\mathcal{A}(\psi_1) = (S^{\psi_1}, s_I^{\psi_1}, \delta^{\psi_1}, \Omega^{\psi_1})$, $\mathcal{A}(\psi_2) = (S^{\psi_2}, s_I^{\psi_2}, \delta^{\psi_2}, \Omega^{\psi_2})$, and by assumption we have $\mathcal{N}(\psi_1) = (S^{\neg\psi_1}, s_I^{\neg\psi_1}, \delta^{\neg\psi_1}, \Omega^{\neg\psi_1})$, $\mathcal{N}(\psi_2) = (S^{\neg\psi_2}, s_I^{\neg\psi_2}, \delta^{\neg\psi_2}, \Omega^{\neg\psi_2})$ and $\mathcal{N}(\psi_3) = (S^{\neg\psi_3}, s_I^{\neg\psi_3}, \delta^{\neg\psi_3}, \Omega^{\neg\psi_3})$. Then we define $\mathcal{N}^{\psi_1 \vee \psi_2} = \mathcal{N}(\psi_1) \cdot \mathcal{N}(\psi_2) = (S^\wedge, s_I^\wedge, \delta^\wedge, \Omega^\wedge)$ and $\mathcal{A}^{\psi_1 \vee \psi_2} = \mathcal{A}(\psi_1) + \mathcal{A}(\psi_2) = (S^\vee, s_I^\vee, \delta^\vee, \Omega^\vee)$. But as we saw above we can also define the ATA $\mathcal{D}(\!|\pi|\!)p\mathcal{U}q\mathcal{T}r = (S', s_I', s_p', s_{\neg p}, s_q', s_{\neg q}, s_f', \delta', \Omega')$, where p, q and r are a triple of distinct propositional variables not in ϕ. We assume that $S^{\psi_i}, S^{\neg\psi_i}, S^\wedge, S^\vee$ and S' are disjoint. Then $\mathcal{A}([\![\pi]\!]\psi_1 \mathcal{U}\psi_2 \mathcal{T}\psi_3) = (S^{\phi_1} \cup S^{\phi_2} \cup S^\vee \cup S^\wedge \cup S^{\neg\phi_2} \cup S^{\neg\phi_3} \cup S', s_I', \delta, \Omega)$ where $\Omega(s) = \Omega^{\phi_i}(s)$ for $s \in S^{\phi_1}, \Omega(s) = \Omega^{\neg\phi_i}(s)$ for $s \in S^{\phi_2}, \Omega(s) = \Omega^\wedge(s)$ for $s \in S^\wedge, \Omega(s) = \Omega^\vee(s)$ for $s \in S^\vee$ and $\Omega(s') = \Omega'(s')$ for $s' \in S'$. The transition function δ is defined as follows:

- $\delta(s) = \delta^{\neg \psi_i}(s)$ if $s \in S^{\neg \psi_i}$ where $i \in \{2,3\}$
- $\delta(s) = \delta^{\psi_2}(s)$ if $s \in S^{\psi_2}$
- $\delta(s) = \delta^{\wedge}(s)$ if $s \in S^{\wedge}$ and $\delta(s) = \delta^{\vee}(s)$ if $s \in S^{\vee}$,
- $\delta(s) = s_I^{\neg \psi_2}$ if $s = s'_p$ and $\delta(s) = s_I^{\psi_2}$ if $s = s'_{\neg p}$
- $\delta(s) = s_I^{\wedge}$ if $s = s'_q$ and $\delta(s) = s_I^{\vee}$ if $s = s'_{\neg q}$
- $\delta(s) = s_I^{\neg \psi_3}$ if $s = s'_f$.

We can prove the following two theorems (proofs ommited due to lack of space):

Theorem 3 *For any pointed Kripke structure $(\mathfrak{M}, w)$ where $\mathfrak{M} = (W, \tau, \kappa)$ and RPTL formula ϕ, $(\mathfrak{M}, w) \Vdash \phi$ if and only if $(\mathfrak{M}, w) \in \|\mathcal{A}(\phi)\|$*

Theorem 4 *For any pointed Kripke structure $(\mathfrak{M}, w)$ where $\mathfrak{M} = (W, \tau, \kappa)$ and RPTL formula $\neg \phi$. Given that the Theorem 3 holds for all formulae of lower complexity than ϕ we have, $(\mathfrak{M}, w) \Vdash \neg \phi$ if and only if $(\mathfrak{M}, w) \in \|\mathcal{N}(\phi)\|$*

This clearly gives us an ATA that is polynomial in the size of our original formula.

3.4. Conclusion

In this paper we have introduced a new logic RPTL and proven its decidability and in so doing have established the complexity of its satisfiability problem. However we have not yet established whether or not RPTL is actually equivalent in expressive power to PDL, i.e., whether or not RPTL can be translated into PDL. It also remains to be seen whether an axiomatisation can be found. We have also yet to explore model checking issues for RPTL.

References

[1] Natasha Alechina, Mehdi Dastani, Brian Logan, and John-Jules Ch. Meyer, 'A logic of agent programs', In *AAAI*, pp. 795–800, (2007).
[2] Ilan Beer, Shoham Ben-David, and Avner Landver, 'On-the-fly model checking of rctl formulas', In *CAV '98: Proceedings of the 10th International Conference on Computer Aided Verification*, pp. 184–194, London, UK, (1998). Springer-Verlag.
[3] Jens Claßen and Gerhard Lakemeyer, 'A logic for non-terminating golog programs', In *Principles of Knowledge Representation and Reasoning: Proceedings of the Eleventh International Conference, KR 2008, Sydney, Australia, September 16-19, 2008*, eds., Gerhard Brewka and Jérôme Lang, pp. 589–599. AAAI Press, (2008).
[4] Mads Dam, 'Ctl* and ectl* as fragments of the modal mu-calculus', *Theor. Comput. Sci.*, **126**(1), 77–96, (1994).
[5] David Harel and David Peleg, 'Process logic with regular formulas', *Theor. Comput. Sci.*, **38**, 307–322, (1985).
[6] M Y Vardi and P Wolper, 'Yet another process logic', In *Logics of Programs LNCS 164*, pp. 501–512, (1983).
[7] Moshe Y. Vardi, 'Alternating automata: Checking truth and validity for temporal logics', in *Proceedings of the 14th International Conference on Automated Deduction (CADE'97)*, ed., William McCune, volume 1249 of *Lecture Notes in Artifcial Intelligence*, pp. 191–206. Springer-Verlag, (July 1997).
[8] Thomas Wilke, 'Alternating tree automata, parity games, and modal μ-calculus', *Bull. Soc. Math. Belg.*, **8**(2), (May 2001).

Confluent Term Rewriting for Only-knowing Logics

Espen H. LIAN [a,1], Einar Broch JOHNSEN [a] and Arild WAALER [a]
[a] *Department of Informatics, University of Oslo, Norway*

Abstract. Combining term rewriting and modal logics, this paper addresses confluence and termination of rewrite systems introduced for only-knowing logics. The rewrite systems contain a rule scheme that gives rise to an infinite number of critical pairs, hence we cannot check the joinability of every critical pair directly, in order to establish local confluence. We investigate conditions that are sufficient for confluence and identify a set of rewrite rules that satisfy these conditions; however, the general confluence result makes it easier to check confluence also of stronger systems should one want additional rules. The results provide a firm logical basis for implementation of procedures that compute autoepistemic expansions.

Keywords. Nonmonotonic reasoning, Term rewriting, Only-knowing logics

1. Introduction

One way of motivating only-knowing logics is through their intended application to nonmonotonic reasoning. Although only-knowing logics have successfully been used to represent autoepistemic and default logics [14,11,21,15], the only-knowing logic addressed in this paper primarily relates to propositional autoepistemic logic, the simplest case in point. Let us, before we motivate and explain the contribution of this paper, briefly summarize autoepistemic logic and the way it is reflected in only-knowing logic.

The language of autoepistemic propositional logic is a modal language with a single belief modality B. The central notion of a stable set is defined as follows: A set Γ of autoepistemic formulae is *stable* if it is closed under propositional logic, $B\psi \in \Gamma$ for each $\psi \in \Gamma$ and $\neg B\psi \in \Gamma$ for each $\psi \notin \Gamma$. The subset of Γ consisting only of propositional formulae (i.e. formulae without modalities) is the kernel of Γ. This kernel is unique; moreover, each deductively closed set of propositional formulae is the kernel of a unique stable set.

Given an autoepistemic formula φ, the autoepistemic consequence relation determines the stable expansions of φ, i.e. stable sets that entail it and that satisfy a specific fixpoint equation. Despite the non-constructive nature of the consequence relation, there are simple algorithms [1,5,14] that for each autoepistemic formula φ compute a set of propositional formulae $\varphi_1, \ldots, \varphi_n$ such that $\text{Th}(\varphi_1), \ldots, \text{Th}(\varphi_n)$ are the kernels of all and only stable expansions of φ, where $\text{Th}(\varphi_i)$ denotes the set of propositional consequences of φ_i. We illustrate a simple algorithm on the so-called *Nixon Diamond*, a well-known example illustrating conflicting defaults.

---

[1]Corresponding Author: Espen H. Lian, E-mail: elian@ifi.uio.no

Example 1. *Assume a knowledge base* KB, *a formula of propositional logic, which entails that Nixon is both a quaker and a republican, formalized as* $q \wedge r$. *"Quakers are normally pacifists" is, when applied to Nixon, expressed as a formula* $\delta_q = (Bq \wedge \neg B \neg p) \supset p$. *It intuitively reads "If I believe that Nixon is a quaker and it is consistent with my beliefs that he is a pacifist, then he is a pacifist." "Republicans are normally not pacifists" applied to Nixon is expressed as* $\delta_r = (Br \wedge \neg Bp) \supset \neg p$. *We want to find the stable expansions of the formula* $\varphi = \text{KB} \wedge \delta_q \wedge \delta_r$.

The algorithm first identifies the modal atoms that occur as subformulae of φ: Bq, Br, Bp, $B \neg p$. *There are potentially 16 different ways in which these may be valuated, each of which is treated separately. Consider the valuation that maps* Bq, Br *and* Bp *to* true *and* $B \neg p$ *to* false. *Take the modal atoms that are valuated to true and determine the propositional consequences of these three and* φ *taken together. The result is* $Th(\text{KB} \wedge p)$, *since the* δ_q *default yields p. This is potentially the kernel of a stable expansion of* φ. *To verify that* $Th(\text{KB} \wedge p)$ *is indeed a stable expansion, we must check that* $\text{KB} \wedge p$ *entails propositions which are believed to hold (i.e.* $q \wedge r \wedge p$*) by the assumed valuation and that it does not entail any proposition that is not believed to hold (i.e.* $\neg p$*). Since both these tests go through,* $Th(\text{KB} \wedge p)$ *is the kernel of a stable expansion of* φ. *It is easy to check that* $Th(\text{KB} \wedge \neg p)$ *is the kernel of another stable expansion of* φ, *and that there are no other stable expansions.*

The algorithm for autoepistemic logic illustrated above manipulates a quite complex construction in the meta-language; enumerating potential valuations, generating consequences and checking for consistencies. It is precisely this reasoning at the meta-level underlying the algorithm, that only-knowing logics can accommodate. Only-knowing logics do not only represent this pattern of reasoning *at the object level* of the logic, they can also replace the construction in the algorithm with a *calculus*.

Example 2. *In only-knowing logic the Nixon Diamond can be represented by the formula* $O\varphi$, *expressing that* φ *is "all I know;" the formula conveys both that "I believe that* φ *holds" and that "whatever I believe is a consequence of* φ*" (the latter statement is formalized by means of a co-belief operator* C *specifically addressed in [21]). By the rules of the logic, the equivalence* $O\varphi \equiv O(\text{KB} \wedge p) \vee O(\text{KB} \wedge \neg p)$ *is a theorem. Note that the disjuncts to the right in the equivalence correspond directly to the stable expansions. The right hand side of the equivalence can be determined from the left hand side in many ways; the procedure addressed in this paper first applies a so-called expand rule and then collapse rules and structural rules. The expand rule can be viewed as a rule that successively builds up valuations of the sort addressed in Example 1. The expand rule will, e.g., map the modal atom* Bq *in* $O\varphi$ *to either* $\top$ *or* $\bot$:

$$O\varphi \to (O\varphi\langle Bq/\top\rangle \wedge Bq) \vee (O\varphi\langle Bq/\bot\rangle \wedge \neg Bq).$$

Here $O\varphi\langle Bq/v\rangle$ *evaluates to* $O(\text{KB} \wedge ((v \wedge \neg B \neg p) \supset p) \wedge \delta_r)$. *We can apply a distribution rule, expand wrt. the remaining modal atoms, and simplify the result to get a formula on DNF, in which one of the 16 disjuncts (corresponding to the potential kernels of stable expansions identified by the procedure in Example 1) is:*

$$O(\text{KB} \wedge p) \wedge Bq \wedge \neg B \neg p \wedge Bp \wedge Br.$$

A consistency check is now implemented using collapse rules (cf. Section 5), in this case leading to $O(\text{KB} \wedge p)$; the collapse rules reduce an O-formula and a modal atom to either the O-formula itself or to $\bot$ (most of the disjuncts in this example reduce to $\bot$). In the end we get a formula with two consistent disjuncts: $O(\text{KB} \wedge p) \vee O(\text{KB} \wedge \neg p)$.

The Modal Reduction Theorem [21] states that for each formula φ, there exists propositional formulae $\psi_1, \ldots, \psi_n$ such that $O\varphi \equiv O\psi_1 \vee \cdots \vee O\psi_n$ is provable, where each $O\psi_i$ has an essentially unique model that corresponds to a stable expansion (it forms a complete theory over the subjective, i.e. completely modalized, fragment of the language). Hence, the theorem guarantees that one can reduce $O\varphi$, representing an autoepistemic theory, to a formula of a form which directly exhibits its models. Note that the validity of the equivalence in the Modal Reduction Theorem shows that only-knowing logic is in itself strong enough to accommodate the reasoning used to determine stable expansions in autoepistemic logic. Also note that only-knowing logics are, in contrast to autoepistemic logic, in themselves monotonic; it is the arguments to O-modalities that exhibit nonmonotonic behaviour. Being normal systems of modal logic they have a standard Kripke semantics that in particular provides autoepistemic logic with increased conceptual clarity compared to its original fixpoint definition of expansions, not least because only-knowing systems sharply separate object-language features from meta-concepts.

Whereas the Modal Reduction Theorem gives an abstract characterization of the expressivity of only-knowing logic, the aim of this paper is to provide a bridge to the design and implementation of procedures for computing expansions. In [21] the Modal Reduction Theorem is proved using a set of equivalence-preserving rewrite rules, providing an easy-to-use calculus for reducing $O\varphi$ to $O\psi_1 \vee \cdots \vee O\psi_n$; we shall refer to the latter as the *canonical form* of the former. Compared to more high-level (pseudo-code) algorithmic specifications, like the one in Example 1, rewrite systems are easier to reason about and may be implemented more directly, for instance using the rewriting logic tool Maude [3]. To pave the way for such principled and high-level approaches to implementation we shall in this paper focus on *conditions for the design of confluent rewrite calculi for only-knowing logics*.

The algorithm in Example 1 is reminiscent of a truth table method for checking propositional satisfiability: list all potential models and check each of them in separation. Clearly, one can do much better, but using the framework of autoepistemic logic the correctness of the algorithm must be checked for each optimization. Adding rules to a confluent system is easier to deal with; all we have to do is to check that confluence is preserved. Once this is done, we get the flexibility to modify search procedures for free. The confluence results in this paper provide a firm logical basis for the implementation of procedures that compute autoepistemic expansions which will, we believe, facilitate the study and comparison of different search strategies. No results like the ones presented in this paper have, to our knowledge, previously been established for a logic that supports nonmonotonic patterns of reasoning.

For standard systems of rewriting modulo an equivalence relation, confluence is proved using the following line of argument:

(i) Local confluence follows from joinability of all critical pairs.
(ii) Confluence follows from local confluence, local coherence with the equivalence relation, and termination.

Hence, one has to check joinability of critical pairs, local coherence and termination; in many cases these follow straightforwardly using standard techniques. The expand rule, illustrated in Example 2, is in fact a rule *scheme* that gives rise to an infinite number of critical pairs, hence we need a systematic method to establish the joinability of every critical pair.

The collapse rules are expensive as they are preconditioned by SAT (propositional satisfiability) tests, a fact which efficient strategies must deal with. The proof of the Modal Reduction Theorem based on formula rewriting uses just the set of rewrite rules that is needed to establish the theorem. The canonical form of an only-knowing formula is derived by first generating a large DNF formula in which each disjunct corresponds to a potential model, and then reducing each disjunct either to $\bot$ or to a satisfiable only-knowing formula. This rule set consists of modal rules and two propositional structural rules: a distribution rule and a contradiction rule. From a computational perspective it is clearly desirable to have more simplification rules at hand, to avoid having to generate the large DNF formula upfront.

What we need is hence not just one confluent system for only-knowing logic, but a systematic method, that can be used to check confluence of rewrite systems with the expand rule. A result of this kind is not straightforward to establish. In Section 4 we suggest a solution by introducing a system R_{Min} and a natural condition that establishes that critical pairs stemming from the use of the expand rule are joinable. In Section 5 we prove that the original rewrite system in [21] equipped with some extra structural rules is indeed confluent.

2. Only-knowing Logic

The only-knowing language we address in this paper slightly generalizes the language discussed in Section 1 in that it is parameterized by an index set I partially ordered by a relation $\preccurlyeq$. Intuitively each index in I denotes a confidence layer of an agent. Relative to each confidence layer, there are the modal operators B_k (belief), C_k (co-belief) and O_k (exact belief). Atomic formula consist of the truth constants $\top$ and $\bot$, and a set $\{p_i\}_{i \geqslant 1}$ of *propositional letters*; we will sometimes write p, q and r for p_1, p_2, and p_3. Formulae are constructed as follows.

$$\varphi, \psi \longrightarrow \top \mid \bot \mid p_i \mid \neg\varphi \mid \varphi \wedge \psi \mid \varphi \vee \psi \mid B_k\varphi \mid C_k\varphi \mid O_k\varphi$$

for all $k \in I$, where I is a finite index set. A formula of the form $B_k\varphi$ or $C_k\varphi$ is called a *modal atom*. A modal *literal* is a modal atom or its negation. We say that a formula with an occurrence of O_k is *tainted*; the reason for discriminating against tainted formulae has to do with confluence issues. A formula is *subjective* if every propositional letter is within the scope of a modal operator. A subjective formula is *prime* if it contains no nested modalities. A formula without any occurrence of a modal operator is called *objective*. A formula is *constant* if it is a Boolean combination of the truth constants. Note that a constant formula is both subjective and objective; subjective because it contains no propositional letters and objective because it contains no modalities. The sets $\mathrm{mod}(\varphi)$ and $\mathrm{pmod}(\varphi)$ consist of the modal atoms and prime modal atoms, resp., occurring in φ.

For further motivation, axiomatization and semantics of the only-knowing logic, cf. [21]. Of special interest are formulae of the form $\bigwedge_{k \in I} O_k \varphi_k$, called O_I-*blocks*. O_I-

blocks intuitively represent the belief state of an agent relative to each confidence level in the index set I. Let $\varphi = \bigwedge_{k \in I} O_k \varphi_k$ and $\psi = \bigwedge_{k \in I} O_k \psi_k$ be two prime O_I-blocks. φ is *cumulative* if $i \prec j$ implies that $\varphi_j \supset \varphi_i$ is a tautology, i.e. that $\{\neg \varphi_i, \varphi_j\}$ is unsatisfiable. Cumulativity reflects the intuition behind the partial order $\prec$ on I. φ and ψ are *independent* if there is an $i \in I$ such that $\varphi_i \equiv \psi_i$ is not a tautology.

A fundamental result in only-knowing logic, the Modal Reduction Theorem (MRT) [21], states that any O_I-block φ is equivalent to a disjunction of prime O_I-blocks $\mu_1 \vee \cdots \vee \mu_n$ for some $n \geq 0$ such that each μ_k is cumulative. Such a disjunction is on *canonical form* if every pair of disjuncts μ_i and μ_j for $i \neq j$ is independent; observe that the empty disjunction $\bot$ is on canonical form. One goal in this paper is to present a confluent rewrite system where the normal form of O_I-blocks is canonical.

As explained in Section 1, the rewrite procedure is based on substituting truth constants for modal atoms. To this end we need some terminology about substitutions. *Bindings* $a, b, c, \ldots$ are ordered pairs $\langle \beta / v \rangle$ such that β is a prime modal atom and v a truth constant. We view a binding $\langle \beta / v \rangle$ as a function that maps (or *binds*) β to v, that is $\beta \langle \beta / v \rangle = v$ using postfix notation. Bindings are extended to arbitrary formulae in the usual way. A *modal substitution* (henceforth just *substitution*, not to be confused with the ground substitutions in Section 3) is a sequence over some set of bindings; the *empty substitution* is written ε. If σ and τ are sequences, the *concatenation* of σ and τ is denoted $\sigma \cdot \tau$ or simply $\sigma \tau$. We let $\varphi(a\sigma) = (\varphi a)\sigma$ for any substitution $a\sigma$. For the sake of simplicity, we define the complement operation on truth constants: $\overline{\top} = \bot$ and $\overline{\bot} = \top$. Observe that bindings are in general not commutative (and not idempotent): If we let $b = \langle Lv/\overline{v} \rangle$ and $c = \langle L\overline{v}/v \rangle$, then $(LLv)bc = v$, while $(LLv)cb = L\overline{v}$. A set of bindings is *consistent* if no subset is of the form $\{\langle \beta/\top \rangle, \langle \beta/\bot \rangle\}$; a *modal valuation* is a consistent set of bindings. We may view a modal valuation V as a function from prime modal atoms to truth constants, hence we may refer to the *domain* of V: $\mathrm{dom}(V) = \{\beta \mid \langle \beta/v \rangle \in V\}$. A straightforward generalization of Lemma 31 in [21] is:

Lemma 3. *If σ and τ are substitutions over a modal valuation V such that $\varphi\sigma$ and $\varphi\tau$ are without occurrences from $\mathrm{dom}(V)$, then $\varphi\sigma = \varphi\tau$.*

We will assume that no formula has nested Os, equivalently that $O_k \varphi$ is a formula iff φ is not tainted, as this complicates the confluence argument unnecessarily. However, this assumption does not decrease expressibility, as any formula $O_k \varphi$ is equivalent to $B_k \varphi \wedge C_k \neg \varphi$, which may occur freely. Hence to express, e.g., $O_1 O_2 p$, we must write $O_1 (B_2 p \wedge C_2 \neg p)$.

3. Order-Sorted Term Rewriting

We want to capture the MRT with a rewrite theory, i.e. we want a rule set R such that for any O_I-block φ, there is a μ on canonical form such that $\varphi \twoheadrightarrow_R \mu$. Additionally, we want this rule set to be confluent.

3.1. General Notions

Cf. [2,17] for details on standard definitions and results. Let Σ be a set of function symbols of given sorts – partially ordered by a subsort relation – and arities, X an unbounded set of variables disjoint from Σ, and denote by T the term algebra over the function symbols Σ and variables X. For a term $\varphi \in T$ and ground substitution θ, we denote by $\theta\varphi$ the application of θ to φ (resulting in a ground term without variables). The set $\mathcal{P}os(\varphi)$ of *positions* and the set $\mathcal{V}ar(\varphi)$ of *variables* in φ are defined in the standard way [2]. Denote by $\varphi|_p$ the subterm of φ at position p and by $\varphi[\psi]_p$ the term φ in which ψ replaces the subterm at position p.

Let R be a set rewrite rules $l \to r$ where $l, r \in T$. We conventionally refer to the *left hand side* l of a rule $l \to r$ as the LHS, and to the *right hand side* r as RHS, and call an instance of a LHS a *redex*. A term φ *reduces* to ψ, written $\varphi \to_R \psi$, if there exists $l \to r \in R$, $p \in \mathcal{P}os(\varphi)$, and $\theta \in Sub(\Sigma)$ such that $\varphi|_p = \theta l$ and $\psi = \varphi[\theta r]_p$. The reflexive transitive closure of $\to_R$ is denoted $\twoheadrightarrow_R$. If the rule set is clear from the context, we simply write $\to$ and $\twoheadrightarrow$. A term φ is on *normal form* if there is no ψ such that $\varphi \to \psi$.

Let AC be a set of equations specifying associativity and commutativity of conjunction and disjunction, and let $\to_{AC}$ denote the rewrite system derived by orienting each equation $l = r \in AC$ as a rule $l \to r$. We write $\varphi \leftrightarrow_{AC} \psi$ if $\varphi \to_{AC} \psi$ or $\psi \to_{AC} \varphi$, while $=_{AC}$ denotes the reflexive transitive closure of $\leftrightarrow_{AC}$. For terms φ and ψ, we write $\varphi \to_{R/AC} \psi$ if there are terms μ and ν such that $\varphi =_{AC} \mu \to_R \nu =_{AC} \psi$. We will simply write R for R/AC throughout. Following [4], R is *terminating* if there is no infinite sequence of the form $\varphi_1 \to_R \varphi_2 =_{AC} \varphi_3 \to_R \varphi_4 =_{AC} \varphi_5 \to_R \cdots$. We say that φ and ψ are *R-joinable*, denoted $\varphi \downarrow_R \psi$, if there are terms μ and ν such that $\varphi \twoheadrightarrow_R \mu =_{AC} \nu \twoheadleftarrow_R \psi$. Furthermore, R is *locally confluent* if $\mu \leftarrow_R \varphi \to_R \nu$ implies $\mu \downarrow_R \nu$; R is *locally coherent with AC* if $\mu \leftarrow_R \varphi \leftrightarrow_{AC} \nu$ implies $\mu \downarrow_R \nu$; and R is *confluent* if $\mu \twoheadleftarrow_R \varphi \twoheadrightarrow_R \nu$ implies $\mu \downarrow_R \nu$.

Lemma 4 ([4,9,10]). *R is confluent if it is terminating, locally confluent and locally coherent with AC.*

If $l \to r$ and $l' \to r'$ are variable-renamed rules such that $\mathcal{V}ar(l,r) \cap \mathcal{V}ar(l',r') = \emptyset$, p is a non-variable position of l, and θ is a most general unifier of $(l|_p, l')$, then $(\theta r_1, (\theta l)[\theta r_2]_p)$ is called a *critical pair* [2].

Critical Pair Lemma ([2,9,18]). *R is locally confluent iff all its critical pairs are joinable.*

3.2. An Order-Sorted Equational Specification

We define a term algebra for the language of only-knowing formulae. It consists of the following sorts: Fml, Subj, Obj, PMA, PML, Const, At and Bool. Let Bool $= \{\top, \bot\}$, and let At be the set of propositional letters. Terms are constructed as follows. Each sort in the upper diamond-shaped part of the subsort hierarchy (Figure 1) is closed under the Boolean connectives, i.e. $\vee, \wedge : X \times X \Rightarrow X$ and $\neg : X \Rightarrow X$ for $X \in \{\text{Fml}, \text{Subj}, \text{Obj}, \text{Const}\}$. Negating a prime modal atom constructs a prime modal literal: $\neg : \text{PMA} \Rightarrow \text{PML}$. We conventionally use infix notation for the connectives and write the index of the modal operators as subscripts, e.g., $O_k\varphi$ for $O(k, \varphi)$. Prefixing an objective formula with B_k or C_k constructs a prime modal atom: $B, C : I \times \text{Obj} \Rightarrow$ PMA; prefixing a general formula with O_k, B_k or C_k constructs a a subjective formula: $O, B, C : I \times \text{Fml} \Rightarrow$ Subj. It is easy to see that the sorts capture the syntax of the only-knowing logic correctly, e.g., Subj corresponds the set of subjective formulae, as it comprises prime modal literals and constant formulae, and is closed under boolean connectives. The correspondence between sorts and fragments of the logical language is listed in Figure 1.

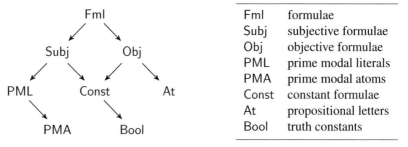

Figure 1. The subsort hierarchy and intended meaning of the sorts.

4. Confluence of Rewrite Systems with the Expand Rule

As we have seen, the rewriting procedure is based on uniformly substituting a truth constant for every occurrence of some prime modal atom β in a formula φ, using the expand rule, which is actually a rule scheme, and as such gives rise to an infinite number of rules. The *expand rule (scheme)* is defined as

$$O_i\varphi \rightarrow_E (O_i\varphi\langle\beta/\top\rangle \wedge \beta) \vee (O_i\varphi\langle\beta/\bot\rangle \wedge \neg\beta) \text{ if } \beta \in \text{pmod}(\varphi).$$

The problem with the expand rule is that it is the source of an infinite number of critical pairs. Hence we need a systematic way to show that critical pairs stemming from the use of the expand rule are joinable. In the rest of this section we investigate the relationship (wrt. joinability) between the expand rule and the *structural rules* in Figure 2. We consider several rule sets with different properties; not all will capture the MRT. All contain the expand rule and additional rules are either a structural rule or the *collapse rules* (Figure 4) introduced in Section 5. The rule set consisting of all of these rules is denoted R_{Only}.

4.1. Permutable Expandability

For $\alpha_1, \ldots, \alpha_n \in \text{PMA}$, let $e(O_i\varphi, \alpha_1, \ldots, \alpha_n)$ be shorthand for

$$\bigvee_{\vec{u}\in\text{Bool}^n} (O_i\varphi\langle\alpha_1/u_1\rangle \cdots \langle\alpha_n/u_n\rangle \wedge \bigwedge_{1\leqslant k\leqslant n} \alpha_k(u_k)),$$

where $\vec{u} = (u_1, \ldots, u_n)$. Using this notation, the expand rule can be written as

$$O_i\varphi \rightarrow_E e(O_i\varphi, \alpha) \text{ if } \alpha \in \text{pmod}(\varphi),$$

in which case we say that $O_i\varphi$ is *expanded* wrt. α. A rule set R satisfies *permutable expandability* if $e(O_i\varphi, \alpha) \downarrow_R e(O_i\varphi, \beta)$ for any $\alpha, \beta \in \text{pmod}(\varphi)$; i.e. if $O_i\varphi$ can be expanded both wrt. α and β, the resulting reducts are joinable. Any rule set containing the expand rule must satisfy this property in order to be confluent. The rule set consisting of just the expand rule, does not satisfy permutable expandability, hence we are interested in stronger systems that do. A minimal (in the sense that we need every rule except A1 to show Lemma 5 below, while A1 is needed to prove Lemma 8) rule set with this property is $R_{\mathsf{Min}} = \{\mathsf{E}, \mathsf{Dt}, \mathsf{Dm}, \mathsf{J}\vee, \mathsf{I}\wedge, \mathsf{Kn}, \mathsf{A1}\}$.

Distribution		$(\psi_1 \vee \psi_2) \wedge \eta \to_{\mathsf{Dt}} (\psi_1 \wedge \eta) \vee (\psi_2 \wedge \eta)$		
Absorption 1		$(\varphi \wedge \beta) \vee (\varphi \wedge \overline{\beta}) \to_{\mathsf{A1}} \varphi$		
Absorption 2		$(\varphi \wedge \beta) \vee (\varphi \wedge \overline{\beta} \wedge \eta) \to_{\mathsf{A2}} (\varphi \wedge \beta) \vee (\varphi \wedge \eta)$		
Absorption 3		$\varphi \vee (\varphi \wedge \eta) \to_{\mathsf{A3}} \varphi$		
Identity of $\wedge$	$\psi \wedge \top \to_{\mathsf{J}\wedge} \psi$		Domination	$\psi \wedge \bot \to_{\mathsf{Dm}} \bot$
Identity of $\vee$	$\psi \vee \bot \to_{\mathsf{J}\vee} \psi$		Contradiction	$\beta \wedge \overline{\beta} \to_{\mathsf{Kn}} \bot$
Idempotency of $\vee$	$\psi \vee \psi \to_{\mathsf{I}\vee} \psi$		Complement of $\top$	$\neg \top \to_{\mathsf{Co}} \bot$
Idempotency of $\wedge$	$\beta \wedge \beta \to_{\mathsf{I}\wedge} \beta$		Complement of $\bot$	$\neg \bot \to_{\mathsf{Co}} \top$

Figure 2. The structural rules. $\psi_1, \psi_2, \psi, \eta \in \mathsf{Subj}$, $\beta \in \mathsf{PML}$, φ is of the form $O_i\mu$ or $O_i\mu \wedge \psi$, and η must be untainted. $\overline{\beta}$ denotes the complement of β, i.e. $\overline{L\psi} = \neg L\psi$ and $\overline{\neg L\psi} = L\psi$. A1, A2 and A3 are called *the absorption rules*.

Repeated application of first the expand rule and then the distribution rule aggregates conjunctions of prime modal atoms. Since we rewrite modulo AC, a conjunction of prime modal literals can be viewed as a multiset. With the aid of the structural rules, such a conjunction can be reduced to a form which corresponds to a consistent set: $\mathsf{I}\wedge$ removes duplicates and Kn/Dm reduce it to the empty disjunction $\bot$ if inconsistent. The following notation is useful for further characterizing conjunctions of prime modal atoms. Let V be a (possibly inconsistent) set of bindings. Define $\phi(V) = \bigwedge\{\beta(v) \mid \langle \beta/v \rangle \in V\}$, where $\beta(\top)$ and $\beta(\bot)$ denote β and $\neg\beta$ resp.

Lemma 5. $O_i\varphi \wedge \phi(V) \twoheadrightarrow_{R_{\mathsf{Min}}} O_i\varphi\sigma \wedge \phi(V)$ *for every substitution σ over V.*

Proof. By induction on the length of σ. The basis step, where $\sigma = \varepsilon$, is trivial. Let σ be some substitution over V, and assume for the induction hypothesis that $O_i\varphi \wedge \phi(V) \twoheadrightarrow_{R_{\mathsf{Min}}} O_i\varphi\sigma \wedge \phi(V)$. Let $\langle \beta/v \rangle \in V$. Then $\phi(V) \wedge \beta(v) \twoheadrightarrow_{R_{\mathsf{Min}}} \phi(V)$ by $\mathsf{I}\wedge$ and $\phi(V) \wedge \beta(\overline{v}) \twoheadrightarrow_{R_{\mathsf{Min}}} \bot$ by Kn and Dm. If $\beta \notin \mathrm{pmod}(\varphi\sigma)$, then $\varphi\sigma\langle \beta/v \rangle = \varphi\sigma$. If $\beta \in \mathrm{pmod}(\varphi\sigma)$, then

$$O_i\varphi\sigma \wedge \phi(V) \to_{\mathsf{E}} ((O_i\varphi\sigma\langle \beta/\top\rangle \wedge \beta) \vee (O_i\varphi\sigma\langle \beta/\bot\rangle \wedge \neg\beta)) \wedge \phi(V)$$
$$\to_{\mathsf{Dt}} (O_i\varphi\sigma\langle \beta/\top\rangle \wedge \phi(V) \wedge \beta) \vee (O_i\varphi\sigma\langle \beta/\bot\rangle \wedge \phi(V) \wedge \neg\beta)$$
$$\twoheadrightarrow_{R_{\mathsf{Min}}} O_i\varphi\sigma\langle \beta/v\rangle \wedge \phi(V) \text{ by the observations above.} \qquad \square$$

If $\alpha \in \mathrm{pmod}(\varphi)$, we may expand $O_i\varphi$ to $e(O_i\varphi, \alpha)$; if in addition $\beta \in \mathrm{pmod}(\varphi\langle\alpha/\top\rangle) \cap \mathrm{pmod}(\varphi\langle\alpha/\bot\rangle)$, we may expand each disjunct once more and apply the distribution rule:

$e(O_i\varphi, \alpha) \twoheadrightarrow_{R_{\mathsf{Min}}} e(O_i\varphi, \alpha, \beta)$. Observe that it may be the case that $\beta \notin \mathrm{pmod}(\varphi)$, and in general it is not the case that $e(O_i\varphi, \alpha, \beta) = e(O_i\varphi, \beta, \alpha)$, nor that $e(O_i\varphi, \alpha) = e(O_i\varphi, \alpha, \alpha)$. What *is* the case, though, is that $e(O_i\varphi, \alpha)$ and $e(O_i\varphi, \beta)$ are R_{Min}-joinable:

Lemma 6. *R_{Min} satisfies permutable expandability.*

Proof. Assume that $\alpha, \beta \in \mathrm{pmod}(\varphi)$, and let $\mu = e(O_i\varphi, \alpha)$ and $\nu = e(O_i\varphi, \beta)$. We show that $\mu \downarrow_{R_{\mathsf{Min}}} \nu$. If $\alpha \neq \beta$, then $\beta \in O_i\varphi\langle \alpha/u\rangle$ and $\alpha \in O_i\varphi\langle \beta/v\rangle$, thus $\mu \twoheadrightarrow_{R_{\mathsf{Min}}} e(O_i\varphi, \alpha, \beta)$ and $\nu \twoheadrightarrow_{R_{\mathsf{Min}}} e(O_i\varphi, \beta, \alpha)$. We have to show that for every u and v, if we let $a = \langle \alpha/u\rangle$ and $b = \langle \beta/v\rangle$, then $O_i\varphi ab \wedge \alpha(u) \wedge \beta(v)$ and $O_i\varphi ba \wedge \alpha(u) \wedge \beta(v)$ are joinable. One can easily construct substitutions σ and τ over $V = \{a, b\}$ – a modal valuation – such that $\varphi ab\sigma$ and $\varphi ba\tau$ are without occurrences of α and β. By Lemma 3, $O_i\varphi ab\sigma = O_i\varphi ba\tau$, and by Lemma 5, $O_i\varphi ba \wedge \phi(V) \twoheadrightarrow_{R_{\mathsf{Min}}} O_i\varphi ba\tau \wedge \phi(V)$ and $O_i\varphi ab \wedge \phi(V) \twoheadrightarrow_{R_{\mathsf{Min}}} O_i\varphi ab\sigma \wedge \phi(V)$. □

4.2. Local Confluence

A rule $l \to r$ satisfies *R-substitutional joinability* if $la \downarrow_{R \cup \{l \to r\}} ra$ whenever l is untainted, for any binding a. We use this property to show joinability when some $O_i\varphi$ is expanded and reduction is performed on some proper subformula of $O_i\varphi$. Some rules satisfy R-substitutional joinability for any R:

- The rules $l \to r$ whose LHS are tainted trivially satisfy the property. If we had allowed nested Os, we would have had to show substitutional joinability for tainted LHS, and this proves much harder than what is presently the case. And as disallowing nested Os does not reduce expressibility, we find it to be worth the sacrifice.
- The rules whose LHS and RHS are objective satisfy the property, as $la = l \to_{R \cup \{l \to r\}} r = ra$ for any R.
- The rules where the only requirement on the variables on the LHS is that they are subjective also satisfy the property, as if $x \in \mathsf{Subj}$, then $x\langle \beta/v\rangle \in \mathsf{Subj}$, hence the rule is still applicable: $la \to_{R \cup \{l \to r\}} ra$.

The only two structural rules that fall outside all three categories are I∧ and Kn. We say that a rule set R satisfies R'-substitutional joinability if every rule in R does; if $R = R'$ we simply say that R satisfies substitutional joinability. R_{Min} does *not* satisfy substitutional joinability, as neither I∧ nor Kn satisfy R_{Min}-substitutional joinability.

Lemma 7. *R_{Only} satisfies substitutional joinability.*

Proof. We show R_{Only}-substitutional joinability for I∧ and Kn. Let $\beta \in \mathsf{PMA}$.

$l \to r$	$l\langle \beta/v\rangle \twoheadrightarrow$	j	$r\langle \beta/v\rangle \twoheadrightarrow$	j
I∧	$\beta \wedge \beta\langle \beta/v\rangle = v \wedge v \to_x$	v	$\beta\langle \beta/v\rangle =$	v
I∧	$\neg\beta \wedge \neg\beta\langle \beta/v\rangle = \neg v \wedge \neg v \to_{\mathsf{Co}} \bar{v} \wedge \bar{v} \to_y \bar{v}$	$\bar{v}$	$\neg\beta\langle \beta/v\rangle = \neg v \to_{\mathsf{Co}} \bar{v}$	$\bar{v}$
Kn	$\beta \wedge \neg\beta\langle \beta/v\rangle = v \wedge \neg v \to_{\mathsf{Co}} \top \wedge \bot \to_z$	$\bot$	$\bot\langle \beta/v\rangle =$	$\bot$

j denotes the common reduct of $l\langle \beta/v\rangle$ and $r\langle \beta/v\rangle$. x, y and z are Dm or J∧, depending on v. The remaining rules satisfy R-substitutional joinability for any R. □

The following lemma gives us joinability when one of the reducts stems from an application of the expand rule, and the other satisfies substitutional joinability (see Figure 3, left).

Lemma 8. *Let $R \supseteq R_{\mathsf{Min}}$. If $O_i\varphi|_p \to_{l \to r} \omega$ for some rule $l \to r$ satisfying R-substitutional joinability, then $e(O_i\varphi, \alpha) \downarrow_{R \cup \{l \to r\}} O_i\varphi[\omega]_p$ for every $\alpha \in \mathsf{pmod}(\varphi)$.*

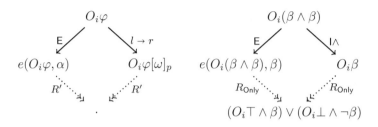

Figure 3. *Left:* Lemma 8: $R' = R \cup \{l \to r\}$-joinability of $e(O_i\varphi, \alpha)$ and $O_i\varphi[\omega]_p$ is guaranteed as long as $l \to r$ satisfies R-substitutional joinability and $R_{\mathsf{Min}} \subseteq R$. *Right:* $e(O_i(\beta \wedge \beta), \beta)$ and $O_i\beta$ are R_{Only}-joinable.

As the expand rule is the source of an infinite number of critical pairs, we have introduced the notion of substitutional joinability in order to show that all critical pairs are joinable. As long as the system contains R_{Min}, it already satisfies permutable expandability.

Theorem 9. *Any rule set R extending R_{Min} is locally confluent if it satisfies substitutional joinability and all critical pairs of $R \setminus \{\mathsf{E}\}$ are joinable.*

Proof. Any critical pair involving the expand rule is joinable by Lemma 6 (as $R_{\mathsf{Min}} \subseteq R$) and Lemma 8 (as $R_{\mathsf{Min}} \subseteq R$ and as long as substitutional joinability holds). Any critical pair not involving the expand rule is joinable by assumption. Hence R is locally confluent by the Critical Pair Lemma. □

5. A Confluent Rule Set Capturing the MRT

In the previous section we gave sufficient properties for a rule set extending R_{Min} to be locally confluent. But what we really want is a rule set that is confluent, not merely locally. By Lemma 4, such a rule set must be locally coherent with AC, which R_{Min} is not, hence we need some additional rules. R_{Min} is not even strong enough to guarantee that there is some normal form that is canonical; the rule set $R_{\mathsf{Comp}} = \{\mathsf{E, Dt, C, Dm, J}\vee\}$ is, however, as was shown in [21]. Note that R_{Comp} does not extend R_{Min}, but extends a subset of it with the collapse rules. The rule set we are primarily interested in is R_{Only}, comprising the expand rule, all of the structural rules, and the collapse rules, i.e. $R_{\mathsf{Only}} = R_{\mathsf{Min}} \cup \{\mathsf{C, I}\vee, \mathsf{A2, A3, J}\wedge, \mathsf{Co}\}$.

Lemma 10. *Any canonical formula is on normal form wrt. R_{Only}.*

Proof. The only LHS that matches a formula $\mu_1 \vee \cdots \vee \mu_n$ on canonical form is that of the very last collapse rule, i.e. $O_i\varphi \wedge O_j\psi$ for some $i \prec j$. However, its side condition requires that $\{\neg\varphi, \psi\}$ is satisfiable, but as each μ_k is cumulative, this cannot be the case. □

By Lemma 10 and the fact that R_{Only} extends R_{Comp}, R_{Only} also captures the MRT. As R_{Only} extends R_{Min}, we may use Theorem 9 to show that it is confluent. The additional rules in $R_{\text{Only}} \setminus R_{\text{Min}}$ are needed for the following reasons:

- We need the collapse rules to obtain canonical normal forms.
- Associativity of disjunction lets us apply A1 in two distinct ways to some formula (cf. Figure 5), resulting in two distinct reducts which can only be joined by applying A2.
- Now we may apply both A1 and A2 to some formula (cf. Figure 5), resulting in two distinct reducts, joinable by A3 (and A1).
- If we apply A3 to $Op \vee (Op \wedge Bp)$, and $Op \wedge Bp \to_C Op$, we obtain the two distinct reducts Op and $Op \vee Op$, joinable by I∨.
- J∧ and Co are needed to show R_{Only}-substitutional joinability.

Although the additional rules are introduced for purely technical reasons (we need A1 to show confluence in a somewhat esoteric case, and because of this, we need A2, and because of this again, we need A3), they are nonetheless useful in practice. Rules structurally similar to the absorption rules are found in [15], where they are called *simplification rules*. In Example 27 of the same paper, all three rules are used when reducing the representation of a default theory with two defaults.

$$O_i\varphi \wedge B_k\psi \to_C O_i\varphi \text{ if } i \preccurlyeq k \text{ and not SAT}(\varphi, \neg\psi)$$

$$O_i\varphi \wedge B_k\psi \to_C \bot \quad \text{ if } k \preccurlyeq i \text{ and SAT}(\varphi, \neg\psi)$$

$$O_i\varphi \wedge \neg B_k\psi \to_C \bot \quad \text{ if } i \preccurlyeq k \text{ and not SAT}(\varphi, \neg\psi)$$

$$O_i\varphi \wedge \neg B_k\psi \to_C O_i\varphi \text{ if } k \preccurlyeq i \text{ and SAT}(\varphi, \neg\psi)$$

$$O_i\varphi \wedge C_k\psi \to_C O_i\varphi \text{ if } k \preccurlyeq i \text{ and not SAT}(\neg\varphi, \neg\psi)$$

$$O_i\varphi \wedge C_k\psi \to_C \bot \quad \text{ if } i \preccurlyeq k \text{ and SAT}(\neg\varphi, \neg\psi)$$

$$O_i\varphi \wedge \neg C_k\psi \to_C \bot \quad \text{ if } k \preccurlyeq i \text{ and not SAT}(\neg\varphi, \neg\psi)$$

$$O_i\varphi \wedge \neg C_k\psi \to_C O_i\varphi \text{ if } i \preccurlyeq k \text{ and SAT}(\neg\varphi, \neg\psi)$$

$$O_i\varphi \wedge O_k\psi \to_C \bot \quad \text{ if } i \preccurlyeq k \text{ and SAT}(\neg\varphi, \psi)$$

Figure 4. The collapse rules. $\varphi, \psi \in$ Obj and SAT : Obj × Obj $\Rightarrow$ Bool. We assume that SAT(φ, ψ) reduces to *true* iff $\{\varphi, \psi\}$ is propositionally satisfiable.

In order to obtain confluence, the structural rules are restricted by requiring that variables are of a more specific sort than Fml. Consider $(Op \wedge Bp) \vee (Op \wedge \neg Bp) \to Op$, which is a typical instance of A1. The reason why we restrict the sort of the variables such that, e.g., $(Bp \wedge Op) \vee (Bp \wedge \neg Op) \to Bp$ is not an instance of A1, is that $Bp \wedge Op \to_C Op$, while $Bp \wedge \neg Op$ is on normal form. Hence a less restrictive rule would generate an instance of a critical pair $(Bp, Op \vee (Bp \wedge \neg Op))$ that is not joinable.

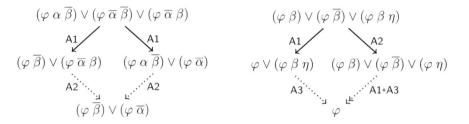

Figure 5. Examples of why the absorption rules A2 and A3 are needed. The conjunction sign ∧ has been omitted to save space. A1 necessitates the inclusion of A2, which again necessitates the inclusion of A3.

Theorem 11. R_{Only} *is confluent.*

Proof. By Lemma 4, R_{Only} is confluent if terminating, locally confluent and locally coherent with AC. By Theorem 9, R_{Only} is locally confluent if it satisfies substitutional joinability and critical pairs (of $R_{\text{Only}} \setminus \{E\}$) are joinable. Hence we need the following properties. *Joinability of critical pairs:* Left to the reader. *Local coherence with AC:* Left to the reader. *Substitutional joinability:* By Lemma 7. *Termination:* We only give an informal argument. Every rule except the expand and distribution rules decreases the length of the formula. The expand rule is only applicable a finite number of times, as $|\text{mod}(\varphi\langle\beta/v\rangle)| < |\text{mod}(\varphi)|$ if $O_i\varphi \to e(O_i\varphi, \beta)$. No rule increases the number of distinct modal atoms. By itself, the distribution rule can only applied a finite number of times, as it pushes conjunctions inwards. If the distribution rule is not applicable and some other rule than the expand rule is applied, then the distribution rule is still not applicable. Thus any rule is only applicable a finite number of times. □

As mentioned, R_{Comp} captures the MRT, i.e. for any O_I-block φ, there is some canonical μ on normal form such that $\varphi \twoheadrightarrow_{R_{\text{Comp}}} \mu$. Being confluent, R_{Only} has the additional property that if $\varphi \twoheadrightarrow_{R_{\text{Only}}} \mu$ and μ is on normal form, then μ is canonical. In relation to the MRT, this can be viewed as a step towards a correctness result. Correctness requires soundness, a property which relies on a formal semantics. To establish soundness one must, relative to an appropriate notion of validity, show that the LHS of the rules are logically equivalent to the resp. RHS, and that substitution of logical equivalents is truth preserving. These properties have been established for R_{Comp} wrt. the formal semantics of the only-knowing logics in [21]. Since the rules in R_{Only} that are not in R_{Comp}, are based on propositional tautologies, R_{Only} is, in the sense of the term just described, correct.

6. Conclusion and Future Work

We have in this paper proved termination and confluence of a rewrite system for one of the most basic only-knowing logics [13,21]. The proof is generic in the sense that it is based on the notion of substitutional joinability, a concept which can be used to show confluence also in cases where one wants to add new rules to the system. Using the rewriting logic tool Maude [3], we are currently experimenting with an implementation of the system, investigating the effect of adding further simplification rules and changing the search strategy.

References

[1] Grigoris Antoniou. *Nonmonotonic Reasoning*. The MIT Press, Cambridge, Massachusetts, 1997.
[2] Franz Baader and Tobias Nipkow. *Term Rewriting and All That*. Cambridge University Press, 1998.
[3] Manuel Clavel, Francisco Durán, Steven Eker, Patrick Lincoln, Narciso Martí-Oliet, José Meseguer, and José F. Quesada. Maude: Specification and Programming in Rewriting Logic. *Theoretical Computer Science*, 285:187–243, August 2002.
[4] Nachum Dershowitz and David A. Plaisted. Rewriting. In *Handbook of Automated Reasoning*, pages 535–610. 2001.
[5] Jürgen Dix, Ulrich Furbach, and Ilkka Niemelä. Nonmonotonic reasoning: Towards efficient calculi and implementations. In *Handbook of Automated Reasoning*, pages 1241–1354. 2001.
[6] Iselin Engan, Tore Langholm, Espen H. Lian, and Arild Waaler. Default Reasoning with Preference Within Only Knowing Logic. In *Proceedings of LPNMR 2005*.
[7] Georg Gottlob. Complexity Results for Nonmonotonic Logics. *J. Log. Comput.*, 2(3):397–425, 1992.
[8] Joseph Y. Halpern and Gerhard Lakemeyer. Multi-agent only knowing. *J. Log. Comput.*, 11(1):41–70, 2001.
[9] Gérard P. Huet. Confluent Reductions: Abstract Properties and Applications to Term Rewriting Systems. *J. ACM*, 27(4):797–821, 1980.
[10] Jean-Pierre Jouannaud and Hélène Kirchner. Completion of a Set of Rules Modulo a Set of Equations. *SIAM J. Comput.*, 15(4):1155–1194, 1986.
[11] Gerhard Lakemeyer and Hector J. Levesque. Only-Knowing: Taking It Beyond Autoepistemic Reasoning. In *Proceedings of AAAI 2005*.
[12] Gerhard Lakemeyer and Hector J. Levesque. Towards an Axiom System for Default Logic. In *Proceedings of AAAI 2006*.
[13] Hector J. Levesque. All I Know: A Study in Autoepistemic Logic. *Artif. Intell.*, 42(2-3):263–309, 1990.
[14] Hector J. Levesque and Gerhard Lakemeyer. *The Logic of Knowledge Bases*. MIT Press, 2001.
[15] Espen H. Lian and Arild Waaler. Computing Default Extensions by Reductions on O^R. In *Proceedings of KR 2008*, pages 496–506. AAAI Press.
[16] Espen H. Lian and Arild Waaler. An Only Knowing Approach to Defeasible Description Logics (extended abstract). In *DL 2009*, 2009.
[17] José Meseguer. Conditional Rewriting Logic as a United Model of Concurrency. *Theoretical Computer Science*, 96(1):73–155, 1992.
[18] Enno Ohlebusch. *Advanced Topics in Term Rewriting*. Springer Verlag, 2002.
[19] Riccardo Rosati. A sound and complete tableau calculus for reasoning about only knowing and knowing at most. *Studia Logica*, 69(1):171–191, 2001.
[20] Arild Waaler. Consistency proofs for systems of multi-agent only knowing. In *Proceedings of AiML 2004*.
[21] Arild Waaler, Johan W. Klüwer, Tore Langholm, and Espen H. Lian. Only knowing with degrees of confidence. *J. Applied Logic*, 5(3):492–518, 2007.
[22] Arild Waaler and Bjørnar Solhaug. Semantics for multi-agent only knowing: extended abstract. In Ron van der Meyden, editor, *Proceedings of the 10th Conference on Theoretical Aspects of Rationality and Knowledge (TARK)*, pages 109–125, 2005.

A much better polynomial time approximation of consistency in the $\mathcal{LR}$ calculus

Dominik LÜCKE [a] and Till MOSSAKOWSKI [a,b]
[a] *SFB/TR 8 Spatial Cognition, Bremen, Germany*
[b] *DFKI GmbH Bremen, Germany*

Abstract In the area of qualitative spatial reasoning, the $\mathcal{LR}$ calculus (a refinement of Ligozat's flip-flop calculus) is a quite simple constraint calculus that forms the core of several orientation calculi like the Dipole calculi and the $\mathcal{OPRA}_1$ calculus by introducing the left-right-dichotomy.

For many qualitative spatial calculi, algebraic closure is applied as the standard polynomial time "decision" procedure. For a long time it was believed that this can decide the consistency of scenarios of the $\mathcal{LR}$ calculus. However, in [8] it was shown that algebraic closure is a bad approximation of consistency for $\mathcal{LR}$ scenarios: scenarios in the base relations "Left" and "Right" are always algebraically closed, no matter if those scenarios are consistent or not. So algebraic closure is completely useless here. Furthermore, in [15] it was proved that the consistency problem for any calculus with relative orientation containing the relations "Left" and "Right" is NP-hard.

In this paper we propose a new and better polynomial time approximation procedure for this NP-hard problem. It is based on the angles of triangles in the Euclidean plane. $\mathcal{LR}$ scenarios are translated to sets of linear inequalities over the real numbers. We evaluate the quality of this procedure by comparing it both to the old approximation using algebraic closure and to the (exact but exponential time) Buchberger algorithm for Gröbner bases (used as a decision method).

Keywords. Qualitative Spatial Reasoning, Consistency, Geometry

1. Introduction

Since the work of Allen [1] on temporal intervals, constraint calculi have been used to model a variety of aspects of space and time in a way that is both qualitative (and thus closer to natural language than quantitative representations) and computationally efficient (by appropriately restricting the vocabulary of rich mathematical theories about space and time). For example, the well-known region connection calculus [9] allows for reasoning about regions in space. Applications include geographic information systems, human-machine interaction, and robot navigation.

Directions in the (Euclidean) plane are described by *orientation* calculi. These directions can be given with respect to a global reference frame like for the Cardinal directions algebra. The Cardinal directions calculus features the (absolute) orientations North, South, East, and West. On the other hand a (relative) reference frame can be given locally at any object of the calculus, like e.g. for the Flip-Flop calculus [7], where the reference frame is given by an oriented line from a start to an end point. The $\mathcal{LR}$-calculus [13] is a refinement of Flip-Flop curing its shortcomings.

These *Relative orientation* calculi are quite important examples of qualitative calculi, because relative orientation is very natural in many real world applications. Just consider the situation that you want to describe the way to some point of interest in your home-town. You will tell your addressee to turn left or right at some crossing with respect to their current orientation. You will neither tell them to change the direction to e.g. North, nor will you tell them to turn by a certain amount of degrees. If you describe the layout of some point of interest, you will most certainly use the same qualitative relations either. But how can we make a machine, e.g. a robot, decide efficiently that a qualitative description is consistent?

This is where the reasoning facilities of the qualitative calculi are needed. Efficient reasoning in them mainly relies on the *algebraic closure* algorithm. Using relational composition and converse, it refines (basic) constraint networks in polynomial time. If algebraic closure detects an inconsistency, the original network is surely inconsistent. If no inconsistency is detected, for some calculi, this implies consistency of the original network — but not for all calculi. For the cardinal direction calculus, it can be easily shown that algebraic closure indeed decides consistency for scenarios. However, in [8] we have shown that the consistency of $\mathcal{LR}$-scenarios cannot be decided by applying the algebraic closure method. This result naturally carries over to the Flip-Flop calculus.

Wolter and Lee [15] give a new explanation of this phenomenon: through a reduction to oriented matroids, they prove that deciding consistency for scenarios in the $\mathcal{LR}$ calculus is NP-hard. Assuming the generally believed hypothesis that P $\neq$ NP, this explains why algebraic closure (a polynomial procedure) does not decide consistency of scenarios: all what we can hope for are *polynomial approximations* of consistency. Here, we develop a polynomial approximation that improves on algebraic closure. Of course, we cannot do this by staying at the level of abstract relation algebras (where algebraic closure operates). Rather, we have to take properties of the "natural" domain of the calculus at hand into account. Our new approach to approximate the consistency of $\mathcal{LR}$-scenarios is based on the properties of triangles in the Euclidean plane, which are formalized algebraically as a set of linear inequalities. Our notion of *triangle consistency* can be decided in polynomial time; this essentially follows from the solvability of the corresponding inequalities in polynomial time [2]. First experiments showed that triangle consistency approximates consistency of $\mathcal{LR}$ scenarios much better than algebraic closure does. We focus on comparing our approach to algebraic closure, since tool-support is available for that method, which is still lacking for e.g. neighborhood-based reasoning. Further experiments gave some evidence that the approach is quite well suited for approximating the consistency of $\mathcal{LR}$ scenarios. This approximation procedure also naturally applies to the $\mathcal{DRA}$-calculi, another family of calculi dealing with relative orientation, as well as to $\mathcal{OPRA}_1$[1].

---

[1]The $\mathcal{OPRA}_n$ calculi with $n > 1$ encode more information than just the left-right-dichotomy and some information about the position of points on a line and therefore need more refined decision procedures.

2. Qualitative Calculi

Qualitative calculi are employed for representing knowledge about a domain using a finite set of labels, so-called base relations. Base relations partition the domain into discrete parts. One example is distinguishing points on the time line by binary relations such as "before", "after" and "same". A qualitative representation only captures membership of domain objects in these parts. For example, it can be represented that time point A occurs before B, but not how much earlier nor at which absolute time. Thus, a qualitative representation abstracts, which is particularly helpful when dealing with infinite domains like time and space that possess an internal structure like for example $\mathbb{R}^n$.

In order to ensure that any constellation of domain objects is captured by exactly one qualitative relation, a special property is commonly required:

Definition 1. Let $\mathcal{B} = \{B_1, \ldots, B_k\}$ be a set of n-ary *base relations* over a domain $\mathcal{D}$. These relations are said to be *jointly exhaustive and pairwise disjoint (JEPD)*, if they satisfy the properties

1. $\forall i, j \in \{1, \ldots, k\}$ with $i \neq j : B_i \cap B_j = \emptyset$
2. $\mathcal{D}^n = \bigcup_{i \in \{1, \ldots, k\}} B_i$

For representing uncertain knowledge within a qualitative calculus, e.g., to represent that objects $x_1, x_2, \ldots, x_n$ are either related by relation B_i or by relation B_j, *general relations* are introduced.

Definition 2. Let $\mathcal{B} = \{B_1, \ldots, B_k\}$ be a set of n-ary base relations over a domain $\mathcal{D}$. The set of *general relations* $\mathcal{R}_\mathcal{B}$ (or simply $\mathcal{R}$) is the powerset $\mathcal{P}(\mathcal{B})$. The semantics of a relation $R \in \mathcal{R}_\mathcal{B}$ is defined as $R(x_1, \ldots, x_n) :\Leftrightarrow \exists B_i \in R.B_i(x_1, \ldots, x_n)$.

In a set of base relations that is JEPD, the empty relation $\emptyset \in \mathcal{R}_\mathcal{B}$ is called the *impossible relation*. Reasoning with qualitative information takes place on the symbolic level of relations $\mathcal{R}$, so we need special operators that allow us to manipulate qualitative knowledge. These operators constitute the algebraic structure of a qualitative calculus.

2.1. Algebraic Structure of Qualitative Calculi

The most fundamental operators in a qualitative calculus are those for relating qualitative relations in accordance to their set-theoretic disjunctive semantics. So, for $R, S \in \mathcal{R}$, intersection ($\cap$) and union ($\cup$) are defined canonically. The set of general relations is closed under these operators. Set-theoretic operators are independent of the calculus at hand, further operators are defined using the calculus semantics.

Qualitative calculi need to provide operators for interrelating relations that are declared to hold for the same set of objects but differ in the order of arguments. Put differently, we need operators which allow us to change perspective. For binary relations this operation is just forming the converse relation.

Definition 3. Permutation operators for ternary calculi:

$$INV(R) := \{\,(y,x,z) \mid (x,y,z) \in R\,\} \quad \text{(inverse)}$$
$$SC(R) := \{\,(x,z,y) \mid (x,y,z) \in R\,\} \quad \text{(shortcut)}$$
$$SCI(R) := \{\,(z,x,y) \mid (x,y,z) \in R\,\} \quad \text{(inverse shortcut)}$$
$$HM(R) := \{\,(y,z,x) \mid (x,y,z) \in R\,\} \quad \text{(homing)}$$
$$HMI(R) := \{\,(z,y,x) \mid (x,y,z) \in R\,\} \quad \text{(inverse homing)}$$

If the set of relations is closed under INV, SC and HM, then SCI and HMI can be defined as compositions of the respective operations (ref. to [3]). A restriction to few operations particularly eases definition of higher arity calculi.

Definition 4 ([3]). Let $R_1, R_2, \ldots, R_n \in \mathcal{R_B}$ be a sequence of n general relations in an n-ary qualitative calculus over the domain $\mathcal{D}$. Then the operation

$$\circ\,(R_1, \ldots, R_n) := \{(x_1, \ldots, x_n) \in \mathcal{D}^n \mid \exists u \in \mathcal{D}, (x_1, \ldots, x_{n-1}, u) \in R_1,$$
$$(x_1, \ldots, x_{n-2}, u, x_n) \in R_2, \ldots, (u, x_2 \ldots, x_n) \in R_n\}$$

is called *n-ary composition*.

Note that for $n = 2$ one obtains the classical composition operation for binary calculi (cp. [11]) which is usually noted as infix operator. Nevertheless different kinds of binary compositions have been used for ternary calculi, too, as e.g. for the $\mathcal{LR}$-calculus.

2.2. Strong and Weak Operations

Permutation and composition operators define relations. Per se it is unclear whether the relations obtained by application of an operation are expressible in the calculus, i.e. whether the set of general relations $\mathcal{R_B}$ is closed under an operation. Indeed, for some calculi the set of relations is not closed, there even exist calculi for which no closed set of finite size can exist, e.g. the composition operation in Freksa's double cross calculus [12].

Definition 5. Let an n-ary qualitative calculus with relations $\mathcal{R_B}$ over domain $\mathcal{D}$ and an m-ary operation $\phi : \mathcal{B}^m \to \mathcal{P}(\mathcal{D}^n)$ be given. If the set of relations is closed under ϕ, i.e. for $\forall \vec{B} \in \mathcal{B}^m \; \exists R' \in \mathcal{R_B} \;:\; \phi(\vec{B}) = \bigcup_{B \in R'} B$, then the operation ϕ is called *strong*.

In qualitative reasoning we must restrict ourselves to a finite set of relations. Therefore, if some operation is not strong in the sense of Def. 5, an upper approximation of the true operation is used instead.

Definition 6. Given a qualitative calculus with n-ary relations $\mathcal{R_B}$ over domain $\mathcal{D}$ and an operation $\phi : \mathcal{B}^m \to \mathcal{P}(\mathcal{D}^n)$, then the operator

$$\phi^\star : \mathcal{B}^m \to \mathcal{R_B} \qquad \phi^\star(B_1, \ldots, B_k) := \{R \in \mathcal{B} \mid R \cap \phi(B_1, \ldots, B_k) \neq \emptyset\}$$

is called a *weak* operation, namely the weak approximation of ϕ.

Note that the weak approximation of an operation is identical to the original operation if and only if the original operation is strong. Further note that any calculus is closed under weak operations. Applying weak operations can lead to a loss of information which may be critical in certain reasoning processes. In the literature the weak composition operation is usually denoted by $\diamond$.

3. Constraint Based Qualitative Reasoning

Qualitative reasoning is concerned with solving constraint satisfaction problems (CSPs) in which constraints are expressed using relations of the calculus. Definitions from the field of CSP are carried over to qualitative reasoning (cp. [4]).

Definition 7. Let $\mathcal{R}$ be the general relations of a qualitative calculus over the domain $\mathcal{D}$. A *qualitative constraint* is a formula $R(X_1, \ldots, X_n)$ (also written $X_1 \ldots X_{n-1} R X_n$) with variables X_i taking values from the domain and $R \in \mathcal{R}$. A *constraint network* is a set of constraints. A constraint network is said to be a *scenario* if it gives base relations for all relations $R(X_1, \ldots, X_n)$ and the base relations obtained for different permutations of variables $X_1, \ldots, X_n$ must be agreeable wrt. the permutation operations.

One key problem is to decide whether a given CSP has a solution or not. This can be a very hard problem. Infinity of the domain underlying qualitative CSPs inhibits searching for an agreeable valuation of the variables.

Definition 8. A constraint network is called *consistent* if a valuation of all variables exists, such that all constraints are fulfilled. A constraint network is called *n-consistent* ($n \in \mathbb{N}$) if every solution for $n-1$ variables can be extended to a solution with n variables involving any further variable. A constraint network is called *strongly n-consistent*, if it is m-consistent for all $m \leq n$.

A fundamental technique for deciding consistency in a classical CSP is to enforce k-consistency by restricting the domain of variables in the CSP to mutually agreeable values. Backtracking search can then identify a consistent variable assignment. If the domain of some variable gets restricted to down to zero size while enforcing k-consistency, the CSP is not consistent. This procedure except for backtracking search (which is not applicable in infinite domains) is also applied to qualitative CSPs [11]. For a JEPD calculus with n-ary relations any qualitative CSP is strongly n-consistent unless it contains a constraint with the empty relation. So the first step in checking consistency would be to test $n+1$-consistency. In the case of a calculus with binary relations this would mean analyzing 3-consistency, also called *path-consistency*. This is the aim of the algebraic closure algorithm which exploits that composition lists all 3-consistent scenarios.

Definition 9. A CSP over binary relations is called *algebraically closed* if for all variables X_1, X_2, X_3 and all relations R_1, R_2, R_3 the constraint relations $R_1(X_1, X_2)$, $R_2(X_2, X_3), R_3(X_1, X_3)$ imply $R_3 \subseteq R_1 \diamond R_2$. To enforce algebraic closure, the operation $R_3 := R_3 \cap R_1 \diamond R_2$ (as well as a similar operation for converses) is applied for all variables until a fixed-point is reached.

Enforcing algebraic closure preserves consistency, i.e., if the empty relation is obtained during refinement, then the qualitative CSP is inconsistent. However, algebraic closure does not mandatorily decide consistency: a CSP may be algebraically closed but inconsistent — even if composition is strong [10].

Algebraic closure has also been adapted to ternary calculi using binary composition [6]. Binary composition of ternary relations involves 4 variables, it may not be able to represent all 4-consistent scenarios though. Scenarios with 4 variables are specified by 4 ternary relations. However, binary composition $R_1 \diamond R_2 = R_3$ only involves 3 ternary relations. Therefore, using n-ary composition in reasoning with n-ary relations is more natural (cp. [3]).

4. The $\mathcal{LR}$-calculus

In this section we introduce the $\mathcal{LR}$-calculus [13], a coarse relative orientation calculus. We use it as our starting point to develop new decision procedures for relative orientation calculi. This calculus defines nine base relations which are depicted in Fig. 1. The $\mathcal{LR}$-calculus deals with the relative position of a point C with respect to the oriented line from point A to point B, if $A \neq B$. The point C can be to the left of (l), to the right of (r) the line, or it can be on a line collinear to the given one and in front of (f) B, between A and B with the relation (i) or behind (b) A; furthermore, it can be on the start-point A (s) or an the end-point B (e). If $A = B$, then we can distinguish between the relations Tri, expressing that $A = C$ and Dou, meaning $A \neq C$. Freksa's double cross calculus $\mathcal{DCC}$ is a refinement of the $\mathcal{LR}$-calculus and, henceforth, our findings for the $\mathcal{LR}$-calculus can be directly applied to the $\mathcal{DCC}$-calculus as well.

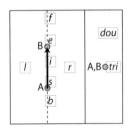

Figure 1. The nine base relations of the $\mathcal{LR}$-calculus; tri designates the case of $A = B = C$, whereas dou stands for $A = B \neq C$.

5. Algebraic Closure is no Decision Procedure for $\mathcal{LR}$

In [8] we have shown that algebraic closure does not decide consistency for the $\mathcal{LR}$-calculus, i.e., not every algebraically closed scenario is consistent. We recall the most crucial results, for the proofs refer to the particular paper. The most staggering result is:

Proposition 10. *All scenarios only containing the relations l and r are algebraically closed wrt. the $\mathcal{LR}$-calculus with binary composition, as soon as they agree on the permutation operations.*

This result almost disqualifies algebraic closure as a decision procedure for $\mathcal{LR}$. Moreover, neither classical binary nor for ternary algebraic closure can decide consistency for $\mathcal{LR}$.

Theorem 11. *Neither classical binary algebraic closure nor algebraic closure wrt. ternary composition enforces scenario consistency for the $\mathcal{LR}$-calculus.*

Proof. Refer to [8]. □

6. Triangle Consistency: A New Approximation of Consistency for $\mathcal{LR}$

Our approach is inspired by the simple observation that any 3 points in the Euclidean plane together with their connecting lines form a (possibly degenerated) triangle. Because of that for any such triple of points and their connecting lines, all well-known properties of triangles need to be fulfilled. We currently restrict ourselves to the interesting cases of the relations l and r for which algebraic closure performs very badly, as we have seen in section 5. This means that we will not have to deal with any degenerate triangles. Our approach works for all base-relations of the $\mathcal{LR}$-calculus, but the restriction to the "interesting" cases is necessary due to space limitations, the extension to all base relations is straightforward.

In our new approach, we translate any $\mathcal{LR}$-scenario (which has to contain base relations between all permutation of all triples of distinct points) into a set of inequalities over triangles in the Euclidean plane. We normalize all angles to the interval $(-\pi, \pi)$ to simplify later calculations. "Left" and "Right" can be distinguished by the orientation (read sectors of a circle) of the involved angles (ref. to. Fig. 2). Let 3 points A, B and C in relation $(A\ B\ r\ C)$ be given. For such a relation, we get a scenario in the plane as in Fig 2. We can derive that the angle from C to B at A, which we call BAC, is in the open

Figure 2. $(A\ B\ r\ C)$ in the plane

interval $(-\pi, 0)$. The derivation for $(A\ B\ l\ C)$ is similar and yields angles in the interval $(0, \pi)$. Further, by a simple geometrical argument, we can show, that:

Lemma 12. *For a non-degenerate triangle in the Euclidean plane with points A, B, C, the properties*

$$0 < BAC < \pi \Leftrightarrow 0 < ACB < \pi \Leftrightarrow 0 < CAB < \pi$$
$$-\pi < BAC < 0 \Leftrightarrow -\pi < ACB < 0 \Leftrightarrow -\pi < CAB < 0$$

are fulfilled.

With this and the well-known properties of triangles in the plane, we can derive our system of inequalities INEQNB (BAC) for any arbitrary angle BAC which is depicted in Fig. 3.

Distinction *l/r*	
$0 < BAC < \pi$	if $(A\,B\,l\,C)$
$-\pi < BAC < 0$	if $(A\,B\,r\,C)$
Opposite angles	
$BAC = -CAB$	
Sum of angles	
$BAC + CBA + ACB = \pi$	if $(A\,B\,l\,C)$
$BAC + CBA + ACB = -\pi$	if $(A\,B\,r\,C)$
Adjacent angles	
$BAC + CAD = BAD + 2 \cdot \pi$ if	$\begin{cases} (A\,B\,l\,C) \\ (A\,C\,l\,D) \\ (A\,B\,r\,D) \end{cases}$
$BAC + CAD = BAD - 2 \cdot \pi$ if	$\begin{cases} (A\,B\,r\,C) \\ (A\,C\,r\,D) \\ (A\,B\,l\,D) \end{cases}$
$BAC + CAD = BAD$	otherwise

Figure 3. INEQNB (BAC)

To the inequalities INEQNB (BAC), we add the ones derived from lemma 12. With them, we obtain the set INEQN (BAC) for any angle BAC. Such sets of inequalities are generated for each triple of points in an $\mathcal{LR}$-scenario. By INEQN we denote the set of all inequalities for such a scenario.

Definition 13. We call an $\mathcal{LR}$-scenario *triangle consistent*, if there is at least one solution for all of its inequalities INEQN.

The "compression" of knowledge is done at this point by not considering any lengths of lines. Considering them would yield non-linear inequalities that cannot be solved efficiently. We want to use as little knowledge in this approach as possible to make it computationally efficient:

Theorem 14. *Systems of linear inequalities can be decided in polynomial time.*

Proof. This follows from [2]. □

Triangle consistency yields a decision procedure consisting of just two steps:

1. Translate the $\mathcal{LR}$-scenario to a system of linear inequalities (this is just a substitution in the number of relations contained in the scenario and can clearly be performed in linear time),
2. Check the solvability of the system with a standard polynomial algorithm. (In fact, also the simplex algorithm can be applied in this step, it has exponential worst-case running time, but often performs very well.)

With Thm. 14 we obtain:

Proposition 15. *Triangle consistency has polynomial running time.*

Each geometric realization of an $\mathcal{LR}$ scenario obviously leads to a system of angles for the involved point triples; it is easy to show that such a system of angles is a solution for the inequalities INEQN. We thus arrive at:

Proposition 16. *Consistency implies triangle consistency.*

By Prop. 15 and the fact that deciding consistency is NP-hard, we obtain that under the assumption P $\neq$ NP, the converse implication (triangle consistency implies consistency) does not hold. However, we have not found a counterexample yet.

7. Experiments

We have conducted intensive experiments evaluating the quality of our approach of triangle consistency. A big issue about doing experiments with relative orientation calculi is the infinite size of their domain. It is basically impossible to list all possible quantitative positions of points in the Euclidean plane. But for restricted numbers of points an upper bound for the number of qualitatively different configurations can be derived. This still leaves the problem that for a certain number of points (6 in our case) the memory consumption of a program listing those different configurations becomes excessive, as well as the running time.

We have implemented a prototype solver in Haskell for deciding whether a given $\mathcal{LR}$-scenario is triangle consistent. This tool can generate all complete $\mathcal{LR}$-scenarios in n-points and calculate the corresponding set of inequalities INEQN. As the reasoning engine this tool currently uses the Yices SMT-solver [5]. We decided to use an external possibly not completely optimal reasoning engine for the prototype to overcome the issue of programming bugs and intensive debugging. However, the performance of the actual equation solver dominates the running time. Further, we have written a Haskell program that enumerates n-point $\mathcal{LR}$-scenarios using a grid of $m \times m$ points. This program starts with a specified value of m_0 and calculates all possible $\mathcal{LR}$-scenarios, then it increases the current bound and calculates again. This is continued until the user requests to terminate it. If the list of scenarios from run l and $l + 1$ differ, the new list of scenarios is displayed, otherwise a message, that the scenarios are the same. To list all 5 point scenarios completely, it turned out, that a grid of 8×8 points already is sufficient, which can be shown by an involved geometric argument. Unfortunately, for scenarios in 6 points we neither had the computation power nor the memory to enumerate all possible configurations. In fact, the memory usage grows double exponentially with the number of points involved as the running time increases in a triple exponential way.

We also have used the Gröbner reasoner that is available in SparQ [14]. It led to the same set of consistent scenarios. However, the exponential runtime of both the grid method and the Gröbner reasoner prevented a computation of all consistent 6 point scenarios. For algebraic closure, we used the tool SparQ [14]. To examine scenarios with more than 5 points, we implemented a Haskell program that constructs algebraically closed scenarios in up to n points (where n is a given parameter). We let the program run for several days with the parameter n set up to 9 (examining thousands of scenarios). Unfortunately in many cases the Gröbner reasoner was not able to decide consistency, but if it was it gave the same answer as triangle consistency. Candidates for failure of the triangle consistency remained problems where the Gröbner reasoner could not decide consistency, but triangle consistency was fulfilled. We double checked dozens of such scenarios by hand, and could deem all of them being consistent.

Since we were able to enumerate all consistent all 5-point scenarios in the relations l and r^2, we can quantify how well our method performs on them. We could identify 1955 consistent $\mathcal{LR}$-scenarios (s_{con}) of this kind, algebraic closure with binary composition yields 3095 scenarios (s_{bin}) while ternary algebraic closure leads to 2355 scenarios (s_{ter}). We found exactly 1955 triangle consistent scenarios ($s_\triangle$), and when inspecting them, we found out that $s_{con} = s_\triangle$. These numbers are depicted in Fig. 4. Please note that the numbers of the scenarios are given modulo swapping of the names of the points. As noted above, we could not identify all consistent 6 point scenarios, mainly because

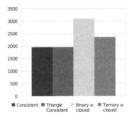

Figure 4. Comparison of algebraic closure with triangle consistency

of hardware restrictions. But we were still be able to identify a subset of consistent $\mathcal{LR}$-scenarios. So far we were able to classify 429449 scenarios with our approach, of which 4698 are deemed triangle consistent. Not all of them are in the list of our pre-calculated scenarios, but we have to remember that that list is incomplete. We took samples from the list of triangle consistent scenarios that were not in the pre-calculated list, and it turned out that we could find a realization for all of them. Many of those samples had a cloud of points lying close together, with at least one point lying very far away from the others. This is a case that could not be found with our grid method in limits that yield a feasible computation time.

Algebraic closure (binary as well as ternary) failed badly when we had scenarios with one more point than the number of points captured by the composition table; this is fortunately not true for triangle consistency.

All of these experimental results imply that triangle consistency approximates better than binary as well as ternary algebraic closure. Compared to Tarski's quantifier elimination and Gröbner Reasoning, it has a much better running time, since it is a polynomial time algorithm. Since we are only using a prototype implementation of our algorithm and since the used Gröbner reasoner can detect patterns in the equations that imply that it cannot decide consistency, quantifying the running time of the programs is in vain. Indeed, the Gröbner reasoner integrated into SparQ often fails to determine consistency for scenarios if the number of points grows. Sometimes it even gives up for quite small scenarios. For scenarios in more than nine or ten points the Gröbner reasoner gives up more often than it can decide. By contrast, triangle consistency works well with scenarios consisting of dozens of points, which is a size that is quite realistic for e.g. robot navigation applications.

---

[2]Smaller scenarios are not really interesting, since we can already detect inconsistencies with algebraic closure with ternary composition for 4 point scenarios, all smaller ones do not need additional consideration, since they are at most base relations. The 14 scenarios in 4 points are detected by our method.

8. Conclusion/Outlook

We have approximated the NP-hard problem of deciding consistency of scenarios in the $\mathcal{LR}$ calculus. Algebraic closure is a tool that has severe limits: for the $\mathcal{LR}$-calculus it approximates consistency in its intended domain (the Euclidean plane) only quite badly. Information provided by the the relations of the relative orientation calculi can be described algebraically by non-linear inequalities. Such systems of non-linear inequalities over $\mathbb{R}$ can of course be decided by Tarski's quantifier elimination. Gröbner reasoning is another applicable procedure, but the running time of both of them is exponential and far too slow for many real world applications, e.g. in mobile robots. In fact, we need a reasoning procedure that is computationally feasible and as accurate as possible. In designing such a procedure, the incorporation of properties of the domain of the calculus at hand for simplifying the problem seems to be a sane way to go. Currently, our method of triangle consistency outperforms algebraic closure by far on $\mathcal{LR}$-scenarios, at least for scenarios of reasonable size. It would be interesting to study the performance of our method on really big scenarios, but a lot of computing power is needed for that.

Future work will extend triangle consistency to the $\mathcal{DRA}$-calculus, which feels very natural, since $\mathcal{DRA}$ is defined using $\mathcal{LR}$-relations.

References

[1] J.F. Allen, 'Maintaining knowledge about temporal intervals', *Communications of the ACM*, 832–843, (1983).

[2] A. R. Bradley and Z. Manna, *The Calculus of Computation*, Springer, 2007.

[3] J.-F. Condotta, M. Saade, and G.F. Ligozat, 'A Generic Toolkit for n-ary Qualitative Temporal and Spatial Calculi', in *Proc. of TIME 06*, pp. 78–86. IEEE Computer Society, (2006).

[4] R. Dechter, 'From Local to Global Consistency', *Artificial Intelligence*, **55**, 87–108, (1992).

[5] B. Dutertre and L. de Moura. The Yices SMT solver. Tool paper at http://yices.csl.sri.com/toolpaper.pdf, August 2006.

[6] F. Dylla and R. Moratz, 'Empirical complexity issues of practical qualitative spatial reasoning about relative position', in *Proc. of the Workshop on Spatial and Temporal Reasoning at ECAI 2004*, (2004).

[7] G.F. Ligozat, 'Qualitative triangulation for spatial reasoning', in *Proc. International Conference on Spatial Information Theory*, pp. 54–68, (1993).

[8] D. Lücke, T. Mossakowski, and D. Wolter, 'Qualitative Reasoning About Convex Relations', in *Spatial Cognition VI*, ed., Christian Freksa et al., (2008).

[9] D. A. Randell, Zhan Cui, and A. Cohn, 'A Spatial Logic Based on Regions and Connection', in *KR'92. Principles of Knowledge Representation and Reasoning*, eds., Bernhard Nebel, Charles Rich, and William Swartout, 165–176, Morgan Kaufmann, (1992).

[10] J. Renz and G.F. Ligozat, 'Weak Composition for Qualitative Spatial and Temporal Reasoning.', in *Principles and Practice of Constraint Programming - CP 2005*, ed., Peter van Beek, volume 3709 of *LNCS*, pp. 534–548. Springer, (2005).

[11] J. Renz and B. Nebel, 'Qualitative spatial reasoning using constraint calculi', in *Handbook of Spatial Logics*, Springer, (2007).

[12] A. Scivos and B. Nebel, 'Double-crossing: Decidability and computational complexity of a qualitative calculus for navigation', in *Spatial Information Theory: Foundations of GIS*, volume 2205 of *LNCS*, pp. 431–446. Springer, (2001).

[13] A. Scivos and B. Nebel, 'The Finest of its Class: The Natural, Point-Based Ternary Calculus $\mathcal{LR}$ for Qualitative Spatial Reasoning', in *Spatial Cognition*, pp. 283–303, (2004).

[14] J. O. Wallgrün, L. Frommberger, D. Wolter, F. Dylla, and C. Freksa, 'A toolbox for qualitative spatial representation and reasoning', in *Spatial Cognition V*, number 4387 in LNCS, pp. 39–58, (2007).

[15] D. Wolter and J. H. Lee, 'Qualitative reasoning about relative point position'. Submitted for publication, 2009.

Fair Mechanisms for Recurrent Multi Unit Combinatorial Auctions

Javier MURILLO, and Beatriz LÓPEZ
University of Girona, Spain

Abstract. Auctions have been used to deal with resource allocation in multi-agent systems. In some environments like service-oriented electronic markets, it is advisable to use recurrent auctions since resources are perishable and auctions are repeated over time with the same or a very similar set of agents. Recurrent auctions are a series of auctions of any kind where the result of one auction may influence the following one. As a drawback some problems do appear that could cause the market to collapse at mid-long term. Previous works have dealt with these problems by adding fairness to the auction outcomes. Those works dealt with multi-unit auctions, in which several units of an item are sold, and they do not assure that agents cannot manipulate the auctions for their own benefit. In this paper, we present new fair mechanisms that goes further. First we focus on combinatorial auctions, in which different items, and several units per item are sold in each auction, which poses additional challenges when they are recurrent. And second, the mechanisms are shown to prevent some agents' manipulation of the auction outcomes.

Keywords. Recurrent auctions, Combinatorial auctions, Fairness

Introduction

Auctions have become a well known mechanism to share resources among agents in distributed environments. Traditionally, the auctioneer or the owner of the resources exhibits an utilitarian behavior in which he tries to maximize his own revenue by giving the resources to the agents that offer the highest bids. Recent work, such as [7,10] has shown that this utilitarian behavior can cause the collapse of the market at the mid-long run when dealing with recurrent markets. Thus, this rational behavior exhibited in a single shot game, becomes unsuccessful when repeating the game or auction several times. The reason for that is that this behavior produces the inevitable starvation of certain buyers that could leave the market [8]. So, when poor agents leave, richer bidders have the power to set the prices, provoking a fall in prices that can collapse the market in the mid-term.

Some authors have equipped the traditional mechanisms with reservation prices, which consist in the auctioneer setting a minimum price for the resources and bids below the reservation price cannot be winners. However this adds a new problem: resource waste. With reservation prices, many resources are not sold, and if the resources cannot be stored, they are lost. This is the case of the domain of network bandwidth allocations with which our work is concerned. Thus, if the auctioneer wishes to obtain the maximum revenue from the resources along all the auctions, he needs to look for alternative mechanisms to solve the auction. Particularly, [7,10] show that if each auction is solved with a fair mechanism, at the end of the recurrent auction the highest revenue is obtained. Thus, all of the agents are behaving selfishly; and particularly the auctioneer, that by exhibiting a fair behavior also obtains the maximum total revenue.

However, such works consider that the auctioneer sells a constant quantity of units of a unique resource and bidders can only send a unique bid to obtain one unit of the resource. The real world, however, is different, and agents can compete for bandwidth of different quality: voice, high quality voice, video, high quality video, and data. Thus, we are dealing with a multi-unit combinatorial auction (MUCA), in which different kinds of resources, and several units of each resources (e.g. two units of data bandwidth) are auctioned. The extension from a unique kind of resources to multiple kinds of resources in a recurrent scenario is not straightforward, and this is the main contribution of this paper.

In this article we propose two new fair mechanisms for MUCA. In this case, the auctioneer auctions several units of several resources and bidders can bid for several resources and several units of each resource. Moreover, we study the impact of fairness regarding agent manipulation. That is, since the auctions are repeated, bidders can learn about the fairness behavior, and act malevolently in order to obtain the resources at lower prices. We prove that our mechanism, unlike to the previous fair ones, avoids some kinds of manipulation.

1. Background

This section shows some necessary background on recurrent multi unit auctions, fairness and trust to understand the following sections.

1.1. Recurrent MUCA

Recurrent auctions are a series of auctions (of any kind) that are solved individually, but the outcomes of the auctions could be influenced by previous auctions. For example, if a bidder wins an auction, it could reduce the bid in the next one, trying to obtain a higher utility. In this paper we use the recurrent multi-unit, multi-item, sealed-bid combinatorial auction. A *combinatorial* auction is an auction in which bidders can place bids on combination of items, or packages, rather than just individual items [3]. In a *multi-unit* auction the auctioneer offers several (identical) units of each auctioned item. In a *multi-item* auction the auctioneer offers several items or resources. Finally a *sealed-bid* auction is one where the auctioneer is the only agent that knows the bids sent by the bidders (i.e., one bidder does not know what other bidders bid).

In an auction process we can distinguish the following three main components. First, the *bidding policies* are the methods used by the agents to decide which items to bid for and the price they are willing to pay for them. Although the auction is sealed bid and bidders do not know the bids of other agents, in a recurrent scenario an agent has information since he knows the result of his previous auctions and the bid that he has sent. From this information the agent can intuit the global state of the market and choose an appropriate bid. So, we assume that agents have a behavior that tries to maximize their profit using the adaptation strategy defined in [8]. This strategy consists in varying the bid price depending on whether they have won or lost in the previous auction, thus trying to get as close as possible to the optimal bid price with which they can obtain the resources. The second component is the *winner determination problem*, that is the method the auctioneer uses to select the winning bids. The third component is the *pricing mechanism*, that is how the auctioneer decides the price to be paid by the winners. In our case each bidder pays the price he bids (*first-price* auction). Our research is concerned mainly with the winner determination, which poses an optimization problem for auctioneers that try to maximize their revenue [11].

The winner determination algorithm strategy is conditioned on the kind of resource being auctioned. In this paper, we focus on perishable resources. A resource is perishable if it vanishes or loses its value when held over an extended period of time (e.g., the network bandwidth not used is not accumulable for the future).

When perishable resources are auctioned in recurrent auctions some problems appear. First, perishable resources cannot be stored in warehouses for future sales; if the resources are not allocated, they lose their value or vanish completely. This is the *resource waste* problem in recurrent auctions, because if the auctioneer does not sell the resource in an auction, it cannot be sold in the forthcoming auctions. The second problem is the *asymmetric balance of negotiation power*. In most traditional auction mechanisms, the bid prices depend only on the customer's willingness to pay for the traded goods. This means that only the intentions of customers, not those of the auctioneers, are reflected in the auction winning prices [7]. In the long run, the effect of this problem may cause the auction to collapse. And third, the *bidder drop* problem occurs when bidder agents participating in many auctions always lose. These bidders could decide to leave the market because they are not making any profit. The reduction in the number of bidders gradually decreases the price competition because the probability of winning increases for the remaining bidders. Bidders can decrease their bids without losing the chance to win, provoking the overall drop in bid price[1].

Finally, an important drawback that can appear in this kind of auction is the manipulation of the mechanism by bidders. That is, different trials of bidders in a recurrent auction could be planned in order to take advantage of the auctioneer's mechanism. This problem is worse when we are dealing with several resources and several units as happens in combinatorial auctions. Thus, the winner determination algorithms should be strategy-proof in the sense that no bidder can manipulate the outcome of the auction. Our mechanisms are based on reinforcement mechanisms, so that agents have priorities and reservation prices that are dynamically adapted according to the auction outcomes, including agent's honesty.

1.2. Fairness

The application of fairness in recurrent auctions can be considered from either a local or a global point of view. A local point of view means treating each auction separately and trying to find a fair solution to each one. With a global point of view we can find that all the solutions of a set of auctions are fair. In this paper we focus on the global point of view. Fairness can also be analyzed in light of the agent who is fair. From the point of view of the bidder agent, fairness means that the objective of the agent is not only to maximize revenue in the short term but also to consider fairness at the time of making decisions. Fairness can benefit the whole society and consequently it allows to obtain

---
[1]We assume that we are working in a closed environment where there are not arrivals of new bidders.

greater individual benefits. In this case the solution to the allocation of resources is given by the interaction, negotiation and coalition between agents, etc. [6]. It is also possible to consider fairness from the point of view of the seller agent. In this case the behavior of bidders could be totally utilitarian and the seller agent imposes fairness to distribute the resources [9]. In this article we focus on the seller point of view. Other fairness studies take the bidder point of view, such as in an envy-free allocation, where none of the agents would prefer to exchange his allocated goods with those allocated to another agent [1]. However, this criteria alone is not sufficient since the efficiency is also important. Other studies [2] have shown how such efficient envy-free allocations can be attained through distributed negotiation among the agents. In such a setting, there is no central agent or authority to decide what the optimal allocation is, but the agents themselves perform a sequence of deals (exchanges of resources and payments) to find an efficient and envy-free allocation. The work presented by these authors, however, deals with an isolated allocation problem, and does not mention how distributed negotiation could be applied when the agents are faced with a sequence of allocation problems. In another study [4] the concept of egalitarian social welfare is defined to measure the degree of fairness in this envy-free scenario, as well as for a general purpose.

2. Related work

There are two main previous works on fair mechanisms. First, Lee and Szymanski proposed a method based on agent classification and reservation prices [7]. Agents are classified into three categories: definite winners, definite losers, and the "winner or loser" ones. This classification varies from auction to auction and depends on a reservation price that defines the separation between definite winners and "winner or loser" class. The reservation price changes according to an *ad hoc* mechanism and is updated in each auction. Based on a dropout probability model maintained by the auctioneer about the agents, resources are assigned to winner agents and "winner or loser" agents with the aim of keeping agents interested in the auction. After Lee and Szymanski's work, in [10] a reinforcement learning method was used to determine the reservation price from run to run, based on the previous reservation prices and the price paid by the bidder. Thus, reservation prices are set one per agent instead of a general value for all the bidders. Both approaches have been tested to demonstrate that fairness is able to reduce the problems of traditional recurrent auctions, but they have been developed for non-combinatorial auctions.

3. Fair MUCA Mechanisms

Our work focuses on developing a recurrent auction mechanism that clears the auction with fairness from the point of view of the auctioneer along time. Thus, after introducing some notation, in this section we first explain the mechanism based exclusively on priorities and then we extend the mechanism with dynamic reservation prices.

3.1. Notation

The recurrent auction A is formed by a succession of one-shot auctions $A = \{a_0, ..., a_{|A|-1}\}$. In each auction a_i, $|R_i|$ resources or items are auctioned where R_i is a set composed by tuples that indicates the resource r_x and the number of units of each resource q_x ($R_i = \{\langle r_0, q_0 \rangle, ..., \langle r_{|R_i|-1}, q_{|R_i|-1} \rangle\}$). A set R_i of an auction a_i can be different of the set R_j corresponding to auction a_j, $i \neq j$.

Auctions are ordered temporally and we associate to each auction a_i a time step t_i where T is the set of time steps in which the auctions of A occur ($T = \{t_0, ..., t_{|A|-1}\}$ where $t_0 < t_1 < ... < t_{|A|-1}$). G is the set of all bidder agents, $G = \{g_0, ..., g_{|G|-1}\}$, that participate in the recurrent auction A. A bidder agent g_i sends to the auctioneer agent a set $V_{i,j}$ of bids in auction a_j. Each bid is composed by a package and the price. A package is formed by one tuple indicating the items required by the agent and the number of units of each item (e.g. $\{\langle bandwidth, 2 \rangle, \langle memory, 5 \rangle\}$). We define as $\mathbb{S}_i$ the set of all packages sent by agent g_i in the recurrent auction, $\mathbb{S}_i = \{S_{i,0}, ..., S_{i,|\mathbb{S}_i|-1}\}$. Therefore a bid is defined as $b_{i,j,x} = \langle S_{i,m}, c_{i,j,x} \rangle$ where x is the number of bid in the auction a_j sent by agent g_i to obtain the package $S_{i,m}$ ($0 \leq m < |\mathbb{S}_i|$) paying $c_{i,j,x}$. We define the functions $\mathcal{S}(b_{i,j,x})$ to know the index of the package of bid $b_{i,j,x}$ and $\mathcal{C}(b_{i,j,x})$ to know the bid price.

We have chosen the XOR bidding language. This language allows to bidders express any preference over resources [3]. The bidder sends a set of bids XOR, consequently only one or none can be winner. Solving a combinatorial auction is NP-hard [11] and in the case of a recurrent auction, an auction must finish after the start of the following one and before the perish of resources too. For the sake of simplicity, we do not deal with the way of solving the combinatorial auctions in this paper.

3.2. Prioritized MUCA (PMUCA)

The PMUCA mechanism takes into account the past history of each agent. The auctioneer assigns to each bidder a set of priorities, one priority for each different package that the bidder agent has bid for in the recurrent auction. The value of each priority depends on the number of lost auctions since the bidder won a package for the last time. The more auctions the bidder has lost the greater the priority. The priority values are calculated by the auctioneer and are only known by him. The priority values are calculated after the reception of bids and are used to solve the auction modifying the prices $c_{i,j,x}$ of the bids $b_{i,j,x}$ generating new bids $b'_{i,j,x}$ with new prices $c'_{i,j,x}$. The auctioneer stores in a set L_i the counters of lost auctions for each bidder g_i, one counter for each element of $\mathbb{S}_i$ ($L_i = \{l_{i,0}, ..., l_{i,|\mathbb{S}_i|-1}\}$).

However, the outcome from such fair winner determination, that is, changing the price from $c_{i,j,x}$ to $c'_{i,j,x}$, could be learnt easily by dishonesty agents. That is, a bidder that is not actually interested in an auction run could send a fake bid with the aim to lose and thus obtain a greater priority in the next auction where the agent is truly interested. Thus, a mechanism should not incentivize the participation in the auctions where the bidder is not actually interested.

On the other hand a mechanism that works with combinatorial auctions must take into account the different nature of items. A bidder could send a bid for an item of little value to obtain a high priority and then use the priority to bid for a high value item. For

```
{1}    for each bidder $g_i$
{2}        if agent $g_i$ has won in current auction $a_j$
{3}            for each bid $b_{i,j,x}$ in $V_{i,j}$
{4}                $l_{i,\mathcal{S}(b_{i,j,x})} \leftarrow 0, k_{i,\mathcal{S}(b_{i,j,x})} \leftarrow \mathcal{C}(b_{i,j,x})$
{5}        else
{6}            for each bid $b_{i,j,x}$ in $V_{i,j}$
{7}                if $(k_{i,\mathcal{S}(b_{i,j,x})} < \mathcal{C}(b_{i,j,x}))$
{8}                    $l_{i,\mathcal{S}(b_{i,j,x})} \leftarrow 0, k_{i,\mathcal{S}(b_{i,j,x})} \leftarrow \mathcal{C}(b_{i,j,x})$
{9}                else
{10}                   $l_{i,\mathcal{S}(b_{i,j,x})} \leftarrow l_{i,\mathcal{S}(b_{i,j,x})} + 1$
```

Figure 1. Algorithm for update the L_i and K_i sets after auction a_j.

example a bidder could send a bid for a pencil until obtaining a high priority assuming the risk of winning the pencil since the cost of the pencil is low. Then, when the bidder obtains a high priority, he can use the priority to bid for a car.

In order to avoid these situations we define a *cycle* as a set of consecutive auctions where the priority of the agent g_i for the package $S_{i,m}$ is not decreasing. Each agent has a different cycle for each package. When a cycle ends the priority is initialized with an initial value. A cycle ends and another starts when a bidder agent wins the package or when the agent sends a bid for the package with a price higher than the bid price that the agent sent at the first auction of the cycle. If a bidder agent sends more than one bid, the agent could have a different priority for each bid since each bid requests a different package. We define $k_{i,m}$ as the price of the bid in the first auction of the current cycle of agent g_i and package $S_{i,m}$. We define K_i as the set of all the $k_{i,m}$ of agent g_i, $K_i = \{k_{i,0}, ..., k_{i,|S_i|-1}\}$.

The priority $p_{i,m}$ of an agent g_i and a package $S_{i,m}$ is calculated with the following equation:

$$p_{i,m} = \begin{cases} l_{i,m} < \gamma & \lambda + \frac{1-\lambda}{\gamma} \cdot l_{i,m} \\ l_{i,m} \geq \gamma & 1 \end{cases} \quad (1)$$

Where λ is the initial priority and γ indicates the number of lost auctions necessary so that the priority arrives to its maximum value (1.0). $l_{i,m}$ is the number of lost auctions in the actual cycle for package $S_{i,m}$. The expression $\frac{1-\lambda}{\gamma}$ shows the increase of priority for each lost auction. After priorities are calculated, the modified bids $b'_{i,j,x}$ are generated. The bid $b'_{i,j,x}$ of an agent g_i that has sent a bid $b_{i,j,x}$ in the auction a_j is:

$$b'_{i,j,x} = \langle S_{i,\mathcal{S}(b_{i,j,x})}, \mathcal{C}(b_{i,j,x}) \cdot p_{i,\mathcal{S}(b_{i,j,x})} \rangle \quad (2)$$

Then the auction is solved in the traditional form with the $b'_{i,j,x}$ bids. When winners are determined, the mechanism updates the sets L_i and K_i (see Algorithm of Figure 1). For each bidder g_i if any of his bids has been winner, the actual cycle is ended for each package $S_{i,m}$ corresponding to the bids sent by agent g_i, therefore all counters $l_{i,m}$ of agent g_i that corresponds to bids sent in the auction are initialized. In the case of all bids being losers, then all counters corresponding to g_i are incremented one unit except if the price is lower than $k_{i,m}$. We assume that there aren't two bids from the same bidder with the same package with different prices in the same auction since one of the bids would be dominated by the other and never will be winner [5,11].

In order to show that our mechanism cannot be affected by the explained manipulation, let us suppose two consecutive auctions: a_0 and a_1. An agent wants to win a package in the auction a_1 but not in a_0. Suppose the following two situations: an agent that is honest (g_h) and an agent that is not ($g_{\neg h}$). So, g_h does not participate in the first auction, and in the second he sends a bid $b_{h,1,1}$ for the package with a price $\mathcal{C}(b_{h,1,1})$. While, $g_{\neg h}$ sends a bid in the first auction with a low price $\mathcal{C}(b_{\neg h,0,1})$ with the aim of losing and raising his priority for the package in the next auction. In the second auction $g_{\neg h}$ sends a bid with a price $\mathcal{C}(b_{\neg h,1,1})$, where $\mathcal{C}(b_{\neg h,0,1}) < \mathcal{C}(b_{\neg h,1,1})$. Assume that the price is the same for both agents in the second auction, $\mathcal{C}(b_{\neg h,1,1}) = \mathcal{C}(b_{h,1,1})$. Thus, in order to analyze which agent has more chances to become a winner, we define $pow_x(y)$ as the probability of winning in the auction a_x with a bid price y. Then the probability of winning for the honest agent in the second auction a_1 is $pow_1(\mathcal{C}(b_{h,1,1}) \cdot pr)$ where pr is the priority of agent g_h. Analogously, the probability of winning for $g_{\neg h}$ is $pow_1(\mathcal{C}(b_{\neg h,1,1}) \cdot \lambda)$. Note that $pr \geq \lambda$ since $\mathcal{C}(b_{\neg h,0,1}) < \mathcal{C}(b_{\neg h,1,1})$ and consequently the priority for $g_{\neg h}$ is initialized with the initial value λ. Then the probability of winning for g_h is equal or greater than for $g_{\neg h}$:

$$pow_1(\mathcal{C}(b_{h,1,1}) \cdot pr) \geq pow_1(\mathcal{C}(b_{\neg h,1,1}) \cdot \lambda) \tag{3}$$

Regarding the price that the agents have to pay, g_h has an expected value of $pow_1(\mathcal{C}(b_{h,1,1}) \cdot pr) \cdot \mathcal{C}(b_{h,1,1})$. On the other hand $g_{\neg h}$ has an expectation of $pow_1(\mathcal{C}(b_{\neg h,1,1}) \cdot \lambda) \cdot \mathcal{C}(b_{\neg h,1,1}) + pow_0(\mathcal{C}(b_{\neg h,0,1}) \cdot pr) \cdot \mathcal{C}(b_{\neg h,0,1})$. Then, assuming the worst case in which the honest agent was also the initial priority value ($pr = \lambda$), we obtain the results shown in Equation 4.

$$\begin{aligned} pow_1(\mathcal{C}(b_{h,1,1}) \cdot \lambda) \cdot \mathcal{C}(b_{h,1,1}) \leq \\ pow_1(\mathcal{C}(b_{\neg h,1,1}) \cdot \lambda) \cdot \mathcal{C}(b_{\neg h,1,1}) + \\ pow_0(\mathcal{C}(b_{\neg h,0,1}) \cdot \lambda) \cdot \mathcal{C}(b_{\neg h,0,1}) \end{aligned} \tag{4}$$

As $\mathcal{C}(b_{h,1,1}) = \mathcal{C}(b_{\neg h,1,1})$ we can see that $g_{\neg h}$ has more chances to pay equal or more than g_h supposing that they win the same number of times. Then, the best strategy for a bidder in not to participate in the auction if the agent is not really interested in winning it.

3.3. Dynamic Reservation Price MUCA (DRPMUCA)

Priorities are fair since they allow bidders from win time to time, independently of their wealth, and keep agents interested in the auction. However fairness can be improved if a minimum price can be defined for each agent according to his wealth. The main purpose of reservation prices is to incentive bidders to pay a higher value for resources. In DRPMUCA the auctioneer has a set RP_i of reservation prices for each bidder agent g_i. In RP_i there is a reservation price for each package sent by g_i ($RP_i = \{rp_{i,0}, ..., rp_{i,|S_i|-1}\}$). The reservation price $rp_{i,m}$ is defined as the minimum price at which the auctioneer is willing to sell the package $S_{i,m}$ to the agent g_i. This means that the auctioneer will not accept a bid of agent g_i for package $S_{i,m}$ with a price lower than $rp_{i,m}$. The reservation prices are dynamically changed according to the bids sent in each auction.

```
{1} For each bidder g_i
{2}    For each package rp_{i,m} in RP_i
{3}       If bidder g_i has sent a bid b_{i,j,x} for S_{i,m}
{4}          If C(b_{i,j,x}) > rp_{i,m} then
{5}             rp_{i,m} = rp_{i,m} + max( (C(b_{i,j,x})-rp_{i,m})/2 , rp_{i,m} + rp_{i,m} · δ)
{6}          else
{7}             rp_{i,m} = rp_{i,m} - rp_{i,m} · δ
{8}       else
{9}          rp_{i,m} = rp_{i,m} - rp_{i,m} · δ
```

Figure 2. Update algorithm of RP_i after a_j auction

DRPMUCA is composed by three phases. In the first phase the auction is solved in the traditional way but only taking into account the bids $b_{i,j,x}$ that fulfils the condition $C(b_{i,j,x}) \geq rp_{i,S(b_{i,j,x})}$. In this first phase the bids are not modified. Once determined the winners of the first phase, the idea of the second phase is to sell the resources that are not being distributed in the first phase between the loser bidders with higher priority without taking into account the bid price. But in order to an agent become a winner in the second phase, the priority of the bid has to be greater than a parameter ξ. This minimum priority value avoids having the rich agents obtaining the resources at low price due to the fair distribution. The priority is calculated using Equation 1. Then each bid $b_{i,j,x}$ that belongs to loser bidders with a priority greater than ξ is modified in order to obtain $b'_{i,j,x}$:

$$b'_{i,j,x} = \langle S(b_{i,j,x}), p_{i,S(b_{i,j,x})} \rangle \qquad (5)$$

A new auction is solved with the modified bids. Finally, in the last phase of DRPMUCA, the information related to priorities (L_i and K_i sets) are updated following the algorithm of Figure 1 and reservation prices as follows. For each agent, if the price of a bid that requires the package $S_{i,m}$ is greater than $rp_{i,m}$, $rp_{i,m}$ will be incremented for the next auction since the bidder is showing that he can pay more for the package. Conversely if the price is lower, $rp_{i,m}$ will be decremented. Note that changes in $rp_{i,m}$ are independent of whether the bids are winners or losers, or they participate or not (if they do not participate is equivalent to send a bid with price 0 for all of the packages, and the reservation price is decreased). We define $\delta \in [0, 1]$ as the minimum percentage of increment or decrement. When $rp_{i,m}$ is incremented, the increment is the maximum between the half of the difference between the price and the $rp_{i,m}$ and $rp_{i,m} \cdot \delta$. When $rp_{i,m}$ is decremented, the new $rp_{i,m}$ is $rp_{i,m} - (rp_{i,m} \cdot \delta)$. Reservation prices are updated at the end of each auction and are used to solve the next auction. Figure 2 shows the update of each RP_i.

In order to show that this mechanism cannot be affected by the explained manipulation too, let us suppose two consecutive auctions: a_0 and a_1. An agent wants to win a package in the auction a_1 but not in a_0. Suppose an honest agent (g_h) and a dishonest agent ($g_{\neg h}$). g_h does not participate in the first auction and in the second sends a bid $b_{h,1,1}$ for the package with a price $C(b_{h,1,1})$. In the second case, $g_{\neg h}$ sends a bid in the first auction with a low price $C(b_{\neg h,0,1})$ with the aim of losing and decreasing the reservation price for the package in the next auction. In the second auction $g_{\neg h}$ sends a bid with a price $C(b_{\neg h,1,1})$, where $C(b_{\neg h,1,1}) = C(b_{h,1,1})$. In both cases the reservation prices are decremented thus the resulting reservation prices are the same and consequently the probability of obtaining the package is the same in both situations.

Regarding the payments, analogously to the case of PMUCA, the honest agent has to pay the same or less than $g_{\neg h}$:

$$pow_1(\mathcal{C}(b_{h,1,1})) \cdot \mathcal{C}(b_{h,1,1}) \leq pow_1(\mathcal{C}(b_{\neg h,1,1})) \cdot \mathcal{C}(b_{\neg h,1,1})$$
$$+ pow_0(\mathcal{C}(b_{\neg h,0,1})) \cdot \mathcal{C}(b_{\neg h,0,1}) \qquad (6)$$

4. Experimentation

In this section we show the experimentation done with the proposed mechanisms. First of all we define a fairness measure to know the level of fairness obtained by the different mechanisms. Then we describe our experimental scenario and finally we show the results obtained in a bandwidth allocation domain.

4.1. Fairness measure

We define a measure that takes into account the sequence of winning and losing bids of an agent in a recurrent auction. This measure provides an aggregation of bidder satisfaction values of each auction round. We assume that if a bidder sends a price $\mathcal{C}(b_{i,j,1})$ in a bid $b_{i,j,1}$ and in other bid $b_{i,j,2}$ he sends a price $\mathcal{C}(b_{i,j,2})$, if $\mathcal{C}(b_{i,j,1}) > \mathcal{C}(b_{i,j,2})$, then we suppose that the bidder is more interested in winning the bid $b_{i,j,1}$. Consequently we assume that if he wins $b_{i,j,1}$, it has a greatest satisfaction degree than winning $b_{i,j,2}$. Then we define the satisfaction of an agent g_i in an auction a_j as the won value divided by the maximum that the agent could win. Formally:

$$s(i,j) = \frac{\sum_{\forall b_{i,j,x} \in V_{i,j}} (\mathcal{C}(b_{i,j,x}) \cdot \mathcal{W}(b_{i,j,x}))}{\mathcal{M}(V_{i,j})} \qquad (7)$$

Where $V_{i,j}$ is the set of bids sent by agent g_i in the auction a_j. $\mathcal{W}(b_{i,j,x})$ indicates whether bid $b_{i,j,x}$ has resulted winner (value 1) or not (value 0) and $\mathcal{M}(V_{i,j})$ returns the highest bid price of the $V_{i,j}$ set. Thus the level of fairness of an auctioneer can be defined as the inverse of the standard deviation of the average satisfaction degree of all of the agents.

4.2. Experimental setup

We have created a bandwidth allocation scenario based on extending the one described in [7] to multi unit combinatorial auctions. Each auctioneer is a bandwidth provider that owns 60 units of bandwidth that are distributed in five groups. The first group is dedicated to voice (20 units), the second group is dedicated to high quality voice (10 units), the third group is dedicated to video (10 units), the fourth group is dedicated to high quality video (10 units) and the fifth group is dedicated to data (10 units). Then the auctioneer can provide five different services or resources: Voice (VO), High Quality Voice (HQVO), Video (VI), High Quality Video (HQVI) and Data (D).

There are 100 bidder agents that are requesting services. Bidders can be classified in six groups. The agents of the first group (20 agents) are doing a video conference and send a bid to obtain the package $\{\langle VI, 1\rangle, \langle VO, 1\rangle\}$. The second group (15 agents) is watching TV and want a good quality, and bid for $\{\langle HQVI, 1\rangle, \langle HQVO, 1\rangle\}$ xor $\{\langle VI, 1\rangle, \langle HQVO, 1\rangle\}$ xor $\{\langle HQVI, 1\rangle, \langle VO, 1\rangle\}$ xor $\{\langle VI, 1\rangle, \langle VO, 1\rangle\}$. Obviously for the first bid they offer the highest price but if they cannot win the first bid they want to win any of the alternatives. The third group (30 agents) is composed by bidders that are doing phone calls and they want $\{\langle VO, 1\rangle\}$. The members of the fourth group (10 agents) want $\{\langle HQVO, 1\rangle\}$ xor $\{\langle VO, 1\rangle\}$ since they are listening to music. In the fifth group there are 15 agents that need $\{\langle D, 1\rangle\}$. Finally the agents of the last group (10 agents) need $\{\langle D, 2\rangle\}$ because they want to download files at a high velocity.

To compare the results of the proposed mechanisms, three unfair auction mechanisms have been considered. First the Traditional MUCA (TMUCA) mechanism in which the winners are the bidders with the highest bids. This is the simplest auction mechanism. Second the Reservation Price MUCA (RPMUCA) in which the auctioneer defines a reservation price (the same for all bidders) that indicates the minimum price the bidders should pay. Only bids higher than the auctioneer's reservation price are considered during the winner selection. And third, the Cancellable MUCA (CMUCA) where if the resulting revenue of an auction does not meet the minimum requirements of the auctioneer, the entire auction is canceled.

In order to implement the bidding policy of bidders we have adapted the strategy proposed in [7] to combinatorial auctions. For each possible package $S_{i,m}$ bidders have a $z_{i,m}$ value that indicates the current price that they offered by the package $S_{i,m}$ and a value $w_{i,m}$ that indicates the maximum price that they can pay for the package. $z_{i,m}$ is dynamic during the auctions while $w_{i,m}$ is chosen at the beginning of the simulation and it maintains its value during all the recurrent auction. The initial value of $z_{i,m}$ is a random value between $w_{i,m}/2$ and $w_{i,m}$. If a bidder loses in an auction a_j, the bidder increments the value of $z_{i,m}$ multiplying $z_{i,m}$ by α for all the packages that the agent has requested in the auction a_j in order to increment the probability of winning in the next auction. We consider that a bidder loses the auction a_j if none of his bids results as winner. In the opposite, if the bidder won in the auction a_j, all the prices of the packages requested are decremented multiplying it by β the 50% of the times. The other 50% the prices remain with the same value. The values of α and β are fixed to 1.2 and 0.8 respectively. The minimum price that a bidder g_i can offer for a package $S_{i,m}$ is the 10% of the $w_{i,m}$ value. Before starting the simulation a value of wealth is assigned to each bidder following several statistical distributions. This value will be used to set the values of $w_{i,m}$. The value for each $w_{i,m}$ is the wealth of the bidder multiplied by the number of units of the package counting twice the high quality items.

In order to model the bidder drop problem we have used the same concept of Tolerance to Consecutive Losses defined in [7]. Each bidder has a TCL value randomly distributed between 2 and 10. If a bidder agent loses more than his TCL consecutive auctions he leaves the recurrent auction.

4.3. Results

Figure 3 shows the average resource price at which each of the 5 auctioneers has sold the resources during the 2000 auctions of one simulation. The x-axis represents the temporal sequence of the auctions, and the y-axis is the average price. The wealth of bidders has been distributed following a uniform distribution in [2, 10]. The numerical data is shown

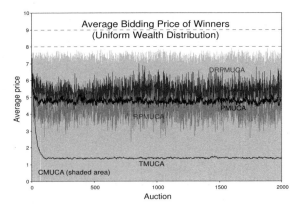

Figure 3. Average bidding price in scenario 1 (uniform wealth distribution). CMUCA appears in the plot as an area because the average prices are 0 when the auction is cancelled.

in Table 1, where the total revenue, the resource waste produced, the fairness level, and the number of bidders remaining with the auctioneer at the end are shown. The table values are the average of 20 simulations with the standard deviation below.

Results on Table 1 show that the bidder drop problem affects in a major way TMUCA, CMUCA and RPMUCA. In the case of TMUCA, the drop of bidders has provoked the collapse of the auction. Figure 3 shows that the average price of TMUCA has fallen to very low prices in less than 100 auctions. The bidders that have not dropped have obtained the power of negotiation and consequently have fixed the price at the minimum possible. The rest of the methods, despite the drop of bidders, has maintained the power of negotiation thanks to the reservation prices. Regarding the resource waste, RPMUCA and CMUCA have been the mechanisms most affected. They have wasted 31.87% and 38.94% of resources respectively. Below these mechanisms, DRPMUCA has lost 15.32% of resources and finally the mechanism non based on reservation prices are the ones that have wasted less resources. Note that these methods can also have resource waste due to the combinatorial nature of the problem. Regarding the total revenue, DRPMUCA has been the mechanism that has obtained the first position followed by RPMUCA, PMUCA and CMUCA. Finally regarding fairness, DRPMUCA is the mechanism with a higher value followed by PMUCA. We can see that the methods with higher fairness obtains the highest revenue.

On the other hand, in a bandwidth communications domain it is feasible to expect malfunctions, technical problems with the network, and maintenance issues that decrease the available supply. In a second experiment we have reduced the supply in the auctions during the time steps between 1000 and 1100 by a 40%. Figure 4 (left) shows the average price in one simulation of this experiment. We can see how prices rise for all methods during the time with scarce units of resource (less supply, prices go up). During this period all methods suffer the drop of the poorest bidders, and as a consequence, some of the mechanisms are not able to return to their same or close steady-state when the supply is restored. Only DRPMUCA and RPMUCA achieve an acceptable average price when the supply is restored. The average total revenue in 20 simulations for RPMUCA is 508869.65 lower than the 635399.09 obtained by DRPMUCA.

In this experiment the effect of bidder drop problem is higher. All the methods have lost more bidders than in the first experiments. In Figure 4 (right) we can see the drop of

Table 1. Results for all mechanisms with a uniform distribution of wealth in scenario 1. Averaged results of 20 simulations

Name	◇	□	△	⋈
PMUCA	550119.74	5729.30	68.60	3.51
	60183.99	1480.90	2.43	0.08
DRPMUCA	666314.48	18384.25	66.50	4.10
	41969.16	2283.99	2.18	0.12
TMUCA	178297.63	2439.00	52.25	2.71
	29690.01	1835.44	1.58	0.08
RPMUCA	549565.30	38255.10	45.25	3.10
	53360.16	6779.03	3.64	0.03
CMUCA	532021.85	46737.40	37.60	3.46
	19758.86	2932.32	1.04	0.06

◇ Total revenue □ Resource Waste △ Number of bidders ⋈ Fairness

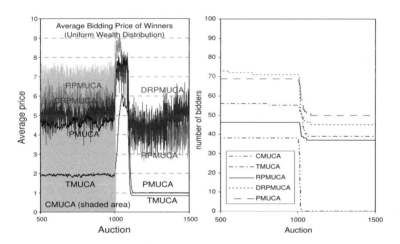

Figure 4. Average bidding price in scenario 2 (left). Number of bidders in the recurrent auction (right). Detail between time step 500 and 1500

bidders produced at time step 1000. PMUCA is the method that has maintained the greatest number of bidders but when the supply has returned to its normal value, the method has collapsed. We can find the explanation on the fair distribution of the resources. This mechanism focus on avoiding resource waste, and it is always trying to sell all the resources. If we classify the bidders in two classes, rich and poor agents, the bidders from the poor class put pressure on the upper class. If bidders from the high class relax, the bidders of the lower class get the resources, and the rich ones do not get the resources, consequently they maintain prices at an acceptable level. When bidders of the upper class get the resources at low prices due to the fair distribution, then they have no incentive to increase their bids, and prices begin to decrease. This does not happen with DRPMUCA, because they sacrifice resource waste for avoiding that rich agents obtain the resources due to the fair distribution thanks to the ξ parameter.

5. Conclusions

In environments where resources are perishable and the allocation of resources is repeated over time with the same set or a very similar set of agents, recurrent auctions come up. A recurrent auction is a series of auctions where the result of one auction can influence the following ones. However, these kinds of auctions have particular problems when the wealth of the agents is unevenly distributed and resources are perishable. Fair mechanisms have already been proposed in order to deal with this problem in non-combinatorial auctions. In this work we have presented two mechanisms for recurrent combinatorial auctions based on priorities and reservation prices that minimize these problems and prevents some kind of bidder's manipulation. The results show that fairness gives bidders incentives to stay in the auction and reservation prices help maintaining the equilibrium in negotiation power. Moreover the DRPMUCA proposed here avoids collapse by introducing a minimum priority value that prevents the fairly distributed resources from arriving to the middle-upper class and presents the highest averaged performance of all the simulated conditions and makes a profit for the auctioneer. However, we need to further explore different manipulation strategies to clearly claim about the impossibility of manipulating our mechanism.

Acknowledgements

This work has been done with the support of the Commissioner for Universities and Research of the Department of Innovation, Universities and Enterprises of the Generalitat of Catalonia, the European Social Funds and the Spanish MICINN project SuRoS (TIN2008-04547).

References

[1] S.J. Brams and A.D. Taylor, *Fair division: From cake-cutting to dispute resolution*, Cambridge University Press, 1996.
[2] Y. Chevaleyre, U. Endriss, J. Lang, and N. Maudet, 'A short introduction to computational social choice', in *SOFSEM-2007*, number 4362 in LNCS. Springer-Verlag, (2007).
[3] *Combinatorial Auctions*, eds., Peter Cramton, Yoav Shoham, and Richard Steinberg, MIT Press, 2006.
[4] U. Endriss, N. Maudet, F. Sadri, and F. Toni, 'Negotiating socially optimal allocations of resources', *JAIR*, **25**, 315–348, (2006).
[5] Y. Fujishima, K. Leyton-Brown, and Y. Shoham, 'Taming the computational complexity of combinatorial auctions: Optimal and approximate approaches', in *IJCAI '99*, pp. 548–553, (1999).
[6] S. De Jong, K. Tuyls, and K. Verbeeck, 'Fairness in multi-agent systems', *Knowledge Engineering Review*, **23**(2), 153–180, (2008).
[7] J-S. Lee and B.K. Szymanski, 'A novel auction mechanism for selling time-sensitive e-services', in *IEEE International Conference on E-Commerce Technology*, pp. 75–82. IEEE Computer Society, (2005).
[8] J-S. Lee and B.K. Szymanski, 'Stabilizing markets via a novel auction based pricing mechanism for short-term contracts for network services', in *Integrated Network Management*, pp. 367–380, (2005).
[9] M. Lemaître, G. Verfaillie, H. Fargier, J. Lang, N. Bataille, and J.-M. Lachiver, 'Equitable allocation of earth observing satellite resources', in *Proc. 5th ONERA-DLR Aerospace Symposium (ODAS 2003)*, (2003).
[10] J. Murillo, V. Muñoz, B. López, and D. Busquets, 'A fair mechanism for recurrent multi-unit auctions', in *Lecture Notes in Computer Science*, volume 5244, pp. 147–158. Springer, (2008).
[11] T. Sandholm, 'Algorithm for optimal winner determination in combinatorial auctions', in *Artificial Intelligence*, pp. 542–547, (2002).

Onto.PT: Automatic Construction of a Lexical Ontology for Portuguese

Hugo GONÇALO OLIVEIRA [1], and Paulo GOMES [2]
CISUC, University of Coimbra, Portugal

Abstract. This ongoing research presents an alternative to the manual creation of lexical resources and proposes an approach towards the automatic construction of a lexical ontology for Portuguese. Textual sources are exploited in order to obtain a lexical network based on terms and, after clustering and mapping, a wordnet-like lexical ontology is created. At the end of the paper, current results are shown.

Keywords. Natural language processing, lexical semantics, knowledge extraction, ontologies

Introduction

In the last decade, besides the increasing amount of Semantic Web [1] applications, we have seen a growing number of systems that perform tasks where understanding the information conveyed by natural language plays an important role. Natural language processing (NLP) tasks, ranging from machine translation or automatic generation of text to intelligent search, are becoming more and more common, which demands better access to semantic knowledge.

Knowledge about words and their meanings is typically structured in lexical ontologies, such as Princeton WordNet [2], which are used in the achievement of the aforementioned tasks. Since this kind of resource is most of the times handcrafted, its creation and maintenance involves time-consuming human effort. So, its automatic construction from text arises as an alternative, providing less intensive labour, easier maintenance and allowing for higher coverage, as a trade-off for lower, but still acceptable, correction.

This paper presents Onto.PT, an ongoing research project where textual resources, more precisely dictionaries, thesaurus and corpora, are being exploited in order to extract lexico-semantic knowledge that will be used in the construction of a public domain lexical ontology for Portuguese. While the first stage of this work deals mainly with information extraction from text, subsequent stages are concerned with the disambiguation of the acquired information and the construction of a structure similar to WordNet. Considering that information is extracted from different sources, one particular point is that we aim to accomplish word

---

[1] E-mail: hroliv@dei.uc.pt
[2] E-mail: pgomes@dei.uc.pt

sense disambiguation (WSD) [3] based not on the context where information is found but on knowledge already extracted. Therefore, clustering over extracted synonymy instances is first used to identify groups of synonymous words that will be used as a conceptual base. The rest of the information, consisting of term-based triples, is then mapped to the conceptual base as each term is assigned to a group of synonyms.

After introducing some background concepts and relevant work, we state the goals of this research. Then, we introduce the stages involved in the approach we are following. Before concluding, current results of this project, as well as their evaluation, when available, are shown.

1. Background knowledge

Besides recognising words, their structure and their interactions, applications that deal with information in natural language need to understand its meaning. This is usually achieved with the help of knowledge bases assembling lexical and semantic information, such as lexical ontologies. Despite some terminological issues, the latter can be seen both as a lexicon and as an ontology [4], and are significantly different from classic ontologies — they provide knowledge structured on lexical items (words) of a language by relating them according to their meanings and are not based on a specific domain. In this context, Princeton WordNet [2] is the most representative lexico-semantic resource for English and also the most common model for representing a lexical ontology. WordNet is structured on synsets, which are groups of synonymous words describing concepts, and connections, denoting semantic relations (e.g. hyponymy, part-of), between those groups.

The success of the WordNet model led to its adoption by many lexical resources in several different languages, such as the wordnets involved in the EuroWordNet [5] project, or WordNet.PT [6], for Portuguese. However, the creation of a wordnet, as well as the creation of most ontologies, is typically manual, thus involving much human effort [7]. To overcome this problem, some authors [8] propose the translation of a target wordnet to wordnets in other languages. This seems to be a suitable alternative for several applications but another problem arises because different languages represent different socio-cultural realities, they do not cover exactly the same part of the lexicon and, even where they seem to be common, several concepts are lexicalised differently [4]. Another popular alternative is to extract lexico-semantic knowledge and learn lexical ontologies from text, which can either be unstructured, as in textual corpora, or semi-structured, as in dictionaries or encyclopedias.

Research on the acquisition of lexico-semantic knowledge from corpora is not new and varied methods, roughly divided into linguistics-based (see [9,10]), statistics or graph-based (see [11,12,13]) or hybrid (see [14,15,16,17,18]), have been proposed to achieve different steps of this task, such as the extraction of relations like hyponymy [9,14,15], meronymy [16,18], causation [17], or the establishment of sets of similar or synonymous words [10,12,11].

Dictionary processing, which became popular during the 1970s [19], is also a good option for the extraction of this kind of knowledge. MindNet [20] is both an extraction methodology and a lexical ontology different from a wordnet, since it was created automatically from a dictionary and its structure is based on such resources. Nevertheless, it still connects sense records with semantic relations (e.g. hyponymy, cause, manner). Most of the research on the automatic creation of lexical resources from electronic dictionaries was made during the 1980s and 1990s, where the advantages and drawbacks of using the later resources were studied and discussed [21]. Still, there are reports of recent works on the automatic extraction of knowledge from dictionaries (see [22,23,24]). For instance, PAPEL [23] is a lexical resource consisting of a set of triples denoting semantic relations between words found in a Portuguese dictionary.

Besides corpora and dictionary processing, in the later years, semi-structured collaborative resources such as Wikipedia or Wiktionary, have proved to be important sources of lexico-semantic information and have thus been receiving more and more attention by the research community (see for instance [25,26,27,24]).

On the one hand, there are clear advantages of using dictionaries — they are already structured on words and meanings, they cover the whole language, and they generally use simple and almost predictable vocabulary. On the other hand, dictionaries are static resources with limited knowledge. Therefore, some authors [9,10] argue that textual corpora should be exploited to extract knowledge that can be found neither in dictionaries nor in lexical ontologies. Also, while language dictionaries are not always available for this kind of research, there is always much text available on the most different subjects, for instance in the Web. The biggest problem concerning lexico-semantic information extraction from corpora is that there are no boundaries on the vocabulary and linguistic constructions used, thus leading to more ambiguity and parsing issues.

Most of the aforementioned works on the extraction of semantic relations from text output related words, identified by their orthographical form. However, since natural language is ambiguous, this representation is not practical for most computational applications, because the same orthographical form might either have completely different meanings (e.g. *bank*, institution or slope) or closely related meanings (e.g. *bank*, institution or building). Furthermore, there are words with completely different orthographical forms denoting the same concept (e.g. *car* and *automobile*). This might lead to serious inconsistencies, for instance when dealing with inference.

Therefore, another challenge on lexical ontology learning from text, often called ontologising, is concerned with moving from knowledge based on simple words to knowledge based on concepts. For English, there are works on the assignment of suitable WordNet synsets to the arguments of relational triples extracted from text, or to other term entities, such as Wikipedia entries [25]. Some of the methods for ontologising term-based triples compute the similarity between the context from where each triple was extracted with the synset glosses [25], terms in synsets, sibling synsets or direct hyponym synsets [28]. Others look for relations established with the argument terms and with the terms of each synset [29], or take advantage of generalisation through hypernymy links [29].

2. Research goals

The main goal of this research is the automatic construction of a broad-coverage structure of Portuguese words according to their meanings, or, more precisely, a lexical ontology.

Regarding information sparsity, it seems natural trying to create such a resource with knowledge extracted from several sources, as proposed in [30] for creating a lexical ontology for German, but for Portuguese. Thus, we are using or planning to use the following sources of knowledge: (i) dictionaries, such as Dicionário da Língua Portuguesa [31], through PAPEL; Dicionário Aberto (DA) [32], an open domain electronic version of a Portuguese dictionary; and the Portuguese Wiktionary[3]; (ii) encyclopedias, such as the complete entries of the Portuguese Wikipedia[4] or just their abstracts; (iii) corpora, yet to decide; and (iv) thesaurus, such as TeP [33], an electronic thesaurus for Brasilian Portuguese; and OpenThesaurus.PT[5], a thesaurus for European Portuguese.

Considering each resource specificities, such as its organisation or the vocabulary used, the extraction procedures might be significantly different, but must have one common output: a set of term-based relational triples. Still, considering the limitations of representations based on the terms, we are adopting a wordnet-like structure which enables the establishment of unambiguous semantic relations between synsets. Moving from a lexical network to a lexical ontology requires the application of several WSD techniques. However, our intention is to achieve WSD based only on knowledge already extracted, because we believe this is the best way to harmoniously integrate knowledge coming from different heterogeneous sources. Another point that should be considered is the attribution of confidence weights on each triple, based on its frequency and also on one or several similarity measures, calculated according to the words distribution in a corpus.

3. Proposed approach

All the stages currently involved in the creation of Onto.PT are represented in Figure 1. Despite their description, this section gives an overview on possible ways to evaluate this work, which, in the future, will be freely available.

3.1. Extraction of relational triples

The first stage on the creation of Onto.PT is the automatic extraction of lexico-semantic knowledge from textual sources. The extracted information is represented as relational triples, $t_1 \ R \ t_2$, where t_1 and t_2 are terms and R is the name of a semantic relation held between possible meanings of t_1 and t_2. These triples establish a lexical network, $L = (N, E)$, with $|N|$ nodes and $|E|$ edges, $E \subset N^2$, where each node $i \in N$ is a term and each edge between nodes i and j, $E(i, R, j)$, means that a relation of the type R between nodes i and j was extracted.

---

[3] http://pt.wiktionary.org
[4] http://pt.wikipedia.org
[5] http://openthesaurus.caixamagica.pt/

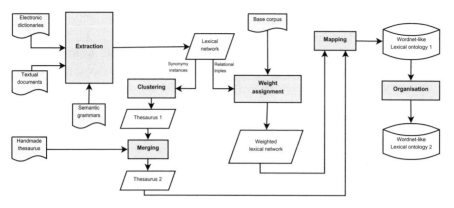

Figure 1. Information flow in the construction of Onto.PT

Table 1. Examples of (Portuguese) patterns frequently indicating semantic relations.

Relation	Example pattern	Rough translation
Hypernymy	tipo|género|variedade|forma de	*type|variety|kind of*
Meronymy	parte|membro de	*part|member of*
Causation	causado|provocado|originado por	*caused|provoked|originated by*
Purpose	usado|utilizado|serve para	*used for*

Hence, each sentence is analysed by a parser according to semantic grammars created specifically for each relation to be extracted. Most of the rules in the semantic grammars are based on textual patterns frequently used to denote each semantic relation, such as the ones presented in Table 1 for well-known relations in Portuguese.

Extraction from dictionaries follows very closely the extraction procedure described in [23]. Despite significant differences in dictionary and corpora text, the general extraction procedure works for both, with slightly differences in the construction of the grammars. For instance, most of the relations extracted from dictionary definitions are established between a word in the definition and the word being defined. Dictionaries are important to obtain synonymy instances (t_1 SYNONYM_OF t_2), since many words are defined by (a list of) their synonyms. On the other hand, despite sharing most of the times the same neighbourhood, synonymy instances may not co-occur frequently in corpora text [13].

In order to find less intuitive patterns, a pattern discovery algorithm [9] can be applied over a corpus: (i) a relation R is chosen; (ii) several pairs of words known to establish R are looked for in a corpus; (iii) everytime both words of the same pair co-occur in a sentence, the text connecting them is collected; (iv) most frequent sentences collected are used as hints for new patterns denoting R. This procedure can also be the seen as the first step to weakly supervised relation extraction [34].

3.2. Clustering for synsets

Since lexical resources based on the words orthographical form are inadequate to deal with ambiguity, we are adopting a wordnet-like structure, where concepts are described by synsets and ambiguous words are included in a synset for each of their meanings. Semantic relations can thereby be unambiguously established between two synsets, and concepts, even though described by groups of words, will bring together natural language and knowledge engineering in a suitable representation, for instance, for the Semantic Web. Moreover, this makes it possible to apply inference rules for the discovery of new knowledge.

From a linguistic point of view, word senses are complex and overlapping structures [35,4]. So, despite word sense divisions in dictionaries and ontologies being most of the times artificial, this trade-off is needed in order to increase the usability of broad-coverage computational lexical resources.

As lexical synonymy networks extracted from dictionaries tend to have a clustered structure [36], clusters are identified in order to establish synsets. A possible way to achieve clustering and deal with ambiguity at the same time, is to use a hard-clustering algorithm, such as the Markov Clustering Algorithm (MCL) [37], and extend it to find unstable nodes, which are most of the times ambiguous words. In this kind of approach [36], clustering is ran with noise several times, a matrix with the probabilities of each node belonging to each cluster is created, and finally, each word is assigned to all the clusters its belonging probability is higher than a threshold.

We are following a very similar procedure: (i) split the original network into sub-networks, such that there is no path between two elements in different sub-networks. Calculate the frequency-weighted adjacency matrix F of each sub-network; (ii) add stochastic noise to each entry of F, $F_{ij} = F_{ij} + F_{ij} * \delta$; (iii) run MCL over F for 30 times; (iv) use the clustering obtained by each one of the 30 runs to create a new matrix P with the probabilities of each pair of words in F belonging to the same cluster; (v) create the clusters based on P and on a given threshold $t = 0.2$. If $P_{ij} > t$, i and j belong to the same cluster; (vi) in order to clean the results, remove: (a) big clusters, B, if there is a group of clusters $C = C_1, C_2, ...C_n$ such that $B = C_1 \cup C_2 \cup ... \cup C_n$; (b) clusters completely included in other clusters.

3.3. Merging with other synset-based resources

In this stage, we take advantage of broad-coverage synset-based resources for Portuguese, such as thesaurus, in order to enrich our synset base. Still, we are more interested in manually created resources of that kind, since they can amplify the coverage, and improve the precision of our synsets at a significantly low cost.

The following procedure is applied for merging two thesaurus: (i) B is the base thesaurus and the other is T; (ii) create an empty thesaurus M and copy all the synsets in B to M; (iii) for each synset $T_i \in T$, find the synsets $B_i \in B$ with higher Jaccard coefficient[6] c, and add them to a set of synsets $J \subset B$. (iv) considering c and J, do one of the following: (a) if $c = 1$, the synset is already in M, so nothing is done; (b) if $c = 0$, T_i is copied to M; (c) if $|J| = 1$, remove J_1 from M and add a new synset $N = J_1 \cup T_i$ to M. (d) if $|J| > 1$, a new set, $N = T_i \cup J'$ where $J' = \cup_{i=0}^{|J|} J_i, J_i \in J$, is added to M and all synsets in J are removed from M.

---

[6] $Jaccard(A, B) = A \cap B / A \cup B$

3.4. Assigning weights to triples

In this stage, weights are assigned to triples based on the number of times they were extracted (frequency) and also on distributional metrics, calculated over a corpus. The later metrics, typically used to retrieve similar documents, assume that similar or related words tend to co-occur or to occur in similar contexts. Nevertheless, several distributional metrics (e.g. latent semantic analysis (LSA) [38]) have also been adapted to measure the similarity of two words, based on their neighbourhoods [15,30]. The weights can thus be used to indicate the confidence for each triple and thresholds can be applied to discard lower-weighted triples and improve precision. For instance, [39] reports high correlations between manual evaluation of hypernymy and part-of triples and their weights according to some distributional measures computed on a corpus.

3.5. Mapping term-based triples to synsets

After the previous stages, a thesaurus T and a term-based lexical network L are available. In order to set up a wordnet, this stage uses the latter to map term-based triples to synset-based triples, or, in other words, assign each term, a and b, in each triple, $(a \ R \ b) \in L$, to suitable synsets of T. This task, often called ontologising [29], can be seen as WSD, but we explicitly aim to achieve disambiguation by taking advantage of knowledge already extracted, and not of the context from where it was extracted. Having this in mind, we have developed two mapping methods. In both methods, when one of the terms (e.g. a) in not in T, it is assigned to a new synset (e.g. $A = (a)$). Also, there might be situations where the term-based triple remains unassigned (e.g. ties).

In the first method, to assign a to a synset A, b is fixed and all the synsets containing a, $S_a \subset T$, are obtained. For each synset $S_{ai} \in S_a$, n_{ai} is the number of terms $t \in S_{ai}$ such that $(t \ R \ b)$ holds. Then, the proportion $p_{ai} = \frac{n_{ai}}{|S_{ai}|}$ is calculated and all the synsets with the highest p_{ai} establish a set C. Finally, (i) if $|C| = 1$, a is assigned to the only synset in C; (ii) if $|C| > 1$, C' is the set of elements of C with the highest n_a and, if $|C'| = 1$, a is assigned the synset in C', unless $p_{ai} < \theta$ [7]; Term b is assigned to a synset using this procedure, but fixing a.

The second mapping method starts by creating a term-term matrix, M, based on the adjacencies of the lexical network. Consequently, M is a square matrix with n lines, where n is the total number of nodes (terms) in the lexical network. If the term in index i and the term in index j are connected by some kind of relation, $M_{ij} = 1$, otherwise, $M_{ij} = 0$. In order to assign synsets to a and b, the first thing to do is, once again, to get all the synsets including the term a, $S_a \subset T$, and also all synsets including b, $S_b \subset T$. Then, the similarity between each synset $A \in S_a$ and each synset $B \in S_b$ is given by the average lexical network based similarity for each term in A with each term in B (expression 1).

$$sim(A, B) = \frac{\sum_{i=1}^{|A|} \sum_{j=1}^{|B|} \cos(A_i, B_j)}{|A||B|} \qquad (1)$$

---

[7] θ is a threshold defined to avoid that a is assigned to a big synset where a, itself, is the only term related to b.

Here, the similarity of two vectors of M gives us the similarity of two words, based on their neighbourhoods in the lexical network, and is calculated by the cosine of their adjacency vectors, A_i and B_j respectively. To conclude, the pair of synsets with a higher similarity is chosen.

3.6. Knowledge organisation

In this stage, routines for knowledge organisation are applied in order both to make it possible to infer new implicit knowledge and also to remove redundant triples. This is achieved by applying some rules to the synset-based triple set, including:

- Transitivity: if R is transitive (e.g. SYNONYMY, HYPERNYMY, ...),
  $(A\ R\ B) \wedge (B\ R\ C) \rightarrow (A\ R\ C)$
- Inheritance: if R is not a HYPERNYMY or HYPONYMY relation,
  $(A\ \text{HYPERNYM\_OF}\ B) \wedge (A\ R\ C) \rightarrow (B\ R\ C)$

Therefore, some behaving properties, such as transitivity, inheritance or inversion, of the extracted relations must be predefined. For instance, to deal with inversion, all relations are only stored in the type defined as the direct one, but, if needed, the system can inverse them.

3.7. Evaluation

Evaluation takes place through all the previous stages. Manual evaluation is a reliable kind of evaluation, but it is also time-consuming and difficult to reproduce, so, when possible, we are willing to explore automatic validation procedures. Automatic evaluation is typically performed by comparing the results obtained with a gold standard, but the later is not always available, especially for a broad-coverage ontology, where freely available gold standards are scarce.

The validation of relational triples can alternatively be perfomed using a collection of documents to find hints on them. For instance, triples can be translated to common natural language patterns, such as the ones in Table 1, and looked for in that form, as in [40] to assign probabilities to semantic triples, or in [23], to validate them.

Moreover, the quality of the ontology will also be assessed when using it to perform NLP tasks, such as question answering or automatic generation of text.

4. Current results

Since the authors of this research are also part of the PAPEL development team, PAPEL can be seen as a seed project. So, in Table 2, we start by presenting the numbers and examples of some of the relations included in PAPEL 2.0, and also the numbers of the relations obtained after applying exactly same extraction procedure, described in [23], to DA. We have taken advantage of the grammatical information provided by the dictionaries to organise each type of relation according to the grammatical category of its arguments.

Some of the relations in a previous version of PAPEL were validated (also in [23]) by searching for natural language sentences denoting the relations in a news-

Table 2. Relations extracted from dictionaries.

Relation	Arguments	PAPEL 2.0	DA	Example	Rough translation
Synonymy	noun,noun	37,452	20,910	auxílio,contributo	support,contribution
	verb,verb	21,465	8,715	tributar,colectar	to_tax,to_charge
	adj,adj	19,073	7,353	flexível,moldável	flexible,moldable
	adv,adv	1,171	605	após,seguidamente	after,next
Hypernymy	noun,noun	62,591	59,887	planta,salva	plant,sage
Part-of	noun,noun	2,805	1,795	cauda,cometa	tail,comet
	noun,adj	3.721	4,902	tampa,coberto	lid,covered
Member-of	noun,noun	5.929	1,564	ervilha,Leguminosas	pea,Leguminosae
	adj,noun	883	59	celular,célula	celular,cell
Causation	noun,noun	1.013	264	fricção,assadura	friction,rash
	adj,noun	498	166	reactivo,reacção	reactive,reaction
	verb,noun	6,399	5,714	limpar,purgação	to_clean,purgation
Purpose	noun,noun	2,886	1,760	defesa,armadura	defense,armor
	verb,noun	5,192	3,383	fazer_rir,comédia	to_make_laugh,comedy
	verb,adj	260	186	corrigir,correccional	to_correct,correctional

Table 3. Relations extracted from Wikipedia abstracts.

Relation	Quant.	Example	Rough translation	Sample	Correct	Agreement
Synonymy	11,862	estupro,violação	rape,violation	286	86,1%	91,2%
Hypernymy	29,563	estilo_de_música,folk	music_style,folk	322	59,1%	93,1%
Part-of	1,287	jejuno,intestino	jejunum,intestine	268	52,6%	78,4%
Causation	520	parasita,doença	parasite,disease	244	49,6%	79,5%
Purpose	743	insecticida,rotenona	insecticide,rotenone	264	57,0%	82,2%

paper corpus. About 20% of the part-of and hypernymy triples were supported by the corpus. On the other hand, these numbers were respectively 10% and 4% for purpose and causation. The results are interesting since there is not as much general knowledge in a newspaper as in a dictionary and because we have used a small set of patterns when there is a huge amount of possibilities to denote these semantic relations in corpora text.

Moving on to other kinds of text, around 37,898 sentences of the Portuguese Wikipedia were processed with the grammars for corpora. All the processed sentences were introducing articles which, in the DBpedia [41] taxonomy, had one of the following types: *species, anatomical structure, chemical compound, disease, currency, drug, activity, language, music genre, colour, ethnic group* or *protein*. A pos-tagger was used in the extraction, but only to identify adjectives. Also, in an additional stage, we have used it to identify the grammatical categories of the arguments of the triples and we noticed that most of the relations extracted were between nouns. The evaluation of the extracted triples was performed by human judges, who classified samples with triples of each relation as correct or incorrect. The quantities of relations extracted, the proportion of correct triples, as well as the agreement values, are shown in Table 3.

To test the synset discovery procedure, we have made several experimentations using the noun synsets of TeP, OpenThesaurus.PT (OT), and also the noun synonymy instances of PAPEL which, after clustering, became the thesaurus CLIP. We have also used TeP (17,158 nouns/8,254 synsets) as the base thesaurus and merged it, first with OT (5,819 nouns/1,872 synsets), and then with CLIP (23,741 nouns/7,468 synsets), giving rise to TOP (30,554 nouns/9,960 synsets). Even though TOP is the biggest thesaurus and has the biggest synset (277 words), the average size of its synsets (6.6) is almost half of CLIP's average synset size (12.5). Other numbers on these experimentations can be found in [42].

Table 4. Results of manual synset validation.

	Sample	Correct	Incorrect	N/A	Agreement
CLIP	519 sets	65.8%	31.7%	2.5%	76.1%
CLIP'	310 sets	81.1%	16.9%	2.0%	84.2%
TOP	480 sets	83.2%	15.8%	1.0%	82.3%
TOP'	448 sets	86.8%	12.3%	0.9%	83.0%

Table 5. Results of triples mapping.

	Hypernym_of	Part_of	Member_of
Term-based triples	62,591	2,805	5,929
Mapped	27,750	1,460	3,962
Same synset	233	5	12
Already present	3,970	40	167
Semi-mapped triples	7,952	262	357
Synset-based triples	23,547	1,415	3,783

519 synsets of CLIP and 480 of TOP were manually validated, each by two human judges who had to classify each synset as: correct, incorrect, or don't know[8]. Besides the average validation results and the agreement rates, Table 4 also contains the results considering only synsets with ten or less words, which are less problematic (CLIP' and TOP').

The last set of results presented here regard using the first mapping method (related proportion) to map all the hypernym-of, part-of and member-of term-based triples of PAPEL to the synsets of TOP. Table 5 shows that 33,172 triples had both of their terms assigned to a synset, and 10,530 had only one assigned. However, 4,427 were not really added, either because the same synset was assigned to both of the terms or because the triple had already been added after analysing other term-based triple.

More information on this mapping can be found in [43] where, in a second stage, established hypernymy links were exploited to map 89 additional triples. Of the latter, 13 had been added in the first stage while other 50 triples were discarded or not attached because they could be inferred.

A first approach to the validation of the mapping (also described in [43]) used Google web search engine to look for evidence on the synset-based triples. Once again, a set of natural language generic patterns, indicative of each relation, was defined. Then, for each triple $A\ R\ B$, each combination of terms $a \in A$ and $b \in B$ connected by a pattern indicative of R[9] was searched for. The validation scores obtained with expression 2 on samples of hypernym-of (419 synsets), part-of (290) and member-of (379) triples were respectively 44.1%, 24.8% and 24.3%. In this expression, $found(A, R, B) = 1$ if evidence is found for the triple or 0 otherwise.

---

[8]In some context, all the words of a correct synset could have the same meaning, while for incorrect synsets, at least one word could never mean the same meaning as the others.

[9]Patterns used for part-of and member-of were the same because these relations can be expressed in very similar ways.

$$score = \frac{\sum_{i=1}^{|A|} \sum_{j=1}^{|B|} found(A_i, R, B_j)}{|A| * |B|} \tag{2}$$

We are currently working on the comparison of both mapping methods with a baseline where each term is attached to a random synset containing it.

5. Concluding remarks

This ongoing research is an answer to the growing demand on semantically aware applications and addresses the lack of public domain lexico-semantic resources for Portuguese. The tools for knowledge extraction and the lexical ontology itself will be useful for researchers and developers of applications in Portuguese. To extend the potential utilisation scenarios we are devising to export the ontology to several data representation formats, including RDF/OWL models, because these are the W3C standard description languages and, therefore, ease the browsing and visualisation of ontologies besides other useful features like reasoning capabilities.

Even though most of the methods presented here are not completely new, some of them have never targeted Portuguese. Nevertheless, we believe their application in the proposed sequence to be a suitable alternative to the manual creation of lexical resources in any language. Most of the tools and resources developed during this work are and will be available through http://ontopt.dei.uc.pt.

Acknowledgements

Hugo Gonçalo Oliveira is supported by FCT scholarship grant SFRH/BD/44955/2008. We would like to thank Hernani Costa and the KDigg team for their participation in project discussions and in the development of the tools for corpora processing.

References

[1] T. Berners-Lee, J. Hendler, and O. Lassila, "The Semantic Web," *Scientific American*, May 2001.
[2] C. Fellbaum, ed., *WordNet: An Electronic Lexical Database (Language, Speech, and Communication)*. The MIT Press, 1998.
[3] R. Navigli, "Word sense disambiguation: A survey," *ACM Computing Surveys*, vol. 41, no. 2, 2009.
[4] G. Hirst, "Ontology and the lexicon," in *Handbook on Ontologies* (S. Staab and R. Studer, eds.), International Handbooks on Information Systems, pp. 209–230, Springer, 2004.
[5] P. Vossen, "Eurowordnet: a multilingual database for information retrieval," in *Proc. DELOS workshop on Cross-Language Information Retrieval*, (Zurich), 1997.
[6] P. Marrafa, "Portuguese Wordnet: general architecture and internal semantic relations," *DELTA*, vol. 18, pp. 131–146, 2002.
[7] C. Brewster and Y. Wilks, "Ontologies, Taxonomies, Thesauri: Learning from Texts," in *Proc. The Use of Computational Linguistics in the Extraction of Keyword Information from Digital Library Content Workshop*, (London, UK), Kings College, 2004.

[8] G. de Melo and G. Weikum, "On the utility of automatically generated wordnets," in *Proc. 4th Global WordNet Conf. (GWC)*, (Szeged, Hungary), pp. 147–161, University of Szeged, 2008.

[9] M. A. Hearst, "Automatic acquisition of hyponyms from large text corpora," in *Proc. 14th Conf. on Computational Linguistics (COLING)*, (Morristown, NJ, USA), pp. 539–545, Association for Computational Linguistics, 1992.

[10] E. Riloff and J. Shepherd, "A corpus-based approach for building semantic lexicons," in *Proc. 2nd Conf. on Empirical Methods in Natural Language Processing*, pp. 117–124, 1997.

[11] P. D. Turney, "Mining the web for synonyms: PMI–IR versus LSA on TOEFL," in *Proc. 12th European Conf. on Machine Learning (ECML)*, vol. 2167, pp. 491–502, Springer, 2001.

[12] D. Lin and P. Pantel, "Concept discovery from text," in *Proc. Intl. Conf. on Computational Linguistics (COLING)*, 2002.

[13] B. Dorow, *A Graph Model for Words and their Meanings*. PhD thesis, Institut fur Maschinelle Sprachverarbeitung der Universitat Stuttgart, 2006.

[14] S. A. Caraballo, "Automatic construction of a hypernym-labeled noun hierarchy from text," in *Proc. 37th annual meeting of the ACL on Computational Linguistics (COLING-ACL)*, (Morristown, NJ, USA), pp. 120–126, Association for Computational Linguistics, 1999.

[15] S. Cederberg and D. Widdows, "Using lsa and noun coordination information to improve the precision and recall of automatic hyponymy extraction," in *Proc. 7th Conf. on Computational Natural Language Learning (CoNLL)*, (Morristown, NJ, USA), pp. 111–118, Association for Computational Linguistics, 2003.

[16] M. Berland and E. Charniak, "Finding parts in very large corpora," in *Proc. 37th Annual Meeting of the ACL on Computational Linguistics*, (Morristown, NJ, USA), pp. 57–64, Association for Computational Linguistics, 1999.

[17] R. Girju and D. Moldovan, "Text mining for causal relations," in *Proc. 15th Intl. Florida Artificial Intelligence Research Society Conf. (FLAIRS)*, pp. 360–364, 2002.

[18] R. Girju, A. Badulescu, and D. Moldovan, "Automatic discovery of part-whole relations," *Computational Linguistics*, vol. 32, no. 1, pp. 83–135, 2006.

[19] N. Calzolari, L. Pecchia, and A. Zampolli, "Working on the italian machine dictionary: a semantic approach," in *Proc. 5th Conf. on Computational Linguistics*, (Morristown, NJ, USA), pp. 49–52, Association for Computational Linguistics, 1973.

[20] S. D. Richardson, W. B. Dolan, and L. Vanderwende, "Mindnet: Acquiring and structuring semantic information from text," in *Proc. 36th Annual Meeting of the Association for Computational Linguistics and 17th International Conference on Computational Linguistics (COLING-ACL)*, pp. 1098–1102, 1998.

[21] N. Ide and J. Veronis, "Knowledge extraction from machine-readable dictionaries: An evaluation," in *Machine Translation and the Lexicon, LNAI*, Springer, 1995.

[22] E. Nichols, F. Bond, and D. Flickinger, "Robust ontology acquisition from machine-readable dictionaries," in *Proc. 19th Intl. Joint Conf. on Artificial Intelligence (IJCAI)*, pp. 1111–1116, Professional Book Center, 2005.

[23] H. Gonçalo Oliveira, D. Santos, and P. Gomes, "Relations extracted from a portuguese dictionary: results and first evaluation," in *Local Proc. 14th Portuguese Conf. on Artificial Intelligence (EPIA)*, 2009.

[24] E. Navarro, F. Sajous, B. Gaume, L. Prévot, S. Hsieh, T. Y. Kuo, P. Magistry, and C. R. Huang, "Wiktionary and nlp: Improving synonymy networks," in *Proc. Workshop on The People's Web Meets NLP: Collaboratively Constructed Semantic Resources*, (Suntec, Singapore), pp. 19–27, Association for Computational Linguistics, 2009.

[25] M. Ruiz-Casado, E. Alfonseca, and P. Castells, "Automatic assignment of wikipedia encyclopedic entries to wordnet synsets," in *Proc. Advances in Web Intelligence 3rd Intl. Atlantic Web Intelligence Conf. (AWIC)*, pp. 380–386, Springer, 2005.

[26] A. Herbelot and A. Copestake, "Acquiring ontological relationships from wikipedia using RMRS," in *Proc. ISWC 2006 Workshop on Web Content Mining with Human Language Technologies*, 2006.

[27] T. Zesch, C. Müller, and I. Gurevych, "Extracting lexical semantic knowledge from Wikipedia and Wiktionary," in *Proc. 6th Intl. Language Resources and Evaluation (LREC)*, (Marrakech, Morocco), 2008.

[28] S. Soderland and B. Mandhani, "Moving from textual relations to ontologized relations," in *Proc. AAAI Spring Symposium on Machine Reading*, 2007.

[29] P. Pantel and M. Pennacchiotti, "Automatically harvesting and ontologizing semantic relations," in *Ontology Learning and Population: Bridging the Gap between Text and Knowledge* (P. Buitelaar and P. Cimmiano, eds.), IOS Press, 2008.

[30] T. Wandmacher, E. Ovchinnikova, U. Krumnack, and H. Dittmann, "Extraction, evaluation and integration of lexical-semantic relations for the automated construction of a lexical ontology," in *Third Australasian Ontology Workshop (AOW)*, vol. 85 of *CRPIT*, (Gold Coast, Australia), pp. 61–69, ACS, 2007.

[31] *Dicionário PRO da Língua Portuguesa*. Porto Editora, Porto, 2005.

[32] A. Simões and R. Farinha, "Dicionário Aberto: Um novo recurso para PLN," *Vice-Versa*, September 2010. forthcoming.

[33] B. C. Dias-Da-Silva and H. R. de Moraes, "A construção de um thesaurus eletrônico para o português do Brasil," *ALFA*, vol. 47, no. 2, pp. 101–115, 2003.

[34] P. Pantel and M. Pennacchiotti, "Espresso: Leveraging generic patterns for automatically harvesting semantic relations," in *Proc. Intl. Conf. on Computational Linguistics/Association (COLING-ACL)*, (Sydney, Australia), pp. 113–120, ACL Press, 17th-21st July 2006.

[35] A. Kilgarriff, ""I don't believe in word senses"," *Computing and the Humanities*, vol. 31, no. 2, pp. 91–113, 1997.

[36] D. Gfeller, J.-C. Chappelier, and P. D. L. Rios, "Synonym Dictionary Improvement through Markov Clustering and Clustering Stability," in *Proc. of Intl. Symposium on Applied Stochastic Models and Data Analysis (ASMDA)*, pp. 106–113, 2005.

[37] S. M. van Dongen, *Graph Clustering by Flow Simulation*. PhD thesis, University of Utrecht, 2000.

[38] S. Deerwester, S. T. Dumais, G. W. Furnas, T. K. Landauer, and R. Harshman, "Indexing by latent semantic analysis," *Journal of the American Society for Information Science*, vol. 41, pp. 391–407, 1990.

[39] H. Costa, H. Gonçalo Oliveira, and P. Gomes, "The impact of distributional metrics in the quality of relational triples," in *Proc. ECAI Workshop on Language Technology for Cultural Heritage, Social Sciences, and Humanities (LaTeCH)*, 2010.

[40] P. Oliveira, "Probabilistic reasoning in the semantic web using markov logic," Master's thesis, University of Coimbra, Faculty of Sciences and Technology, Department of Informatics Engineering, July 2009.

[41] C. Bizer, J. Lehmann, G. Kobilarov, S. Auer, C. Becker, R. Cyganiak, and S. Hellmann, "Dbpedia – a crystallization point for the web of data," *Web Semantics: Science, Services and Agents on the World Wide Web*, vol. 7, pp. 154–165, September 2009.

[42] H. Gonçalo Oliveira and P. Gomes, "Automatic creation of a conceptual base for portuguese using clustering techniques," in *Proc. 19th European Conf. on Artifical Intelligence (ECAI 2010)*, IOS Press, 2010.

[43] H. Gonçalo Oliveira and P. Gomes, "Towards the automatic creation of a wordnet from a term-based lexical network," in *Proc. ACL Workshop TextGraphs-5: Graph-based Methods for Natural Language Processing*, 2010.

MEC - Monitoring Clusters' Transitions

Márcia OLIVEIRA [a,1], João GAMA [a]

[a] *LIAAD, Faculty of Economics, University of Porto, Portugal*

Abstract. In this work we address the problem of monitoring the evolution of clusters, which became an important research issue in recent years due to our ability to collect and store data that evolves over time. The evolution is traced through the detection and categorization of transitions undergone by clusters' structures computed at different points in time. We adopt two main strategies for cluster characterization - representation by enumeration and representation by comprehension -, and propose the MEC (Monitor of the Evolution of Clusters) framework, which was developed along the lines of the *change mining* paradigm. MEC includes a taxonomy of various types of clusters' transitions, a tracking mechanism that depends on cluster representation, and a transition detection algorithm. Our tracking mechanism can be subdivided in two methods, devised to monitor clusters' transitions: one based on graph transitions, and another based on clusters' overlap. To demonstrate the feasibility and applicability of MEC we present real world case studies, using datasets from different knowledge areas, such as Economy and Education.

Keywords. Change Mining, Clusters, Evolution, Monitoring, Transitions

Introduction

The celerity at which the evolution takes place, typically characterized by breaks and shifts, has increased exponentially in the last decades. The rapid progress made in science and technology has contributed to the emergence of a volatile and fast pace evolving world, which demands new perspectives in knowledge discovery upon data, such as time-oriented perspectives. The paradigm of *change mining* arises as a consequence of this evolution and encompasses Data Mining mechanisms that monitor models and patterns over time, compare them, detect and describe changes, and quantify them on their interestingness [1]. The challenge of *change mining* goes beyond the adaptation of models to changes in data distribution, and is mainly focused in the understanding of changes. In this paper we propose MEC (Monitor of the Evolution of Clusters) framework, which is built along these lines, to tackle the problem of monitoring clusters' transitions over time, through the identification of temporal relationships among them. We assume that clusters can be represented in two different ways - by enumeration and by comprehension - and we adopt two main strategies to monitor and classify changes experienced by clusters, to each possible representation. The proposed methods were devised to deal only with clusters characterized by numerical attributes, however it is our intention to extend them to categorical attributes in the near future. Thus, our framework

---

[1] Corresponding Author: Márcia Oliveira, LIAAD - INESC Porto L.A., Rua de Ceuta 118, 6th, 4050-190 Porto, Portugal; E-mail: marcia@liaad.up.pt

encompasses a taxonomy of various types of clusters' transitions, that may be external or internal, a tracking mechanism that depends on cluster representation, and a transition detection algorithm.

The monitoring of the dynamics of clusters' structures is very important in many real world applications, since it fosters the creation of sustainable knowledge about the studied phenomena and, consequently, the adoption of pro-active attitudes. Besides, it may correlate to some important or critical events in the real applications or unveil the emergence of new ones. For these reasons, this study can benefit several areas, such as Marketing, Fraud Detection, Economy and Health. For instance, the study of the evolution of customers' segments allow the detection of shifts in preferences and consumer habits, which can sustain the forecast of trends and consequent redefinition of Marketing's strategies and policies. The domain knowledge acquired by these means can act as a powerful differentiating factor in the market and strongly contributes to the creation, or reinforcement, of the company's competitive advantages. Traditional data mining is not able to help companies achieve these goals since it relies on static data and does not take into account its evolving nature. Therefore, the study of the dynamics of clusters contributes to the achievement of a greater understanding of cluster's evolutionary processes, broadening horizons and opening new paths in the way of thinking problems.

This paper is organized as follows. In Section 1 we provide a brief overview of the current state of the art. In Section 2 we distinguish two types of cluster representation and highlight their advantages and drawbacks. In Section 3 we formally introduce our MEC framework. In this section we present our taxonomy for clusters' transitions and explain the foundations of our tracking mechanism, for each type of representation. In Section 4 we show and discuss two real world case studies. Section 5 concludes our study.

1. Related Work

Despite the extensive study of the clustering problem [2,3], there is not much work conducted in the monitoring of clusters' transitions. In this context of change, the research endeavor has been mainly directed to the adaptation of clusters to changed populations. However, the dynamic nature of most datasets encouraged new directions in research. This effort is clearly present in the areas of machine learning and data analysis.

There are several algorithms that directly or indirectly aim to capture and, especially, understand the dynamic nature of these datasets, particularly susceptible to the occurrence of changes in the underlying structure. The last decade has been especially profuse in the design of transition detection algorithms. Based on recent literature, it was possible to deduce a preliminary classification for algorithms built in this context. In general, there are algorithms designed to operate in relatively static (snapshots) or highly dynamic (data streams) environments. The first may be focused on transitions experienced by generic patterns [4,5,6], clusters [7,8,9,10] or association rules [11,12]. In the context of data streams, approaches focusing unclassified data are quite common (here we include clustering algorithms for mobile objects or spatio-temporal objects). These approaches [14,15,16,17,18,19,20] elect clusters as its main data structure and are concerned with the efficiency and scalability of algorithms.

Based on our knowledge, currently there are two research works that address a problem related to ours [7,8]. The framework proposed in [7] models the evolution of clusters by a weighted bipartite graph. MONIC framework [8] also proposes a cluster transition model to track cluster changes, supporting cluster comparisons across the time axis. MONIC uses a data ageing function that assigns lower weights to older observations and computes the overlap of clusters to capture its evolution. However, both frameworks only apply to clusters represented by enumeration, contrary to MEC, which is not restricted by the adopted method to represent clusters. MEC proposes a more complete framework to study the evolution of clusters which applicability to real world problems is much wider, since it can also consider clusters represented using summary statistics. This is the major contribution of our work, compared to the referred ones. Somewhat related is the work on novelty detection that can identify new concepts (in our terminology, the birth of new clusters), from unlabeled data (see for example [24]). These kind of methods are restricted to cluster's births, contrary to our framework, which is able to capture a much wider variety of concepts, such as splits, merges, deaths and survival.

2. Cluster Characterization

MEC framework assumes that clusters can be represented using two main strategies or representation schemes: **representation by enumeration** and **representation by comprehension** (can also be called **extensional** and **intensional** representation, using the mathematical nomenclature). The most used and straightforward way to define clusters is what we call **representation by enumeration**. In this kind of representation a cluster is characterized by its elements, ie, by the observations that were assigned to it by a given clustering algorithm (see Definition 1).

Definition 1 - Representation by Enumeration:
Let $\vec{x}_i$, $(i = 1, ..., N)$ be the ith observation defined as a vector of real numbers in a d-dimensional space $\vec{x}_i = (x_{i,1}, x_{i,2}, x_{i,3}, ..., x_{i,d})$. A possible temporal representation of a cluster is defined as follows:

$$C_j(t) = \{\vec{x_1}, ..., \vec{x_m}\}$$

where m is the number of observations assigned to cluster $C_j(t)$, $j = (1, ..., k)$, k is the number of clusters and $t = (1, ..., T)$, where T corresponds to the last analyzed timestamp.

This type of representation does not involve information loss and enables the monitoring of each observation over time, which contributes to the achievement of more reliable and accurate transition results. Though, it is not always possible to define clusters using this representation method, e.g. due to storage demands or privacy issues.

Alternatively, a cluster can be characterized through summary data, ie, using statistics that summarize its internal characteristics [24]. This is the idea behind **representation by comprehension** (see Definition 2), which is inspired by the notion of conceptual clustering.

Definition 2 - Representation by Comprehension:
According to this representation a cluster C_j is a temporal object characterized by the following statistics:

$$C_j = \{ID, t, m, sup, r, \rho, \vec{c}\}$$

where ID is the unique identifier of C_j ($j = 1, ..., k$), t is the time point where the cluster first appears ($t = 1, ..., T$), m is the number of observations assigned to C_j, sup is the support of a cluster, used to assess the relative importance of the cluster, r is the cluster's radius, ρ represents the density of cluster and $\vec{c}$ represents cluster's centroid.

To summarize the contents of each isolated cluster, within the comprehension representation scheme, we considered a centrality measure, a dispersion measure and a density measure. Due to simplicity issues, we adopted the cluster's centroid as our measure of centrality, the cluster's radius as our measure of dispersion and we use a definition of density that assumes spherical d-dimensional objects [24,25]. Other measures could have been used, e.g. Mahalanobis metrics, but this would lead to more complex computations. The drawback of these measures is that they can only describe spherical or ball-shaped clusters [2]. This kind of compact representations are very appealing to several real world applications, especially to those whose information are restricted due to privacy issues. However, it implies information loss, which may compromise the accuracy of the *mapping* process [3].

To implement the transitions detection algorithm we have considered the definitions of **radius** and **centroid** presented in [21]. Thereby, in this work, the **radius** of a cluster is the average distance from member points to the centroid.

3. MEC Framework

We developed MEC framework in order to monitor the evolution of clusters' structures (also referred to as *clustering*) obtained at different time points. In this context, the concept of evolution refers to transitions undergone by clusters during time interval under observation $[t_i, t_{i+\Delta t}]$ ($\Delta t = 1, ..., T-i$). Since there are, at least, two strategies to represent clusters, we designed a flexible tracking mechanism that is able to efficiently detect transitions experienced by clusters, regardless of how they are represented. Therefore, our tracking mechanism can be subdivided in two different methods, each one adapted to a distinct cluster representation. In the next subsections we present our taxonomy of transitions and the two developed methods.

---

[2] In this work, we restrict to numerical features. For non-numerical features we will need appropriate measures for centrality and dispersion.
[3] *Mapping* is the process of discovering the matches of clusters between two distinct time points

3.1. Taxonomy of Transitions

There are at least eight taxonomic schemes for the classification of transitions in clusters, patterns or concepts that evolve over time, in the literature [9,14,16,15,22,20,8,10]. To capture the changes likely to occur in clusters' structures we considered the following taxonomy:

- **Birth** - a new cluster emerges
- **Death** - a previous discovered cluster disappears
- **Split** - one cluster is separated into two or more clusters
- **Merge** - two or more clusters fuse, or merge, into one cluster
- **Survival** - a cluster that does not suffer none of the above transitions

These transitions are external, as they relate to changes in the whole *clustering*. The key concept for the detection and evaluation of these transitions is the concept of *mapping*, which can be defined as the process of discovering the matches between clusters obtained at time point t_i and clusters obtained at a later time point $t_{i+\Delta t}$, in case they still exist. On the other hand, it is also possible to categorize internal transitions, ie, changes concerning the contents of each isolated cluster. For this purpose, we considered size and compactness transitions [8]. Size transitions encompasses **Expansion** or **Shrinkage**, depending on the increase or decrease of the surviving cluster's cardinality. Compactness transitions include **Compression** or **Dispersal**, which depends on the increase or decrease of the surviving cluster's density. These type of transitions can be easily traced through the monitoring of summary data, such as the cardinality and the density of the surviving clusters.

3.2. Method for Clusters Represented by Enumeration

In this method, the *mapping* process explores the concept of conditional probability and is restricted by a pre-defined threshold - **survival threshold** τ -, which assumes the minimum of $\tau = 0.5$ (intuitively, this means that a match must contain at least half of the objects of the previous cluster). The use of conditional probabilities requires structurally identical datasets, ie, datasets composed by observations of the same objects, in each time point under analysis. These conditional probabilities are computed for every pair of possible connections between clusters obtained at different time points and they represent the edge's weights in a bipartite graph. The use of bipartite graphs is related to its usefulness in modeling matching problems and the fact that graph based representations are visually appealing, exploiting the power of the eye and human intuition. The foundations of our transition detection algorithm are based in this idea, which can be defined as follows (Definition 3).

Definition 3 - Weighted Bipartite Graphs:
Given the clusterings ξ_i, $\xi_{i+\Delta t}$, obtained at t_i, $t_{i+\Delta t}$, a graph $G = (U, V, E)$ can be constructed, where U represents the first subset of vertices (clusters of t_i), V represents the second subset of vertices (clusters of $t_{i+\Delta t}$), and E denotes a set of weighted edges between any pair of clusters belonging to ξ_i and $\xi_{i+\Delta t}$. Formally, the weight assigned to the edge connecting clusters $C_m(t_i)$ and $C_u(t_{i+\Delta t})$ ($m = (1, ..., k_{t_i})$ and $u = (1, ..., k_{t_{i+\Delta t}})$, where k_{t_i} and $k_{t_{i+\Delta t}}$ are the number of clusters returned by a given

clustering algorithm in time points t_i and $t_{i+\Delta t}$, respectively) are estimated in accordance with the conditional probability:

$$weight(C_m(t_i), C_u(t_{i+\Delta t})) = P(X \in C_u(t_{i+\Delta t}) | X \in C_m(t_i)) =$$

$$= \frac{\sum P(x \in C_m(t_i) \cap C_u(t_{i+\Delta t}))}{\sum P(x \in C_m(t_i))}$$

where X is the set of observations assigned to cluster $C_m(t_i)$ and $P(X \in C_u(t_{i+\Delta t}) | X \in C_m(t_i))$ represents the probability of X belonging to cluster C_u from $t_{i+\Delta t}$ knowing that X belongs to cluster C_m obtained at a previous timestamp t_i.

To detect changes, we formally define the transitions that a cluster $C \in \xi_i$ can experience, with respect to $\xi_{i+\Delta t}$. It was introduced a new threshold to help the definition of these transitions: the **split threshold** λ. This formal design is based on MONIC's framework's external transitions [8] and is depicted in Table 1. The drawback of this method boils down to the fact that monitoring based on graph transitions only allow the detection of external transitions. However, internal transitions can be detected in this method through the computation of statistics, like density and cardinality of clusters.

Table 1. Formal definition of the external transitions of a cluster represented by enumeration

Transitions' Taxonomy	Notation	Formal Definition
Cluster's Birth	$\emptyset \to C_u(t_{i+\Delta t})$	$0 < weight(C_m(t_i), C_u(t_{i+\Delta t})) < \tau \forall m$
Cluster's Death	$C_m(t_i) \to \emptyset$	$weight(C_m(t_i), C_u(t_{i+\Delta t})) < \lambda \forall u$
Cluster's Split	$C_m(t_i) \overset{\subseteq}{\to} \{C_1(t_{i+\Delta t}), ..., C_r(t_{i+\Delta t})\}$	$(\exists u \exists v : weight(C_m(t_i), C_u(t_{i+\Delta t})) \geq \lambda \wedge$ $weight(C_m(t_i), C_v(t_{i+\Delta t})) \geq \lambda) \wedge$ $\sum_{u=1}^{r} weight(C_m(t_i), C_u(t_{i+\Delta t})) \geq \tau$
Cluster's Merge	$\{C_1(t_i), ..., C_p(t_i)\} \overset{\subseteq}{\to} C_u(t_{i+\Delta t})$	$(weight(C_m(t_i), C_u(t_{i+\Delta t})) \geq \tau) \wedge$ $\exists C_p \in \xi_i \setminus \{C_m\} : weight(C_p(t_i), C_u(t_{i+\Delta t})) \geq \tau$
Cluster's Survival	$C_m(t_i) \to C_u(t_{i+\Delta t})$	$(weight(C_m(t_i), C_u(t_{i+\Delta t})) \geq \tau) \wedge$ $\nexists C_p \in \xi_i \setminus \{C_m\} : weight(C_p(t_i), C_u(t_{i+\Delta t})) \geq \tau$

3.3. Method for Clusters Represented by Comprehension

For compact representations of clusters, we developed a method to assess the similarity between clusters through the discovery of an intersection region in the feature space, formed by pairs of clusters from different timestamps. This procedure allows us to know if cluster $C_m(t_i)$ in clustering ξ_i is the match of cluster $C_u(t_{i+\Delta t})$ in the later clustering $\xi_{i+\Delta t}$. To accomplish this task, we compute the Euclidean distance between clusters' centroids (see Definition 4) for every pair of clusters belonging to clusterings generated at different time points.

Definition 4 - Centroid Euclidean Distance:
Let C_m and C_u be two clusters obtained at t_i and $t_{i+\Delta t}$, respectively, and let $\vec{c_m} = (c_{m,1}, c_{m,2}, ..., c_{m,d})$ and $\vec{c_u} = (c_{u,1}, c_{u,2}, ..., c_{u,d})$ be the corresponding centroids. The Centroid Euclidean Distance is used to measure the similarity between $C_m(t_i)$ and $C_u(t_{i+\Delta t})$, and is defined as:

$$d(\vec{c_m}, \vec{c_u}) = \sqrt{\sum_{j=1}^{d}(c_{m,j} - c_{u,j})^2} \tag{1}$$

Posteriorly, to assess the existence of overlap (or intersection) between clusters, we compare the centroids' distance with the sum of the radius of clusters. If the centroids' distance is equal or greater than the sum of clusters' radius (Eq. 2), then we can deduce that clusters don't intersect and, therefore, the cluster of t_i cannot be the match of the cluster of $t_{i+\Delta t}$. Otherwise (Eq. 3), we can assume that these pair of clusters intersect in the feature space and conclude that they form a match.

$$d(C_m(t_i), C_u(t_{i+\Delta t})) \geq r_{C_m(t_i)} + r_{C_u(t_{i+\Delta t})} \tag{2}$$

$$d(C_m(t_i), C_u(t_{i+\Delta t})) < r_{C_m(t_i)} + r_{C_u(t_{i+\Delta t})} \tag{3}$$

To detect external and internal transitions and discover the changes undergone by clusters, we formally define the transitions, using the presented concepts. The formal design is depicted in Table 2 and Table 3. Note that internal transitions are only monitored for surviving clusters and, also, that the usage of Euclidean distance recommends the standardization of the attributes.

Table 2. Formal definition of the external transitions of a cluster represented by comprehension

Transitions' Taxonomy	Notation	Formal Definition
Cluster's Birth	$\emptyset \rightarrow C_u(t_{i+\Delta t})$	$d(C_m(t_i), C_u(t_{i+\Delta t})) \geq r_{C_m(t_i)} + r_{C_u(t_{i+\Delta t})} \forall m$
Cluster's Death	$C_m(t_i) \rightarrow \emptyset$	$d(C_m(t_i), C_u(t_{i+\Delta t})) \geq r_{C_m(t_i)} + r_{C_u(t_{i+\Delta t})} \forall u$
Cluster's Split	$C_m(t_i) \overset{\subseteq}{\rightarrow} \{C_1(t_{i+\Delta t}), ..., C_r(t_{i+\Delta t})\}$	$(d(C_m(t_i), C_u(t_{i+\Delta t})) < r_{C_m(t_i)} + r_{C_u(t_{i+\Delta t})}) \wedge \exists C_r \in \xi_{i+\Delta t} \setminus \{C_u\} : d(C_m(t_i), C_r(t_{i+\Delta t})) < r_{C_m(t_i)} + r_{C_r(t_{i+\Delta t})}$
Cluster's Merge	$\{C_1(t_i), ..., C_p(t_i)\} \overset{\subseteq}{\rightarrow} C_u(t_{i+\Delta t})$	$(d(C_m(t_i), C_u(t_{i+\Delta t})) < r_{C_m(t_i)} + r_{C_u(t_{i+\Delta t})}) \wedge \exists C_p \in \xi_i \setminus \{C_m\} : d(C_p(t_i), C_u(t_{i+\Delta t})) < r_{C_p(t_i)} + r_{C_u(t_{i+\Delta t})}$
Cluster's Survival	$C_m(t_i) \rightarrow C_u(t_{i+\Delta t})$	$(d(C_m(t_i), C_u(t_{i+\Delta t})) < r_{C_m(t_i)} + r_{C_u(t_{i+\Delta t})}) \wedge \nexists C_p \in \xi_i \setminus \{C_m\} : d(C_p(t_i), C_u(t_{i+\Delta t})) < r_{C_p(t_i)} + r_{C_u(t_{i+\Delta t})}$

The implementation of the transitions detection algorithm, in software R 2.10.0, was supported by the definitions presented in Table 1, Table 2 and Table 3.

To better understand this framework, in next section we present real world case studies.

4. Real World Case Studies

In order to show the feasibility and application of the proposed framework and glean insights about the evolution of clusters, we experimented MEC in real datasets extracted from Banco de Portugal's Central Balance-Sheet Database (CBSD) and from the Portuguese Institute of Statistics (INE).

Table 3. Formal definition of the internal transitions of a cluster represented by comprehension

Transitions' Taxonomy	Notation	Formal Definition
Cluster's Expansion	$C_m(t_i) \nearrow C_u(t_{i+\Delta t})$	$\#C_m(t_i) < \#C_u(t_{i+\Delta t})$
Cluster's Shrinkage	$C_m(t_i) \searrow C_u(t_{i+\Delta t})$	$\#C_m(t_i) \geq \#C_u(t_{i+\Delta t})$
Cluster's Compression	$C_m(t_i) \xrightarrow{\bullet} C_u(t_{i+\Delta t})$	$\lambda_{C_m(t_i)} < \lambda_{C_u(t_{i+\Delta t})}$
Cluster's Dispersal	$C_m(t_i) \xrightarrow{*} C_u(t_{i+\Delta t})$	$\lambda_{C_m(t_i)} > \lambda_{C_u(t_{i+\Delta t})}$

4.1. Representation by Enumeration

4.1.1. First Experiment - Portuguese Activity Sectors

For the first experiment, we extracted three datasets from CBSD. Each dataset corresponds to a year (2005, 2006 and 2007) and consists of 439 observations characterized by 10 continuous attributes. The objects represent activity sectors, according to the higher granularity level of CEA (Portuguese Classification of Economic Activities), and the attributes are financial and economic aggregated indicators (e.g. net income, investment rate and labor productivity). It should be noted that the activity sectors and performance indicators are exactly the same, for all periods under analysis, which is a requirement for the application of MEC framework. The attributes were normalized using Z-scores, due to significant differences on scale and dispersion.

In order to discover the clusters (input of MEC) from the CBSD' datasets, we conducted experiments using two different algorithms for clustering: the agglomerative hierarchical algorithm using Ward's method, and K-means algorithm. Although there were experiments with other algorithms, the mentioned ones have achieved good quality levels. In both algorithms, the determination of the critical clustering structure, through the identification of the best number of clusters (best k), was supported by the analysis of an internal validation measure: the silhouette width [23]. Afterwards, we applied our transitions detection algorithm, setting a fixed $\lambda = 0.2$ and $\tau = 0.5$, whose choice was guided by a thresholds' sensitivity analysis. These parameters are more relaxed and allow the detection of a wider variety of transitions. The resulting graphs, showing the transitions between clusters, are depicted in Figure 1.

On the left-hand side of Figure 1 we observe two bipartite graphs, one corresponding to transitions experienced during the time interval $[2005, 2006]$ and another one corresponding to transitions occurred during $[2006, 2007]$. In the former, there were two surviving clusters ($C_3(2005) \rightarrow C_2(2006)$ and $C_6(2005) \rightarrow C_3(2006)$), a merge of three clusters ($\{C_1(2005), C_2(2005), C_4(2005)\} \xrightarrow{\supsetneq} C_1(2006)$) and a split ($C_5(2005) \xrightarrow{\subsetneq} \{C_1(2006), C_2(2006), C_3(2006)\}$). In the latter, all clusters survived ($C_1(2006) \rightarrow C_1(2007)$, $C_2(2006) \rightarrow C_3(2007)$ and $C_3(2006) \rightarrow C_4(2007)$) and a new one has emerged ($\emptyset \rightarrow C_2(2007)$). The right-hand side of Figure 1 corresponds to the K-means algorithm's bipartite graphs. Using the same strategy and the silhouette width validation measure, K-means algorithm resulted in a different partition (five clusters to all time points under analysis). The detected transitions also differ from the ones obtained for the agglomerative hierarchical algorithm, as expected. Thereby, during $[2005, 2006]$ we detect the survival of two clusters ($C_1(2005) \rightarrow C_3(2006)$ and $C_5(2005) \rightarrow C_2(2006)$), a merge of three clusters ($\{C_2(2005), C_3(2005), C_4(2005)\} \xrightarrow{\supsetneq} C_5(2006)$) and two births ($\emptyset \rightarrow C_1(2006)$ and $\emptyset \rightarrow C_4(2006)$). At period $[2006, 2007]$, four clusters sur-

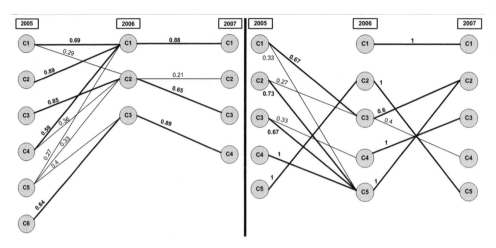

Figure 1. Bipartite graphs, corresponding to timestamps 2005, 2006 and 2007, for the CBSD' datasets. The thickness of the edges indicate weights that are equal or greater to survival threshold; the edges whose weights are below the split threshold were removed from the graphs, due to their insignificance. The left-hand side graph corresponds to the agglomerative hierarchical clustering and the right-hand side to the K-means clustering.

vived ($C_1(2006) \rightarrow C_1(2007)$, $C_2(2006) \rightarrow C_5(2007)$ and $C_4(2006) \rightarrow C_3(2007)$), two clusters merged ($\{C_3(2006), C_5(2006)\} \overset{\hookrightarrow}{} C_2(2007)$) and a new one has emerged ($\emptyset \rightarrow C_4(2007)$).

In this experiment, the differences in terms of transitions between the hierarchical and the K-means algorithm are explained by the different number of clusters assumed by each algorithm. If k was the same for each algorithm, transitions results would converge. The merge occurred in $[2005, 2006]$ was captured by both clustering algorithms, so we assumed this was an important transition. The inspection of the dataset suggested that these three clusters were grouped into one because the activity sectors assigned to them experienced a worsening in their economic and financial performance, which was reflected in the mitigation of their initial differences. But why did this happen? To answer this question we searched for relevant information about the topic and we found out that, in 2006, there has been a homogenization of the information process within the SIMPLEX portuguese program, which aimed to incorporate in one document (the Simplified Business Information) and a single delivery operation the information that companies are required to provide to public institutions. Moreover, the reporting of the Business information became mandatory, which contributed to the increase of the coverage degree of CBSD. For this reason, the data became more reliable and complete, reflecting a more realistic image of the country, which may be the cause of the detected cluster's merge.

4.1.2. Second Experiment - Students Enrolled in Non-Higher Education

The second experiment was designed using datasets extracted from the Portuguese Institute of Statistics (INE). These datasets focus on the number of students enrolled in non-higher education, which are available for years 2001, 2002 and 2003, and are useful for the analysis of a country's Education. Each dataset consists of 30 observations, corresponding to the units of analysis of NUTS III (Nomenclature of territorial units for statistics level III), and 5 continuous attributes that are expressed in terms of the number of enrolled students in each non-higher school stage. Similarly to the first experiment,

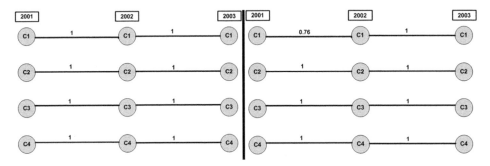

Figure 2. Bipartite graphs, corresponding to timestamps 2001, 2002 and 2003, for the INE datasets. The left-hand side graph corresponds to the agglomerative hierarchical clustering and the right-hand side to the K-means clustering.

the observations and attributes are exactly the same for both years. Experimental conditions are also the same. The resulting graphs, that illustrate the transitions, are depicted in Figure 2.

The analysis of Figure 2 allows the diagnosis of changes between three snapshots of data (2001, 2002 and 2003). As evident from the bipartite graphs, all clusters survived. It is also evident that both clustering algorithms agree that there were no structural changes over the years. This clearly indicates that there were no significant changes in the number of enrolled students, in the time period under analysis. From this we can deduce that Portugal didn't implement remarkable Education reforms during the considered time horizon.

4.2. Representation by Comprehension

To test the tracking mechanism for compact representations of clusters we use the same dataset from CBSD. Since the data contain information on all observations, when applying the clustering algorithm we transformed the original representation into a comprehension representation scheme, according to Definition 2. We show the results using the same clustering algorithms - hierarchical algorithm and K-means -, and briefly compare the solutions obtained for each representation scheme (by enumeration and by comprehension).

During $[2005, 2006]$, and using the hierarchical agglomerative clustering algorithm (partition in six, three and four clusters, for each year), the transitions detection algorithm detected the merge of three groups of clusters ($\{C_1(2005), C_2(2005)\} \subsetneq C_1(2006)$, $\{C_1(2005), C_3(2005)\} \subsetneq C_2(2006)$ and $\{C_5(2005), C_6(2005)\} \subsetneq C_3(2006)$), a split ($C_1(2005) \subsetneq \{C_1(2006), C_2(2006)\}$) and the death of one cluster ($C_4(2005) \to \emptyset$). At time interval $[2006, 2007]$ we observe the split of two groups of clusters ($C_1(2006) \subsetneq \{C_1(2007), C_4(2007)\}$ and $C_2(2006) \subsetneq \{C_1(2007), C_2(2007), C_3(2007), C_4(2007)\}$) and two merges ($\{C_1(2006), C_2(2006)\} \subsetneq C_1(2007)$ and $\{C_1(2006), C_2(2006), C_3(2006)\} \subsetneq C_4(2007)$). Using the K-means algorithm we obtain a partition in five clusters, and different transitions results. During $[2005, 2006]$ a cluster was born ($\emptyset \to C_1(2006)$), four clusters died ($C_3(2005) \to \emptyset$, $C_4(2005) \to \emptyset$, $C_5(2005) \to \emptyset$ and $C_6(2005) \to \emptyset$) and two clusters survived ($C_1(2005) \to C_3(2006)$ and $C_2(2005) \to$

$C_2(2006)$). For the surviving clusters we investigated the possible existence of internal transitions. The detected internal transitions were only related to changes in clusters' size. Thus, we found that cluster $C_1(2005)$ shrinks ($C_1(2005) \searrow C_3(2005)$), reducing the number of observations assigned to it, and that cluster $C_2(2005)$ suffers the reverse process - *expansion* - increasing its cardinality ($C_1(2005) \nearrow C_2(2006)$). During [2006, 2007], we detect the death of one cluster ($C_1(2006) \rightarrow \emptyset$), the birth of two clusters ($\emptyset \rightarrow C_2(2007)$ and $\emptyset \rightarrow C_4(2007)$) and the survival of another two clusters ($C_2(2006) \rightarrow C_3(2007)$ and $C_3(2006) \rightarrow C_1(2007)$). Both surviving clusters shrink ($C_2(2006) \searrow C_3(2007)$ and $C_3(2006) \searrow C_1(2007)$).

Comparing the results obtained for the two different representation schemes we can deduce that the transitions detection algorithm's behavior differs. The most obvious difference is the number of deaths and births, which is much higher in the method based in cluster's overlap. These differences are related to the foundations of each method and the different strategies used for mapping the clusters. In fact, if one cluster moves abruptly in the feature space from one year to another, the method won't be able to detect an intersection region and, therefore, a survival, and will consider this situation as a death and birth of a cluster.

5. Conclusions

In this paper we introduced a framework for addressing the problem of monitoring and detecting transitions in clusters' structures, over time. We define and propose two different strategies to represent clusters. We also propose two methods, adapted to each type of cluster representation. These methods rely in solid concepts such as conditional probabilities, bipartite graphs, radius and centroid. Two real world case studies are presented to illustrate the applicability and feasibility of MEC. In these illustrative examples the framework proved its ability to provide an effective diagnosis of clusters' transitions. It was also demonstrated how these results can be interpreted and explored in order to better understand the studied problem.

The main contribution of this work lies in the use of bipartite graphs and conditional probabilities to monitor the transitions of clusters represented by enumeration, and in the computation and assessment of clusters' overlap, for compact representation of clusters.

As future work we intend to extend the application domain of MEC to categorical attributes, create more complex intensional representation schemes and explore the information provided by the dendrogram, in hierarchical clustering, in order to apply MEC to nested clusters. It is also our intention to develop a similar framework to monitor the evolution of social networks.

Acknowledgements

Thanks to the support of the project *Knowledge Discovery from Ubiquitous Data Streams* (PTDC/EIA-EIA/098355/2008).

References

[1] Bottcher, M., Hoppner, F., Spiliopoulou, M. : On exploiting the power of time in data mining. SIGKDD Explorations (10), 3–11 (2008)

[2] Jain, A. K. : Data Clustering: 50 Years Beyond K-means. In: Daelemans, W., Goethals, B., Morik, K. (eds.) ECML/PKDD 2008. LNCS, vol. 5211. Springer, Belgium (2008)

[3] Jain, A. K., Murty, M. N., Flynn, P. J. : Data Clustering: A Review. ACM Comput. Surv. (31), 264–323 (1999)

[4] Ganti, V., Gehrke, J., Ramakrishnan, R. : A Framework for Measuring Changes in Data Characteristics. In: Proceedings of the 18th ACM SIGACT-SIGMOD-SIGART Symposium on Principles of Database Systems, pp. 126–137. ACM Press, Pennsylvania (1999)

[5] Bartolini, I., Ciaccia, P., Ntoutsi, I., Patella, M., Theodoridis, Y. : The Panda framework for Comparing Patterns. Data Knowl. Eng. (68), 244–260 (2009)

[6] Chawathe, S. S., Garcia-Molina, H. : Meaningful Change Detection in Structured Data. In: Peckham, J. (ed.) Proceedings ACM SIGMOD International Conference on Management of Data, pp. 26-37. ACM Press, Arizona (1997)

[7] Oliveira, M., Gama, J.: Bipartite Graphs for Monitoring Clusters Transitions. In: Proceedings of the Ninth International Symposium on Intelligent Data Analysis. LNCS, vol. 6065, pp. to appear. Springer, Arizona (2010)

[8] Spiliopoulou, M., Ntoutsi, I., Theodoridis, Y., Schult, R.: MONIC: modeling and monitoring cluster transitions. In: Eliassi-Rad, T., Ungar, L. H., Craven, M., Gunopulos, D. (eds.) ACM SIGKDD 2006, pp. 706–711. ACM, Philadelphia (2006)

[9] Falkowski, T., Bartelheimer, J., Spiliopoulou, M. : Mining and Visualizing the Evolution of Subgroups in Social Networks. In: IEEE / WIC / ACM International Conference on Web Intelligence, pp. 52-58. IEEE Computer Society, China (2006)

[10] Yang, H., Parthasarathy, S., Mehta, S. : A generalized framework for mining spatio-temporal patterns in scientific data. In: Grossman, R., Bayardo, R. J., Bennett, K. P. (eds.) Proceedings of the 11th ACM SIGKDD International Conference on Knowledge Discovery and Data Mining, pp. 716–721. ACM, Illinois (2005)

[11] Baron, S., Spiliopoulou, M. : Monitoring Change in Mining Results. In: Kambayashi, Y., Winiwarter, W., Arikawa, M. (eds.) Data Warehousing and Knowledge Discovery, Third International Conference. LNCS, vol. 2114. Springer, Germany (2001)

[12] Baron, S., Spiliopoulou, M. : Monitoring the Evolution of Web Usage Patterns. In: Berendt, B., Hotho, A., Mladenic, D., Someren, M., Spiliopoulou, M., Stumme, G. (eds.) Web Mining: From Web to Semantic Web, First European Web Mining Forum. LNCS, vol. 3209. Springer, Croatia (2004)

[13] Lu, Y-H., Huang, Y. : Mining data streams using clustering. In: Proceedings of the 4th International Conference on Machine Learning and Cybernetics, pp. 2079-2083. IEEE Computer Society, China (2005)

[14] Aggarwal, C. C. : On Change Diagnosis in Evolving Data Streams. IEEE Trans. Knowl. Data Eng. (17), 587–600 (2005)

[15] Chen, K., Liu, L. : Detecting the Change of Clustering Structure in Categorical Data Streams. In: Ghosh, J., Lambert, D., Skillicorn, D. B., Srivastava, J. (eds.) Proceedings of the 6th SIAM International Conference on Data Mining. SIAM, USA (2006)

[16] Aggarwal, C. C., Han, J., Wang, J., Yu, P. S. : A Framework for Change Diagnosis of Data Streams. In: Halevy, A. Y., Ives, Z. G., Doan, A. : Proceedings of the 2003 ACM SIGMOD International Conference on Management of Data, pp. 575–586. ACM, California (2003)

[17] O'Callaghan, L., Meyerson, A., Motwani, R., Mishra, N., Guha, S. : Streaming-Data Algorithms for High-Quality Clustering. In: Proceedings of the 18th International Conference on Data Engineering. IEEE Computer Society, California (2002)

[18] Elnekave, S., Last, M., Maimon, O. : Incremental Clustering of Mobile Objects. ICDE Workshops (2007)

[19] Kalnis, P., Mamoulis, N., Bakiras, S. : On Discovering Moving Clusters in Spatio-temporal Data. In: Medeiros, C. B., Egenhofer, M. J., Bertino, E. (eds.) Advances in Spatial and Temporal Databases, 9th International Symposium. LNCS, vol. 3633, pp. 364–381. Springer, Brazil (2005)

[20] Li, T., Ma, S., Ogihara, M. : Entropy-based criterion in categorical clustering. In: Proceedings of the 21th international conference on Machine learning. ACM, New York (2004)

[21] Zhang, T., Ramakrishnan, R., Livny, M. : BIRCH: An Efficient Data Clustering Method for Very Large Databases. In: Proceedings of the 1996 ACM SIGMOD International Conference on Management of

Data, pp. 103–114. ACM Press, Canada(1996)
[22] Kaur, S., Bhatnagar, V., Mehta, S., Kapoor, S.: Concept Drift in Unlabeled Data Stream. Technical Report, University of Delhi (2009)
[23] Rousseeuw, P. J. : Silhouettes: a graphical aid to the interpretation and validation of cluster analysis. Journal of Computational and Applied Mathematics, 53–65 (1987)
[24] Spinosa, E. J., Ponce de Leon Ferreira de Carvalho, A., Gama, J.: OLINDDA: a clusterbased approach for detecting novelty and concept drift in data streams. In: Proceedings of the 22nd Annual ACM Symposium of Applied Computing. SAC, vol. 1, pp. 318–332. ACM, Seoul, South Korea (2007)
[25] Fanizzi, N., d'Amato, C., Esposito, F.: Conceptual clustering and Its Application to Concept Drift and Novelty Detection. In: Proceedings of the 5th European semantic web conference on the semantic web (ESWC). LNCS, vol. 5021, pp. 448–452. Springer-Verlag, Tenerife, Spain (2008)

Dealing with the dynamics of proof-standard in argumentation-based decision aiding

Wassila OUERDANE [a,1], Nicolas MAUDET [a] and Alexis TSOUKIAS [a]

[a] *LAMSADE, University Paris-Dauphine, France*

Abstract. Usually, in argumentation, the proof-standards that are used are fixed a priori by the procedure. However decision-aiding is a context where these may be modified dynamically during the process, depending on the responses of the client. The expert indeed needs to adapt and refine its choice of an appropriate method of aggregation, so that it fits the preference model inferred from the interaction. In this paper we examine how this aspect can be handled in an argumentation-based decision-aiding framework. The first contribution of the paper is conceptual: the notion of a concept lattice based on simple properties and allowing to navigate among the different proof-standards is put forward. We then show how this can be integrated within the Carneades model while still preserving its essential properties; and illustrates our proposal with a detailed example.

Keywords. Argumentation Theory, Knowledge representation, Decision Making, Preferences

Introduction

From the seminal work of [7] to recent accounts (see e.g. [2]), argumentation has been advocated as a relevant approach to account for decision-aiding. Under such a perspective, an agent faced with several possible candidate actions (or alternatives) will seek a decision which is "sufficiently" justified in the light of the arguments which can be constructed for or against the considered alternative. One (important) aspect of argumentation is to define what valid justifications (sets of arguments) can be considered, for instance whether reinstatement should be used or not [12]. On top of that, though, a proper definition of what "sufficiently" means should be given, for in most situations conflicting justifications may typically be built for and against the considered decision. Doing that amounts to defining a *proof standard* [10]. In most applications (for example those dealing with legal issues), the proof standard to be used is fixed a priori, given exogenously by the procedure.

In this paper, the context we are interested in is that of a specific case of decision-aiding: an expert helps a decision maker in choosing a single decision to be undertaken, given that the different actions may be evaluated on several dimensions (criteria) which

---

[1]Corresponding Author: Ouerdane Wassila, LAMSADE, Universtity Paris-Dauphine, France; E-mail: wassila.ouerdane@lamsade.dauphine.fr

then need to be aggregated. By interpreting criteria as dimensions against which arguments can be constructed (we shall discuss this point later on) we see that the problem is very similar to the one discussed above. Except in trivial cases, these different criteria will indeed conflict and promote different decisions, and we should define what makes a decision sufficiently justified. What makes the problem challenging here is the following feature: part of the job of the expert is precisely to choose a given aggregation method and adapt it to the responses provided by the client during the course of interaction. It is indeed important to realize that not all the methods may be meaningfully used for a given choice problem. The preference model of the decision maker inferred from the interaction with him discards or instead reinforce the reasons that the expert have to select a given method. For instance, the expert may realize during the process that a given criterion plays a prominent role. The purpose of this paper is precisely to provide a formal account of how this can be done conceptually and in practice in an argumentation-based setting.

The remainder of this paper is as follows. In the next section, we briefly overview the related works, either in the domain of argumentation-based decision-making, or in the field of multiple criteria decision-aiding. In Section 2 we present a motivating example which illustrates the need to cater for proof standards dynamic modification, in our context of decision-aiding dialogues. Our conceptual contribution is explicited in Section 3: we show how different properties can be used to indicate how proofs vary in the process. More specifically, we propose a concept lattice which will allow to navigate among the different aggregation techniques. In Section 4, we show more specifically how this proposal can be integrated in the recent Carneades model [9] . Section 5 concludes.

1. Related Work

In multicriteria decision-aiding, the question of how to chose or adapt the aggregation method is a central issue, which is typically left under the expert's responsibility. Decision-aiding tools rarely address this aspect of the problem. Even in the case of *interactive methods* [16] which emphasize the need to take into account the client's feedback, the objective is to explore the neighborhood of a given solution, not to modify the aggregation method itself. In fact, whether formal guidelines to help the expert in this process can be proposed is still a matter of intense discussions. The ambitious research program of *conjoint measurement* [4] is dedicated to the axiomatic study of aggregation methods: by providing characterization of the different aggregation methods under the form of sets of axioms, it provides a theoretically sound framework which may serve as a foundation for the interactive method selection procedures. Unfortunately, the different axioms used in such characterisations do not necessarily easily appeal to intuition. In particular, they do not give rise to "natural" ways to invalidate or reinforce them during the interaction. Although this approach inspires our work, we opted for a set of simple properties that do not necessarily match exactly such axioms. One approach which shares with us the objective to provide a simple and intuitive to discriminate can be found in [11]. However, such a work does not provide any operational way to guide the selection process.

In the domain of argumentation, the notion of proof standard has recently received much attention (see [10] for a recent survey). The notion of *accrual of arguments* [15] essentially tackles the same issue: how to aggregate different arguments together. Usually in argumentation, as mentioned above, the notion of proof standard that should be used is determined by a given context. This is especially true in the legal domain, where the proof standards that should be used are well identified. For instance, under the *"scintilla of evidence"* proof standard, a small piece of evidence is enough to make the claim justifiable. Under the *"preponderance of the evidence"*, the available evidence should make the claim more probable than not. The strongest requirement is attached to the *"beyond reasonable doubt"*, whose definition is clear from the name. Depending on the nature of the case, the proof standard required may be different. In a criminal case for instance, this latter definition is appropriate.

The use of proof standard is not restricted to legal field and can be used in a context of decision-making. For instance, *Hermes*, a groupe decision support system where argumentation is used to enhance group decision making, used proof standards to calculate an *activation label* associated to the component of the system [13]. Indeed, the *Hermes* system organized the knowledge under the form of a discussion graph, which consists of: *issues* (decision to be made, or goal to be achieved), *alternatives* (different choices attached to an issue), *position* (proposition or claims that defend the selection of an alternative) and *constraints* (a qualitative way to weight reasons for and against the selection of an alternative). Thus, the activation label associated to each alternative, position and constraint is used to indicate their *status (active or not active)*. This status allows to accept (or reject) a position and to distinguish the recommended alternatives from the rejected one.

A more recent account, in the same vein, is proposed in the Carneades framework [9]. A distinctive and very appealing feature of this approach is that the acceptability of claims is computed on the way an argument is attacked or defended in a given argument graph, but also on the *dialectical status* of the different moves that brought the arguments, as well as on the proof standards attached to them. The approach will be detailed further in Section 4, when we give the detail of how our notions can be integrated in this framework.

Finally, we note that the notion is seldom discussed in the context of Dung's abstract framework [6]. This is certainly due to the fact that this framework does not model explicitly arguments in favour of a given claim. However, there may some way to provide an interpretation of this notion, based for instance on the type of extensions arguments belong to [3].

A final word is useful on the exact relation between these two notions. It is certainly possible to "retrieve" many multicriteria aggregation procedures by means of argumentation. This is done for example in [1]. However, as noted by these authors, only the most simple aggregation procedures can be captured this way. This is essentially due to the (mostly) qualitative nature of the argumentation process. On the other hand, multicriteria aggregation makes (typically) assumption that argumentation would *not* do when defining proof-standards. In particular, argumentative approaches emphasize that the reasons in favour and the reasons against some conclusion should be treated separately. Proof standards as usually proposed in argumentation are intrinsically *bipolar*, in other words they constitute techniques to aggregate *pros* and *cons* (see [5]).

2. A Motivating Example

We assume that a decision maker specifies his evaluation model, comprising of four actions $A=\{a_0, a_1, a_2, a_3\}$, five criteria $H=\{h_0, h_1, h_2, h_3, h_4\}$, and the following performance table:

	h_0	h_1	h_2	h_3	h_4
a_0	7	6	2	3	5
a_1	6	4	8	4	7
a_2	3	2	5	5	3
a_3	7	7	2	0	2

(1) S: I recommend a_1 as being the best choice
(2) U: Why is that the case?
(3) S: because a_1 is globally better than all other alternatives
(4) U: Why?
(5) S: Because a_1 is prefered to each other alternatives by a majority of criteria: it is ranked first on h_2 and h_4, and is only beaten by a_2 on h_3. But a_1 beats a_2 on h_0.
(6) U: I see, but I would prefer a_0 to a_1
(7) S: Why?
(8) U: Because a_0 is better on $\{h_0, h_1\}$
(9) S: Fine. But then why is not a_3 prefered?
(10) U: No. a_3 is too bad on h_3. This would not be justifiable.

Let us briefly analyze this dialogue. We follow [14] and assume that different types of arguments can be constructed to capture different aspects of these dialogues. In turn (1), the system suggests that the action a_1 is the best one, without giving further information. In turn (2), the user challenges this proposition and asks for a justification, which is given by the system in the turn (3). The justification given explains that a_1 is better than any other action (technically, this is a Condorcet winner). Not satisfied with this explanation, the user asks for more explanations.

The system offers the detailed explanation on turn (5). Now on turn (6) the decision maker puts forward the alternative that he feels intuitively as being the best here. The system challenges this claim and at turn (8) the decision maker gives an explanation based on the fact that a_0 is better on two criteria: h_0 and h_1. The system again challenges the claim by emphasizing that on this basis a_3 should then be preferred. Finally the decision maker gives a reason for *not* accepting a_3: a very low score on criteria h_3.

From (1) to (5) the dialogue amounts to revealing an increasingly detailed evidence for a specific recommendation. The dialogue moves that are of interest for us come right after. In both turn (8) and (10) the responses of the decision maker would trigger a difficult task for the system, since the assumptions made at the beginning of the dialogue turn out to be inadequate, and then invalidate the method initially chosen to compute the recommendation. More precisely, in turn (5), the system used the majority principle to justify the recommendation a_1. However, in turn (8) the user does not seem to follow the same reasoning, since he proposed a coalition of two criteria to support his best choice.

3. Navigating Through Proof Standards

Dealing with such dynamics of the proofs poses a number of challenges. The first one is to define a principled way to identify an adequate proof standard, given the current state of the interaction. The second one is to design a mechanism that will allow to automatically update the proof as a result of the client's responses. We now discuss these two issues in turn.

3.1. How to identify a proof?

The key idea here is to identify a set of properties that will help us to discriminate each procedure. Such properties will correspond to some characteristics of the decision maker's preferences, corresponding to a set of conditions supporting the use of a given proof.

First of all, we assume that each proof obeys the following principle: *sufficiently supporting reasons must be provided, and no strong opposing reasons should be provided*. This principle is sometimes called concordance/discordance in the multicriteria decision aiding literature [4]. A proof standard instantiates this principle by applying different (separate) proofs on each side (leaving maybe the discordance side void in case this principle does not apply). Note that this dichotomy does not necessarily correspond to bipolarity, as each side may involve arguments *pro* and *con*. Instead, the concordance side provides necessary conditions for reasons to support a given claim, whereas the discordance side provides sufficient reasons to discard a given claim.

We now propose and briefly discuss three simple properties. These properties are by no means exhaustive, and there are clearly many other which could be proposed (for instance to cater more specifically for bipolar aggregation methods or proof standards used in argumentation, see *e.g.* [5]). These properties permit nevertheless to illustrate our purpose as they allow to distinguish a large variety of methods practically used in multicriteria decision aiding.

- *Ordinality* (ORD.). Only the ordering of actions is relevant for comparison, in particular the specific difference of performance values is not.
- *Anonymity* (ANO.). It suggests that all criteria are exchangeable;
- *Independence* (INDEP.). Preferences expressed on a criterion do not depend on preferences expressed on another criterion.

Take the *weighted sum*. Each criteria separately has a different weight assigned, so anonymity is not satisfied. The preferential information is also not only ordinal, since the numerical values of the performance are used to compute the overall score. Finally, preferential independence is satisfied since it is possible for the decision maker to express his preferences on a given criterion regardless of other criteria.

As a second example consider now *simple majority*. Here we just count the number of criteria in favour a given claim, so the proof is anonymous. It is also purely ordinal, and satisfies preferential independence.

Table 1 provides more examples of classical aggregation methods which can be taken as proof standards in our context. Again, they should just be taken for illustrative purpose. In particular, they are not necessarily independent, which means that not all combinations is necessarily meaningful. We shall come back on that point later.

Table 1. Some proof standards and their properties

Methods	ORD.	ANO.	INDEP.	NO VETO
Simple majority	✓	✓	✓	✓
Weighted Majority	✓		✓	✓
Outranking method	✓		✓	
Mean		✓	✓	✓
Additive value model			✓	✓
Non linear value model				✓
Oligarchies	✓			✓

An interesting but difficult question is whether different proofs can conceivably instantiate the concordance and discordance side. For instance, if the decision maker exhibit an ordinal method to establish supporting reasons, can he use a completely different way to decide when a reason is sufficient to discard a claim? The practice suggests that this may indeed be the case, the typical case being the use of a *veto* specifying a threshold (on a criteria) above/below which a claim is judged unacceptable. For simplicity reasons, we shall assume in what follows that the proof for the discordance can be a veto, if any. To sum up, in the Table 1 the three first properties will help to identify proofs for the concordance side (such as simple majority) and the last one to specify the existence of a veto.

3.2. How to choose a proof?

The difficulty of choosing a procedure is mainly due to the fact that at the beginning of the process, it is virtually impossible to have all the preferential information of the decision maker. Moreover, such preferences may change and evolve during the interaction, leading to corrections or new information being provided. Despite such difficulties, the system should be able to decide on the fly whether a procedure is appropriate or not.

We assume a set $R=\{r_0, r_1, \ldots r_n\}$ of potential proofs to be used by the system, and a set $P=\{p_0, \ldots, p_k\}$ of properties as identified previously. At each time step of the dialogue t we denote by $\mathcal{I}_t$ the available preferential information and by R_t the methods that are compatible with I_t, that is, methods that are still eligible to be used by the system.

However, defining the set of compatible methods is not good enough, as the system should select *one* method as being its favoured method, the one it will base its current reasoning on. The idea here is just to opt for methods that are *simple* for the user to understand. In theory this is a tricky problem to rank the proof standard according to a simplicity criteria which is certainly difficult to grasp. The solution proposed here allows in a sense to circumvent the problem: the system requires to start with a favorite proof to be used: this can be provided by the expert, or sometimes the decision maker himself (who may be familiar with a specific proof). This would typically be, for instance, a *weighted sum* or *simple majority*. Technically, when the system makes this first choice among the set R, the properties corresponding to this procedure are assumed to be true *by default*. Now as the user provides more preferential information (during the interaction), the system should be able to adapt and jump to the new favoured method. To do that, the system will be based on the one hand on the *set of properties* identified previously and on the other hand on the *decision maker's responses*.

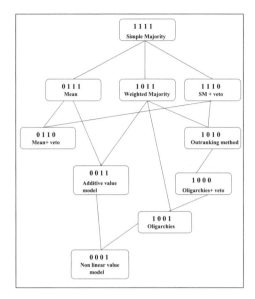

Figure 1. An example lattice for navigating among proofs.

The mechanism is almost in place. We just need to specify how to guide the navigation among the different candidate proof standards, depending on the properties that are currently satisfied or contradicted. To account for that, we propose to formalise the relationship between the set of properties and the set of proofs by a *Concept Lattice* as proposed in *Formal Concept Analysis* (FCA) [8].

In our context, a *formal concept* corresponds to a pair (R_i, P_i), such that $R_i \subseteq R$ the set of proofs and $P_i \subseteq P$ the set of properties. Let prop(p_k,r) a boolean function returning true when the property p_k indeed belong to the set of properties attached to r. The navigation works as follows: position yourself in the lattice at the initially chosen proof (attached to this proof the property vector with values assumed to be as required by the corresponding proof). Then, depending on the response of the decision maker, the system will "slide" to the next reachable proof. This gives a natural interpretation of how simple is a proof standard, namely how close (in terms of the number of properties that differ) it stands from the initially chosen proof standard. For instance, the Figure 1 gives an example of such a lattice by considering that the first chosen procedure is the Simple Majority with the vector (1111).

Usually, the *concept lattice* is a complete lattice such that the concepts are partially ordered by inclusion: the lattice is composed of nodes that are formal concepts and edges that represent the links of specialization/generalization. However, in our context this is not necessarily the case as some combination of properties do not necessarily specify any procedure, see *e.g* Figure 1). A further difficulty which may occur is that it may also be the case that a given response is ambiguous as to what property is concerned, as it is illustrated in the following example, in which case a heuristics should be used.

Example 1 *We have only a performance table, we can admit that the most simple procedure is the simple majority without any veto (1111). Now, the update of the procedure will depend on the user's responses during the dialogue. For instance, if the answers refer to a difference in performance between two actions we can have two ways to interpret that.*

The first one is that such difference represents a penalty that can not be compensated. In other terms, it represents a strong negative reason against a given conclusion. Thus, in this case we are in presence of a kind of a veto in the discordance and the corresponding combination is (1110). In the second case, such difference is interpreted as the existence of a compensation, and therefore the ordinality of the supporting side is challenged. In this case, we move towards the combination (0111), corresponding to the mean.

This, finally, gives us a procedure *update_proof(.)* which takes as parameters the responses and the current information state. To be able to specify more precisely how this will proceed, we need a more detailed representation of the current state of the interaction, more explicit on how the properties can be modified. The Carneades model provides a framework upon which this can be built.

4. Integration in the Carneades Model

We now show how this mechanism can be integrated in the state-of-the art Carneades model for [9].

4.1. Acceptability in the Carneades model.

The acceptability of a statement in the Carneades model is determined in an arguments graph. Two kinds of nodes are used: *statement* nodes and *argument* nodes. Statements are declarative sentences (in a given language) and argument nodes are (instantiatied) argument schemes. Furthermore, arguments graph have different kinds of edges that link the premises and conclusions of the arguments. The acceptability of the statement depends essentially on three elements: its dialectical status during the dialogue (*stated*, *questioned*, *accepted* and *rejected*), its proof standard and its *premises types*. Indeed, depending on their type, different requirement are attached to the premises considered. *Ordinary premises* must be supported with further ground, *assumptions* can be assumed to hold until they are questioned, and finally *exceptions* don't hold in the absence of evidence to the contrary. Determining the acceptability of a statement is eventually the result of a procedure which recursively determine the acceptability of its premises on the basis of the elements mentioned above (for more details see [9]).

4.2. An extended acceptability function.

In our case, an argument graph is constructed with the arguments exchanged during the decision aiding process. We consider the same types of nodes, such that the statements are constructed on the basis of preferential information provided by the user and the argument nodes are instantiation of different types of argument schemes for the decision aiding context (see [14] for more details). Now what is missing is a way to represent explicitly the proof standard, so that it can be (indirectly) discussed and challenged as any other statement in the graph. Specifically, it should have its own dialectical status during the dialogue and thus its own acceptability. We draw the attention of the reader that the dialectical status of a proof can be either "*stated*" or "*rejected*". The practice of decision-aiding indeed tells us that the decision-maker is not able to explicitly accept a proof-standard.

Technically, a new link is added to represent the fact that a given proof is assigned to a statement. The proof standard itself is a statement of a special type, to which are attached the different properties discussed in the previous section (graphically, such a link is represented by a double line edge with no arrowhead, see Figure 2).

The acceptability function of [9] is extended in an obvious way: now the system requires that the statement satisfies the proof standard attached to it, and also that the proof standard is itself acceptable:

$$acceptable(s, G) = satisfies(s, ps(s), G) \wedge acceptable(ps(s), G) \qquad (1)$$

There is theoretically a risk of infinite recursion here, as the acceptability of a proof may itself obey to a different proof, etc. However, this case does not occur: for the statement nodes of type "proof standard", a unique way to assess the acceptability is imposed, as a single argument will be considered to support the use of this proof (This assumes of course that no other argument are advanced pro or against the use of a specific proof standard—we leave this issue open for future works). Hence this argument must be defensible. Indeed if the properties discussed in Section 3 are conceived as a set of premises of an argument supporting "theoretically" the use of a specific proof standard, then contradicting one of this property will invalidate the acceptability of the proof standard. More precisely, Table 1 specifies the content of the premises that the argument supporting the use of the proof standard uses as assumption premises. Take for instance the *weighted majority*: the content of the property premises will be "ordinality", "not anonymous" and "independence of criteria".

The question of the dialectical status of these premises is now raised. In practice, most of the aspect of this proof standard is transparent to the decision-maker, as he is not supposed to discuss these concepts. To account for this, we suppose that the dialectical status of these premises is "assumed true", to differentiate with stated which is supposed to be made explicit in the dialogue.

4.3. Critical responses, positive and negative evidence.

To each of these premises is now attached a list of possible *critical responses*, which play the same role as critical questions (a set of questions that represent attacks, challenges or criticisms to a given argument scheme). Critical responses play the same role, except that the decision maker is typically not aware that it constitutes a counter-argument to some claim. These responses correspond to typical manners that the decision maker may contradict a given property. There is an important difference to make between two types of responses:

- *Positive Evidence (PE)*—these responses provide supporting evidence to the fact that the property is satisfied. This would typically consist of general statements that the decision maker may make, *e.g.* "the difference between x and y is not significant for me" would be positive evidence for ordinality.
- *Negative Evidence (NE)*—these responses provide an explicit counter-example to a specific property, *e.g.* "frankly the score of this alternative x is so much better than the one of y that I can't take y" would be negative evidence for ordinality.

The reader must bear in mind here that the decision maker is *not* supposed to be competent to state general features of his preference. The only thing that the decision-maker is expected to do is to express some preference by comparing alternatives. This means that the two types of evidence have very different consequences, and this will be made explicit in what follows.

Following [9], the critical responses will be modeled as premises (Table 2 provides an example of some possible critical responses). The type of premises used here depends on the kind of evidence required. As explained earlier, negative evidence is sufficiently convincing since it provides an explicit counter-example. They will be modeled as *assumptions*. On the other hand, positive evidence may require further ground to be acceptable. They will be modeled as *ordinary premises*. The system may subsequently test the decision-maker with a series of question to establish some grounds upon which the validity of the claim may be granted via a *property testing subdialogue*.

Table 2. Examples of Critical responses.

Property	Positive and Negative Evidences
Ordinality	*PE:* the difference between x and y is not significant for me.
	NE: the difference between x and y on the criterion h_i is too small, large, ...
Anonymity	*PE:* replacing the criterion h_i by h_j is the same result; all the criteria play the same role
	NE: the criterion h_i is more important than the criterion h_j
	x is better than y on the coalition of criteria $\{h_i, h_j\}$
Independence	*PE:* Every thing being equal on the rest of criteria, I prefer x to y
	on the criterion h_i because $h_i(x) > h_i(y)$ (Ceteris Paribus sentence)
	NE: if x is preferred to y on the criterion h_i it should be the same on the criterion h_j
	if x is preferred to y on h_i then w should be preferred to z on h_j
No Veto	*PE:* any difference of performances is meaningful of preferences
	NE: comparing x to y on the criterion h_i, x is not acceptable, x is too bad, x is not satisfactory

4.4. Property testing subdialogues.

The idea of a property testing (PT) subdialogue is that the system enters into an embedded dialogue with the objective to back a positive evidence claim. Again, as the decision maker himself is not in a position to provide some reasons to back this claim, the process will be guided by the system. Typically, the system will generate some test questions specifically designed to perform some sort of verification. Let us take a very simple example. Suppose that the decision maker claimed that "all criteria play exactly the same role", a positive evidence for the *anonymity* property. Now the system performs some permutations on the names of the criteria (leaving the the values of actions unchanged) and checks:

(S): Would you still prefer alternative x now?

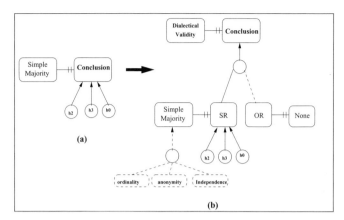

Figure 2. Example of explicit proof in an argument graph.

This can be repeated a number of times. In the end the system has gained sufficient knowledge to decide whether this property can indeed continue to be considered true in the rest of the interaction (although there is no way to formally establish this of course). Typically, a PT subdialogue then terminates with either the system having established sufficient evidence for the claim (in which case the status of the property will move to *stated*), or the decision maker having provided an answer explicitly contradicting the disputed property (in which case the status of the complement of the property will move to *accepted*.) We can come up with similar types of dialogues for other properties, possibly involving fictive alternative.[2]

4.5. Integrating the procedure.

It is now time to gather the different pieces mentioned so far into a general procedure (see Algorithm 1)which makes explicit how our proposal can be integrated into a Carneades-based dialogue game. The general algorithm is as follows and supposes that the *update_proof(.)* procedure given in Section 4 takes as input the current state of the argument graph (G) and a given critical response (CR) and $\overline{p_i}$ stands for the complement of p_i. Moreover, termination (as long as the dialogue game it is inserted in also terminates) is guaranteed. It relies in particular on the fact that we do not allow contradictory positive evidence to be put forward, otherwise we will have an *inconsistency*. Thus, navigation in the lattice allows only a finite number of moves.

Let us give an example of how such a procedure can be used. Consider again the example of Section 2. In this example, on the basis of the performance table, the system has selected a first proof in order to construct a recommendation, which is the *Simple Majority* (it is explicitly given on turn (5) of the dialogue). This can be illustrated by the arguments graph [3] of the Figure 2 (a), where we can observe that an explicit proof is attached to the claim. Such a link allows to conclude that we have effectively enough supporting reasons for the claim according to some aggregation procedure $r_i \in R$. However, as it was mentioned before in this paper, the proof standard is a combination of two

---

[2]Although there is debate in decision-aiding on the fact that a counter-example on a fictive example really constitutes an evidence that some property is violated.

[3]For the sake of simplicity, we depicted only the elements of the graph that are relevant for the discussion.

Algorithm 1. General Procedure
  chose $c_r \in R$;
  for all prop(p_i,r)=true **do**
    status(p_i) $\leftarrow$ assumed_true;
  end for
  while dialogue game not terminated **do**
    play dialogue move;
    if CR identified **then**
      if $CR = \langle NE, p_i \rangle$ **then**
        if $status(p_i) = accepted$ **then**
          return inconsistency;
        else
          status($\overline{p_i}$) $\leftarrow$ accepted;
        end if
      else
        if $status(p_i) = accepted\ or\ stated$ **then**
          return inconsistency;
        else
          $status(\overline{p_i}) leftarrow questioned$;
          property testing subdialogue();
        end if
      end if
    end if
    $c_r \leftarrow update\_proof(CR, G)$;
  end while

distincts proofs (concordance vs. discordance), therefore, we can distinguish two sides in the graph, as it is indicated in the Figure 2 (b), where the Simple Majority is the proof for the supporting reasons. At this point, the acceptability of such a proof is true. Indeed, it is supported by a defensible Pro argument, because the status of all the premises (corresponding to the properties describing the proof) is assumed true. However, on turn (6) the user keeps refusing the recommendation, and argues that a_0 should be prefered. The system challenges this choice, and the user says that a_0 is better on h_1 and h_2 (on turn (8)). *This not only attacks the previous recommendation of the system, but also attacks the proof-standard currently used.* In fact, such a claim is interpreted as a NE against the property *anonymity* (see Table 2). Thus, according to our previous procedure, we have status (non anonymous)= accepted, and therefore the current proof is no longer warranted (because the argument is not defensible). Given this new information (see Figure 1), the current proof-standard becomes a Weighted majority consisting of $\{h_1,h_2\}$, enforcing the system to use this proof-standard. Hence, although a_1 continues to satisfy the *majority*, the proof-standard itself is invalidated. However, on turn (9), the system informs the user that a_3 should be the best according to this new proof. The user rejects the proposal by putting forward a negative reason against it (10). More precisely, the user gives a NE for the absence of a veto. Therefore, the new proof corresponds to the *weighted majority* for the supporting reasons and a veto for the opposing reasons (i.e. (1010)). Finally, the consequence on the graph is that to the statement "OR" we link the proof "veto".

5. Conclusion

We proposed in this this work a mechanism to deal with the problem of choosing a proof standard within a decision aiding process, and showed how such a mechanism can be integrated into the Carneades model. It is clear that the identification of set of properties is a difficult task, one that goes much beyond our ambition in this paper. We plan to focus more specifically on bipolar methods in forthcoming works. We believe that an experimental study aiming at analyzing the behavior of the decision maker in a situation of decision support should allow to refine the types of reactions that the system should be prepared to deal with.

References

[1] L. Amgoud, J.-F. Bonnefon, and H. Prade. An argumentation-based approach to multiple criteria decision. In *Proc. of the 8th European Conf. on Symbolic and Quantitative Approaches to Reasoning and Uncertainty*, pages 269–280, 2005.

[2] L. Amgoud and H. Prade. Using arguments for making and explaining decisions. *Journal of Artificial Intelligence*, 173:413–436, 2009.

[3] K. Atkinson and T Bench-Capon. Argumentation and standards of proof. In *Proc. of the 11th Inter. Conf. on Artificial Intelligence and law*, pages 107–116, 2007.

[4] D. Bouyssou, Th. Marchant, M. Pirlot, A. Tsoukiàs, and Ph. Vincke. *Evaluation and decision models with multiple criteria: Stepping stones for the analyst.* 2006.

[5] D. Dubois, H. Fargier, and J-F Bonnefon. On the qualitative comparison of decisions having positive and negative features. *Journal of Artificial Intelligence Research*, 32:385–417, 2008.

[6] P. M. Dung. On the Acceptability of Arguments and its Fundamental Role in Nonmonotonic Reasoning, Logic Programming and n-person games. *Artificial Intelligence*, 77(2):321–358, 1995.

[7] J. Fox and S. Parsons. On Using Arguments for Reasoning about Actions and Values. In *Proc. of the AAAI Spring Symposium on Qualitative Preferences in Deliberation and Practical Reasoning*, pages 55–63, 1997.

[8] B. Ganter and R. Willer. *Formal concept Analysis.* Springer, 1999.

[9] T. Gordon, H. Prakken, and D. Walton. The Carneades model of argument and burden of proof. *Artificial Intelligence*, 171(4):875–896, 2007.

[10] T.F. Gordon and D. Walton. Proof burdens and standards. In I. Rahwan and G. Simari, editors, *Argumentation in Artificial Intelligence*. 2009.

[11] A. Guitouni and J.M. Martel. Tentative guidelines to help choosing an appropriate MCDA method. *European Journal of Operational Research*, 109(2):501–521, 1998.

[12] J. F. Horty. Argument construction and reinstatement in logics for defeasible reasoning. *Artificial Intelligence and Law*, 9(1):1–28, 2001.

[13] N. I. Karacapilidis and D. Papadias. Hermes: Supporting argumentative discourse in multi-agent decision making. In *Proc. of the 15th National Conf. on AI and 10th Innovative Applications of Artificial Intelligence Conference*, pages 827–832, 1998.

[14] W. Ouerdane, N. Maudet, and A. Tsoukiàs. Argument schemes and critical questions for decision aiding process. In *Proc. of the 2nd Inter. Conf. on Computational Models of Argument*, pages 285–296, 2008.

[15] H. Prakken. A study of accrual of arguments, with applications to evidential reasoning. In *Proc. of the 10th Inter. Conf. on Artificial intelligence and law*, pages 85–94, 2005.

[16] D. Vanderpooten. The interactive approach in mcda: a technical framework and some basic conceptions. *Mathematical and Computer Modelling*, 12:1213–1220, 1989.

Domain Independent Goal Recognition

David PATTISON [a] and Derek LONG [a]

[a] *Department of Computer and Information Science,*
University of Strathclyde, Glasgow G1 1XH, UK

Abstract. Goal recognition is generally considered to follow *plan* recognition. The plan recognition problem is typically defined to be that of identifying which plan in a given library of plans is being executed, given a sequence of observed actions. Once a plan has been identified, the goal of the plan can be assumed to follow. In this work, we address the problem of goal recognition directly, without assuming a plan library. Instead, we start with a domain description, just as is used for plan construction, and a sequence of action observations. The task, then, is to identify which possible goal state is the ultimate destination of the trajectory being observed.

We present a formalisation of the problem and motivate its interest, before describing some simplifying assumptions we have made to arrive at a first implementation of a goal recognition system, AUTOGRAPH. We discuss the techniques employed in AUTOGRAPH to arrive at a tractable approximation of the goal recognition problem and show results for the system we have implemented.

Keywords. Goal recognition, Plan recognition, Planning

Introduction

Goal Recognition (GR) is the process of inferring an agent's end goals given a series of observed actions. This is clearly related to the *Plan Recognition* (PR) problem which aims to also find the plan being executed. *Planning* is simply the generation of these plans in an efficient and sensible manner. Yet despite both being based on *actions*, *states* and *goals*, and effectively mirroring one another, advances in research have rarely overlapped.

Previous work has often focused on a single application of the recognition problem, such as identification of human goals through observation of behaviour [15], giving speech/text context [9] or responding with natural dialogue [20]. These have all resulted in systems and algorithms that lack generality or widespread application.

AUTOGRAPH (AUTOmatic Goal Recognition with A Planning Heuristic), is a new approach to Goal Recognition which makes use of Planning techniques. The system uses a standard planning domain model, avoiding the construction of a goal/plan library.

1. Motivation and Prior Approaches

Plan and Goal Recognition problems are motivated by the desire to anticipate the actions or objectives of an agent that is being observed. There are many situations in which this could be useful, including detection and prevention of crime, in teaching, in monitoring the elderly or infirm in their own homes, in military operations and in games. In computer games, intelligent responses to human player activity depend on recognising what that activity might be. Creating a believable and responsive environment that allows players to participate in a truly immersive experience requires that computer controlled agents react to human players with plausible levels of understanding of the human players' actions. This context, in particular, motivates two assumptions underlying our work: first, that the actions are fully observable (game software mediates every action on behalf of the players) and, second, that we are interested in identifying goals as early as possible during the execution of the plan.

Kautz [17] defines the plan recognition problem as minimising the number of top-level, hierarchical plans which explain a sequence of observed actions. Plans were taken from a *plan graph* and every action is assumed to be *relevant* to the plan being executed. The library containing known, valid plans has remained a key element of plan recognition ever since. This structure presents several drawbacks such as the time, effort and space required to construct it and its inevitable incompleteness and irrelevant content. AUTO-GRAPH attempts to address these problems in three areas: *Completeness*, *Scalability* and *Domain Independence*.

Completeness: It is impossible to generate and store every valid plan in a library for non-trivial problems. Previous work has often made use of tree-like structures to represent a large number of plans efficiently but cannot hold *all* possible plans or goals. In our work, any conjunction of literals may form a hypothesis.

Scalability: The scaling behaviour of plan recognition systems is highly dependent on library sizes. This and the previous problems combine to create a tension between scalability and completeness.

Domain Independence: Generating plan libraries is time-consuming and restricts application to domains for which libraries are available.

The goal recognition system of Blaylock and Allen [1] does allow unseen plans to be recognised but must first be *trained* using valid plans *and* explicitly defined goals. Lesh and Etzioi have also explored adapting recognition to a previously unseen plan with the *ADAPT* system [18,19]. The recogniser is trained using recent behaviour which has **not** been annotated with the true goal. This data is then used to try and find the combination which provides the best results. Unlike the previous system, this work does not assume access to training data or require a policy to be constructed for recognition.

We are not the first to propose using *planning* for recognition. Hong [14] proposes an approach in which, as actions are observed, a *goal graph* is constructed similarly to a *plan graph*, with propositions which are recognised goals being linked into a goal layer. The system scales well, but must be provided with an explicit set of valid goals to be used in the graph construction and analysis processes.

Most recently Ramírez and Geffner [22] make use of *heuristic estimation* to eliminate goals from a candidate set, due to an increasing heuristic distance from the current state. The authors present two approaches, assuming *optimal* or *suboptimal* plans, with goals that have become impossible being removed from the *possible* set. Once candidate goals have been eliminated they are never reconsidered. Ramírez and Geffner assume a (small) set of possible goal states is supplied explicitly and they work with an assumption of *partial* observability, so that only a subsequence of the plan is observed.

2. Problem Definition

We now formally define the goal recognition problem. We start with the same framework that is used in classical planning, based on a propositional action model structure. A goal recognition problem is based on a standard planning problem (the facts, actions and initial state). Of course, the goal recognition problem does not contain a goal specification — the problem is to find this specification.

Definition 1. *Goal Recognition Problem Base*
A goal recognition problem base is a triple $\langle F, A, I \rangle$, where F is a set of primitive (propositional) facts, A is a set of actions and $I \subseteq F$ is the initial state for the problem. Each action $a \in A$ is a triple $\langle pre_a, add_a, del_a \rangle$, where $pre_a, add_a, del_a \subseteq F$ are the preconditions, add effects and delete effects of a, respectively.

In addition to the base, a goal recognition problem requires observations: a sequence of actions. We assume that all actions and states are fully observable, but we want to identify the goals as early as possible during execution of the plan. Before we define the goal recognition problem, however, we briefly consider the nature of the solutions we seek and the implications this has on the problem itself. Our expectation is that we should be presented with a goal recognition problem base and a series of actions, with the objective being to identify the target goals of the agent performing the actions. We assume that the agent actually has a target and is not simply executing actions at random. However, even though the agent has an objective, it is not clear that the actions we observe will be unambiguously leading the agent towards this. To simplify things, we begin by assuming that the agent is sufficiently intelligent to make optimal choices in planning for its goal. This is a strong assumption and we consider the implications of weakening it shortly. Even under this assumption, identifying goals is hard. A further problem is that goals can be any subset of facts that is achievable from the initial state so, as we observe actions, each new state could be the goal — the path taken to reach it will be the shortest path (if there were a shorter path then it would contradict our assumption that the agent is executing an optimal plan) and, therefore, it will be consistent with the observations that this is precisely what the agent intended to achieve.

In general, there are many goal sets consistent with a sequence of observed actions, ranging from the possibility that the most recent state was in fact the goal state to the possibility that there are many goals towards which the agent has not yet even begun to act. However, these possibilities are not all equally likely: in most domains there is a clear bias towards certain kinds of goals. This motivates the following definition:

Definition 2. *Goal Hypothesis and Goal Hypothesis Space*
Given a goal recognition problem base, G, with facts F, a goal hypothesis for G is a probability distribution over subsets of F reachable from the initial state using actions in G. The goal hypothesis space for G, $\mathbb{H}$, is the set of all such goal hypotheses for G.

Note that as a special case a goal hypothesis might assign equal non-zero probabilities to some subset of reachable sets of facts and zero to all others (that is, a uniform distribution over a subset of the candidate goals). We will refer to this case as the uniform goal hypothesis over this subset of goals.

Definition 3. *Goal Recognition Problem*
A goal recognition problem is a triple, $\langle G, H_I, (o_1, o_2, ..., o_n) \rangle$, where G is a goal recognition problem base, H_I is an initial goal hypothesis and $(o_1, ..., o_n)$ is the sequence of actions observed one-by-one during the problem.

Each observation in a goal recognition problem updates the hypothesis space, such that candidate goals that are further away from the new state than the previous state are assigned an updated probability of 0, while the remaining probability mass is renormalised across the other states. Nothing observable in the sequence can lead us to modify the relative probabilities of goals that have a common shortest path following the observations made so far. It is interesting to note that actions are transitions between goal hypotheses in an analogous way to their behaviour as transitions between states.

Unfortunately, a goal hypothesis is potentially exponentially large in the size of the set of facts for the underlying planning problem. This is generally far too large to make it possible to represent goal hypotheses explicitly. However, in the work of Ramírez and Geffner [22], the initial goal hypothesis *is* described explicitly, by enumeration (although in their work they do not refer to probabilities). Their work can be interpreted as offering a way to handle the special case of uniform goal hypotheses, but restricted to small (that is, explicitly enumerated) subsets of candidate goal sets.

Explicit representation of $\mathbb{H}$ for anything other than trivial problems is impossible, due to its exponential size. We therefore introduce an approximation of the space which is tractable, but at the price that we cannot accurately represent all possible goal hypotheses.

Definition 4. *Approximate Goal Hypothesis*
An nth order approximation to a goal hypothesis, H, is a goal hypothesis, $\hat{H}$, where $\hat{H}(f) = H(f)$ when $|f| \leqslant n$ and, $\hat{H}(f) = \min_{x \in f} \hat{H}(f \setminus \{x\}) \cdot \hat{H}(\{x\})/N$, where N is an appropriate normalising factor to ensure that $\hat{H}$ is a probability distribution.

An approximate goal hypothesis is not necessarily a member of the same goal hypothesis space as the goal hypothesis it approximates, because the approximation can assign non-zero probabilities to unreachable sets of facts. Identifying unreachable sets is as hard as planning, so allowing these sets to be assigned non-zero values is a useful efficiency measure. The method by which probabilities are combined in the recursive extension of the approximation to the whole space of possible goals is somewhat arbitrary and alternative approximations are certainly possible. In our current work we only consider 1st order approximations, so the probability of sets of facts is the product of the probabilities of the individual facts they include. This is equivalent to assuming that the individual goals have independent probabilities of appearing. Although 1st order approximations are poor in domains where goals are strongly correlated, in many domains we see goals falling into independent selections of states of a collection of objects (such as packages in a delivery domain).

This independence assumption clearly does not hold for all domains, for example BLOCKSWORLD problems often have the same numbers of goal and initial-state literals. We currently focus on problems which do exhibit this property, although we also consider the performance of the approximation on other benchmark domains.

Within the framework we have now defined, it is apparent that each successive observation implies an update of the current goal hypothesis reducing the probabilities of reachable facts that are subsets of those states which are now no closer in the state than the prior state. However, it is impractical to identify exactly which states these are. Furthermore, the assumption that the agent that is being observed has the capability to identify the shortest path to its goal, without error, is unreliable. For this reason, we work with 1st order approximations and update by reducing the probability associated with *facts* that get further away following observed actions and increasing the probabilities of *facts* that get closer.

3. Recognition without Libraries

AUTOGRAPH performs goal recognition in four stages: *Analysis*, wherein the problem is instantiated and analysed to reveal useful aspects of the domain; *Observation*, in which a single, ordered action is fed into the recogniser and the current state updated to reflect its effects; *Intermediate Hypothesis Generation*, in which a single hypothesis is produced after each observation[1]; and, lastly, a *Final Hypothesis* is generated once the plan is known to have finished.

3.1. Analysis

Domain analysis can provide rich information to aid subsequent search [6,10,11], lowering search time and shortening plan length. We apply relevant prior research to GR and develop new techniques that allow the recogniser to make more informed hypotheses.

3.1.1. Problem Representation

We use domains encoded in PDDL2.1 [7] and then apply Helmert's translator [12] to translate these into a SAS+ formalism. Two key products of this translation process are Domain Transition Graphs (DTGs) and a Causal Graph (CG), both of which encode aspects of the original PDDL problem in another form. We use both the PDDL and SAS+ representations of the problem during analysis, as they can each reveal aspects of the domain that aid in recognition. The Causal Graph reveals how objects influence others within the domain through actions: of particular interest are the *leaf nodes*, corresponding to objects with no influence on others.

Definition 5. *CG Leaves*
*A node, v, in the causal graph with $|v_{out}| = 0$ is a **leaf variable** and any fact which contains a leaf variable in its parameters is a **leaf proposition**.*

Should a causal graph contain leaf nodes, any leaf proposition that is **not** true in the initial state can be seen as a likely goal, as it can play no role other than to be altered.

Modern planners typically use a *grounded problem* that contains **all** possible fact and action combinations, often including some that are unreachable (e.g. (on crate1 crate1)). We filter this set to include only reachable facts which can then be further analysed to reveal certain domain characteristics that aid in recognition.

By using an action-centred model to define domains we lose the knowledge present in more structured hierarchical models, but note that such information can often be extrapolated through domain analysis. It is also the case that, while our first-order approximation will reduce the size of the goal-space, it often makes determining the true goal state of an object difficult. Where object goal states are modelled by properties drawn from several sets, the first-order approximation will not explicitly link these properties. However, plans achieving such collections will show correlated increases in probabilities for all of the goal properties, so the linkage is implicit in the treatment of the updates.

3.1.2. Predicate Partitioning

Geib [8] proposes the concept of *plan heads* in Plan Recognition as a way to highlight important plan actions and allowing lazy commitment to plans, resulting in faster runtimes. We adapt this idea for GR through the concept of *predicate partitioning*. By auto-

---

[1] If the plan has further actions to be observed, steps 2 and 3 are repeated until this is no longer the case.

matically classifying propositions into mutually-exclusive sets it can often become clear which are more or less likely to be goals. For example, in a standard Logistics problem it is unlikely that the goal will be to simply have a package inside a truck and far more likely that it must be delivered to a warehouse. Facts can be placed in the following sets through analysis of the two domain representations, which can then be applied to the initial probability distribution.

Definition 6. *Predicate Partitions – A fact f is:*

1. **strictly activating** *iff $f \in I$ and $\forall a \in A$, $f \notin eff_a$ and $\exists a \in A$, $f \in pre_a$, where A is the set of grounded actions and $eff_a = add_a \cup del_a$. Strictly activating (SA) facts are often referred to as* static. *These facts can never be removed from the state and therefore extremely unlikely to be goals.*
2. **unstably activating** *iff $f \in I$ and $\forall a \in A$, $f \notin add_a$ and $\exists a \in A$, $f \in pre_a$ and $\exists a \in A$, $f \in del_a$. Unstably Activating facts differ from SA facts in that they can be deleted by at least one action, but once removed from the current state, cannot be re-added. Once deleted they can be removed from future hypotheses.*
3. **strictly terminal** *iff $\exists a \in A$, $f \in add_a$ and $\forall a \in A$, $f \notin pre_a$, $f \notin del_a$. These facts are assigned a high initial probability. Once added to the current state, they will not be removed, meaning they must appear in the final state.*
4. **unstably terminal** *iff $\exists a \in A$, $f \in add_a$ and $\forall a \in A$, $f \notin pre_a$, but $\exists a \in A$, $f \in del_a$. Unlike strictly terminal facts, these can be removed once they have been added, but they are never used as preconditions to any actions. They may simply be an uninteresting side-effect of an action, or involved in a mutex-relation.*
5. **waypoint** *iff f has predicate symbol $pred_f$ and $\forall q \in dtg(f)_{out}$, $|dtg(f)_{out}| \geqslant 2$, and $\bigcup_{i=1}^{n} pred_{q_i} = pred_f$, where $dtg(f)_{out}$ is the set of DTG vertices to which f is connected by at least two outgoing edges. It is common for problems to involve transforming objects through a chain of related states, all defined by the same predicate. The facts located within this predicate-chain (excluding end-points) are waypoint facts, and are assigned a low initial probability.*
6. **transient** *iff the predicate symbol for f is $pred_f$ and $\forall q \in dtg(f)_{out}$, $\bigcup_{i=1}^{n} pred_{q_i} = pred_{q_1}$ and $pred_{q_1} \neq pred_f$, where $dtg(f)_{out}$ is the set of DTG vertices to which f is connected by at least two outgoing edges. While waypoints form chains of facts sharing the same predicate, transient facts are intermediate values in a transition that use a different predicate. Furthermore, objects entering the transient state must return to a state with the same predicate as the one they originally left. It is generally unlikely that the goal will be to leave the object within this intermediate state so we assign them a low probability in the initial-probability distribution.*
7. **binary** *iff $\forall dtg \in DTG$, $|dtg(f)| = 2$. As a special case, facts that have a DTG of size 1 are also considered binary, by including the negated literal. Binary facts are assigned low initial probabilities as it is difficult to assess which of them might be relevant to the goal.*

In addition to these sets, a further *neutral* set is defined, containing all facts that have not been partitioned into one of the above sets.

The population of the various partitions is dependent on the domain being analysed. For example the ROVERS domain populates 6 partitions, while others such as ZENO-

Table 1. Abbreviated results indicating partition totals for the problem files associated with each domain.

Problem	T	W	UT	ST	UA	SA	B	N
Driverlog	403	4880	0	0	0	2114	67	741
Depots	560	5513	0	0	0	231	121	372
Rovers	0	1518	0	395	188	3943	75	349
Zenotravel	78	1022	0	0	0	120	0	34
Storage	930	319	202	0	0	890	234	340

TRAVEL largely categorise facts in the *waypoint* and *transient* sets. Overall results of this partitioning process on the testing domains can be seen in Table 1. The populations of these partitions are used during construction of the *initial-probability distribution*.

3.1.3. Landmarks

The use of *landmarks* in heuristic search has shown that they can be a powerful guide through the search-space [21,24]. We detect landmarks for all $f \in \mathcal{H}$, where $\mathcal{H}$ is the set of all facts within the goal-space, and store these in lists of the form $(Lm_1, Lm_2...Lm_n, f)$. These landmark-lists show which facts are "stepping-stones" to the final goal. For instance, if (in truck1 package3) is added to the current state after an observation and that same fact is in two landmark lists, it is sensible to increase the probability of propositions which follow this landmark as being goals – or a the very least not lower their probability. This is covered in further detail during the *Execution* section.

3.1.4. Unhelpful Facts

While Helmert's SAS+ translation also approximates the set of all *reachable* facts, it is likely that some will never appear as a goal. We begin to reduce the set of facts by first observing that it is extremely unlikely that a problem will be considered a planning problem if its goals can be achieved in a single step, since this could be achieved by purely greedy action selection. Therefore, any action applicable in the initial state is considered *unhelpful* and its effects are assigned negligible probability in the initial hypothesis. Additionally, if the domain contains *strictly-terminal* facts, we assign negligible probability to the preconditions of any action which achieves them by reasoning that the enabling conditions for achievement of a *strictly-terminal* fact are very unlikely to be goals instead of the terminal itself.

Definition 7. *Unhelpful Facts*
*Given an initial state I, the set of **unhelpful effects** is equivalent to $\bigcup_{m=1}^{|A_I|} add_{a_m}$ where A_I is the set of actions applicable in I. Furthermore, if a domain exhibits strictly-terminal facts F_{sTerm}, the set of **unhelpful preconditions** is equivalent to $\bigcup_{n=1}^{|A_{ST}|} pre_{a_n}$ where A_{ST} is the the set of all actions that achieve any member of F_{sTerm}.*

3.1.5. Initial Probability Distribution

Once the analysis phase has been completed, each fact f in the approximate hypothesis space $\mathcal{H}$ can be assigned an initial probability. This figure is dependent on which, if any, of the previous domain analysis criteria the fact has met.

The values assigned during this phase are selected directly according to which partition facts belong to among those described above. For example, *strictly terminal* and *unstably terminal* facts are given very high values because they only exist to be achieved, i.e. they do not appear as a precondition to any action. Conversely, *strictly activating* facts are given a probability of 0 as they will remain true throughout execution, making their appearance in the goal futile. *Waypoint, transient* and *binary* facts must be treated with more caution, as it is conceivable that they could be a goal, but more likely to be used as a means of achieving other goal propositions. Furthermore, *leaf propositions* which are not true in the initial state are all assigned the same value, as it is equally likely that the *leaf variable* contained within them could appear in any one of them in the goal state. The values selected for each partition are somewhat arbitrary and we have not yet explored the effect of a wide range of alternative assignments. Our initial experiments suggest that the system is not particularly sensitive to the precise choice of values.

3.2. Execution

Once the domain has been analysed and the initial goal-space populated, plan observation can begin. After each observation we record the *heuristic estimate* to each fact in the *approximate hypothesis space*.

By observing the estimated distance to each fact after action observations, it is possible to determine those which are being moved towards and away from. Each fact which has a lower heuristic estimate at time t than it did at $t - 1$ has its probability of being a goal increased, while those which now have a larger estimate have their probability set to 0. Facts whose estimate remains unchanged do not have their probability updated as they may be goals which have been achieved at time t.

3.2.1. Landmark-Linked Facts

The above probability increments and decrements apply to all propositions in the goal space, with the exception of those which appear as *landmarks* of other goals. If a fact L_f is classified as a landmark of another fact and is getting closer, then it is reasonable to assume any facts ordered *after* L_f are more likely to appear than other facts.

Landmarks which succeed L_f have their probabilities increased as it is possible they may be the true goal. The increment value of these successors is lower than a standard fact increment, with this decreasing linearly over any successor landmarks until 0 or the end of the list is reached. However, if the predecessor of L_f is being moved away from then L_f and successor landmarks do not have their probability modified. This is due to the possibility of search "turning around" towards L_n once L_{n-1} is achieved.

3.3. Hypothesis Generation

By using a 1st order approximation of a goal hypothesis we rely on goal sets being small. However, it would be naïve to assume that all domains only contain a single literal as their goal. We therefore construct an *intermediate greedy hypothesis* h_i from the approximate goal hypothesis constructed at each timestep i, representing the single most likely goal of the agent being observed.

To produce this set, facts are considered in mutually exclusive clusters (the sets that make up the nodes in a single DTG). The fact with highest probability within each cluster is selected, provided it has probability higher than a specified threshold (this eliminates highly unlikely candidates from the set).

Definition 8. *Greedy-Hypothesis*
Given an approximate hypothesis space $\mathcal{H}$, *a* **greedy-hypothesis** h_{gr} *is the set of facts with the highest probabilities above a base threshold,* T_{min}, *with ties broken randomly. If a fact* f *is chosen, then all facts that are mutex with it will not be added to* h_{gr}.

3.4. Final Hypothesis

Once the plan is known to have terminated and the final state is known, a more accurate final hypothesis can be produced. This is simpler than generating an *intermediate hypothesis* since $G \subseteq S_n$, and the state is certainly mutex-free. Along with the final probability distribution, this can produce a very accurate goal hypothesis.

4. Evaluation

We now present empirical results of several tests performed on the techniques presented previously. While others have previously expressed a desire for plan and goal recognition to have a standard evaluation method [4], there is still no agreement on standard benchmarks. Therefore, we have used classical planning benchmarks as an alternative. The system is evaluated using *precision and recall*, a technique used to score database document-retrieval which has also previously been applied to a GR context [2], where the number of required facts in each hypothesis is the *precision* and the number of correct facts is the *recall*.

The test system is written in Java and makes extensive use of a Java implementation of the FF planner [5]. SAS+ translation is performed using Helmert's standard Python scripts [12], which is then converted into a Java representation. Tests were conducted in Ubuntu 9.10 on a quad core 2.8GHz Intel i5 with 4GB of RAM using the latest Java Virtual Machine (1.6.0_14), and were given as much time as necessary to complete each stage of the recognition process.

The domains used in testing are taken from the 2002 and 2006 International Planning Competitions – specifically the propositional/STRIPS versions of DRIVERLOG, DEPOTS, ZENOTRAVEL, ROVERS and STORAGE, along with their best-known-solutions.

All of the domains have 20-40 associated problem files[2] which become increasingly difficult for planners to solve. Harder problems have much larger goal-spaces than trivial problems, which means that the recogniser has a much wider *hypothesis space* to work with. However, in compliance with our expectations, the number of facts in the goal state of these problems does not increase at the same rate as the number of *grounded facts*.

We have tested the system using the *Max* (h_{max}), *FF* (h_{ff}) and *Causal Graph* (h_{cg}) heuristics [3,13,23] in order to determine how this choice affects performance. We note that in testing with these heuristics in combination with solutions produced by planners which also use the heuristic there is the possibility of *heuristic bias*, but that this should not adversely affect the results.

4.1. Intermediate Hypothesis Results

The results of precision versus recall for *intermediate hypotheses* over all domains and heuristics can be seen in Table 2. Also included are the average precision and recall over all problems using h_{ff} at various timepoints. These latter results show *heuristic convergence* as precision and recall increase at over the course of plan execution.

---

[2] All problems were tested with the exceptions of DEPOTS 21 and 22, ROVERS 37-40, STORAGE 24-30 which could not be grounded correctly.

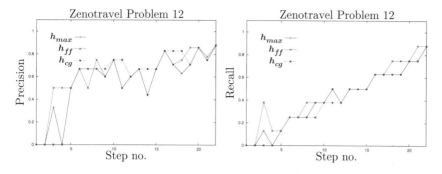

Figure 1. Intermediate P+R results for a single problem instance in ZENOTRAVEL.

Table 2. The total normalised intermediate precision and recall results for each heuristic, and the average precision and recall for h_{ff} over all problems at 25%, 50%, 75% and 100% plan completion.

Domain	h_{max}	h_{ff}	h_{cg}	Domain	h_{ff} 25%	h_{ff} 50%	h_{ff} 75%	h_{ff} 100%
Depots	**0.22 / 0.3**	0.22 / 0.28	0.22 / 0.28	Depots	0.15 / 0.07	0.2 / 0.21	0.34 / 0.5	0.52 / 0.93
Driverlog	0.42 / 0.32	**0.47 / 0.32**	**0.47 / 0.32**	Driverlog	0.43 / 0.12	0.56 / 0.29	0.72 / 0.5	0.94 / 0.73
Rovers	0.78 / 0.54	0.82 / 0.5	**0.86 / 0.56**	Rovers	0.62 / 0.22	0.81 / 0.42	0.93 / 0.66	0.96 / 1
Zenotravel	0.46 / 0.32	**0.49 / 0.33**	0.48 / 0.31	Zenotravel	0.3 / 0.1	0.42 / 0.26	0.61 / 0.48	0.81 / 0.7
Storage	**0.19 / 0.42**	**0.22 / 0.39**	**0.22 / 0.39**	Storage	0.17 / 0.14	0.29 / 0.49	0.27 / 0.64	0.3 / 0.91
Total	0.54 / 0.43	0.58 / 0.4	**0.6 / 0.43**	Average	0.33 / 0.13	0.46 / 0.33	0.57 / 0.56	0.7 / 0.85

The process of *heuristic-convergence* is more clearly visible in Figure 1 which contains the results of a typical ZENOTRAVEL problem. All three heuristics move towards the true goal, but with occasional dips in accuracy. This is a result of all three heuristics chosen being *inadmissible*. By being able to both over and under-estimate the distance to a goal, facts may be incorrectly classed as becoming further away after an observation. In the future it may be of use to apply an *admissible* heuristic which would guarantee never to over-estimate the distance, and thus possibly remove these fluctuations. Note that h_{cg} provides the fewest drops in accuracy, but not the quickest convergence rate.

Perhaps of most interest is that there is no clear leader in terms of heuristic chosen to generate estimates. While h_{cg} has the highest overall P+R results, this is primarily caused by the results of ROVERS, which contains more tests than other domains. The normalised results in Table 2 show the difference between this and h_{ff} is minor, while Figure 1 shows how close the estimates are on an individual problem.

4.2. Final Hypothesis Results

Once the plan being observed is known to have finished, the *final hypothesis* can be generated. Table 3 shows the total normalised P+R values for the final hypotheses in each problem. We note that the seeming indifference of heuristic choice is further reinforced by these results, as all three heuristics produce identical final P+R results.

With the exception of DEPOTS and STORAGE, the recogniser produces highly accurate hypotheses for all problems in terms of both precision and recall. ROVERS shows particularly accurate results due to the presence of *strictly-terminal* facts, which produces a perfect score for recall, and 95% average for precision.

Table 3. Normalised total values for precision and recall values associated with the final hypothesis for each domain

Domain	Depots	Driverlog	Rovers	Zenotravel	Storage
Precision	0.52	0.94	0.96	0.86	0.32
Recall	0.93	0.73	1	0.7	0.95

Table 4. Differences in P+R if the initial probability distribution is used during generation of a final hypothesis.

Improvement	Depots	Driverlog	Rovers	Zenotravel	Storage
Precision	40.57%	-3.95%	4.10%	4.77%	49.63%
Recall	6.73%	-15.95%	0.00%	13.91%	10.05%

In the case of DEPOTS and STORAGE, precision scores average only 52% and 32% respectively. This is caused by the large number of facts which become true during execution of a typical plan, which along with a small goal set combine to form a large hypothesis with extraneous facts. For instance, the location of certain trucks is often not a required goal in DEPOTS, but will be put forward as a goal because trucks will stop moving once the last package has been delivered to its destination.

4.2.1. Accuracy of Initial Hypothesis After Final Observation

In the *Analysis* section we described the generation of an *initial probability distribution* using only domain analysis. At the time it this generated, it is unlikely that construction of a *greedy-hypothesis* would produce an accurate result as no observations have been seen. However, if this initial, unmodified probability distribution is combined with the final state it can often produce an accurate hypothesis. Table 4 shows the difference in overall P+R when this is compared with the true final hypothesis. These results show that, in the case of DEPOTS, precision can be increased by over 40% whilst also increasing recall, while ZENOTRAVEL also shows this to a lesser extent. Moreover, the presence of *terminal* facts in STORAGE and ROVERS shows that it is possible to achieve almost 100% accuracy on both precision and recall without modifying the *initial probability distribution*. Only DRIVERLOG shows a reduction of both precision and recall.

For some domains the risk of lowering of P+R is not preferable, but in a situation where computing resources are limited and the domain is known to exhibit this property, it may be preferable to accept a small loss in recall and save any processing-time related to the updating of probabilities after each observation.

5. Conclusions and Future Work

We have presented AUTOGRAPH, a new method of tackling Goal Recognition by applying Planning technology. The approach and empirical evidence presented has successfully shown that libraries are not required to achieve online recognition of an agent's activities.

The work presented offers a novel approach to the problem in the form of *heuristic estimation*, as well as several new methods of refining valid goal facts. Perhaps most importantly it offers a viable solution to the problem of offline library construction and allows **any** domain to be recognised without prior analysis.

5.1. Strengths

AUTOGRAPH demonstrates an effective and efficient performance in goal recognition. It is **complete** in the sense that it can construct a hypothesis from *any* conjunction of literals within $\mathcal{H}$. The system is **scalable** because it is based on a 1st order approximation of the true goal hypothesis, meaning that the hypothesis grows only linearly with the size of the grounded problem. Finally, it is **domain-independent** because it only relies on the use of a standard problem definition schema and use of generic heuristics and algorithms.

Several new and interesting aspects of GR have also been observed. For example, the ability to accurately predict goals purely from initial domain analysis and the current state is an interesting avenue of research which could make the system more applicable in low-resource environments.

5.2. Limitations

A drawback of the system is the inability to know if a hypothesis is valid, due to the problem of detecting all mutually-exclusive propositions. The detection of these mutexes is an NP-Hard problem, meaning that other methods must be used to estimate propositions which cannot exist together in the same state. Undetectable mutexes are a domain-specific feature, with only DEPOTS showing this trait from the set of test domains. Future work will explore the *approximation* of mutex information by recording facts which never appear together during intermediate plan-states.

The current linear convergence rate of the recogniser is to be expected from the heuristic estimation process, but a faster convergence rate would obviously be preferable. One method of increasing convergence rates could be to rule out any facts which cannot be reached within n steps, where $n > |P|$. However, in order to do this the problem of plan-length estimation would need to be solved first, along with the detection of accurate goal-conjunctions. Additionally, automating the process of selecting initial probabilities for each partition and during updates on a domain-by-domain basis using a system such as Hoos *et al* [16] would reveal the optimal set of values for generating fast and accurate hypotheses.

Acknowledgements

Thanks go to Bram Ridder for access to his Java SAS+ translator and Causal Graph heuristic code.

References

[1] Nate Blaylock and James F. Allen, 'Corpus-based, statistical goal recognition', in *Proc. Int. Joint Conf. AI*, pp. 1303–1308, (2003).
[2] Nate Blaylock and James F. Allen, 'Fast hierarchical goal schema recognition', in *Proc. Nat. Conf. on AI (AAAI)*, pp. 796–801, (2006).
[3] Blai Bonet and Hector Geffner, 'Planning as heuristic search', *J. AI Res.*, **129**(1-2), 5–33, (2001).
[4] Sandra Carberry, 'Techniques for plan recognition', *User Modeling and User-Adapted Interaction*, **11**(1-2), 31–48, (2001).
[5] Andrew Coles, Maria Fox, Derek Long, and Amanda Smith, 'Teaching forward-chaining planning with JavaFF', in *Colloquium on AI Education, 23rd Nat. Conf. on AI (AAAI)*, (2008).
[6] Maria Fox and Derek Long, 'The automatic inference of state invariants in TIM', *J. AI Res.*, **9**, 367–421, (1998).
[7] Maria Fox and Derek Long, 'PDDL2.1: An extension to PDDL for expressing temporal planning domains', *J. AI Res.*, **20**, 61–124, (2003).
[8] Christopher W. Geib, 'Delaying commitment in plan recognition using combinatory categorial grammars', in *Proc. Int. Joint Conf. on AI*, pp. 1702–1707, (2009).

[9] Peter Gorniak and Deb Roy, 'Probabilistic grounding of situated speech using plan recognition and reference resolution', in *Proc. 7th Int. Conf. on Multimodal Interfaces*, pp. 138–143, (2005).
[10] Malte Helmert, 'A planning heuristic based on causal graph analysis', in *Proc. Int. Conf. on Automated Planning and Scheduling*, pp. 161–170, (2004).
[11] Malte Helmert, 'The fast downward planning system', *J. AI Res.*, **26**, 191–246, (2006).
[12] Malte Helmert, 'Concise finite-domain representations for PDDL planning tasks', *Artif. Intell.*, **173**(5-6), 503–535, (2009).
[13] Jörg Hoffmann and Bernhard Nebel, 'The FF planning system: Fast plan generation through heuristic search', *J. AI Res.*, **14**, 253–302, (2001).
[14] Jun Hong, 'Goal recognition through goal graph analysis', *J. AI Res.*, **15**, 1–30, (2001).
[15] Alexander Huntemann, Eric Demeester, Hendrik van Brussel, and Marnix Nuttin, 'Can Bayes help disabled users? A Bayesian approach to plan recognition and shared control for steering an electrical wheelchair', in *Proc. ACM/IEEE Human-Robot Interaction Conf.*, pp. 67–70, (2008).
[16] Frank Hutter, Domagoj Babic, Holger H. Hoos, and Alan J. Hu, 'Boosting verification by automatic tuning of decision procedures', in *FMCAD '07: Proc. Formal Methods in CAD*, pp. 27–34, (2007).
[17] Henry A. Kautz, *A formal theory of plan recognition*, Ph.D. dissertation, University of Rochester, 1987.
[18] Neal Lesh, 'Adaptive goal recognition', in *Proc. Int. Joint Conf. on AI*, pp. 1208–1214, (1997).
[19] Neal Lesh and Oren Etzioni, 'A sound and fast goal recognizer', in *Proc. Int. Joint Conf. on AI*, pp. 1704–1710, (1995).
[20] Bradford Mott, Sunyoung Lee, and James Lester, 'Probabilistic goal recognition in interactive narrative environments', in *Proc. Nat. Conf. on AI (AAAI)*, pp. 187–192, (2006).
[21] Julie Porteous, Laura Sebastia, and Jörg Hoffmann, 'On the extraction, ordering, and usage of landmarks in planning', in *Proc. European Conf. on AI*, pp. 37–48, (2001).
[22] Miquel Ramírez and Hector Geffner, 'Plan recognition as planning', in *Proc. Int. Joint Conf. on AI*, pp. 1778–1783, (2009).
[23] Silvia Richter, Malte Helmert, and Matthias Westphal, 'Landmarks revisited', in *Proc. Nat. Conf. on AI (AAAI)*, pp. 975–982, (2008).
[24] Matthias Westphal and Silvia Richter. The LAMA planner. using landmark counting in heuristic search, 2008. Short paper for IPC 2008.

Maintaining Arc Consistency in Non-Binary Dynamic CSPs using Simple Tabular Reduction

Matthieu QUÉVA [a], Christian W. PROBST [a] and Laurent RICCI [b]
[a] DTU Informatics, Technical University of Denmark, email: {mq, probst}@imm.dtu.dk
[b] Microsoft Development Center Copenhagen, email: lricci@microsoft.com

Abstract. Constraint Satisfaction Problems (CSPs) are well known models used in Artificial Intelligence. In order to represent real world systems, CSPs have been extended to Dynamic CSPs (DCSPs), which support adding and removing constraints at runtime. Some approaches to the NP-complete problem of solving CSPs use filtering techniques such as arc consistency, which also have been adapted to handle DCSPs with binary constraints. However, there exists only one algorithm targeting non-binary DCSPs (*DnGAC4*). In this paper we present a new algorithm *DnSTR* for maintaining arc consistency in DCSPs with non-binary constraints. Our algorithm is based on Simple Tabular Reduction for Table Constraints, a technique that dynamically maintains the tables of supports within the constraints. Initial results show that our algorithm outperforms *DnGAC4* both for addition and removal of constraints.

Keywords. Dynamic Constraint Satisfaction Problems, Arc consistency, Table constraints, Simple Tabular Reduction

Introduction

One of the many interesting topics in Artificial Intelligence is the use of Constraint Programming to solve combinatorial problems. Those problems are usually modeled as Constraint Satisfaction Problems (CSPs), where the number of constraints in the system is known beforehand. However, many problems involve dynamic behaviours: user requirements may for example evolve during interactive design, or the set of tasks to be performed in a scheduling problem may be modified due to external factors. Dynamic Constraint Satisfaction Problems (DCSPs) have thus been introduced to permit the addition and removal (or retraction) of constraints at runtime.

The task of finding solutions in CSPs is NP-complete, and thus solvers usually apply filtering techniques to reduce the search space and simplify the problem. Filtering techniques can also be used in interactive problems, such as product configuration, in order to reduce the set of values available for each variable. The most used techniques are the ones achieving arc consistency.

There has been a considerable amount of work in designing arc consistency algorithms for CSPs with binary constraints. Among them are the well-known AC3 [10], AC4 [12] and AC6 [6]. Most authors have generally not extended their work to achieve arc consistency on non-binary problems, as any non-binary CSP can potentially always be transformed into an equivalent binary CSP, although it is sometimes impracticable [1]. However, non-binary constraints have been proved to be practically relevant (e.g. in configurators or database systems), and dedicated algorithms are essential to handle them.

Among existing algorithms for non-binary CSPs are GAC3 [11] and GAC4 [13]. These algorithms are extensions of binary algorithms, and are much more expensive than their counterparts. Indeed, the best worst-case time complexity with such generic algorithms is exponential in the greatest constraint arity. Other algorithms have then been designed to achieve arc consistency for specific problems, containing only table constraints for instance. This is the case for Simple Tabular Reduction (STR) [15,9], which can achieve arc consistency in linear time in the size of the table.

Arc consistency algorithms are well suited for growing constraint problems, and thus can easily handle the addition of constraints in a problem. However, this is not true for constraint retraction. The problem is still arc consistent, but some solutions may be lost as result of the retraction, and thus the system has to find out which values should be restored, in order to achieve *maximal* arc consistency. Several techniques have been proposed to maintain arc consistency in binary Dynamic CSPs. The most recent ones are DnAC4 [4], DnAC6 [8], and AC|DC and its extensions [3,14,2]. Those algorithms are based on static arc consistency algorithms, respectively AC4, AC6 and AC3. For non-binary DCSPs, however, DnGAC4 [5] is currently the only algorithm that has been extended to handle them. This algorithm is an extension of DnAC4, and has thus the same time complexity as GAC4.

In this paper we propose a new algorithm *DnSTR* for solving Dynamic CSPs with non-binary constraints, described as (extensional) table constraints. Table constraints are commonly used in applications where databases are involved, for example product configuration systems. Our algorithm is based on STR, one of the most efficient approaches for maintaining arc consistency on table constraints, instead of the generic GAC4 algorithm.

The paper is organized as follows. Section 1 recalls the definitions of Dynamic CSPs and arc consistency, then presents GAC4 and the most used method for maintaining arc consistency in DCSPs. The algorithm DnSTR is described in detail in Section 2, and is analyzed in Section 3. Finally, an experimental study is presented in Section 4, while Section 5 gives a summary along with some final remarks.

1. Definitions and Preliminaries

We will now define what a CSP and a Dynamic CSP are, as well as the concept of arc consistency. We will then introduce the current algorithms for solving non-binary CSPs, and the method to maintain arc consistency in DCSPs.

1.1. Dynamic Constraint Satisfaction Problems

A Constraint Satisfaction Problem (CSP) is a triple $\mathcal{P} = \langle X, D, C \rangle$ where: $X = \langle x_1, x_2, ..., x_n \rangle$ is an n-tuple of variables, $D = \langle D(x_1), D(x_2), ..., D(x_n) \rangle$ is an n-tuple of *domains*, representing, for each variable x_i, the set of possible values it can take, and $C = \langle c_1, c_2, ..., c_t \rangle$ is a t-tuple of constraints restricting the values that the variables can

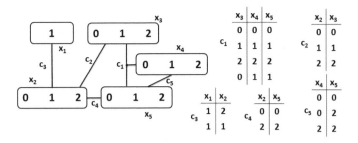

Figure 1. Example of CSP. Each node represents a variable whose domain is explicitly indicated. The constraints are defined in extension to specify the set of allowed tuples.

simultaneously take. A constraint c involves a subset $scp(c)$ of variables from X and can be defined by the set of all tuples of values allowed (extensional table constraint) or by a relation between variables (in intension). Solving a CSP consists in assigning a value to each variable such that all constraints are satisfied. The example of a CSP can be seen in Figure 1.

A Dynamic Constraint Satisfaction Problem (DCSP) is a sequence of CSPs $\mathcal{P}_0, \mathcal{P}_1, ..., \mathcal{P}_m$ where each problem results from an addition or removal of a constraint c in its predecessor. More precisely, if $\mathcal{P}_i = \langle X, D, C_i \rangle$, then $\mathcal{P}_{i+1} = \langle X, D, C_{i+1} \rangle$ where $C_{i+1} = C_i \pm c$.

1.2. Arc Consistency

Constraint satisfaction problems on finite domains are typically solved using a form of search. However, since finding solutions in a CSP is an NP-complete task, filtering techniques can be used to simplify the problem during search. The most used algorithms are the ones achieving arc consistency.

> **Definition.** For a constraint c on $(x_1, ..., x_i, ..., x_p)$, a tuple $\tau = (d_1, ..., d_i, ..., d_p)$ is a **support** of c if it is an allowed tuple ($\tau \in c$) and $\forall x_i \in scp(c), \tau(x_i) = d_i \in D(x_i)$. A pair (x_i, d_{x_i}) is said to be **arc consistent** iff, for each $c \in C$ constraining x_i, there exists a support $\tau \in c$ such as $\tau(x_i) = d_{x_i}$. A problem $\mathcal{P}_k$ is arc consistent iff $\forall x_i \in X, \forall d_{x_i} \in D(x_i)$, (x_i, d_{x_i}) are arc consistent. $\mathcal{P}_k$ is **maximally arc consistent** if enlarging the domain of any of its variables makes it not arc consistent.

1.3. Arc Consistency in DCSPs

Maintaining arc consistency in Dynamic CSPs is equivalent to making the problem $\mathcal{P}_i$ maximally arc consistent, provided that $\mathcal{P}_0, ..., \mathcal{P}_{i-1}$ are maximally arc consistent. Handling constraint *addition* is fairly straightforward: the new problem can indeed be made maximally arc consistent just by applying GAC algorithms again. However, the task of *removing* a constraint is a bit different. In fact, when removing a constraint, the problem stays arc consistent, but not necessary maximally arc consistent. This is due to the fact that some solutions can be lost, and formerly inconsistent values may need to be restored to re-establish maximal arc consistency.

Existing algorithms for arc consistency in DCSPs are working in three phases during constraint removal: first the values deleted by the removed constraints are restored (initialization phase); then those restorations are propagated to other variables connected through existing constraints (propagation phase); finally, the values are filtered again (filtering phase). The last phase ensures that all wrongly restored values are removed. The latest and most efficient algorithms for binary constraints are AC|DC-2i and AC3.1|DC-2i [2].

1.4. CSPs with Non-Binary Constraints

Enforcing arc consistency on CSPs with non-binary constraints is NP-complete [7], and the best worst-time complexity obtained by generic algorithms such as GAC4 is $O(erd^r)$, with e the number of constraints, r the greatest constraint arity and d the greatest domain size. Many other algorithms have been designed to enforce arc consistency in a more efficient way for specific problems, for example non-binary CSPs with table constraints. Tables can actually be considered as the most explicit way to represent constraints, as in theory any constraints in intension can be transformed into a table constraint. However, this may in practice lead to time and space explosion when solving the problem.

Among the work on table constraints, one particular method of interest is Simple Tabular Reduction (STR) [15,9]. This algorithm differs from previous methods as it dynamically maintains the tables in order only to go through the supporting tuples when enforcing arc consistency. More precisely, when the domain of a variable is reduced, each table constraining that variable is updated, by removing all invalid tuples. The variables' values that are not arc consistent are then removed from their domain. STR uses arrays of indexes to avoid moving tuples in memory, and is enforcing arc consistency in $O(er(d + t'))$, where t' is the maximum size of the current tables. Worst-case space complexity of STR is $O(e(n + rt))$, with t the greatest original table size. STR has been shown to be one of the most efficient approaches when dealing with table constraints. A more detailed description of STR can be found in [9].

2. The Algorithm DnSTR

In this section, we will describe our new DnSTR algorithm. This algorithm can be used to solve DCSPs with table constraints. It relies on a timeline of events, which is composed by timestamps. Each timestamp t is defined by two integers (dp, lt), which represent the *depth* of the timestamp (the depth is increased every time a constraint is added) and the *local time* at a given depth. The timestamps can also be compared: $\forall t_1, t_2 : t_1 < t_2 \Leftrightarrow (t_1.dp < t_2.dp \lor (t_1.dp = t_2.dp \land t_1.lt < t_2.lt))$.

Like the other algorithms targeting DCSPs, DnSTR is working in three phases (as described in Section 1.3). However, the filtering phase in DnSTR is performed incrementally during constraint retraction, in order to keep the timeline consistent and use it to restore only specific tuples. Indeed, during constraint retraction, wrongly restored tuples need to be put back at the depth they would have been deleted at if the removed constraint had never been added to the problem. Thanks to this mechanism, when a value is restored at a certain depth, only tuples at this same depth have to be restored during propagation (except if the constraint associated to those tuples was added later, in which case the depth considered is this constraint addition's depth).

The algorithm works with the following data structures:

- A global depth counter $gdepth$, as well as an array $lastLTime$ that for each depth dp associates the last local time lt in the current timeline.
- Two justifications arrays $justif_t$ and $justif_c$ that, for each pair (x, d_x), keep track of when and by which constraint the value d_x has been removed from x's domain. Each constraint is also associated with the time of addition, recorded in the array $time_c$.
- As we already pointed out, the algorithm DnSTR is based on Simple Tabular Reduction. It thus shares similar data structures for each table constraint, including an initial set of tuples $c.table$, the index of the first tuple in the current table $c.first$ (i.e. the table of valid tuples), an array $c.next$ that links lists of tuples (by their indexes), and two arrays $c.removedHead$ and $c.removedTail$ that give the index of the first and last invalid tuples at each depth. Note that $c.next[i] = -1$ if i is the position of the last tuple, either in the current table if i is a valid tuple or in the removed list if i has been removed. For each constraint c, we also store the index of the last restored tuple in $c.restoredTail$, and an array $c.removed_t$ that records the removal time (or timestamp) of each tuple.

2.1. Constraint Addition

Adding a constraint to the DCSP is done by filtering the system through the function ADDCONSTRAINT described in Algorithm 1.

Algorithm 1: ADDCONSTRAINT(c: Constraint): Bool

1   add c to C ;
2   $gdepth = gdepth + 1$; $lastLTime[gdepth] = 0$;
3   $time_c[c] = (gdepth, 0)$;
4   $revise[gdepth] = \{c\}$;
5   **return** FILTER($revise, D, (gdepth, 0)$) ;

Algorithm 2: FILTER($revise, values$: Arrays, (dp_i, lt_i): Time): Bool

1   **while** $revise[dp_i] \neq \emptyset$ **do**
2   select and remove c from $revise[dp_i]$;
3      $changed = \emptyset$;
4   **if not** GACSTRDYN($c, changed, (dp_i, lt_i), values$) **then**
5   **return** false;
6   **foreach** $(x, jt_x) \in changed$ **do**
7          $c_{revise} = \{c_r \in C$ s.t. $c_r \neq c, x \in scp(c_r), time_c[c_r] \leq (dp_i, lt_i)\}$;
8   **if** $jt_x.dp > dp_i$ **then**
9   add c_{revise} to $revise[jt_x.dp]$;
10   **else**
11   add c_{revise} to $revise[dp_i]$;

12   **return** true;

Algorithm 3: GACSTRDYN(*c*: Constraint, *changed*: Set, (dp_i, lt_i): Time, *values*: Array): Bool

1 $S_{sup} = \emptyset$;
2 **foreach** $x \in scp(c)$ **do**
3 $\quad$ $gacValues[x] = \emptyset$;
4 $\quad$ **if** $values[x] \neq NIL$ **then**
5 $\quad\quad$ add x to S_{sup} ;

6 $prev = -1$;
7 $curr = c.first$;
8 **while** $curr \neq -1$ **do**
9 $\quad$ $\tau = c.table[curr]$;
10 $\quad$ $nextT = c.next[curr]$; $rTail = c.restoredTail$;
11 $\quad$ **if** ISVALID$(c, \tau, (dp_i, lt_i))$ **then**
12 $\quad\quad$ **foreach** $x \in S_{sup}$ **do**
13 $\quad\quad\quad$ **if** $(\tau[x] \notin gacValues[x]$ **and** $\tau[x] \in values[x])$ **then**
14 $\quad\quad\quad\quad$ add $\tau[x]$ to $gacValues[x]$;
15 $\quad\quad\quad\quad$ **if** $|gacValues[x]| = |values[x]|$ **then**
16 $\quad\quad\quad\quad\quad$ remove x from S_{sup};

17 $\quad\quad$ $prev = curr$;
18 $\quad$ **else**
19 $\quad\quad$ $c.removed_t[curr] = (dp_i, lt_i)$;
20 $\quad\quad$ **if** $c.restoredTail = curr$ **then** $c.restoredTail = prev$;
21 $\quad\quad$ REMOVETUPLE$(c, prev, curr, dp_i)$;
22 $\quad$ **if** $curr = rTail$ **then break**;
23 $\quad$ $curr = nextT$;

24 **foreach** $x \in S_{sup}$ **do**
25 $\quad$ **foreach** $d_x \in values[x]$ **do**
26 $\quad\quad$ **if** $d_x \notin gacValues[x]$ **then**
27 $\quad\quad\quad$ remove d_x from $values[x]$;
28 $\quad\quad\quad$ **if** $|D[x]| \neq |values[x]|$ **then** remove d_x from $D[x]$;
29 $\quad\quad\quad$ **if not** $(justif_c[x, d_x] = c$ **and** $justif_t[x, d_x] > (dp_i, lt_i))$ **then**
30 $\quad\quad\quad\quad$ $justif_c[x, d_x] = c$;
31 $\quad\quad\quad\quad$ $justif_t = (dp_i, lt_i)$;
32 $\quad\quad\quad$ add $(x, justif_t[x, d_x])$ to $changed$;
33 $\quad$ **if** $|D[x]| = 0$ **then return false**;
34 $lastLTime[dp_i] = lt_i + 1$;
35 **return true**;

Algorithm 4: ISVALID(*c*: Constraint, τ: Tuple, (dp_i, lt_i): Time): Bool

1 **foreach** $x \in scp(c)$ **do**
2 $\quad$ **if** $(\tau[x] \notin D[x])$ **and** $(justif_t[x, \tau[x]] \leq (dp_i, lt_i))$ **then**
3 $\quad\quad$ **return false**;
4 **return true**;

The *revise* structure contains for each depth the constraints to evaluate at filtering. FILTER iterates over the constraints to revise at the given depth (the latest for constraint addition) and applies a modified version of STR (Algorithm 3), where only the elements in the list *values* are taken into account (*values* represents the full domain D for constraint addition, but only the restored values for constraint retraction). GACSTRDYN also differs from [9] as it handles the restored tuples (for constraint retraction) and the update of the justifications. Those are computed at lines 30-31, except if the pair (x, d_x) had been removed by the same constraint at a later stage (line 29) — in which case another support for (x, d_x) is still valid at this time but will be removed later in time. ISVALID also differs as it checks the value's justification time, while REMOVETUPLE is identical to the one described in [9], and is thus not shown. FILTER then updates *revise* with potentially affected constraints. The timestamp parameter (dp_i, lt_i) is used to specify when the filtering occurs (line 7), so that the constraints added *after* that time are not filtered yet (but will be later, at the incremental filtering used during constraint retraction). If x was changed at a later depth (lines 8-9), the constraint to revise is inserted at that specific depth $jt_x.dp$ instead of the current one.

2.2. Constraint Removal

Constraint retraction is performed by the function REMOVECONSTRAINT (Algorithm 5).

Algorithm 5: REMOVECONSTRAINT(c: Constraint): Bool

    // Initialization phase
1   $restoredValues = \emptyset$;
2   **foreach** $x \in \text{scp}(c)$ **do**
3   **foreach** $d_x \in D_0[x] \setminus D[x]$ **do**
4   **if** $justif_c[x, d_x] = c$ **then**
5   add d_x to $D[x]$;
6   add d_x to $restoredValues[x]$;

7   Remove c from C ;

    // Propagation phase
8   $revise = \emptyset$;
9   $tcr = \text{PROPAGATE}(restoredValues, revise, time_c[c].depth)$;

    // Filtering phase
10 **for** $dp_i \leftarrow time_c[c].dp$ **to** $gdepth$ **do**
11   FILTER($revise, restoredValues, (dp_i, lastLTime[dp_i])$);

    // Cleaning phase
12 **foreach** $c_j \in tcr$ **do**
13      $c_j.restoredTail = -1$;
14 **foreach** $x \in restoredValues$ **do**
15   **foreach** $d_x \in restoredValues[x]$ **do**
16         $justif_t[x, d_x] = NIL$;
17         $justif_c[x, d_x] = NIL$;
18      $restoredValues[x] = NIL$;
19 **return** true;

Algorithm 6: PROPAGATE(*restoredValues*: Set, *revise*: Array , dp_{rem}: Int): Set

1   $restore = \emptyset$;
2   **foreach** $x \in restoredValues$ **do**
3   UPDATELISTS($x, restoredValues[x], revise, restore, dp_{rem}$)
4   **while** $restore \neq \emptyset$ **do**
5   select and remove $(c, minRestoredTimes)$ from $restore$;
6      $newRestored = \emptyset$; add c to tcr ;
7   **foreach** $(dp, lt) \in minRestoredTimes$ **do**
8         $curr = c.removedHead[dp]$; $prev = -1$;
9         $rtail = c.removedTail[dp]$;
10   **if** $c.restoredTail = -1$ **then** $c.restoredTail = rtail$;
11   RESTORETUPLES(c, dp) ;
12   **while** $curr \neq -1$ **do**
13           $nextT = c.next[curr]$;
14   **if** $c.removed_t[curr] < (dp, lt)$ **then**
15   **if** $c.restoredTail = curr$ **then**
16                 $c.restoredTail = prev$;
17   REMOVETUPLE($c, prev, curr, dp$);
18   **else**
19              $\tau = c.table[curr]$; $jTimes = \emptyset$;
20   **foreach** $x \in \text{scp}(c)$ **do**
21   **if** $\tau[x] \notin D[x]$ **then**
22   **if** $justif_c[x, \tau[x]] \neq c$ **then**
23   add $justif_t[x, \tau[x]]$ to $jTimes$;
24   **else**
25   add $\tau[x]$ to $D[x]$;
26   add $\tau[x]$ to $newRestored[x]$;
27   **if** $jTimes \neq \emptyset$ **then**
28   add c to $revise[\mathbf{min}(jTimes)]$;
29              $c.removed_t[curr] = NIL$; $prev = curr$;
30   **if** $curr = rTail$ **then break**;
31           $curr = nextT$;
32   **foreach** *($x \in newRestored$)* **do**
33   UPDATELISTS($x, newRestored[x], dp_{rem}, revise, restore$) ;
34   add $newRestored[x]$ to $restoredValues[x]$;
35   **return** tcr;

Algorithm 7: UPDATELISTS(x: Var, $restored\_x$: Set, dp_{rem}: Int, $revise, restore$: Arrays)

1   **foreach** $c_x \in C$ *constraining* x **do**
2   **if** *($\exists d_x \in restored\_x$ s.t. $justif_t[x, d_x].dp \leq time_c[c_x].dp$)* **then**
3   add c_x to $revise[\mathbf{max}(time_c[c_x].dp, dp_{rem})]$;
4      $jtimes = \{\mathbf{max}(justif_t[x, d_x], time_c[c_x])$ s.t. $d_x \in restored\_x$ **and** $justif_c[x, d_x] \neq c_x\}$;
5   add $\{t \in jtimes$ s.t. $t = \mathbf{min}(t_1 \in jtimes, t_1.dp = t.dp)\}$ to $restore[c_x]$;

During the initialization stage, all pairs (x, d_x) that were removed by the retracted constraints are restored. Notice that all restored values are placed in a list *restoredValues* so that only those values are considered in the filtering stage.

During the propagation stage in function PROPAGATE, tuples from constraints connected to restored variables are restored. The list *minRestoredTimes* contains the minimum times (dp, lt) for each depth where tuples need to be restored. After tuples have been restored for a specific depth (line 11), the ones that have been deleted before the time (dp, lt) considered are immediately removed (lines 14-17). For each tuple, only values that had been deleted by the current constraint are restored. The function RESTORE-TUPLES(c, t) is identical to the one described in [9]. In case another constraint has made a tuple invalid, the table is added to *revise* at the time when a value first invalidated the tuple (line 27-28). Thanks to the strictly maintained timeline, only the tuples that have been removed after a pair (x, d_x) and in the same depth need to be restored. This is done through the update of *restore* in function UPDATELISTS: depending whether the value d_x was deleted before the constraint c_x was added, the justification time or the constraint addition time is retrieved (line 4) and the minimum for each depth is added to *restore* (line 5). The array *revise* is also updated at the beginning of the propagation and after each restoration to include constraints that were added after the restored values were deleted (line 2-3 in UPDATELISTS). Note that the PROPAGATE algorithm returns the set *tcr* of table constraints that have been modified during restoration.

Finally, filtration is performed on the constraints in *revise* (line 12-13 in REMOVE-CONSTRAINT). This is done incrementally so that constraints are evaluated in the same order as they were added, keeping the new problem's timeline consistent with what it would be if the retracted constraint had never been added. Although it may introduce redundancy in the constraint evaluation process, this type of filtering is necessary to guarantee that all invalid tuples restored in the propagation stage are put back at the correct depth.

2.3. Example

An example of constraint removal can be seen in Figure 2, after adding all constraints in the CSP from Figure 1. It is interesting to note that although the last tuple of table c_1 is restored, it is potentially invalid, as $(x_5, 1)$ has been removed by c_4: $(x_5, 1)$ is thus not restored, and the table c_1 is put in $revise$ for the filtering phase. The two tables c_4 and c_5 are also added to $revise$, as the restored $(x_2, 0)$ and $(x_4, 1)$ had been deleted before the addition of those tables: they might be deleted again in the filtering stage.

3. Analysis

In this section, we will discuss the correctness of DnSTR, and describe the time and space complexity of the algorithm.

3.1. Correctness

During constraint addition, the filtering depth is the global depth $gdepth$, and the whole domain values are checked when using the STR algorithm. As the second check in IS-VALID is always true, the STR algorithm used is equivalent to the original algorithm. All

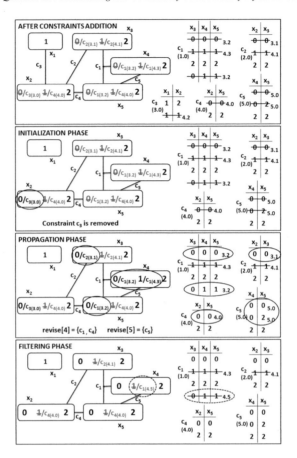

Figure 2. Removing constraint c3 in the CSP example from Figure 1. Associated timestamps are written as "3.1" for ($dp = 3, lt = 1$) next to each added constraint and removed tuple. Justifications (constraint and time) are also shown next to each deleted value. Plain circles show the values and tuples restored since the previous phase, while dashed circles represent values and tuples re-filtered.

constraints to revise are put back in $revise[gdepth]$ in FILTER as the check of line 8 is always false with $dp_i = gdepth$, so the correctness directly comes from the correctness of STR.

For constraint removal, let us consider a problem $\mathcal{P}_n$, resulting of the addition of $(c_0, ..., c_n)$, and where we are removing constraint c_i. Before the removal of c_i, problem $\mathcal{P}_n$ is arc consistent, so for all $\mathcal{P}_j$ with $j < n$, all justifications arrays are coherent with the actual timeline, all tuples have been removed at the correct depth and always at a local time greater than any justification of deleted value that might have caused its removal.

First, consider that c_i was added at $t_i = (d_i, 0)$, and $t_i + t_0$ is the first time that a value from a variable $x \notin scp(c_i)$ has been removed. All the removal of values before $t_i + t_0$ are caused by c_i, and so those values are directly restored during the initialization phase, thanks to having c_i as justification constraint. For each constraint, the tuples impacted by a value removed at t_r are tuples deleted at a later time $t > t_r$. Moreover, the only impacted tuples are the ones deleted in the same depth, as $\mathcal{P}_i$ was made consistent before any new constraint addition (and change of depth), *except* if they are from a constraint c_j

added *after* c_i, as they may have been removed because of values deleted in $[t_i, t_i + t_0[$ at $d_j > d_i$. All those tuples are considered for restoration in UPDATELISTS (line 4-5) and restored in PROPAGATE (line 11). All values supported by those restored tuples of any table c and which had been removed by c are restored in PROPAGATE (line 25-26). The propagation of these restorations (via the *restore* list) ensures that a superset of all impacted values is restored.

We need now to make sure that all restored tuples that are removed during the filtering phase are put back at the correct depth and time. The incremental filtering is performed chronologically, so constraints just need to be added in revise at the correct depth. The local time is always increased during filtering using STR, so any removed tuple will always be placed after the first value responsible for its deletion. There are two cases when table constraints must be revised. The first one occurs when invalid tuples are restored. The tuples must then be placed at the earliest time when one of its value were deleted from its domain. This is taken care of in PROPAGATE (line 28). In the second case, a value restored during propagation may actually have to be deleted by another constraint that had been added later (line 2-3 in UPDATELISTS).

Finally, justifications need to be maintained throughout the filtering process. When a restored value (x, d_x) is filtered by a constraint c_m at t_1, its justification constraint is obviously c_m. However, if d_x had been removed (prior to restoration) because of c_m but at a later time $t_2 > t_1$, it means that there is still another supporting tuple for (x, d_x) valid at t_1 (that will be removed only at t_2), and thus the justification time should stay equal to t_2 (GACSTRDYN line 29).

3.2. Time and Space Complexity

The worst-case time complexity of the STR is $O(er(d + t'))$ (the number of constraints e is added because the whole constraint system is considered). In the case of DnSTR, the worst-case time complexity of the initialization and propagation phases is $O(er(d+t'))$, where t' represents the size of the removed tuples list. However, the incremental filtering in the filtering phase may introduce a factor e, as the filtering could occur in the worst case as many times as there are constraints (or depths). The worst-case time complexity for DnSTR is thus $O(e^2 r(d + t'))$. The space complexity of STR is $O(e(n + rt))$. For DnSTR, justifications arrays are in $O(nd)$. For each constraint, as for STR, *table* is in $O(rt)$ and *next* in $O(t)$. The arrays *removedHead* and *removedTail* are each in $O(e)$, as they can be filled for each depth, and $removed_t$ is in $O(t)$, which makes a worst-case space complexity of $O(e + rt)$ for each constraint, and $O(nd + e(e + rt))$ for DnSTR.

4. Experimental Results

In order to evaluate the practical behaviour of the proposed algorithm, we have implemented DnSTR in C# and compared it to DnGAC4 and the classic STR (where backtracking is used to remove constraints). The experiments were conducted using Random CSPs with model B [16]. Each instance is characterized by a tuple $\langle r, n, d, m, p_2 \rangle$ where r is the arity of each constraint, n the number of variables, d the uniform domain size, m the number of constraints and p_2 the tightness of the constraints. The tightness defines the number $t = (1 - p_2)d^k$ of allowed tuples in each constraint. For each arity

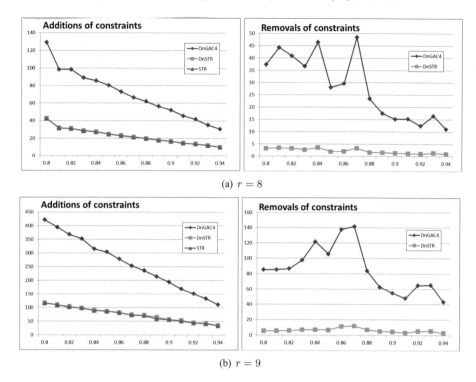

Figure 3. Runtime (in ms) as a function of p_2

$r \in \{8, 9\}$, we did the experiments with 10 instances of RCSP $\langle r, 20, 3, 100, p_2 \rangle$, where $p_2 \in [0.8 - 0.94]$. The constraints were first added one by one (inconsistent systems were discarded). In order to see some real change in the variables' domain with such a low density (a more suitable density for a problem with arity 8 requires many more constraints), 10% random unary constraints were then added. Then 10% of all the constraints were removed. This protocol was applied 10 times per instance. The mean values of the runtime for adding and removing constraints are shown in Figures 3(a) and 3(b).

The experiments show that when adding a constraint, STR and DynSTR are almost identical and faster than DnGAC4. This is not surprising, as the STR algorithm, also used in DnSTR, has been shown more efficient than GAC4 in [9]. For constraint removal, DnSTR outperforms both STR and DnGAC4. The results for the STR algorihms are not shown, as it performs more than 20 times worse than DnGAC4. The poor performance of STR is explained by the important amount of work it has to perform again after backtracking all the way to the removed constraint. DnGAC4 performs better than the classic STR, as it only checks restored values and updates justifications arrays. However, DnSTR beats DnGAC4 again, thanks to the interaction with the dynamic tables of valid tuples. Note that the overhead of the incremental filtering necessary for preserving the timeline does not seem to have an important impact on performance.

We also measured the memory consumption of DnSTR, STR and DnGAC4 with RCSP $\langle 8, 20, 3, 100, p_2 \rangle$. To use as much memory as possible, we added all the constraints and assigned values to random variables until the problem stopped being consistent. Table 1 shows the mean memory consumption of the algorithms for different values of $p2$, just before the system became inconsistent. As we can see, the memory consump-

Table 1. Memory consumption for RCSP $\langle 8, 20, 3, 100, p_2 \rangle$ (in MB)

p_2	0.82	0.84	0.86	0.88	0.9	0.92	0.94
DnSTR4	8.3	8.2	7.6	7.4	7.3	6.7	5.1
STR	3.2	3	2.7	2.5	2.5	1.7	1.1
DnGAC4	12.5	12.3	10.4	8	7.1	6.9	5.7

tion between DnGAC4 and DnSTR is close, also DnSTR performs a bit better, while STR uses much less memory, as it has much less data structures to maintain.

5. Conclusion

In this paper, we propose a new algorithm (DnSTR) to solve Dynamic CSPs with non-binary constraints, described as (extensional) table constraints. Table constraints are commonly used in applications where databases are involved, for example product configuration systems. Our algorithm uses a timeline to record when and why values from domains have been removed. This timeline allows to decide the consequences of retracting constraints. While similar algorithms are based on the generic GAC4 algorithm, our algorithm is based on Simple Tabular Reduction for table constraints. DnSTR as a result performs better than the only other existing algorithm for such problems, DnGAC4. It is also worth noting that DnSTR uses the same justifications data structures as the best algorithms for DCSPs with binary constraints (AC|DC-2i and AC3.1|DC-2i [2]). Our approach can thus easily be adapted to deal with binary constraints defined in intension.

References

[1] F. Bacchus, X. Chen, P. Beek, and T. Walsh, 'Binary vs. non-binary constraints', *Artificial Intelligence*, **140**, 1–37, (2002).
[2] R. Bartak and P. Surynek, 'An improved algorithm for maintaining arc consistency in dynamic constraint satisfaction problems', *Proc. FLAIRS'05*, 161–166.
[3] P. Berlandier and B. Neveu, 'Arc-consistency for Dynamic Constraint Satisfaction Problems: a RMS free approach', *Proc. ECAI'94 Workshop on Constraint Satisfaction Issues raised by Practical Applications*.
[4] C. Bessiére, 'Arc-consistency in Dynamic Constraint Satisfaction Problems', *Proc. AAAI'91*, 221–226.
[5] C. Bessiére, 'Arc-consistency for non-binary CSPs', *Proc. ECAI'92*, 23–27.
[6] C. Bessiére, 'Arc-consistency and arc-consistency again', *Artificial Intelligence*, **65**, 179–190, (1994).
[7] C. Bessiére, E. Hebrard, B. Hnich, and T. Walsh, 'The complexity of reasoning with global constraints', *Constraints*, **12**, 239–259, (2007).
[8] R. Debruyne, 'Arc-consistency in Dynamic CSPs is no more prohibitive', *Proc. ICTAI'96*, 239–267.
[9] C. Lecoutre, 'Optimization of Simple Tabular Reduction', *Proc. CP'08*, 128–143.
[10] A. K. Mackworth, 'Consistency in networks of relations', *Artificial Intelligence*, **8**, 99–118, (1977).
[11] A. K. Mackworth, 'On reading sketch maps', *Proc. IJCAI'77*, 598–606.
[12] R. Mohr and T. C. Henderson, 'Arc and Path consistency revisited', *Artificial Intelligence*, **28**, 225–233, (1986).
[13] R. Mohr and G. Masini, 'Good old discrete relaxation', *Proc. ECAI'88*, 651–656.
[14] M. Mouhoub, 'Arc-consistency for Dynamic CSPs', *Proc. KES'03*, 393–400.
[15] J. R. Ullmann, 'Partition search for non-binary constraint satisfaction', *Information Science*, **177**, 3639–3678, (2007).
[16] K. Xu, F. Boussemart, F. Hemery, and C. Lecoutre, 'Random constraint satisfaction: Easy generation of hard (satisfiable) instances', *Artificial Intelligence*, **171**, 514–534, (2007).

User-based Collaborative Filtering: Sparsity and Performance

Jennifer REDPATH[a,1], David H. GLASS[a], Sally MCCLEAN[a] and Luke CHEN[a]
[a] *Computer Science Research Institute, University of Ulster, Newtownabbey, Northern Ireland*

Abstract. It is generally assumed that all users in a dataset are equally adversely affected by data sparsity and hence addressing this problem should result in improved performance. However, although all users may be members of a sparse dataset, they do not all suffer equally from the data sparsity problem. This indicates that there is some ambiguity as to which users should be identified as suffering from data sparsity, referred to as sparse users throughout this paper, and targeted with new recommendation improvement strategies. This paper defines sparsity in terms of number of item ratings and average similarity with nearest neighbours and then goes on to look at the impact of sparsity so defined on performance. Counterintuitively, it is found that in top-N recommendations sparse users actually perform better than some other categories of users when a standard approach is used. These results are explained, and empirically verified, in terms of a bias towards users with a low number of ratings. The link between sparsity and performance is also considered in the case of predictions rather than top-N recommendations. This work provides the motivation for targeting improvement approaches towards distinct groups of users as opposed to the entire dataset.

Keywords. Collaborative Filtering, Recommender Systems, Evaluation

1. Introduction

Recommender systems [1] are typically employed to assist users with the discovery of items that may be of interest. A commonly-used approach for generating personalised recommendations is User-based Collaborative Filtering (*CF*) [2], in which a database of user ratings profiles is searched for the closest matches to the active user, the user's Neighbourhood (*NN*). The process is modelled on how people naturally interact with each other i.e. sharing opinions. Early User-based *CF* systems were semi-automated, requiring the individual user to discriminate between useful and interesting items and have knowledge about the community of people. These systems were known as either pull-active [2] or push-active [18]. Current systems are automated and use either memory-based or model-based learning algorithms [3]. These algorithms are evaluated in various ways, with a popular approach being the Leave-N-Out (also known as All-But-N) protocol [3]. Any items that are withheld from the recommender algorithm for the purpose of evaluation are referred to as the *hidden* set (H). The items remaining after H has been removed is referred to as the training set (T); this is the information that the system has available regarding the active user a. Either the Top-N items in the

---

[1] Corresponding Author: Jennifer Redpath, Computer Science Research Institute, University of Ulster, Newtownabbey, Northern Ireland, email: redpath-j@email.ulster.ac.uk

neighbourhood are selected to form the recommendations or predictions are generated for *H*.

The central components of a recommender system are the dataset and the recommender algorithm. The dataset can be thought of as a set of items that are available for recommendation to a set of users. Information stored on the users is usually in the form of ratings collected, either implicitly or explicitly, although there could also be other information, such as user demographics. If many of the hidden items occur in the recommendations or the algorithm can accurately predict ratings for unknown items, the system is considered to be successful. Providing user-centric recommendations has proved difficult for many reasons, chiefly, that certain areas of the dataset are very sparse. This occurs as the dataset increases, as even the most active of users will only have rated a small percentage of the product catalogue. As a result, user preferences and overlaps are difficult to infer. Approaches to alleviate the problem have been researched extensively with many different approaches being suggested: including item-based [10, 11], graph-based [19], clustering [20], hybrid recommenders [5] and various dimensionality reduction techniques [21]. Dimensionality reduction methods, such as Singular Value Decomposition (SVD) and Latent Semantic Indexing (LSI) tend to lead to a reduction in accuracy, compared to using the entire dataset, as valuable information is discarded. [5] suggests a hybrid approach: using content to "boost" the *CF* by predicting ratings for empty spaces in the user-ratings matrix and then applying *CF* to the dense pseudo-user ratings matrix. This approach still suffers from the sparsity problem, as users that have fewer than 50 items rated produce less reliable pseudo-user rating vectors.

Some researchers suggest that the only means for assessing a system is via on-line user studies [4]. These can record how the system recommendations are used by the individual, in other words, did the user continue to use the system? Unfortunately these studies are expensive in terms of time and finding a diverse test group. It must also be noted that a test group of users can be more sympathetic than real users and this must be taken into account.

There is an abundance of offline evaluation metrics, which are uncorrelated [12], not standardised for ease of comparison and not widely available as reusable resources [14]. Comparative studies have been conducted [12; 22; 7; 3] to evaluate different collaborative recommender algorithms. The metrics used have differed and therefore the degree of improvement in the end results is not transparent. The research community recognises that the problems with current evaluation methods and measures must be addressed [23]. In response to this, new and modified metrics have started to appear in the literature [7, 24]. [7] introduces a modified precision, whereby any recommendation generated which is not rated by the test user counts negatively towards the result. [24] introduced the Intra-List Similarity Metric to measure the diversity of recommendations within a list.

This paper does not attempt to address the problems of traditional evaluation metrics, but seeks to provide an explanation of a problem in the evaluation of Top-N recommendations using traditional evaluation protocols and metrics. It is demonstrated that the problem of data sparsity, as identified in the literature [5; 6], does not affect users in a uniform manner and in fact the users that suffer most are the users deemed to be in the least sparse area of the dataset. Research focused on improving Top-N recommendations [7; 8] has not identified this problem, but has instead concentrated on addressing issues with the traditional evaluation metrics. Those users who perform worst when an algorithm has been evaluated are the users who require attention. The paper also shows that this problem does not affect evaluation of rating predictions for H.

The problem identified is a result of the protocols being biased towards users with a low number of item ratings. This problem is compounded by problems with common evaluation metrics: for instance, recall only measures how many previously viewed items are found in the hidden set, but not how likely a user is to rate these items highly [9]. In contrast, mean absolute error (MAE) provides the error rate for items that are rated but ignores recommended items that have no user rating; therefore they have no effect on the MAE result (this is only an issue when predicting ratings for items other than H).

The remainder of this paper is organised as follows; Section Two provides a definition for sparse users. This is followed by a detailed description of the methodology in Section Three for both Top-N recommendation and prediction generation; including the methods and metrics for evaluation. Section Four presents the results obtained from running the experiments, demonstrating well that the sparse users are not the worst performers for Top-N recommendation. A discussion, explanation and verification of the results are provided in Section Five. Finally, Section Six completes the report with conclusions and suggestions for future work.

2. Sparsity in User-based CF

While there is generally agreement that sparsity is a problem in recommender systems, the term itself is often used in slightly different ways. An obvious way to characterise sparsity is in terms of number or ratings so that a user who has only a few ratings is considered to be a sparse user. The same approach can be applied not only to individual users, but to a dataset as a whole so that if a high proportion of user-item pairs have not been rated the dataset is sparse. The Sparsity Level measure [10], which will be considered later, is of this kind.

It also seems clear, however, that a user could have a low number of ratings and yet a high proportion of the items rated might also have been rated by other users. In this case the user might well have a high similarity with other users. By contrast, another user might have a high number of ratings yet only a small proportion of the items rated might have been rated by other users. In this case the user might have a low similarity with other users. In order to take this into account, the approach in this paper will be to consider both the number of ratings and the average similarity with nearest neighbours as contributing to sparsity. This will be discussed further in section 4.

In terms of addressing sparsity, a common approach is to consider the performance of an algorithm while the ratio of the number of items used in training to that used in testing is varied [10; 11]. The idea is that sparsity corresponds to the case where this ratio is low and so approaches for alleviating sparsity can be assessed in this case. This approach corresponds to the idea that sparsity is considered as a property of the dataset and so the focus is on the dataset as a whole rather than distinctly identified sparse users.

The approach adopted here is to identify sparse users in terms of their number of ratings and average similarity with nearest neighbours as noted above. The goal then is to investigate the performance of such users in standard recommendation tasks and to compare it with the performance of less sparse users.

3. Methodology

The core recommendation generation tasks are to suggest good items to users and/or make predictions that indicate the expected level of user satisfaction [12]. This paper concentrates on these two tasks, namely Recommending Some Good Items and Predicting Ratings. The well known MovieLens dataset [13] was used. There were 6,040 visitors with 1,000,199 ratings on 3,706 movies.

There is a wide variety of metrics used in the literature to assess the accuracy of a recommender algorithm. In fact, [14] reports that this abundance of metrics is what makes it so difficult for researchers to evaluate recommender systems. It is important to select the most appropriate metric for evaluating the corresponding recommendation task [15]. Recommender Algorithms can be evaluated in terms of predictive, classification or rank accuracy [12]. In this report, recall is the choice for evaluating the classification of Recommending Some Good Items and MAE was chosen for the Predicting Ratings task.

3.1. Recommending Some Good Items

It is assumed that there are many good items that could be of interest to the user. A user-centric approach to recommendation is to provide a small number of good suggestions, to prevent the user from having to search through a large set in order to find a handful of good ones. The recommended items at the top of the list should be the items of most interest to the user, Top-N. In this report N is set to 20.

3.1.1. Collaborative Filtering Algorithm

The neighbourhoods throughout this paper are formulated using a standard user-based collaborative filtering approach with cosine as the similarity measure, which is defined in Eq. (1),

$$sim(u,v) = \frac{u \cdot v}{\parallel u \parallel \parallel v \parallel} \quad (1)$$

Cosine is the measure of the cosine angle between two user rating vectors, in this case u and v. When including non co-rated items [9] the denominator is able to account for the number of movies each user has rated individually. This ensures that users with a high number of ratings do not swamp the neighbourhood selections.

The approach adopted uses the Most-Frequently-Rated (*MFR*) [16] recommendation generation method. *MFR* is a simple incremental count of movie occurrences; movies are counted regardless of the rating attributed to them and all *NN* contribute equally, the Top-N *MFR* items that do not occur in the active user's test set are then recommended.

3.1.2. Evaluation of top-N

Recall is classified as a *Successful Decision Making Capacity* [17] metric, as its role is to measure the ability of a recommender algorithm to make successful decisions. It is the ratio of true positives to the number of hidden items H (Eq. 2), i.e. this metric measures the proportion of successful recoveries from H. The number of true positives

(TP) is a count of the number of times a recommendation has been found in the hidden items.

$$recall = \frac{TP}{H} \tag{2}$$

The interpretation of the evaluation method's result depends on whether the intention is to maximise the prediction of previously watched items, or to uncover the greatest number of movies the user has expressed a favoured opinion towards. In order to distinguish between these two different assessments, two evaluation methods are used: *Complete* (*COM*), where any recommendation that corresponds to a hidden item is considered a *TP* and *Positive* (*POS*), where only items found with a rating above a predefined threshold [8] contribute to the measurement of accuracy. In this paper the rating threshold is set to 3.

An additional measure used in the assessment of the recommender algorithm's decision-making success was User Coverage (UC), which is the proportion of users that receive one or more true positive recommendations.

3.1.3. Evaluation Protocols

The commonly used Leave-*N*-Out evaluation protocol can be applied to the dataset in two ways, (1) select a fixed number of items from every user to withhold, or (2) conceal a fixed percentage of each user profile. In this report these different dataset divides are referred to as *10Hidden* and *80/20*, respectively.

In *10Hidden*; the hidden items are selected by randomly withholding 10 items from each user's profile. The remainder of the data is used for training purposes. Each user receives a set number of recommendations. This approach is biased towards users with small rating sets (explained further in section 5). When using the *10Hidden* evaluation protocol and *COM* evaluation technique there were 60,400 possible *TPs* to find, whereas with the *POS* approach only 37,575 movies were available. While using the *POS* approach, 27 users were completely omitted as none of these had any highly rated movies in their hidden set.

For *80/20*; 80 % of the data is retained for training and 20% of each user's profile is hidden from the algorithm. The mean number of hidden items is 33.11 and the standard deviation of hidden items is 38.56. This approach deals with users with a high number of ratings more equally than *10Hidden*. As before, each user receives a set number of recommendations. The problem with this approach is apparent when the hidden set is greater than the recommendation set (explained further in section 5).

3.2. Predicting Ratings

For this particular task, a set of predicted ratings needs to be generated for items not rated by the active user. The use of predicted ratings is common when generating a set of recommendations. In this report, predictions are generated for all the hidden items.

Predictions are calculated as a weighted average deviation from the neighbour's mean (Eq.3):

$$p_{a,i} = \bar{r}_a + \frac{\sum_{u=1}^{n}(r_{u,i} - \bar{r}_u) \times S_{a,u}}{\sum_{u=1}^{n} S_{a,u}} \qquad (3)$$

where $p_{a,i}$ is the prediction for the active user a for item i; $r_{u,i}$ is the rating for item i by neighbour u; $\bar{r}_u$ and $\bar{r}_a$ are the mean rating of user u and a, respectively; $S_{a,u}$ is the similarity between users a and u; and n is the number of users in the neighbourhood. For the experiments in this paper the top 30 neighbours who had rated the item i were considered. If less than 10 neighbours had rated the item then the average rating for that item in the dataset was used instead, known as the background rating.

3.2.1. Evaluating Predictions

Mean Absolute Error (*MAE*) is a prediction evaluation metric used for measuring the average absolute deviation from each predicted rating to each actual rating. It is formulated in Eq. 4. *MAE* concentrates on the accuracy of a predicted rating as opposed to the accuracy of the recommendation [8]. Other metrics related to *MAE* are *Mean Squared Error*, *Root Mean Squared Error* and *Normalised Mean Absolute Error*.

$$\frac{\sum_{i=1}^{N} |f_i - y_i|}{N} \qquad (4)$$

Where, f_i is the predicted or background rating, y_i is the actual rating the active user assigned to item i and N is the number of hidden items. The lower the *MAE* score obtained, the better the performance of the algorithm.

[7] argue that because *MAE* evaluates each predicted recommendation independently the results are biased towards algorithms that predict all items well, as opposed to predicting the top items well. The top items, usually 10 or 20, are the items of most interest to the user. This report suggests that if the algorithm can accurately predict some hidden items then this is an indication of the quality of the recommendation set, even if they are not found in the hidden set.

4. Results

A sparse user is defined as a user with few overlapping ratings and a small number of items rated. To identify these users the dataset was divided into quadrants, see figure 1, with the sparsest users in the low average nearest-neighbour similarity and low number of ratings quadrant, Quadrant 1, and the least sparse users in the high average nearest-neighbour similarity and high number of ratings quadrant, Quadrant 4. Quadrants 2 and 3 represent intermediate levels of sparsity. The ranges for the quadrants were defined using the similarity results from *COSINE*, and the number of movies in the active user's training set. For example when using *10Hidden*, quadrant one is users with an average similarity value below 0.3475 and number of training ratings below 86.

Quadrant One:	Quadrant Three:
Low NN Similarity	High NN Similarity
Low Number of Ratings	Low Number of Ratings
Quadrant Two:	**Quadrant Four:**
Low NN Similarity	High NN Similarity
High Number of Ratings	High Number of Ratings

Figure 1. Quadrants for Categorising Users

Sarwar et al. define the Sparsity Level [10] as follows,

$$1 - \frac{nonzero\ entries}{total\ entries} \tag{5}$$

It measures the proportion of zero entries in the user-ratings matrix and so takes into account the number of ratings, but it does not take into account the similarity between users. The sparsity level of the entire MovieLens dataset is calculated as 1 − 1,000,199 / 6040 * 3706, which is 0.96.

4.1. Recommendation Results

COM and *POS* recall and *UC* (as defined in section 3.1.2) is shown in table 1 and 2, respectively. The number of users followed by the sparsity level of each quadrant is shown in brackets after the quadrant number. The results shown in tables 1 and 2 would indicate that the worst performing users are in Quadrants 2 and 4; users with a high number of training ratings. Surprisingly, it is Quadrant 3 that does best overall. Quadrant 1, assumed to be the sparse users, is the second best group of users. In fact the users that would be expected to perform best, Quadrant 4, are in 3rd place.

Table 1. *COM* and *POS* Recall using 10 Hidden, 20 Recommendations and *COSINE*; (number of users: quadrant sparsity level)

Quadrant 1 (2425 : 0.99)		Quadrant 3 (594 : 0.97)	
COM	POS	COM	POS
0.3159	0.2521	0.3980	0.3012
Quadrant 2 (595 : 0.96)		**Quadrant 4 (2426 : 0.91)**	
COM	POS	COM	POS
0.2311	0.1931	0.2596	0.2115

Table 2. COM UC and POS UC using 10 Hidden, 20 Recommendations and COSINE; (number of users: quadrant sparsity level)

Quadrant 1 (2425 : 0.99)		Quadrant 3 (594 : 0.97)	
COM UC	POS UC	COM UC	POS UC
96%	89%	99%	94%
Quadrant 2 (595 : 0.96)		**Quadrant 4 (2426 : 0.91)**	
COM UC	POS UC	COM UC	POS UC
86%	77%	91%	81%

It is worth noting that sparsity level scores correspond with the ordering of the quadrants as noted earlier, i.e. Quadrant 1 is the most sparse, Quadrant 4 least sparse and Quadrants 2 and 3 are intermediate. Table 2 supports the findings in table 1 demonstrating that more users in Quadrants 1 and 3 are receiving *TPs* than users in Quadrants 2 and 4.

The evaluation results when using *80/20* are displayed in tables 3 and 4. The quadrants for this data split are defined as <0.3370 ≥ for the average similarity, and <77 ≥ for the numbers of ratings.

Table 3. COM and POS Recall using 80/20, 20 Recommendations and COSINE; (number of users: quadrant sparsity level)

Quadrant 1 (2235 : 0.99)		Quadrant 3 (784 : 0.98)	
COM	POS	COM	POS
0.2990	0.3453	0.3986	0.4574
Quadrant 2 (780 : 0.97)		**Quadrant 4 (2241 : 0.91)**	
COM	POS	COM	POS
0.1813	0.2237	0.1791	0.2322

Table 4. COM UC and POS UC using 80/20, 20 Recommendations and COSINE; (number of users: quadrant sparsity level)

Quadrant 1 (2235 : 0.99)		Quadrant 3 (784 : 0.98)	
COM UC	POS UC	COM UC	POS UC
92%	84%	98%	94%
Quadrant 2 (780 : 0.97)		**Quadrant 4 (2241 : 0.91)**	
COM UC	POS UC	COM UC	POS UC
99%	97%	100%	99%

The results in table 3 are similar to table 1 in that the users with smaller rating vectors perform better with recall. The main differences are that when using *COM* Quadrant 4 becomes the worst group, but as shown by the sparsity level these are the users in the dense area of the dataset. Table 4 is different from table 2, as it is shown that the users in Quadrants 2 and 4 are covered better than users with smaller rating vectors (1 and 3). This would suggest that fixing the size of the hidden set has an effect on the number of users that will receive *TP*s.

4.2. Prediction Results

Table 5 shows the results when using *MAE* as the evaluation metric.

Table 5. MAE using 10Hidden; (number of users: quadrant sparsity level)

Quadrant 1 (2425 : 0.99)	Quadrant 3 (594 : 0.97)
0.7902	0.7402
Quadrant 2 (595 : 0.96)	Quadrant 4 (2426 : 0.91)
0.7649	0.7194

When using predictions and evaluating the hidden items using *MAE* it is found that the sparse users (Quadrant 1) do perform worse. As expected the users in Quadrant 4, high similarity and high number of items rated, receive the best *MAE* results, followed by the users with high similarity and low number of ratings (Quadrant 3).

5. Discussion

As noted in section 4, Quadrant 1 represents the sparsest users within the dataset and Quadrant 4 the least sparse (or most dense) users. Correspondingly, we would expect performance to be worst for the former and best for the latter and this is indeed the case for prediction results evaluated using *MAE*. Quadrants 2 and 3 are intermediate cases with the former having a low average neighbourhood similarity and high number of ratings and the latter a high average neighbourhood similarity and low number of ratings. And as would be expected, the performance for the prediction experiments yields intermediate values for these quadrants. Interestingly, the results are slightly better for Quadrant 3 than Quadrant 2 even though the sparsity level as defined in equation (5) indicates that Quadrant 3 is sparser than Quadrant 2. This shows that a greater degree of sparsity does not necessarily correspond to poorer performance in the case of prediction if sparsity is quantified in terms of the sparsity level. However, the sparsity level only takes into account the proportion of non-zero entries in a dataset and does not incorporate the degree of similarity between users. The results in section 4 suggest that the latter has a greater impact on performance since the average similarity in Quadrant 3 is greater than that in Quadrant 2. Hence, if sparsity is to be correlated with performance, sparsity must be taken to include degree of similarity and not just number of ratings.

Much more surprising are the results for recommendation of the Top-*N* items. In particular, performance, as measured by recall, is best for Quadrant 3, even though it is sparser than Quadrant 4. Worse still, Quadrant 1 performs second best even though it is the sparsest quadrant by any reckoning. The expected correlation between degree of similarity and performance does hold since Quadrants 3 and 4 outperform Quadrants 1 and 2 respectively in the case of *10Hidden* presented in table 1. In the case of *80/20* and *COM* Quadrant 4 performs worse than Quadrant 2, but this may be an artefact of the number of hidden items being greater than the number of recommendations in some cases.

However, since Quadrants 1 and 3 outperform Quadrants 2 and 4 respectively in both *10Hidden* and *80/20* it is clear that a greater number of ratings *adversely* affects performance. This is an extremely counterintuitive result and deserves explanation.

In an attempt to make sense of these results, it is worth recalling that for an active user u the approach involves selecting items from the set of items rated by the nearest neighbours of u, the candidate set of u, CS_u, in the hope that they will also be in u's hidden set, H_u. For this reason it is instructive to consider $P(i \in H_u \mid i \in CS_u)$, the probability than an item i is in the hidden set given that it is in the candidate set. Of course, in reality items are not selected randomly from the candidate set, but on the basis of how frequently they have been rated. Nevertheless, this probability helps to shed light on the problem since it draws attention to the difficulty of finding hidden items in large candidate sets. Via Bayes' theorem, the probability of interest can be expressed as

$$P(i \in H_u \mid i \in CS_u) = \frac{P(i \in CS_u \mid i \in H_u)}{P(i \in CS_u)} \times P(i \in H_u). \qquad 6)$$

Since $P(i \in H_u)$, the probability that a randomly selected item will be in the hidden set depends only on the size of the hidden set, this probability will be the same for all users and so need not be considered further. $P(i \in CS_u)$, the probability that a randomly selected item will belong to the candidate set, is just the ratio of the number of items in the candidate set to the total number of items. Finally, $P(i \in CS_u \mid i \in H_u)$, can be estimated in terms of the probability that an item will be in the set of items rated by the nearest neighbours of u given that it is in the non-hidden items rated by u, which in turn can be estimated by ratio of the corresponding frequencies.

Consider now a typical user in Quadrant 1, v say, and a typical user in Quadrant 2, w say. Since the cosine similarity behaves in a similar way to a simple overlap measure [see 9] and since the average cosine similarity would be the same for these two users, the ratio of items co-rated by v and v's neighbours to the number of items rated by v would be similar to the corresponding ratio for w. This means that the estimates for $P(i \in CS_v \mid i \in H_v)$ and $P(i \in CS_w \mid i \in H_w)$ would be similar. By contrast, the candidate set for w will be much larger than that for v since w has a larger number of ratings and so w's neighbours will also have a larger number of ratings than v's neighbours since v and w have the same average similarity. This means that $P(i \in CS_w)$ will be greater than $P(i \in CS_v)$ and so, via Eq. 6, $P(i \in H_v \mid i \in CS_v)$ will be greater than $P(i \in H_w \mid i \in CS_w)$. That is, the probability of finding an item in v's hidden set given that it is in v's candidate set is greater than the corresponding probability for w. See table 6 for an illustration of the above example using the mean values of the users in Quadrants 1 and 2 to estimate the relevant probabilities.

Table 6. Estimated Probabilities for Quadrants 1 and 2

	Quadrant 1 Mean Values	Quadrant 2 Mean Values
$P(i \in CS_u \mid i \in H_u)$	32.69/35.09 = 0.9316	127.78/131.73 = 0.97
$P(i \in CS_u)$	902/3706 = 0.2434	1918/3706 = 0.5175
$\dfrac{P(i \in CS_u \mid i \in H_u)}{P(i \in CS_u)}$	0.9316 / 0.2434 = 3.83	0.97 / 0.5175 = 1.87

This goes some way to explaining why the performance is better for Quadrant 1 than Quadrant 2. Basically, since users in Quadrant 2 have a greater number of ratings than users in Quadrant 1 they have a larger candidate set and hence it is much more difficult to find the 10 hidden items. Exactly the same kind of reasoning helps explain why Quadrant 3 outperforms Quadrant 4. The size of the candidate set is not so crucial when comparing Quadrants 1 and 3 since they have approximately the same number of ratings. In this case, it is the greater similarity in Quadrant 3 which makes it easier to find a hidden item from a given user's candidate set and hence Quadrant 3 outperforms Quadrant 1. The same reasoning explains why Quadrant 4 outperforms Quadrant 2.

In summary, the greater number of ratings in the case of Quadrants 2 and 4 results in a larger candidate set and hence makes it more difficult to find a small number of hidden items. In effect, there is a bias towards users with a small number of ratings. This is closely related to research by Redpath et al [9] who argued that using standard evaluation metrics when recommending the Top-N items indicates how good algorithms are at identifying items that users have previously rated rather than how likely users are to rate items highly.

6. Conclusions and Future Work

A widely accepted assumption in the research community is that because sparsity is a property of the ratings matrix and all users are considered sparse, that it follows that all users suffer from the sparsity problem. The results in this paper demonstrate that this is not always the case. By defining sparse users in terms of low average similarity with nearest neighbours and low number of ratings, it has been demonstrated that while sparse users do perform worse for prediction generation, they do not perform worse for Top-N recommendation when using the current evaluation protocols. This counterintuitive result has been explained and empirically verified in terms of a bias towards users with smaller rating vectors.

This result has important consequences for attempts to address the problem of sparsity. In the context of Top-N recommendation when using the current evaluation protocols, attempts to improve results for sparse users are unlikely to be very successful since sparse users actually perform quite well. This, of course, highlights a problem with current approaches to Top-N recommendation which needs to be addressed. In particular, steps are required to develop evaluation protocols and metrics that treat all users fairly.

Future work includes evaluating the quality of the recommendation sets from different algorithms in terms of, not just how many known items or ratings can be predicted correctly but how good the items that were not in the hidden set were.

The results in this paper are based on a single run of each protocol, *10Hidden* and *80/20*; future work will include cross-fold validation of the results by running 10 test sets per user per protocol. It should be noted that by changing the training set some users will be assigned to different quadrants as the average neighbourhood similarity and number of test ratings will vary.

The conclusion of this report, that not all users suffer from the data sparsity problem, provides the motivation for targeting improvement approaches towards distinct groups of users as opposed to the entire dataset. Work is underway to provide predictions and Top-N recommendations to the appropriate sparse users using content-based, item-based and hybrid approaches.

A combined content and collaborative similarity measure that uses the ratings for co-rated items and calculates a content divergence for all other movies rated, is being developed. It is hypothesized that the combined measure will provide a more detailed measure of similarity for users in Quadrant 1 when generating item predictions: whereas, when producing top-N recommendations for users in Quadrants 2 and 4 an item-based method is being tested to prune candidate item sets of unlikely *TPs*.

References

[1] Resnick, P., Varian, H.: Recommender Systems. CACM. 40(3), 56--58 (1997)
[2] Goldberg, D., Nichols, D., Oki, B. M., Terry, D.: Using Collaborative Filtering to Weave an Information Tapestry. Commun. ACM 35(12), 61--70 (1992)
[3] Breese, J., Heckerman, D., Kadie, C.: Empirical Analysis of Predictive Algorithms for Collaborative Filtering. In: UAI-98, 43--52 (1998)
[4] Hayes, C., Massa, P., Avesani, P., Cunningham, P.: An On-line Evaluation Framework for Recommender Systems. In: Workshop on Personalization and Recommendation in E-Commerce (2002)
[5] Melville, P., Mooney, R. J., and Nagarajan, R. Content-boosted collaborative filtering for improved recommendations. In *Eighteenth National Conference on Artificial intelligence* R. Dechter, M. Kearns, and R. Sutton, Eds. American Association for Artificial Intelligence, Menlo Park, CA, 187-192. (2002)
[6] Anand, S.S., Mobasher, B.: Intelligent Techniques for Web Personalization. In: Mobasher, B., Anand, S.S. (eds.) LNCS, vol. 3169, pp. 1--37. Springer-Verlag, Berlin, Germany (2005)
[7] McLaughlin, M.R., Herlocker, J.L.: A Collaborative Filtering Algorithm and Evaluation Metric that Accurately Model the User Experience. In: SIGIR '04. ACM, New York, 329--336 (2004)
[8] Symeonidis, P., Nanopoulos, A., Papadopoulos, A., Manolopoulos, Y.: Collaborative Filtering Process in a Whole New Light. In: IDEAS'06. IEEE Computer Society, Washington, DC, 29--36. (2006)
[9] Redpath, J., Glass, D. H., McClean, S., Chen, L.: Collaborative Filtering: The Aim of Recommender Systems and the Significance of User Ratings. InGurrin et al. (Eds): ECIR 2010, LNCS 5993, pp. 394—406, Springer-Verlag, Berlin, Heidelberg (2010)
[10] Sarwar, B., Karypis, G., Konstan, J., Riedl, J.: Item-based Collaborative Filtering Recommendation Algorithms. In: WWW'01. ACM, New York, 285—295. (2001)
[11] Yildirim, H. and Krishnamoorthy, M. S.: A random walk method for alleviating the sparsity problem in collaborative filtering. In: RecSys '08. ACM, New York, NY, 131-138. (2008)
[12] Herlocker, J., Konstan, J., Terveen, L., Riedl, J.: Evaluating Collaborative Filtering Recommender Systems. ACM TOIS. 22(1), 5--53 (2004)
[13] MovieLens Dataset, 2006, http://www.grouplens.org/
[14] Konstan, J.A., Riedl, J.: Research Resources for Recommender Systems. In: CHI'99. (1999)
[15] Gunawardana, a., Shani, G.: A Survey of Accuracy Evaluation Metrics of Recommendation Tasks. Journal of Machine Learning Research. Vol. 10, 2935--2962. (2009)
[16] Sarwar, B., Karypis, G., Konstan, J., Riedl, J.: Analysis of Recommendation Algorithms for E-commerce. In: EC '00. ACM, New York, 158--167. (2000a)

[17] Hernandezdelolmo, F., Gaudioso, E.: Evaluation of recommender systems: A new approach. Expert Systems with Applications 35(3):790-804 (2008)
[18] Maltz, D and Ehrlich, K.: Pointing the way: Active Collaborative Filtering. Human Factors in Computing Systems: Proceedings of CHI'95, May 1995, pp. 202--209
[19] Aggarwal, C. C., Wolf, J. L., Wu, K., and Yu, P. S.: Horting hatches an egg: a new graph-theoretic approach to collaborative filtering. In: ACM SIGKDD'99. ACM, New York, NY, 201-212. (1999)
[20] Ungar, L., Foster, D.: Clustering methods for Collaborative Filtering. In: AAAI Workshop on Recommendation Systems. California: AAAI. (1998)
[21] Sarwar, B., Karypis, G., Konstan, J., Riedl, J.: Application of Dimensionality Reduction in Recommender System - A Case Study. In Proceedings of the ACM WebKDD Workshop. Boston, MA, USA, 82--90. (2000b)
[22] Huang, Z., Zeng, D., Chen, H.: A Comparison of Collaborative-Filtering Recommendation Algorithms for E-commerce. IEEE IS, 22(5), 68-78 (2007)
[23] McNee, S. M., Riedl, J., Konstan, J. A.: Being Accurate is Not Enough: How Accuracy Metrics have hurt Recommender Systems, In CHI '06. ACM, New York, 1097-1101 (2006)
[24] Ziegler, C., McNee, S. M., Konstan, J. A., Lausen, G.: Improving recommendation lists through topic diversification. In: WWW '05. ACM, New York, 22-32 (2005)

Merging and Splitting for Power Indices in Weighted Voting Games and Network Flow Games on Hypergraphs

Anja REY [a] and Jörg ROTHE [a,1]
[a] *Institut für Informatik, Heinrich-Heine-Universität Düsseldorf, Germany*

Abstract. The Banzhaf power index is a prominent measure of a player's influence for coalition formation in weighted voting games, an important class of simple coalitional games that are fully expressive but compactly representable. For the normalized Banzhaf index, Aziz and Paterson [1] show that it is NP-hard to decide whether merging any coalition of players is beneficial, and that in unanimity games, merging is always disadvantageous, whereas splitting is always advantageous. We show that for the *probabilistic* Banzhaf index (which is considered more natural than the normalized Banzhaf index), the merging problem is in P for coalitions of size two, and is NP-hard for coalitions of size at least three. We also prove a corresponding result for the splitting problem. In unanimity games and for the probabilistic Banzhaf index (in strong contrast with the results for the normalized Banzhaf index), we show that splitting is always disadvantageous or neutral, whereas merging is neutral for size-two coalitions, yet advantageous for coalitions of size at least three. In addition, we study the merging and splitting problems for threshold network flow games [3,4] on hypergraphs.

Keywords. Agents and multiagent systems, weighted voting games, Banzhaf index, Shapley-Shubik index, merging und splitting.

1. Introduction

Weighted voting games are an important class of simple coalitional games; their importance is mainly due to the fact that they are fully expressive but at the same time compactly representable.

Power indices measure how influential a player is for forming winning coalitions in weighted voting games. The Banzhaf and the Shapley-Shubik power indices are most prominent among such measures. Roughly speaking, they indicate, respectively, in how many ways and in how many "orders of support" a player can swing the outcome of a coalition by joining or leaving it. For the Shapley-Shubik index, Bachrach and Elkind [2] study the problem of whether a player can increase its power by splitting into several new players and distributing its weight among them; such a player may have incentive to manipulate the game via introducing false names. Bachrach and Elkind also ask whether merging their weights can help any two players to increase their power. For the normal-

---
[1]Corresponding Author: Jörg Rothe, Institut für Informatik, Heinrich-Heine-Universität Düsseldorf, Universitätsstraße 1, 40225 Düsseldorf, Germany; E-mail: rothe@cs.uni-duesseldorf.de.

ized Banzhaf index, Aziz and Paterson [1] show that it is NP-hard to decide whether merging any coalition of players is beneficial, and that in unanimity games, merging is always disadvantageous and splitting is always advantageous.

We show that for the *probabilistic* Banzhaf index (which Dubey and Shapley [6, p. 102] call "in many respects more natural" than the normalized Banzhaf index), the merging problem is in P for coalitions of size two, and is NP-hard for coalitions with at least three players. We also prove a corresponding result for the splitting problem. In unanimity games and with respect to the probabilistic Banzhaf index, we show that splitting is always disadvantageous or neutral, whereas merging is neutral for size-two coalitions, yet advantageous for coalitions with at least three players. This strongly contrasts with Aziz and Paterson's result [1] for unanimity games with respect to the normalized Banzhaf index.

We also consider the merging and splitting problems for threshold network flow games, which have been introduced by Bachrach and Rosenschein [3,4]. However, it seems that merging and splitting cannot be reasonably defined on graphs in such games. We propose to study threshold network flow games on hypergraphs where merging and splitting can be sensibly defined. Though our results here are rather preliminary, we hope to propose an interesting model and to obtain more results in future work.

2. Banzhaf Indices in Weighted Voting Games

A *simple coalitional game* consists of a set $N = \{1,\ldots,n\}$ of players and a function $v : \mathfrak{P}(N) \to \{0,1\}$ such that $v(\emptyset) = 0$, $v(N) = 1$, and $v(R) \leq v(S)$ whenever $R \subseteq S$ for coalitions $R, S \subseteq N$. A weighted voting game $G = (w_1,\ldots,w_n; q)$ is a special form of simple coalitional game with a threshold q and nonnegative integer weights w_i, $1 \leq i \leq n$, where w_i is the ith player's weight. A coalition $S \subseteq N$ is *successful* (i.e., $v(S) = 1$) if $\sum_{i \in S} w_i \geq q$, and not successful (i.e., $v(S) = 0$) otherwise. An essential term is that of a pivotal (or "crucial" or "critical") player. A player i is *pivotal for a coalition* $S \subseteq N - \{i\}$ if $S \cup \{i\}$ is successful, but S is not. Letting $d_G(S,i) = v(S \cup \{i\}) - v(S)$, we have $d_G(S,i) = 1$ if player i is pivotal for S, and $d_G(S,i) = 0$ otherwise.

A power index measures a player's influence in a weighted voting game. The *raw Banzhaf power index* was introduced in [5] and indicates the number of coalitions in which a player is pivotal:

$$\text{Banzhaf}^*(G,i) = \sum_{S \subseteq N - \{i\}} d_G(S,i)$$

for a weighted voting game G and a player i in G. However, since the ratios of these indices are more important than their magnitudes, it has become common to normalize them so as to add up to one. In fact, two different ways of normalization have been proposed for the Banzhaf index. The original definition of the *normalized* Banzhaf power index [5] was analyzed by Dubey and Shapley [6], who introduced another normalization, which they dubbed the *probabilistic* Banzhaf power index and which they viewed as being "in many respects more natural" than the normalized Banzhaf index.[2]

---

[2] As pointed out by an ECAI-2010 reviewer, the normalized Banzhaf power index has its advantages as well, depending on which setting one considers.

In a nutshell, Dubey and Shapley [6] consider various natural and useful properties (or axioms) of power indices in simple games, and they show as Theorem 1 in [6, p. 104] that there exists a unique function φ on the set of simple games satisfying Axioms A1 through A4. In particular, Axiom A4 can be stated as follows: For any two simple games v and w on the set $N = \{1, 2, \ldots, n\}$ of players, it holds that

$$\varphi(v \vee w) + \varphi(v \wedge w) = \varphi(v) + \varphi(w),$$

where the games $v \vee w$ and $v \wedge w$ are defined by $(v \vee w)(S) = \max(v(S), w(S))$ and $(v \wedge w)(S) = \min(v(S), w(S))$. Moreover, $\varphi(v) = \eta(v)$ for each simple game v, where $\eta(v) = (\eta_1(v), \eta_2(v), \ldots, \eta_n(v))$ and $\eta_i(v)$ gives the number of coalitions for which player i is pivotal in game v (i.e., $\eta_i(v)$ is the raw Banzhaf index of player i in v). It is beyond the purpose of this paper to give a full explanation of these axioms (and even of A4), but we refer the reader to [6] for a careful, detailed discussion (including proofs of various equivalent conditions for Axiom A4, which show that this axiom can be presented in a variety of mathematical guises). However, we note here that Dubey and Shapley show that the probabilistic Banzhaf index satisfies Axiom A4, whereas the normalized one does not. As the normalized Banzhaf index lacks Axiom A4, they conclude: "This may be taken as an initial sign of trouble with the normalization [of the normalized Banzhaf index]" (see [6, Footnote 21]). They also note that the probabilistic Banzhaf index "is better behaved when analyzing convergence" [6, p. 116]. To cite another source, Bachrach and Rosenschein [4, p. 126] note that the normalized Banzhaf index "has certain undesirable qualities."

Formally, the *normalized Banzhaf power index* is defined as

$$\text{Banzhaf}'(G, i) = \frac{\text{Banzhaf}^*(G, i)}{\sum_{j=1}^{n} \text{Banzhaf}^*(G, j)},$$

and the *probabilistic Banzhaf power index* is defined as

$$\text{Banzhaf}(G, i) = \frac{\text{Banzhaf}^*(G, i)}{2^{n-1}}.$$

The *raw Shapley-Shubik power index* [12]:

$$\text{Shapley-Shubik}^*(G, i) = \sum_{S \subseteq N - \{i\}} \|S\|! \cdot (n - \|S\| - 1)! \cdot d_G(S, i)$$

describes in how many coalitions a player is pivotal with respect to the order in which players enter coalitions. Normalizing the raw Shapley-Shubik power index by

$$\text{Shapley-Shubik}(G, i) = \frac{\text{Shapley-Shubik}^*(G, i)}{n!}$$

we obtain the *Shapley-Shubik power index*

We assume that the reader is familiar with the basic notions of complexity theory such as the complexity classes P, NP, #P (the class of functions that map instances of NP problems to the number of their solutions, see [14]), and PP ("probabilistic polynomial time," see [9]) and with the notions of hardness and completeness (with respect to the polynomial-time many-one reducibility) for complexity classes. For more background and details we refer to, e.g., the textbooks [8,10,11].

Our reductions will make use of the following well-known NP-complete problem (see, e.g., [8]):

	PARTITION
Given:	A nonempty sequence $A = (a_1, a_2, \ldots, a_k)$ of positive integers summing up to an even number.
Question:	Is there a subset $I' \subseteq I = \{1, 2, \ldots, k\}$ such that $\sum_{i \in I'} a_i = \sum_{i \in I - I'} a_i$?

Let #PARTITION denote the function that maps any given instance A of PARTITION to the number of solutions of A, i.e.,

$$\text{\#PARTITION}(A) = \left\| \left\{ I' \;\middle|\; \begin{array}{l} A = (a_1, a_2, \ldots, a_k) \text{ and } I' \subseteq I = \{1, 2, \ldots, k\} \\ \text{and } \sum_{i \in I'} a_i = \sum_{i \in I - I'} a_i \end{array} \right\} \right\|.$$

#PARTITION is the counting variant of the decision problem PARTITION and is one member of the function class #P.

3. Beneficial Merging and Beneficial Splitting

Bachrach and Elkind [2] asked about the complexity of the problem of whether two players in a given weighted voting game can benefit from merging their weights by forming a single new player, i.e., of whether their joint power will increase in this new weighted voting game. For both the Shapley-Shubik power index and the normalized Banzhaf power index, Aziz and Paterson [1] provided an NP-hardness lower bound for the more general problem of whether any given *coalition* of players can benefit from merging (i.e., can increase their joint power by forming a new player whose weight is the sum of the coalition members' weights). To define this problem formally for the probabilistic Banzhaf power index, we need the following notation. For a weighted voting game $G = (w_1, \ldots, w_n; q)$ and a coalition $S \subseteq N = \{1, \ldots, n\}$, define the new weighted voting game

$$G_{\&S} = (\sum_{i \in S} w_i, w_{j_1}, \ldots, w_{j_{n-\|S\|}}; q),$$

where $\{j_1, \ldots, j_{n-\|S\|}\} = N - S$.[3] BENEFICIALMERGE$_{\text{Banzhaf}}$ is the problem of whether a coalition can increase its power by merging their weights to form one new player. Formally, letting f be one of the power indices defined in Section 2, define the following problem:

---
[3] Note that the players' order doesn't matter when considering the normalized or probabilistic Banzhaf index.

	BENEFICIALMERGE$_f$
Given:	A weighted voting game $G = (w_1,\ldots,w_n; q)$ and a coalition $S \subseteq \{1,\ldots,n\}$.
Question:	Is it true that $f(G_{\&S}, 1) > \sum_{i \in S} f(G, i)$?

Aziz and Paterson [1] have proved NP-hardness of BENEFICIALMERGE$_{\text{Banzhaf}}$. Considering the probabilistic Banzhaf index, we now show that the complexity of BENEFICIALMERGE$_{\text{Banzhaf}}$ depends on whether the input coalition S contains either two players or more than two players.

Theorem 3.1 BENEFICIALMERGE$_{\text{Banzhaf}}$ *is in P for instances* (G,S) *with* $\|S\| = 2$, *and is NP-hard for instances* (G,S) *with* $\|S\| \geq 3$.

Proof. Given an instance (G,S) of BENEFICIALMERGE$_{\text{Banzhaf}}$, suppose $\|S\| = 2$. Without loss of generality (see Footnote 3), we may assume that $S = \{1,2\}$. Thus $G_{\&S} = (w_1 + w_2, w_3, \ldots, w_n; q)$. It is easy to see that

$$\text{Banzhaf}(G_{\&S}, 1) = \text{Banzhaf}(G, 1) + \text{Banzhaf}(G, 2),$$

so a coalition of two players can never benefit from merging.

To prove NP-hardness of BENEFICIALMERGE$_{\text{Banzhaf}}$ for $\|S\| \geq 3$, we give a reduction from the NP-complete problem PARTITION. From a given instance $A = (a_1,\ldots,a_k)$ of PARTITION we construct in polynomial time the following instance (G,S) of BENEFICIALMERGE$_{\text{Banzhaf}}$:

$$G = (w_1,\ldots,w_n, 1,1,1,1; q) = (8a_1,\ldots,8a_k,1,1,1,1; 1 + 4\sum_{\ell=1}^{k} a_\ell);$$

$$S = \{k+2, k+3, k+4\}.$$

The last three players' *raw* Banzhaf indices each are equal to

$$\text{Banzhaf}^*(G, k+4) = \|\{S' \subseteq \{1,\ldots,k+3\} \mid k+4 \text{ is pivotal for } S'\}\|. \quad (1)$$

The set of coalitions S' in (1) can be divided into four disjoint subsets: For any $\tilde{S} \subseteq \{1,\ldots,k\}$ and any two distinct $a,b \in \{k+1, k+2, k+3\}$, distinguish between the set of coalitions S' with

(i) $S' = \tilde{S}$,
(ii) $S' = \tilde{S} \cup \{a\}$,
(iii) $S' = \tilde{S} \cup \{a,b\}$, and
(iv) $S' = \tilde{S} \cup \{k+1, k+2, k+3\}$.

By construction of G, player $k+4$ cannot be pivotal for any coalition S' in cases (ii), (iii), or (iv) but only for those in case (i): Player $k+4$ is pivotal for those $S' = \tilde{S} \subseteq \{1,\ldots,k\}$ such that

$$1 + \sum_{j \in \tilde{S}} 8a_j \geq 1 + 4\sum_{\ell=1}^{k} a_\ell \text{ and } \sum_{j \in \tilde{S}} 8a_j < 1 + 4\sum_{\ell=1}^{k} a_\ell,$$

which is true if and only if $\sum_{j \in \tilde{S}} 8a_j = 4\sum_{\ell=1}^{k} a_\ell$, which in turn is true exactly if A is a yes instance of PARTITION. Thus, the number of coalitions for which player $k+4$ is pivotal equals the number of solutions of the PARTITION instance A. Denote this number by $X_A = \#\text{PARTITION}(A)$. Thus, the probabilistic Banzhaf index of player $k+4$ (and, analogously, of players $k+3$ and $k+2$) is

$$\text{Banzhaf}(G, k+4) = \text{Banzhaf}(G, k+3) = \text{Banzhaf}(G, k+2) = \frac{X_A}{2^{k+3}}.$$

Similarly, the probabilistic Banzhaf index of the first player in the new game

$$G_{\&S} = (3, 8a_1, \ldots, 8a_k, 1; 1 + 4\sum_{\ell=1}^{k} a_\ell)$$

can be calculated to be $\text{Banzhaf}(G_{\&S}, 1) = X_A/2^{k+1}$. Thus, $X_A > 0$ if and only if

$$\text{Banzhaf}(G_{\&S}, 1) = \frac{X_A}{2^{k+1}} = \frac{4X_A}{2^{k+3}} > \frac{3X_A}{2^{k+3}} = \sum_{i=2}^{4} \text{Banzhaf}(G, k+i),$$

which in turn is true if and only if A is a yes instance of PARTITION. □

Now, to formally define the splitting problem, let f be one of the power indices from Section 2, and define the following problem:

BENEFICIALSPLIT$_f$	
Given:	A weighted voting game $G = (w_1, \ldots, w_n; q)$, a player $i \in \{1, \ldots, n\}$, and an integer $m \geq 2$.
Question:	Can player i split into m players $i_1, \ldots i_m$ such that $\sum_{j=1}^{m} f(G', i_j) > f(G, i)$, where $G' = (w_1, \ldots, w_{i-1}, w_{i_1}, \ldots, w_{i_m}, w_{i+1}, \ldots, w_n; q)$ with $\sum_{j=1}^{m} w_{i_j} = w_i$?

By similar methods as above we can prove the following theorem.

Theorem 3.2 BENEFICIALSPLIT$_{\text{Banzhaf}}$ *is in P for instances* $(G, i, 2)$, *and is NP-hard for instances* (G, i, m) *with* $m \geq 3$.

For the lower bounds for BENEFICIALMERGE$_{\text{Banzhaf}}$ and BENEFICIALSPLIT$_{\text{Banzhaf}}$ stated in Theorems 3.1 and 3.2, a natural question arises: What about the upper bounds? Faliszewski and Hemaspaandra [7] established an upper bound for the beneficial merging problem originally proposed by Bachrach and Elkind [2] ("Can any two players increase their joint Shapley-Shubik index via merging?"): This problem is in the complexity class PP. Their proof technique can be used to show that BENEFICIALMERGE$_{\text{Banzhaf}}$ also belongs to PP.[4] The proof is omitted. We conjecture that both BENEFICIALMERGE$_{\text{Banzhaf}}$ and BENEFICIALSPLIT$_{\text{Banzhaf}}$ are PP-complete.

Theorem 3.3 BENEFICIALMERGE$_{\text{Banzhaf}}$ *is in* PP.

4. Merging and Splitting in Unanimity Games

A weighted voting game $G = (w_1, \ldots, w_n; q)$ is called a *unanimity game* if $q = \sum_{i=1}^{n} w_i$, i.e., if only the grand coalition can reach the threshold and win. Aziz and Paterson [1] show that for the normalized Banzhaf index in unanimity games, merging is always disadvantageous, whereas splitting is always advantageous. (Thus one can decide in polynomial time whether or not merging/splitting is beneficial.) In strong contrast, we show that in unanimity games with respect to the probabilistic Banzhaf index, splitting is always disadvantageous or neutral, whereas merging is neutral for size-two coalitions, yet advantageous for coalitions with at least three players.

Theorem 4.1 *Let G be a unanimity game with player set N.*

1. $(G, S) \notin$ BENEFICIALMERGE$_{\text{Banzhaf}}$ *for each* $S \subseteq N$ *with* $\|S\| = 2$,
2. $(G, S) \in$ BENEFICIALMERGE$_{\text{Banzhaf}}$ *for each* $S \subseteq N$ *with* $\|S\| \geq 3$.
3. $(G, i, m) \notin$ BENEFICIALSPLIT$_{\text{Banzhaf}}$ *for each* $i \in N$ *and* $m \geq 2$.

Proof. The first statement follows immediately from Theorem 3.1.

To prove the second statement, note that in a unanimity game, any player i can be pivotal only for the coalition $S = N - \{i\}$, and i always is pivotal for this coalition. Thus the raw Banzhaf index of each i is always equal to one. It follows that Banzhaf$(G, i) = 1/2^{n-1}$ for each player i. If an arbitrary coalition S merges, the new game $G_{\&S} = (\sum_{i \in S} w_i, w_{j_1}, \ldots, w_{j_{n-\|S\|}}; \sum_{i=1}^{n} w_i)$, where $\{j_1, \ldots, j_{n-\|S\|}\} = N - S$, is also a unanimity game. Thus, Banzhaf$(G_{\&S}, i) = 1/2^{n-\|S\|}$. Since $\|S\| \geq 3$, we have

$$\text{Banzhaf}(G_{\&S}, 1) - \sum_{i \in S} \text{Banzhaf}(G, i) = \frac{(2^{\|S\|-1} - \|S\|)}{2^{n-1}} > 0.$$

The third statement can be shown by similar arguments. In particular, for any possible split into players with integer weights, it holds that

$$\sum_{j=1}^{m} \text{Banzhaf}(G', i_j) - \text{Banzhaf}(G, i) = \frac{m - 2^{m-1}}{2^{n+m-2}} \leq 0.$$

This completes the proof. □

---

[4]We note that the same proof cannot be transferred immediately to the beneficial merging problem with respect to the normalized Banzhaf index, since the normalization in the original game G differs from that in the game $G_{\&S}$.

5. Threshold Hypergraph Weighted Voting Games

In this section, we consider another representation of weighted voting games, namely, *threshold network flow games on hypergraphs*.

Bachrach and Rosenschein introduced and analyzed network flow games (on graphs) [3,4]. A *threshold network flow game* $\mathcal{G}$ is defined as a weighted graph $G = (V, E, w : E \to \mathbb{N})$ with n agents[5] that each control one edge in E, a source node $s \in V$ and a target node $t \in V$, and a threshold $k \in \mathbb{R}$ representing the data flow. The coalitional function is the success function $\text{succ}_\mathcal{G} : \mathfrak{P}(N) \to \{0, 1\}$, where a coalition of agents is *successful* if and only if a dataflow of size k can be sent from s to t over the edges represented by the agents in the coalition.

Power indices can be defined analogously as in the case of weighted voting games (see Section 2). Determining the raw Banzhaf index is #P-complete [3], while the Shapley-Shubik index is only known to be at least as hard as problems in NP [4].

If one wants to analyze the problems of merging and splitting in network flow games, the question arises of how these problems can be defined in that setting. Since agents control single edges, merging two or more agents would yield one new agent who has control over more than one edge and so would be different than the remaining agents. Similarly, splitting an agent into several subagents would mean to "split" the original agent's edge, and it is unclear how that could be defined.

Our approach for solving this issue is to consider threshold network flow games on hypergraphs rather than on graphs.[6] A hyperedge in a hypergraph is any subset of the vertex set (so a graph is the special case of a hypergraph with hyperedges of size two only). This makes it possible that, in a game defined on a hypergraph, a coalition of agents can be merged into a single new agent who controls the edge that corresponds to the union of vertices belonging to the edges of the coalition's original agents. Similarly, if we consider such a game on a hypergraph, it is possible for an agent to split into several subagents by partitioning this agent's edge into subsets that each are controlled by one of the new subagents.

Definition 5.1 (Threshold hypergraph network flow games) *A threshold hypergraph network flow game (a THNFG, for short) $\mathcal{G}$ consists of a weighted hypergraph $H = (V, E)$ with vertex set V and a set $E = \{e_1, \ldots, e_n\}$ of n hyperedges, which represent the n agents, and a weight function $w : E \to \mathbb{N}$, where we write $w_i = w(e_i)$, a source node $s \in V$ and a target node $t \in V$, and a threshold $k \in \mathbb{R}$ representing the data flow.*

The success function $\text{succ}_\mathcal{G} : \mathfrak{P}(N) \to \{0, 1\}$ *is defined by*

$$\text{succ}_\mathcal{G}(S) = \begin{cases} 1 & \text{if a dataflow of size } k \text{ from } s \text{ to } t \text{ is possible} \\ & \text{in } H|_{\{e_i \mid i \in S\}}, \\ 0 & \text{otherwise.} \end{cases}$$

---

[5] We use "agent" and "player" synonymously.

[6] It might be tempting—and, indeed, an anonymous STAIRS reviewer suggested this approach—to allow an agent to control more than a single edge, and if one does so, merging and splitting for threshold network flow games could be formulated on graphs rather than on hypergraphs. However, Bachrach and Rosenschein's model [3,4] allows each agent to control only a single edge. We feel it is more natural to extend their model to hypergraphs—keeping their restriction—to be able to define merging and splitting in terms of threshold network flow games.

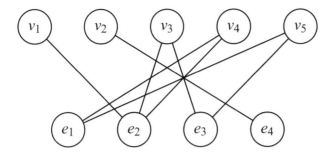

Figure 1. A THNFG for Example 5.2

where $H|_{\{e_i \mid i \in S\}}$ denotes the subhypergraph of H induced by the edge set $\{e_i \mid i \in S\}$.
Power indices in THNFGs can be defined analogously to those in weighted voting games.

Example 5.2 *The THNFG with four agents in Figure 1 may help to visualize the definitions and theorems given below. It shows the hypergraph (in the standard bipartite graph representation for hypergraphs) related to the following game:*

$$\mathscr{G} = (H, s, t, w, k)$$
$$= ((\{v_1, \ldots, v_5\}, \{\{v_4, v_5\}, \{v_1, v_3, v_4\}, \{v_3, v_5\}, \{v_2\}\}), v_1, v_5, (1, 2, 3, 4), 5).$$

Possible applications of THNFGs can be found in grid computing where many—often thousands of—computers collaborate to solve a common task by distributing various subtasks to certain clusters of computers (which represent the agents, respectively the hyperedges). Connecting a number of such computer clusters corresponds to forming a coalition of agents. Modeled as a game, a coalition (i.e., a set of clusters) is successful if it is connected and its total weight (i.e., the sum of the computing power of the computers in the clusters) exceeds a certain threshold so as to allow a sufficient network flow from the source to the target, and in this case these clusters can be assigned the desired subtask.

As another example of a possible application of THNFGs, we propose to use this model for smart power grids that deliver electricity from suppliers to consumers. Success of a coalition would mean here that a certain threshold need be exceeded according to the consumers' current demands, thus allowing a sufficiently large power flow.

For functions, there are several notions of reducibility and consequently there are several notions of hardness and completeness for complexity classes of functions such as #P. We define below parsimonious reductions [13] and the more flexible many-one reductions [15] (see [7] for a more detailed discussion). Intuitively, parsimonious reductions preserve the number of solutions, whereas many-one reductions are the functional analogue of (polynomial-time) many-one reductions between sets.

Definition 5.3 *Let f and g be two functions mapping from Σ^* to $\mathbb{N}$.*

1. *We say f parsimoniously reduces to g if there exists a polynomial-time computable function φ such that for each $x \in \Sigma^*$, $f(x) = g(\varphi(x))$.*

2. We say f many-one-reduces to g if there exist two polynomial-time computable functions, φ and ψ, such that for each $x \in \Sigma^*$, $f(x) = \psi(g(\varphi(x)))$.
3. We say g is #P-parsimonious-hard if every function $f \in$ #P parsimoniously reduces to g. If g is #P-parsimonious-hard and $g \in$ #P, then g is #P-parsimonious-complete. The notions of #P-many-one-hardness and #P-many-one-completeness are defined analogously.

Theorem 5.4 *Computing the raw Banzhaf power index in THNFGs is #P-parsimonious-complete.*

Proof. Given a THNFG $\mathscr{G} = ((\{v_1,\ldots,v_m\},\{e_1,\ldots,e_n\}),s,t,(w_1,\ldots,w_n),k)$ and an agent i in $\mathscr{G}$, the raw Banzhaf power index can be computed in #P, since there exists a nondeterministic Turing machine M that, on input $(\mathscr{G},i)$, nondeterministically guesses a coalition $S \subseteq N - \{i\}$ and verifies deterministically whether $\text{succ}_\mathscr{G}(S \cup i) - \text{succ}_\mathscr{G}(S) = 1$. For each coalition S guessed, this verification is successful exactly if i is pivotal for S. Thus, the number of accepting paths in $M(\mathscr{G},i)$ is exactly the raw Banzhaf index Banzhaf*$(\mathscr{G},i)$. M is an NP machine, since the success of a coalition S can be determined by testing the following three properties in polynomial time each:

1. The hypergraph $H|_{\{e_i \mid i \in S\}}$ contains s and t.
2. There exists a path from s to t in $H|_{\{e_i \mid i \in S\}}$, i.e., there exists a subset $T \subseteq S$, such that $H|_{\{e_i \mid i \in S\}}$ contains s and t and is connected.
3. The sum of weights is not below the threshold, i.e., $\sum_{i \in T} w_i \geq k$ with T as in (2).

#P-parsimonious-hardness can be shown by a reduction from the raw Banzhaf power index in weighted voting games, which is #P-parsimonous-complete [7]. Given a weighted voting game $G = (w_1,\ldots,w_n,q)$ and a player i in G, create the THNFG

$$\mathscr{G} = ((\{v_0,v_1,\ldots,v_{n+1}\},\{e_1,\ldots e_n\}),v_0,v_{n+1},(w_1,\ldots,w_n),q),$$

where $e_i = \{v_0, v_i, v_n + 1\}$ for each i, $1 \leq i \leq n$, with the same weights and threshold, and consider the same player i in $\mathscr{G}$. Since for every nonempty coalition S the corresponding subhypergraph $H|_{\{e_i \mid i \in S\}}$ always contains $s = v_0$ and $t = v_{n+1}$ and is connected, it obviously holds that $\text{succ}_G(S) = \text{succ}_\mathscr{G}(S)$. Therefore, Banzhaf*$(G,i) =$ Banzhaf*$(\mathscr{G},i)$.

Consequently, computing the raw Banzhaf is #P-parsimonious-complete. $\square$

Similarly, the following results that are known for weighted voting games also hold for THNFGs.

Theorem 5.5 *Computing the Shapley-Shubik power index in THNFGs is #P-many-one-complete.*

Proof. That the problem is in #P follows from similar argumentats as those in Theorem 5.4. By means of the same reduction as in Theorem 5.4, a weighted voting game G and a player i are mapped to a THNFG $\mathscr{G}$ and the same player i. It holds that

$$\text{Shapley-Shubik}^*(G,i) = \text{Shapley-Shubik}^*(\mathscr{G},i).$$

This reduction is parsimonious. Since it is #P-many-one-complete to compute the Shapley-Shubik index in weighted voting games [7], computing the Shapley-Shubik index in THNFGs is #P-many-one-hard, and thus #P-many-one-complete. ❏

Faliszewski and Hemaspaandra [7] studied the power compare problem POWERCOMPARE$_f$ in weighted voting games, where f is some power index. This problem can be defined analogously for THNFGs:

	THNFG-POWERCOMPARE$_f$
Given:	Two THNFNGs $\mathscr{G} = (H,s,t,w,k)$, and $\mathscr{G}' = (H',s',t',w',k')$, and a player i occurring in both games.
Question:	Is is true that $f(\mathscr{G},i) > f(\mathscr{G}',i)$?

Theorem 5.6 THNFG-POWERCOMPARE$_f$ is PP-hard for $f \in \{$Shapley-Shubik, Banzhaf$\}$.

Proof. For both the probabilistic Banzhaf and the Shapley-Shubik index, PP-completeness of POWERCOMPARE$_f$ in weighted voting games has been shown by Faliszewski and Hemaspaandra [7]. Using the reduction from the proof of Theorem 5.4, we obtain PP-hardness of THNFG-POWERCOMPARE$_f$. An instance (G,G',i) of POWERCOMPARE$_f$ in weighted voting games is mapped to an instance $(\mathscr{G},\mathscr{G}',i)$ of THNFG-POWERCOMPARE$_f$, where $\mathscr{G}$ and $\mathscr{G}'$ are constructed as in Theorem 5.4. Since succ$_G$ = succ$_\mathscr{G}$ and succ$_{G'}$ = succ$_{\mathscr{G}'}$, it follows that

$$f(G,i) > f(G',i) \iff f(\mathscr{G},i) > f(\mathscr{G}',i).$$

This completes the proof. ❏

Now, for a given power index f, the problems THNFG-BENEFICIALMERGE$_f$ and THNFG-BENEFICIALSPLIT$_f$ can be defined for THNFGs as follows:

	THNFG-BENEFICIALMERGE$_f$
Given:	A THNFG $\mathscr{G} = (H,s,t,w,k)$ and a coalition $S \subseteq \{1,\ldots,n\}$.
Question:	Defining a new agent Merge(S) controlling the edge $e_{\&S} = \bigcup_{i \in S} e_i$ with $w_{\&S} = \sum_{i \in S} w_i$ and the corresponding new game $\mathscr{G}_{\&S} = (H_{\&S},s,t,w_{\&S},k)$ with $H = (V, E - \{e_i \mid i \in S\} \cup e_{\&S})$, does it hold that $f(\mathscr{G}_{\&S}, \text{Merge}(S)) > \sum_{i \in S} f(\mathscr{G},i)$?

THNFG-BENEFICIALSPLIT$_f$
Given: A THNFG $\mathcal{G} = (H,s,t,w,k)$, an agent $i \in \{1,\ldots,n\}$, and an integer $m \geq 2$.
Question: Can agent i split into m agents $\{i_1,\ldots,i_m\}$ such that $\sum_{j=1}^{m} f(\mathcal{G}',i_j) > f(\mathcal{G},i)$, where $\mathcal{G}' = (H',s,t,w',k)$ with $H = (V,(E-\{e_i\}) \cup \{e_{i_1},\ldots,e_{i_m}\})$, $\bigcup_{j=1}^{m} e_{i_j} = e_i$, $e_{i_j} \cap e_{i_k} = \emptyset$ for $j \neq k$, and w_{i_j}, $1 \leq j \leq m$, such that $\sum_{j=1}^{m} w_{i_j} = w_i$?

Analyzing the complexity of these two problems, in contrast to weighted voting games, merging and splitting might be advantageous for the probabilistic Banzhaf index, also for size-two coalitions, or, respectively, a split into two players.

As an example, consider the THNFG in Example 5.2. When merging the players of coalition $S = \{1,2\}$, neither of the power indices increases in the new game

$$\mathcal{G}_{\&\{1,2\}} = ((\{v_1,\ldots,v_5\},\{\{v_1,v_3,v_4,v_5\},\{v_3,v_5\},\{v_2\}\}),v_1,v_5,(3,3,4),5)$$

in comparison to the sum of power indices of the first two players in $\mathcal{G}$. However, merging the agents of coalition $S = \{1,4\}$ is beneficial for all three power indices. The new game is

$$\mathcal{G}_{\&\{1,4\}} = ((\{v_1,v_2\ldots,v_5\},\{\{v_4,v_5\},\{v_1,v_3,v_4\},\{v_3,v_5\}\}),v_1,v_5,(5,2,3),5).$$

For comparison, letting $G = (1,2,3,4;5)$ be the corresponding weighted voting game, and, respectively, $G_{\&\{1,4\}} = (5,1,3;5)$, merging the agents of $S = \{1,4\}$ is neutral.

Analogously to weighted voting games, unanimity games can be defined on hypergraphs. In order to satisfy the property that only the grand coalition $S = N$ is successful, an adequate definition is the following.

Definition 5.7 *A THNFG $\mathcal{G} = (H,s,t,w,k)$ is called a* unanimity game *if $k = \sum_{i=1}^{n} w_i$ and H is connected.*

It is easy to see that Thereom 4.1 also holds for unanimity THNFGs.

6. Conclusions and Future Work

In this paper, we complemented the results of Aziz and Paterson [1] for the normalized Banzhaf power index to the probabilistic Banzhaf power index in weighted voting games. The latter was introduced by Dubey and Shapley [6], who argued that, in certain ways, it is more natural than the normalized Banzhaf power index originally defined by Banzhaf [5]. In particular, we showed that for the probabilistic Banzhaf power index the merging problem is in P for coalitions of size two, and is NP-hard for coalitions of size at least three, and we provided corresponding results for the splitting problem. The most interesting open question in this regard is to close the gap between NP-hardness (Theorem 3.1) and membership in PP (Theorem 3.3) for BENEFICIALMERGE$_{\text{Banzhaf}}$.

In addition, we studied these two problems for threshold network flow games on hypergraphs.

Acknowledgments

We are grateful to the anonymous ECAI-2010 and STAIRS-2010 reviewers for their helpful comments on this paper. This work was supported in part by the EUROCORES program LogICCC of the ESF and DFG grants RO 1202/11-1 and RO 1202/12-1. The results of Sections 3 and 4 appeared in the proceedings of the *19th European Conference on Artificial Intelligence* (ECAI'10), August 2010.

References

[1] H. Aziz and M. Paterson, 'False name manipulations in weighted voting games: Splitting, merging and annexation', in *Proceedings of the 8th International Joint Conference on Autonomous Agents and Multiagent Systems*, pp. 409–416. IFAAMAS, (May 2009).
[2] Y. Bachrach and E. Elkind, 'Divide and conquer: False-name manipulations in weighted voting games', in *Proceedings of the 7th International Joint Conference on Autonomous Agents and Multiagent Systems*, pp. 975–982. IFAAMAS, (May 2008).
[3] Y. Bachrach and J. Rosenschein, 'Computing the banzhaf power index in network flow games', in *Proceedings of the 7th International Joint Conference on Autonomous Agents and Multiagent Systems*, pp. 323–329. IFAAMAS, (2007).
[4] Y. Bachrach and J. Rosenschein, 'Power in threshold network flow games', *Journal of Autonomous Agents and Multi-Agent Systems*, **18**(1), 106–132, (2009).
[5] J. Banzhaf III, 'Weighted voting doesn't work: A mathematical analysis', *Rutgers Law Review*, **19**, 317–343, (1965).
[6] P. Dubey and L. Shapley, 'Mathematical properties of the Banzhaf power index', *Mathematics of Operations Research*, **4**(2), 99–131, (1979).
[7] P. Faliszewski and L. Hemaspaandra, 'The complexity of power-index comparison', *Theoretical Computer Science*, **410**(1), 101–107, (2009).
[8] M. Garey and D. Johnson, *Computers and Intractability: A Guide to the Theory of NP-Completeness*, W. H. Freeman and Company, 1979.
[9] J. Gill, 'Computational complexity of probabilistic Turing machines', *SIAM Journal on Computing*, **6**(4), 675–695, (1977).
[10] C. Papadimitriou, *Computational Complexity*, Addison-Wesley, 1994.
[11] J. Rothe, *Complexity Theory and Cryptology. An Introduction to Cryptocomplexity*, EATCS Texts in Theoretical Computer Science, Springer-Verlag, 2005.
[12] L. Shapley and M. Shubik, 'A method of evaluating the distribution of power in a committee system', *American Political Science Review*, **48**, 787–792, (1954).
[13] J. Simon, *On Some Central Problems in Computational Complexity*, Ph.D. dissertation, Cornell University, Ithaca, NY, January 1975. Available as Cornell Department of Computer Science Technical Report TR75-224.
[14] L. Valiant, 'The complexity of enumeration and reliability problems', *SIAM Journal on Computing*, **8**(3), 410–421, (1979).
[15] V. Zankó, '#P-completeness via many-one reductions', *International Journal of Foundations of Computer Science*, **2**(1), 76–82, (1991).

Cancer Classification using SVM-boosted Multiobjective Differential Fuzzy Clustering

Indrajit Saha [a,1], Ujjwal Maulik [b] Sanghamitra Bandyopadhyay [c] and Dariusz Plewczynski [a]

[a] *ICM, University of Warsaw, Warsaw, Poland.*
[b] *Dept. of Comp. Sci. and Engg., Jadavpur University, Kolkata, West Bengal, India.*
[c] *Machine Intelligence Unit, Indian Statistical Institute, Kolkata, West Bengal, India.*

Abstract. Microarray technology facilitates the monitoring of the expression profile of a large number of genes across different experimental conditions or tissue samples simultaneously. Microarray technology is being utilized in cancer diagnosis through the classification of the tissue samples. In this article, we have presented an integrated unsupervised technique for cancer classification. The proposed method is based on multiobjective differential fuzzy clustering of the tissue samples. In this regard, real coded encoding of the cluster centres is used and two fuzzy cluster validity indices are simultaneously optimized. The resultant set of near-Pareto-optimal solutions contains a number of non-dominated solutions. Each such solution has been improved by a novel technique based on Support Vector Machine (SVM) classification. Thereafter, the final clustering solution is produced by majority voting ensemble technique of all improved solutions. The performance of the proposed multiobjective clustering method has been compared to several other microarray clustering algorithms for three publicly available benchmark cancer data sets, viz., leukemia, Colon cancer and Lymphoma data to establish its superiority. Also statistical significance tests have been conducted to establish the statistical superiority of the proposed clustering method.

Keywords. Cancer classification, multiobjective optimization, differential evolution, statistical test

Introduction

The advent of microarray technology has made it possible to study the expression profile of a huge number of genes across different experimental conditions or tissue samples simultaneously. This has significant impact on cancer research. Microarray technology is being utilized in cancer diagnosis through the classification of the tissue samples. When microarrays are organized in gene versus sample fashion, then they are very helpful in classification of different types of tissues and identification of those genes whose expression levels are good diagnostic indicators. The microarrays where tissue samples are

---

[1]Corresponding Authors: Indrajit Saha and Dariusz Plewczynski, ICM, University of Warsaw, 02-089 Warsaw, Poland; E-mail: { indra, draman } @icm.edu.pl

represent cancerous (malignant) and non-cancerous (benign) cells, then the classification of them will result in binary cancer classification. Most of the researches in the area of cancer diagnosis have focused on supervised classification of cancer data sets through training, validation and testing to classify the tumor samples as malignant or benign, or their subtypes [1,2]. However, unsupervised classification or clustering of tissue samples should also be studied since in many cases, labeled tissue samples are not available. In this article, we explore the application of the multiobjective differential fuzzy clustering (MODEFC) for unsupervised classification of cancer data.

A microarray gene expression data, consisting of n genes and $\mathcal{T}$ time points, is typically organized in a **2D** matrix $E = [g_{ij}]$ of size $n \times \mathcal{T}$. Each element g_{ij} gives the expression level of the ith gene at the jth time point. Clustering [7] is an important microarray analysis tool, is used to identify the sets of genes with similar expression profiles. Clustering methods partition the input space into K regions depending on some similarity/dissimilarity metric where the value of K may or may not be known $a\ priori$. The main objective of any clustering technique is to produce a $K \times n$ partition matrix $U(X)$ of the given data set X, consisting of n patterns, $X = \{x_1, x_2, \ldots, x_n\}$. The partition matrix may be represented as $U = [u_{kj}]$, $k = 1, 2, \ldots, K$ and $j = 1, 2, \ldots, n$, where u_{kj} is the membership of pattern x_j to the kth cluster. For fuzzy clustering of the data, $0 \leq u_{kj} \leq 1$, i.e., u_{kj} denotes the degree of belongingness of pattern x_j to the kth cluster.

Differential Evolution (DE) [9] has been effectively used to develop single objective clustering techniques [8]. However, a single cluster validity measure is seldom equally applicable for different kinds of data sets. This article poses the problem of fuzzy partitioning as one of multiobjective optimizations (MOO) [5]. Unlike single objective optimization, in MOO, search is performed over a number of, often conflicting, objective functions. The final solution set contains a number of Pareto-optimal solutions, none of which can be further improved on any one objective without degrading it in another. The proposed multiobjective differential fuzzy clustering (MODEFC) algorithm has been optimized the Xie-Beni (XB) index [11] and the fuzzy C-means (FCM) error function J_m [3] simultaneously. Usually, a fuzzy clustering solution is defuzzified by assigning each point to the cluster to which the point has the highest membership degree. In general, it has been observed that for a particular cluster, among the points that are assigned to it based on maximum membership criterion, some have higher membership degree to that cluster, whereas the other points of the same cluster may have lower membership degree. Thus the points in the latter case are not assigned to that cluster with high confidence. This observation motivates us to improve the clustering result obtained by multiobjective fuzzy clustering method using some supervised classification tool, such as Support Vector Machine (SVM) [10], which is trained by the points with high membership degree in a cluster. The trained classifier thereafter can be used to classify the remaining points.

A characteristic of any MOO approach is that it often produces a large number of Pareto optimal solutions, from which selecting a particular solution is difficult. The existing methods use the characteristics of the Pareto optimal surface or some external measure for this purpose. However, these approaches almost always pick up one solution from the Pareto optimal set as the final solution, although evidently all the solutions in this set have some information that is inherently good for the problem in hand. Motivated by this observation, this article describes a novel method to obtain the final solution by combining the information of all the non-dominated solutions produced in the final generation. In this approach, first each solution (fuzzy membership matrix) of the final non-dominated front is considered one by one and each of them is improved using SVM classifier [10] as discussed above. Finally, the improved clustering solutions are ensembled to create final optimal clustering solution based on majority voting technique.

The superiority of the proposed MODEFC-SVM algorithm is compared with multi-objective genetic algorithm (non-dominated sorting genetic algorithm-II [5]) based fuzzy clustering algorithm (MOGAFC), integrated version of MOGAFC with SVM and a well-known fuzzy c-means (FCM) [3] algorithm for three publicly available benchmark cancer data sets: Leukemia, Colon cancer, and Lymphoma data. The performance of the proposed clustering scheme is also demonstrated both quantitatively and visually. The superiority of the MODEFC-SVM clustering technique has also been proved to be statistically significant through statistical significance tests.

1. Fundamentals of Differential Evolution and SVM Classifier

1.1. Differential Evolution

Differential Evolution [9] is a relatively recent heuristic designed to optimize problems over continuous domains. In DE, each decision variable is represented in the vector by a real number. As in any other evolutionary algorithm, the initial population of DE is generated randomly, and then evaluated. The kth individual vector of the population at time-step (generation) t has d components (dimensions), i.e.,

$$G_k(t) = [G_{k,1}(t), G_{k,2}(t), \ldots, G_{k,d}(t)] \quad (1)$$

For each target vector $G_k(t)$ that belongs to the current population, three randomly selected vectors from the current population are used. In other words, the dth component of each trial offspring is generated as follows.

$$\vartheta_k(t+1) = G_i(t) + F(G_n(t) - G_m(t)) \quad (2)$$

Here F is a mutation factor. In order to increase the diversity of the perturbed parameter vectors, crossover is introduced. To this end, the trial vector:

$$Q_k(t+1) = [Q_{k,1}(t+1), Q_{k,2}(t+1), \ldots, Q_{k,d}(t+1)] \quad (3)$$

is formed, where

$$Q_{jk}(t+1) = \begin{cases} \vartheta_{jk}(t+1) \\ \quad if\ rand_j(0,1) \leq CR\ or\ j = rand(k) \\ G_k(t) \\ \quad if\ rand_j(0,1) > CR\ and\ j \neq rand(k) \end{cases} \quad (4)$$

In Eqn. (4), $rand_j(0,1)$ is the jth evaluation of a uniform random number generator with outcome $\in [0, 1]$. CR is the crossover rate $\in [0, 1]$ which has to be determined by the user. $rand(k)$ is a randomly chosen index $\in \{1, 2, \ldots, d\}$ which ensures that $Q_k(t+1)$ gets at least one parameter from $\vartheta_k(t+1)$. The following condition decide whether or not it should become a member of next generation $(t+1)$,

$$G_k(t+1) = \begin{cases} Q_k(t+1) \\ \quad if\ f(Q_k(t+1)) > f(G_k) \\ G_k(t) \\ \quad if\ f(Q_k(t+1)) \leq f(G_k) \end{cases} \quad (5)$$

where $f(.)$ is the objective function to be minimized in this article. The processes of mutation, crossover and selection are executed for a fixed number of iterations. The best vector seen up to the last generation provides the solution to the clustering problem. The algorithm of DE is described at here can be used for single objective optimization whereas in multiobjective optimization multiple $f(.)$ are to be optimized simultaneously.

1.2. SVM Classifier

Support Vector Machines (SVM) is a learning algorithm originally developed by Vapnik [10]. It has been used extensively for the purpose of classification in a wide variety of fields. Support Vector Machines classifier is inspired by the statistical learning theory and they perform structural risk minimization on a nested set structure of separating hyperplanes [10]. Fundamentally the SVM classifier is designed for two-class problems. It can be extended to handle multi-class problems by designing a number of one-against-all or one-against-one two-class SVMs.

Suppose a data set consists of n feature vectors $< x_i, y_i >$, where $y_i \in \{+1, -1\}$, denotes the class label for the data point x_i. The problem of finding the weight vector w can be formulated as minimizing the following function:

$$L(w) = \frac{1}{2} \| w \|^2 \quad (6)$$

subject to

$$y_i[w.\phi(x_i) + b] \geq 1, \quad i = 1, \ldots, n. \quad (7)$$

Here, b is the bias and the function $\phi(x)$ maps the input vector to the feature vector. The SVM classifier for the case on linearly inseparable data is given by,

$$f(x) = \sum_{i=1}^{n} y_i \beta_i K(x_i, x) + b \quad (8)$$

Where K is the kernel matrix, and n is the number of input patterns having nonzero values of the Langrangian multipliers(β_i). In case of categorical data, x_i is the ith sample, and y_i is the class label. These n input patterns are called support vectors, and hence the name support vector machines. The Langrangian multipliers(β_i) can be obtained by maximizing the following:

$$Q(\beta) = \sum_{i=1}^{n} \beta_i - \frac{1}{2} \sum_{i=1}^{n} \sum_{j=1}^{n} y_i y_j \beta_i \beta_j K(x_i, x_j), \quad (9)$$

subject to

$$\sum_{i=1}^{n} y_i \beta_i = 0\ and\ 0 \leq \beta_i \leq C,\ i = 1, \ldots, n \quad (10)$$

Only a small fraction of the β_i coefficients are nonzero. The corresponding pairs of x_i entries are known as support vectors and they fully define the decision function. Geometrically, the support vectors are the points lying near the separating hyperplane. $K(x_i, x_j) = \phi(x_i).\phi(x_j)$ is called the *kernel function*. The kernel function may be linear or non-linear, like polynomial, sigmoidal, radial basis functions (RBF), etc. RBF kernels are of the following form:

$$K(x_i, x_j) = e^{-w|x_i - x_j|^2} \qquad (11)$$

where x_i denotes the ith data point and w is the weight. In this article, the above mentioned RBF kernel is used. Also, the extended version of the two-class SVM that deals with multi-class classification problem by designing a number of one-against-all two-class SVMs, is used here.

2. Multiobjective Optimization and Existing Tools

2.1. Mathematical Background

The multiobjective optimization can be formally stated as following: Find the vector $\bar{x}^*$ = $[x_1^*, x_2^*, \ldots, x_n^*]^T$ of decision variables which will satisfy the m inequality constraints:

$$g_i(\bar{x}) \geq 0, \quad i = 1, 2, \ldots, m, \qquad (12)$$

the p equality constraints

$$h_i(\bar{x}) \geq 0, \quad i = 1, 2, \ldots, p, \qquad (13)$$

and optimizes the vector function

$$\bar{f}(\bar{x}) = [f_1(\bar{x}), f_2(\bar{x}), \ldots, f_k(\bar{x})]^T \qquad (14)$$

The constraints given in Eqns. 12 and 13 define the feasible region $\mathcal{F}$ which contains all the admissible solutions. Any solution outside this region is inadmissible since it violates one or more constraints. The vector $\bar{x}^*$ denotes an optimal solution in $\mathcal{F}$. In the context of multiobjective optimization, the difficulty lies in the definition of optimality, since it is only rare that we will find a situation where a single vector $\bar{x}^*$ represents the optimum solution to all the objective functions.

The concept of *Pareto optimality* comes handy in the domain of multiobjective optimization. A formal definition of Pareto optimality from the viewpoint of minimization problem may be given as follows: A decision vector $\bar{x}^*$ is called Pareto optimal if and only if there is no $\bar{x}$ that dominates $\bar{x}^*$, i.e., there is no $\bar{x}$ such that

$$\forall i \in \{1, 2, \ldots, k\}, \ f_i(\bar{x}) \leq f_i(\bar{x}^*) \qquad (15)$$

and

$$\exists i \in \{1, 2, \ldots, k\}, \ f_i(\bar{x}) < f_i(\bar{x}^*) \qquad (16)$$

In other words, $\bar{x}^*$ is Pareto optimal if there exists no feasible vector $\bar{x}$ which causes a reduction on some criterion without a simultaneous increase in at least another. In this context, two other notions viz., *weakly non-dominated* and *strongly non-dominated* solutions are defined [4]. A point $\overline{x}^*$ is a weakly non-dominated solution if there exists no $\overline{x}$ such that $f_i(\overline{x}) < f_i(\overline{x}^*)$, for $i = 1, 2, \ldots, k$. A point $\overline{x}^*$ is a strongly non-dominated solution if there exists no $\overline{x}$ such that $f_i(\overline{x}) \leq f_i(\overline{x}^*)$, for $i = 1, 2, \ldots, k$, and for at least one i, $f_i(\overline{x}) < f_i(\overline{x}^*)$. In general, Pareto optimum usually admits a set of solutions called non-dominated solutions.

2.2. Non-dominated Sorting

In this approach, every solution from the population is checked with a partially filled population of dominance. To start with, the first solution from the population is kept in the set S. Thereafter, each solution p (the second solution onwards) is compared with all members of the set S one by one. If the solution p dominates any member q of S, then solution q is removed from S. These way non-members of the non-dominated front get deleted from S. Otherwise, if solution p is dominated by any member of S, then solution p is ignored. If solution p is not dominated any member of S, it is entered in S. This is how the set S grows with non-dominated solutions. When all solutions of the population are checked, the remaining members of S constitute the non-dominated set. To find the other fronts, the members of S will be discounted and the above procedure is repeated. After getting the different fronts, they are assigned through different ranks. The maximum computational complexity of this approach to find the non-dominated front is $O(\log(M \times N^2))$ where M is the number of objective and N is the size of the population [5].

2.3. Crowding Distance

For estimating the density of the solutions surrounding a particular solution in the population, the average distance of two points on either sides of this point along each of the objectives are computed. This quantity $j_{distance}$ serves as an estimate of the size of the largest cuboid enclosing the point j without including any other point in the population, is called *crowding distance*. In Fig. 1, the crowding distance of the jth in its front is the average side-length of the cuboid. The crowding distance computation requires sorting of the population according to each objective function value in their ascending order of magnitude. Thereafter, for each objective function, the boundary solutions are assigned as infinity distance value. All other intermediate solutions are assigned a distance value equal to the absolute difference in the functional values of two adjacent solutions. This computation is continued with other objective functions. The overall crowding distance value is calculated as the sum of individual distance values corresponding to each objective. Computational complexity of crowding distance is $O(M \times N \times \log(N))$ [5].

3. Proposed Multiobjective Algorithm

3.1. Multiobjective Differential Evolution based Fuzzy Clustering

3.1.1. Vector Representation and Initial Population

In Multiobjective Differential Evolution based Fuzzy Clustering (MODEFC), each vector is a sequence of real numbers representing the K cluster centres. For an d-

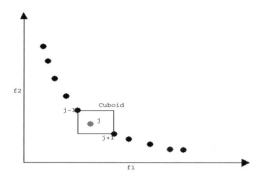

Figure 1. The crowding distance calculation is shown.

dimensional space, the length of a vector is $l = d \times K$, where the first d positions represent the first cluster centre, the next d positions represent those of the second cluster centre, and so on. The K cluster centres encoded in each vector are initialized to K randomly chosen points from the data set. This process is repeated for each of the P vectors in the population, where P is the size of the population.

3.1.2. Evaluation of the Objectives

For computing the objective functions, first the centres $V = \{v_1, v_2, \ldots, v_K\}$ encoded in a given chromosome are extracted. The fuzzy membership values u_{ki}, $k = 1, 2, \ldots, K$, $i = 1, 2, \ldots, n$ are computed using the following equation:

$$u_{ki} = \frac{\left(\frac{1}{D(v_k, x_i)}\right)^{\frac{1}{m-1}}}{\sum_{j=1}^{K}\left(\frac{1}{D(v_j, x_i)}\right)^{\frac{1}{m-1}}}, \quad for\ 1 \leq k \leq K,\ 1 \leq i \leq n \tag{17}$$

where $D(v_k, x_i)$ and $D(v_j, x_i)$ are the distances between x_i and v_k, and x_i and v_j respectively. The value of m, the fuzzy exponent, is taken as 2. Note that while computing u_{ki} using Eqn. 17, if $D(v_j, x_i)$ is equal to zero for some j, then u_{ki} is set to zero for all $k = 1, \ldots, K, k \neq j$, while u_{ki} is set equal to one. Based on the membership values, the cluster centres are recomputed using the following equation

$$v_k = \frac{\sum_{i=1}^{n} u_{ki}^m x_i}{\sum_{i=1}^{n} u_{ki}^m} \quad 1 \leq k \leq K \tag{18}$$

The membership values are then recomputed using Eqn. 17. The XB index is defined as a function of the ratio of the total variation σ $(\sigma(U, Z; X) = \sum_{k=1}^{K} \sum_{i=1}^{n} u_{ki}^2\, D^2(v_k, x_i))$ to the minimum separation sep $(sep(Z) = min_{k \neq j} D^2(v_k - v_j)$ of the clusters. The XB index is then written as:

$$XB(U, Z; X) = \frac{\sigma(U, Z; X)}{n \times sep(Z)} \tag{19}$$

Note that when the partitioning is compact and the clusters are well separated, value of σ should be low while sep should be high, thereby yielding lower values of the XB index.

The objective is therefore to minimize it.

The other objective is the J_m validity measure that is optimized by the FCM algorithm. This computes the global fuzzy variance of the clusters and this is expressed by the following equation:

$$J_m = \sum_{i=1}^{n} \sum_{k=1}^{K} u_{ki}^m D^2(v_k, x_i) \qquad (20)$$

J_m is to be minimized to get compact clusters.

XB and J_m indices are used as they are contradictory in nature. XB index is responsible for both compactness and separation for the clusters, whereas J_m only represents the global compactness of the clusters.

3.1.3. Other processes

After evaluating the fitness of each vector, it goes through mutation (described in Eqn. 2) to generate the new offspring and crossover (described in Eqn. 4) for increasing the diversity of the mutant vector. The created offspring pool combined with its parent pool for performing the non-dominated sort in the next step. Thereafter, the selection process has been performed based on the lowest rank assigned by the non-dominated sort as well as least crowding distance. These processes are executed for a fixed number of iterations and final non-dominated front is used in the next section for further processing.

3.2. Integrating MODEFC with SVM and Voting Ensemble

Step1: Apply MODEFC on the given data set to obtain a set $S = \{s_1, s_2, \ldots, s_N\}$, $N \leq P$, (P is the population size) of non-dominated Pareto-optimal solution strings consisting of cluster centres.

Step2: Substeps of Step 2 are repeated N times depending on the size of non-dominated solutions s_i, $1 \leq i \leq N$.

  a) Select 50% of data points from each cluster which are nearest to the respective cluster centres for each s_i.
  b) Train the SVM classifier by the selected training points.
  c) Predict the class labels for the remaining points (test points) using the trained SVM classifier.
  d) Combine the label vectors corresponding to training and testing points to obtain the label vector δ_i for the complete data set corresponding to the non-dominated solution s_i.

Step3: Reorganize the data points to make them consistent with each other, i.e., cluster j in the first solution should be equivalent to cluster j in all the other solutions. For example, the solution string $\{(p, q, r), (a, b, c)\}$ is equivalent to $\{(a, b, c), (p, q, r)\}$. The reorganization is done in such way that each δ_i, $i \neq 1$, becomes consistent with δ_1.

Step4: Apply majority voting on the label vectors δ_i, $i = 1, \ldots, N$ to obtain the final clustering label vector δ. The majority voting is done as follows: assign each point $k = 1, \ldots, n$ to the cluster j where the label j appears the maximum number of times among all the labels for the point k in all the δ_i.

4. Data Sets and Preprocessing

In this article, three publicly available benchmark cancer data sets, viz., Leukemia, Colon cancer and Lymphoma data sets have been used for experiments. The data sets and their pre-processing are described in this section.

4.1. Leukemia Data

The Leukemia data set [6] consists of 72 tissue samples. The samples consist of two types of leukemia, 25 of AML and 47 of ALL. The samples are taken from 63 bone marrow samples and 9 peripheral blood samples. There are 7,129 genes in the data set. The data set is publicly available at http://www.genome.wi.mit.edu/MPR.

The data set is subjected to a number of pre-processing steps to find out the genes with most variability. As this article considers the problem of unsupervised classification, hence the gene selection steps followed here are also completely unsupervised. However, more sophisticated methods for gene selection could have been applied. First we select the genes whose expression levels fall between 100 and 15000. From the resulting 1015 genes, the 100 genes with the largest variation across samples are selected, and the remaining expression values are log-transformed. The resultant data set is of dimension 72 × 100.

4.2. Colon Cancer Data

The Colon cancer data set [2] consists of 62 samples of colon epithelial cells from colon cancer patients. The samples consists of tumor biopsies collected from tumors (40 samples), and normal biopsies collected from healthy part of the colons (22 samples) of the same patient. The number of genes in the data set is 2000. The data set is publicly available at http://microarray.princeton.edu/oncology.

This data set is pre-processed as follows: first the genes whose expression levels fall between 10 and 15000 are selected. From the resulting 1756 genes, the 100 genes with the largest variation across samples are selected, and the remaining expression values are log-transformed. The resultant data set is of dimension 62 × 100.

4.3. Lymphoma Data

The diffuse large B-cell lymphoma (DLBCL) dataset [1] contains expression measurements of 96 normal and malignant lymphocyte samples each measured using a specialized cDNA microarray, containing 4,026 genes that are preferentially expressed in lymphoid cells or which are of known immunological or oncological importance. There are 42 DLBCL and 54 other cancer disease samples. The data set is publicly available at http://genome-www.stanford.edu/lymphoma.

The pre-processing steps for this data sets are as follows: As the data set contains some missing values, we select only those genes which do not contain any missing value. This results in 854 genes. Next each gene is normalized to have expression value between 0 and 1. Thereafter top 100 genes with respect to variance are selected. Hence the data set contains 96 samples each described by 100 genes.

5. Experimental Results

5.1. Performance Metric

Silhouette index is a cluster validity index that is used to judge the quality of any clustering solution C. Suppose a represents the average distance of a gene from the other genes of the cluster to which the gene is assigned, and b represents the minimum of the average distances of the gene from the genes of the other clusters. Now the silhouette width s of the gene is defined as:

$$s = \frac{b-a}{max\{a,b\}} \qquad (21)$$

Silhouette index $s(C)$ is the average Silhouette width of all the genes and it reflects the compactness and separation of clusters. The value of Silhouette index varies from -1 to 1 and higher value indicates better clustering result.

5.2. Distance Measure

Pearson Correlation: Given two sample vectors, α_i and α_j, Pearson correlation coefficient $Cor(\alpha_i, \alpha_j)$ between them is computed as:

$$Cor(\alpha_i, \alpha_j) = \frac{\sum_{l=1}^{p}(\alpha_{il} - \mu_{\alpha_i})(\alpha_{jl} - \mu_{\alpha_j})}{\sqrt{\sum_{l=1}^{p}(\alpha_{il} - \mu_{\alpha_i})^2}\sqrt{\sum_{l=1}^{p}(\alpha_{jl} - \mu_{\alpha_j})^2}}. \qquad (22)$$

Here μ_{α_i} and μ_{α_j} represent the arithmetic means of the components of the sample vectors α_i and α_j respectively. Pearson correlation coefficient defined in Eqn. 22 is a measure of similarity between two samples in the feature space. The distance between two samples α_i and α_j is computed as $1 - Cor(\alpha_i, \alpha_j)$, which represents the dissimilarity between those two samples.

5.3. Input Parameters

The population size and number of generation used for MODEFC and MOGAFC are 50 and 100 respectively. The crossover probability and mutation factors (F) for MODEFC are set to be 0.8 and 0.7, respectively. The crossover and mutation probabilities for MOGAFC are taken to be 0.8 and 0.3, respectively. The FCM algorithm is executed till it converges to the final solution. For all the fuzzy clustering algorithms m, the fuzzy exponent, is set to 2.0. The results provided corresponding to the MODEFC and MOGAFC are obtained by selecting the solution of the final non-dominated front that provides the best Silhouette index. Results reported in the tables are the average values obtained over 50 runs of the algorithms.

5.4. Performance

Table 1 reports the average $s(C)$ index scores over these 50 runs, for the Leukemia, Colon cancer and Lymphoma data sets. As is evident from the table, the MODEFC-SVM clustering produces the best $s(C)$ index scores compared to the other algorithms. For

Table 1. Average $s(C)$ values over 50 runs for the three microarray data sets.

Algorithms	Leukemia	Colon cancer	Lymphoma
MODEFC-SVM	0.3942	0.5173	0.4083
MODEFC	0.3601	0.4284	0.3682
MOGAFC-SVM	0.3129	0.4357	0.3253
MOGAFC	0.2851	0.4006	0.2902
FCM	0.2453	0.1649	0.2239

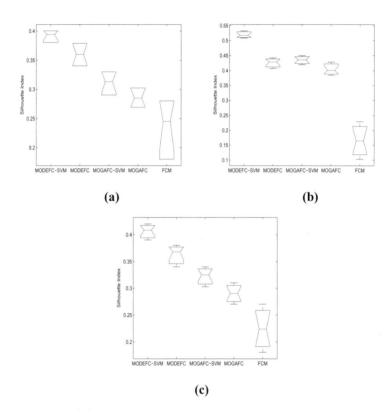

Figure 2. Boxplot of $s(C)$ produces by different clustering algorithms over 50 runs for (a) Leukemia (b) Colon cancer (c) Lymphoma data sets.

example, for the leukemia data set, MODEFC-SVM produces average $s(C)$ index score of 0.3942, whereas the next best $s(C)$ score is 0.3601, provided by MODEFC. Similar results are obtained for all the data sets. In general, it can be noted that MODEFC-SVM consistently outperforms the other algorithms for each of the Leukemia, Colon cancer and Lymphoma data sets in terms of $s(C)$. From the table, it appears that MODEFC-SVM also outperforms single objective counterpart FCM. FCM minimizes the J_m measure. On the other hand MODEFC-SVM minimizes J_m and XB objectives simultaneously. As MODEFC-SVM performs better in terms of cluster validity index ($s(C)$), it is establishes that optimizing multiple criteria simultaneously can yield better clustering rather than the cases when the objectives are optimized separately.

For the purpose of illustration, Fig. 2 shows the boxplot representing the $s(C)$ index

Table 2. $P-values$ produced by $t-test$ comparing MODEFC-SVM with other algorithms.

Data Set	P-value			
	MODEFC	MOGAFC-SVM	MOGAFC	FCM
Leukemia	0.0313	1.5151e-003	1.4147e-004	5.1307e-005
Colon cancer	0.0406	1.6336e-003	1.5303e-004	5.9084e-005
Lymphoma	0.0382	1.5372e-003	1.4815e-004	4.8203e-005

values, over 50 runs of the algorithms for the three data sets considered here. It is evident from the figure that the boxplot corresponding to the MODEFC-SVM clustering method is situated to the upper side of the figure, which indicates that MODEFC-SVM produces higher $s(C)$ index values compared to the other algorithms in all the runs.

6. Statistical Significance Test

To establish that MODEFC-SVM is significantly superior compared to the other algorithms, a statistical significance test called $t-test$ has been conducted at the 5% significance level. Six groups, corresponding to the seven algorithms (1. MODEFC-SVM, 2. MODEFC, 3. MOGAFC-SVM, 4. MOGAFC, and 5. FCM) have been created for each data set.

Each group consists of the $s(C)$ index scores produced by 50 consecutive runs of the corresponding algorithm. As evident from the Table 2, the average values of $s(C)$ values for MODEFC-SVM are better than those for the other algorithms. To establish that this goodness is statistically significant, Table 2 reports the $P-values$ produced by $t-test$ for comparison of two groups (group corresponding to MODEFC-SVM and a group corresponding to some other algorithm) at a time. As a null hypothesis, it is assumed that there are no significant differences between the mean values of two groups. Whereas, the alternative hypothesis is that there is significant difference in the mean values of the two groups. All the $P-values$ reported in the table are less than 0.05 (5% significance level). This is strong evidence against the null hypothesis, indicating that the better mean values of the $s(C)$ index produced by MODEFC-SVM is statistically significant and has not occurred by chance.

7. Conclusion

In this article, an unsupervised cancer data classification technique based on multiobjective differential fuzzy clustering has been developed. Real coded encoding of the cluster centres has been used and two cluster validity measures, namely XB validity index and FCM measure J_m have been simultaneously optimized. The non-dominated solutions produced at the final generation are improved through SVM classification. A novel technique for producing the final clustering result by combining the clustering information of the improved solutions through a majority voting ensemble method is proposed. Results on three publicly available benchmark cancer data sets, viz., Leukemia, Colon cancer and Lymphoma, have been demonstrated. The performance of the proposed technique has been compared with that of MODEFC, MOGAFC-SVM, MOGAFC and FCM clustering methods. The results have been demonstrated both quantitatively and visually. The developed MODEFC-SVM clustering technique consistently outperformed the other algorithms considered here. Also statistical superiority has been established through statistical significance test.

Acknowledgements

This work was supported by the Polish Ministry of Education and Science (grants: N301 159735, N518 409238).

References

[1] A. A. Alizadeh, M. B. Eisen, R. Davis, C. Ma, I. Lossos, A. Rosenwald, J. Boldrick, R. Warnke, R. Levy, W. Wilson, M. Grever, J. Byrd, D. Botstein, P. O. Brown, and L. M. Straudt, 'Distinct types of diffuse large b-cell lymphomas identified by gene expression profiling', *Nature*, **403**, 503–511, (2000).
[2] U. Alon, N. Barkai, D. A. Notterman, K. Gish, S. Ybarra, D. Mack, and A. J. Levine, 'Broad patterns of gene expression revealed by clustering analysis of tumor and normal colon tissues probed by oligonucleotide arrays', *in Proceedings of National Academy of Science, Cell Biology*, **96**, 6745–6750, (1999).
[3] J. C. Bezdek, *Pattern Recognition with Fuzzy Objective Function Algorithms*, Plenum, New York, 1981.
[4] C. A. Coello Coello, 'A comprehensive survey of evolutionary-based multiobjective optimization techniques', *Knowledge and Information Systems*, **1**(3), 129–156, (1999).
[5] K. Deb, A. Pratap, S. Agrawal, and T. Meyarivan, 'A fast and elitist multiobjective genetic algorithm: NSGA-II', *IEEE Transactions on Evolutionary Computation*, **6**(6), 182–197, (2002).
[6] T. R. Golub, D. K. Slonim, P. Tamayo, C. Huard, M. Gassenbeek, J. P. Mesirov, H. Coller, M. L. Loh, J. R. Downing, M. A. Caligiuri, D. D. Bloomeld, and E. S. Lander, 'Molecular classification of cancer: class discovery and class prediction by gene expression monitoring', *Science*, **286**, 531–537, (1999).
[7] A. K. Jain and R. C. Dubes, *Algorithms for Clustering Data*, Prentice-Hall, Englewood Cliffs, NJ, 1988.
[8] U. Maulik and I. Saha, 'Modified differential evolution based fuzzy clustering for pixel classification in remote sensing imagery', *Pattern Recognition*, **42**(9), 2135–2149, (2009).
[9] R. Storn and K. Price, 'Differential evolution - A simple and efficient heuristic strategy for global optimization over continuous spaces', *Journal of Global Optimization*, **11**, 341–359, (1997).
[10] V. Vapnik, *Statistical Learning Theory*, Wiley, New York, USA, 1998.
[11] X. L. Xie and G. Beni, 'A validity measure for fuzzy clustering', *IEEE Transactions on Pattern Analysis and Machine Intelligence*, **13**, 841–847, (1991).

Performance Analysis of Class Noise Detection Algorithms

Borut SLUBAN [a,1], Dragan GAMBERGER [b] and Nada LAVRAČ [c,d]

[a] Jožef Stefan International Postgraduate School, Ljubljana, Slovenia
[b] Rudjer Bošković Institute, Zagreb, Croatia
[c] Jožef Stefan Institute, Ljubljana, Slovenia
[d] University of Nova Gorica, Nova Gorica, Slovenia

Abstract. In real-world datasets noisy instances and outliers require special attention of domain experts. While noise filtering algorithms are usually used to improve the accuracy of induced classification models, our aim is to detect noisy instances to be inspected by human experts in the phase of data understanding, data cleaning and outlier detection. As a result, new algorithms for explicit noise detection have been developed aiming at highest possible precision of noise detection within a reasonable recall threshold. The best performing noise detection algorithms are therefore selected based on a variant of the F-measure combining precision and recall. We use the $F_{0.5}$-score, which weights precision twice as much as recall. New variants of ensemble noise filtering approaches to noise detection, using a consensus voting scheme, have been developed. They proved to be significantly better than elementary noise filters in supporting the domain expert at identifying potential outliers and/or erroneous data instances.

Keywords. class noise, noise handling, performance analysis

Introduction

The quality of real-world data is inevitably subject to errors and other irregularities that are usually referred to as noise. While data measurement errors represent noise which should best be repaired or discarded from the data, other irregularities such as outliers[2] may actually lead to the discovery of intriguing new information. For instance, outlier mining has already proved to have important applications in fraud detection and network intrusion detection [1].

Both types of irregularities, errors and outliers, appear in the data as class noise (errors in class labels) and/or attribute noise (errors in one or more attribute values). Regardless of the type of noise, noise may have an adverse impact on the quality of information retrieved from the data, models created from the data, and decisions made based on the data. A qualitative study of the impacts of both types of noise on reduced classi-

---

[1] Corresponding Author: E-mail: borut.sluban@ijs.si.
[2] In statistics, an outlier is an observation that is numerically distant from the rest of the data, or more formally, it is an observation that lies outside the overall pattern of a distribution.

fication accuracy, increased time complexity and size of the constructed classification or representation models was performed by Zhu & Wu [2].

The main concern of standard noise handling approaches used in machine learning is improved classification accuracy of models induced from the data. In contrast, the focus of this work is on detecting noisy instances to be inspected by human experts in the phase of data understanding and data cleaning. Therefore, our approach should result in highest possible precision of noise detection. Moreover, it should detect a relatively small set of data instances for which one can claim—with high certainty—that they are indeed noisy and worth the expert's inspection time and effort.

This paper presents several variations of elementary algorithms for noise detection as well as ensembles of elementary noise detection algorithms. The main novelty of the paper is the redesign and reimplementation of these algorithms, using new algorithm combinations and settings. Several new instantiations of consensus-based ensemble filtering approaches to noise detection prove to be the best approaches to noise detection, as shown in the experimental evaluation on two noiseless and two real-world datasets with randomly injected artificial noise. Since new noise detection approaches should result in highest possible precision of noise detection and reasonable recall of noisy instances, a variant of the F-measure combining precision and recall is used in the experimental evaluation of the noise detection methods presented in this work. We use the $F_{0.5}$-score, which weights precision twice as much as recall.

The paper is structured as follows. Section 1 presents the related work. Section 2 presents three motivating cases showing the practical utility of expert evaluation of noisy examples. Section 3 describes the experimental setting used in this work. Our experiments started by evaluating several elementary noise filtering approaches. For this purpose, we have intentionally inserted different levels of noise into different datasets and measured the precision and the $F_{0.5}$-score of noise detection for these known sets of noisy examples. The elementary noise filtering algorithms and their results are presented in Section 4. After that we tested several ensemble filtering approaches using the majority and consensus voting schemes; the results presented in Section 5 are very good, both in the sense of achieved precision and $F_{0.5}$-score. Finally, Section 6 presents a comparison of performance of elementary and ensemble filters, where a significant improvement of noise detection performance by the ensemble filters using a consensus voting scheme can be observed over the elementary filters. A summary and ideas for further work are presented in Section 7.

1. Related Work

A lot of attention in data mining and machine learning has been devoted to the topic of noise handling. One of the first approaches was to make inductive learning algorithms resistant to noise in the data. In order to avoid overfitting noisy training data, constructed models (decision trees and rule sets) were pruned so they can get a more general form, thereby reducing the chance of their performance being influenced by noise [3,4,5,6]. However, pruning alone can not avoid all the damaging effects of noise on the structure of the constructed model.

Another common approach to dealing with noise is to eliminate it by filtering of noisy instances before model construction; this has the advantage that noisy instances will not adversely affect the structure of the induced model. In the filtering approach by Brodley & Friedl [7] multiple learning algorithms are applied to induce classifiers which are then used for noise identification. In this approach, a data instance is denoted as noise if it is incorrectly classified by one or more classifiers. A cross-validation approach is used: a training set is partitioned into n subsets and repeatedly $n - 1$ subsets are used for classifier induction and the complementary subset for evaluating the classifiers where misclassified instances are identified as noise. This approach is referred to as the *Classification Filter* approach. In the case of multiple classifiers used, a majority or consensus scheme can be used for noise elimination, meaning that an instance is identified as noise only if it is incorrectly classified by the majority or by all of the classifiers, respectively.

A substantially different filtering approach, the so-called *Saturation Filter* by Gamberger & Lavrač [8], is based on the observation that the elimination of noisy examples reduces the Complexity of the Least Complex correct Hypothesis (*CLCH*) value of the training set. The *CLCH* measure is used to find a saturated training set enabling the induction of a hypothesis that correctly captures the generally valid concept of the domain presented by the available data.

An approach to classification filtering using different levels of agreement among multiple classifiers was proposed by Khoshgoftaar et. al [9] and is referred to as the *Ensemble Filter*. For large and distributed datasets a *Partitioning Filter* was presented by Zhu et. al [10] which initially splits the dataset into n partitions and a learning algorithm is induced on each of them. The n predictions are evaluated on the whole dataset. In the end, voting is used to identify noisy examples. Two modifications of the partitioning scheme were introduced by Khoshgoftaar & Rebours [11]. First, the *Multiple-Partitioning Filter* combines the predictions of multiple classifiers learned on each partition. And second, the *Iterative-Partitioning Filter* builds only one model on each subset, but iterates the filtering process until a given stopping criterion is reached.

All of the mentioned filtering algorithms are mainly used for detecting class noise which should be removed from the data to improve its quality. Teng [12] describes a different approach called *Polishing*. When the noisy instances are identified, instead of removing them, they are repaired by replacing the corrupted values with more appropriate ones. The corrected instances are then reintroduced into the data set.

2. Motivation

Expert evaluation of detected noise can be very useful for domain understanding as well as for the identification of data collection problems. The following real-world cases have been encountered during expert evaluation of patient records, detected as potentially noisy examples during the process of modeling coronary heart disease diagnosis by supervised machine learning methods [13].

- Data measured in a laboratory for two female patients with the same name were accidentally swapped, leading to wrong diagnoses assigned.
- For patients unable to follow a complete testing procedure, test values have been recorded as actual values at the time of test interruption instead of as unknown values.
- There existed a very small set of patients especially strongly reacting to the prescribed drug therapy.

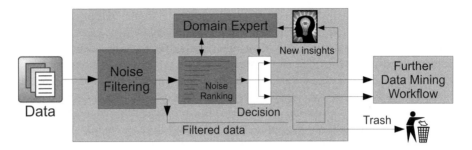

Figure 1. An expert guided filtering tool used in a data mining workflow.

These cases have been recognized due to the fact that available patients' anamnestic, laboratory, and measurement data have suggested a diagnosis different from the diagnosis given by medical practitioners and saved in patient records. These cases indicate that explicit detection and expert evaluation of noisy examples may help in detecting mistakes in data collection, in the detection and correction of inappropriate data collection procedures, and in distinguishing of a very small number of important exceptions (outliers) from a general concept. The real medical domain in which the described cases have been recognized is included in the experimental part of this work under the name Medical-CHD (where CHD stands for Coronary Heart Disease diagnosis problem, explored in collaboration with medical experts). Obviously, the same methodology may be relevant also for other non-medical domains.

Motivated by the above described cases, we have developed a tool which can support the expert in inspecting the data by finding and explicitly presenting noisy instances. The tool offers the expert a choice of noise filtering algorithms, and returns a set of noisy data instances detected. The scheme of the system is shown in Figure 1.

As in our experiments, described later in this paper, consensus-based ensemble filters proved to be the best noise filtering approaches, it was decided that in order to better support the user, visual output can be provided, which ranks instances according to the agreement of being noisy by the majority/consensus of filtering approaches. A visual representation of the list of detected noisy examples, ranked according to the agreement of filtering approaches, is shown in Figure 2.

3. Experimental Setting

In our work we examined different filtering approaches, starting with few basic settings of *Classification Filters* and *Saturation Filters*. For experimental evaluation of their performance we chose two noiseless and two real-world datasets that are specified in Table 1. In all the datasets we injected three different levels of class noise: in 2%, 5% and 10% of the dataset size, class values of instances were replaced.[3] We intentionally chose two artificial noiseless UCI datasets containing instances of all feasible attribute-value configurations of these domains, as a starting point to evaluate the filtering algorithms' ability to detect injected noise. The other two datasets are real-world datasets, containing their own noisy instances. All the datasets have two different class values.

---

[3] Alternatively, attribute noise could have been inserted, but we were motivated by medical domains where false diagnostics is the main concern.

```
Filtering was done on dataset: medical-CHD.tab
Noisy examples (class, id, detected by):

non-CHD  38  __Bayes____RF100____RF500_____SVM____SVMEasy__SatFilt__PruneSF_
--------------------------------- "Consensus Filter" END -------------------
non-CHD  14  __RF100____RF500___SVMEasy__SatFilt__PruneSF_
CHD      29  __RF500____SVM____SVMEasy__PruneSF_
non-CHD 207  __Bayes____SVM____SatFilt__PruneSF_
CHD     210  __RF100____RF500_____SVM____SVMEasy_
---------------- "Majority  Filter" END --------------------------------
non-CHD  26  __Bayes_____SVM____SVMEasy_
non-CHD  37  ___SVM____SVMEasy__PruneSF_
non-CHD  45  __Bayes____SatFilt__PruneSF_
CHD      82  __RF100____RF500___PruneSF_
non-CHD 148  __Bayes____RF100___SVMEasy_
CHD     157  __Bayes____SVM____SVMEasy_
CHD     177  __Bayes____SVM____SVMEasy_
non-CHD  24  ___SVM____SVMEasy_
non-CHD  48  __Bayes_____SVM___
non-CHD 104  __Bayes_____SVM___
non-CHD 119  ___SVM____SVMEasy_
non-CHD 154  _SatFilt__PruneSF_
CHD     162  __Bayes___PruneSF_
CHD     194  __RF500_____SVM___
CHD     212  __Bayes____RF100__
non-CHD   3  __Bayes__
non-CHD  34  _SatFilt_
CHD      74  _SVMEasy_
CHD      93  _PruneSF_
non-CHD 165  _SVMEasy_
CHD     173  _SVMEasy_
CHD     175  _SVMEasy_
CHD     186  ___SVM___

Noise detected by filtering algorithm:
        __Bayes__  detected 12 noisy examples.
        __RF100__  detected  6 noisy examples.
        __RF500__  detected  6 noisy examples.
        ___SVM___  detected 14 noisy examples.
        _SVMEasy_  detected 15 noisy examples.
        _SatFilt_  detected  6 noisy examples.
        _PruneSF_  detected 10 noisy examples.
        Consensus  detected  1 noisy examples.
        Majority   detected  5 noisy examples.
```

Figure 2. Visual representation of noise filtering output. Instances are ranked by the number of filtering algorithms identifying them as noise.

For each of the four datasets and for each noise level we made ten datasets with randomly injected noise. This was done to get more reliable noise filtering results, meaning that each result presented in this work for a specific domain and a specific noise level is the average value of the results obtained from ten separate experiments, each on a dataset with different randomly injected noise. In this way each filtering algorithm was tested not only on four different datasets but actually on 120 datasets, allowing for massive testing of noise detection algorithms despite the relatively small number of selected domains.

Table 1. Datasets used for experimental evaluation of noise filtering algorithms. Datasets TTT and KRKP are taken from the UCI machine learning repository [14], MCHD is described in [13], and NA is described in [15].

Dataset		Instances	Attributes	Type
TTT:	Tic Tac Toe	956	9	noiseless
KRKP:	King-Rook vs. King-Pawn	3196	36	noiseless
MCHD:	Medical-CHD	219	37	real-world
NA:	News Articles	464	500	real-world

4. Elementary Noise Filtering Algorithms

This section presents our reimplementations and the settings of elementary filtering approaches previously mentioned in the literature [7,8].

4.1. Classification Filters

The idea behind the so-called classification filtering approach, presented by Brodley & Friedl [7], is to use a classifier as a tool for detecting noisy instances in data. In this work the simple classifiers used in [7] were replaced by new, best performing classifiers, as the noise filter should, as much as possible, trust the classifier that it is able to correctly predict the class of a data instance. In this way the incorrectly classified instances are considered to be noise. We performed classification filtering in a ten-fold cross-validation manner with the following five different classifiers:

Bayes: Naïve Bayes classifier (used as a baseline filtering algorithm)
RF100: Random forest classifier with 100 decision trees
RF500: Random forest classifier with 500 decision trees
SVM: Support vector machine classifier (with a radial basis kernel function)
SVMEasy: Support vector machine classifier which performs data scaling and parameter optimization

Precision (Pr) and $F_{0.5}$-score ($F_{0.5}$) values of noise detection by different classification filters on the datasets with injected noise are presented in Table 2. In the table the values for noise level and precision are expressed in percentages (%) and the $F_{0.5}$-score is a value on the interval $[0, 1]$.

Table 2. Results of different noise filtering algorithms on four datasets with various levels of injected class noise, where *Pr* stands for precision of detected artificially injected class noise and $F_{0.5}$ for the *F*-measure which weights precision twice as much as recall. The best precision results are shown in italics and the best $F_{0.5}$-score results in bold.

		Classification filters								
	NL	Bayes		RF100		RF500		SVM		SVMEasy	
Dataset	(%)	Pr (%)	$F_{0.5}$	Pr (%)	$F_{0.5}$	Pr (%)	$F_{0.5}$	Pr (%)	$F_{0.5}$	Pr (%)	$F_{0.5}$
TTT	2	4.23	0.052	14.84	0.178	15.65	0.187	54.36	0.597	*54.91*	**0.603**
	5	10.96	0.132	30.98	0.357	32.19	0.370	75.58	**0.793**	75.36	0.791
	10	20.61	0.240	44.17	0.492	45.89	0.508	*86.71*	**0.888**	*86.71*	**0.888**
KRKP	2	12.44	0.150	60.10	0.652	60.20	0.653	18.92	0.225	*79.25*	**0.826**
	5	26.02	0.303	75.98	0.796	77.80	0.812	37.80	0.428	*83.41*	**0.861**
	10	40.93	0.457	84.20	0.866	84.92	0.872	56.97	0.616	*85.00*	**0.873**
MCHD	2	19.73	0.234	36.32	0.416	*41.61*	**0.471**	17.36	0.208	19.64	0.234
	5	40.16	0.454	60.15	0.650	*61.05*	**0.659**	36.51	0.415	37.56	0.427
	10	54.66	0.595	76.24	0.795	*79.10*	**0.822**	52.29	0.572	50.73	0.556
NA	2	18.78	0.224	24.90	0.292	24.65	0.289	27.25	0.318	*33.40*	**0.385**
	5	36.35	0.413	44.91	0.502	46.21	0.515	49.64	0.550	*55.93*	**0.611**
	10	53.13	0.580	64.37	0.685	64.37	0.686	67.42	0.715	*70.33*	**0.740**

The results in Table 2 show that the classification filter with the SVMEasy classifier achieves best precision of noise detection results on all domains, except for the MCHD domain where RF100 and RF500 perform much better. The results in terms of the $F_{0.5}$-score are similar.

4.2. Saturation Filters

Gamberger & Lavrač [8] introduced a concept of a *saturated* training set enabling the induction of a simple hypothesis correctly capturing the concept of the domain presented by the data. By the elimination of noisy examples a non-saturated training set can be transformed into a saturated one. In a saturation filtering algorithm noisy examples are recognized as those enabling the reduction of the complexity of the resulting hypothesis measured by the Complexity of the Least Complex correct Hypothesis (*CLCH* value) of the training set. A practical problem of the saturation filter implementation is to find a complexity measure for a classification model (constructed from a training set) which corresponds to the *CLCH* value and is sensitive enough to enable the filtering algorithm to distinguish between noisy and non-noisy instances.

The saturation filter is constructed from two basic methods. The first one is a *saturation test*. At first it computes the complexity of the classification model for the given training set, then it iteratively excludes only one training example and computes the complexity of a classification model induced from the rest of the training examples. The examples which have the largest effect on reducing the complexity of the classification model by their exclusion are labeled as the *most noisy* and are passed on to the second method. The second method, the *filter*, randomly chooses one among the most noisy examples and finally excludes it from the training dataset, while the others are reused as training examples. These steps are repeated as long as the saturation test finds noisy examples (meaning that a saturated subset has not yet been obtained).

In our implementation a decision tree learner is used to construct models and the number of all nodes in the decision tree is used as the *CLCH* measure of model complexity. The saturation filtering algorithm has to construct as many decision trees as there are instances in the dataset and this is repeated as many times as there are potentially noisy instances. Consequently, this implementation is very time consuming. Therefore we also tested an implementation, named *PruneSF*, that prunes all the leaves of the decision tree supporting only one instance of the first constructed model, removes these instances, and only then starts the filtering phase. This works as a speed up to our first saturation filter implementation. Performance results of noise detection of these two saturation filtering methods can be found in Table 3.

The comparison of results in Table 2 and 3 show that the two saturation filters do not succeed to outperform the best results obtained by the best classification filters on a given dataset, but they do perform better than some of the classification filters. They perform better than SVM, SVMEasy and Bayes (except 10% noise level) on the MCHD domain, and better than SVM and Bayes on the KRKP domain. However, their performance is worse in every aspect on the News Articles domain.

On the other hand, when comparing the two saturation filters, the *SatFilt* has higher precision of noise detection than *PruneSF*, but despite this, the $F_{0.5}$-scores of the *PruneSF* in three cases even exceed those of the *SatFilt*, which means that *PruneSF* achieves better recall than *SatFilt*.

Table 3. Results of two saturation filters on four datasets with various levels of injected class noise.

Data	Noise level (%)	Saturation Filters			
		SatFilt		PruneSF	
		Pr (%)	$F_{0.5}$	Pr (%)	$F_{0.5}$
TTT	2	22.58	0.261	13.52	0.162
	5	38.98	0.422	25.93	0.300
	10	46.63	0.476	34.18	0.379
KRKP	2	81.06	0.818	45.99	0.513
	5	73.74	0.711	48.04	0.531
	10	60.74	0.557	49.11	0.531
MCHD	2	35.16	0.393	25.90	0.300
	5	51.73	0.523	48.53	0.525
	10	61.78	0.557	61.17	0.621
NA	2	23.03	0.256	14.89	0.174
	5	33.05	0.325	29.05	0.319
	10	40.89	0.351	38.87	0.397

4.3. Comparison of performance of elementary filters

To simplify the overview of noise detection results obtained by the two groups of elementary filters, Figures 3 and 4 are introduced to present a comparison of precision of noise detection and the $F_{0.5}$-score obtained by different elementary noise filtering algorithms, respectively. Figures 3 and 4 present results obtained on four domains with 5% injected noise.

By inspecting Figures 3 and 4 we can see that among the elementary noise filters the classification filter using the SVMEasy classifier achieves the best results in terms

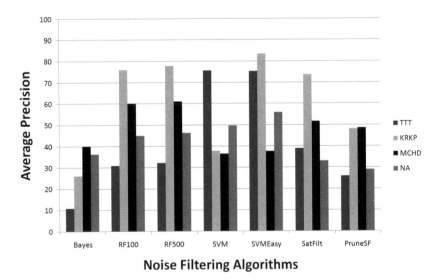

Figure 3. Comparison of precision of noise detection results of different elementary filtering algorithms on four datasets with 5% injected noise.

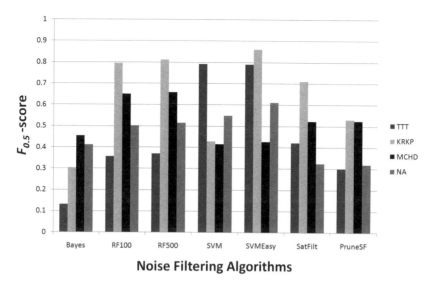

Figure 4. Comparison of $F_{0.5}$-score results of different elementary filtering algorithms on four datasets with 5% injected noise.

of precision and the $F_{0.5}$-score on three out of four domains, whereas for the MCHD domain the classification filter with RF500 performs the best.

The saturation filters on the other hand seem to perform poorly at first, however closer inspection reveals that they perform better on the MCHD domain than Bayes, SVM and SVMEasy, and better than Bayes and SVM on the KRKP domain. *SatFilt* also outperforms Bayes, RF100 and RF500 on the TTT domain.

5. Ensemble Filters

The filtering algorithms presented so far were quite accurate at detecting the injected noise, but they identified as noisy also a lot of regular (non-noisy) instances, therefore having low precision of injected noise detection. To be more convinced that an instance is noisy, predictions of an ensemble of different filtering algorithms should be considered when deciding if an instance should be identified as noise.

We experimented with ensemble filtering in a majority and in a consensus voting scheme. The novelty of this approach is that ensemble filters were constructed from combinations of classification and saturation filters, forming four different groups of filtering algorithms:

Ens1: Bayes, RF100, RF500, SVM, SVMEasy
Ens2: Bayes, RF100, RF500, SVM, SVMEasy, SatFilt, PruneSF
Ens3: Bayes, RF500, SVMEasy, SatFilt
Ens4: Bayes, RF500, SVMEasy, PruneSF

Ensemble filtering using a majority voting scheme (a simple majority of votes of filters in the given ensemble) did not outperform the precision of injected noise detection

Table 4. Results of four ensemble filters use in a consensus voting scheme (made from four different groups of elementary filters) on four datasets with various levels of injected class noise. The best precision results are shown in italics and the best $F_{0.5}$-score results in bold.

Data	NL (%)	Group of filters							
		Ens1		Ens2		Ens3		Ens4	
		Pr (%)	$F_{0.5}$	Pr (%)	$F_{0.5}$	Pr (%)	$F_{0.5}$	Pr (%)	$F_{0.5}$
TTT	2	60.30	0.612	96.89	0.819	91.72	0.794	95.71	**0.849**
	5	79.36	0.770	98.70	0.783	96.15	0.800	95.32	**0.844**
	10	89.09	**0.836**	*100.00*	0.723	98.63	0.753	97.87	0.809
KRKP	2	90.08	0.884	93.59	0.870	*93.88*	0.892	92.50	**0.903**
	5	91.88	0.897	96.82	0.812	*97.09*	0.832	96.70	**0.930**
	10	94.34	**0.911**	97.87	0.696	97.76	0.727	97.27	0.892
MCHD	2	64.38	0.683	89.50	0.832	84.50	0.811	*90.00*	**0.872**
	5	84.85	**0.853**	90.08	0.763	85.08	0.746	88.90	0.851
	10	92.12	**0.904**	96.32	0.685	93.07	0.688	95.89	0.851
NA	2	48.39	0.533	*79.71*	**0.677**	76.68	0.675	60.77	0.597
	5	69.83	**0.730**	77.15	0.550	73.19	0.559	76.03	0.684
	10	83.02	**0.837**	*89.75*	0.510	89.10	0.544	85.15	0.710

achieved by the best elementary filtering algorithms alone.[4] On the other hand, with consensus filtering we significantly improved the precision of noise detection as well as the $F_{0.5}$-scores. Therefore, from now on, when we talk about ensemble filters in this paper we actually refer to ensemble filters using a consensus voting scheme.

An overview of noise detection results of ensemble filters is given in Table 4. The results show that the ensemble filter made of classification filters (Ens1) has the lowest precision of noise detection among all ensemble filters on all domains with all noise levels. But nevertheless it achieves the highest $F_{0.5}$-score (in bold) in half of the experimental settings, for the MCHD and NA domains with 5 and 10% noise level and for the TTT and KRKP domains with 10% noise level. The other three ensemble filters (Ens2-4) used also one or two saturation-based filters, which use a different approach to noise filtering and thereby contribute to the diversity among filters that get to vote on noise identification. If more filters from different filtering approaches agree on an instance being noisy, the precision of noise detection is increased (see the precision results of filters Ens2 to Ens4). This also contributes to best $F_{0.5}$-scores on the TTT and KRKP domains with 2 and 5% noise level and on the MCHD and NA domains with 2% noise level.

6. Comparison of Ensemble and Elementary Filtering Approaches

Ensemble filters constructed from different groups of elementary noise filters presented in Section 5 proved to be a significant improvement over the elementary filters in terms of high precision of noise detection and higher $F_{0.5}$-scores. Figures 5 and 6 present a comparison of the performance results obtained by different elementary and ensemble filters for the case of 5% noise level.

---

[4]Tabular results are available by request from the authors. Due to space limitations they are not presented in this paper.

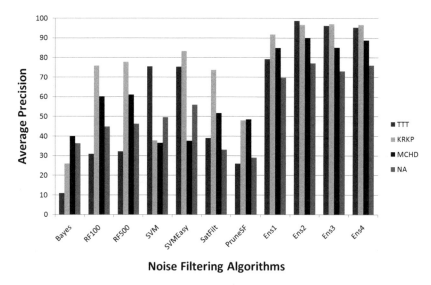

Figure 5. Comparison of precision of noise detection results of different elementary filtering algorithms and ensemble filters on four datasets with 5% injected noise.

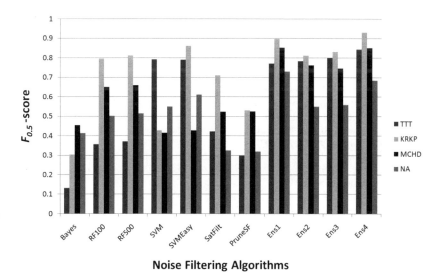

Figure 6. Comparison of $F_{0.5}$-score results of different elementary filtering algorithms and ensemble filters on four datasets with 5% injected noise.

7. Summary and Further Work

We proposed several new elementary and ensemble noise filtering algorithms and evaluated their performance based on their precision of noise detection and their $F_{0.5}$-scores. The evaluation shows that consensus-based ensemble filters composed of a mixture of classification and saturation filters outperform the elementary filters and can thus better support the domain expert in identifying potentially interesting outliers and/or erroneous data instances. In further work we will focus on further development of ensemble filtering approaches and evaluate their capacity for filtering massive amounts of data.

Acknowledgements

The research presented in this paper was supported by the Slovenian Ministry of Higher Education, Science and Technology (grant no. P-0103) and the EU FP7 projects e-LICO and BISON.

References

[1] C. C. Aggarwal, P. S. Yu, 'Outlier Detection for High Dimensional Data', in *Proceedings of the 2001 ACM SIGMOD International Conference on Management of Data*, 37–46, (2001).

[2] X. Zhu and X.Wu, 'Class noise vs. attribute noise: A quantitative study' of their impacts, *Artificial Intelligence Review*, **22**, 177–210, (2004).

[3] J. R. Quinlan, 'Simplifying decision trees', *International Journal of Man-Machine Studies*, **27**, 221–234, (1987).

[4] T. Niblett and I. Bratko, 'Learning decision rules in noisy domains', in *Research and Development in Expert Systems*, ed., M. Bramer. Cambridge University Press, (1987).

[5] J. Mingers, 'An empirical comparison of pruning methods for decision tree induction', *Machine Learning*, **4**, 227–243, (1989).

[6] J. Fürnkranz, 'Pruning algorithms for rule learning', *Machine Learning*, **27**, 139–171, (May 1997).

[7] C. E. Brodley and M. A. Friedl, 'Identifying mislabeled training data', *Journal of Artificial Intelligence Research*, **11**, 131–167, (1999).

[8] D. Gamberger and N. Lavrač, 'Conditions for Occam's razor applicability and noise elimination', in *Lecture Notes in Artificial Intelligence: Machine Learning: ECML-97*, volume 1224, pp. 108–123, (1997).

[9] T. M. Khoshgoftaar, S. Zhong, and V. Joshi, 'Noise elimination with ensemble-classification filtering for software quality estimation', *Intelligent Data Analysis*, **9**(1), 3–27, (2005).

[10] X. Zhu, X.Wu, and Q. Chen, 'Eliminating class noise in large datasets', in *Proc. of the Int. Conf. on Machine Learning*, pp. 920–927, (2003).

[11] T. M. Khoshgoftaar and P. Rebours, 'Generating multiple noise elimination filters with the ensemble-partitioning filter', in *Proceedings of the 2004 IEEE International Conference on Information Reuse and Integration*, pp. 369–375, (2004).

[12] C. M. Teng, 'Correcting noisy data', in *Proceedings of the Sixteenth International Conference on Machine Learning*, pp. 239–248, (1999).

[13] D. Gamberger, N. Lavrač, and G. Krstačić, 'Active subgroup mining: A case study in a coronary heart disease risk group detection', *Artificial Intelligence in Medicine*, **28**, 27–57, (2003).

[14] A. Asuncion and D.J. Newman. UCI machine learning repository, 2007. http://www.ics.uci.edu/~mlearn/MLRepository.html

[15] S. Pollak, 'Text classification of articles on kenyan elections', in *Proceedings of the 4th Language & Technology Conference: Human language technologies as a challenge for computer science and linguistics*, pp. 229–233, (2009).

Relational Graph Mining for Learning Events from Video[1]

Muralikrishna Sridhar, Anthony G Cohn and David C Hogg
University of Leeds, UK, {krishna,agc,dch}@comp.leeds.ac.uk

Abstract. In this work, we represent complex video activities as one large activity graph and propose a constraint based graph mining technique to discover a partonomy of classes of subgraphs corresponding to event classes. Events are defined as subgraphs of the activity graph that represent what we regard as *interesting* interactions, that is, where all objects are actively engaged and are characterized by frequent occurrences in the activity graph. Subgraphs with these two properties are mined using a level-wise algorithm, and then partitioned into equivalence classes which we regard as event classes. Moreover, a taxonomy of these event classes naturally emerges from the level-wise mining procedure. Experimental results in an aircraft turnaround apron scenario show that the proposed technique has considerable potential for characterizing and mining events from video.

Keywords. Video Event Analysis, Unsupervised Learning, Graph Mining

Introduction

An important problem in computer vision is to learn a high level understanding of *complex activities* from videos starting with low level visual analysis. Such an understanding involves learning the *events* which are the natural building blocks of activities, and also their structural partonomic relationships. Complex activities are usually composed of multiple events that may occur in parallel, and overlapping events may share participating objects. Complex activities also contain spurious and missing objects and spatial relationships, arising either due to instability in image processing or due to coincidental occurrences. We address the problem of *unsupervised discovery* of an event partonomy from such complex video scenes.

An important problem in graph mining is to mine interesting subgraphs from a graph database or a single graph. Several techniques [2] have been developed to mine subgraphs that are interesting either because of their frequency or for satisfying certain constraints. In this work, we represent activities as a single large *activity graph*. The key hypothesis is that events (in contrast to noise and coincidental occurrences) correspond to interesting subgraphs of this activity graph and are hence called *event graphs*.

Our earlier work [9] introduced a relational qualitative spatio-temporal representation called an *activity graph* to represent interactions between all objects in a scene. Two measures of interestingness - *frequency* and *a manually defined focus mechanism* were

---

[1] This work is supported by the EPSRC (EP/D061334/1) and the EU FP7 (Project 214975, Co-Friend). We also thank colleagues in the Co-friend project.

Figure 1. Aircraft handling scenario. The highlighted ellipses shows some groups of interacting objects.

used to drive the mining process for discovering event graphs. We have very recently improved the representation in [11] with a more robust variable free activity graph and a generic focus mechanism called *interactivity*, bo.h of which we adopt in this work. In [11], we focussed on learning the most probable interpretation of a video using a generative model. In this work, we adopt a complementary graph mining approach of learning an event partonomy by characterizing *events* as sufficiently *frequent* and *interactive* subgraphs of the activity graph. The underlying hypothesis is that non-events which may be observation noise or coincidences do not tend to possess these systematic properties. This hypothesis is validated on large video data set capturing activities in an aircraft apron.

This paper presents a more formal treatment of the graph mining technique that has been very briefly introduced in our recent short paper in [10], where also a HMM for robustly computing the activity graph is introduced. This paper also formalizes the interactivity measure in terms of graphs, which was originally formulated in terms of tracks [11].

1. Related Work

Much previous work on event analysis represents activities as propositional sequences rather than in a more expressive relational form such as logic or graphs. Sequential representation has been used for unsupervised learning of events using standard frameworks such as pattern recognition techniques [14], graphical models [13] and grammars [7]. However, activities that are composed of events happening in parallel or with shared objects are challenging to mine with sequence based representations [3] or even those that may use logical sequences[1], since sequences do not form a natural representation for such parallel overlapping activities.

These problems are addressed in [9], where we introduced a relational graph based representations of activities for representing interactions between objects. This representation has been further modified in [11] with a more robust variable free activity graph where graph mining frameworks can be directly applied. We also introduced a generic focus mechanism called *interactivity*, both of which we adopt in this work. The following paragraphs provide an overview of graph mining approaches related to this work.

Much of the initial work on graph based learning [15] focussed on frequent subgraphs since the isomorphism of graphs is combinatorially expensive [6]. Despite this restriction, many solutions that efficiently search the space of candidate frequent graphs

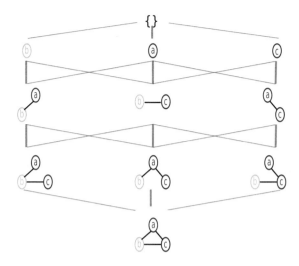

Figure 2. This edge expansion lattice is the search space for mining graphs. In this lattice, each level k corresponds to graphs with k edges.

have been developed. The search space of frequent candidate graphs can be organized as an edge expansion lattice shown in Fig. 2 and graph mining techniques tend to exploit the structure of this lattice in order to efficiently steer the search for frequent or more generally interesting subgraphs.

The authors in [4] introduced SUBDUE, which is a greedy beam search based technique that uses the MDL principle for obtaining a compressed representation of an input graph(s). However, this approach is prone to getting struck in a local optimum as Subdue is based on a greedy search with no backtracking. Depth first approaches such as Gspan[17] dramatically improves the performance by reorganizing the edge expansion lattice into a DFS code tree, where the nodes at the level k corresponds to a candidate subgraph with k edges.

In this work, we adopt a breadth first approach. These approaches, such as AGM [5], FSG [8], tend to search the space to generate candidate $k + 1$ sized graphs by combining *only* pairs of frequent k sized graphs, that share a common $k - 1$ size graph. The frequency of a $k + 1$ size candidate graph is computed by scanning the graph data base or a single graph. By using only frequent graphs to generate candidates at the next level, the search space is kept under control.

The techniques above have been developed mainly for improving scalability on subgraph mining. However, when the graphs are dense, the extraction is not always tractable and results in many uninteresting graphs being generated. CabGin [12] and gprune [19] were paradigms that were introduced to mine constraints in order to reduce the cost of mining and increase the focus on interesting patterns.

However, from a literature survey [2] and experimentation with existing techniques for constraint based graph mining, we have not found that these existing constraints allow us to naturally mine for the desired structures in our domain of application In this work we use the breadth first approach for searching a lattice of candidate event graphs using two interestingness measures – frequency and interactivity – to drive the search.

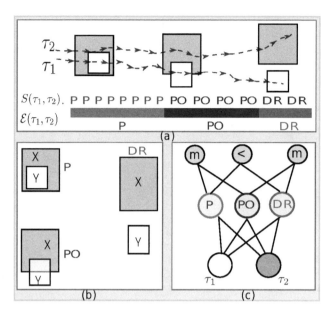

Figure 3. (a) Two tracks, τ_1, τ_2, sequence of spatial relations $S(\tau_1, \tau_2)$ and episodes $\mathcal{E}(\tau_1, \tau_2)$. (b) Spatial relations $\{P, PO, DR\}$. (c) Activity graph for the interaction between τ_1, τ_2.

2. Qualitative Spatio-Temporal Graphs

This section describes the representation of a video activity in terms of an activity graph. The activity graph that represents interactions between all the tracks in a scene. The *key feature* of the activity graph is that it abstracts the spatio-temporal relationships between tracks, away from other metric details of their interaction, such as the spatial locations, temporal duration and object features. Thus, the activity graph facilitates comparison of interactions, since spatio-temporally identical (resp. similar) interactions induce isomorphic (resp. similar) subgraphs in the activity graph.

Tracks. Given a video, object tracks $T = \{..., \tau_i, ...\}$ (e.g. τ_1, τ_2 in Fig. 3.a) are obtained using techniques in [18]. For the purpose of expositional simplicity, we use a scene with just two tracks τ_1, τ_2 shown in Fig. 3.a and represent their interaction in an activity graph shown in Fig. 3.c.

Spatial Relations. For each pair of tracks (e.g. τ_1, τ_2), a sequence (e.g. $S(\tau_1, \tau_2)$ in Fig. 3.a) of qualitative spatial relations, which are either $\{P, PO, DR\}$ (Fig. 3.b) are computed using a HMM, as detailed in [10].

Episodes. For each pair of tracks τ_i, τ_j, the sequence of spatial relations is aggregated to a sequence of *episodes* (e.g. $\mathcal{E}(\tau_1, \tau_2)$ in Fig. 3.a), such that within the temporal interval of each episode, the same spatial relation holds, but a different spatial relation holds immediately before and after this interval. The set of all episodes between the tracks for an activity is given by $\mathcal{E}$.

We define the following functors on episodes (e, e') for later use: (i) $Tracks(e) = \langle \tau_i, \tau_j \rangle$ maps to the respective pair of tracks for e; (ii) $\mathcal{I}(e)$ maps to the temporal interval for e; (iii) $Spatial(e) \in \Re$ maps to the spatial relation for e; (iv) $Temporal(\mathcal{I}(e), \mathcal{I}(e'))$ maps to Allen's temporal relationship between the intervals corresponding to two episodes e, e'.

Activity Graph. An activity graph $G = (V, E, \rho, \eta, \Re, \Im)$ is a directed edge-labelled *layered graph* in which the vertices V are partitioned into 3 layers V^1, V^2, V^3 and edges E exists only between adjacent layers. All our relations are binary, so there are exactly two edges from each node to nodes in the layer below. The function ρ maps the nodes in the second layer to labels which are spatial relations in $\Re$. The function η maps nodes in the third layer to labels which are Allen's temporal relations in $\Im$. The activity graph is described more precisely below.

Layer 1 nodes of the activity graph correspond to tracks (e.g. τ_1, τ_2 in Fig. 3.a). That is, there is a 1-1 mapping $\gamma_1 : V^1 \leftrightarrow \mathcal{T}$. However, these nodes are not explicitly labelled with any details of these tracks, in order to abstract away information specific to these tracks.

Layer 2 nodes of the activity correspond to episodes (e.g. $\mathcal{E}_{\tau_1,\tau_2}$ in Fig. 3.a). That is, there is a 1-1 mapping $\gamma_2 : V^2 \leftrightarrow \mathcal{E}$ where $\mathcal{E}$ is the set of episodes generated by the tracks $T = \gamma_1(V^1)$. These nodes are labelled with spatial relations between the respective pairs of tracks pointed to at layer 1 as shown in Fig. 3.c. So we define a mapping $\rho : V^2 \to \Re$ such that for $v \in V^2$, $\rho(v) = s \in \Re$ is equivalent to:

$$s = Spatial(\gamma_2(v)) \wedge Tracks(\gamma_2(v)) = (\gamma_1(v'), \gamma_1(v''))$$
$$\wedge\, v' \in V^1 \wedge v'' \in V^1 \wedge \langle v, v' \rangle \in E \wedge \langle v, v'' \rangle \in E$$

Layer 3 nodes of the activity graph relate pairs layer 2 episode nodes. That is, there is a 1-1 mapping $\gamma_3 : V^2 \times V^2 \leftrightarrow V^3$. These nodes are labelled with Allen's temporal relations (e.g. m : meets, <: before in Fig. 3.c) between intervals corresponding to the episodes for pairs of layer 2 nodes. So we define a mapping $\eta : E \to \Im$ such that for any $v \in V^3$, $\eta(v) = t \in \Im$ is equivalent to:

$$t = Temporal(\mathcal{I}(\gamma_2(v')), \mathcal{I}(\gamma_2(v''))) \wedge \gamma_3(v) = (v', v'')$$
$$\wedge\, v' \in V_2 \wedge v'' \in V_2 \wedge \langle v, v' \rangle \in E \wedge \langle v, v'' \rangle \in E$$

Graphs or Logic ? In this work, we have adopted a graph based representation of interactions, since several frameworks for efficiently mining from graphs have been developed [2] in the data mining research community. Equivalently, interactions can also be expressed as logical formulae and logic based relational data mining techniques could be potentially applied. For example, the interaction in Fig. 3.a with X, Y as object variables and I_1, I_2, I_3 as temporal variables can be represented logically as:

$$holds(\mathsf{P}(X,Y), I_1) \wedge holds(\mathsf{PO}(X,Y), I_2) \wedge holds(\mathsf{DR}(X,Y), I_3)$$
$$\wedge\ \mathsf{meets}(I_1, I_2) \wedge \mathsf{meets}(I_2, I_3) \wedge \mathsf{before}(I_1, I_3)$$

Note the need for variable repetition in the textual formula compared to the variable free graphical representation where variable co-occurence is represented implicitly by the unique nodes for each object/episode and multiple parent nodes.

3. Event Definition

The activity graph represents an exhaustive set of spatio-temporal relationships between all the tracks from a video. We are interested only in candidate event graphs which are defined as those subgraphs of the activity graph that correspond to semantically meaningful interactions between a set of tracks. Event graphs are defined as those candidate event graphs which are also *maximally frequent* and *sufficiently interactive*. We apply a breadth first graph mining technique detailed in section 3.2 to discover classes of isomorphic event graphs, which are regarded as event classes. The following paragraphs describe candidate event graphs and event graphs before proceeding to the mining technique.

3.1. Candidate Event Graphs.

Candidate event subgraphs of the activity graph are intended to correspond to the conceptual notion of an interaction between a set of tracks. A subgraph of the activity graph is a candidate event subgraph if there exists some interval $\mathcal{I}$ such that it describes all of the spatio-temporal interactions between a set of tracks during $\mathcal{I}$ (and only those interactions). That is to say that, firstly every episode (layer 2 node) involving any of the tracks and temporally connected to $\mathcal{I}$ is present in the subgraph.

$$\forall e \in \mathcal{E} : Tracks(e) \in T \wedge \mathcal{I}(e) \cap \mathcal{I} \neq \emptyset \Rightarrow \exists v \in V^2 : \gamma_2(v) = e$$

Secondly, all temporal relationships involving these episodes are represented as layer 3 nodes in the subgraph, except between those pairs of episodes which are both either (i) initial episodes $\mathcal{E}_i$ for a pair of tracks, or (ii) both final episodes $\mathcal{E}_f$ for a pair of tracks.

$$\forall v', v'' \in V^2 : \langle v', v'' \rangle \notin \mathcal{E}_i \wedge \langle v', v'' \rangle \notin \mathcal{E}_f \Rightarrow \exists v \in V^3 : \gamma_3(v) = \langle v', v'' \rangle$$

This latter condition is necessary to ensure isomorphism of similar events, which only differ in when the initial and final episodes respectively start and end[2].

Maximally Frequent. A candidate event graph H is *frequent* with respect to an activity graph, iff the number of node-isomorphic instances of H in the activity graph is greater than a threshold λ_1. A frequent layered graph H is also *maximally frequent* if there is no other proper super graph H' of H, which is as frequent as H. The value of the thresholds λ_1 for maximally frequent and λ_2 for sufficiently interactive criterion as detailed below, are described further in section 3.2.

Sufficiently Interactive. As already identified in the introduction, we are more interested in candidate events in which all participating tracks are actively engaged uniformly over time. More precisely, we prefer those candidate event graphs in which spatial relations are distributed uniformly (i) *across all subsets of tracks* (for e.g. Fig. 4 (a) rather than Fig. 4 (b)) (ii) *temporally* (for e.g. Fig. 4 (a) rather than Fig. 4 (c)). Preference (i)

---

[2]Note that this does not preclude any of the objects involved in the candidate event graph being involved in other interactions during $\mathcal{I}$ - e.g. answering the telephone while cooking a meal.

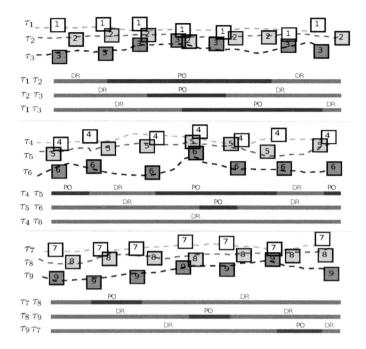

Figure 4. (a) Interactions between all three tracks τ_1, τ_2, τ_3 are uniformly distributed between all subsets of tracks and over the temporal period. (b) Interactions between tracks τ_4, τ_5 are far more than between the other subsets $\{\tau_5, \tau_6\}$ and $\{\tau_4, \tau_6\}$. (c) While interactions are evenly distributed between subsets of tracks, they are less evenly distributed temporally. Here, τ_7, τ_8 interact initially, while τ_9 is a *bystander*, and then τ_7, τ_9 interact while τ_8 is a *bystander*.

means preferring candidate events with fewer tracks involved ignoring extraneous ones. (ii) means preferring candidate events in which interactions between pairs of tracks are tightly interleaved. The following details may be omitted on a first reading.

Pointwise mutual information (PMI)[16] is a well suited measure to model the degree of association between a subset of outcomes belonging to random variables. We model the degree of interaction between a subset of tracks for a candidate event, in terms of the PMI between them. Then we express *interactivity* in terms of pointwise total correlation [16], which is just a weighted sum of PMIs over all subsets of tracks for a candidate event graph. Pointwise total correlation is highest when interactions between the tracks for the candidate event graph H are well distributed, both temporally and amongst subsets of tracks.

Let U_1, U_2, U_3 be the nodes corresponding to the three layers of the a candidate subgraph H of the activity graph. PMI measures the strength of association between a set of tracks ε corresponding to U_1, by comparing the joint probability of interaction $P(\varepsilon)$ between tracks in ε, to the joint probabilities of interactions $P(\varepsilon')$, of all its respective subsets[3] of tracks $\varepsilon' \subseteq \varepsilon$.

---

[3] When ε is a set of two outcomes $\{x, y\}$, we have the well known form $PMI(x, y) = \log(P(x, y)P(x)^{-1}P(y)^{-1})$. This form is generalized to more than 2 variables in equation 1. Note that joint probabilities of subsets $\varepsilon' \subseteq \varepsilon$ with odd cardinality (e.g. $P(x), P(x, y, z)$) are in the denominator since $q_{\varepsilon'} = -1$, while those of even cardinality (e.g. $P(x, y)$) are in the numerator, since $q_{\varepsilon'} = 1$.

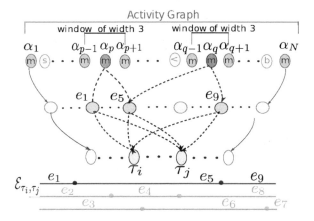

Figure 5. Windows on a sequence of layer 3 meets nodes $\alpha_1, ..., \alpha_N$ of an activity graph are used to measure the joint probabilities for a set of tracks - here just τ_i and τ_j.

$$PMI(\varepsilon) = \log \left(\prod_{\varepsilon':\varepsilon' \subseteq \varepsilon} P(\varepsilon')^{q_{\varepsilon'}} \right) \text{ where } q_{\varepsilon'} = (-1)^{\|\varepsilon'\|} \quad (1)$$

We adopt a well known procedure for estimating the joint probabilities $P(\varepsilon')$ in equation 1, by measuring the proportion of contexts (which is appropriately defined below) in which the interaction between all tracks in the subset ε' are observed, to the total number (N) of all possible contexts. We have found that a window of width w that captures w consecutive interactions of the activity is an appropriate context for our purpose[4]

We formulate the window in terms of the activity graph by first noting that the layer 3 nodes labelled by *meets* capture (points of) interactions between all pair of tracks for the entire activity. We order these nodes temporally (by the end of each initial episode of the *meets* relation) to get a sequence $A = (\alpha_1, ..., \alpha_N)$ as shown in Fig 5, where N is the total number of interactions for an entire activity. A window of width w is simply defined as a subsequence $(\alpha_k, ..., \alpha_{k+w-1})$ of length w.

The probability of interaction $P(\tau_i)$ for a single track $\tau_i \in \varepsilon$, with respect to a candidate event graph H, is just the fraction of the total number of windows $N - w + 1$, in which τ_i interacts with any other track in U_1. We estimate $P(\tau_i)$ from the activity graph, by counting the number windows ω, which contain layer 3 nodes labelled by *meets* in H, such that its descendants in layer 1 contain τ_i and all the layer 2 nodes are in H, and then normalizing by $N - w + 1$.

In a similar manner, the joint probability $P(\varepsilon)$ for any set of tracks ε, with respect to a candidate event graph H, is estimated by counting the number of windows ω of width w, which contain layer 3 *meets* nodes in H, the set of all layer 1 descendants of which are equal to ε and all the descendants in layer 2 are in H, and then finally normalizing

---

[4] A sliding *window* of a fixed width w (e.g. a window of w words) has been regarded as a good context in the statistical natural language processing community, where it is used to compute the association between co-occurring words (e.g. *bread and butter*) by computing their co-occurrence within such windows.

by $N - w + 1$. Let $Desc_1(\bar{\alpha})$ and $Desc_2(\bar{\alpha})$ be the set of all descendants of $\bar{\alpha} \in A$ in layer 1 and layer 2 respectively of the activity graph G. We define the probability $P(\varepsilon) = \frac{\|\beta\|}{N-w+1}$, where β as follows.

$$\beta := \{\bar{\alpha} = \omega \cap U^3 \neq \emptyset \wedge Desc_2(\bar{\alpha}) \subseteq U^2 \wedge Desc_1(\bar{\alpha}) \in U^1\}$$

In Fig. 5, the leftmost sample window of width 3 captures the interaction $meets(e_1, e_5)$ between τ_i, τ_j as shown below the activity graph, as represented by the layer 3 node α_p. Similarly, the rightmost window captures the interaction $meets(e_5, e_9)$ between τ_i, τ_j as shown below the activity graph, and as represented by the layer 3 node α_q. All the descendants of α_p and α_q in layer 1 are equal to $\{\tau_i, \tau_j\}$.

We insert the probabilities of interaction for all subsets $\varepsilon' \subseteq \varepsilon$ in equation 1 to obtain $PMI(\varepsilon)$, and thus measure the PMI for all subsets ε that correspond to the respective layer 1 nodes (tracks) for the candidate event graph H. The PMI for scenarios such as shown in Fig. 4 (a), in which interactions are temporally well interleaved, tend to be higher than scenarios such as Figs. 4 (b),(c), since the former kind are likely to induce more windows, for larger subsets of tracks (and therefore a greater PMI score).

We now compute pointwise total correlation $\xi(H)$ [16], which is the sum of all the pointwise mutual information $PMI(\varepsilon)$ over all subsets ε of tracks H_1 of a candidate event, weighted by their respective joint probabilities $P(\varepsilon)$.

$$\xi(H) = \sum_{\varepsilon : \varepsilon \subseteq H_1} P(\varepsilon) PMI(\varepsilon)$$

The value of $\xi(H)$ is highest when interactions between the tracks for the candidate event graph H are well distributed, both temporally and amongst subsets of tracks. Therefore we regard $\xi(H)$ as a good measure of *interactivity*. We define a candidate event graph H as being *sufficiently interactive* if $\xi(H)$ is greater than a threshold λ_2.

3.2. Mining an Event Taxonomy

We apply a level-wise mining procedure [2] to obtain a hierarchy of event classes, where level i contains event classes with i layer 1 nodes. Initially $i = 2$, and the activity graph is searched to find *frequent* candidate event graphs which are *sufficiently interactive*. Instead of a threshold on frequency and interactivity, the top $k\%$ of frequent and interactive event classes are regarded as the initial set of event classes with 2 nodes in layer 1. The resulting event class graphs form a partonomy ordered by a part of relation between sets of layer 1 nodes, as indicated in the *vertical dimension* of figure 6.

Level 3 event class graphs are found in the same way, by extending the event class graphs from level 2 and so on for each successive level until no maximally frequent and sufficiently interactive event class graphs can be found at the new level. By using the results of level i to form level $i + 1$, efficiency is improved over a search for level $i + 1$ graphs *de novo*.

However there is a second way in which one event class graph can be a subevent of another: the number of layer 1 nodes is identical, but the superclass contains more interactions. This aspect of the hierarchy is indicated in the *horizontal dimension* within each plane in Fig 6. In both cases the subclass is a subgraph of the superclass.

Once the level-wise search terminates, all event classes which are *non-maximal* are eliminated, i.e. those classes all of whose instances appear as instances of a subgraph of its respective superclass. We also eliminate those graphs from the remaining event classes, which are not a subgraph of any graph of the respective superclasses. This way, we obtain event classes all of whose graphs naturally compose their respective superclasses and thus contribute to the entire structure of the taxonomy.

4. Experiments

4.1. Synthetic Data.

We perform experiments with synthetic data where (i) we artificially generate event classes; (ii) simulate tracks that interact according to relations given by these event classes (iii) add noise in these interactions; (iv) try to re-discover these original event classes using the proposed technique by varying the thresholds. These experiments suggested that retaining the top 30% of graphs at each level recovers most of the interesting patterns.

4.2. Evaluation on Real Data.

Experimental Setup. We evaluated the proposed method on approximately 12 hours of video showing servicing of aircraft between flights. There are eight turnarounds consisting of several classes of events such as unloading of luggage and bridge attaching to the plane etc. This dataset was chosen since it clearly contains structured events and these may occur in parallel with objects shared between events (e.g. the plane). The camera positioning for all the eight turnarounds is the same, so we obtain the same view. We first learned models for six visual appearance based object classes (1.Plane 2.Trolley 3.Carriage 4.Loader 5.Bridge 6.Plane Puller) from two turnarounds and then use the tracking techniques from [18] to generate tracks T for the other 6 turnarounds. Note that although the tracked objects have types as a result of the tracking technique we use, the event learning procedure deliberately ignores these in order not to be dependent on them. In principle, it could work equally with untyped tracks.

The Activity Graph We applied the proposed event learning framework to the tracks obtained from the test data of 6 turnarounds of aircraft handling videos. Using the tracks, we obtained the corresponding activity graph which consists of 749700 nodes.

The Event Taxonomy We applied the proposed level wise mining technique to the activity graph and obtained an event taxonomy shown in Fig. 6. The taxonomy represents a hierarchy of event classes, where level i contains event classes (shown as boxes) that represent spatio-temporal relations between i layer 1 nodes (tracks). Within each level i of the taxonomy, events are further organized as a hierarchy, where each sub-level j contain j meets relations, that is to say that they represent j *interactions* between the i tracks. A pair of numbers (i, j) indicating i tracks and j interactions are shown along side each level of the taxonomy. The part-of relations between the event classes are shown using connecting lines which span both *within* and *across* the levels of the event taxonomy.

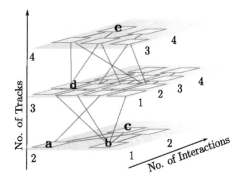

Figure 6. Sample events *a–e* from the taxonomy on the left are shown on the right. In the image sequences on the right, next to the respective bounding boxes are symbols that stand for the object types : b - bridge, p - plane, pp - plane puller, t - trolley, l - loader.

In order to visualize the events in taxonomy, we have sampled some of the event classes marked using letters *a* to *j*, an event graph from each of these classes, and then displayed the corresponding interactions which are also marked with the respective letters *a* to *j*, in Fig. 7.

Qualitative Evaluation by Inspection. From an examination of the taxonomy and the sample interactions shown in Fig. 7, we can make the following observations. To start with, the taxonomy has been able to capture very simple interactions, such as between just two tracks given by the letters *a* and *b*, and their combination (attach-detach) in *c*, as captured by level 2 of the taxonomy. At the next level 3, interactions between trolley,plane and loader in *d,e* represent events that are typical for aircraft handling scenarios, as these interactions are central to the loading operation. The event indicated by *f* typically happens in the beginning of the turnover, when the bridge attaches itself to the plane, followed by the loader attaching itself to the plane, before the loading operations commence. The event given by letter *j* usually takes place in the middle of a turnover when multiple trollies arrive and depart with baggage. Finally, while the event given by *h* spans an entire turnaround, *g,i* take place towards the end as the plane puller attaches to the plane and the bridge detaches from the plane. It can also be seen that the taxonomy in Fig. 6 captures both within-level relations, for example *e* and *d* are a part-of *h*, and across-level relations, for example *d* is a part-of *i*.

From an inspection, as described above, we conclude that the proposed technique has discovered intuitive events in a natural taxonomic relation, that represent *commonly occurring* and *significant* interactions that take place in aircraft handling scenarios.

Quantitative Evaluation with a Pre-defined Set of Events We evaluate the performance of our event mining framework with respect to a pre-determined set of event classes - 1.Unloading 2.Bridge attaches and detaches from the plane 3.Plane Puller(PP) attaches to the plane. These classes were predefined as *interesting* with respect to monitoring tasks that were prescribed by domain experts. A ground truth of the 6 turnarounds for these three classes was defined by domain experts.

The proposed technique was able to discover (i) 51% of the unloading occurrences without and 73% with the HMM developed in our previous work [9] for obtaining robust qualitative spatial relationships; (ii) 66% of the Bridge attach-detach occurrences without the HMM and 83.3% with the HMM; (iii) 83.3% of the plane puller attach occurrences

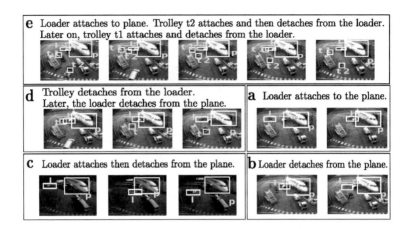

Figure 7. Sample events *a–e* from the taxonomy on the left are shown on the right. In the image sequences on the right, next to the respective bounding boxes are symbols that stand for the object types : b - bridge, p - plane, pp - plane puller, t - trolley, l - loader.

without the HMM and 100% with the HMM; We conclude that despite the imperfect inputs from tracking and absence of any supervision for each of these event classes, the proposed technique has discovered these pre-defined events with a reasonably high accuracy. We also conclude that the proposed HMM based technique for obtaining qualitative spatial relations from potentially noisy tracking output offers a robust alternative for using qualitative spatio-temporal relations to discover events.

5. Summary and Future Work

In this work we have proposed a framework for unsupervised discovery of event class taxonomy from videos with the following features: (i) activity graph – a variable free graph based representation of spatio-temporal relationships for an activity; (ii) interactivity and frequency – two criteria to steer the search for subgraphs of the activity graph which are event-like; (iii) a level wise procedure for automatically constructing an event taxonomy; Experiments to evaluate the proposed technique have shown that the event taxonomy represents intuitive events in a natural taxonomic relations on real video data which are complex due to multiple overlapping events that may share participating objects.

In the future, we plan to use the learned event class taxonomy in several ways. First, the learned classes may be used for detecting events in an unseen video or classifying unseen events as normal or abnormal. We also plan to experiment with techniques described in [9] showing how to learn functional object classes. Further challenges include combining object appearance features as a part of event definitions.

References

[1] Laura-Andreea Antanas, Ingo Thon, Martijn van Otterlo, Niels Landwehr, and Luc De Raedt, 'Probabilistic logical sequence learning for video', in *Preliminary Proceedings of the International Conference on Inductive Logic Programming (ILP-2009)*, (July 2009).

[2] D J Cook and L B Holder, *Mining Graph Data*, Wiley-Interscience, 2007.
[3] Raffay Hamid, Siddhartha Maddi, Amos Johnson, Aaron Bobick, Irfan Essa, and Charles Isbell, 'A novel sequence representation for unsupervised analysis of human activities', *Art. Int. Journal*, (2009).
[4] L. B. Holder, D. J. Cook, and S. Djoko, 'Substructure discovery in the subdue system', in *Proc. of the AAAI Workshop on Knowledge Discovery in Databases*, pp. 169–180, (1994).
[5] A Inokuchi, T Washio, and H Motoda, 'An apriori-based algorithm for mining frequent substructures from graph data', in *PKDD '00: Proc. 4th Eur. Conf. on Principles of Data Mining and Knowledge Discovery*, pp. 13–23, London, UK, (2000). Springer-Verlag.
[6] J. Kabler, U. Schaning, and J. Toran, 'The graph isomorphism problem: Its structural complexity', *Birkhauser*, (1993).
[7] Kris M. Kitani, Yoichi Sato, and Akihiro Sugimoto, 'Recovering the basic structure of human activities from noisy video-based symbol strings', *IJPRAI*, **22**(8), 1621–1646, (2008).
[8] M Kuramochi and G Karypis, 'Frequent subgraph discovery', in *ICDM*, pp. 313–320, (2001).
[9] Muralikrishna Sridhar, Anthony G. Cohn, and David C. Hogg, 'Learning functional object-categories from a relational spatio-temporal representation', in *Proc. ECAI 2008*, pp. 606–610, Amsterdam, The Netherlands, The Netherlands, (2008). IOS Press.
[10] Muralikrishna Sridhar, Anthony G. Cohn, and David C. Hogg, 'Discovering an event taxonomy from video using qualitative spatio-temporal graphs', in *Proc. ECAI 2010*. IOS Press, (2010).
[11] Muralikrishna Sridhar, Anthony G. Cohn, and David C. Hogg, 'Unsupervised learning of event classes from video', *Proc. AAAI*, (2010).
[12] C Wang, Y Zhu, T Wu, W Wang, and B Shi, 'Constraint-based graph mining in large database'.
[13] Xiaogang Wang, Xiaoxu Ma, and Grimson, 'Unsupervised activity perception in crowded and complicated scenes using hierarchical bayesian models', *IEEE TPAMI*, **31**(3), 539–555, (2009).
[14] Xiaogang Wang, Kinh Tieu, and Eric Grimson, 'Learning semantic scene models by trajectory analysis', in *In ECCV (3) (2006*, pp. 110–123, (2006).
[15] Takashi Washio and Hiroshi Motoda, 'State of the art of graph-based data mining', *SIGKDD Explorations*, **5**(1), 59–68, (2003).
[16] S. Watanabe, 'Information theoretical analysis of multivariate correlation', *IBM Journal of Research and Development*, **4**, 66+, (1960).
[17] Xifeng Yan and Jiawei Han, 'gspan: Graph-based substructure pattern mining', in *ICDM '02: Proceedings of the 2002 IEEE International Conference on Data Mining*, p. 721, Washington, DC, USA, (2002). IEEE Computer Society.
[18] Qian Yu and Gerard Medioni, 'Integrated detection and tracking for multiple moving objects using data-driven mcmc data association', *Motion and Video Computing, IEEE Workshop on*, **0**, 1–8, (2008).
[19] Feida Zhu, Xifeng Yan, Jiawei Han, and Philip S. Yu, 'gprune: A constraint pushing framework for graph pattern mining', in *PAKDD*, eds., Zhi-Hua Zhou, Hang Li, and Qiang Yang, volume 4426 of *Lecture Notes in Computer Science*, pp. 388–400. Springer, (2007).

A Workbench for Anytime Reasoning by Ontology Approximation

With a case study on instance retrieval

Gaston TAGNI [1], Stefan SCHLOBACH, Annette TEN TEIJE,
Frank VAN HARMELEN and Giorgios KARAFOTIAS

Department of Computer Science, Vrije Universtiteit Amsterdam, The Netherlands

Abstract. Reasoning is computationally expensive. This is especially true for reasoning on the Web, where data sets are very large and often described by complex terminologies. One way to reduce this complexity is through the use of approximate reasoning methods which trade one computational property (eg. quality of answers) for others, such as time and memory. Previous research into approximation on the Semantic Web has been rather ad-hoc, and we propose a framework for systematically studying such methods. We developed a workbench which allows the structured combination of different algorithms for approximation, reasoning and measuring in one single framework. As a case-study we investigate an incremental method for instance retrieval through ontology approximation, and we use our workbench to study the computational behaviour of several approximation strategies.

Keywords. Approximate Reasoning, Anytime Reasoning, Description Logics, Ontologies, Semantic Web

1. Introduction

Motivation: Since the introduction of anytime algorithms in [1] it has become widely accepted that they are attractive for many reasoning tasks in AI [9]. Instead of producing the perfect answer after a long period of computation, they allow a reasoning task to progress gradually, producing output of increasing quality as runtime progresses. This allows to produce meaningful output under time-pressure, and to save time for applications where an approximate answer is already sufficient.

A recent set of reasoning challenges has been posed to AI by Semantic Web applications. These applications typically use large and complex ontologies for searching information on the Web, personalising Web sites, matchmaking between web-services, etc. They rely on reasoning in languages based on Description Logics [3], such as the retrieval of instances of a specified class (called instance-retrieval). Many of these Semantic Web applications are performed under time pressure (eg. because of user-interaction). Often approximate answers are sufficient, given the incomplete and noisy nature of the

---

[1]Corresponding Author: Gaston Tagni, Vrije Univesiteit Amsterdam, De Boelelaan 1081a, 1081 HV Amsterdam, The Netherlands; E-mail: gtagni@few.vu.nl.

data on the Web. Clearly approximate anytime reasoning is an important step towards a scalable Semantic Web.

A workbench for studying ontology approximation: The need for approximation on the Semantic Web raises the challenge to develop algorithms for anytime Semantic Web reasoning, and several attempts have been made to find suitable approximation strategies and study their effects in practice [7,2,6,8]. Until now, this work has been limited in scope, has had a rather ad-hoc character (lacking a general framework for theory and application), and most importantly, results have often been inconclusive and show a need for a more thorough experimental analysis. A systematic evaluation of strategies and heuristics is challenging, and the results until now have been difficult to reproduce and compare. In this paper, we introduce a framework and a workbench for testing approximation algorithms systematically that will make the development of such methods more easy, and thus increases their chances of adoption and deployment.

To this end, we design a workflow consisting of a number of independent modules, which can be instantiated for different reasoning tasks and approximation strategies. The crucial elements of this workflow are separate modules for *approximation*, *reasoning* and *evaluation*. The first allows implementing approximation strategies based on subsetting (eg. subsets of axioms, or of vocabulary), the second allows to specify a specific reasoning task (eg. instance retrieval, ontology classification, or consistency checking), and the final module allows to implement a suitable evaluation metric. This metric results in a novel type of gain diagrams, which are a further contribution of this paper. This 3-step design is the basis for an adaptable workbench, which is implemented and made available online.

A case-study in Instance Retrieval: We evaluated our framework with a study of a particular Semantic Web reasoning task: Instance Retrieval. For this exercise we studied the behaviour of half a dozen different approximation strategies on over 30 different real-world ontologies available on the Web.

Finding instances of a concept with respect to a complex ontology is known to be a computationally difficult task. Very often users are satisfied with an algorithm that returns some, but maybe not all, answers very fast, instead of waiting for the full answer-set to be returned after a longer wait. This makes instance retrieval an interesting case-study for our anytime approximation framework.

The basic idea of our approach is to select a subset of the vocabulary of an ontology, use this set to create a new, approximate version of the ontology by rewriting the set of terminological axioms and to gradually increase the size of the vocabulary. Instances of the ontology can then be retrieved using the approximate version of the ontology. This mechanism yields an anytime algorithm for retrieving instances of an ontology that produces sound but incomplete results where completeness increases as time progresses and the size of the vocabulary increases. This paper presents the results of a series of experiments aimed at empirically evaluating a number of selection strategies in order to discover how each strategy affects the anytime retrieval of instances.

Related work: The idea of selecting a subset of the vocabulary has been formalised as approximate deduction in [5]. These results hace been used in earlier work on approximate subsumption by [2] and [7], and we will apply a rewrite procedure defined in [7]. The essential difference with our approach is that in [2,7] the approximation is used to reformulate the *queries*, whereas we use it to approximate the *ontology*. The results in [2] are mostly negative, while [7] does not report any empirical results. Our experiments

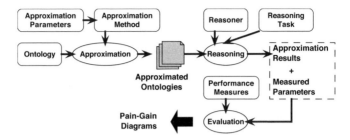

Figure 1. 3-step workflow for approximate reasoning experiments; every square box can be changed per experiment

show that approximating the ontology produces much better anytime behaviour then the reported results on approximating the query. Related to the topic of approximate Abox reasoning is also the work by [4] where the authors propose a soundness-preserving approximate reasoning approach for OWL2 ontologies. The main difference with our work is that such approach is based on a language weakening technique.

Findings: An observation that confirmed previous, less thorough studies, is that structural syntactic approximation can work astonishingly well in a number of case, but not in all. Although we believe to have tested the most natural selection strategies we have not found a strategy that works universally. Whether or not approximation works at all depends mostly on the ontology and seems mostly independent of the strategy used, while the actual amount of gains are strongly dependent on the particular strategy that is being used.

What to expect from this paper: This paper has two major contributions, a domain specific one, where we provide an assessment of approximation strategies for a particular Semantic Web reasoning task, and a methodological one by introducing a standardised way to perform comparative experiments for related reasoning problems in a greatly simplified fashion through our workbench.

In the following we will first describe our framework in Section 2, before describing our case-study on approximate instance retrieval in Section 3, including the necessary theory, the experimental setup and results, as well as our findings. We will analyse the pros and cons of our framework in Section 4 before we conclude in Section 5.

2. Framework

Our framework consists of a pipeline of three steps (see Figure 1), resulting in a new type of gain diagrams. These three steps allow to define (i) the particular approximation heuristic to be used, (ii) the reasoning task to which it should be applied, and (iii) the definition of a performance measure for evaluating the heuristic. This section describes each of these steps and the resulting gain diagrams.

2.1. Approximation Step

The foundational results from [5] show that performing an approximate reasoning task on a logical theory can be transformed into executing a classical reasoner on a suitably approximated theory. Hence, the purpose of the approximation step is to take an ontology O, an approximation method M and to return a sequence of approximations $O_1, O_2, ..., O_n$ computed according to M and sorted according to some criterion. Approximation methods can take as input multiple parameters that drive the approximation method. For instance, the approximation method used in our experiments takes as input a parameter that indicates the specific vocabulary selection strategy to be used for computing the approximations. Approximations can be sorted according to different criteria such as their completeness w.r.t the original ontology (from less complete approximations to more complete ones) or their size in terms of axioms. The framework imposes no restrictions on the criteria used for sorting approximations. The only restriction imposed in this respect is that such an ordering scheme reflects the complexity of the problem one is trying to solve. Very often, such approximations can be phrased in terms of a selection method, operating on either the symbols appearing in an ontology (vocabulary selection), or on the set of axioms in an ontology (axiom selection), operating on either or both of the A-box and T-box of the ontology. Our framework does not depend on a particular strategy: the only requirement is that for a given ontology, the approximation module returns a sequence of approximations that follow a certain ordering schema.

Although our framework imposes no further constraints on the approximation step except that it produces ontologies that can be used in the reasoning step, some formal properties of such selection steps are desirable. Let O^* denote the semantic closure of an ontology, ie. all facts that can be derived according to its semantics. We then have *soundness* if each $O_i^* \subseteq O^*$, ensuring that the approximate results are correct (although possibly incomplete); *monotonicity* if $O_i^* \subseteq O_{i+1}^*$ for all $i = 1, ..., n-1$, ensuring that the successive approximations get more correct; and *completeness* if $O^* = O_n^*$, at which point the approximation has reached perfect quality.

2.2. Reasoning Step

Approximation can be applied to different reasoning problems such as Instance retrieval or Classification. All that our framework requires is that the reasoning step takes as input an ontology, and returns *answer-sets*. These answer sets could be instance-class memberships (for instance retrieval) or class-class subsumptions (for classification). It is these answer-sets that determine the quality of the approximation, and the computational efforts which determine the price one has to pay.

2.3. Evaluation Step

In the analysis step of our framework we specify the notions of success and costs. These performance measures can be eg. the standard notions of recall (the number of retrieved facts in relation to all possible findings), or precision (the correctness of the given answers), or some more non-standard notion of semantic proximity of the approximate answers to the perfect answers. More generally, we propose a notion of *gain*, which abstracts over the detailed measures and describes the results as ratios between possible and actual findings. *Pain* is the orthogonal notion describing the ration between the costs of reasoning over an approximate ontology versus the non-approximate one. For specific examples of pain one could think of costs in terms of runtime or other computational resources, such as memory, user-interaction, database access, etc.

Gain-Pain diagrams: Obviously, we are interested in whether the gain (success-ratio

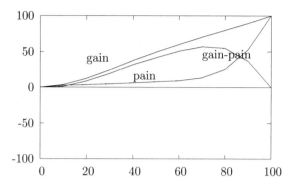

Figure 2. Gain, Pain and Gain-Pain curves

of current answers against perfect answers) outweighs the pain (cost-ratio of current answers against perfect answers), in other words in the gain-pain difference. This ratio is plotted in our gain-pain diagrams which show at which point of the anytime computation the gain outweighs the pain (or not, as the case may be, and by how much). Figure 2 illustrates these measures. As the quality of the approximation increases along the x-axis from $0 - 100\%$, in this example the gain increases linearly while the pain increases much more slowly initially, and rises more sharply in the final 20%. The combined performance measure (pain-gain curve) is calculated as the difference between these two, with the best performance achieved at about 75% of the approximation where the proportional gain maximally outweighs the proportional pain.

The ideal gain-pain curve rises sharply for the initial approximations of the input representing the desired outcome of a high gain and low pain in the early stages of the algorithm. Although such a convex gain-curve is the most ideal, even a flat gain curve at $y = 0$ is already attractive, because it indicates that the gains grow proportionally with costs, giving still an attractive anytime behaviour.

Notice that gain-curves always start in $(0, 0)$, since for the empty input both gain (eg. recall) and pain (eg. runtime) are 0, hence their difference is 0. Gain curves always ends in $(100, 0)$, since for the final perfect approximation both recall and runtime are 100%, hence their difference is again 0. Also notice that gain-pain curves can be negative when the proportional pain outweighs the proportional gain for certain approximations.

In our experiments in section 3, we will run different approximation heuristics on an ontology, and we will report their results in terms of gain-pain curves. It is not obvious how to compare such curves. Higher curves are to be preferred over low curves, and curves with an early peak are to be preferred over curves with a late peak. In order to compare the curves of multiple strategies we associate the curve G with a *gain-score*, defined as the product of the area under the gain-curve and the point at which the absolute gain is maximal, more specifically $gainscore = area * (1 - P)$, where P is the percentage of vocabulary at which the absolute gain is maximal. In this way we reward strategies with a flat gain-curve that reach maximum gain earlier in the reasoning process (and of course, gain-scores can be negative in case the pain outweighs the gain).

3. Approximate Instance Retrieval

In this section we report on a series of experiments aimed at studying a specific reasoning task, namely: instance retrieval. This is done by using the framework introduced in the previous section and instantiating its three main components. In particular, the *approximation* component is instantiated with a variety of vocabulary selection strategies to produce different sound but incomplete approximations of the same ontology. The *reasoning task* component is instance retrieval, and the *evaluation* module is instantiated with comparing recall of instance retrieval against runtime.

3.1. A Sound Approximation for Instance Retrieval

In this section we will define a sound and incomplete approximation for anytime instance-retrieval. An ontology is a set of axioms. To simplify the presentation in the paper these axioms have the form $A_i \sqsubseteq B_i$, with A_i and B_i built from atomic concepts and a number of logical operators, eg. conjunction, disjunction, negation, role and number restrictions, etc. Range and domain restrictions can be translated into this form. Axioms not involving classes exist, but remain unchanged in the approximation. The semantics of an ontology is given as a set of interpretations, ie. functions with domains that satisfy all its axioms, called *models*.

Given an ontology $O = (\mathcal{T}, \mathcal{A})$, consisting of a terminological part (called TBox), and an assertional part (called ABox), the task of instance retrieval is to find all individuals i in O which belong to a particular concept C for all models of O, written as $O \models i : C$. The basic intuition of our approximation is that if we rewrite a terminology $\mathcal{T}$ to a weaker $\mathcal{T}'$ then establishing $\mathcal{T}', \mathcal{A} \models i : C$ is sufficient to establish $\mathcal{T}, \mathcal{A} \models i : C$ for any individual i of an ABox $\mathcal{A}$ and concept C. In other words, entailment under $\mathcal{T}'$ is a sound (but incomplete) approximation of entailment under $\mathcal{T}$.

We will now define a rewrite procedure that we will apply to every axiom $A_i \sqsubseteq B_i$ of $\mathcal{T}$ in order to obtain $\mathcal{T}'$. Following the ideas [5] we define an *approximation set* S consisting of a subset of the vocabulary used in $\mathcal{T}$. In this paper we will only approximate concept names. Role and individual names will remain unchanged. The rewrite procedure will restrict the vocabulary of $\mathcal{T}$ only to atoms that appear in S.

Definition 1 ([7]) *The rewrite procedures* $(\cdot)^S$, $(\cdot)^{S+}$ *and* $(\cdot)^{S-}$ *are defined as follows*[2]:
$(A \sqsubseteq B)^S = A^{S-} \sqsubseteq B^{S+}$,

$$
\begin{aligned}
A^{S-} &= A \text{ if } A \in S & A^{S+} &= A \text{ if } A \in S \\
A^{S-} &= \bot \text{ if } A \notin S & A^{S+} &= \top \text{ if } A \notin S \\
(\neg C)^{S-} &= \neg C^{S+} & (\neg C)^{S+} &= \neg C^{S-} \\
(C \sqcap D)^{S-} &= C^{S-} \sqcap D^{S-} & (C \sqcap D)^{S+} &= C^{S+} \sqcap D^{S+} \\
(C \sqcup D)^{S-} &= C^{S-} \sqcup D^{S-} & (C \sqcup D)^{S+} &= C^{S+} \sqcup D^{S+} \\
(\exists R.C)^{S-} &= \exists R.C^{S-} & (\exists R.C)^{S+} &= \exists R.C^{S+} \\
(\forall R.C)^{S-} &= \forall R.C^{S-} & (\forall R.C)^{S+} &= \forall R.C^{S+}
\end{aligned}
$$

---
[2] Only the rewrite rules for the operators in $\mathcal{ALC}$ are reproduced here. They can easily be extended to full OWL.

Both $(\cdot)^{+^S}$ and $(\cdot)^{-^S}$ terminate as the complexity of the formula decreases in any application of the rules. The TBox $\mathcal{T}^S$ is obtained by applying this rewrite procedure to every axiom in $\mathcal{T}$.

We will use a small example to illustrate our idea.

Example 1 *Let* $\mathcal{T} = \{A \sqsubseteq B \sqcap C, B \sqsubseteq D, C \sqsubseteq E \sqcup D\}$. *If we take as successive approximation sets* $\emptyset, \{B\}, \{A, B\}, \{A, B, D\}, \{A, B, C, D\}, \{A, B, C, D, E\}$, *then rewriting produces approximate TBoxes as follows:*

$$
\begin{aligned}
\mathcal{T}^{\emptyset} &= \{\bot \sqsubseteq \top \sqcap \top, \bot \sqsubseteq \top, \bot \sqsubseteq \top \sqcup \top\} \\
\mathcal{T}^{\{B\}} &= \{\bot \sqsubseteq B \sqcap \top, B \sqsubseteq \top, \bot \sqsubseteq \top \sqcup \top\} \\
\mathcal{T}^{\{A,B\}} &= \{A \sqsubseteq B \sqcap \top, B \sqsubseteq \top, \bot \sqsubseteq \top \sqcup \top\} \\
\mathcal{T}^{\{A,B,C\}} &= \{A \sqsubseteq B \sqcap C, B \sqsubseteq \top, C \sqsubseteq \top \sqcup \top\} \\
\mathcal{T}^{\{A,B,C,D\}} &= \{A \sqsubseteq B \sqcap C, B \sqsubseteq D, C \sqsubseteq \top \sqcup D\} \\
\mathcal{T}^{\{A,B,C,D,E\}} &= \mathcal{T}
\end{aligned}
$$

This rewrite procedure is taken from [7]. The essential difference is that in [7] the procedure is used to approximate the *queries* (ie. $\mathcal{T} \models \phi^S$), whereas we use it to approximate the *ontology* (ie. $\mathcal{T}^S \models \phi$).

The following property is crucial to establish that $\mathcal{T}^S$ is a sound approximation of $\mathcal{T}$:

Theorem 1 (From [7]) *For any axiom* $C \sqsubseteq D$: *if* $C^{\mathcal{I}} \subseteq D^{\mathcal{I}}$ *then* $(C^{S-})^{\mathcal{I}} \subseteq (D^{S+})^{\mathcal{I}}$ *for any interpretation* $(\cdot)^{\mathcal{I}}$.

The intuition behind this is that $(C^{S-})^{\mathcal{I}} \subseteq C^{\mathcal{I}}$ (since the atoms in C not listed in S have been replaced by $\bot$), and $D^{\mathcal{I}} \subseteq (D^{S+})^{\mathcal{I}}$ (since the atoms in B_i not listed in S have been replaced by $\top$). The full proof of this is given in [6]. From this the following is immediate:

Corrolary 1 (Soundness) *For any subset S of the concept-names occurring in $\mathcal{T}$, and individual names i occurring in an ABox $\mathcal{A}$: if* $(\mathcal{T}^S, \mathcal{A}) \models i : C$ *then* $(\mathcal{T}, \mathcal{A}) \models i : C$

If $S = \emptyset$, $\mathcal{T}^S$ is reduced to the empty (trivial) TBox, entailing only tautologies. Similarly, if S contains all atoms from $\mathcal{T}$ then the rewrite operation is the identity, and the consequences of $\mathcal{T}^S$ equal those of $\mathcal{T}$. Note that in these experiments we do not approximate the ABox. Although risking to overload notation we will use D^S to abbreviate $\{i \in \mathcal{A} \mid (\mathcal{T}^S, \mathcal{A}) \models i : D\}$, ie. the set of all individuals classified as instances of D wrt. the approximated TBox $\mathcal{T}^S$. In general, if S grows, the entailments from $\mathcal{T}^S$ become more complete:

Theorem 2 (Monotonicity) *If* $S_1 \subseteq S_2$ *then* $(\mathcal{T}^{S_1}, \mathcal{A}) \models i : C$ *entails* $(\mathcal{T}^{S_2}, \mathcal{A}) \models i : C$. *In other words,* $C^{S_1} \subseteq C^{S_2}$ *for any C.*

This is because any model for $(\mathcal{T}^{S_2}, \mathcal{A})$ is necessarily also a model for $(\mathcal{T}^{S_1}, \mathcal{A})$.

Anytime instance retrieval We can now obtain an anytime algorithm for instance-checking wrt. a TBox $\mathcal{T}$ and an ABox $\mathcal{A}$ by starting out with finding instances wrt. $\mathcal{T}^S$ and $\mathcal{A}$ for an initial (typically small) set S. We then increase S and repeat the procedure until either the number of retrieved instances is sufficient for our purposes, or we run out of available computing time, or S contains all atoms from $\mathcal{T}$. Theorem 2 guarantees that the output of this algorithm monotonically improves during the iteration, as is typically required of anytime algorithms [9]

Example 2 *Let* $\mathcal{T} = \{A \sqsubseteq B \sqcap C, B \sqsubseteq D, C \sqsubseteq E \sqcup D\}$ *be defined as above, and* $\mathcal{A} = \{i : A, j : C \sqcap \neg E, k : B\}$. *Retrieving all instances of* D *returns the set* $\{i, j, k\}$. *Taking the ordering from the previous example we get*

$D^{\emptyset} = D^{\{B\}} = D^{\{A,B\}} = D^{\{A,B,C\}} = \emptyset$
$D^{\{A,B,C,D\}} = \{i, k\}$
$D^{\{A,B,C,D,E\}} = \{i, j, k\}$

This example illustrates that for small values of S, $\mathcal{T}^S$ is a very incomplete approximation of $\mathcal{T}$; with increasing S, $\mathcal{T}^S$ becomes a less incomplete approximation; and when S contains all atoms from $\mathcal{T}$, $\mathcal{T}^S$ equals $\mathcal{T}$. The instance-retrieval algorithm given above increases S in successive iterations. The choice of how to increment S determines how quickly the approximation approaches the classical result. This is shown in the following example:

Example 3 *Let* $\mathcal{T}$ *be the same as in ex. 1, but now with the sequence* $S = \emptyset, \{B\}, \{B, D\}, \{A, B, D\}, \{A, B, C, D\}, \{A, B, C, D, E\}$. *This yields the following set retrieved instances for* D:

$D^{\emptyset} = D^{\{B\}} = \emptyset$
$D^{\{B,D\}} = \{k\}$
$D^{\{A,B,D\}} = D^{\{A,B,C,D\}} = \{i, k\}$
$D^{\{A,B,C,D,E\}} = \{i, j, k\}$

3.2. Experimental Setup

The example from the previous section illustrates that different approximation strategies result in different anytime behaviours of the retrieval algorithm. This raises the question on what would be a good approximation strategy. In this section, we will define different strategies and we will use the 3-step framework from section 2 to investigate their resulting anytime behaviour on a number of realistic ontologies.

3.2.1. Selection Strategies

Given a vocabulary set V of atomic concept names, a selection function returns a subset $V_i \subseteq V$. In an anytime setting, the set V_i is computed from those concepts in V that were not selected previously. In our experiments we tested six selection functions, namely:

- *Random (R):* This function randomly selects a set of atomic concept names.
- *Most Referenced (MR):* This function selects concept names according to the number of times they are appear in terminological axioms.
- *Most Members (MM):* In each approximation step concept names are sorted according to the number of instances that were retrieved in the previous step. Initially, concepts are sorted according to the Most References strategy. The rationale behind this strategy is to select as early as possible those concepts that can produce the largest number of instances.

- *Restriction Class (RC):* This function gives higher priority to the fillers of quantified concept expressions and to their respective sub concepts. If the number of such elements is less than desired number M the additional concepts are chosen based on the number of instances asserted in the assertional part of the ontology. The rationale of this strategy is that property restrictions are used for defining classes implicitly. Consequently, these classes may contribute to retrieving a large number of instances. The main disadvatange of this strategy is that not every class in an ontology is defined through property restrictions, a characteristic that makes this strategy incomplete. Therefore, as with the previous strategy this one needs to be complemented with another strategy for selecting classes that are not defined through property restrictions.
- *Most Direct Subclasses (MDS):* This function selects atomic concepts based on the number of direct subclasses they have. The first time this strategy is used, atomic concepts are sorted in decreasing number of direct subclasses and each successive call to this function returns the next set of concepts. As with the Most Referenced strategy concepts can be sorted only once at the beginning of the anytime reasoning process.
- *Least Direct Subclasses (LDS):* This function is the opposite of the MDS function. The rationale for this strategy is that concepts with the least number of subclasses are more specific and tend to be used to annotate large number of individuals.

3.2.2. Reasoning Step

Most of our tests were performed using Pellet (v2.0.0rc7) [3], a well-known open source DL reasoner capable of dealing with OWL 2 ontologies. Although Pellet performed well with many of the ontologies tested it showed some problems when reasoning with some of them, eg. LKIF, for which the reasoner was unable to classify the ontology even after a long period of time. To overcome these issues we used FaCT++ (v1.3.0) [4], another standard DL reasoner. All the tests were performed on a dual-core AMD Opteron processor at 2.8Ghz. with 32Gb of RAM running Linux and Java runtime 1.6 Update 12.

Given an ontology $O = (T, A)$ with Tbox T and Abox A and a selection strategy F we generated a number of approximations T_i^S of T, each of them based on a vocabulary set S with a fixed 10% step-size. For each pair (T_i, A) we ran the reasoner ten times and measured the average value of several parameters such as recall, classification time, approximation time and instance retrieval time, among others. All experiments were run as "contract algorithms" [9], that is: creating fresh runs for each iteration, not incrementing from the previous iteration (which would constitute an "interruptable algorithm").

3.2.3. Performance Measures

In order to evaluate how each strategy influences the instance retrieval process we need to define a performance measure. Notice that since the approximation algorithm is sound we only need to measure completeness. Measuring the degree of completeness is equivalent to measuring recall, ie. the ratio between the number of instances retrieved and the total number of instances in the ontology (see Eq. (1)).

---

[3] http://clarkparsia.com/pellet/
[4] http://owl.man.ac.uk/factplusplus/

Table 1. Some properties of the ontologies used in our experiments

	DL expressivity	#Axioms	#∀	#∃	#⊓	#⊔	#¬
Galen-100	SHOIQ(D)	874	3734	5606	1951	784	0
BVA	SHIF	1485	0	5	16	2	1
FHHO	ALCHIF(D)	2216	0	0	72	0	0
GRO	ALCHIQ(D)	2433	236	37	67	16	1
LKIF	SHIN	1014	47	97	23	7	2
myGrid-v1	SHOIN	2204	0	289	274	12	1
Brenda	ALE	54212	0	948	0	0	0

$$Recall = \frac{\#InstancesRetrieved}{\#Instances} \quad (1)$$

Cost is measured in terms of the runtime. This time includes classification, instance retrieval and approximation time.

3.2.4. Datasets

In our experiments we used an extensive collection of well-known ontologies among which we included: LKIF, an ontology of basic legal concepts; BVA, a basic vertebrate anatomy ontology ; the Family Health History Ontology (FHHO), which facilitates the representation of health histories of persons related by biologial and/or social family relationships; the Gene Regulation ontology, a conceptual model for the domain of gene regulation; the Brenda ontology, a structured controlled vocabulary for the source of an enzyme; Galen, an ontology of medical concepts; and myGrid, an ontology describing the bioinformatics research domain. The complete list of over 30 ontologies together with several related information including test results can be found on our website [5].

Table 1 summarises some properties of these ontologies: the number of axioms, their expressivity and the number of occurrences of operators. This table shows that we have chosen a dataset of realistic ontologies of different size (ranging from hundreds of axioms to tens of thousands of axioms), and of different logical expressivity.

3.3. Experimental Results

In this section, we will investigate (1) in which cases anytime instance retrieval is effective, and (2) which of the selection strategies is most effective.

Table 2 summarises the results of our experiments: for each ontology it indicates how attractive the anytime behaviour is under the various strategies. Each column shows the *gain-score* of each strategy, calculated as defined in Section 2. Unfortunately, due to space restrictions we can not show the results of all the experiments. For the complete set of results including the gain-pain curves for all the experiments the interested reader is referred to the website of our framework. From these results we can observe the following:

Anytime instance retrieval benefits some cases: Figure 3 illustrates the case of the GRO ontology that exhibits very attractive anytime behaviour. The figure shows that for

---

[5] http://www.few.vu.nl/~gtagni/aboxreasoning

Table 2. Summary of success and failure of the different strategies.

ontology	R	MM	LDS	MDS	RC	MR
Galen-100	-16.86	-15.69	-50.69	-4.62	-8.88	-10.67
BVA	-12.22	-18.89	-40.26	-0.40	-18.21	-16.44
FHHO	-3.65	-18.18	-44.35	-2.19	-15.40	-15.46
GRO-250	1.62	6.97	0.80	6.63	3.99	7.29
LKIF	3.95	2.53	3.52	6.69	5.95	2.94
myGrid-v1	1.67	6.98	3.04	10.90	27.49	6.57
Brenda	-0.18	-5.78	-17.23	7.72	12.19	4.92

this complex ontology all strategies have an almost always-positive gain-curve. Other ontologies with attractive anytime behaviour are myGrid-v1, where all strategies have positive gains everywhere and LKIF (also Figure 3), where all strategies except MM and MR have positive gains; the last two strategies have positive gains up to the 80% and 90% point respectively.

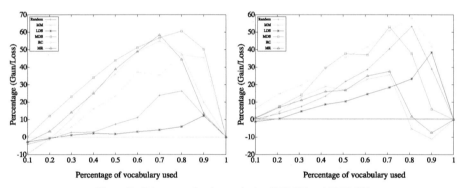

Figure 3. Gain-curves for the ontologies GRO-250 and LKIF-100

Anytime instance retrieval benefit some but not all cases: Some ontologies allow for very high gain-scores under many strategies, but we also see cases with less attractive anytime behaviour. For example, on some versions of Galen and FHHO, almost all strategies have negative gains almost everywhere (see Figure 4). This means that more (percentage of) time is spent than (percentage of) correct answers are found. The same behaviour is observed in BVA where almost all strategies have negative gain. The results show that whether anytime instance retrieval is beneficial or not depends very much on the selection strategy used and the complexity and structure of the ontology at hand.

Which strategy performs best? The data is inconclusive on the question which strategy performs best. While some of the strategies perform well on some of the ontologies, their performance is rather poor on others; the only exception being LDS which was outperformed by every other strategy in 14 out of 20 ontologies and was the best strategy in only one ontology. As an example take the case of the RC strategy which strongly dominates all the others when applied to myGrid-v1 but is outperformed by MM, MDS and MR when applied to GRO-250 (see Table 2). Another example that illustrates this behaviour is the MR strategy that outperforms all others on GRO-250 but it is outperformed by almost every other strategy on myGrid-v1. An interesting case is the

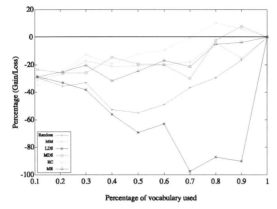

Figure 4. Gain-curves for the ontology Galen-100

behaviour of the MM strategy which, given how the strategy works, should perform well in most of the ontologies but that is not the case. The reason for this is that the strategy has a much bigger impact on the runtime (due to the sorting process) than the impact it has on the recall, and thus it reduces the gain significantly. What these experiments have shown us is that ultimately the choice of a selection strategy depends on the complexity and structure of the ontology at hand. This opens the door to future research targeted to finding better selection strategies that are able to exploit regularities in the environment (ontologies), ie. strategies or heuristics that are *ecologically valid*.

4. Analysing the Framework

Our case-study on Instance Retrieval showed the benefit of our framework for systematically analysing approximation methods. The following observations worth mentioning.

- *Reproducibility*: previous work on approximation is considerable, but the impact of published results has often been hampered by the difficulty to reproduce results, as implementing an approximation method is non-trivial, and the tuning even more so. Our framework and implementation should simplify the reuse of published results.
- *Scalability of experiments*: previously, running experiments of the kind presented in the previous section were painful experiences: combining different strategies with various reasoners on numerable ontology formats often results in incompatibilities. Experiments at the scale of our case-study, in numbers of ontologies and strategies, are made much easier in our workbench.
- *Tunability*: earlier results have shown that experiments involving reasoning with ontologies and approximation are difficult in nature. Small differences in strategy can have large impact on the results. This makes it paramount to systematically study the influence of often very subtle choices in strategy. In our framework this can now be done systematically.
- *Comparability*: often, performance measures are difficult to compare. The pain/gain diagrams introduced in Section 2 allow comparison of different approximation strategies across application problem and domain, approximation strategy and reasoning task.

5. Conclusion

Reasoning with complex ontologies on the Semantic Web is computationally difficult, and approximate anytime reasoning is required in many applications. In previous research it had become apparent that developing approximate methods is very difficult, there is no unique strategy to suit all ontologies, and it is not even clear whether for all ontologies approximation strategies exist.

This emphasises the need for the more systematic approach for studying approximated ontology reasoning which we provide in this paper. To this end we describe a systematic framework for studying approximate methods, and present an implementation that is publicly available on our website. A further contribution is to develop approximation and domain independent performance measures based on so-called pain/gain diagrams, which summarise the quality of an approximation in a natural way.

We have used our systematic evaluation approach and its implementation to perform a study on instance retrieval as a prototypical case where approximation is paramount. The findings confirm previous results: none of the more structural approximations introduced in this paper work on all ontologies, and even stronger, for many ontologies all our strategies fail.

This implies that future research needs an even more fine-grained experimental setups, which is now simplified by our evaluation framework. We will use the workbench in future research for studying more task-driven or *ecologically valid* heuristics, ie. strategies that are based on an extensive knowledge about the ontology itself and the task for which it is being used. Doing this has become a realistic perspective due to the framework presented in this paper.

References

[1] Mark S. Boddy and Thomas Dean, 'Solving time-dependent planning problems', in *IJCAI*, pp. 979–984, (1989).
[2] Perry Groot, Heiner Stuckenschmidt, and Holger Wache, 'Approximating description logic classification for semantic web reasoning.', in *ESWC*, eds., Asunción Gómez-Pérez and Jérôme Euzenat, volume 3532 of *Lecture Notes in Computer Science*, pp. 318–332. Springer, (2005).
[3] Ian Horrocks, Peter F. Patel-Schneider, and Frank van Harmelen, 'From SHIQ and RDF to OWL: The making of a web ontology language', *Journal of Web Semantics*, **1**(1), 7–26, (2003).
[4] Yuan Ren, Jeff Pan, and Yuting Zha, 'Towards soundness preserving approximation for abox reasoning of owl2', in *Proceedings of the International Description Logic Workshop (DL2010)*, (2010).
[5] Marco Schaerf and Marco Cadoli, 'Tractable reasoning via approximation', *Artificial Intelligence*, **74**(2), 249–310, (1995).
[6] S. Schlobach, E. Blaauw, M. El Kebir, A. ten Teije, F. van Harmelen, S. Bortoli, M. Hobbelman, K. Millian, Y. Ren, S. Stam, P. Thomassen, R. van het Schip, and W. van Willigem, 'Anytime classification by ontology approximation', in *Proceedings of the workshop on new forms of reasoning for the Semantic Web: scalable, tolerant and dynamic*, ed., Ruzica Piskac et al., pp. 60–74, (2007).
[7] Heiner Stuckenschmidt, 'Partial matchmaking using approximate subsumption', in *Proceedings of the Twenty-Second Conference on Artificial Intelligence (AAAI-07)*, (2007).
[8] H Wache, P Groot, and H Stuckenschmidt, 'Scalable instance retrieval for the semantic web by approximation', *Lecture notes in computer science*, **3807**, 245, (2005).
[9] Shlomo Zilberstein, 'Using anytime algorithms in intelligent systems', *AI Magazine*, **17**(3), 73–83, (1996).

Obligationes as Formal Dialogue Systems

Sara L. UCKELMAN [a,1,2]

[a] *Institute for Logic, Language, and Computation*

Abstract. Formal Dialogue Systems (FDSs) model rule-based interaction between agents. Their conceptual roots go back to Hamblin's [11,12], which cites the medieval theory of *obligationes* as inspiration for his development of a formal system of argumentation. In an *obligatio*, two agents, Opponent and Respondent, engage in an alternating-move dialogue, where Respondent's actions are governed by certain rules, and the goal of the dialogue is establishing the consistency of a proposition. We implement *obligationes* in the formal dialogue system framework of [20] using Dynamic Epistemic Logic [26]. The result is a new type of inter-agent dialogue, *consistency-checking*, and analyzing *obligationes* in this way also sheds light on interpretational and historical questions concerning their use and purpose in medieval academia.

Keywords. dialogue protocol, disputation, Formal Dialogue Systems, *obligationes*

1. Introduction

Rule-based interactions such as dialogues are ubiquitous and diverse; they are the basic method of communication between agents. In the context of AI and computer science, formal dialogue systems (FDSs) such as those developed in, e.g., [14,20] give formal, and hence potentially implementable, methods for modeling real-life dialogue situations, for example the complex reasoning in legal domains. The conceptual roots of FDSs are found in philosophical logic, argumentation theory, and, more broadly, the role of dialogue or argumentation in law and philosophy. One of the earliest attempts to provide a theory of formal dialogues is Hamblin's [12,11]. In [12], Hamblin locates part of the motivation for his development of formal argumentation in historical formal dialogue systems, that is, dialogical or disputational settings where explicit rules are given governing the actions of the participants. One such system that he considers in particular is the medieval theory of *obligationes*, developed in the 13th and 14th centuries. In an *obligatio*, two agents, Opponent and Respondent, engage in an alternate-move dialogue, where Respondent's actions are governed by certain rules, and the goal of the dialogue is, in the most basic case, to establish the consistency of a proposition. We argue that *obligationes* are best modeled by FDSs because of their intrinsic dialogical nature, and

---

[1] Institute for Logic, Language, and Computation, University of Amsterdam, The Netherlands, email: S.L.Uckelman@uva.nl

[2] This research was funded by the project "Dialogical Foundations of Semantics" (DiFoS) in the ESF EuroCoRes programme LogICCC (LogICCC-FP004; DN 231-80-002; CN 2008/08314/GW). The author would like to thank the anonymous referees for helpful comments on an earlier version of this paper.

that they determine a new type of dialogue system different from those discussed in the AI literature.

The plan of the paper is as follows. In §2 we present the medieval theory of *obligationes*, focusing specifically on the works of one author, Walter Burley. In §3 we briefly survey previous work on *obligationes*, both formal and philosophical, and motivate modeling *obligationes* as FDSs by showing how they can make sense of King's interpretation of *obligationes* as a meta-disputational framework. In §4 we introduce formal dialogue systems and show generally how *obligationes* fit within this set-up. In order to give a precise specification, we must first outline the logic used in the argumentation, which we do in §5. In §6 we then give a precise characterization of *obligationes* as FDSs. In §7, we compare the result with standard types of FDSs, and define a new dialogue protocol for *consistency-checking*.

2. The medieval theory of *obligationes*

An *obligatio* is a dialogue between two agents, Opponent and Respondent, where Opponent puts forward a sequence of propositions, and Respondent is obligated (hence the name) to follow certain rules in his responses to Opponent's propositions. More precisely, Opponent puts forward an initial statement, called the *positum*, which Respondent can either accept or refuse to accept. If he accepts, the *obligatio* begins. If he does not, no *obligatio* begins. If the *obligatio* begins, Opponent puts forward propositions and Respondent has three ways that he can respond: He can grant or concede the proposition, he can deny the proposition, or he can doubt it, where 'doubt' should be understood as 'remain agnostic about'; doubting φ does not entail any commitment to $\neg\varphi$. (Some authors, such as the anonymous author of the *Obligationes Parisienses* [7], mention a fourth option, which is to 'draw distinctions', that is, to clarify an ambiguity on the part of Opponent.) The *obligatio* continues until Opponent calls "*Cedat tempus*" ("Time's up"), whereupon the responses of Respondent are analysed with respect to Respondent's obligations, to determine whether he has responded well or badly.

The earliest texts on *obligationes* date from the beginning of the 13th century [6,7,8], and many of the leading logicians from that century and the next wrote treatises on the subject. While the roots of obligational disputations are clearly grounded in Aristotle's discussion of dialectical exchanges in the *Topics* VIII, 4 (159a15–24) and in the *Prior Analytics* I, 13 (32a18–20) (cf. [29, §II.A]), the systematic development of the theory of *obligationes* over the course of the 13th and 14th centuries tends to show little adherence to the Aristotelian definitions. While the specific details vary from author to author, a number of distinct types of *obligationes* discussed by multiple authors can be identified. The six most common are *positio*, *depositio*, *dubitatio*, *sit verum* or *rei veritatis*, *institutio*, and *petitio*. Of these six, *positio* is universally the most widely studied, both by medieval and modern authors; as a result, it is the focus of the current paper. For further information on *obligationes*, including a discussion of their purpose and their role in medieval philosophy, see [29].

To make the above more precise, we look at the theory of *obligationes* of a specific writer, Walter Burley. Burley's treatise *De obligationibus*, written around 1302, gives a standard treatment of *positio*. The text of this treatise is edited in [10] and a partial translation of the text, including the section on *positio* in its entirety, is found in [4]. Burley defines the general goal of an *obligatio* as follows:

The opponent's job is to use language in a way that makes the respondent grant impossible things that he need not grant because of the *positum*. The respondent's job, on the other hand, is to maintain the *positum* in such a way that any impossibility seems to follow not because of him but rather because of the *positum* [4, p. 370].[3]

Thus, it is clear that in an *obligatio* the goal is consistency, not logical truth or validity. In *positio*, the primary obligation of Respondent is to grant, that is, to hold as true, the *positum*. If Respondent accepts the *positum* and the *obligatio* begins, he is obliged to follow the following rules:

Rule 1 Everything that is posited and put forward in the form of the positum during the time of the positio must be granted [4, p. 379].[4]

Rule 2 Everything that follows from the positum must be granted. Everything that follows from the positum either together with an already granted proposition (or propositions), or together with the opposite of a proposition (or the opposites of propositions) already correctly denied and known to be such, must be granted [4, p. 381].[5]

Rule 3 Everything incompatible with the positum must be denied. Likewise, everything incompatible with the positum together with an already granted proposition (or propositions), or together with the opposite of a proposition (or the opposites of propositions) already correctly denied and known to be such, must be denied [4, p. 381].[6]

In Rule 1, 'in the same form as' should be understood syntactically; if the *positum* is 'Marcus is Roman', then Respondent doesn't have an obligation to accept 'Tullius is Roman' unless it is explicit (either through common knowledge or through previous concessions) that Marcus is Tullius.

Burley also defines a notion of relevance of propositions which applies to all types of *obligatio*. A proposition is *irrelevant* or *impertinent* if neither it nor its negation follows from the set of propositions which have already been conceded (which includes the negations of propositions which have been denied).

Rule for Irrelevant Propositions One must reply to what is irrelevant in accordance with its own quality [4, p. 375].[7]

I.e., Respondent should concede the proposition if it is true, deny if it is false, and doubt if he is not sure.

A simple example illustrating Burley's rules for *positio* is given in Figure 1. Suppose φ does not imply $\neg\psi$ and φ is known to be contingently false. In the first round, the Opponent puts forward a contingent (but false) proposition; the Respondent grants it in

---

[3] *Opus opponentis est sic inducere orationem ut faciat respondentem concedere impossibilia quae propter positum non sunt necessaria concedere. Opus autem respondentis est sic sustinere positum ut propter ipsum non videatur aliquod impossibile sequi, sed magis propter positum* [10, p. 34].

[4] *Omne positum, sub forma positi propositum, in tempore positionis, est concedendum* [10, p. 46].

[5] *Omne sequens ex posito est concedendum. Omne sequens ex posito cum concesso vel concessis, vel cum opposito bene negati vel oppositis bene negatorum, scitum esse tale, est concedendum* [10, p. 48].

[6] *Omne repugnans posito est negandum. Similiter omne repugnans posito cum concesso vel concessis, vel opposito bene negati vel oppositis bene negatorum, scitum esse tale, est negandum* [10, p. 48].

[7] *[A]d impertinens respondendum est secundum sui qualitatem* [10, p. 42].

	Opponent	Respondent	
1	φ.	I admit it.	$\Phi_0 := \{\varphi\}$.
2	$\neg\varphi \vee \psi$.	I concede it.	$\Phi_1 := \{\varphi, \neg\varphi \vee \psi\}$.
3	ψ	I concede it.	

Figure 1. An example *obligatio*.

accord with Rule 1. In the second round, either φ implies ψ, then the sentence is relevant and follows from Φ_0 (the set of propositions conceded so far along with the negations of propositions denied to this point); or it doesn't, in which case it is irrelevant and true (since φ is false). In both cases, the rules require the Respondent to concede; in the first case, Rule 2 is operational, in the second, the Rule for Irrelevant Propositions. In the third round, the Respondent likewise must concede because ψ follows from Φ_1. This example *obligatio* shows how, given a *positum* which is false, but not necessarily inconsistent, Opponent can force Respondent to concede any other consistent proposition.

Other examples commonly found in *obligationes* treatises are more interesting, because they involve *posita* that are not propositional but instead include statements about the players obligations in the games (e.g., the example discussed in [29, pp. 152–155]).

3. Previous work on *obligationes*

Green's Ph.D. dissertation [10], containing an edition of and commentary on two treatises on *obligationes*, now generally ascribed to William of Sherwood and Walter Burley, marks the beginning of modern research on *obligationes*. Hamblin is the first modern author to attempt to formalize *obligationes* [12, pp. 260–263]. Given his interest in formalizing argumentation generally, he focuses on the dialogical aspects of *obligationes*. His formalization is rudimentary and models only one variant, that given by William of Sherwood[8], but it marks the beginning of modern scholarship on the formal properties of *obligationes*. More recent scholarship has focused on the game-like nature of *obligationes*, e.g., [7,9,29]. It may therefore seem natural to look to game-based structures in logic to provide a general framework for modeling different types of *obligationes*. However, despite the strongly logical component of *obligationes*, to date relatively little work has been done on the formal properties of the logic and few attempts have been made to provide an explicit specification of the game(s) involved[9], and there are a number of aspects which do not immediately lend themselves nicely to a game-like interpretation (e.g., the notion of a winning strategy for an *obligatio* is difficult to define[10]).

---

[8]Hamblin routinely questions the attribution to Sherwood of the text he is considering; however, more recent scholarship is agreed that the text was almost certainly written by Sherwood, sometime in the middle of the 13th century [2].

[9]The most extensive attempt is [9], which contains analyses of the obligational theories of Walter Burley, Richard Swyneshed (c.1330), and Ralph Strode (second half of the 14th C). However, Dutilh Novaes's framework is not very *game*-like; there are players and winning conditions, but no concept of, e.g., strategy. Other drawbacks of her framework for modeling *obligationes* are discussed in [24].

[10]Yrjönsuuri mentions the possibility of modeling *obligationes* as games, but he says that "defining the results of the game in any manner appropriate to modern game-theory seem utterly problematic" though despite this "[i]n the following I will keep to the English word *game*, assuming that the problems pointed out above can just be left unsolved" [29, pp. 9–10].

In the last four decades, many philosophers and historians have devoted themselves to the question of the goal or purpose of obligational disputations and the role they played in medieval academic life, while somewhat fewer have focused on the logical properties of *obligationes*. Despite this, the purpose of *obligationes* and their role in medieval academic life remains stubbornly unclear [23,30,29]. One particularly interesting interpretation is given by King [15], who takes his starting point from Spade, who, in [22], looked to the textual evidence for actual uses of *obligationes* to understand how they were used by the medievals. While to date there is no historical record for actual obligational disputations, we have many examples of philosophers using obligational techniques as part of their argumentation [15, p. 1]. King explains the apparent "content-freeness" of obligational disputations by pointing out that "they operate at a higher level of logical generality than that at which substantive debate occurs. If this is correct, then actual obligational moves—perhaps even recognized as such—are the vehicle whereby real argument takes place" [15, p. 6], and thus *obligationes* provide a "meta-methodology" for reasoning [15, p. 7]. We use this suggestion as the motivation for our approach to modeling *obligationes*. An *obligatio* is essentially a dialogue; and any dialogue can be seen as a game played according to the rules specified by an FDS [17]. We believe that viewing *obligationes* as FDSs, which require that we explicitly specify the logic of argumentation/inference and the models against which the dialogue is to be evaluated, provide a more fruitful approach to modeling *obligationes*. On this view, Hamblin's modeling approach has the advantage over others proposed in recent literature because it takes the dialogical nature of the disputation seriously. By varying the rules governing the disputation, radically different types of *obligationes* arise, which result in radically different types of dialogues/disputations. Despite the wide range of difference that can be found, the basic structure of an *obligatio* remains the same, making the general framework of FDSs an appropriate modeling choice. Specifying *obligationes* from within the context of FDSs allows us to situate them formally in current research on formal dialogues, which in turn can help to clarify the interpretational question, by helping us understand the possible purposes to which *obligationes* could be disposed. In particular, we argue that the naturalness of modeling *obligationes* as formal dialogue systems supports King's suggestion that *obligationes* provide agents with a meta-methodology for argumentation. That is, *obligationes* give frameworks within which dialectical argumentation can take place.

4. Formal dialogue systems

In this section, we follow the presentation of formal dialogue systems given by Prakken in [20], an overview paper which discusses different formal argumentation systems that have been proposed for the analysis of persuasion dialogues and provides a unified approach within which each of these different systems can be modeled. While Prakken focuses on persuasion dialogues, his framework is in fact general enough to handle other types as well [20, pp. 170, 173]. Thus, it is appropriate to use it to consider *obligationes*.

A *formal dialogue system* contains the following elements [20, p. 166]:

- A *topic language* $\mathcal{L}_t$, closed under classical negation.
- A *communication language* $\mathcal{L}_c$. We denote the set of *dialogues*, that is, the set sequences of $\mathcal{L}_c$, by $M^{\leq \infty}$, and the set of finite sequences of $\mathcal{L}_c$ by $M^{<\infty}$. For a dialogue $d = m_0, \ldots, m_n, \ldots$, the subsequence $m_0, \ldots, m_i$ is denoted d_i.

- A *dialogue purpose* or *goal*.
- A set $\mathcal{A}$ of *agents* (participants) and a set $\mathcal{R}$ of *roles* that the participants can occupy. Each participant a has a (possibly empty) *belief base* $\Sigma_a \subseteq \mathcal{L}_t$ and a (possibly empty) *commitment set* $C_a(d_n) \subseteq \mathcal{L}_t$. The belief base may or may not change during the dialogue; the commitment set usually does.
- A *context* $K \subseteq \mathcal{L}_t$, representing the (shared, consistent, and unchanging) knowledge of the agents specified at the outset.
- A *logic* L for $\mathcal{L}_t$.
- A set E of *effect rules* $C_a(d_n) : M^{<\infty} \to \mathcal{P}(\mathcal{L}_t)$ for $\mathcal{L}_c$, specifying how utterances $\varphi \in \mathcal{L}_c$ in the dialogue affect the commitment stores of the agents. The effect rules are such that if $d = d'$ then $C_a(d, m) = C_a(d', m)$, that is, the changes in commitments are determined solely by the most recent move in the dialogue along with the commitments at that step.
- A *protocol* P for $\mathcal{L}_c$, specifying the legal moves of the dialogue, which is a function from the context and a non-empty $D \subseteq M^{<\infty}$ to $\mathcal{P}(\mathcal{L}_c)$, satisfying the requirement that if $d \in D$ and $m \in P(d)$, then $d, m \in D$. The elements of D are called *legal finite dialogues*, and $P(d)$ is the set of moves allowed after move d. At any stage, if $P(d) = \emptyset$, then the dialogue has *terminated*. A protocol will often be accompanied by a *turn-taking* function $T : D \to \mathcal{P}(\mathcal{A})$, which takes a finite dialogue d_n and specifies who governs move m_{n+1}, and *termination* conditions, which specify when $P(d) = \emptyset$.
- A set of *outcome rules* O.

We can identify a number of properties of protocols [20, p. 170]:

- A protocol has *public semantics* iff the set of legal moves is always independent from the agents' belief bases.
- A protocol is *context-independent* iff the set of legal moves and the outcome is always independent of the context, that is, $P(K, d) = P(\emptyset, d)$.
- A protocol is *fully deterministic* iff P always returns a singleton or the empty set.
- A protocol is *unique-move* iff the turn shifts after each move; it is *multiple-move* otherwise.

Protocols which are not fully deterministic are *permissive*, that is, they specify what moves are *legal* or *allowed* for the agent, rather than specify what moves are *required*. Thus, *obligationes* are a type of FDS where the protocol for Respondent is fully deterministic.

We now show how generically *obligationes* can be viewed as FDSs; we give precise examples in §6. In *obligationes*, there are two designated roles O (Opponent) and R (Respondent) that members of $\mathcal{A}$ can have; those members of $\mathcal{A}$ which do not fill either role are irrelevant for modeling the disputation. We explain below how Σ_O, Σ_R, C_O, C_R, and the context K are generated. In Burley-style *positio*, the dialogue purpose is consistency: If we take R's commitment set to be the set of formulas he has conceded along with the negation of those that he's denied over the course of a *positio*, then the goal for R is to maintain the consistency of his commitment set, and the goal for O is to force R into contradiction.

In general, the topic language $\mathcal{L}_t$ and the communication language $\mathcal{L}_c$ are the same. This allows, among other things, the participants in an *obligatio* to dispute about the allowed moves of the other players. (For example, O may ask R to respond to the claim

"You deny φ".) The turn-taking protocol in an *obligatio* is unique-move: $T(\emptyset) = \mathsf{O}$, $T(d_n) = \mathsf{O}$ if n is odd, and $T(d_n) = \mathsf{R}$ if n is even. (Throughout we assume that we label the steps in the sequence from 0, so in an *obligatio* it is always O that goes first.) The protocol P will be such that the moves of O are not constrained in any way, but R's moves must be made in reaction to the move of O at the previous stage. The same will be true for the effect rules E; in a disputation, O makes a series of claims or assertions, but these actions have no effect on his commitment store. On the other hand, R is constrained to be reactive only: He can only concede statements claimed by O, concede their negations, or remain ambivalent. R never asserts any statement of his own devising, he only ever responds to propositions put forward by O. Thus, *obligationes* are essentially asymmetric, in that the rules governing the behavior of the O and R are disjoint[11], and so are their actions.

The outcome rules for *obligationes* are simple: If R realizes the goal, then he wins. If O realizes the goal, then he wins. There is nothing further that hinges upon winning or losing an obligational disputation (except, of course, the individual prestige or embarrassment of the participants!).

Above we noted that in an arbitrary FDS, the commitment set of an agent will generally change during the course of the dialogue. It can either strictly grow, so that the agents are only adding new propositions to their commitment-base at each turn, or they can also revise their commitments by rejecting previous commitments in favor of new ones. This later case arises in ordinary circumstances when agents utilize a form of default reasoning, which is defeasible and non-monotonic, in that an agent can be forced to accept information which contradicts his previous commitments, requiring that his commitments be revised in order to maintain consistency (cf. [1,3]). In AI contexts, the ability to simulate non-monotonic reasoning is of great importance; in philosophical contexts, dialogues and disputations are more likely to be monotonic. One of the benefits of Prakken's approach to FDS is that it can handle both approaches, merely by the specification of the underlying logic [20, p. 173].

5. The underlying logic

By specifying the logic L and its underlying models, we are able to explicitly generate $\Sigma_\mathsf{O}, \Sigma_\mathsf{R}, C_\mathsf{O}, C_\mathsf{R}$, and K satisfying desired properties. In our approach to modeling *obligationes* as FDSs, the underlying logic is multi-agent Dynamic Epistemic Logic (DEL, [26]). This logic is monotonic and not argument based (we discuss below our motivations for selecting this type of logic for our underlying logic). An epistemic logic is an extension of propositional logic with a family of modal operators K_a for $a \in \mathcal{A}$. We are interested in a particular extension of standard epistemic logic, namely, *epistemic logic with common knowledge*, which has a further family of operators C_G, for $G \subseteq \mathcal{A}$. For a set Φ_0 of propositional letters and set $\mathcal{A}$ of agents, the set $\Phi_{\mathrm{EL}}^{\mathcal{A}}$ of wffs of EL is defined as follows:

$$\varphi := p \in \Phi_0 \mid \neg\varphi \mid \varphi \vee \varphi \mid K_a\varphi : a \in \mathcal{A} \mid C_G\varphi : G \subseteq \mathcal{A}$$

---

[11]In fact, in most texts, no rules for O are given. One exception is the early text *Tractatus Emmeranus* [6], which gives some rules (better thought of as guidelines, or strategic advice) to Opponent.

$K_a\varphi$ is read 'agent a knows that φ'. $C_G\varphi$ is read 'it is common knowledge amongst the group of agents G that φ'. We can use C_G to represent explicitly the knowledge of the two agents at the beginning of the disputation, if so required.

Epistemic logic is interpreted on Kripke frames. A structure $\mathfrak{M} = \langle W, w^*, \{\sim_a : a \in \mathcal{A}\}, V \rangle$ is an *epistemic model* if

- W is a set (of possible worlds), with a designated point $w^* \in W$ (representing the actual world).
- $\{\sim_a : a \in \mathcal{A}\}$ is a family of equivalence relations on W, one for each member of $\mathcal{A}$. The relation $w \sim_a w'$ is interpreted as 'w and w' are epistemically equivalent for agent a'. $\sim_G : G \subseteq \mathcal{A}$ is defined as the reflexive and transitive closure of $\bigcup_{a \in G}\{\sim_a\}$.
- $V : \Phi_0 \to 2^W$ is a valuation function associating atomic propositions with subsets of W. For $p \in \Phi_0$, if $w \in V(p)$, we say that 'p is true at w'.

The semantics for the propositional connectives are as expected. We give just the semantics for the epistemic operators.

$$\mathfrak{M}, w \vDash K_a\varphi \text{ iff } \forall w'(\text{if } \langle w, w' \rangle \in \sim_a \text{ then } \mathfrak{M}^E, w' \vDash \varphi)$$
$$\mathfrak{M}, w \vDash C_G\varphi \text{ iff } \forall w'(\text{if } \langle w, w' \rangle \in \sim_G \text{ then } \mathfrak{M}^E, w' \vDash \varphi)$$

EL models cover the knowledge of the agents; to model their actions, we add dynamics, via Propositional Dynamic Logic (PDL, [13]). PDL is an extension of propositional logic by a family of modal operators $[\alpha]$ for $\alpha \in \Pi$, a set of programmes (or more generally, a set of actions or events). The language of PDL is two-sorted, with a set Φ_0 of atoms and a set Π_0 of atomic actions. We do not need the full expressivity of PDL to model *obligationes*, so we introduce only the fragment we require. We let $\Pi_0 = \emptyset$, and the sets Φ_{Ob} and Π_{Ob} of complex well-formed formulas and programmes are defined by mutual induction:

$$\varphi := \varphi \in \Phi_{EL}^{\mathcal{A}} \mid [\alpha]\varphi : \alpha \in \Pi_{Ob}$$
$$\alpha := \varphi? : \varphi \in \Phi_{EL}^{\mathcal{A}}$$

The programme φ? is similar to the ordinary test operator in PDL, in that it tests for the truth of φ, but it differs in that it does not, as the truth conditions below make clear, require the truth of φ at the actual world. Note that the only programmes that we allow are testing of formulas which do not themselves contain any programmes. The semantics for the new $[\varphi?]$ operator are given in terms of model reduction. Let $\mathfrak{M} \upharpoonright \varphi := \langle W^{\mathfrak{M},\varphi}, \{\sim_a^{\mathfrak{M},\varphi} : a \in \mathcal{A}\}, V^{\mathfrak{M},\varphi} \rangle$, where $W^{\mathfrak{M},\varphi} := \{w \in W : \mathfrak{M}, w \vDash \varphi\}$, and the relations and valuation functions are just restrictions of the originals. For a set of ordered propositions Γ_n, let $\mathfrak{M} \upharpoonright \Gamma_n = \mathfrak{M} \upharpoonright \gamma_0 \upharpoonright \cdots \upharpoonright \gamma_n$, that is, $\mathfrak{M} \upharpoonright \Gamma_n$ is the result of the sequential restriction of $\mathfrak{M}$ by the elements of Γ_n. Then:

$$\mathfrak{M}, w \vDash [\varphi?]\psi \text{ iff } \forall v \in \mathfrak{M} \upharpoonright \varphi, v \vDash \psi$$

One advantage of using an epistemic logic for our disputation logic is that it allows us to model the epistemic bases of the agents, and the context of the disputation, explicitly (for other advantages see [24]). We are in general not interested in the *belief* bases of the agents, but rather their *knowledge* bases; while beliefs may be false, we follow the standard definition of knowledge, on which it is veridical. Given an epistemic model $\mathfrak{M}$, the knowledge bases of O and R are defined as follows:

$$\Sigma_O^{\mathfrak{M}} := \{\varphi : \mathfrak{M}, w^* \vDash K_O \varphi\}$$
$$\Sigma_R^{\mathfrak{M}} := \{\varphi : \mathfrak{M}, w^* \vDash K_R \varphi\}$$

In an arbitrary model $\mathfrak{M}$, the set of propositions which are common knowledge amongst a group of agents is not explicitly specified. In an *obligatio*, the set of common knowledge, against which the truth of irrelevant propositions is evaluated, is likewise often left implicit. In some cases, before the *obligatio* begins, a *casus* is introduced. A *casus* is a hypothesis about how the world is, or extra information about how the *positum* should be analyzed [28]. In the first sense, the *casus* can be understood as a set of literals expressing the *explicit common knowledge* at the start of the dialogue, so the *casus* can be implemented by a restriction on V.

Definition 5.1. (*Casus*). Let Lit_{Φ_0} be the set of literals formed from Φ_0, and $K \subseteq \text{Lit}_{\Phi_0}$ be the *casus*. Then $\mathfrak{M}$ *models the casus* if there is a $P_c \subseteq P$ of W with $w^* \in P_c$, such that if $w \sim_R w^*$, then $w \in P_c$, if $v \sim_O w^*$, then $v \in P_c$, and for all $w, v \in P_c$, $w \sim_R v$ and $w \sim_O v$; and for every positive literal $p \in K$ and every $w \in P_c$, $w \in V(p)$, and for every negative literal $\neg q \in K$ and every $w \in P_c$, $w \notin V(q)$.

Unlike contexts in FDS, it is not assumed that the *casus* of an *obligatio* is consistent, but if it is not, then R should not accept the *positum*, since O could easily force him into conceding a contradiction. However, if the *casus* is consistent, we can easily show that if $\mathfrak{M}$ models a *casus* K, then for every $\varphi \in K$, $\mathfrak{M} \vDash C_{\{O,R\}}\varphi$, and so $K \subseteq \Sigma_O^{\mathfrak{M}}$ and $K \subseteq \Sigma_R^{\mathfrak{M}}$.

We close this section by briefly commenting on our choice of DEL for the underlying logic, as opposed to an argument-based logic or one that allows for nonmonotonicity. First, as we noted above, one advantage of using an epistemic logic rather than an argument-based logic is that we can explicitly discuss the knowledge bases of the agents, and the context. While the applications that we discuss in this paper do not exploit this expressivity, dealing with individual knowledge and common knowledge, other types of *obligationes* which we do not consider here make crucial use of this information during the disputation. Building epistemic characteristics into our underlying logic from the start means that this framework can be used to model a much wider range of types of *obligationes* than we consider in this paper (cf. [24,25] for two further applications).

Second, a general characteristic shared by almost all types of *obligationes*, both *positio* and otherwise, is that if R follows the rules correctly, the only time he is required to give different answers to the same proposition at different rounds of the disputation is if he first doubts the proposition, and then at a later stage concedes or denies it. Thus, the obligational systems are monotonic in so far as the only change in R's response is moving from doubt concerning a specific proposition to certainty (that is, concession or denial). Thus, since the rules are monotonic, we do not need to consider defeasibility.

6. Protocols, effect rules, and outcomes

Different types of *obligationes* can be modeled by changing the protocols, effect rules, and outcome conditions. First, we specify the general properties shared by all *obliga-*

tiones. We identify our set of agents with their roles, i.e., our set of agents is $\mathcal{A} = \{\mathsf{O}, \mathsf{R}\}$, and our topic language and commitment language is the language of dynamic epistemic logic $\mathcal{L}_{\mathrm{DEL}}$ introduced in the previous section. Let α be a designated formula representing "*cedat tempus*". We can identify two types of protocols used in *obligationes*. The first type of protocol is uniform throughout all different systems; the second varies from author to author and type to type. The uniform protocol P_u is invariant over all contexts and is defined for a finite dialogue d_n:

$$\mathrm{P}_u(\emptyset) = \mathcal{L}_c$$
if $m_n = \alpha$ $\quad \mathrm{P}_u(d_n) = \emptyset$
otherwise, if n is odd, $\mathrm{P}_u(d_n) = \mathcal{L}_c$
and if n is even, $\quad \mathrm{P}_u(d_n) = \{[m_n?]\top, [\neg m_n?]\top, [\top?]\top\}$

That is, if it is O's turn, he is allowed to assert any statement in the communication language (we allow repetitions). If it is R's turn, he must either concede, deny, or doubt O's statement from the previous round. Since m_n, the move of O, will always be a statement in the communication language $\mathcal{L}_c$, and the communication language allows for the embeddings of the test programme, this protocol is well-defined. This protocol has public semantics and is context-independent, but it is not fully deterministic, since whenever it is R's turn, he has a choice of actions. For ease of future reference, we introduce meta-names for the actions of R: **concede**:$\varphi := [\varphi?]\top$, **deny**:$\varphi := [\neg\varphi?]\top$, and **doubt**:$\varphi := [\top?]\top$. The last clause is equivalent to saying "I don't know"; $[\top?]\top$ will always be valid, in any model.

The rules governing the commitment sets $\mathrm{C_O}$ and $\mathrm{C_R}$ are defined as follows:

for all n $\quad \mathrm{C_O}(d_n) = \emptyset$
if n is even $\mathrm{C_R}(d_n) = \mathrm{C_R}(d_{n-1})$
if n is odd $\mathrm{C_R}(d_n) = \mathrm{C_R}(d_{n-1}) \cup \{m_n\}$

That is, O has no commitments, O's moves do not change R's commitments, and R's commitment store strictly grows on the basis of his actions, and thus obligational dialogues are monotonic (cf. above). As above, since $\mathcal{L}_c$ and $\mathcal{L}_t$ coincide, the final clause of the definition is well-defined. Note that in general, $\mathrm{C_R}$ and Σ_R will be disjoint, and similarly for $\mathrm{C_R}$ and K (contra, e.g., [19, §3]).

The general protocol defined above specifies what the possible moves of R are. In an *obligatio*, however, we want to say more than what moves are *allowed*, we also want to specify a set of possible moves which are in fact *required*, since in an obligational disputation R is under obligation to respond to O in certain ways. This is done by specifying a more refined protocol. Such a protocol, because it makes reference to the agents' knowledge bases, will always be defined with respect to a particular DEL model $\mathfrak{M}$. We give as an example Burley's protocol $\mathrm{P}^{\mathrm{Bur}}$ for *positio*, introduced in §2. Let Γ_n be the sequence of R's move in a dialogue d_n. For a DEL model $\mathfrak{M}$ and context K, $\mathrm{P}^{\mathrm{Bur}}(K, \emptyset) = \mathrm{P}_u(\emptyset)$ and if n is odd, $\mathrm{P}^{\mathrm{Bur}}(K, d_n) = \mathrm{P}_u(d_n)$. For n even,

- For $d_0 = m_0 =$ the *positum*,

$$\mathrm{P}^{\mathrm{Bur}}(K, d_0) = \begin{cases} \textbf{concede}{:}m_0 & \text{iff } \exists w \in W, \mathfrak{M}, w \models m_0 \\ \textbf{deny}{:}m_0 & \text{iff } \forall w \in W, \mathfrak{M}, w \not\models m_0 \end{cases}$$

- For $d_n, n > 0$:

  If $\mathfrak{M} \upharpoonright \Gamma_n \vDash m_n$: $\quad$ $P^{Bur}(K, d_n) = $ **concede**:m_n
  If $\mathfrak{M} \upharpoonright \Gamma_n \vDash \neg m_n$: $\quad$ $P^{Bur}(K, d_n) = $ **deny**:m_n
  Otherwise:
  If $\mathfrak{M}, w^* \vDash K_R m_n$: $\quad$ $P^{Bur}(K, d_n) = $ **concede**:m_n
  If $\mathfrak{M}, w^* \vDash K_R \neg m_n$: $\quad$ $P^{Bur}(K, d_n) = $ **deny**:m_n
  If $\mathfrak{M}, w^* \vDash \neg(K_R m_n \vee K_R \neg m_n)$: $P^{Bur}(K, d_n) = $ **doubt**:m_n

This protocol is semi-public, as it depends on R's knowledge, but does not depend on O's; context-dependent; and fully deterministic. It also meets all but four of the 13 desiderata for agent argumentation protocols given in [18].[12] It thus scores as well, or better, than the protocols that they analyse.

We can define two outcome rules for Burley-style *positio*, governing who wins. Generally speaking, O wins if he can force R into inconsistency, and R wins otherwise. Since any individual *obligatio* $= d_n$ for some finite n, we can define a weak notion of "local" winning: If $m_n = \alpha$, then O *wins* if $\mathfrak{M} \upharpoonright \Gamma_n = \langle \emptyset, \{\sim_a^{\mathfrak{M},\Gamma_n} : a \in A\}, V^{\mathfrak{M},\Gamma_n}\rangle$ and R wins otherwise. But even though individual *obligationes* are finite, they are all potentially infinite. This view gives rise to a "global" winning condition: O *wins* if there is some n such that $\mathfrak{M} \upharpoonright \Gamma_n = \langle \emptyset, \{\sim_a^{\mathfrak{M},\Gamma_n} : a \in A\}, V^{\mathfrak{M},\Gamma_n}\rangle$. R wins otherwise. In both cases, the only time W will be empty is when $C_R \vDash \varphi \wedge \neg\varphi$, that is, over the course of the disputation R has conceded an inconsistent set, and has thus "responded badly". Thus, protocol P^{Bur} ensures the dialogical consistency of R (cf. [20, p. 171] and [9, ch. 3]).

There are also two ways that "responded badly" can be explicated, a broad-grained way and a fine-grained way. On the broad-grained view, we are only interested in whether O or R has locally won, that is, whether O has been able to force R to concede a contradiction, or whether R has remained consistent in his answers. This is the view generally considered by medieval authors.

7. Discussion

7.1. Understanding obligationes

We have now seen how at least one type of medieval obligational theory can be interpreted as giving rise to a formal dialogue system; it is straightforward to extend this analysis to the theories of other medieval authors (and we intend to do so in future work). The result of such an analysis shows that, just as a particular dialogue can be viewed as a game played according to a set of rules specified by an FDS (cf. §3), so too *obligationes* can be naturally understood as giving the participants a methodology of argu-

---

[12] Because the topic language and the communication language coincide, it is not clear to what extent *obligationes* satisfy the requirement of the separation of syntax and semantics (7), and because O can continually put forward the same proposition and, on some obligational theories, R can always doubt, they do not satisfy rule-consistency (8) and discouragement of disruption (10) as they define them. As we note in the final section, the computational complexity of certain decision problems that can be extracted from this protocol is not yet known, so we do not know yet if it satisfies computational simplicity (13).

mentation or reasoning to follow. In particular, the two-tiered nature of the protocols involved in *obligationes*, with both the general uniform protocol P_u and then a specific protocol for a particular type of *obligationes*, such as P^{Bur} for Burley-style *positio*, helps us understand King's analysis of *obligationes* as a meta-methodology of argumentation. The specific protocol is the methodology—it tells R how to respond within a particular disputation—while the general protocol constrains the types of specific protocols that are allowed, and hence can be understood as a meta-methodology (a higher order method). Thus, this new approach to *obligationes* provides formal support for King's interpretation of *obligationes* as functioning at the meta-level, rather than at the content level. That is, by specifying the protocols and rules of an FDS, a particular obligational theory gives participants a framework within which to do philosophical analysis.

7.2. Comparison

Walton and Krabbe in [27] give a typology for dialogues, identifying six different basic types: information seeking, inquiry, persuasion, negotiation, deliberation, and eristic. Cogan et al. extend this division by introducing four new types of dialogues, verification and three types of queries, as they argue that "there remain several situations in which it seems natural to engage in dialogues, but to which the basic Walton and Krabbe dialogue types do not apply" [5, p. 161]. (Their new classification is based on the preconditions for dialogues.) A natural question to ask is where do *obligationes* fit in these schemes? The decempartite division of [5] does not accommodate *obligationes*. Because they are about the consistency of a formula, *obligationes* are not negotiation or deliberation dialogues. Because the truth value of the proposition in dispute is known to both, and the Opponent is not trying to persuade the Respondent of anything, they are not information-seeking, inquiry, or persuasion dialogues. Since they are not pugilistic in nature, they are not eristic dialogues. Nor are they any of the four new kinds introduced in [5], since those types require as well that at least one party not know the truth-value of the proposition.

Obligationes are somewhat similar to the 'elicit-inform' dialogue game of [16,21]. These dialogues, between a tutor system and a student, were developed in the context of collaborative e-learning. In an elicit-inform dialogue, the student is questioned by the tutorial system, and "after reasoning about the learner's contributions, the tutor system either *sanctions* their explanations by informing them they were correct, or points out that they were 'incorrect' and so *informs* them of a consistent, or 'correct' answer" [21, p. 96]. This resembles the behavior of the Opponent when he calls *Cedat tempus* and evaluates the actions of the Respondent to determine whether he has responded well or badly. However, as elicit-inform dialogues have as their goal the persuasion of the student to adopt a certain belief, they are not a complete match for *obligationes*, since persuasion is not at issue in obligational dialogues.

We conclude that the type of protocol that are generated by *obligationes* are best understood on their own merits, and not shoehorned into a type of dialogue already identified. Thus, one of the contributions of the current paper is the introduction of a new type of inter-agent dialogue, which we can term *consistency-checking*.

References

[1] A. Bondarenko, P. M. Dung, R. A. Kowalski, and F. Toni, 'An abstract, argumentation-theoretic approach to default reasoning', *Artificial Intelligence*, **93**, 63–101, (1997).

[2] H.A.G. Braakhuis, 'Obligations in early 13th century Paris: the *Obligationes* of Nicholas of Paris (?)', *Vivarium*, 36(2), 152–233, (1998).
[3] G. Brewka, 'Dynamic argument systems', *Journal of Logic and Computation*, 11(2), 257–282, (2001).
[4] W. Burley, 'Obligations (selections)', in *Cambridge Translations of Medieval Philosophical Texts*, eds., N. Kretzmann and E. Stump, volume 1, 369–412, Cambridge University Press, (1988).
[5] E. Cogan, S. Parsons, and P. McBurney, 'New types of inter-agent dialogues', in *Argumentation in Multi-Agent Systems*, eds., S. Parsons, N. Maudet, P. Moraitis, and I. Rahwan, LNAI 4049, 154–168, Springer, (2006).
[6] L. M. de Rijk, 'Some thirteenth century tracts on the game of obligation', *Vivarium*, 12(2), 94–123, (1974).
[7] L. M. de Rijk, 'Some thirteenth century tracts on the game of obligation II', *Vivarium*, 13(1), 22–54, (1975).
[8] L. M. de Rijk, 'Some thirteenth century tracts on the game of obligation III', *Vivarium*, 14(1), 26–49, (1976).
[9] C. Dutilh Novaes, *Formalizing Medieval Logical Theories*, Springer, 2007.
[10] R. Green, O.F.M., *An Introduction to the Logical Treatise 'de Obligationibus'*, Université Catholique Louvain, 1963.
[11] C. Hamblin, 'Mathematical models of dialogue', *Theoria*, 37, 130–155, (1971).
[12] C. L. Hamblin, *Fallacies*, Methuen, [1970].
[13] D. Harel, D. Kozen, and J. Tiuryn, 'Dynamic logic', in *Handbook of Philosophical Logic*, eds., D.M. Gabbay and F. Guenther, volume 4, Kluwer, 2 edn., (2002).
[14] N. C. Karunatillake, N. R. Jennings, I. Rahwan, and P. McBurney, 'Dialogue games that agents play within a society', *Artificial Intelligence*, 173, 935–981, (2009).
[15] P. King, 'Opposing and responding: comments on Paul Spade'. Preprint, http://individual.utoronto.ca/pking/presentations/Spade_Comments.pdf, 2004.
[16] M. Matheson and A. Ravenscroft, 'Evaluating and investigating learning through collaborative argumentation: An empirical study', Technical Report DDRG-01-01, The Open University, Milton Keynes, (2001).
[17] N. Maudet, 'Negotiating dialogue games', *Autonomous Agents and Multi-Agent Systems*, 7, 229–233, (2003).
[18] P. McBurney, S. Parsons, and M. Wooldridge, 'Desiderata for agent argumentation protocols', in *AAMAS'02*, pp. 402–409, (2002).
[19] S. Parsons, M. Wooldridge, and L. Amgoud, 'An analysis of formal inter-agent dialogues', in *AAMAS'02*, pp. 394–401, (2002).
[20] H. Prakken, 'Formal systems for persuasion dialogue', *Knowledge Engineering Review*, 21(2), 163–188, (2006).
[21] A. Ravenscroft and M. P. Matheson, 'Developing and evaluating dialogue games for collaborative e-learning', *Journal of Computer Assisted Learning*, 18(1), 93–101, (2002).
[22] P. V. Spade, 'Unpublished talk on *obligationes* presented at the Midwestern Division of the American Philosophical Association'. 1993.
[23] P. V. Spade, 'Why don't medieval logicians ever tell us what they're doing? or, what is this, a conspiracy?'. Preprint, http://pvspade.com/Logic/docs/Conspiracy.pdf, 2000.
[24] S. L. Uckelman, "A unified dynamic framework for modeling *obligationes*". Working paper, 2010.
[25] S. L. Uckelman, 'Deceit and nondefeasible knowledge: The case of *dubitatio*'. Working paper, 2010.
[26] H. van Ditmarsch, W. van der Hoek, and B. Kooi, *Dynamic Epistemic Logic*, Springer, 2007.
[27] D. N. Walton and E. C. W. Krabbe, *Commitment in Dialogue: Basic Concepts of Interpersonal Reasoning*, State University of New York Press, 1995.
[28] M. Yrjönsuuri, 'The role of casus in some fourteenth century treatises on sophismata and obligations', in *Argumentationstheorie*, ed., K. Jacobi, 301–321, Brill, (1993).
[29] M. Yrjönsuuri, *Obligationes: 14th Century Logic of Disputational Duties*, Societatis Philosophia Fennica, 1994.
[30] M. Yrjönsuuri, ed., *Medieval Formal Logic*, Kluwer, 2001.

On-line ADL Recognition with Prior Knowledge

Jonas ULLBERG [a], Silvia CORADESCHI [a] Federico PECORA [a]

[a] *Center for Applied Autonomous Sensor Systems*
Örebro University
Örebro, SE - 70182, Sweden

Abstract. This paper addresses the problem of recognizing activities of daily living. The novelty lies in the use of an existing knowledge base (ConceptNet) to introduce prior knowledge into the system in order to reduce the amount of learning required to deploy the system in a real environment. The use of household objects is central in the recognition of activities that are being performed, and we attach semantic meaning to both the objects and activities that are being recognized. The paper describes a framework which is specifically geared towards realizing activity recognition systems which leverage prior knowledge. A preliminary implementation of a neural network based recognition system built on this framework is shown, and the added value of prior knowledge is evaluated through the use of various data sets.

Keywords. Activity recognition, Knowledge representation, Machine learning, Commonsense knowledge, Stream-based architecture

Introduction

The ability to recognize activities of daily living (ADLs) is pivotal for developing intelligent home environments since it enables them to provide proactive contextualized services that help the resident concretely and in a timely fashion. For instance, if an intelligent home environment is aware of the fact that the resident is taking a shower, it could turn off the TV in order to save electricity. Many approaches to the problem of recognizing ADLs have been studied. However, these approaches have focused mainly on the challenging pattern recognition aspects of the problem, while disregarding some key practical aspects of the proposed solutions. While systems described throughout the literature often have a high rate of success and can in some cases recognize both concurrent and interleaved activities as well as fine grained activities [12], this efficacy inevitably comes at a cost. Specifically, the proposed systems tend to require extensive model training with significant amounts of annotated data before being deployed in real environments. Furthermore, the training data used in the process is difficult to reuse for training models in other settings. In addition, the performance of these systems is often evaluated on the entire data set at once, which says little about how well such systems would be able to detect the activities in a timely fashion.

In this paper we draw inspiration from previous attempts and try to overcome these weaknesses by shifting the focus slightly from the pattern recognition aspects of the problem to a more practical one that focuses on recognizing basic ADLs in a generic way that can be more easily accepted by the end-user.

The main goal of our work is to develop a system that provides two key features that have not gained much attention in the activity recognition literature. Specifically, we want our system to; (1) be flexible enough to be deployed in many different settings without any prior training, and (2) allow modular enhancements to accommodate functionalities that make existing systems adaptable and precise (e.g., through the use of learning).

We accomplish this by: (a) developing a stream-based framework, inspired by Digital Signal Processing (DSP) techniques which leverages prior knowledge and is able to accommodate both event-based and continuous input, (b) accepting a coarser level of detail on the recognized activities, and (c) representing as output the estimated probabilities of performed activities rather than the best match. The latter point is particularly beneficial since it allows us to represent uncertainty in the output of the activity recognition process.

The activity recognition system presented in this paper takes as input objects that are being used in the environment and uses information retrieved from the freely available ConceptNet [8] commonsense knowledge base (KB) to detect activities as they occur. ConceptNet contains knowledge about objects and their respective uses which we use to create rough estimates about which activity is being performed at any given time. The claim is that in so doing we can reduce the dependency of our system on training, thus allowing a non-trained, out-of-the-box deployment of the system which already provides coarse ADL recognition capabilities.

This paper is organized as follows. Section describes related work in the field of activity recognition which is either relevant or complementary to ours. Section gives an overview of the architecture of our system and the parts of ConceptNet that are relevant to our work. Section describes some preliminary experimental results. Finally, Section presents our conclusions and lists some possible future work.

Related work

Prior approaches to the problem of recognizing activities of daily living can roughly be categorized by how the input data is processed. A common solution is the *data-driven* approach in which models of human behavior are learned from large sets of sensory data recorded over time. These models often employ Hidden Markov Models (HMM) or variations thereof to process the data. A notable example is described in [12], in which activities are being recognized with the help of an RFID-based glove and a series of probabilistic graphical models. Also, [10] shows how location data and Relational Markov Networks (RMR) can be used for this purpose. More recently, [4] has described the use of Switching Hidden Semi Markov Models (SHSMM) to recognize activities. Activity recognition systems which employ Neural Networks are more uncommon but a few exist, such as the one described in [7], where human motion patterns are used to recognize activities. Also, some unique approaches exist such as in [6], where a data mining technique called emerging patterns is used to discriminate concurrent and interleaved activities.

A complementary set of approaches to ADL recognition can be categorized as *knowledge-driven*. Such approaches are based on sets of rules that define constraints on the activities to be recognized. These rules can be specified by a knowledge engineer explicitly, as in [13] and [3], where the activity recognition problem is solved by finding patterns of events in the sensory input that conform to a set of temporal constraints. It has been shown that temporal constraints provide a useful and flexible language for specifying requirements for ADL recognition (e.g., Allen's temporal relations) [1]. Other knowledge-based models can be trained as in [2], where temporal constraints are employed to recognize activities outside the home with the help of the Bluetooth neighborhood and the current Cell ID of a mobile phone. In this case, learning is based on the computation of common time-use sub-graphs.

Data and knowledge driven approaches have complementary advantages and drawbacks. The former requires extensive data collection and subsequent training prior to being deployed in a specific setting. The latter category of approaches suffers from a similar drawback, namely the extensive work necessary to model discriminatory rules and consequent portability of the knowledge. It appears that no approach so far described in the literature has contributed to addressing the trade-off between knowledge modeling requirements and the need to re-learn from scratch once the setting is (re)defined.

There are, however, a few examples of hybrid approaches in the literature. Among these, [15] has shown that it is possible to obtain an accuracy of 42% over 26 activities using activity models mined without supervision from the web. The input to their system was a set of words describing the activities to be recognized. These words were then used in combination with the discriminating phrase "how to" to locate pages in the instructional genre from which they extract relevant objects with the help of WordNet. In a later work [14], it has also been shown that is it possible to use a statistical smoothing technique called hierarchical shrinkage to counteract the incompleteness of mined models. The main difference with our work lies in the fact that we bootstrap the activity recognition process with the objects available in the environment and then recognize all possible activities which they can take part in, providing a probabilistic rather than crisp output. Also relevant is LifeNet [11], a computational model of human life that attempts to anticipate and predict what humans do in the world. This approach is in some ways similar to ours. However, their system is different from an architectural point of view, and most importantly their emphasis is on forecasting what will happen in space and time in a typical person's life, being able to show this in human language, and to a lesser extent recognize human activities as they occur.

Stream based architecture

Our activity recognition approach is inspired by Digital Signal Processing (DSP), in that we cascade a series of interconnected *operators* acting on multi-channel data streams. The streams represent sensor data, and each operator acts as a *source* of data, a *sink* of data, or both. A data stream is not a construct in our system per-se but a terminological convenience to denote a connection between a source and a sink. Thus, an operator which implements the source interface can be connected to an operator implementing the sink interface, and if the latter also implements the source interface it can transform the data received from its connected source and provide it to another component.

The data emitted by the sources in our system are time-stamped data packages in the form $D = \{t, \langle a_1, a_2, \ldots, a_n \rangle\}$, where t is the time stamp of the package and $\langle a_1, a_2, \ldots, a_n \rangle$ is a ordered set of real-valued *activation factors*. Each source also has an ordered set of *keys* $K = k_1, k_2, \ldots k_n$ associated with it, where $k_1, k_2, \ldots k_n$ are symbols that provide *semantic meaning* to the activation factors of the data. Even though it is not an inherent property in the formalism described here, the intended use of the activation factors is probabilistic in the sense that $a_i = P(k_i)$ so that a_i defines to which extent k_i holds true at time t.

When the system is initialized, and before any data is sent, each source operator dynamically generates its key set, thereby defining its "topic". For instance, a source operator that is not a sink but provides data from an external source such as a log file in CSV format might scan the file and generate its key set based on the column headers in the file. In contrast, if the source operator is a sink as well (which is the most common situation) this is typically achieved by applying some semantic transformation on the parent's key set. The set of keys will then remain the same during the lifespan of the system as the data is relayed between the sources and the sinks. An operator that always provides the same set of keys as its parent will be referred to as a *transparent* operator in this text.

As a consequence, an operator that implements both the source and the sink interface is able to act as a causal[1] filter F on the data stream during run time and on the keys at start up. Furthermore, operators can be composed so that $G \circ F \circ \ldots = G(F(\ldots))$, both with respect to keys and activation values.

ConceptNet

ConceptNet [8] is a freely available commonsense knowledge base trained by ordinary people who have contributed content via the web. From our perspective the most relevant constructs in ConceptNet are the *concepts*. An example of concept is an item `stove` or an activity such as `cooking`. ConceptNet also contains *relations*, for example `UsedFor`, and *assertions* that connect two concepts together with the help of one relation, for example ⟨`stove, UsedFor, cooking`⟩. In addition, each assertion has a score that determines its reliability and a polarity that defines if the assertion is made in a positive or negative way. For instance, a reliability score of 0 indicates that an assertion is considered to be irrelevant or nonsensical by the user community, while an assertion using the relation `UsedFor` with a polarity of -1 defines that a concept is not `UsedFor` some other concept.

In the current system we use the concepts in ConceptNet as keys for the stream operators. This allows us to mine an ever increasing amount of user contributed data, and thus to create operators that use information about relations between concepts to provide new, different sets of keys with other interpretations than the operators' parent's keys. For instance, given a parent operator whose keys represent objects in our domain, we can construct an operator that casts objects into activities with the help of the `UsedFor` relation mentioned earlier.

Compared to other KBs in widespread use such as WordNet [5] or CyC [9], ConceptNet was chosen due to the fact that it contained more information about objects and activities than CyC, and more relevant relations than the structurally similar WordNet, which contains only limited information about usage and is more exclusively a semantic network. Also, both CyC and ConceptNet are both largely handcrafted by knowledge

---

[1] In DSP terminology the word causal means that the output only depends on past and present inputs and not future ones.

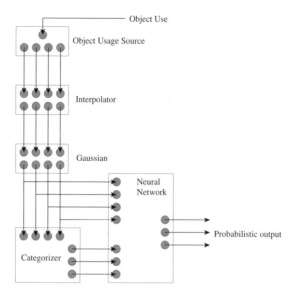

Figure 1. A basic activity recognition system realized in our architecture.

engineers, a fact that we perceive as a drawback since the growth of information can be assumed to be slower, and the information itself less inspired by the real-world.

System structure

A basic setup of the system that is able to provide an estimate about a user's activity can be constructed with the help of a few operators and is illustrated in Figure 1.

The topmost operator in the connection hierarchy (labeled "Object Usage Source") is a source of object use events which provides a key set consisting of ConceptNet concepts that correspond to objects in a physical environment. The key set is generated at start up and contains all objects that can be used in the environment. Thus, the set of object concepts that can appear in the domain has to be known in advance or derived in some way at start up. The object usage source itself can take its input from different sources, for example from a file that contains logged usage data or on-line from a physical environment as objects are being used. When an object is being used or stops being used, this source emits a data package with a monotonically increasing time stamp that corresponds to the current time in milliseconds where $a_i = 1$ if the object that corresponds to k_i is being used, otherwise $a_i = 0$. As mentioned, the activation factors are probabilistic and the choice of values here reflects the fact that we treat the incoming data as the ground truth. This operator is designed to be able to be plugged into various data sources. It provides an abstraction layer between a physical, artificially generated or logged source of object use information and the activity recognition system itself.

The second operator (labeled *Interpolator*) is a sink and source of concepts which discretizes time into regularly sized time-steps with a user defined time span of $\triangle T$. When this operator's parent source emits data with a time stamp t, this data gets aggregated if $t \leq t_* + \triangle T$ where t_* is the last emit time, otherwise the data is emitted with the time stamp t_* and t_* is set to $t_* + \triangle T$ subsequently. Since the activation values are continuous, aggregation consists of a piecewise max operation (a fuzzy OR operation), which allows to represent concurrent object use within the time frame $[t_*, t_* + \triangle T]$

The output of the second operator is semi-continuous in time but binary in value since each activation factor can only take a value of either 0 or 1. To model how the significance of object use in the past decreases over time we add a third operator that applies a Gaussian decay function to the data stream. This operator implements both the sink and the source interface, and adds a decay time to the activation peaks in the data stream. This is done to bridge the gap between single-use objects (events) and continuous-use objects so that we can use both types of sensor readings in the same framework. The operator's output activations are calculated from the input activations as $a_{now} = a_{max} * e^{\frac{(t_{max} - t_{now})^2}{c^2}}$ where c is a predefined width factor of the Gaussian, t_{now} is the current time and t_{max} and a_{max} are the last time when the input activation was greater than the output activation produced by the Gaussian and the input activation at that time. However, since the input to this operator in the current setup is always 0 or 1, the effect is equal to applying a Gaussian decay to the output when the input is 0 from the last point the input was 1 and peak the output directly to 1 as the input changes to 1 from 0. An example of the output of this operator can be seen in Figure 2, which shows how the activation factors of different concepts corresponding to objects that are being used in the domain vary over time. The width factor c of the Gaussian is set to some reasonable value depending on the objects in the domain, for example 60000 (ms^{-1}). Naturally this operator is transparent to its parents keys as well.

In order to cast the estimated probabilities of objects being active into probabilities of activities occurring, we define an operator called a *Categorizer*. The Categorizer uses ConceptNet to change the domain of the data stream. It is both a sink and a source of concepts, but is not transparent to the parent's key set. When initialized, the Categorizer takes a ConceptNet relation R as an argument and uses this to cast the keys and the streaming data of the parent into a new dimension. At start up the operator checks the keys of the parent operator and for each key k_i it mines ConceptNet to find assertions of the form $A_{ij} = \langle k_i, R, x_{ij} \rangle$. The key x_{ij} is added to the operator's key set if the assertion meets a certain goodness criterion which is determined by the reliability score of the assertion (indicated in ConceptNet), and optionally the number of keys of the parent that are involved in the same assertion. The assertions that meet the criteria are then used to build a $n * m$ matrix where n is the number of keys of the parent and m is the number of output keys. In this matrix, w_{ij} determines how much the parent key k_i influences the output key k_j. These weights are initialized to the reliability score of the assertion multiplied by the total number of assertions made on the target concept with the relation R and then normalized so that $\forall i, \sum_{j=0}^{m} a_{ij} = 1$. The matrix is then used to (linearly) transform the input data to the output dimension. Also, before the data is sent it is normalized so that $\sum_{i=0}^{m} a_i = 1$.

By using this setup and by parameterizing the Categorizer with a `UsedFor` relation, we create a basic activity recognition system that is able to provide educated guesses about which activities are being performed. Figure 3 shows the results of transforming the data illustrated in Figure 2 into a domain of activity concepts. Due to the fact that ConceptNet is built up by the user community, the data is inherently noisy and contains many irrelevant assertions.

In order to give an impression about the amount of irrelevant assertions provided by ConceptNet, we can state that when mining all possible activities for the 18 common household objects shown in Figure 2, we ended up with 367 possible activity concepts. Among these, 94.5% were only referenced by one object, while the remaining 5.5% shared two or more objects in common. We can expect that the activity concepts that are relevant fall within the latter category in most domains. We can thus reduce the noise to a large extent by pruning the set of activities using a simple reliability criteria as mentioned above and/or demand that activity concepts should be referenced by at least two object concepts in our domain, which is effective in practice but makes an unwarranted assumption on the domain. However, the operator will still choose some irrelevant or duplicate concepts as can be seen in Figure 3. For instance, sit and sit down have the same meaning and can in addition be considered to be more basic than for example cook; or the presence of the concept butter, which is not an activity.

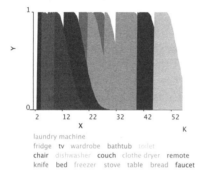 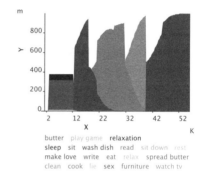

Figure 2. Output of the Gaussian operator, which indicates estimated probabilities of object use over time.

Figure 3. Estimated probabilities of activities being performed over time.

In those cases where the activities that should be monitored are fairly different in terms of object use, this setup can provide adequate results by letting the end user or an automated system pick the relevant concepts. In the remaining cases there is a need for further refinement. In order to overcome the coarseness of this out-of-the-box, untrained system, we resort to another type of operator that can be trained by the user on-line.

On-line learning

In order to adapt the noisy result produced by the chain of operators described earlier, we have provided interfaces for an operator that can be trained by the user on-line. Currently we have implemented one such operator that contains a fairly standard three layer neural network (NN) with a linear input layer, a sigmoid hidden layer and a Softmax output layer. The neural network is a source of concepts corresponding to activities and a sink of object use information. The size of the neural network's hidden layer is determined by its key set which is a parameter defined at start up. Currently, we use the key set computed by the Categorizer with the UsedFor relation. The neural network operator can also provide an arbitrary number of additional "pseudo" sinks which can be connected to other sources to provide auxiliary input to the network. This is very useful since it enables us to attach a number of Categorizers that mine additional information from ConceptNet, using for instance the relation AtLocation, which enables the neural network to generalize its training. That is, if the user explicitly trains the neural network to recognize that a `stove` is used for the activity `cook`, it also relates the training to the mined location property `kitchen` of the object. When an untrained object later appears as used in the data stream, the neural network is able to classify its usage on these futures as well. For instance, an untrained `knife` which shares the mined location property `kitchen` would make use of the training given for the `stove` object and be classified to be `UsedFor cook` to some degree depending on the features it shares with the other trained objects in the domain.

The motivation for using a neural network to provide the adaptability is that it enables us to implement operators that perform adaptations and different kinds of feature extraction on the data stream outside the (modular) scope of the classifier and that it is able to provide a continuous output as any other operator in our system. Naturally this means that we can not easily disambiguate different activities with the help of historical information, we will however implement such functionality in our system in the near future.

Experimental results

We have performed an initial evaluation of our system using the data set described in [12]. The set contains usage data on 60 different RFID-equipped objects such as "cupboard", "faucet", "saucepan" or "vanilla_syrup", which are used for 11 different annotated fine-grained household activities which can take place concurrently (for example "Making oatmeal" and "Eating breakfast"). The data set describes a morning household routine which consists of going to the bathroom, preparing breakfast and then eating it. This sequence of actions is repeated by a human user ten times with slight variations.

The evaluation was carried out without employing the neural network component in our system. Our goal here is to assess whether it is possible to employ the prior knowledge in ConceptNet (specifically, the relevance scores for the assertions in ConceptNet) to select activities to monitor in an unsupervised manner. It should be noticed that a system exhibiting this capability is by construction unaffected by the introduction of additional activities, nor does its accuracy depend on the size of the domain.

Since our aim is not to perform fine-grained activity recognition, nor to recognize concurrent activities, we have chosen to evaluate how well our unsupervised approach is able to give a high activation of important concepts and how well the activities can be identified. We have done this by considering all instances of preparing any kind of meal as a `cook` activity, and all instances of eating breakfast as an `eat` activity. This downscaling makes the activities disjoint in this data set so that there is no time instant which has both the `cook` and `eat` activities as ground truth at the same time. We then proceed and classify these two activities while leaving out the "Use The Bathroom" activity since it is quite short and too vague to be translated into a meaningful concept. It should be mentioned explicitly that this changes the activity recognition problem described in [12]: on one hand, it simplifies the problem as we only need to distinguish between two activities; on the other hand, the problem becomes more difficult since we consider any time instant in which the user is cooking as a cooking activity exclusively, thus we are negatively penalized by the influence of some concurrent activities. Although not fully suited for our needs, we have decided to use this data set to perform a simple evaluation of our system since it contains many instances of object use while at the same time being relatively long.

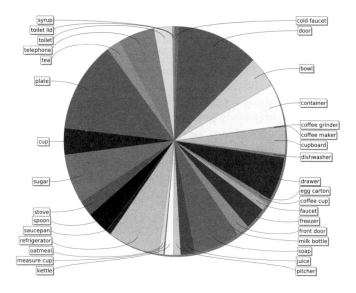

Figure 4. ConceptNet concepts used to represent objects. The relative sizes of the portions in the pie chart are determine by the amount of knowledge ConceptNet contains on each object.

We have manually mapped the 60 object names in this data set into 36 ConceptNet concepts which we use as keys in the input by using a best-match-first principle. This means that we choose a concept in ConceptNet that has the same name as the given object label in the data set when possible, which was the case for most labels. The downscaling comes from the fact that the data set contains different instances of the same types of objects which we do not take into account currently and that it also tags different parts of the same object. From this data, our system automatically selects 44 activity concepts to use as outputs. The concepts which correspond to objects in the domain are visible in Figure 4, here scaled by the number of assertions made on them in ConceptNet.

When classifying the data and trying to classify the cooking and eating activity without any prior information, our system selects 44 activity concepts to use as outputs and the cooking concept is the output with the maximum activation 19.8% of the time during the cooking activity, while the eating concept is the likeliest activity 33.8% of the time during the eating activity, both well above the baseline of 2.2%. This proves that it is possible to use the relevance score for the assertions in ConceptNet to pick activities to monitor. Also, due to the fact that the set of activities we classify is generated automatically from the set of objects, this result would be unaffected by the introduction of additional objects used for other activities. Thus we are always able to provide this accuracy on these two activities regardless of the domain size.

It should also be mentioned that with prior knowledge of the fact that we should only distinguish between the cooking and the eating activity, the answer is only correct in 47.2% percent of the cases for the cooking activity and 98.5% of the time for the eating activity (compared to the baseline of 50%). This bias is due to the fact that the cooking activity in this data set involves some objects that are more intuitively used for eating and also because the person is setting the table (thus touching forks, knives and dishes) while cooking. This shows the need for user adaptability to distinguish between different activities, and/or taking into account the location of the person. These results are calculated as a mean over all 10 instances in the data set.

We can however expect that these types of classification errors will not grow when classifying additional activities which have a more disjoint object use such as taking a shower. In such cases, the baseline would be reduced and the static classification would be able to provide an interesting prior into an adaptable system with little effort. When taking into account the current quality and coverage of ConceptNet, the most realistic application of it today is as a source of prior knowledge that interacts positively with more sophisticated and adaptable operators such as a NN as proposed above

Generator of object use events

Due to the lack of publicly available long term object use data sets that suit our needs, we have resorted to implementing a virtual source of object use events in order to test our system. The motivation for doing this rather than creating our own custom data set is that we want to be able to quickly and repeatedly try with different variations in object use behavior in different scenarios containing different objects in order to pinpoint any problems. The use of data sets obtained through the generator during development allows us to training against a fixed data set would make our approach vulnerable to over-customization in the sense that we choose operators and their configurations to get good results in a particular data set.

For example, by utilizing operators that make use of and enforce temporal ordering information mined from ConceptNet, e.g., $\langle$eat, HasPrerequisite, cook$\rangle$, we have been able to get almost perfect results on the data set presented in [12]. However such configurations are only possible if we were able to make rough assumptions in advance about the length of the `cook` activity and define a corresponding parameter accordingly. The generator of object use information makes it simple for us to pinpoint these kinds of problems and evaluate different solutions for them.

The generator is a source of concepts that corresponds to objects as described previously. When the generator is instantiated, it presents the user with a graphical user interface such as the one seen in Figure 5, which uses an image of a floor plan and an accompanying XHTML image map to define a home along with regions containing objects. The user can then mimic different activities by hovering the mouse over any object to produce object-use events. If the user clicks the objects, they become continuously activated until the user deactivates them. The user can also specify the ground truth activity that is being performed at any given time in order to train any adaptable operator such as the neural network present in the set of operators. This would correspond to a user giving feedback in a real environment. The user interface also allows the user to inspect different aspects of the activity recognition system, such as the estimated probability of different activities occurring as in Figure 6, the number of assertions made on different concepts as in Figure 4, or the correlation between instances of object use (e.g., the `stove` tends to be used together with the `saucepan`).

According to our observations, the system is able to provide correct results in about 50% of the cases without any modifications. For instance, it classifies correctly that the

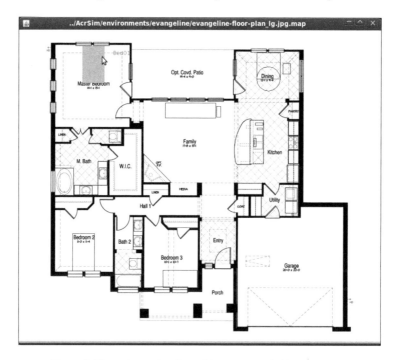

Figure 5. The main user interface of the generator of object use events.

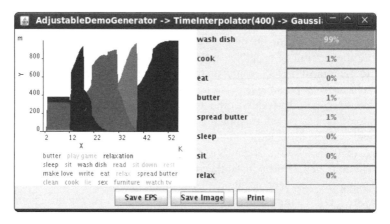

Figure 6. GUI that enables the user to inspect the probabilities of different hypotheses.

stove is used for cooking, the faucet is used for the activity wash dish, and that the table is used for eating (amongst other things). In the remaining cases, the relevant concept is usually ranked at the second place among the top rated approximations. The most common problem is that some ConceptNet concepts lack associated usages, or the provided usages are few and unintuitive. This is mostly the case for (intuitively) uncommon objects such as a clothes dryer, but can also occur for more common objects such as a laundry machine. Furthermore, the user community seems to be inclined to add assertions on concepts such as make love rather than on sleep, giving the former activity concept a higher reliability than the latter when using the bed.

Conclusions and future work

Being able to recognize ADLs is a fundamental capability for any intelligent home environment that provides contextualized services to its residents. However, prior solutions to this problem either require extensive model training or disproportionate modeling effort in order to be deployed in real environments. In this paper, we have presented the first step of a work in progress that aims to provide on-line ADL recognition in a way that is both practical and non-intrusive. The novelty of our approach lies in how we overcome the extensive training requirements of previous activity recognition systems by integrating easily accessible knowledge about the possible usages of household objects into our system. This integration is realized through the implementation of different modular operators which simplifies the task of configuring the system for deployment in new environments and at the same time allows us to attach semantic meaning to our sensory input which is made available for reasoning in all parts of our system.

We acknowledge the need for experimental comparisons of the proposed system to previous ones, such evaluations will be performed as more elaborate classifiers are integrated as operators in the framework and will also serve as evaluations of the respective strengths and weaknesses of different approaches. This will include taking into account the temporal relations between instances of object use and activities. At the same time, we will develop methods for interacting with the user and explore how the user provided feedback can be seamlessly combined with the estimate provided by the knowledge base. We will also evaluate the benefits of using multiple aspects of the data to achieve abstraction over different categorizations of objects in the domain. Finally, we also plan to integrate the ADL recognition system in a intelligent home environment maintained in our labs.

Acknowledgements

This work was supported by Vetenskapsrådet (the Swedish Research Council) on grant 621-2008-4308.

References

[1] J.F. Allen. Towards a general theory of action and time. *Artificial Intelligence*, 23(2):123–154, 1984.
[2] D. Choujaa and N. Dulay. Tracme: Temporal activity recognition using mobile phone data. In *EUC '08: Proceedings of the 2008 IEEE/IFIP International Conference on Embedded and Ubiquitous Computing*, pages 119–126, Washington, DC, USA, 2008. IEEE Computer Society.
[3] C. Dousson, P. Gaborit, and M. Ghallab. Situation recognition: Representation and algorithms. In *Proceedings of the Thirteenth International Joint Conference on Artificial Intelligence (IJCAI)*, pages 166–174, 1993.
[4] T. Duong, D. Phung, H. Bui, and S. Venkatesh. Efficient duration and hierarchical modeling for human activity recognition. *Artificial Intelligence*, 173(7-8):830–856, 2009.
[5] C. Fellbaum, editor. *WordNet An Electronic Lexical Database*. The MIT Press, Cambridge, MA ; London, May 1998.
[6] T. Gu, Z. Wu, X. Tao, P.H. Keng, and J. Lu. epSICAR: An emerging patterns based approach to sequential, interleaved and concurrent activity recognition. In *Proceedings of the 2009 IEEE International Conference on Pervasive Computing and Communications (PERCOM '09)*, pages 1–9, Washington, DC, USA, 2009. IEEE Computer Society.

[7] N. Györbíró, Á. Fábián, and G. Hományi. An activity recognition system for mobile phones. *Mob. Netw. Appl.*, 14(1):82–91, 2009.
[8] C. Havasi, R. Speer, and J. Alonso. Conceptnet 3: a flexible, multilingual semantic network for common sense knowledge. In *Recent Advances in Natural Language Processing*, Borovets, Bulgaria, September 2007.
[9] D.B. Lenat. CYC: a large-scale investment in knowledge infrastructure. *Commun. ACM*, 38(11):33–38, 1995.
[10] L. Liao, D. Fox, and H. Kautz. Location-based activity recognition using relational markov networks. In *Proceedings of the Nineteenth International Joint Conference on Artificial Intelligence (IJCAI)*, 2005.
[11] B. Morgan and P. Singh. Elaborating sensor data using temporal and spatial commonsense reasoning. In *BSN*, pages 187–190, 2006.
[12] D.J. Patterson, D. Fox, H. Kautz, and M. Philipose. Fine-grained activity recognition by aggregating abstract object usage. *Wearable Computers, IEEE International Symposium*, 0:44–51, 2005.
[13] F. Pecora and M. Cirillo. A Constraint-Based Approach for Plan Management in Intelligent Environments. In *Proc. of the Scheduling and Planning Applications Workshop at ICAPS09*, 2009.
[14] E.M. Tapia, T. Choudhury, and M. Philipose. Building reliable activity models using hierarchical shrinkage and mined ontology. In *Proceedings of PERVASIVE 2006*. Springer-Verlag, 2006.
[15] D. Wyatt, M. Philipose, and T. Choudhury. Unsupervised activity recognition using automatically mined common sense. In *Proceedings of the Twentieth National Conference on Artificial Intelligence (AAAI)*, pages 21–27. AAAI Press, 2005.

Subject Index

access control	114	lexical semantics	199
active perception	50	machine learning	1, 354
activity recognition	354	Markov logic network	63
agent societies	101	merging und splitting	277
agents and multiagent systems	277	monitoring	212
alternating tree automata	151	multiobjective optimization	290
anytime reasoning	328	music tracking	24
approximate reasoning	328	natural language processing	199
arc consistency	251	noise handling	303
argumentation theory	225	nonmonotonic reasoning	162
autonomous agents	101	obligationes	341
Banzhaf index	277	only-knowing logics	162
Bayesian networks	127	ontologies	13, 199, 328
cancer classification	290	optimization criterion	50
change mining	212	PDL	151
class noise	303	performance analysis	303
clusters	212	personalization	13
collaborative filtering	264	plan recognition	238
combinatorial auctions	186	planning	238
commonsense knowledge	354	POMDP	50
computational model	140	preferences	225
conditional independence	127	probabilistic logic	127
consistency	175	prototypicality	13
CTL	151	qualitative spatial reasoning	175
decision making	225	real-time systems	24
description logics	328	recommender systems	264
dialogue protocol	341	recurrent auctions	186
differential evolution	290	regular path temporal logic	151
difficulty rating	140	relational learning	63
disputation	341	reputation	101
dynamic constraint satisfaction problems	251	Semantic Web	328
evaluation	264	semiotic	13
evolution	212	Shapley-Shubik index	277
fairness	186	simple tabular reduction	251
formal dialogue systems	341	SimpleAPL	151
geometry	175	Sokoban puzzle	140
goal recognition	238	state space	140
graph mining	315	statistical test	290
inductive logic programming	1	stream-based architecture	354
intuitionistic modal logic	114	structure learning	63
knowledge extraction	199	subgroup discovery	1
knowledge representation	225, 354	table constraints	251
		term rewriting	162

theorem proving	114	unsupervised learning	315
transitions	212	video event analysis	315
trust	101	weighted voting games	277

Author Index

Abudawood, T.	1	Lücke, D.	175
Ågotnes, T.	v	Maudet, N.	225
Aimé, X.	13	Maulik, U.	290
Arzt, A.	24	McClean, S.	264
Bandyopadhyay, S.	290	Mossakowski, T.	175
Blom, M.L.	37	Murillo, J.	186
Carmo, J.	101	Oliveira, M.	212
Chanel, C.P.C.	50	Ouerdane, W.	225
Chen, L.	264	Pattison, D.	238
Cohn, A.G.	315	Pearce, A.R.	37
Coradeschi, S.	354	Pecora, F.	354
da Costa Pereira, C.	76, 89	Pelánek, R.	140
Dinh, Q.-T.	63	Plewczynski, D.	290
Dragoni, M.	76, 89	Prada, R.	101
Exbrayat, M.	63	Probst, C.W.	251
Farges, J.-L.	50	Quéva, M.	251
Figueiredo, R.	101	Redpath, J.	264
Flach, P.	1	Rey, A.	277
Fürst, F.	13	Ricci, L.	251
Gabbay, D.M.	114	Rispoli, D.	114
Gama, J.	212	Rothe, J.	277
Gamberger, D.	303	Saha, I.	290
Genovese, V.	114	Schlobach, S.	328
Giese, M.	127	Sluban, B.	303
Glass, D.H.	264	Sridhar, M.	315
Gomes, P.	199	Tagni, G.	328
Gonçalo Oliveira, H.	199	Teichteil-Königsbuch, F.	50
Hogg, D.C.	315	ten Teije, A.	328
Infantes, G.	50	Tettamanzi, A.G.B.	76, 89
Ivanovska, M.	127	Trichet, F.	13
Jarušek, P.	140	Tsoukias, A.	225
Johnsen, E.B.	162	Uckelman, S.L.	341
Karafotias, G.	328	Ullberg, J.	354
Khan, F.	151	van der Torre, L.	114
Kuntz, P.	13	van Harmelen, F.	328
Lavrač, N.	303	Vrain, C.	63
Lian, E.H.	162	Waaler, A.	162
Long, D.	238	Widmer, G.	24
López, B.	186